Lecture Notes in Computer Science　14590

Founding Editors

Gerhard Goos
Juris Hartmanis

The series Lecture Notes in Computer Science (LNCS), including its subseries Lecture Notes in Artificial Intelligence (LNAI) and Lecture Notes in Bioinformatics (LNBI), has established itself as a medium for the publication of new developments in computer science and information technology research, teaching, and education.

LNCS enjoys close cooperation with the computer science R & D community, the series counts many renowned academics among its volume editors and paper authors, and collaborates with prestigious societies. Its mission is to serve this international community by providing an invaluable service, mainly focused on the publication of conference and workshop proceedings and postproceedings. LNCS commenced publication in 1973.

Bedir Tekinerdoğan · Romina Spalazzese ·
Hasan Sözer · Silvia Bonfanti · Danny Weyns
Editors

Software Architecture

ECSA 2023 Tracks, Workshops, and Doctoral Symposium

Istanbul, Turkey, September 18–22, 2023
Revised Selected Papers

 Springer

Editors
Bedir Tekinerdoğan
Wageningen University
Wageningen, The Netherlands

Romina Spalazzese 🆔
Malmö University
Malmö, Sweden

Hasan Sözer 🆔
Ozyegin University
İstanbul, Türkiye

Silvia Bonfanti 🆔
University of Bergamo
Dalmine, Italy

Danny Weyns 🆔
Katholieke Universiteit Leuven
Leuven, Belgium

Linnaeus University
Växjö, Sweden

ISSN 0302-9743 ISSN 1611-3349 (electronic)
Lecture Notes in Computer Science
ISBN 978-3-031-66325-3 ISBN 978-3-031-66326-0 (eBook)
https://doi.org/10.1007/978-3-031-66326-0

This Springer imprint is published by the registered company Springer Nature Switzerland AG
The registered company address is: Gewerbestrasse 11, 6330 Cham, Switzerland

If disposing of this product, please recycle the paper.

Preface

The European Conference on Software Architecture (ECSA) is the premier European conference aimed at bringing together leading researchers and practitioners to present and discuss the most recent, innovative, and significant findings and experiences in the field of software architecture research and practice. ECSA 2023 was held at Yeditepe University in Istanbul, Türkiye, during September 18–22, 2023, with attendees from all over the world. Accepted contributions for the main research track are included in the conference proceedings, published in Springer Lecture Notes in Computer Science volume 14212. In addition to the main research track, ECSA 2023 included an Industry Track, a Diversity, Equity and Inclusion Track (DE&I), a Doctoral Symposium, and a Tools and Demonstrations Track. ECSA 2023 also offered six workshops on diverse topics related to the software architecture discipline:

- CASA 2023: The 6th Context-Aware, Autonomous and Smart Architectures International Workshop
- AMP 2023: The 4th International Workshop on Agility with Microservices Programming
- FAACS 2023: The 7th International Workshop on Formal Approaches for Advanced Computing Systems
- DeMeSSA 2023: The 3rd International Workshop on Designing and Measuring Security in Software Architectures
- QUALIFIER 2023: The 1st International Workshop on Quality in Software Architecture
- TwinArch 2023: The 2nd International Workshop on Digital Twin Architecture

This volume contains a selection of revised and extended contributions from all these satellite events of ECSA 2023.

We received 32 submissions for the tracks and doctoral symposium. From this list, after selection by the Program Committee, 29 papers are included in the postproceedings. Each submission was reviewed by multiple referees. We used the EasyChair conference system to manage the submission and review process.

We thank the Program Committee members of all the tracks and the additional reviewers that reviewed the revised and extended versions of papers.

We acknowledge Springer's prompt and professional support, which published these proceedings as part of the Lecture Notes in Computer Science series. Finally, we would like to thank the authors of all these submissions for their contributions.

March 2024

Bedir Tekinerdoğan
Romina Spalazzese
Hasan Sözer
Silvia Bonfanti
Danny Weyns

Organization

General Chair

Bedir Tekinerdogan   Wageningen University, The Netherlands

Workshops Co-chairs

Hasan Sözer   Özyeğin University, Türkiye
Romina Spalazzese   Malmö University, Sweden

Program Committee

Abdessalam Elhabbash	Lancaster University, UK
Adam Bachorek	Fraunhofer IESE, Germany
Alfredo Goldman	University of São Paulo, Brazil
Amleto Di Salle	Gran Sasso Science Institute, Italy
André van Hoorn	University of Hamburg, Germany
Andreas Wortmann	University of Stuttgart, Germany
Angelika Musil	Vienna University of Technology, Austria
Antinisca Di Marco	University of L'Aquila, Italy
Antónia Lopes	University of Lisbon, Portugal
Antonino Sabetta	SAP Security Research, France
Apostolos Ampatzoglou	University of Macedonia, Greece
Barbora Buhnova	Masaryk University, Czechia
Bedir Tekinerdogan	Wageningen University, The Netherlands
Bernhard J. Berger	University of Rostock, Germany
Carlo Vallati	University of Pisa, Italy
Christopher Gerking	Karlsruhe Institute of Technology, Germany
Claudia Szabo	University of Adelaide, Australia
Daniel Strüber	Chalmers University of Technology	University of Gothenburg, Sweden; Radboud University Nijmegen, The Netherlands
Danny Weyns	Katholieke Universiteit Leuven, Belgium
Dharini Balasubramaniam	University of St Andrews, UK
Diego Perez-Palacin	Linnaeus University, Sweden
Dimitri Van Landuyt	Katholieke Universiteit Leuven, Belgium

Eduardo B. Fernandez   Florida Atlantic University, USA
Elena Lisova   Mälardalen University, Sweden
Elena Navarro   University of Castilla-La Mancha, Spain
Elisa Yumi Nakagawa   University of São Paulo, Brazil
Emmanuel Letier   University College London, UK
Enis Karaarslan   MSKU, Türkiye
Fabio Moretti   ENEA, Italy
Florian Rademacher   RWTH Aachen University, Germany
Frank Schnicke   Fraunhofer IESE, Germany
Geylani Kardas   Ege University, Türkiye
Giovanni Quattrocchi   Politecnico di Milano, Italy
Gregor Engels   Paderborn University, Germany
Hasan Sözer   Özyeğin University, Türkiye
Heiko Koziolek   ABB Corporate Research, Germany
Henry Muccini   University of L'Aquila, Italy
Ilias Gerostathopoulos   Vrije Universiteit Amsterdam, The Netherlands
J. Andres Diaz-Pace   ISISTAN Research Institute, Argentina
Jacopo Soldani   University of Pisa, Italy
James Ivers   Carnegie Mellon University, USA
Jan Bosch   Chalmers University of Technology, Sweden
Jasmin Jahic   University of Cambridge, UK
João Daniel   Free University of Bozen-Bolzano, Italy
John Doe   Mercedes-Benz AG, Germany
Juha Röning   University of Oulu, Finland
Klara Borowa   Politechnika Warszawska, Poland
Kwabena Bennin   Wageningen University, The Netherlands
Liliana Dobrica   University Politehnica of Bucharest, Romania
Luciana Santos   Gran Sasso Science Institute, Italy
Manuel Wimmer   Johannes Kepler University Linz, Austria
Marcello M. Bersani   Politecnico di Milano, Italy
Marco Jahn   Eclipse Foundation, Germany
Marion Wiese   Universität Hamburg, Germany
Mark van den Brand   Eindhoven University of Technology,
                                        The Netherlands
Matteo Camilli   Politecnico di Milano, Italy
Mert Ozkaya   Yeditepe University, Türkiye
Mirko D'Angelo   Ericsson Research, Sweden
Muhammad Ali Babar   University of Adelaide, Australia
Norha M. Villegas   ICESI University, Colombia
Nour Ali   Brunel University London, UK
Nuno Laranjeiro   University of Coimbra, Portugal
Paolo Arcaini   National Institute of Informatics, Japan

Contents

AMP

Tools Reconstructing Microservice Architecture: A Systematic Mapping
Study 3
   Alexander Bakhtin, Xiaozhou Li, Jacopo Soldani, Antonio Brogi,
   Tomas Cerny, and Davide Taibi

Analysis, Design, Test, and DevOps in Microservice-Based Software
Architectures: Results from Pakistan 19
   Hüseyin Ünlü, Görkem Kılınç Soylu, Isra Shafique Ahmad,
   and Onur Demirörs

DevOps Patterns: A Rapid Review 33
   Sebastian Copei and Jens Kosiol

CASA

MAPE-K Based Guidelines for Designing Reactive and Proactive
Self-adaptive Systems 53
   Hendrik Jilderda and Claudia Raibulet

DE & I Track

Stakeholder Inclusion and Value Diversity: An Evaluation Using an Access
Control System 71
   Razieh Alidoosti, Martina De Sanctis, Ludovico Iovino, Patricia Lago,
   and Maryam Razavian

Data-Driven Analysis of Gender Fairness in the Software Engineering
Academic Landscape 89
   Giordano d'Aloisio, Andrea D'Angelo, Francesca Marzi,
   Diana Di Marco, Giovanni Stilo, and Antinisca Di Marco

DeMeSSA

Sarch-Knows: A Knowledge Graph for Modeling Security Scenarios
at the Software Architecture Level 107
   Jeisson Vergara-Vargas, Felipe Restrepo-Calle, Salah Sadou,
   and Chouki Tibermacine

Threat Modeling: A Rough Diamond or Fool's Gold? 120
    Anh-Duy Tran, Koen Yskout, and Wouter Joosen

FAACS

Declarative Representation of UML State Machines for Querying
and Simulation 133
    Zohreh Mehrafrooz, Ali Jannatpour, and Constantinos Constantinides

Towards Behavior-Based Analysis of Android Obfuscated Malware 151
    Zakaria Sawadogo, Muhammad Taimoor Khan, George Loukas,
    Jean-Marie Dembele, Georgia Sakellari, and Gervais Mendy

QUALIFIER

Towards a Prediction of Machine Learning Training Time to Support
Continuous Learning Systems Development 169
    Francesca Marzi, Giordano d'Aloisio, Antinisca Di Marco,
    and Giovanni Stilo

Performance Comparison of Monolith and Microservice Architectures:
An Analysis of the State of the Art 185
    Helena Rodrigues, António Rito Silva, and Alberto Avritzer

Towards a Sustainability-Aware Software Architecture Evaluation
for Cloud-Based Software Services 200
    Iffat Fatima and Patricia Lago

Technical Debt in Microservices: A Mixed-Method Case Study 217
    Roberto Verdecchia, Kevin Maggi, Leonardo Scommegna,
    and Enrico Vicario

TQPropRefiner: Interactive Comprehension and Refinement
of Specifications on Transient Software Quality Properties 237
    Sebastian Frank, Julian Brott, Alireza Hakamian, and André van Hoorn

TwinArch

Architecture for Digital Twin-Based Reinforcement Learning Optimization
of Cyber-Physical Systems 257
    Elias Modrakowski, Niklas Braun, Mehrnoush Hajnorouzi,
    Andreas Eich, Narges Javaheri, Richard Doornbos, Sebastian Moritz,
    Jan-Willem Bikker, and Rutger van Beek

Towards an Urban Digital Twins Continuum Architecture 272
*Sergio Laso, Lorenzo Toro-Gálvez, Javier Berrocal, Javier Troya,
Carlos Canal, and Juan Manuel Murillo*

Designing a Future-Proof Reference Architecture for Network Digital
Twins 287
*Roberto Verdecchia, Leonardo Scommegna, Enrico Vicario,
and Tommaso Pecorella*

Tools and Demos

Evolution and Anti-patterns Visualized: MicroProspect in Microservice
Architecture 309
*Lauren Adams, Amr S. Abdelfattah, Md Showkat Hossain Chy,
Samantha Perry, Patrick Harris, Tomas Cerny,
Dario Amoroso d'Aragona, and Davide Taibi*

An Approach and Toolset to Semi-automatically Recover and Visualise
Micro-Service Architecture 326
*Nour Ali, Nuha Alshuqayran, Rana Fakeeh, Thoybur Rohman,
and Carlos Solis*

An Extensible Framework for Architecture-Based Data Flow Analysis
for Information Security 342
*Nicolas Boltz, Sebastian Hahner, Christopher Gerking,
and Robert Heinrich*

Studying the Evolution of Library Utilization in Maven Projects:
A Metric-Based Approach 359
*Maria Kolyda, Eirini Kostoglou, Nikolaos Nikolaidis,
Apostolos Ampatzoglou, and Alexander Chatzigeorgiou*

Slicing and Visualizing F' Topologies with F'Prism 375
*Jialong Li, Christos Tsigkanos, Toshihide Ubukata,
Elisa Yumi Nakagawa, Zhenyu Mao, Nianyu Li, and Kenji Tei*

Maestro: A Deep Learning Based Tool to Find and Explore Architectural
Design Decisions in Issue Tracking Systems 390
Jesse Maarleveld, Arjan Dekker, Sarah Druyts, and Mohamed Soliman

Industry Track

Demeter: An Architecture for Long-Term Monitoring of Software Power
Consumption 409
  Lylian Siffre, Gabriel Breuil, Adel Noureddine, and Renaud Pawlak

Experience of the Architectural Evolution of a Big Data System 426
  Felipe Cerezo and Belén Vela

Parallel and Distributed Architecture for Multilingual Open Source
Intelligence Systems 438
  Alper Karamanlioglu, Gokhan Yurtalan, and Yahya Bahadir Karatas

HITA: An Architecture for System-level Testing of Healthcare IoT
Applications 451
  Hassan Sartaj, Shaukat Ali, Tao Yue, and Julie Marie Gjøby

Doctoral Symposium

Pragmatic Architectural Framework to Design for Sustainability in Cloud
Software Services 471
  Sahar Ahmadisakha and Vasilios Andrikopoulos

Author Index 489

AMP

Tools Reconstructing Microservice Architecture: A Systematic Mapping Study

Alexander Bakhtin[1]([⊠]), Xiaozhou Li[1], Jacopo Soldani[2], Antonio Brogi[2], Tomas Cerny[3], and Davide Taibi[1,4]

[1] University of Oulu, Oulu, Finland
alexander.bakhtin@oulu.fi
[2] University of Pisa, Pisa, Italy
[3] University of Arizona, Tucson, AZ, USA
[4] Tampere University, Tampere, Finland

Abstract. Various tools have been developed to reconstruct the microservice system architecture. Some of the main reasons to build yet another architectural reconstruction tool are the lack of features to satisfy the current needs or the fact that researchers are often unaware of the existing tools. To shed light on the available tools, we performed a review of the literature in the form of a systematic mapping study to identify the different architectural reconstriction tools adopted in research works, classifying their purpose, input, and output. This paper compares 37 tools. Out of these, 19 are based on static analysis, 10 on dynamic, and 8 using a combination of them. The study shows a significant overlap among tools, with several unmaintained, abandoned, or unavailable. This work will help researchers identify the architectural reconstruction tools that fit their purposes rather than developing another similar tool. This work includes an online appendix [1].

Keywords: Microservice · Software Architecture · Architectural Reconstruction

1 Introduction

Microservices bring significant benefits to stakeholders involved in software development and deployment. Development teams work in smaller, autonomous units focused on specific services, which enables decentralization. However, there come times when we need to see the system as a whole to make informed decisions on maintenance and evolution. The problem with the decentralization that allows teams to work more independently is that teams understand microservice bounded context but do not see beyond. With access to a system-centered view, they could better strategize for optimization, patches, and new features, not introducing changes that could deteriorate system design and its operability [2].

We typically look into the system architecture to understand the system as a whole. However, there is no guarantee that the planned architecture matches

© The Author(s), under exclusive license to Springer Nature Switzerland AG 2024
B. Tekinerdoğan et al. (Eds.): ECSA 2023, LNCS 14590, pp. 3–18, 2024.
https://doi.org/10.1007/978-3-031-66326-0_1

the actual architecture since the system is developed decentrally and constantly evolves without the means to assess whether the architecture maintains the prescribed format. For example, Baabad et al. [3] synthesize work by Taylor et al. [4] and Perry and Wolf [5] and conclude that they *described the architectural degradation as a process of the persistent inconsistency between the descriptive software architecture as implemented and the prescriptive software architecture as intended.* Thus, to understand systems, we typically perform software architecture reconstruction [6]. However, the challenge with microservices and decentralized teams is determining the system-centered view of separately designed parts, possibly involving different codebases and separate issue-tracking systems. While system monitoring offers certain means to discover service dependencies, these have limits to the extent of uncovered detail and completeness [2,7].

This work aims to identify available tools for reconstructing the system architecture from microservice systems. For this reason, we perform a Systematic Mapping Study [8] (SMS) identifying 37 tools, categorizing them based on common goals, supported platforms, benefits, and outputs behind such reconstructions, along with the common inputs to such tools to provide the community with a comprehensive overview to exiting tools to apply or extend rather than reinventing the wheel.

This paper is structured as follows: Sect. 2 discusses the related works, Sect. 3 describes the adopted SMS method, Sect. 4 presents the results and describes what information we gather about the discovered tools, Sect. 5 goes into further discussion of results, and Sect. 6 concludes the paper. This paper also has an online appendix [1] that provides tables with detailed information about the discovered tools as well as a list of all papers that came from the SMS.

2   Related Works

Various secondary studies try to organize the ever-growing body of research on microservices. The first attempts, to our knowledge, were [9,10]. In [9], authors considered what was proposed by Academic literature concerning microservices up until that point (2016), focusing on proposed views and metrics but not on tools providing them. In [10], authors conduct an SMS to identify different types of microservice architectures as well as tools enabling to create projects with microservice architectures, but not tools extracting them.

Another notable attempt in this direction is [11], which analyzed the state-of-the-art on Microservice Architectures (MSAs). The goal of [11] was indeed to report on the evolution of software architectures into microservices and to describe open research challenges. Other examples are [12–14]: [12] presents the results of a Grey Literature Review aimed at analyzing the practitioners' view on the "pains and gains" of microservices; [13,14] instead elicit the architectural/security smells for MSAs and the refactorings, allowing to resolve them by conducting Multivocal Literature Reviews. However, the four studies mentioned above all differ from our review in the aim of the study and in the method exploited to pursue that aim. Similar considerations apply to [15,16], which run

Systematic Literature Reviews to pursue different aims than ours. [15] actually focuses on the deployment/communication patterns used in MSAs, while [16] focuses on failure detection and root cause analysis in MSAs.

Other secondary studies worth mentioning are the Systematic Mapping Studies in [17–19] and the Rapid Review in [20]. [17,20] both consider the reconstruction of MSAs as part of the broader scopes of analyzing and reasoning on MSAs. [18,19] instead classify the existing techniques for visualizing antipatterns in MSAs and service interactions in running MSAs, respectively. Despite the fact that [17,18,20] touch the topic of MSA reconstruction and visualization, they are not eliciting nor classifying the existing tools for running such tasks, which is instead the aim and scope of this study.

The work by Cerny et al. [6] is perhaps the closest study to ours. The Systematic Literature Review in [6] elicits and classifies the existing techniques for reconstructing the architecture of existing MSAs by distinguishing between static and dynamic reconstruction techniques and by also commenting on how reconstructed MSAs can be visualized. The focus of [6] is, however, on the *techniques* for reconstructing and visualizing architectures, assuming that they are already designed as MSAs, and the work only mentions whether/how they have been implemented.

Similar considerations apply when relating our work to existing primary studies for reconstructing and visualizing MSAs, e.g., [21–24]. The existing primary studies indeed typically focus on proposing *techniques* for reconstructing and visualizing architectures, which are sometimes released also through prototypical implementations.

The focus of our study is, therefore, different: we indeed review the existing *tools* for reconstructing MSAs, including both the migration of monoliths to microservices, the reconstruction of existing MSAs, and the possibility to visualize the obtained results.

3   Methods

This section describes the method we applied to identify and classify the existing tools reconstructing MSAs.

3.1   Research Questions

Our goal is to catalog existing tools that have been introduced to the community with a scientifically published work. We, therefore, formulated the following research questions:

RQ$_1$ *What tools for microservice reconstruction have been developed?*

RQ$_2$ *What languages/platforms are currently supported by the tools?*

RQ$_3$ *What is the purpose of the reconstruction?*

RQ$_4$ *What is the input/output of the tools?*

In order to answer our RQs, we adopt a Systematic Mapping Study of the literature according to [8]. We also perform snowballing on the found papers according to guidelines by Wohlin [25]. Both original and snowballed papers are filtered with the use of Inclusion and Exclusion criteria. We then extract the tools from the selected papers.

3.2   The Search Process

To answer our research questions, we searched for scientific literature introducing tools for reconstructing MSAs. Following the guidelines provided in [8], we identified the search string by structuring it guided by our research questions. More precisely, we defined the search string based on the terms characterizing our research questions, picking keywords in order to cover the four main aspects of our research question. As a result, we obtained the following search string:

```
(Microservice* OR Micro-service* OR "micro-service*") AND Architect*
AND (Reconstr* OR Mining OR Reverse engineering OR Recover* OR Extract* OR
                              Discover*)
AND (Tool* OR Prototype OR Implementation OR GitHub OR Proof of concept OR POC OR
                           Proof-of-concept)
```

(where "*" matches lexically related terms, e.g., plurals and conjugations). In the search string, the first OR-group accounts for different spellings of the term "Microservice", and the third provides additional synonyms to the term "Reconstruction". The fourth OR group was applied to search in-text if permitted by the database's search syntax/filters.

The search string was used to search for literature on the following scientific databases by converting it to the appropriate syntax: SCOPUS,[1] IEEEXPLORE,[2] ACM DIGITAL LIBRARY,[3] and the citation database WEB OF SCIENCE.[4] Initially, only the SCOPUS search was performed on **7th of February 2023**. The decision to include other databases occurred after a team discussion of initial results, and the queries were performed on **23rd of February 2023**.

The counts of obtained papers are: SCOPUS - 369, IEEE - 71, ACM - 28, WEB OF SCIENCE - 114; Total excluding duplicates is 387.

3.3   Selection of Papers

After compiling the initial list of 387 papers found by the query, we proceeded with a read of the title and abstract of each paper to determine if it was in the scope of our research and worthy to be investigated for tools. We used the following inclusion and exclusion criteria to guide the paper selection process:

- **Inclusion criteria**
  - Mentions a tool in the context of microservice reconstruction
- **Exclusion criteria**
  - Material not in English

---

[1] The SCOPUS database: https://www.scopus.com.
[2] The IEEEXPLORE database: https://ieeexplore.ieee.org/.
[3] The ACM DIGITAL LIBRARY: https://dl.acm.org.
[4] WEB OF SCIENCE: https://www.webofscience.com/wos/woscc/basic-search.

– Out of topic - terms used with different meanings
– Different aspects of microservice reconstruction (not dealing with tools)

The inclusion of the paper was determined by two authors separately (from the first three authors of the paper). In case of disagreements, a third author (from the last three authors) resolved the disagreement. After looking at some initial pool of results, we decided to be as inclusive as possible towards papers mentioning some kind of tool in order to create a more comprehensive catalog of proposed tools in the context of MSA reconstruction.

In particular, during piloting, we noticed that three distinct areas use the term 'Microservice Reconstruction' with different meanings:

– Microservice Architecture Reconstruction, i.e., construction of a 'map' of Microservice systems, showing how different microservices connect to each other. *Main interest of this study.*
– Monolith to Microservice Migration, i.e., clustering of methods/classes of monolithic applications into distinct microservices. These papers frequently say, "We *reconstruct* the Microservice architecture from a Monolithic system," even though the correct word to use here would be *construct*, since a novel architecture is created.
– Microservice recovery, i.e., redeploying microservices that crashed due to an error. These papers say that "Microservices are *reconstructed* from a failed state," using *reconstruct* as a synonym for *recover*.

After observing these results during piloting, we decided to accept papers from the first and second contexts but reject papers from the third context. The decision to include, during this stage, Monolith to Microservice migration tools is explained by the hope that some of these tools might be 'tricked' to accept a Microservice system as input and get its real architecture as output.

The number of papers selected from 387 in our case was 81.

3.4   Tool Extraction/Snowballing

After selecting the papers in the previous step, we proceeded with a full read in order to extract the existing tools for MSA reconstruction. We extracted the tools that were directly employed by each paper (e.g., the paper introduces the tool or the tool is studied/applied in the paper), as well as any other tools with similar functionalities that are mentioned in the selected papers' sections (e.g., in their introduction, background, or related work discussion). As such, this process was combined with backward and forward snowballing on the papers, namely finding additional resources by following citations [25]. Backward snowballing was performed on citations in the selected papers, as well as forward snowballing using Google Scholar to find papers that cite the selected papers. Since the process was combined with extracting the tools, we could quickly see that despite finding additional papers using snowballing, the tools they mention are the same tools we find from the originally selected papers.

For each paper, one person extracted the tools. However, if he reported that no tools are found, another author stepped in to read the paper and confirm that. In the online appendix [1], we report for each tool all the papers among the selected papers that cite the tool.

In our case, we added 14 papers by snowballing and extracted a total of 37 tools.

3.5 Tool Coding

For each tool, we collect information on the development activity, license, supported languages, platforms or frameworks, input, and output. We also assessed the architectural recovery method and the existence of visualizations that make information about certain system aspects accessible to users. One author extracted each piece of information in a shared spreadsheet. Then, at least three authors collaboratively classified them using a collective coding method. Incongruences were discussed until disagreements were resolved.

The final coding process led to the collection and classification of the information included in the following taxonomy:

– `Tool name`
– The `reference` of the paper introducing the tool
– All selected papers that `cite` the tool
– `Tool repository` information:
    – `Availability`[5]
    – Indicated `license`
    – `Last update/commit date` (as of 23rd of June 2023)
    – `Total amount of commits`
    – `Number of stars`
    – `Number of forks`
    – `Number of contributors`
– `Supported language/platform/framework`
– `Input`:
    – `Input type`:
        – `Source code (Source)` - original source code in plaintext form; can also refer in particular to git repositories if git history is studied
        – `Model-generatable from source (Model-GFS)` - Some intermediate representation of code/repository/infrastructure/etc. that can be automatically generated by existing tools as it adheres to a standardized format
        – `Model-manual custom format (Model-MCF)` - Some intermediate representation of code/repository/infrastructure/etc. that needs to be manually generated (or a custom generator written) since authors define the format themselves

---

[5] We do not provide links to save space in the table. If the repository is indicated as available, its name in Table 1 is a hyperlink in the electronic version of the paper. Additionally, it can be found in the introductory paper of the tool from Table 4 of the online appendix [1].

  - Traces - Special type of logs, usually implemented using OpenTracing standard[6]
  - Deployment files - Files necessary for Docker/Kubernetes deployment, such as Dockerfile, docker-compose.yml, Kubernetes manifest
 - Input format - Free-form clarification of the particular case
- Output
  - Output type:
    - Smells, patterns, anti-patterns
    - Architectural views [22, 26]- target system aspects to describe, i.e., service view (describing the service models that specify microservices, interfaces, and endpoints), domain view (describing the entity objects of the system as well as the data source connections of those objects.), operational view (describing service deployment and infrastructure, such as containerization, service discovery, and monitoring), etc.
    - Health metrics - For monitoring tools, data they provide that can be used to infer the status and health of the project
    - Tests
    - Refactorings, violations
  - Output sub-category - Free-form clarification of a particular case, common values are:
    - Service Dependency Graph (SDG) - a graph that shows which services call one another
    - Class to Microservice mapping (C2M) - for monolith to microservice migration tools, the proposed grouping/refactoring of existing classes/methods into microservices
  - Output format - The particular format (JSON, CSV, microTOSCA, etc.) that the tool produces
  - Recovery method - One of the following:
    - Static - source code/repository is analyzed without building and running the project
    - Dynamic - project is run, and runtime data (logs, metrics) are collected to perform the analysis
    - Hybrid - data from both stages are used
  - Tool aims - Overall purpose of the tool, common values are:
    - Microservice Reconstruction (MR) - mapping out the SDG of a microservice system
    - Monolith to Microservice Migration (M2M) - proposal of grouping methods/classes of a monolithic system into microservices
    - Vulnerability detection (VD)
    - Smell detection (SD)
    - Pattern detection (P)
    - Monitoring (MO)
  - Visualization - whether the tool produces some kind of visualization

---

[6] A couple of tools use actual logs and not traces, but we decided not to introduce another category for this case.

4   Results

A total of 81 papers are selected by a full read from 387 obtained by search, to which an additional 14 are added by snowballing; a total of 37 tools are identified. The summary of results is reported in Table 1. Detailed information about the tools is provided in the online appendix [1]. We also provide the introductory paper as well as all referencing papers for each tool in Table 4 of the appendix.

4.1   RQ$_1$ - What Tools for Microservice Reconstruction Have Been Developed?

This question concerns a general description of discovered tools. We can summarize the following aspects:

Repository: Of 37 discovered tools, 2 are commercial and proprietary and do not share the code repository. Among the remaining 35 tools, 6 do not provide any kind of open repository.

Of the available tools, 2 were uploaded to Zenodo. This makes 'activity' metrics such as the number of Commits, Stars, and Forks impossible to infer and complicates potential development ('forking') by other researchers. Another 2 tools host codes on GitLab, with the remaining 25 on GitHub.

License: The 2 commercial projects are covered by proprietary licenses, while 5 projects are not available at all.

The majority (17) of openly available projects do not indicate any license, which is a bad practice since it creates legal ambiguity about how the project can be used by third parties, which critically, in our case, includes other researchers.

The other 3 tools specify that they are available 'For Academic Use Only,' which is better than not specifying any license, but also potentially ambiguous.

One project uses a Creative Commons By-Attribution license while CC licenses are not considered suitable for software even by the license authors[7].

The remaining are permissive OSS licenses - 7 instances of MIT License and 1 Apache 2.0 License. Also, 1 instance of 'copyleft' GPLv3 license is represented.

Activity: Most publicly available projects have not been updated since the tool/paper publication. Only 4 tools have commits in the first half of 2023, and additionally, 2 commercial tools are continuously supported. Another 8 tools were last updated in 2022. The earliest abandoned tool is Decomposer, which has not been updated since December 2016.

Another way to measure the activity of development is through commits. Most (16) tools for which we could gather such information have less than 100 commits. We exclude from this 4 projects that have been pushed to a public repository without preserving the git history; thus, they had 1–2 commits.

The largest amount of commits are in VMAMV (798) and mono2micro (609); however, they are not that popular with the community as judged by Stars,

---

[7]   https://creativecommons.org/faq/#can-i-apply-a-creative-commons-license-to-software.

Table 1. Summary of results

Tool name	RQ₁ Repo	License[a]	Last update	RQ₂ Platform[b]	Recovery[e]	RQ₃ Tool aims[f]	RQ₄ Input[c]	Output[d]	Visualization
Arcan	✓	P	-	Many[7]	S	SD	S	S, LV	✓
ARCHI4MOM	✓	-	06/22	OT	D	MR	T	OV	✓
Aroma	✓	M	04/23	OT	D	MR, SD	T	OV	✓
attack-graph-generator	✓	-	01/21	D	S	VD	D	HM	✓
Code2DFD	✓	AP	06/23	J	S	MR, VD	S	OV	✓
Decomposer	✓	-	12/16	J	S	M2M	MG	LV	-
IdentificationApproach	✓	-	01/22	J	S	M2M	S	SV	-
ImpactAnalysis	✓	-	01/19	J	S	Test	MG	T	✓
istio-log-parser	✓	-	05/22	I	D	MR	T	SV	✓
MAIG	-	-	-	OT	D	MR, P	T	SV, AP	✓
MicADO	✓	M	06/22	Any	H	MR	T, MC	SV	✓
microART	✓	A	04/17	D	H	MR	S,D,T	SV	-
MicroDepGraph	✓	-	11/21	J	S	MR	S	SV	✓
microFreshener	✓	M	11/22	Any	S	SD	MG	SV	✓
Microlyze	✓	-	07/18	EU, OT	D	MR	T	SV	✓
MicroMiner	✓	M	11/20	KU	H	MR	D	SV	✓
MAAT	-	-	-	J	D	MR, P	T	SV	✓
microserviceExtraction	✓	A	-	J	S	M2M	S	SV	✓
microTOM	✓	M	01/23	KU	H	MR	D	SV	✓
monitoring_ms	✓	-	08/18	EU,D	D	MR, MO	T	SV, HM	✓
mono2micro (socialsoftw.)	✓	M	06/23	J	H	M2M	S	SV	✓
Mono2Micro (IBM)	✓	P	-	J	D	M2M	T	SV	✓
MonoToMicro [27]	-	-	-	J	S	M2M	S	SV	-
MS-MDE-RL	✓	G	01/22	J	S	M2M	MG	SV	✓
MSA-Nose	✓	-	04/21	J	S	SD	S	S	-
MSDesigner	-	-	-	J	S	M2M	MC	SV	✓
MSExtractor	-	-	-	J	S	M2M	S	SV	-
Rademacher et al. [23]	✓	-	03/20	J	S	MR	S	DV, OV, SV	-
De Alwis et al. [28]	✓	-	07/19	J	H	M2M	S,T	SV	-
Ntentos et al. [29]	✓	CC	02/21	Any	S	MO	MC	Ref., Vio	-
OpenTracingProcessor	✓	M	07/19	OT	D	MR, MO	T	SV, HM	✓
Prophet	✓	-	09/21	J	S	MR	S	SV	-
RAD	✓	-	01/21	J,P	S	MR, SEC	S	SV	-
ServiceCutter	✓	A	05/21	J	S	M2M	MG	SV	✓
Subtype	✓	-	05/18	Any	H	M2M	MG	SV	-
VECROSim	✓	-	12/22	KU	D	MO	MC	HM	-
VMAMV	✓	-	01/22	J	H	MO	S	HM	-

[a] P - Proprietary, M - MIT, AP - Apache v.2, A - Academic Use Only, G - GPL v.3, CC - CC BY 4.0

[b] OT - OpenTracing, D - Docker, J - Java, EU - Eureka, KU - Kubernetes, P - Python

[c] S - Source, T - Traces, D - Deployment files, MG - Model-generatable from source, MC - Model-custom manual format

[d] S - Smells, LV - Logical View, OV - Operational View, SV - Service View, DV - Domain View, HM - Health Metrics, T - Tests, AP - Anti-Patterns, Ref. - Refactorings, Vio. - Violations

[e] S - Static, D - Dynamic, H - Hybrid

[f] SD - Smell Detection, MR - Microservice Reconstruction, VD - Vulneraibility Detection, M2M - Monolith to Microservice, Test - Test Generation, P - [Anti-]Pattern Detection, MO - Monitoring, SEC - Security Analysis

[g] Java, C, C++, C#, Python

Forks, as well as the number of citations among our papers in the online appendix
[1].

The most popular by a huge margin, both in terms of GitHub stats and
citations, is the `ServiceCutter`, which is one of the oldest projects in our list
and is used as a reference implementation in many M2M papers. However, the
project is now abandoned, and the build is broken, with only surviving Docker
images making it possible to run it.

4.2   RQ$_2$ What Languages/Platforms are Currently Supported by Tools?

The overwhelming majority of tools cover Java (21), most as the only supported
language (19). Other represented languages include Python (2 tools), as well as
C, C++, and C# (1 tool - Arcan is multiplatform). Apart from that, certain
tools target a certain framework rather than a language - 6 tools use OpenTracing
logs, 2 leverage Eureka, and 1 Istio. Some tools study deployments, with 3 tools
studying Docker containers and another 3 Kubernetes pods. Additionally, 4 tools
use some intermediate model representation as input, thus potentially being
applicable to any language.

Figure 1 groups all available platforms hierarchically by corresponding input
type (see Sect. 3.5/Table 1). It shows, for each specific platform (outer ring),
how many tools support this platform. Note that, as explained above, some
tools support several platforms, so numbers along the ring do not sum up to 37,
and it is thus not possible to deduce intermediate categories from the figure and
we do not put numbers to intermediate categories.

4.3   RQ$_3$ What is the Purpose of Reconstruction?

When it comes to Reconstruction approaches, 19 tools use Static methods and
10 Dynamic, with another 8 using a combination of both (Hybrid).

Some tools handle systems already using Microservice Architecture (17 in
total). For some (10), reconstructing the architecture by providing the SDG is
the only purpose. Another 2 tools couple this with Monitoring of the Microservice
system, 2 with Pattern and 1 with Smell Detection, and 2 more with Vulnerability detection/Security Analysis; also 3 of found tools are concerned purely with
Monitoring of the health of the system, and 3 more purely with Smell Detection.

Additionally, results included 12 tools that deal with Monolith to Microservice migration by analyzing the legacy monolithic system and proposing a grouping/refactoring of methods/classes into separate microservices.

4.4   RQ$_4$ What is the Input/Output of the Tools?

The mapping between different types of inputs and outputs among the tools is
presented in Fig. 2.

As for the **input**, the majority (13) of the tools use source code as input
directly, meaning they can be potentially integrated into IDEs or CI/CD

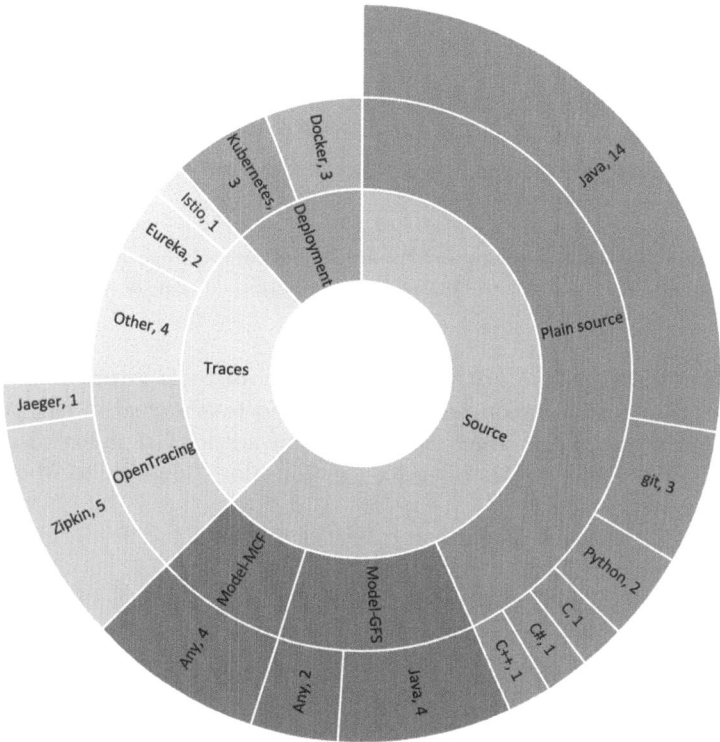

Fig. 1. Sunburst chart showing the correspondence between input types and platforms (languages). Some tools cover several languages, so numbers along the ring exceed 37.

pipelines. Further, 6 tools use some kind of generatable model that can be inferred from the Source, which can also be an automatic step in a pipeline (examples of models are `OpenAPI`, `microTOSCA`). Another 3 tools use a custom-defined Model format, which means that adoption is harder since tools to construct such models need to be developed first because manual model creation for large projects is impractical.

Additionally, 3 tools do not study the Source directly but instead use the Deployment files, which are usually checked into the same repository.

Most of the tools that perform Dynamic Analysis use Traces (9), in particular, OpenTracing, with particular tools using either Jaeger[8] or Zipkin[9] as the tracing tool of choice, while others use Eureka[10] or Istio[11].

Furthermore, some tools combine different inputs (e.g., Traces and Sources).

---

[8] Jaeger https://www.jaegertracing.io.

[9] Zipkin https://zipkin.io.

[10] Spring Eureka Server https://cloud.spring.io/spring-cloud-netflix/multi/multi_spring-cloud-eureka-server.html.

[11] Istio Service Mesh https://istio.io.

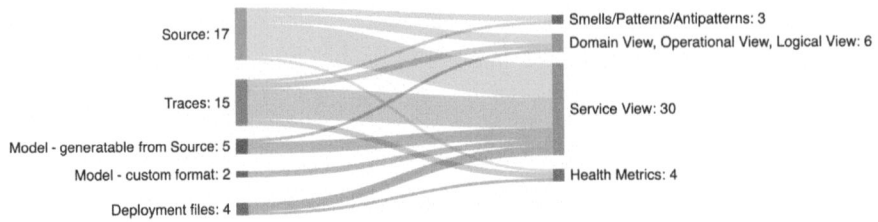

Fig. 2. Sankey diagram mapping tool Inputs to Outputs. Categories that appear only once are excluded; Views except Service View are grouped together.

When it comes to the **output**, the majority of tools return some kind of view (28), the most common being (as expected by the goal of this research) service view (26), which is either the Service Dependency Graph for Microservice systems (15) or Class to Microservice grouping for Monolith to Microservice migration systems (13^{12}).

Additionally, 4 tools provide an operational view, 2 tools - a logical view, and 1 tool a domain view.

Out of 6 tools that deal with smell/pattern/anti-pattern detection (see previous RQ), 4 provide a list of detected smells/patterns/anti-patterns. However, the remaining 2 tools only report these detections on top of the provided SDG as part of the visualization, so we do not mark it as separately obtained input.

5 tools provide health metrics, which in particular can take the form of a system response to injected faults (2), an attack graph (1), or simply metrics given for different parts of the system (2). Another tool concerned with vulnerability detection returns a dataflow diagram and yet another a breakdown of roles required to access different endpoints to monitor potential privilege escalation problems.

Also, 2 tools aim to improve existing code - one by suggesting refactorings that solve detected violations, another by suggesting which CRUD-operations tests to implement.

Different tools use different output formats to provide the results - common include Neo4j, JSON, and microTOSCA to report SDGs or C2M mappings. Some tools only provide the reconstructed SDG as a graphic or web visualization in their front-end application. With 11 papers, we could not determine from the paper text or repository description what formats were used. Additionally, we could confirm that 23 tools provide some kind of visualization for their results while the remaining 15 either do not provide it or did not mention such support in documentation or source publication.

---

[12] Note: one tool (MicADO) is reported with the aim being MR, but output being C2M because it studies an existing Microservice system and proposes a new, optimized grouping of methods into microservices.

5   Discussion

Different architectural reconstruction tools, often with similar features, have been developed in the last few years. The analysis of the literature identified in the SMS indicates that while there is a need for MSA reconstruction tools, there is a limited amount of them actively developed, and in particular, there are no widely adopted tools.

Such tools are commonly built from scratch instead of extending previous ones. Some of the reasons why researchers are developing new tools might be the unavailability of tools meeting their requirements. Often, tools require particular resources, input, or configuration that discourage other research teams from using them. Another reason might be the impossibility of running them. Often, tools are not easily executable or require access to some libraries, databases, or specific hardware not available in the research group trying to run them. Moreover, not all the tools were available in source code repositories. To increase the availability of the tools, we recommend hosting the tools both on GitHub and archival platforms like Zenodo or Software Heritage, the latter providing easy integrations with the former.

It should also be emphasized that, when considering static analysis tools, only a limited number of tools are directly applicable to the industry, mainly because they parse a very limited number of languages or technologies. Most of the research-developed tools parse Java code, thus making them inapplicable in the industry where microservices are developed with a large number of technologies.

5.1   Future Research Directions

Based on the discussion of the research questions (RQs) above, we propose the following directions for future research in this field:

- Focus on validating existing tools and their outcomes to enhance their credibility and facilitate their adoption in the industry. While some tools already exist, our findings suggest that they have not undergone thorough validation in terms of precision and recall of the components of the SDGs, resulting in limited application.
- Center the tools around inputs that produce outcomes of genuine interest to stakeholders and explore the possibility of utilizing inputs from widely accepted technologies, both for static and dynamic analysis tools.

5.2   Threats to Validity

Various sources of bias or error could potentially impact the validity of our study's results. The research questions and classification schema used in our study may be subject to construction validity. To minimize this risk, the authors independently reviewed and discussed the research questions. As for the classification schema, we classified tools and their categories based on objective enumerated categories (e.g., language, license, etc.).

Also, to ensure replicability, we carefully identified and reported the bibliographic sources used to identify peer-reviewed literature. We also provided the search strings and the inclusion and exclusion criteria. Potential issues in the selection process could, however, arise from the choice of search terms, which may lead to an incomplete set of results. To mitigate this risk, we expanded the search string by including possible synonyms. Moreover, to address the limitations of search engines, we queried academic literature from four different bibliographic sources, and we performed both forward and backward snowballing [25] to increase the coverage of possible sources.

Other possible threats may apply to the reliability and generalizability of our results. As for reliability, all primary sources underwent review by at least two authors to mitigate bias in data extraction, with any disagreements resolved through consensus involving a third author. As generalizability, instead, we mapped the academic literature on MSA reconstruction tools. However, we cannot claim to have screened all possible literature, as some documents may not have been appropriately indexed or may be subject to copyright restrictions or limited availability.

6   Conclusion

In this work, we performed a Systematic Mapping Study to classify the tools for MSA reconstruction. We classified 37 tools from 95 primary studies, comparing their input and output, which will be useful to researchers and practitioners to have a quick overview of the existing tools. It is interesting to note that the vast majority of tools are implemented from scratch without extending previous ones. Moreover, most tools are based on static analysis and can parse only a limited set of technologies.

We plan to extend this work by comparing the detection accuracy of the tools that can be executed on a set of microservice projects and conducting an industrial survey to investigate their applicability and the usefulness of the output provided.

Acknowledgements. This material is based upon work supported by grants from the Research Council of Finland (grants n. 349487 and 349488 - MuFAno) and 6GSoft project from Business Finland (grant n. 24304494 - 6GSoft); National Science Foundation (grant n. 2245287); and partly supported by the projects "FREEDA" (PRIN MUR, Italy, CUP: I53D23003550006) and "OSMWARE" project UNIPI_PRA 2022 64.

References

1. Bakhtin, A., et al.: Appendix to: tools reconstructing microservice architecture: a systematic mapping study. Zenodo. https://zenodo.org/doi/10.5281/zenodo.8207331
2. Cerny, T., Abdelfattah, A.S., Maruf, A.A., Janes, A., Taibi, D.: Catalog and detection techniques of microservice anti-patterns and bad smells: a tertiary study. J. Syst. Softw. **206**, 111829 (2023)

3. Baabad, A., Zulzalil, H.B., Hassan, S., Baharom, S.B.: Software architecture degradation in open source software: a systematic literature review. IEEE Access **8**, 173681–173709 (2020)
4. Medvidovic, N., Taylor, R.N.: Software architecture: foundations, theory, and practice. In: Proceedings of the 32nd ACM/IEEE International Conference on Software Engineering-Volume 2, pp. 471–472 (2010)
5. Perry, D.E., Wolf, A.L.: Foundations for the study of software architecture. ACM SIGSOFT Softw. Eng. Notes **17**(4), 40–52 (1992)
6. Cerny, T., et al.: Microservice architecture reconstruction and visualization techniques: a review. In: 2022 IEEE International Conference on Service-Oriented System Engineering (SOSE), pp. 39–48 (2022)
7. Abdelfattah, A.S., Cerny, T.: Roadmap to reasoning in microservice systems: a rapid review. Appl. Sci. **13**(3), 1838 (2023)
8. Petersen, K., Vakkalanka, S., Kuzniarz, L.: Guidelines for conducting systematic mapping studies in software engineering: an update. Inf. Softw. Technol. **64**, 1–18 (2015)
9. Alshuqayran, N., Ali, N., Evans, R.: A systematic mapping study in microservice architecture. In: 2016 IEEE 9th International Conference on Service-Oriented Computing and Applications (SOCA), pp. 44–51 (2016)
10. Pahl, C., Jamshidi, P.: Microservices: a systematic mapping study. In: Proceedings of the 6th International Conference on Cloud Computing and Services Science - Volume 1 and 2. CLOSER 2016, Setubal, PRT, pp. 137-146. SCITEPRESS - Science and Technology Publications, Lda (2016)
11. Dragoni, N., et al.: Microservices: yesterday, today, and tomorrow. In: Mazzara, M., Meyer, B. (eds.) Present and Ulterior Software Engineering, pp. 195–216. Springer, Cham (2017). https://doi.org/10.1007/978-3-319-67425-4_12
12. Soldani, J., et al.: The pains and gains of microservices: a systematic grey literature review. J. Syst. Softw. **146**, 215–232 (2018)
13. Neri, D., et al.: Design principles, architectural smells and refactorings for microservices: a multivocal review. SICS **35** (2020)
14. Ponce, F., et al.: Smells and refactorings for microservices security: a multivocal literature review. J. Syst. Softw. **192**(C) (2022)
15. Karabey Aksakalli, I., et al.: Deployment and communication patterns in microservice architectures: a systematic literature review. J. Syst. Softw. **180**, 111014 (2021)
16. Soldani, J., Brogi, A.: Anomaly detection and failure root cause analysis in (micro) service-based cloud applications: a survey. ACM Comput. Surv. **55**(3) (2022)
17. Bushong, V., et al.: On microservice analysis and architecture evolution: a systematic mapping study. Appl. Sci. (Switzerland) **11**(17) (2021)
18. Gortney, M.E., et al.: Visualizing microservice architecture in the dynamic perspective: a systematic mapping study. IEEE Access **10**, 119999–120012 (2022)
19. Parker, G., et al.: Visualizing anti-patterns in microservices at runtime: a systematic mapping study. IEEE Access **11**, 4434–4442 (2023)
20. Abdelfattah, A.S., Cerny, T.: Roadmap to reasoning in microservice systems: a rapid review. Appl. Sci. **13**(3) (2023)
21. Cerny, T., et al.: Microvision: static analysis-based approach to visualizing microservices in augmented reality. In: 2022 IEEE International Conference on Service-Oriented System Engineering (SOSE), pp. 49–58 (2022)
22. Walker, A., Laird, I., Cerny, T.: On automatic software architecture reconstruction of microservice applications. In: Kim, H., Kim, K.J., Park, S. (eds.) Information Science and Applications. LNEE, vol. 739, pp. 223–234. Springer, Singapore (2021). https://doi.org/10.1007/978-981-33-6385-4_21

23. Rademacher, F., Sachweh, S., Zündorf, A.: A modeling method for systematic architecture reconstruction of microservice-based software systems. In: Nurcan, S., Reinhartz-Berger, I., Soffer, P., Zdravkovic, J. (eds.) BPMDS/EMMSAD -2020. LNBIP, vol. 387, pp. 311–326. Springer, Cham (2020). https://doi.org/10.1007/978-3-030-49418-6_21

24. Kleehaus, M., Uludağ, Ö., Schäfer, P., Matthes, F.: MICROLYZE: a framework for recovering the software architecture in microservice-based environments. In: Mendling, J., Mouratidis, H. (eds.) CAiSE 2018. LNBIP, vol. 317, pp. 148–162. Springer, Cham (2018). https://doi.org/10.1007/978-3-319-92901-9_14

25. Wohlin, C.: Guidelines for snowballing in systematic literature studies and a replication in software engineering. In: International Conference on Evaluation and Assessment in Software Engineering. Ease '14, pp. 1–10 (2014)

26. Cerny, T., Abdelfattah, A.S., Bushong, V., Al Maruf, A., Taibi, D.: Microservice architecture reconstruction and visualization techniques: a review. In: 2022 IEEE International Conference on Service-Oriented System Engineering (SOSE), pp. 39–48. IEEE (2022)

27. Zaragoza, P., Seriai, A.D., Seriai, A., Bouziane, H.L., Shatnawi, A., Derras, M.: Refactoring monolithic object-oriented source code to materialize microservice-oriented architecture, pp. 78–89 (2021)

28. De Alwis, A.A.C., Barros, A., Fidge, C., Polyvyanyy, A.: Availability and scalability optimized microservice discovery from enterprise systems. In: Panetto, H., Debruyne, C., Hepp, M., Lewis, D., Ardagna, C.A., Meersman, R. (eds.) OTM 2019. LNCS, vol. 11877, pp. 496–514. Springer, Cham (2019). https://doi.org/10.1007/978-3-030-33246-4_31

29. Ntentos, E., Zdun, U., Plakidas, K., Geiger, S.: Semi-automatic feedback for improving architecture conformance to microservice patterns and practices, pp. 36–46 (2021)

Analysis, Design, Test, and DevOps in Microservice-Based Software Architectures: Results from Pakistan

Hüseyin Ünlü[(✉)] [iD], Görkem Kılınç Soylu [iD], Isra Shafique Ahmad,
and Onur Demirörs [iD]

Izmir Institute of Technology, Izmir 35430, Turkey
{huseyinunlu,gorkemkilinc,israshafique,onurdemirors}@iyte.edu.tr

Abstract. In today's software industry, Microservice-based Software Architecture (MSSA) has been a common practice and has been adopted by many companies. MSSA differs from traditional object-oriented architecture in several ways. The architecture moved away from being data-driven and evolved into a behavior-oriented structure. The usage of a single database is replaced by the structures in which each microservice is developed independently and has its own database. Therefore, adaptation demands software organizations to transform their culture. However, there is no de facto method for analyzing, designing, and testing systems for these architectures, similar to object-oriented analysis and design practices. This study aimed to understand how Pakistani software organizations undertake analysis, design, test, and DevOps processes in software projects adopting the MSSA paradigm. To achieve this goal, we surveyed 49 participants from various agile organizations in Pakistan, encompassing different roles and domains. The results reveal that Pakistani software organizations continue using familiar object-oriented analysis and design approaches. However, they have already started exploring event-oriented analysis and design methods for MSSA projects.

Keywords: Microservices · Analysis · Design · Test · DevOps · Pakistan · Survey

1 Introduction

The software industry has been experiencing a paradigm shift for the last ten years: microservice-based software architectures (MSSA) [1, 2]. Today, many software organizations, including both small-scale and large-scale, such as Amazon, LinkedIn, Netflix, SoundCloud, and Uber, have adopted the MSSA paradigm [3].

MSSA comprises multiple microservices that exhibit high cohesion and loose coupling. The degree of functional dependence among the elements within each microservice is high, while the degree of interdependence among microservices is as low as possible. In such a system, each microservice is designed as an isolated, autonomous application with a small bounded context and a single responsibility [4]. On the other hand, to perform more complicated tasks, microservices communicate with each other through

B. Tekinerdoğan et al. (Eds.): ECSA 2023, LNCS 14590, pp. 19–32, 2024.
https://doi.org/10.1007/978-3-031-66326-0_2

asynchronous communication channels through messages over lightweight mechanisms, such as event queues. In this form, MSSA has also been associated with event-based asynchronous service communication and ledger-style data persistence to reveal real-world benefits regarding scalability, reliability, and performance [3, 5–7].

Organizations that develop software using Service-Oriented Architecture (SOA) can observe that they apply similar concepts when working with microservices. Similarly, agile software development organizations may observe that they have already started adapting their culture to the microservices world [8]. However, this transition is not as easy as it may seem. It comes with unprecedented challenges, such as the high coupling level, difficulties in identifying the boundaries of services, and system decomposition [9–12].

Agile organizations that start developing software using MSSA face the challenge of dealing with decentralization and autonomy on the one hand and efficient management and integration of the output of all teams on the other. We have previously observed that traditional modeling notations used for the analysis and design are not effective when working with microservices [7]. Even the most fundamental abstraction we use today, the 'object' of the Object-oriented Analysis and Design (OOAD) methodologies, has to change.

On the other hand, organizations implementing DevOps practices may observe that they have already begun adopting automated deployment processes. Some studies also argue that there is an inherent evolution in adopting DevOps within MSSA [13]. DevOps enhances productivity in MSSA by employing a toolchain and establishing a swift feedback mechanism [14].

We previously performed a survey [15, 16] and an interview [9] to explore the organizational choices and the challenges of the agile development process, agile tools, software analysis, design, test, size measurement, and effort estimation. We presented the views, experiences, and challenges over different roles, domains, and countries. The global results showed that organizations continue to use the same analysis, design, size measurement, and effort estimation approaches that they were using previously in traditional architectures. However, they face unique challenges in the management of MSSA projects.

As a developing country, Pakistan's market for computer software has seen steady growth for the past several years. Much of the growth is driven by the work of freelancers who earned subpar certifications from local institutions and support specialized fields in the local market. Pakistan is currently the fourth largest freelance provider after India, Bangladesh, and the United States, with gaming software development [17].

In this study, we aimed to explore how Pakistani Agile organizations perform analysis, design, and test in their projects developed with MSSA. For this purpose, we performed our previous survey of over 49 Pakistani participants from different organizations, roles, and domains. In addition to our previous survey, we added a section that explores the common DevOps practices in MSSA. We compared the results of Pakistani organizations with our previous studies with participants from different countries to see whether software management practices differ based on regional demographics.

The remainder of this paper is structured as follows. Section 2 summarizes the related work. Section 3 explains our research methodology behind the survey. Section 4 summarizes our results. Section 5 discusses our findings. Lastly, Sect. 6 concludes our study by stating the future work.

2 Related Work

In the literature, several studies analyze migration or technical issues for converting monoliths to MSSAs. In our previous paper, we obtained that only a few studies explored the issues from the project management perspective and for building new MSSA systems [9]. To the best of our knowledge, no study reveals Pakistani organizational practices in these management practices.

3 Research Method

In this work, we conducted a survey, following the guidelines proposed by [18, 19], to investigate how organizations in Pakistan apply analysis, design, and test their software projects adopting the MSSA paradigm. We conducted the survey anonymously online to ensure confidentiality and encourage open sharing. This approach served multiple purposes. Firstly, it respects organizations' privacy, allowing them to freely provide information without hesitation. Secondly, it facilitated efficient outreach to a large number of participants within a short period. Lastly, we sought a platform to enable easy organization and analysis of the collected data. In line with these objectives, we selected Google Forms as our survey platform due to its user-friendly interface, free availability, convenient export of results in XLSX format, and its ability to present the collected data in an informative manner.

While the questionnaire-based survey method offers the benefit of efficiently reaching numerous practitioners and quickly collecting substantial data, it can occasionally lead to misunderstandings regarding the questions [18]. In order to address this concern, we conducted three pilot interviews with individuals from different companies. During these interviews, we read the questions aloud to the participants and observed their comprehension of the content. This process allowed us to identify any ambiguities present in the questions and subsequently refine the questionnaire based on the feedback received from the interviews.

3.1 Goals and Research Questions

The primary goal of this work is to gain a deeper understanding of how software organizations in Pakistan carry out analysis, design, and testing in their MSSA projects. By collecting responses from industry practitioners, we aim to identify patterns in the methods and technologies employed in executing MSSA projects. The research questions addressed in this study are as follows:

RQ1. What analysis techniques do Pakistani organizations utilize while applying agile methodologies in MSSA projects?

RQ2. Which design principles do Pakistani organizations follow while applying agile methodologies in their MSSA projects?

RQ3. How do Pakistani organizations test their MSSA projects while applying agile methodologies?

RQ4. How do Pakistani organizations implement DevOps in MSSA projects while applying agile methodologies?

RQ5. Are Pakistan's analysis, design, and test approaches and technologies different from those employed globally? If there are differences, what sets them apart?

3.2 Sampling Method

For our survey, we employed the accidental nonprobabilistic sampling method [19]. Our focus was on professionals in the software industry who had experience in MSSA. To locate and reach out to suitable participants, we utilized various channels such as personal and company contacts, online forums, mailing groups, and LinkedIn. During the participant selection process, we ensured representation from diverse companies operating in different domains.

3.3 Designing Survey Questions

To gather information about analysis, design, and testing in software projects that embrace the MSSA paradigm, we developed a comprehensive set of survey questions. These questions were carefully designed to address our research objectives and provide valuable insights into the practices employed by organizations in Pakistan. The survey encompasses inquiries about the participants' demographics and their respective organizations, as well as inquiries specifically focused on the application of agile methodologies in MSSA projects. Our primary focus was understanding how Pakistani organizations perform analysis, design, and testing in their MSSA projects while incorporating agile methodologies. We aimed to uncover the methods, techniques, and tools utilized in this context, enabling us to gain a deeper understanding of the practices organizations adopt to effectively perform analysis, design, and testing in their MSSA projects.

While our main focus in this paper centers around analysis, design, and testing, our survey investigates a broader range of topics. In addition to these key areas, we also include questions about size measurement, effort estimation, and DevOps. The survey is divided into a total of 7 sections. The initial section provides an overview of the survey and seeks participants' consent regarding its content. The second section is dedicated to gathering demographic information, including details about the participants, their organizations, and their experiences. The third section aims to gather insights into the organization's domain, team dynamics, adoption of agile methodologies, and experience with MSSA projects. The fourth section investigates specific details regarding agile methodologies. The fifth section focuses on how the organization applies size measurement and effort estimation. The sixth section is dedicated to gathering information about how organizations analyze, design, and test and which techniques and tools are used for this aim. The last section includes questions dedicated to DevOps practices. While designing the questions, we considered the following key aspects: relevance, clarity and understandability, coverage, and an unbiased approach.

3.4 Survey Piloting and Execution

Before distributing the survey, we conducted a pilot study to ensure the clarity and effectiveness of the questions. The pilot study took the form of interviews with three participants, each from a different company involved in a MSSA project. These participants possessed varying levels of experience. We read the survey questions aloud to the participants during the interviews while displaying the questionnaire on a screen. As the participants provided their responses, we took notes that were visible to them. We carefully observed and collected participant feedback, which helped us refine and improve the survey accordingly.

Once we received approval from the Human Subjects Ethics Committee (HSEC) at İzmir Institute of Technology (IZTECH), we proceeded to distribute the survey to our intended participants. The survey was completed by 50 participants with diverse levels of experience and represented companies operating in various industries. Following the completion of the survey, we carefully evaluated the collected answers to generate a comprehensive report.

3.5 Criteria for Validation

In order to ensure the validity and reliability of the data gathered from our survey, we implemented specific validation criteria. These criteria were developed to evaluate the survey responses' reliability, accuracy, and overall quality of the survey responses. A key criterion for participant inclusion was their experience in the field of MSSA. Throughout the process of selecting and distributing the survey, we ensured to target individuals who were actively engaged in MSSA projects. Once the survey was concluded, we carefully reviewed the answers provided by all 50 participants to ensure their validity. It should be noted that a few participants did not complete the entire survey, and as a result, their incomplete responses were not saved and did not impact the final results. All the completed surveys were contributed by individuals actively involved in MSSA projects. However, one participant acknowledged their lack of experience in MSSA projects despite their current involvement as a new beginner. Due to their limited experience, their responses were considered inappropriate for an unbiased evaluation of the subject and were therefore excluded from the analysis. Consequently, the survey results from a total of 49 participants were accepted as valid and considered in our findings.

4 Results

In this section, we give a summary of the survey results of 49 participants regarding the demographics, experience with Agile methodology, analysis, design, testing, and DevOps in MSSA projects.

4.1 Participant Demographics and Experience

The majority, i.e., 60%, of the participants who contributed to our survey have an undergraduate degree in computer science, while 30% graduated from software engineering,

4% from information systems, and 6% from other fields (see Fig. 1a). 68% of our participants have a graduate degree, i.e., 38% in computer science, 20% in software engineering
and 10% in other fields (see Fig. 1b).

The survey participants have a range of roles within their respective companies,
including developer, senior developer, software architect, test engineer, software engineer, and other positions such as software test engineer, analyst, and chief executive offi-
cer, among others. Most of the participants, i.e. 38%, hold the role of a senior developer,
followed by 26% as developers, 6% as software engineers, 6% as software architects,
6% as software test engineers, and the remaining 18% occupying various other roles
(see Fig. 1c).

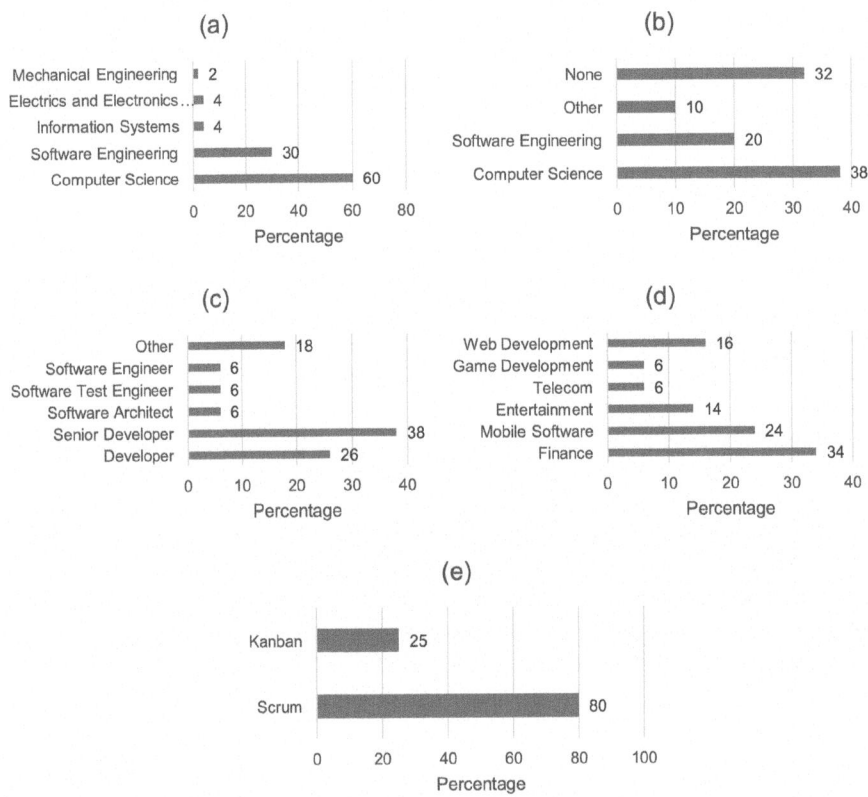

Fig. 1. The percentage of the responses regarding (a) participants' undergraduate education, (b)
participants' graduate education, (c) participants' role in the organization, (d) the domain of the
organization, and (e) the adopted Agile methodology.

Our participants represent organizations from diverse industry sectors. In order to
achieve more readable and informative charts, we grouped some specific answers into
broader domains, allowing for more meaningful deductions from the results, such as
combining "Banking" and "Finance" together as "Finance." Based on the responses, 34%

of our participants are employed in the finance sector, 24% work in mobile software-related fields, 16% are engaged in web development, 14% work in the entertainment sector, 6% are involved in game development, and 6% are employed in the telecom industry (see Fig. 1d).

The participants in our study have a range of experience in their current roles, spanning from 1 to 10 years. This distribution's average (mean) experience is 2.74 years, with a median of 2.5 years. Similarly, their experience in software engineering-related fields varies from 1 to 10 years. The average experience in this domain is 4.29 years, with a median of 4 years. Our results show that the participants' organizations' experience in MSSA ranges from 1 to 9 years, whereas their experience with agile methodologies ranges from 1 to 23 years. The mean and the median of the organizations' experience in MSSA are 4.03 and 3, whereas the mean and the median of the organizations' experience in agile methodologies are 7.81 and 5. The distribution can be found in Table 1.

Table 1. Descriptive statistics of participant experience (years).

	Software field	Current role	Agile methodology	MSSA
Minimum	1	1	1	1
Maximum	10	10	23	9
Mean	4.29	2.74	7.81	4.03
Median	4	2.5	5	3
Mode	3	3	3	3
Standard Deviation	2.01	1.71	6.12	2.45

In our survey, we asked participants about the agile methodologies used in their organizations. The findings reveal that SCRUM is the most preferred methodology as the majority of participants replied with SCRUM. Some participants mentioned using Kanban, while no other methodologies were mentioned. Notably, there were instances where participants indicated using both SCRUM and Kanban in conjunction. According to our results, 80% of participants employ SCRUM, while 25% utilize Kanban. It is worth noting that there is an overlap between the two methodologies (see Fig. 1e).

4.2 Analysis, Design, and Test

In this study, we conducted a comprehensive survey to gain insights into the analysis, design, and testing techniques employed by organizations within Pakistan's software industry for the development of MSSA projects. By exploring the practices utilized in this context, we aimed to contribute to the understanding of software analysis and design approaches specific to MSSA. Our study aimed to identify the techniques implemented by organizations in Pakistan's software industry.

Our results show that 84% of our participants utilize a standard process for software analysis for MSSA projects (see Fig. 2a). The functional requirements are represented using traditional approaches, as shown in Fig. 2b. When asked about the utilized notation,

70% of the participants responded with user stories, while 48% use use-case scenarios, 34% depict the functional requirements with use-case diagrams, and 20% use unstructured/natural language. As seen from the responses, a notable amount of participants utilize a combination of methods.

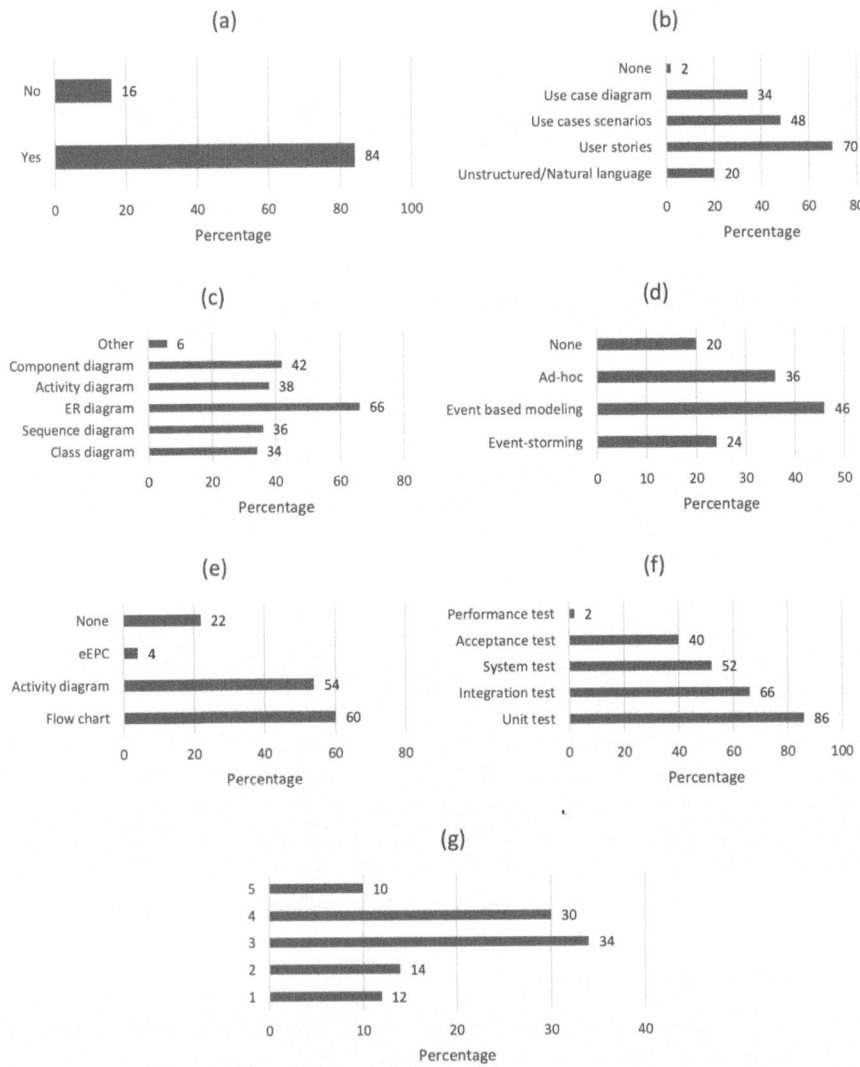

Fig. 2. The percentage of the responses regarding (a) whether the organization utilizes a standard process for software analysis, (b) the notation used to depict the functional requirements, (c) the notation used to represent the design, (d) the method used to analyze the problem, (e) the notation used to show the analysis of the project, (f) focused test paradigms, and (g) the level of test automation.

Our survey inquired about the design notation used in MSSA projects. We have seen that organizations commonly (60%) use ER diagrams, whereas 42% use component diagrams. The other widely used design notations are activity diagrams at 38%, sequence diagrams at 36%, and class diagrams at 34%. 6% of participants mentioned other less common notations. As seen from the results, many organizations combine these notations (see Fig. 2c).

We also asked how our participants perform problem analysis in their projects. The responses show that organizations mainly adopt event-based and ad-hoc analysis techniques. 46% perform event-based modeling, while 36% follow ad-hoc techniques. Event storming is used by 24%, whereas 20% do not perform problem analysis in their MSSA project while utilizing agile methodologies (see Fig. 2d).

As for the notation used for the analysis of the MSSA projects; our results show that flow charts are the most commonly used notation, i.e., 60% of our participants responded with flow charts. Activity diagrams with 54% follow it, whereas 22% of the participants stated that they do not use any specific notation for analysis. According to the responses we received, only 4% of the participants utilize eEPC (see Fig. 2e).

Within MSSA architectures, multiple services coexist and interact with each other asynchronously. While loose coupling is a crucial aspect of such architectures, the communication complexity between microservices is unavoidable. Consequently, testing in this context can become more intricate. Our survey included test-related questions to gain insight into how testing is applied in MSSA projects. We asked our participants what tests they performed in their MSSA projects. Our results indicate the focus is on unit testing since 86% of our participants stated that they perform it. It is followed by integration testing with 66%. The system test is applied by 52% of the participants, whereas the acceptance test is used by 40%. The responses show that only 2% perform a performance test in their MSSA projects (see Fig. 2f).

We inquired about the level of test automation in MSSA projects. We asked our participants to choose a number between 1 and 5, where 1 is the lowest and 5 is the highest level of automation. Most participants (34%) responded with 3, meaning they have a medium level of test automation in their projects. 30% of the participants chose 4, meaning there is a high level of automation, while 10% find the level of automation very high (level 5). 14% of the participants responded with 2, meaning there is some level of automation, whereas 12% indicated that testing is not automated (see Fig. 2g).

4.3 DevOps

We dedicated a section of the survey to inquire about the DevOps tools and technologies used in the MSSA projects in the industry. The first question was to inquire whether the participants' organizations have a dedicated DevOps team. The results show that the majority (82%) have such a team in their organization, whereas the remaining 18% do not. (see Fig. 3.a).

We asked the participants which tools and/or technologies they use for developing, testing, and deploying MSSA. We saw that it is very common to utilize more than one tool. Most participants (54%) stated that they use Jenkins. GitLab was the second most used tool, with 48%. These tools were followed by Circle CI with 18%, while 12% of the participants stated that they use Bamboo. 12% of the participants use other tools, including Azure DevOps and Bitbucket CI, whereas 12% do not use any tools for this purpose (see Fig. 3.b).

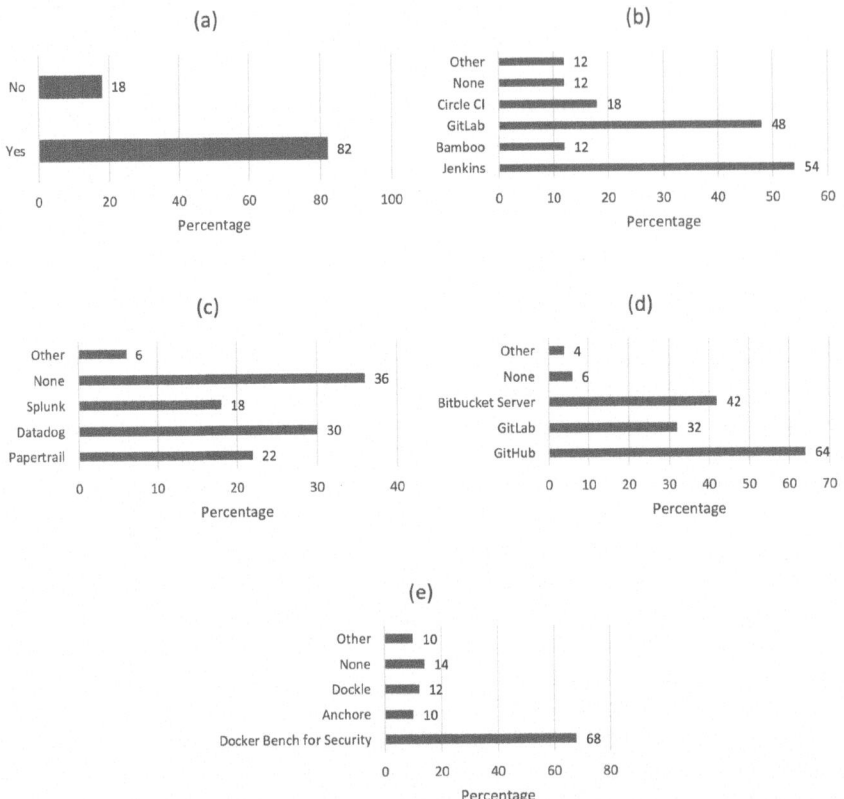

Fig. 3. The percentage of the responses regarding (a) whether the organization has a DevOps team, (b) the tool used for developing, testing, and deploying microservices, (c) the tool used to monitor and troubleshoot the environment, (d) the tool used to manage releases and version control, and (e) the tool used to ensure the security and compliance.

The next question was to inquire about the tools used to monitor and troubleshoot the environment. The results show that a big portion, 36%, stated that they do not use any tool for this purpose. The most used tool was Datadog, as 30% of the participants reported using it. 22% of the participants stated to use Papertrail while 18% stated to use Splunk. 6% of the participants use other tools such as Cloud Watch and Sentry (See Fig. 3.c).

We asked the participants which tools they use to manage releases and version control. The results show that GitHub is used by the majority of the participants, i.e., 64% use it. Bitbucket Server is the second most used tool, with 42%. According to the answers, GitLab is used by 32% of the participants. 4% answered that they use other tools, such as Azure DevOps, whereas only 6% of the participants stated that they do not use any tool for release management and version control (See Fig. 3.d).

The last question of the section was concerning security and compliance. The results show that the majority of the participants (68%) use Docker Bench for Security. 12% use Dockle, and 10% use Anchore. 10% of the participants use other tools, including Clair, whereas 14% do not use any tool for ensuring security and compliance in an MSSA project (See Fig. 3.e).

5 Discussion

Over the last three decades, the software industry has witnessed significant advancements in object-oriented projects. Consequently, Object-Oriented Analysis and Design (OOAD) techniques have become the prevailing standard worldwide. Despite the minimal documentation approach in agile development, OOAD has maintained its popularity. However, with the emergence of MSSA, we have started deviating from object-based decomposition principles. Even the fundamental abstraction we rely on today, known as the 'object,' is now subject to potential modifications.

This paper presented how Pakistani organizations perform analysis, design, test, and DevOps in their MSSA projects. Our results show that there is no standard approach, as proposed by the studies in the literature to be used on microservice decomposition [4, 20], utilized for these tasks among the participants. Pakistani organizations use what they are familiar with; they utilize traditional object-oriented analysis and design notations for their MSSA projects. On the other hand, they started to use some event-based methods to analyze the problem. Therefore, organizations have started exploring new analysis and design methods for MSSA projects.

The structural decompositions required by MSSA are quite different from those of OOAD-based decomposition. MSSA's analysis and design approach should meet characteristics such as small bounded context, asynchronous communication, loose coupling, cohesion, isolation, autonomy, composability, single responsibility, scalability, and fault tolerance. Overall, by its nature, OOAD may not have useful viewpoints to analyze and design an MSSA that meets these essential characteristics. Thus, we believe there is a need for new modeling approaches for the analysis and design that are compatible with the building blocks of MSSA, such as events [4, 20]. In [7], we proposed an event-oriented analysis and design (EOAD) methodology for MSAA.

Another interesting finding of our survey was that Pakistani organizations use mostly ER diagrams to represent the design. However, the usage of a single database is replaced by the structures in which each microservice is developed independently and has its own database. Furthermore, MSSA mainly adopts non-relational NoSQL databases as the nature of their distributed structures. The relational database was replaced with structures such as event queues. Therefore, a question arises: Have Pakistani organizations not fully migrated to MSSA yet?

We also compared the analysis and design methods utilized in Pakistan with those employed globally [9, 16] (see Table 2). The comparison shows that the results are parallel in general. This showed us that the methods in software management do not differ based on different regional demographics. Software management methods are employed globally.

As we added DevOps questions to the survey for the first time in this study, we couldn't compare the DevOps tools used by Pakistani organizations with the global

Table 2. Comparison between Pakistan's and global results.

Question	Pakistan	Global [9, 16]
Utilizing a standard process for software analysis	Yes (84%)	Yes (60%)
The notation used to depict the functional requirements	User story (70%)	User story (69%)
The notation used to represent the design	ER diagram (66%)	Sequence diagram (58%)
The method used to analyze the problem	Event-based modeling (46%)	Event storming (36%)
The notation used to show the analysis of the project	Flow chart (60%)	Flow chart (53%)
Focused test paradigm	Unit test (86%)	Unit test (90%)
The level of test automation	3 (34%)	4 (55%)

community. However, we observed that a significant majority of Pakistani organizations implement DevOps processes and have established a dedicated team for this purpose. Furthermore, we obtained that there are some de facto DevOps tools used in Pakistan. The literature discusses the relationship between MSSA and DevOps processes. Therefore, in future studies, a detailed DevOps survey could be globally employed in organizations that develop projects using MSSA in the industry.

Lastly, our study is not without limitations. The survey's participant size could be viewed as a limitation. We tried expanding the sample size while avoiding dominance by a single organization. This constraint stems from various factors, including the consideration of participants' experience, role, and organization size to ensure a diverse range. Consequently, we achieved a respectable representation, although the number of participants remained limited. Although it is difficult to generalize the results as best practices, we believe we provide a meaningful snapshot of Pakistan's software industry that utilizes MSSA.

6   Conclusion

MSSA is considered a popular and effective approach in software development. However, adopting microservices requires organizations to change their cultures. Software analysis and design techniques differ in MSSA projects. No de facto analysis and design process is similar to OOAD in the literature.

In this study, we surveyed to explore the analysis, design, test, and DevOps practices employed by organizations in Pakistan's software industry when developing MSSA projects. The results indicate that there is generally no consistent approach adopted for the analysis and design of MSSA projects among the participating organizations. It is observed that traditional object-oriented analysis and design methods are predominantly used in developing MSSA projects within these organizations. Weinberg stated,

'People choose the familiar over the comfortable' [21]. However, we believe there is a need to explore new analysis and design methods that result in a natural decomposition strategy for developing MSSA considering bounded context and event-based asynchronous communication. Therefore, further studies may explore a new analysis and design methodology for MSSA.

Supplementary Material

The survey questions and the raw survey data can be found at https://bit.ly/3rQAlAC.

Acknowledgments. This research is supported by The Scientific and Technological Research Council of Turkey (TUBITAK) ARDEB 1001 [Project number: 121E389] program.

References

1. Fowler, M., Lewis: Microservices. https://martinfowler.com/articles/microservices.html. Accessed 11 Mar 2021
2. Alshuqayran, N., Ali, N., Evans, R.: A systematic mapping study in microservice architecture. In: 2016 IEEE 9th International Conference on Service-Oriented Computing and Applications (SOCA), pp. 44–51 (2016). https://doi.org/10.1109/SOCA.2016.15
3. Larrucea, X., Santamaria, I., Colomo-Palacios, R., Ebert, C.: Microservices. IEEE Softw. **35**, 96–100 (2018). https://doi.org/10.1109/MS.2018.2141030
4. Bonér, J.: Reactive Microsystems. O'Reilly Inc, Sebastopol (2017)
5. Thönes, J.: Microservices. IEEE Softw. **32**, 116 (2015). https://doi.org/10.1109/MS.2015.11
6. Sampaio, A.R., et al.: Supporting microservice evolution. In: 2017 IEEE International Conference on Software Maintenance and Evolution (ICSME), pp. 539–543 (2017). https://doi.org/10.1109/ICSME.2017.63
7. Unlu, H., Tenekeci, S., Yıldız, A., Demirors, O.: Event oriented vs object oriented analysis for microservice architecture: an exploratory case study. In: 2021 47th Euromicro Conference on Software Engineering and Advanced Applications (SEAA), pp. 244–251 (2021). https://doi.org/10.1109/SEAA53835.2021.00038
8. Dragoni, N., et al.: Microservices: yesterday, today, and tomorrow. In: Mazzara, M., Meyer, B. (eds.) Present and Ulterior Software Engineering, pp. 195–216. Springer International Publishing, Cham (2017). https://doi.org/10.1007/978-3-319-67425-4_12
9. Ünlü, H., Kennouche, D.E., Soylu, G.K., Demirörs, O.: Microservice-based projects in agile world: a structured interview. Inf. Softw. Technol. **165**, 107334 (2024). https://doi.org/10.1016/j.infsof.2023.107334
10. Velepucha, V., Flores, P.: Monoliths to microservices - migration problems and challenges: A SMS. In: 2021 Second International Conference on Information Systems and Software Technologies (ICI2ST), pp. 135–142 (2021). https://doi.org/10.1109/ICI2ST51859.2021.00027
11. Doležal, J., Buchalcevová, A.: Migration from monolithic to microservice architecture: research of impacts on agility. IDIMT-2022 (2022)
12. Di Francesco, P., Lago, P., Malavolta, I.: Migrating towards microservice architectures: an industrial survey. In: 2018 IEEE International Conference on Software Architecture (ICSA), pp. 29–2909 (2018). https://doi.org/10.1109/ICSA.2018.00012
13. Waseem, M., Liang, P., Shahin, M.: A systematic mapping study on microservices architecture in DevOps. J. Syst. Softw. **170**, 110798 (2020). https://doi.org/10.1016/j.jss.2020.110798

14. Stahl, D., Martensson, T., Bosch, J.: Continuous practices and DevOps: beyond the buzz, what does it all mean? In: 2017 43rd Euromicro Conference on Software Engineering and Advanced Applications (SEAA), pp. 440–448 (2017). https://doi.org/10.1109/SEAA.2017. 8114695

15. Bilgin, B., Unlu, H., Demirörs, O.: Analysis and design of microservices: results from Turkey. In: 2020 Turkish National Software Engineering Symposium (UYMS), pp. 1–6 (2020). https:// doi.org/10.1109/UYMS50627.2020.9247022

16. Ünlü, H., Bilgin, B., Demirors, O.: A survey on organizational choices for microservice-based software architectures. Turkish J. Elect. Eng. Comput. Sci. **30**, 1187–1203 (2022). https://doi. org/10.55730/1300-0632.3843

17. Pakistan - Computer Software. https://www.trade.gov/country-commercial-guides/pakistan-computer-software. Accessed 22 July 2023

18. Shull, F., Singer, J., Sjøberg, D.I.K. (eds.): Guide to Advanced Empirical Software Engineering. Springer, London (2008). https://doi.org/10.1007/978-1-84800-044-5

19. Linåker, J., Sulaman, S.M., Maiani de Mello, R., Höst, M.: Guidelines for conducting surveys in software engineering (2015)

20. Richardson, C.: Microservices patterns: with examples in Java. Simon and Schuster (2018)

21. Weinberg, G.M.: Quality software management, vol. 1, systems thinking. Dorset House Publishing Co., Inc. (1992)

DevOps Patterns: A Rapid Review

Sebastian Copei[✉] and Jens Kosiol

Kassel University, Kassel, Germany
{sco,jens.kosiol}@uni-kassel.de

Abstract. The `DevOps` tool and technology landscape is large and complex. According to the CNCF Landscape, there are about 1196 Tools grouped into five categories, and 20 sub-categories. While CNCF also provides guidelines for each main category, patterns for `DevOps` are not covered. In this Rapid Review, we collect patterns that can be used for `DevOps` and map them onto the phases of the `DevOps` cycle for a better overview of when to use which pattern. In our primary search, we initially identified 193 papers, out of which we eventually selected eight for pattern extraction. We detected 52 patterns, which we grouped into seven categories. Moreover, we mapped these categories onto the phases of the `DevOps` cycle. We find that in each phase, at least one category maps. Furthermore, there is a near even distribution from patterns onto the phases except for one phase, to which only a single pattern could be mapped. Finally, we investigate whether the patterns can be flawlessly combined and which patterns are needed to provide a minimal technology stack to support the usage of `DevOps`. We also introduce a concrete sample stack for a simple scenario.

Keywords: DevOps · design patterns · architecture patterns · rapid review

1   Introduction

Referring to Ramtin Jabbari et al., *"DevOps is a development methodology aimed at bridging the gap between Development (Dev) and Operations emphasizing communication and collaboration, continuous integration, quality assurance, and delivery with automated deployment utilizing a set of development practices."* [17] Besides its technical aspects, `DevOps` is also an organizational pattern for company development and operation teams. To use `DevOps` in a company, the employees must be grouped into multi-functional teams and adopt agile development methods. In contrast to the traditional team layout where the developer and operator are strictly separated, the `DevOps` Engineer combines both roles. He can develop and roll out his software independently [1,16]. `DevOps` is associated with benefits like faster time to market or improved cross-team collaboration and communication [14,20]. The `DevOps` process is summarized in the `DevOps` development cycle (Fig. 1), based on the already known CI/CD cycle.

© The Author(s), under exclusive license to Springer Nature Switzerland AG 2024
B. Tekinerdoğan et al. (Eds.): ECSA 2023, LNCS 14590, pp. 33–50, 2024.
https://doi.org/10.1007/978-3-031-66326-0_3

Motivation. Despite the benefits of DevOps, its adoption is still ongoing and DevOps is not broadly applied. The greatest barriers for a broader adoption are a *lack of collaboration and communication, criticism practices, lack of management,* or *trust and confidence problems* on the cultural side. From the technical side, challenges could be a *lack of skill and knowledge,* a *lack of DevOps approach, complicated or legacy infrastructure, poor software,* or *security issues* [13,18]. There exists material designed to support the DevOps onboarding process. Process models like the DevOps maturity model try to support the general DevOps adoption process [8]. Moreover, the CNCF (Cloud Native Computing Foundation) provides a landscape map[1] for dozens of technologies grouped by categories like databases, logging, or service mesh. The landscape should help conceptualize a technology stack in a cloud environment. Still, the landscape only summarizes technologies and tools, and without general knowledge about DevOps and cloud architectures, it is challenging to select the appropriate technology for an application, as the technologies can have strong interdependencies and the general complexity is very high [30]. Thus, the difficulty of choosing the right technology for a certain set of requirements while adopting DevOps remains a pressing problem.

We conjecture that *design patterns*, rather than tools, provide a helpful approach for getting started with DevOps. Design patterns, popularized by the Gang of Four [15], provide solutions to recurring problems and tasks in software engineering on a higher level of abstraction than tools or coding guidelines. In the long run, we imagine an onboarding process, where engineers are suggested patterns that meet the (architectural) requirements of their project and are helped with building a technology stack that allows to implement the needed patterns.

In this work, we want to investigate whether the foundation for such a system has already been developed. While empirical evidence for their benefits could be more comprehensive [38], describing new patterns for emerging technologies has become a relevant topic in software engineering research. Thus, we expect a reasonable collection of patterns for DevOps to already exist in the academic literature. We perform a Rapid Review (RR) [10] to collect these patterns and investigate their interconnections and the respective roles they can play with reference to the DevOps cycle (see Fig. 1). Furthermore, we investigate whether it is already possible to assemble a minimal blueprint stack needed for DevOps from the extracted patterns. Besides the minimal stack, we also define a small use case and derive possible tools that implement the minimal stack to investigate the practicability of the identified patterns.

Related Work. With DevOps consolidating itself as a field, secondary studies, in particular, Systematic Literature Reviews (SLR), on various aspects of DevOps are a timely topic. A whole range of recent publications review the benefits of applying DevOps [14,20,28] or the challenges of a successful adoption [2–5,18,21,29]. There are also recent SLRs on the usage of DevOps in a specific application area, e.g., [23] (medicine), in combination with a certain technique/

---

[1] https://landscape.cncf.io/.

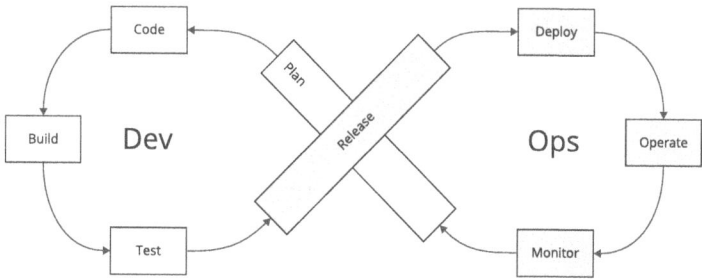

Fig. 1. DevOps cycle

technology, e.g. [36] (microservices) and [31] (machine learning), or with reference to a desired property, e.g., [22] (security). For the usage of patterns, there is an SLR to identify architectural patterns for Microservices [34]. However, no SLR specifically addresses patterns for `DevOps`.

Structure. The following section describes the methodology used for this paper. In Sect. 3, we present the results of the RR and discuss them. In Sect. 4, we examine the threats to the study's validity. Finally, Sect. 5 concludes and highlights our next steps.

2   Methodology

For the methodology of our work, we draw inspiration from the well-established guideline for conducting SLRs by Kitchenham and Charters [19]. As, for the time being, our goals are exploratory rather than analytical, we follow a simplified approach and perform a Rapid Review [10]. The main differences to Kitchenham and Charters' guideline are the following.

– Our research questions are exploratory rather than analytical. In particular, we do not follow the PICO (population, intervention, comparison, outcomes) structure for our questions.
– We use a rather basic search string for our search.
– Study selection and data extraction is performed by a single person. A second person merely performs a consistency check for a subset of the data.
– Instead of developing and applying quality criteria for study selection, we restrict ourselves to academic literature and exclude grey literature (as common for Rapid Reviews [10]). Moreover, we restrict our search to the relevant digital libraries for software engineering and perform snowballing but do not search pre-print servers like arXiv[2] or contact established researchers from our field of study.
– Consequently, we present a simplified research protocol [11] that provides an overview over all extracted studies, reasons for exclusion, and extracted data but cannot give, e.g., quality criteria.

---

[2] https://arxiv.org/.

2.1   Research Questions

In this study, we want to collect patterns that help to create minimal technology stacks to apply DevOps. To reach this goal, we will answer the following research questions:

RQ1 What patterns are described in the literature that can be used for DevOps?

    RQ1a Does the literature already group the patterns?

    RQ1b Can patterns without a group be added to existing categories, or must additional categories be defined?

RQ2 Can the identified patterns be combined, or are there any that mutually exclude each other?

RQ3 Are the identified patterns or categories related in any form to the phases of the DevOps cycle?

We want to summarize the existing research for DevOps patterns by answering the first question. To also address a categorization of these patterns, we added the two subquestions, RQ1a and RQ1b. With the second question, RQ2, we want to ensure that at least a single selection of the patterns exists to derive a blueprint stack for DevOps. With the third research question, RQ3, we aim to investigate whether the identified patterns cover the entire DevOps cycle or only a part of it. We aim to identify a set of patterns that are at least necessary to assist in implementing DevOps.

2.2   Search Strategy and Search String

Figure 2 shows our steps during the search process. Beginning with the initial search, we merged the results and eliminated duplicates. To the resulting set of papers, we have applied our inclusion and exclusion criteria. We read the full text of the remaining papers and decided which papers should be used in the study. As a last step, we have done snowballing on the finally picked papers. For the initial search, a combination of the keywords *devops pattern(s)* and *devops design pattern(s)* builds the used search string, shown in Listing 3.1.

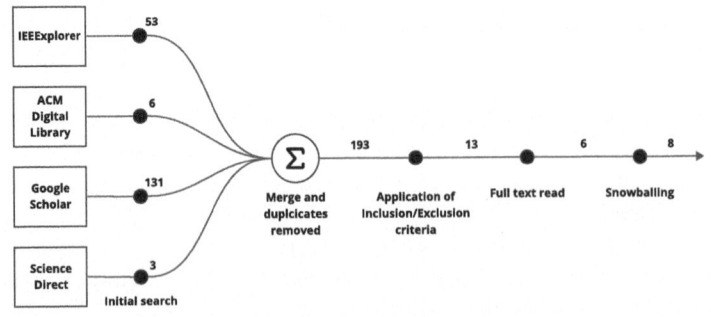

Fig. 2. Overview of the search process and selection process

Listing 3.1. Search string

```
"devops  pattern"  OR  "devops  patterns"  OR
"devops  design  pattern"  OR  "devops  design  patterns"
```

A first test with this simple search string already retrieved papers that use near-synonyms like *architecture* instead of *(design) pattern* in the abstract and/or title. Therefore, we confined ourselves to that search string. We searched the following digital libraries, which are the relevant digital libraries for Software Engineering [19], for this string:

1. IEEExplore (www.ieeexplore.ieee.org)
2. ACM Digital library (www.dl.acm.org)
3. Google Scholar (www.scholar.google.com)
4. ScienceDirect (www.sciencedirect.com)

2.3   Inclusion and Exclusion Criteria

We defined inclusion and exclusion criteria to decide whether we consider a paper for our study. We include a paper if it fulfills each of the following criteria:

– Published between 2007 and October 2023.
– Written in English.
– Peer-reviewed paper.
– The paper describes or introduces one or more patterns that could be useful for `DevOps`.

Concerning publication date, we only include papers published between January 2007 and October 2023. Patrick Debois coined the term `DevOps` around 2007 [9,12,26], so we have used 2007 as the earliest time constraint. We performed the search in October 2023, which provides the upper bound for publication of considered papers. We identify a procedure as a *pattern* if the authors provide a clear problem description and a replicable solution for the corresponding problem. The authors should either describe their patterns in the known structure of context, problem, forces, and solution [24,37], or they can develop the patterns in the context of a use case and describe the usage and the problem that was solved. Finally, to be considered for extraction, a pattern must have a clear connection to `DevOps`. For example, the well-known singleton pattern is not directly associated with `DevOps`. In contrast, the design pattern Circuit Breaker is related to web services and resiliency, which provides an association to `DevOps`. We exclude a paper if it fulfills one of the following criteria:

– The paper presents or demonstrates tools and technologies without any abstraction into a reusable pattern.
– The paper presents a tutorial or example for implementing `DevOps`, again without abstracting the taken approach into a reusable pattern.

With regard to these criteria, we first read the title and abstract of each paper (and sometimes the introduction and conclusion) to pre-select the dataset. Subsequently, we read the full text of the remaining papers and rechecked the criteria. The first author of this paper performed this selection process. The second author reevaluated the criteria on a randomly selected set of 9 extracted papers to prevent selection bias and validate our decisions. No conflicting decisions occurred.

2.4   Data Extraction

From the finally selected papers, we first extracted the categories the authors used to group their patterns if categories were present. Afterwards, we collected all the described patterns. If the authors did not directly categorize patterns, we sorted them into the categories we extracted beforehand. To better understand the connection between the identified patterns and DevOps, we tried to map the patterns onto the different phases of the DevOps cycle (see Fig. 1). For clarity, we mapped the categories and not the patterns.

3   Results and Discussion

Table 1 presents the outcomes of the initial search. Upon applying the search string to the digital libraries, 193 papers were identified. Our first screening phase reduced the number of papers to 13. After thoroughly reading the complete papers, the count was narrowed down to six. Via snowballing, we identified two additional papers and received a final count of eight papers in the study. Table 2 displays the identified papers, denoted by paper IDs P[1–8], for improved readability in subsequent descriptions. The patterns described in the papers do not relate directly to DevOps but to microservices architecture. Nevertheless, the identified patterns can also be applied in DevOps. The papers P1 and P2 describe pattern languages for the cloud and microservices. The paper P3 introduces a pattern map for software orchestration on the cloud. Paper P4 collects the architectural patterns used in open-source projects realized with microservices. In paper P5, the authors describe a single pattern to handle the changes of software specifications during the software lifecycle. Paper P6 describes the

Table 1. Paper sources

Library	Found	Criteria applied	Full text	Snowballing
IEEExplore	53	6	0	
ACM Digital library	6	3	3	
Google Scholar	131	4	3	
ScienceDirect	3	0	0	
Total	193	13	6	**8**

usage of the micro-frontends pattern. The steps to migrate from a monolithic architecture to a microservice-based architecture are described in paper P7. The authors of paper P8 perform a Systematic Mapping Study on architectural patterns for microservices.

Table 2. Included papers

Title	ID/Reference
Overview of a Pattern Language for Engineering Software for the Cloud	P1 [33]
Implementation Patterns for Microservices Architecture	P2 [7]
Patterns for Software Orchestration on the Cloud	P3 [32]
Actual Use of Architectural Patterns in Microservices-Based Open Source Projects	P4 [25]
Specification in Continuous Software Development	P5 [35]
Micro-frontends: application of microservices to web front-ends	P6 [27]
Microservice migration pattern	P7 [6]
Architectural Patterns for Microservices: a Systematic Mapping Study	P8 [34]

3.1 Research Question 1: What Patterns are Described in the Literature that Can Be Used for DevOps?

In total, we identified 52 patterns. Table 3 shows the number of patterns per category, which we introduce in the following. At first, we collected all already grouped patterns, as described in Sect. 3.2. We combined patterns with different names but identical meanings during this step. For example, in P3, the authors describe the pattern *API Management*. In P4 and P8, this pattern is called *API Gateway*; in P7, it is described as *Introduce edge server*. We list the pattern only once (under the name *API Gateway*). After extracting the patterns that had already been categorized in the literature, we proceeded with the remaining patterns from P5, P6, and P7. We present the final list of all identified categories, patterns, and source papers in Table 4. A short description of each pattern is available as part of our research protocol [11].

Table 3. Absolute count of pattern per category

Category	Number of patterns
(C1) Automated Infrastructure Management	6
(C2) Development	9
(C3) Discovery and Communication	5
(C4) Isolated Execution	4
(C5) Monitoring	8
(C6) Orchestration and Supervision	19
(C7) Requirements	1
Total	52

Table 4. Identified patterns grouped by categories

Category	Pattern	Paper
(C1) Automated Infrastructure Management		
	Automated Orchestration	P3, P7
	Automated Scalability	P1
	Complete Code Ownership	P3
	Continuous Deployment	P3
	Continuous Integration	P3, P4, P7
	Infrastructure as Code	P1, P3
(C2) Development		
	Backend for Frontend	P2, P4
	Circuit Breaker	P4, P7
	Micro-Frontends	P6
	Microservices	P2
	Native Mobile Application	P2
	Near Cache	P2
	Page Cache	P2, P4
	Results Cache	P2, P4
	Single Page Application	P2
(C3) Discovery and Communication		
	Automated Master Election	P3
	Local Reverse Proxy	P1, P3
	Message System	P1, P3, P8
	Service Discovery	P4
	Service Registry	P2, P4, P7, P8
(C4) Isolated Execution		
	Environment-based Configuration	P3
	Locale Volumes	P3
	One Container per Application	P3
	Single service per Host	P8
(C5) Monitoring		
	Alarms	P3, P7
	Correlation ID	P2
	External Monitoring	P1, P4
	Health Check	P4
	Log Aggregation	P1, P2, P3, P4
	Monitor Everything	P3, P7
	Preemptive Logging	P1
	Real Time Analytics	P3
(C6) Orchestration and Supervision		
	API Gateway	P3, P4, P7, P8
	Automated Recovery	P1
	Containerization	P1, P3, P4, P7
	Database cluster	P8
	Database per Service	P4, P8
	Deployment Manager	P3
	Deployment Strategies	P3
	Document Store	P2
	Fault Injection	P1, P3
	Job Scheduling	P1, P3, P4
	Key Value Store	P2, P4
	Load Balancer	P4, P7
	Multiple service per Host	P8
	Orchestration by Resource Offering	P3
	Orchestration Manager	P1
	Scalable Store	P2, P4
	Shared database server	P8
	Self-Healing	P3
	System-wide Resiliency	P3
(C7) Requirements		
	Continuous Software Design Specification	P5

3.2   Research Question 1a: Does the Literature Already Group the Patterns?

The papers P1, P2, P3, P4, and P8 use categories to group their identified/described patterns. We extracted all named categories and compared them and the patterns grouped by them. We reused seven from the 28 named categories for our study to categorize our identified patterns. Table 5 lists all categories and briefly describes whether or not we used the category and why not. The originally extracted 28 categories are *Automated Infrastructure Management, Orchestration and Supervision, Monitoring* and *Discovery and Communication* from P1, *Modern Web Architecture, Microservices Architecture, Scalable Store* and *Microservices DevOps* from P2, *Development, Deployment, Supervision, Monitoring, Discovery and Application Support* and *Isolated Execution* from P3, *IoT, DevOps, Front-End, Back-End, Orchestration, Migration, Communication, Behaviour, Design, Mitigation, Deployment* from P4 and *Orchestration and Coordination, Deployment* and *Data Storage* from P8.

We used the four categories from P1 as a starting point for our grouping. We dismissed the categories from P2 and moved the patterns to the categories *Development* from P3 and *Orchestration and Supervision* and *Monitoring* from P1. The original categories from P2 were *Modern Web Architecture Patterns, Microservices Architecture Patterns, Scalable Store Patterns,* and *Microservices DevOps Patterns.* Since the other papers presented more suitable categories for the patterns, we decided to drop the categories from paper P2. We combined the other categories, *Deployment,* and *Supervision,* with the category *Orchestration and Supervision* and *Discovery and Application Support,* with the category *Discovery and Communication* both from P1. The last categories from P3, *Monitoring* and *Isolated Execution,* are used for the study. Since the authors of P4 do not provide patterns for their categories *IoT, DevOps, Front-End, Behaviour,* and *Design,* we neither used these categories. Patterns from the category Back-*End* are moved to *Development* from P3, patterns from *Orchestration* to *Orchestration and Supervision, Migration* and *Communication* to *Discovery and Communication* from P1, and *Mitigation* to *Monitoring* from P3. In contrast to the *Deployment* category from P3, we moved the pattern from this *Deployment* category to the *Development* category from P3. The authors of P4 grouped patterns in the *Deployment* category, which the authors of the other papers grouped into the *Development* category. Finally, we moved the pattern from the categories *Orchestration and Coordination* and *Deployment* to *Orchestration and Supervision* from P1 and *Data Storage* to *Development* from P3. This procedure leads at this point to the six categories *Automated Infrastructure Management, Development, Discovery and Communication, Isolated Execution, Monitoring, Orchestration and Supervision,* which we will use to group our identified patterns. To give more insight into our grouping process, we briefly describe each category we extracted and provide examples of patterns for the categories.

Table 5. Named categories by papers

Paper	Category	Used in study
P1		
	Automated Infrastructure Management	Yes
	Orchestration and Supervision	Yes
	Monitoring	Yes
	Discovery and Communication	Yes
P2		
	Modern Web Architecture	No, patterns moved to Development
	Microservices Architecture	No, patterns moved to Development
	Scalable Store	No, patterns moved to Development
	Microservices DevOps	No, patterns moved to Development
P3		
	Development	Yes
	Deployment	No, patterns moved to Orchestration and Supervision
	Supervision	No, patterns moved to Orchestration and Supervision
	Monitoring	Yes
	Discovery and Application Support	No, patterns moved to Discovery and Communication
	Isolated Execution	Yes
P4		
	IoT	No, no patterns in this category
	DevOps	No, no patterns in this category
	Front-End	No, no patterns in this category
	Back-End	No, patterns moved to Development
	Orchestration	No, patterns moved to Orchestration and Supervision
	Migration	No, patterns moved to Discovery and Communication
	Communication	No, patterns moved to Discovery and Communication
	Behaviour	No, no patterns in this category
	Design	No, no patterns in this category
	Mitigation	No, patterns moved to Monitoring
	Deployment	No, patterns moved to Development
P8		
	Orchestration and Coordination	No, patterns moved to Orchestration and Supervision
	Deployment	No, patterns moved to Orchestration and Supervision
	Data Storage	No, patterns moved to Development

Automated Infrastructure Management (C1) combines patterns to set up the infrastructure needed for a cloud. They help by tackling issues like scalability, reliability, and resilience. For instance, the *Infrastructure as Code* (IaC) pattern is widely used for automating the creation of virtual machines and infrastructure deterministic behavior akin to containers.

Development (C2) groups patterns that can be used directly during the development of applications intended to be deployed in a cloud environment. The patterns can be used for frontends, backends, or service-based applications. The *Microservices* pattern in this category represents a software architecture for service-oriented systems, marking the next evolutionary step after the service-oriented architecture. With this pattern, services are deployed as independent and separate artifacts.

Discovery and Communication (C3) patterns are essential for a distributed service architecture. In contrast to the *Development* patterns, these patterns aim to resolve issues regarding the data exchange between services. For example, the *Message System* pattern should be combined with the *Microservices* pattern to ensure service independence. The advantages of *Microservices* can be exploited by utilizing an asynchronous event-based message system.

Isolated Execution (C4) contains patterns for creating containerized applications. In a cloud environment, multiple applications are hosted. The *Environment-based Configuration* pattern can be employed to guarantee the isolation of these applications. This pattern necessitates the separation of applications using, for instance, namespaces, with each namespace having its own set of configurations, such as database credentials. This approach significantly enhances the security of all applications.

Monitoring (C5) contains patterns to optimize applications' operation and help find bugs and failures during runtime. Collecting log data alone is insufficient for detecting fraud within an application or a large system comprising thousands of services. However, implementing the *Log Aggregation* pattern makes it possible to extract valuable information regarding the status of individual services or applications. For instance, by leveraging AI techniques, anomalies can be detected by analyzing the log message stream.

Orchestration and Supervision (C6) bundles patterns for the distribution and management of containerized applications. This also includes patterns that increase resilience and reliability. The patterns within this category exhibit emergent effects. A *Deployment Manager*, in isolation, is not functional without *Deployment Strategies* or a *Job Scheduler*. However, when combined with the *Containerization* and *Orchestration Manager* patterns, these patterns demonstrate the advantages of a cloud-based environment, exemplified by technologies like Kubernetes.

3.3 Research Question 1b: Can Patterns Without a Group Be Added to Existing Categories, or Must Additional Categories Be Defined?

By collecting and summarizing these categories, we implicitly grouped the patterns from the papers P1, P2, P3, P4, and P8. We then sorted the patterns described in P6 and P7 into these six categories. Since the pattern described in P5 does not fit into any of the extracted categories, we group it into a new seventh category that we call *Requirements*. For completeness, we describe this new category in the same way as the other ones.

Requirements (C7) groups patterns that support the communication between all affected stakeholders during a software development project, like *Continuous Software Design Specification*.

All in all, we reused six categories from the literature and added a seventh. The seventh was added because we could not correctly group the *Continuous Software Design Specification* pattern into the existing ones.

3.4   Research Question 2: Can the Identified Patterns Be Combined, or Are There Any that Mutually Exclude Each Other?

Comparing the individual patterns, we detected conflicting ones. From C6, the patterns *Database cluster*, *Database per Service*, and *Shared database server* mutually exclude each other. The three patterns describe different ways to provide a database. In a *Database cluster*, data is replicated on multiple nodes to provide high availability of the stored data. These clusters can be hosted on-cloud or on-premise. Multiple services could use the *Database cluster* to read and write data. With a *Shared database server*, multiple services also use the same database, but the data are not replicated onto multiple nodes. When developing a microservice-based application, the *Database per Service* pattern can prevent the mixing up of data that does not belong to the same service. Inside of each category, the other patterns are combinable. Across the categories, the patterns *Single service per Host* and *Multiple service per Host* exclude each other. While the *Single service per Host* pattern requires that on each host, only a single service or application is hosted, on the other hand, the *Multiple service per Host* allows the hosting of multiple services and applications on a single host. We could not detect further conflicts between patterns.

3.5   Research Question 3: Are the Identified Patterns or Categories Related in Any Form to the Phases of the DevOps Cycle?

Because we could not identify papers investigating the relationship between patterns and the DevOps Cycle, we tried to map each of the found patterns from Table 4 onto one of the phases of the DevOps cycle (see Fig. 1). Because of the number of patterns, we decided to map the categories. Figure 3 shows a possible mapping of the pattern categories onto the DevOps cycle. While we could map *C2*, *C3*, *C4*, *C5*, and *C7* onto exactly one phase, *C1* and *C6* could be mapped onto multiple phases. The mapping of the categories *C2*, *C5*, and *C7* emerged from the naming of categories and phases. The categories *C3* and *C4* contain patterns used to operate an application in a cloud environment. For this reason, we mapped these categories onto the *Operate* phase. In category *C6*, the patterns are helpful for deployment, like *Deployment Manager*, *Deployment Strategies*, or *Job Scheduling* and operation, like *Load Balancer*, *Self-Healing*, or *System-wide Resiliency*. Therefore, we mapped the category *C6* onto the phases *Deploy* and *Operate*. Category *C1* contains patterns for the process of CI/CD. Thus, we mapped this category on the *Build*, *Test* (CI), *Release*, and *Deploy* (CD) phases.

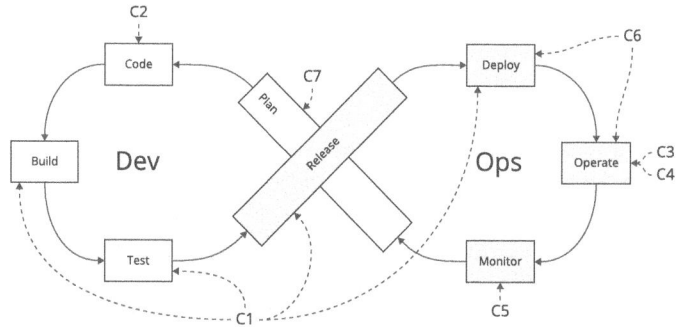

Fig. 3. DevOps cycle with pattern category mapping

The categories *C1* and *C6* could be further divided into sub-categories and then mapped to individual phases. However, despite the distribution seeming to be near even, the phase of *Plan* only has mapped a single pattern. From this, we conclude that there is a need for more patterns applicable to the *Plan* phase.

3.6 Discussion: What is a Possible Minimal Stack to Apply DevOps?

In Table 6, we present the patterns minimally needed in each phase according to our opinion to create a minimal stack. As we have only a single pattern for the *Plan* phase, a minimal stack requires a sufficient project management tool, like *Scrum* or *Kanban*. Although we have identified patterns in the *Code* phase,

Table 6. Patterns minimally needed to enable DevOps

Phase	Patterns	Comment
Plan		Not enough patterns identified in study
Code		Should not be generalized to maintain flexibility
Build		
	Continuous Integration	
Test		
	Continuous Integration	
Release		
	Continuous Deployment	
Deploy		
	Automated Orchestration	
	Containerization	
	Continuous Deployment	
Operate		
	Load Balancer	
	Local Reverse Proxy	
	Locale Volumes	
	Orchestration Manager	
Monitor		
	Alarms	
	Health Check	
	Log Aggregation	

we do not want to fixate any patterns for the development. Patterns used in the following phases depend on decisions made during the *Code* phase. For example, if a team decides to use *Microservices*, more patterns are needed for communication and orchestration of these services. These patterns would not be required if the team used a monolithic architecture. With the patterns *Continuous Integration* and *Continuous Deployment*, the phases of *Build*, *Test*, and *Release* are covered. In the *Deploy* phase, the *Automated Orchestration* and *Containerization* patterns need to be applied besides the *Continuous Deployment* pattern. A deployed workload must be able to be deployed with other services available as containers. During the *Operate* phase, incoming traffic must be directed to the correct service. Therefore, the *Load Balancer* and *Local Reverse Proxy* patterns are needed. The *Local Volumes* pattern should be used to preserve the state of any databases. The *Orchestration Manager* pattern is also crucial for deploying a service on a host with sufficient hardware resources for the *Operate* phase. *Alarms*, *Health Check*, and *Log Aggregation* patterns must be used in the *Monitor* phase to detect errors as soon as possible. With this minimal set of patterns, it is now possible to define technology stacks for scenarios with different complexity.

Example application A team wants to implement a simple application that collects data from soccer games and visualizes the ratio between attempts to make a goal and actual goals for each match in a session. The team uses a monolithic architecture with a single backend and a separate frontend application. To apply the *Continuous Integration* and *Continuous Deployment* pattern, they may use the integrated tool *GitHub Actions* if they use *GitHub* as their repository tool. To enable the patterns *Automated Orchestration*, *Containerization*, *Health Check*, and *Orchestration Manager*, *Docker* would be suitable. For traffic routing, *nginx* could be used for the *Load Balancer* and *Local Reverse Proxy* patterns. Finally, the ELK (*elasticsearch*, *logstash* and *kibana*) stack could be used to apply *Alarms* and *Log Aggregation* patterns.

However, it is important to note that aspects such as resilience, scalability, and security still need to be fully addressed in this minimal scenario. The identified patterns can be instrumental in addressing these concerns. For example, patterns like *Circuit Breaker*, *Automated Recovery*, *Self-Healing*, and *System-wide Resilience* can be employed to enhance resilience. Like the example, it is now possible to define further stacks for other complex scenarios.

4 Threats to Validity

Our threats to validity arise from the taken simplified approach that was laid out at the beginning of Sect. 2. Our simple search string and restriction to digital libraries make it possible that we missed research papers reporting relevant patterns. However, we additionally performed snowballing, controlled our search string to also retrieve papers that use (near) synonyms, and searched Google Scholar that covers pre-print servers like HAL and arXiv. Thus, we deem the risk of missed papers to be minimal.

Next, the first author performed study selection and data extraction alone, which is considered to be a practice that might introduce selection bias. To reduce the risk, the second author double checked a randomly selected set of papers for inclusion and we obtained perfect accordance. Moreover, given the exploratory nature of our research questions, the risks of wrongly excluding papers or making mistakes in data extraction seem to be minimal.

Our greatest threat to validity is the exclusion of grey literature. As `DevOps` is a topic where practice rushes ahead of academia, it is quite possible that we missed trends from the industry.

Summarizing, by design of our study it is possible that we missed individual relevant patterns. In particular, we might have missed patterns that are employed in practice without having been presented in academic publications. However, additional patterns just support our idea that approaching the `DevOps` onboarding problem via patterns might be a viable option.

5 Conclusion and Future Work

In this paper, we conducted a Rapid Review to identify patterns that can help to create stacks for implementing `DevOps`. We extracted a set of categories and used these for grouping the identified patterns. After that, we named patterns that mutually exclude each other. Further, we mapped the categories to the `DevOps` cycle to identify any relations between the patterns and the `DevOps` cycle. We observed a relation between the extracted patterns and the `DevOps` cycle. With this knowledge, we defined a minimal set of patterns to apply `DevOps`. With a short example, we derived a simple technology stack that could be used to implement the minimal set of patterns. However, the actual usability of possible derivable stacks needs to be investigated. Also, whether these patterns can help apply `DevOps` still needs to be determined. Our next step will be to identify a set of tools for each pattern. We aim to create best practice guides for `DevOps` migration or initial onboarding by mapping these tools to the corresponding patterns. By mapping these tools to the related patterns, we intend to refine these guides into tool and technology stacks that can be readily implemented. These stacks should address a range of project sizes and business scales, from small to large.

Acknowledgements. We are very thankful for the constructive criticism of the anonymous reviewers that helped us to considerably improve the presentation of this paper.

References

1. Agrawal, P., Rawat, N.: DevOps, a new approach to cloud development & testing. In: 2019 International Conference on Issues and Challenges in Intelligent Computing Techniques (ICICT), vol. 1, pp. 1–4 (2019). https://doi.org/10.1109/ICICT46931.2019.8977662

2. Akbar, M.A., Rafi, S., Alsanad, A.A.-A., Qadri, S.F., Alsanad, A., Alothaim, A.: Toward successful DevOps: a decision-making framework. IEEE Access **10**, 51343–51362 (2022). https://doi.org/10.1109/ACCESS.2022.3174094

3. Amaro, R., Pereira, R., da Silva, M.M.: Capabilities and practices in devops: a multivocal literature review. IEEE Trans. Softw. Eng. **49**(2), 883–901 (2023). https://doi.org/10.1109/TSE.2022.3166626

4. Azad, N., Hyrynsalmi, S.: DevOps critical success factors – a systematic literature review. Inf. Softw. Technol. **157**, 107150 (2023). https://doi.org/10.1016/j.infsof.2023.107150

5. Badshah, S., Khan, A.A., Khan, B.: Towards process improvement in DevOps: a systematic literature review. In: Li, J., Jaccheri, L., Dingsøyr, T., Chitchyan, R. (eds.) EASE '20: Evaluation and Assessment in Software Engineering, Trondheim, Norway, 15–17 April 2020, pp. 427–433. ACM (2020). https://doi.org/10.1145/3383219.3383280

6. Balalaie, A., Heydarnoori, A., Jamshidi, P., Tamburri, D.A., Lynn, T.: Microservices migration patterns. Softw. Pract. Exp. **48**(11), 2019–2042 (2018). https://doi.org/10.1002/spe.2608

7. Brown, K., Woolf, B.: Implementation patterns for microservices architectures. In: Proceedings of the 23rd Conference on Pattern Languages of Programs. PLoP '16. The Hillside Group, USA (2016)

8. Bucena, I., Kirikova, M.: Simplifying the DevOps adoption process. In: BIR Workshops (2017). https://api.semanticscholar.org/CorpusID:10430574

9. Buchanan, I.: History of DevOps. https://www.atlassian.com/devops/what-is-devops/history-of-devops. Accessed 11 Mar 2024

10. Cartaxo, B., Pinto, G., Soares, S.: Rapid reviews in software engineering. In: Felderer, M., Travassos, G.H. (eds.) Contemporary Empirical Methods in Software Engineering, pp. 357–384. Springer, Cham (2020). https://doi.org/10.1007/978-3-030-32489-6_13

11. Copei, S., Kosiol, J.: Research Protocol for "DevOps Patterns: A Systematic Literature Review", December 2023. https://doi.org/10.5281/zenodo.10224501

12. Debois, P.: Patrick Debois – Speaker Bio. https://www.jedi.be/bio/. Accessed 11 Mar 2024

13. Erich, F.M.A., Amrit, C., Daneva, M.: A qualitative study of DevOps usage in practice. J. Softw. Evol. Process. **29**(6), e1885 (2017). https://doi.org/10.1002/smr.1885

14. Faustino, J.P., Adriano, D., Amaro, R., Pereira, R., da Silva, M.M.: DevOps benefits: a systematic literature review. Softw. Pract. Exp. **52**(9), 1905–1926 (2022). https://doi.org/10.1002/spe.3096

15. Gamma, E., Helm, R., Johnson, R., Vlissides, J.: Design Patterns: Elements of Reusable Object-Oriented Software. Addison-Wesley, Boston (1994)

16. Gokarna, M., Singh, R.: DevOps: a historical review and future works. In: 2021 International Conference on Computing, Communication, and Intelligent Systems (ICCCIS), pp. 366–371 (2021). https://doi.org/10.1109/ICCCIS51004.2021.9397235

17. Jabbari, R., bin Ali, N., Petersen, K., Tanveer, B.: What is DevOps? A systematic mapping study on definitions and practices. In: Proceedings of the Scientific Workshop Proceedings of XP2016. XP '16 Workshops, New York, NY, USA. Association for Computing Machinery (2016). https://doi.org/10.1145/2962695.2962707
18. Khan, M.S., Khan, A.W., Khan, F., Khan, M.A., Whangbo, T.K.: Critical challenges to adopt DevOps culture in software organizations: a systematic review. IEEE Access **10**, 14339–14349 (2022). https://doi.org/10.1109/ACCESS.2022.3145970
19. Kitchenham, B., Charters, S.: Guidelines for performing systematic literature reviews in software engineering (2007). https://www.elsevier.com/__data/promis_misc/525444systematicreviewsguide.pdf
20. Lazuardi, M., Raharjo, T., Hardian, B., Simanungkalit, T.: Perceived benefits of DevOps implementation in organization: a systematic literature review. In: ICSIE 2021: 10th International Conference on Software and Information Engineering, Cairo, Egypt, 12–14 November 2021, pp. 10–16. ACM (2021). https://doi.org/10.1145/3512716.3512718
21. Leite, L.A.F., Rocha, C., Kon, F., Milojicic, D.S., Meirelles, P.: A survey of DevOps concepts and challenges. ACM Comput. Surv. **52**(6), 127:1–127:35 (2020). https://doi.org/10.1145/3359981
22. Leppänen, T., Honkaranta, A., Costin, A.: Trends for the DevOps security. A systematic literature review. In: Shishkov, B. (ed.) BMSD 2022. LNBIP, vol. 453, pp. 200–217. Springer, Cham (2022). https://doi.org/10.1007/978-3-031-11510-3_12
23. Lie, M.F., Sánchez-Gordón, M., Palacios, R.C.: DevOps in an ISO 13485 regulated environment: a multivocal literature review. In: Baldassarre, M.T., Lanubile, F., Kalinowski, M., Sarro, F. (eds.) ESEM '20: ACM/IEEE International Symposium on Empirical Software Engineering and Measurement, Bari, Italy, 5–7 October 2020, pp. 9:1–9:11. ACM (2020). https://doi.org/10.1145/3382494.3410679
24. Meszaros, G.: A pattern language for pattern writing. https://hillside.net/index.php/a-pattern-language-for-pattern-writing. Accessed 11 Mar 2024
25. Márquez, G., Astudillo, H.: Actual use of architectural patterns in microservices-based open source projects. In: 2018 25th Asia-Pacific Software Engineering Conference (APSEC), pp. 31–40 (2018). https://doi.org/10.1109/APSEC.2018.00017
26. Odazie, D., Iheanacho, A.: A Brief History of DevOps and Its Impact on Software Development (2023). https://everythingdevops.dev/a-brief-history-of-devops-and-its-impact-on-software-development/. Accessed 11 Mar 2024
27. Pavlenko, A., Askarbekuly, N., Megha, S., Mazzara, M.: Micro-frontends: application of microservices to web front-ends. J. Internet Serv. Inf. Secur. **10**(2), 49–66 (2020)
28. Plant, O.H., van Hillegersberg, J., Aldea, A.: How DevOps capabilities leverage firm competitive advantage: a systematic review of empirical evidence. In: Almeida, J.P.A., Bork, D., Guizzardi, G., Montali, M., Proper, H.A., Sales, T.P. (eds.) 23rd IEEE Conference on Business Informatics. CBI 2021, Bolzano, Italy, 1–3 September 2021, vol. 1, pp. 141–150. IEEE (2021). https://doi.org/10.1109/CBI52690.2021.00025
29. Rafi, S., Wu, Y., Akbar, M.A.: RMDevOps: a road map for improvement in DevOps activities in context of software organizations. In: Li, J., Jaccheri, L., Dingsøyr, T., Chitchyan, R. (eds.) EASE '20: Evaluation and Assessment in Software Engineering, Trondheim, Norway, 15–17 April 2020, pp. 413–418. ACM (2020). https://doi.org/10.1145/3383219.3383278

30. Rosilier, A., Demir, M.A., Prevost, J.J.: Automated consulting for cloud native architectures. In: 2022 17th Annual System of Systems Engineering Conference (SOSE), pp. 472–477 (2022). https://doi.org/10.1109/SOSE55472.2022.9812695

31. Rzig, D.E., Hassan, F., Kessentini, M.: An empirical study on ML DevOps adoption trends, efforts, and benefits analysis. Inf. Softw. Technol. **152**, 107037 (2022). https://doi.org/10.1016/j.infsof.2022.107037

32. Sousa, T.B., Correia, F.F., Ferreira, H.S.: Patterns for software orchestration on the cloud. In: Proceedings of the 22nd Conference on Pattern Languages of Programs. PLoP '15. The Hillside Group, USA (2015)

33. Sousa, T.B., Ferreira, H.S., Correia, F.F.: Overview of a pattern language for engineering software for the cloud. In: Proceedings of the 25th Conference on Pattern Languages of Programs. PLoP '18. The Hillside Group, USA (2020)

34. Taibi, D., Lenarduzzi, V., Pahl, C.: Architectural patterns for microservices: a systematic mapping study. In: Muñoz, V.M., Ferguson, D., Helfert, M., Pahl, C. (eds.) Proceedings of the 8th International Conference on Cloud Computing and Services Science. CLOSER 2018, Funchal, Madeira, Portugal, 19–21 March 2018, pp. 221–232. SciTePress (2018). https://doi.org/10.5220/0006798302210232

35. Theunissen, T., Van Heesch, U.: Specification in continuous software development. In: Proceedings of the 22nd European Conference on Pattern Languages of Programs. EuroPLoP '17. Association for Computing Machinery, New York, NY, USA (2017). https://doi.org/10.1145/3147704.3147709

36. Waseem, M., Liang, P., Shahin, M.: A systematic mapping study on microservices architecture in DevOps. J. Syst. Softw. **170**, 110798 (2020). https://doi.org/10.1016/j.jss.2020.110798

37. Wellhausen, T., Fiesser, A.: How to write a pattern? A rough guide for first-time pattern authors. In: Proceedings of the 16th European Conference on Pattern Languages of Programs. EuroPLoP '11. Association for Computing Machinery, New York, NY, USA (2011). https://doi.org/10.1145/2396716.2396721

38. Zhang, C., Budgen, D.: What do we know about the effectiveness of software design patterns? IEEE Trans. Softw. Eng. **38**(5), 1213–1231 (2012). https://doi.org/10.1109/TSE.2011.79

CASA

MAPE-K Based Guidelines for Designing Reactive and Proactive Self-adaptive Systems

Hendrik Jilderda[1] and Claudia Raibulet[1,2]([✉]) [iD]

[1] Vrije Universiteit Amsterdam, De Boelelaan 1111, Amsterdam, The Netherlands
h.jilderda@student.vu.nl, c.raibulet@vu.nl
[2] DISCo - Dipartimento di Informatica, Sistemistica e Comunicazione, Universita'
degli Studi di Milano-Bicocca, Viale Sarca 336, 20126 Milan, Italy
claudia.raibulet@unimib.it

Abstract. The rapid evolution of complex software systems claims for
novel approaches, such as self-adaptive systems that can autonomously
adjust their behavior to meet changing requirements and dynamic contexts. This paper proposes guidelines for the development of reactive and
proactive approaches to self-adaptive systems. The guidelines concern
architectural based approaches using explicitly the MAPE-K (Monitor,
Analyze, Plan, Execute using Knowledge) control feedback loop. The
proposed guidelines are organized into five parts, one for each step of the
MAPE-K loop including the knowledge with the goal to provide guidance
when designing and implementing self-adaptive systems from a software
engineering point of view. Three self-adaptive artifacts (i.e., OCCI Monitoring, DingNet, and SWIM) from different application domains (i.e.,
cloud computing, Internet of Things, Web application) have been analyzed by considering the proposed guidelines. Their reactive and proactive characteristics are compared.

Keywords: Self-Adaptive Systems · Reactive · Proactive · MAPE-K ·
Software Design

1 Introduction

The continuously changing technological landscape has created a demand for
Self-Adaptive Systems (SAS) [1,7,25]. Modern systems are getting more complex and dynamic, making it challenging for traditional static systems to stay
effective and efficient [8,21,26]. Changes in the environment, requirements, or
resources in such systems might result in unanticipated behavior or failures which
can be costly or even catastrophic. To overcome these problems, SAS have been
developed. SAS adjust to changes while maintaining functionality and performance. They have usually a managed part, which provides the functionally of
the system, and a managing part, which ensures the adaptation of the managed
one based on its current state and execution environment. SAS may be either

B. Tekinerdoğan et al. (Eds.): ECSA 2023, LNCS 14590, pp. 53–68, 2024.
https://doi.org/10.1007/978-3-031-66326-0_4

reactive, i.e., changing their behavior triggered by a change in their execution context, or *proactive*, i.e., anticipating changes based on historical knowledge about the systems and their execution environments and observing trends that may trigger changes in the next future [25]. Proactive approaches are typically also reactive. While there are changes or uncertainties that cannot be predicted, so reactive approaches may not be also proactive.

The aim of this paper is to research the differences and similarities between reactive and proactive approaches in SAS from a software engineering point of view and define guidelines which can be used for designing and implementing such systems. Its main contributions are:

- comparison of SAS from a reactive and proactive point of view;
- comparison of SAS artifacts based on their reactive and proactive features;
- design guidelines for developing SAS from a software engineering perspective.

Overall, this paper shows the similarities and differences between reactive and proactive SAS from a software engineering perspective, and aims to outline their strengths and weaknesses together with guidelines for their design and implementation. These guidelines enable and promote consistency, reproducibility, standardization, and collaboration for SAS.

Related Work: Significant and constant research effort has been invested in various aspects concerning the development of SAS [2,9,10,26] from the uncertainties they address [23], the control feedback loop they use [27], until their implementation in various application domains and evaluation from various points of view [22]. However, as far as concerns our knowledge, there is no similar work focusing on guidelines for UML-based designing reactive and proactive SAS.

Our Previous Work: Our attention has been focused on facets of self-adaptation [19], criteria and metrics for the evaluation of self-adaptation [6,11,18], as well as on the quality assessment of SAS from various points of view as for any other type of software (e.g., design patterns, code and architectural smells, software metrics, quality attributes) [22]. We also analyzed MAPE-K based solutions in dynamic environments [16,20].

The rest of the paper is organized as follows. Section 2 compares reactive and proactive approaches for SAS. Section 3 compares various SAS artifacts based on their reactive and proactive nature. Section 4 outlines the findings and guidelines. Conclusions and further work are dealt in Sect. 5.

2   MAKE-K Based Comparison of Reactive and Proactive Approaches

This section compares reactive and proactive SAS approaches based on their use of MAPE-K through a three-part examination: *what, when, how.*

- **what** focuses on defining each component and its role in SAS; this provides a clear understanding of the purpose of each step and how it contributes to the overall SAS.

- **when** examines when each step is executed; this provides insight into the temporal aspects of SAS, and how each step operates in real-time.
- **how** delves into the details of how each step is implemented in reactive and proactive approaches; this provides a more detailed understanding of the differences between the two types of approaches.

To further extend the comparison between reactive and proactive MAPE-K based approaches, each subsection includes a UML class diagram and its description. The goal of these diagrams is to show more of the context of the self-adaptation loop, and concurrently the similarities and differences between reactive and proactive approaches. The class diagrams use two colors. **Black:** common elements for both approaches, **Blue:** elements specific to proactive approaches.

2.1 Monitoring

What: The primary goal of this MAPE-K component is executed by both approaches roughly the same. Both approaches make use of real time data from the host system, with the proactive approach commonly saving the realtime data. This results in a history of the system [4]. This history is used for training the proactive part of the implementation.

When: There are three common time frames in which to execute the monitoring: continuous, periodically (pre-defined window), or by signal indicating a finished cycle [26]. Both implementations work the most optimal with continuous monitoring. However, this may result in higher resource usage. Periodic monitoring can be more efficiently used by proactive implementations. Because of the usage of historic data a proactive implementation can shorten the interval based on the predicted pattern of the data making it a suiting middle ground between alertness of the system and resource usage. Assuming a static interval for periodic may result the implementation having a higher detection time.

How: The monitoring component in both implementation collects data from sensors, and performs (if needed) the necessary preprocessing. Here are no specific differences between reactive and proactive implementations.

The primary class is *Monitor* (see Fig. 1). It uses *Sensor(s)* to monitor the *Context* of the system. *Sensors* and *Context* are very important for the system, since they contain the information needed for SAS to be able to achieve self-awareness and context-awareness. Because of the different possible temporal characteristics of monitoring inside of SAS, the *Monitor* class sets a *Strategy* which can be either *Continuous*, *Periodical*, or *Triggered*. Using both *Sensor* and *Strategy*, the *Monitor* generates *Data* which is stored in *Knowledge*. *Data* contains all of the monitored data, including when the data has been monitored. It is important to note that the *Monitor* might implement some sort of data processing function. However, since this is not always included in SAS implementations, it is not shown in Fig. 1.

The *HistoricData* class is the only difference between reactive and proactive approaches on a class level, with *HistoricData* used only by proactive approaches.

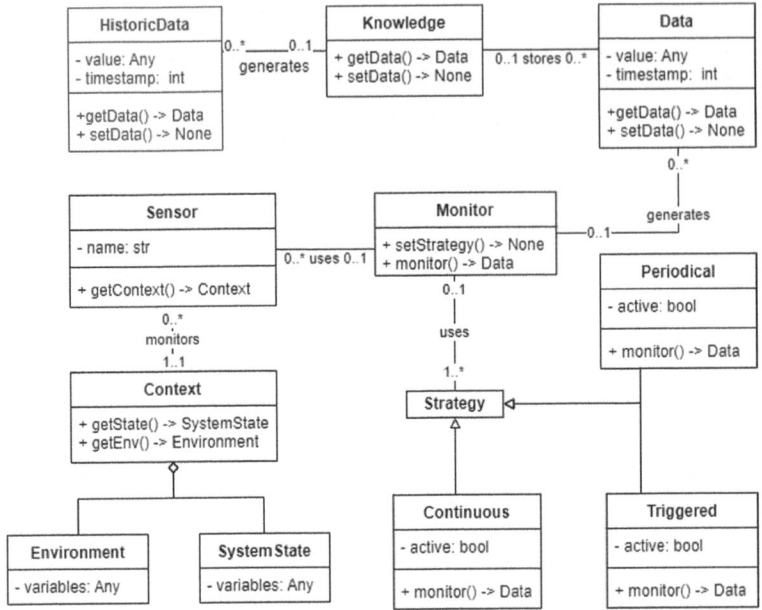

Fig. 1. Class diagram of the Monitoring step

2.2   Analyzing

What: The main differences between the two approaches is essentially in the analysis component. It assesses the data received from the monitoring component and determines if the system needs adaptation [26]. A proactive implementation is primarily focused on prediction. Because this implementation makes use of not only real time data, but also historic data, this approach has the ability to act before the time of change need. This can be important in cases where changes might need time to be effective.

When: In both approaches the analysis step is called at the end of the monitoring step.

How: Reactive approaches commonly consist of rule or policy based implementations to determine how the system should adapt and react in different situations. These rules and policies are commonly defined at design time which makes them a non-dynamic approach [7]. Proactive approaches make use of models (e.g., a machine learning model). To be able to use and train this model, data is used from the knowledge base where the monitoring step deposits it.

Analyzer is the primary class (see Fig. 2). It has the same available strategies as *Monitor*. Since proactive approaches are to a certain extend also reactive, the *Threshold* class is considered used by both approaches. The *Model* class contains some sort of machine learning implementation which uses the *HistoricData* gathered by the *Monitor* step. This is stored within the *Knowledge*.

To summarize the overall Analyzing step, *Analyzer* uses the data, and potentially the historic data, in combination with an *AnalysisType* and a *Strategy* to generate an *OutputAnalysis*, which in turn is stored in the *Knowledge* such that the Planning step can make use of this information.

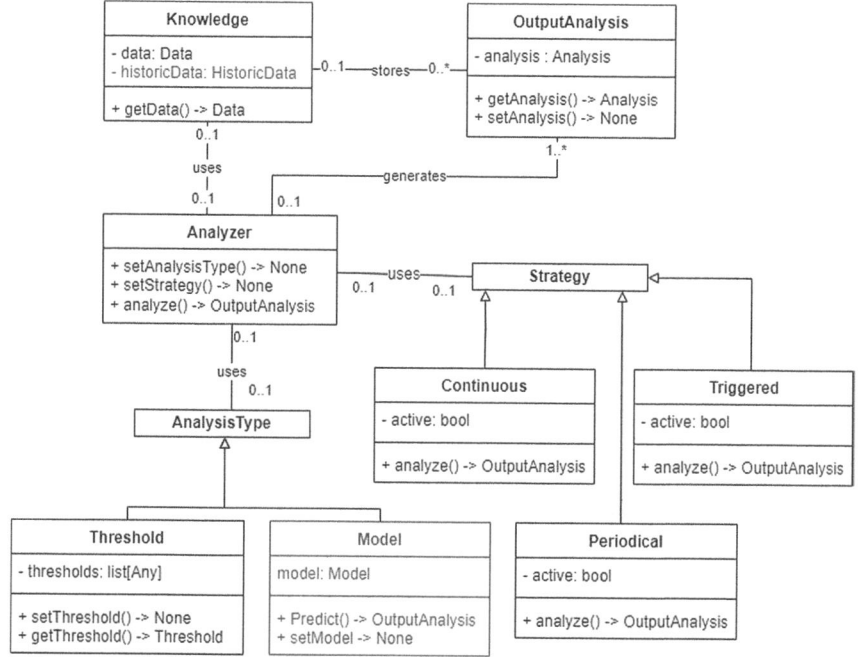

Fig. 2. Class diagram of Analyzing step

2.3   Planning

What: Reactive SAS focus primarily on selecting the best adaptation option to conform to adaptation goals, and generate a plan for adapting the managed system [26]. While proactive does most of this step the same, it anticipates adaptation needs which can lead to more efficient decision making and adaptation.

When: Execution is for both implementations triggered by the Analysis step.

How: Both implementations have the option to perform either static or dynamic decision making. In SAS implementations where the adaptation goals are listed as rules, all the possible adaptation options are ranked, thus turning this step into an optimization problem [26]. Ranking the options is commonly done by running a cost-benefit analysis at runtime.

The planning class diagram is similar to the Analysis one, but with few key differences. Since reactive approaches may not have any historical knowledge, it is not possible for them to consistently predict when a plan should be made and are thus reliant on a strategy in which the planning step gets triggered. With proactive approaches having the historic data, it is possible for them to either monitor *Periodical* or *Continuous* making them blue in this class diagram.

Because an adaptation strategy can consist of multiple strategies, a Composite design pattern [24] is used. The plan that gets generated by the *Planner* class, consists of either one or smaller steps and thus implementing the Composite design pattern once again (Fig. 3).

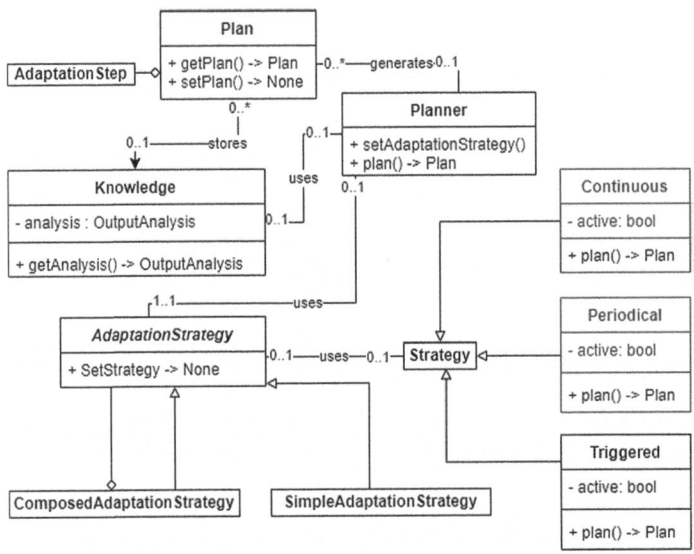

Fig. 3. Class diagram of Planning step

2.4   Executing

What: The execution step in MAPE-K is for both implementations the same. Both have the options for either closed or open adaptation actions. The adaptation plan can consist of multiple steps, in these cases the system can decide to either execute them all together, or rerun MAPE-K after each step in the plan to potentially withdraw the further steps since the goal has been reached.

When: The executing step is triggered by the planning step of MAPE-K.

How: After being triggered, this step selects an adaptation action given by the planning step and enacts this action on the managed system by means of an effector [26].

The *Executor* uses the plan to generate an *Action*, which itself uses *Effector(s)* to implement the changes to the *Context* of the system (see Fig. 4).

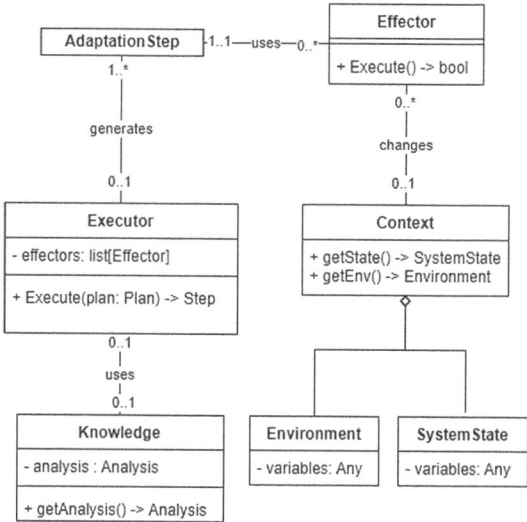

Fig. 4. Class diagram of Executing step

2.5 Knowledge

What: The Knowledge base stores relevant gathered information, and potentially the adaptation goals set by the user. Knowledge acts as a central hub that combines and organizes the information for all the steps of MAPE-K [4,5].

When: There is no specific time when the knowledge base is used. It is used during the whole cycle of the loop.

How: The monitoring step acquires information from the managed system and its environment and updates the knowledge if needed. The analysis step uses this information from the knowledge base and determines if there is a need for adaptation with respect to the adaptation goals [4].

As stated before, Knowledge functions as the basis of the MAPE-K loop (see Fig. 5). All the different classes are linked through the knowledge. It also becomes obvious that, while there are differences between reactive and proactive approaches, they are mostly similar with the proactive approach having some additions on top of a reactive approach. However, these additions do make the whole implementation more complex.

3 Artifact Based Comparison of Reactive and Proactive Approaches

This section investigates the characteristics of reactive and proactive SAS by means of the following artifacts: OCCI Monitoring [3], DingNet [17], and SWIM

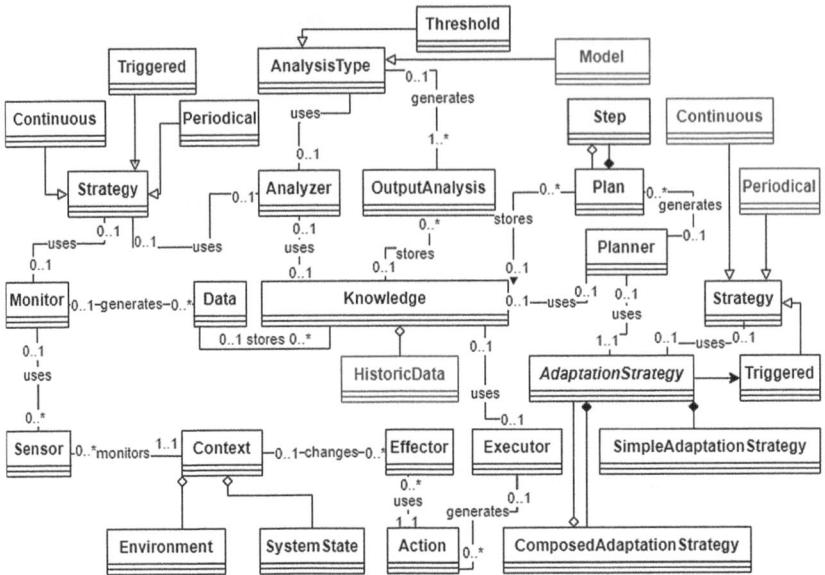

Fig. 5. The overall class diagrams of MAPE-K

[15] made available by the SEAMS community[1]. It examines the differences in quantity, and quality of input data between these two types of approaches. It explores whether the approaches reason about the data, or gain extra knowledge from it. It investigates when an approach executes the analysis, and whether it employs closed or open decision-making. It indicates whether an approach is model-based or not, and whether it makes use of atomic or multiple steps for the execution of an adaptation plan. It outlines whether adaptation is applied immediately, or over time/programmed when a SAS is not overloaded. These aspects aim to provide a deeper understanding of the differences between the two approaches and their underlying processes. OCCI Monitoring and DingNet are reactive, while SWIM is both reactive and proactive.

3.1   Artifacts

OCCI Monitoring: The OCCI Monitoring artifact, as proposed by Erbel et al. [3], is primarily an extension of the Open Cloud Computing Interface (OCCI) specification [12]. It consists of a set of guidelines and standards that define a standardized and open interface for managing cloud computing resources with the intend to provide a common language for cloud providers and its users to interact with each other. The monitoring extension for OCCI allows the OCCI implementation to manage sensors over a standardized interface, and reflect the gathered data within OCCI [3].

---

[1] https://www.hpi.uni-potsdam.de/giese/public/selfadapt/exemplars/.

DingNet: The DingNet artifact, presented by Provoost and Weyns [17], is a reference implementation with the goal to support research of self-adaptation in the Internet of Things (IoT) domain. DingNet offers a simulator that directly maps to a physical IoT system in the area of Leuven, Belgium. DingNet focuses on supporting the design and evaluation process of smart city applications, which can consist of a large number of motes that can be deployed in city areas to collect and send data to gateways.

DingNet makes use of a Long Range Wide Area Network (LoRaWAN) which covers a large part of Leuven. LoRaWAN[2] is a communication protocol that is designed to allow low-powered motes to communicate with Internet-connected applications. To ensure good coverage, DingNet consists of 14 gateways located on high buildings throughout the city. Due to the fact that testing implementations such as DingNet physically can be error-prone and time consuming, simulations can be used to test solutions before deploying them.

SWIM: The SWIM artifact, by Moreno et al. [15], simulates a generic multitier web application. SWIM consists of two tiers, namely web server tier which receives requests from user clients and a database tier which stores data needed to render the page with dynamic content. SWIM also has the ability to use a load balancer, which gives SWIM support for multiple web servers.

The goal of SWIM is to be able to self-adapt to changing request arrival rates and work with the trade-off between cost and revenue. The system is able to deal with changes in two ways. First, it has the ability to add/remove a server to/from the pool of servers connected to the load balancer [15]. Second, the system has the ability to control the amount of optional content send to the user.

3.2   Which Characteristics Do Input Data Have?

For all the considered SAS artifacts both reactive and proactive, the monitored data is used to verify that quality requirements are fulfilled.

– For OCCI Monitoring this results in monitoring the CPU utilization (on one or multiple nodes within a cluster).
– DingNet's primary requirement is low packet loss and energy consumption.
– SWIM monitors the arrival rate of requests, throughput, server utilization.

To summarize, (1) the data to be monitored are derived from the requirements specification for a SAS, and (2) they may consider one aspect (e.g., CPU utilization) or multiple aspects (e.g., arrival rate, throughput server utilization).

3.3   Does the Quantity and the Quality of the Input Data Differ?

The considered artifacts have a low quantity of data used to verify the status and the appropriate working of the system.

---

[2] LoRaWAN - https://www.thethingsnetwork.org/docs/lorawan/.

- OCCI Monitoring monitors its data periodically, in combination with only one value being monitored, it results in a low quantity of data.
- DingNet sends its drones signal home every 10 m with limited amount of data. The quantity of the data is largely reliant on the amount of drones used in the system.
- Between the reactive and proactive implementation of SWIM, there is no difference in quality of data. The quantity of the monitored data is the same, however, the proactive implementation does process a higher quantity of data because of the model used to predict adaptation needs.

To summarize, the quantity of data is limited in the reactive approaches, while it may be significantly higher in proactive approaches due to the historic data needed for prediction. No significant differences in the quality of data.

3.4 Does SAS only Reason About the Data or Does It Gain Extra Knowledge from It?

The considered SAS reason with data directly gathered through monitoring.

- OCCI Monitoring reasons about CPU utilization. In cases where nodes are fully using their RAM in combination with 'normal' CPU usage, the node won't scale, resulting in somewhat of a blind spot in the adaptation. Therefore, OCCI monitoring uses only directly acquired data.
- DingNet uses the signal strength. No extra knowledge is derived to be used for adaptation.
- This is also the case for the reactive implementation of SWIM. The proactive implementation does gain extra knowledge from the system by observing the distribution of data in time and identifying trends meaningful for adaptation.

Generally, reactive approaches use directly monitored data, while proactive approaches aim to find relations among the data by means of a model.

3.5 When is Analysis Executed?

All of the implementations used for this comparison have implemented a periodic approach for gathering and analyzing data.

- OCCI Monitoring makes its nodes send status updates every 3 s.
- Every drone in DingNet has as its requirement to send a status update every 10 m with a speed of 0.5 m/s, this results in a periodic monitoring and analysis every 20 s.
- SWIM has in both its implementations a different philosophy to OCCI Monitoring and DingNet, namely it combines the analysis and planning steps into one making it the first big difference between the artifacts.

To summarize, in reactive approaches, analysis is performed as soon as new data becomes available from the monitoring step. Monitoring and analysis are dependent of each other, i.e., if monitoring is performed periodically then also the analysis is performed periodically.

3.6 Closed (Existing List of Defined Adaptations Strategies) or Open (Generating) Decision Making?

The considered SAS perform the planning as follows:

- Since OCCI Monitoring only monitors the CPU usage of node(s), it is limited in its options to safely adapt the system (i.e., to increase core count of a node or increase the amount of nodes).
- DingNet has two distinct ways to adapt; a signal based adaptation or a distance based adaption. In these cases the system either incrementally adapts power based on signal strength or based on distance from gateway.
- The reactive SWIM implementation has two variables it is able to optimize. One of these variables is on a continuous scale between 0 and 1, with the other variable being the up- or down scaling of the amount of VMs used by the system. The proactive SWIM implementation also has the same two variables to optimize, but it goes a different way in doing so.

Current approaches use closed adaptation strategies. An advantages is the short reaction time to adaptation needs. Open adaptation strategies are not frequently applied due to their potential complexity in the identification process, and a significant response time increase over the closed approach.

3.7 Is the SAS Model-Based or Not?

All the reactive artifacts have a similar approach to adaptation: they make use of conditional statements to enforce thresholds. The proactive artifacts indeed use a model.

- OCCI Monitoring scales vertically or horizontally based on CPU utilization making this a model free implementation.
- The adaptation in DingNet is based on a limited number of conditional statements making this implementation also model-free.
- The reactive implementation of SWIM uses conditional statements which are based on thresholds set in the initial stages of development. One of the proactive SWIM approaches uses both CobRA and PLA. CobRA is a requirements based approach which applies control theory, while PLA provides architecture based stochastic analysis [14]. A different proactive implementation of SWIM uses a Markov Decision Process [13].

To summarize, all reactive approaches are model free, while proactive approaches apply a model-based approach. While machine learning models are commonly used, also other models are suitable, e.g., from control theory.

3.8 Does the Artifact Make Use of Atomic Steps or Multiple Steps?

All the considered artifacts use atomic steps to execute the adaptation plan.

- In the MAPE-K cycle, OCCI Monitoring uses an atomic step to execute the adaptation. However, there exists a chance in which one extra core or node is not sufficient, so the next cycle further increases the core size or node size.
- Since DingNet has a straight forward implementation with two adaptation options and is periodically monitored, it uses atomic adaptation steps.
- Both SWIM implementations use atomic steps. However, steps from different time periods can be executed asynchronously as long as they do not interfere.

Generally, both reactive and proactive approaches apply atomic steps when implementing the adaptation plan. This leads to a lower complexity of the implementation, and an easier way to evaluate the results of the adaptation.

3.9   Is Adaptation Applied Immediately or over Time?

Adaptation plans may be applied immediately after they have been established or scheduled for the next iterations.

- OCCI Monitoring executes the adaptation immediately after is chosen in the planning step.
- Like OCCI Monitoring, the adaptation for DingNet is immediately executed after receiving the adaptation plan.
- SWIM also implements the changes as soon as they become available to the execution step. However, finishing the adaptation step might take some time to complete in the proactive approaches.

All the artifacts implement the adaptation plan as soon as possible. This is also needed since reactive approaches only make use of realtime data making it necessary to instantly adapt to ensure best overall performance.

4   Findings and Guidelines

Based on the taxonomy of Salehie et al. [25], and on the theoretical and practical comparisons between reactive and proactive SAS, several guidelines for each step of the MAPE-K loop can be identified.

Monitoring Guidelines

- **The data monitored as input for the adaptation should concern non-functional requirements.** This leads to a straightforward implementation of the MAPE-K loop. Practical hints can be found in all the considered artifacts. They all monitor one to few values meaningful for the non-functional requirements.
- **Quality over quantity for monitored data.** This leads to reduced need to process the monitored data, and to a reduced reaction time. All the considered artifacts monitor a low amount of data periodically.

– **Continuous monitoring is useful for reactive approaches.** Proactive approaches have the ability to predict, resulting in no significant differences in the exact detection time of the adaptation need. Continuous monitoring is best suited to reactive approaches in comparison to proactive approaches. All considered artifacts use periodical monitoring with different time intervals.

Analyzing Guidelines

– **Focus analysis on the explicitly gathered data.** As stated in the monitoring guidelines, the monitored data should concern non-functional requirements. This makes it unnecessary to reason about the data to gain more insight from it, since the non-functional requirements can already be derived.
– **Proactive approaches must aim to implement some sort of model to predict.** While proactive approaches do have a reactive implementation incorporated, and thus use a threshold implementation, prediction is possible using models based on historic data for trends.
– **Reactive SAS may be developed with a model-free implementation.** Because of the reactive nature of this type of SAS, there is no need to increase the complexity of the system with additional models. It is sufficient for the system to just react based on thresholds. The considered reactive artifacts do not implement any model.

Planning Guidelines

– **Adopt closed decision making.** While open decision making may be implemented, it increases complexity, computation, and power usage.
– **Reactive approaches make no use of continuous or periodical planning.** Since reactive approaches only have the ability to react, and thus only use real time data, the planning step does not have the ability to predict and propose potential future adaptations. Hence, there is no need for continuous, or periodical strategies, which lead to waste computation time and power.

Executing Guidelines

– **Atomic steps over multiple steps.** Executing multiple steps makes it difficult to check if partial changes were sufficient. Further, because of potential delays on adaptions several adaptations might get executed simultaneously.
– **Execute the plan as soon as possible.** The best moment to execute the adaptation plan is as soon as possible. This ensures a reduced reaction time and an efficient application for the context for each it has been designed.
– **Keep execution context in mind when executing plan.** Some adaptations take time to be executed (e.g., start a server). Not accounting for such aspects can result in the same adaptation being executed multiple times, and can therefore result in overcompensation.

Knowledge Guidelines

- **Data should be stored in the knowledge.** Knowledge is the center of MAPE-K. Having each steps reading and writing only from/to the knowledge results in a easy to understand system with reduced chances of missing data. Adaptation goals should also be stored in the knowledge for easy access.
- **Historic data should be used by proactive approaches.** For proactive approaches it is important to consider the amount of historic data stored and used. The amount of data can become too high and waste storage space.

5   Conclusion and Further Work

This paper presents guidelines for developing SAS from a software engineering perspective considering both a theoretical (Sect. 2) and a practical (Sect. 3) comparison. The theoretical comparison based on MAPE-K shows that the differences are not as significant as one might expect. Since proactive approaches are inherently reactive, most of the guidelines coincide, with proactive approaches extending the functionality of reactive ones (see Fig. 5). While the reviewed artifacts are implemented in different domains, a lot of their characteristics are similar. The characteristics, quality, and quantity of the data show no significant differences between approaches other than domain specific differences. The differences between reactive and proactive approaches concern mostly how and when the analysis step is performed. Additionally, the complexity of this step may significantly differ between reactive and proactive approaches.

Guidelines for monitoring essentially concern what the data should look like as well as when it should be gathered. The analysis guidelines focus on how the analysis should be executed and the limitations it should have. For planning the guidelines go into the temporal aspects and suggested complexity limitation for the implementation. Comparable to the planning guidelines the execution guidelines focus on when this step should be executed in combination with suggested limitations. While knowledge plays a key role in the self-adaptation MAPE-K based process, it is important to follow guidelines. These guidelines focus on location and storage of the data as well as limiting the use of historic data.

Further work will concern the extension of the theoretical comparison to other aspects proposed by the SAS taxonomy [25], as well as of the practical comparison to other available artifacts in various application domains. This will extend the guidelines and validate them.

Acknowledgement. This research is partially supported by ExtremeXP, a project co-funded by the European Union Horizon Programme under Grant Agreement No. 101093164.

References

1. Arcelli, F., Raibulet, C., Tisato, F., Adorni, M.: Architectural reflection in adaptive systems. In: Maurer, F., Ruhe, G. (eds.) 16th International Conference on Software Engineering and Knowledge Engineering (SEKE'2004), pp. 74–79 (2004)
2. Cheng, B.H.C., de Lemos, R., Giese, H., Inverardi, P., Magee, J. (eds.): Software Engineering for Self-adaptive Systems [Outcome of a Dagstuhl Seminar]. LNCS, vol. 5525. Springer, Heidelberg (2009). https://doi.org/10.1007/978-3-642-02161-9
3. Erbel, J., Brand, T., Giese, H., Grabowski, J.: OCCI-compliant, fully causal-connected architecture runtime models supporting sensor management. In: 2019 IEEE/ACM 14th International Symposium on Software Engineering for Adaptive and Self-Managing Systems (SEAMS), pp. 188–194. IEEE (2019)
4. Iglesia, D.G.D.L., Weyns, D.: MAPE-k formal templates to rigorously design behaviors for self-adaptive systems. ACM Trans. Auton. Adapt. Syst. (TAAS) **10**(3), 1–31 (2015)
5. Jiang, M., Zheng, L., Ding, Z., Jin, Z.: A software-defined MAPE-k architecture for unmanned systems. Sci. China Inf. Sci. **66**(5), 159101 (2023)
6. Kaddoum, E., Raibulet, C., George, J., Picard, G., Gleizes, M.: Criteria for the evaluation of self-* systems. In: de Lemos, R., Pezzè, M. (eds.) 2010 ICSE Workshop on Software Engineering for Adaptive and Self-managing Systems. SEAMS 2010, pp. 29–38. ACM (2010). https://doi.org/10.1145/1808984.1808988
7. Krupitzer, C., Roth, F.M., VanSyckel, S., Schiele, G., Becker, C.: A survey on engineering approaches for self-adaptive systems. Pervasive Mob. Comput. **17**, 184–206 (2015). https://doi.org/10.1016/J.PMCJ.2014.09.009
8. Krupitzer, C., Temizer, T., Prantl, T., Raibulet, C.: An overview of design patterns for self-adaptive systems in the context of the internet of things. IEEE Access **8**, 187384–187399 (2020). https://doi.org/10.1109/ACCESS.2020.3031189
9. de Lemos, R., Garlan, D., Ghezzi, C., Giese, H. (eds.): Software Engineering for Self-Adaptive Systems III. LNCS, vol. 9640. Springer, Cham (2017). https://doi.org/10.1007/978-3-319-74183-3
10. de Lemos, R., Giese, H., Müller, H.A., Shaw, M. (eds.): Software Engineering for Self-adaptive Systems II. LNCS, vol. 7475. Springer, Heidelberg (2013). https://doi.org/10.1007/978-3-642-35813-5
11. Masciadri, L., Raibulet, C.: Frameworks for the development of adaptive systems: evaluation of their adaptability feature through software metrics. In: Boness, K., Fernandes, J.M., Hall, J.G., Machado, R.J., Oberhauser, R. (eds.) The Fourth International Conference on Software Engineering Advances. ICSEA 2009, pp. 309–312. IEEE Computer Society (2009). https://doi.org/10.1109/ICSEA.2009.51
12. Metsch, T., Edmonds, A., Parák, B.: Open cloud computing interface-infrastructure. In: Standards Track, no. GFD-R in The Open Grid Forum Document Series, Open Cloud Computing Interface (OCCI) Working Group, Muncie (IN) (2010)
13. Moreno, G.A., Cámara, J., Garlan, D., Schmerl, B.: Efficient decision-making under uncertainty for proactive self-adaptation. In: 2016 IEEE International Conference on Autonomic Computing (ICAC), pp. 147–156. IEEE (2016)
14. Moreno, G.A., Papadopoulos, A.V., Angelopoulos, K., Cámara, J., Schmerl, B.: Comparing model-based predictive approaches to self-adaptation: Cobra and PLA. In: 2017 IEEE/ACM 12th International Symposium on Software Engineering for Adaptive and Self-Managing Systems (SEAMS), pp. 42–53. IEEE (2017)

15. Moreno, G.A., Schmerl, B., Garlan, D.: Swim: an exemplar for evaluation and comparison of self-adaptation approaches for web applications. In: Proceedings of the 13th International Conference on Software Engineering for Adaptive and Self-Managing Systems, pp. 137–143 (2018)

16. Oh, J., Raibulet, C., Leest, J.: Analysis of MAPE-K loop in self-adaptive systems for cloud, IoT and CPS. In: Troya, J., et al. (eds.) CSOC 2022. LNCS, vol. 13821, pp. 130–141. Springer, Cham (2022). https://doi.org/10.1007/978-3-031-26507-5_11

17. Provoost, M., Weyns, D.: Dingnet: a self-adaptive internet-of-things exemplar. In: 2019 IEEE/ACM 14th International Symposium on Software Engineering for Adaptive and Self-Managing Systems (SEAMS), pp. 195–201. IEEE Computer Society (2019)

18. Raibulet, C., Arcelli Fontana, F., Capilla, R., Carrillo, C.: Chapter 13 - an overview on quality evaluation of self-adaptive systems. In: Mistrik, I., Ali, N., Kazman, R., Grundy, J., Schmerl, B. (eds.) Managing Trade-Offs in Adaptable Software Architectures, pp. 325–352. Morgan Kaufmann, Boston (2017). https://doi.org/10.1016/B978-0-12-802855-1.00013-7

19. Raibulet, C.: Facets of adaptivity. In: Morrison, R., Balasubramaniam, D., Falkner, K. (eds.) ECSA 2008. LNCS, vol. 5292, pp. 342–345. Springer, Heidelberg (2008). https://doi.org/10.1007/978-3-540-88030-1_33

20. Raibulet, C., Arcelli, F., Mussino, S., Riva, M., Tisato, F., Ubezio, L.: Components in an adaptive and QoS-based architecture. In: International Workshop on Self-adaptation and Self-managing Systems, pp. 65–71. ACM (2006). https://doi.org/10.1145/1137677.1137690

21. Raibulet, C., Drira, K., Fornaro, C., Fugini, M.: Introduction to special issue on software architectures for smart and adaptive systems (SASAS). Inf. Softw. Technol. **157**, 107158 (2023). https://doi.org/10.1016/J.INFSOF.2023.107158

22. Raibulet, C., Fontana, F.A., Carettoni, S.: A preliminary analysis of self-adaptive systems according to different issues. Softw. Qual. J. **28**(3), 1213–1243 (2020). https://doi.org/10.1007/S11219-020-09502-5

23. Ramirez, A.J., Jensen, A.C., Cheng, B.H.C.: A taxonomy of uncertainty for dynamically adaptive systems. In: Müller, H.A., Baresi, L. (eds.) 7th International Symposium on Software Engineering for Adaptive and Self-managing Systems. SEAMS 2012, pp. 99–108. IEEE Computer Society (2012). https://doi.org/10.1109/SEAMS.2012.6224396

24. Riehle, D.: Composite design patterns. In: Proceedings of the 12th ACM SIGPLAN Conference on Object-Oriented Programming, Systems, Languages, and Applications, pp. 218–228 (1997)

25. Salehie, M., Tahvildari, L.: Self-adaptive software: landscape and research challenges. ACM Trans. Auton. Adapt. Syst. (TAAS) **4**(2), 1–42 (2009)

26. Weyns, D.: An Introduction to Self-adaptive Systems: A Contemporary Software Engineering Perspective. Wiley, Hoboken (2020)

27. Weyns, D., et al.: On patterns for decentralized control in self-adaptive systems. In: de Lemos, R., Giese, H., Müller, H.A., Shaw, M. (eds.) Software Engineering for Self-Adaptive Systems II. LNCS, vol. 7475, pp. 76–107. Springer, Heidelberg (2013). https://doi.org/10.1007/978-3-642-35813-5_4

DE & I Track

Stakeholder Inclusion and Value Diversity: An Evaluation Using an Access Control System

Razieh Alidoosti[1,2(✉)], Martina De Sanctis[2], Ludovico Iovino[2], Patricia Lago[1], and Maryam Razavian[3]

[1] Vrije Universiteit Amsterdam, Amsterdam, The Netherlands
{r.alidoosti,p.lago}@vu.nl
[2] Gran Sasso Science Institute, L'Aquila, Italy
{martina.desanctis,ludovico.iovino}@gssi.it
[3] Eindhoven University of Technology, Eindhoven, The Netherlands
m.razavian@tue.nl

Abstract. Software systems bring great benefits to people's lives. Nevertheless, they can cause issues in terms of social and ethical implications toward individuals and society, and compromise their ethical values. Therefore, it is crucial to consider all potentially-concerned stakeholders during the system design process, as they are the primary source of value and requirements identification. In this study, we aim to evaluate the effect that two ethics-driven instruments we have created (*i.e.,* a stakeholder map and a value model) may have on supporting ethical considerations (such as stakeholder and ethical value), using the case of an Access Control System. The paper presents the insights gained from this evaluation, performed as a retrospective study.

Keywords: Stakeholder · Ethical value · Software system · ACS

1 Introduction

With the growing digitalization and the increasing reliance on software systems, ethics in software engineering has gained significant attention. This is because of the social and ethical implications these systems have on individuals and society. Software systems can undermine ethical values, leading to issues such as restrictions on personal freedom and violations of privacy. Such issues, therefore, reinforce the need to focus on software systems and architectures from an ethical standpoint. As pointed out in [1], it is essential to focus on ethical considerations, such as stakeholder, ethical concern, ethical value, and ethical decision, at the early stages of system design (*e.g.,* when making architecture design decisions).

With these premises, stakeholders play a critical role in incorporating an ethical perspective in software systems, as they are the primary source for value and requirements elicitation [3]. Accordingly, it is important to account for the

B. Tekinerdoğan et al. (Eds.): ECSA 2023, LNCS 14590, pp. 71–88, 2024.
https://doi.org/10.1007/978-3-031-66326-0_5

plurality of values in design decision-making, especially when there are various stakeholders who software systems may directly or indirectly impact. For instance, consider the case of facial recognition technology in Access Control Systems used at airports [6]. In such cases, there is a tendency to overlook the needs of specific groups, such as people of color or those with disabilities, as the focus is primarily on security benefits. This can result in discrimination and potential biases against these individuals. Thus, it is crucial to equip software designers with instruments that facilitate the inclusion of a wide range of stakeholders and their values by focusing on software systems' ethical and social implications. These instruments should enable designers to explore various potential stakeholders of the system, either affecting or being affected by it, and prompt designers to explore different aspects and scenarios in which they can be affected by the system from an ethical perspective.

To this end, we introduced two ethics-driven instruments, namely a *stakeholder map* and a *value model* [2]. The stakeholder map outlines the three overarching stakeholder roles that may directly or indirectly receive benefit/harm from the system. The value model is a classification of values usually considered in software design and a representation of relations among values. In this work, we evaluate these instruments with a retrospective study examining the effects of utilizing them on stakeholder inclusion and value diversity within the context of an Access Control System (ACS) [4] (Sect. 2). The selection of the ACS as the case of our evaluative reflective study is justified by its critical role in controlling users' access to resources and services, which can have significant ethical implications, such as privacy violations and threats to autonomy [9]. Specifically, this study investigates the ethical considerations associated with the ACS and evaluates which considerations could have been supported if the instruments had been employed during the system design process. We conducted two focus group sessions involving pertinent stakeholders (Sect. 3). Results indicate that the instruments effectively facilitated the identification of stakeholders with different roles, their ethical concerns and values, and ethical decision making (Sect. 4). We further discuss threats to the validity of our results (Sect. 4.3), and we conclude the paper with future directions (Sect. 5).

2   Background

In this Section, we introduce the ACS that we used as the case of the retrospective study, as well as the two ethics-driven instruments we created in our previous study [2].

An Access Control System. An ACS supports to check entries via controlled gates (*e.g.*, doors equipped with a lock mechanism) to restricted access areas [8]. We selected, as our case, an ACS implementing an approach enabling the communication between an IoT infrastructure (*e.g.*, Near Field Communication (NFC) readers and tags, relays, led, alarms) and an access management platform to authenticate users [4]. The ACS has been deployed and evaluated in a fitness center (in L'Aquila, Italy). The ACS architecture aligns with the conventional access control framework [14] and its components (see Fig. 1), reported in *italic* in this section. The user requests access via an NFC tag through the *Policy Enforcement Point (PEP)* embedded in a NFC reader installed on the gate. The PEP will forward the request to the *Policy Decision Point (PDP)* that evaluates the access request against the authorization policy, by querying a policies repository and replying to the PEP. The PEP will then grant or deny access to the user for the specified resource, *i.e.*, a room. A *Policy Information Point (PIP)* can optionally be used to enrich the authorization request, *e.g.*, with user rights. Lastly, the *Policy Administration Point (PAP)* manages the authorization policies. We refer to [4] for the detailed ACS architecture.

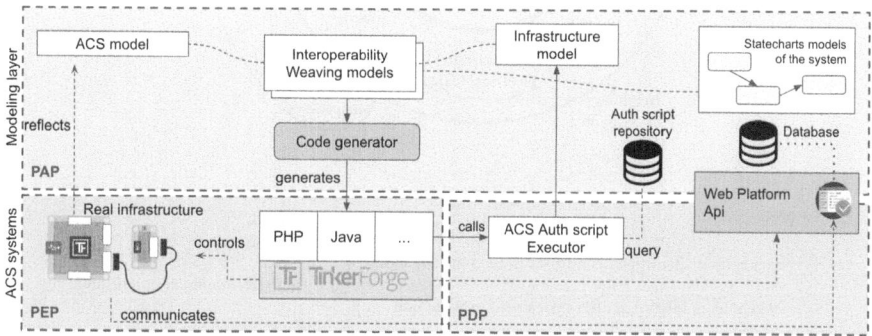

Fig. 1. An overview of the ACS architecture and its components adapted from [4]

Ethics-Driven Instruments. Our Systematic Literature Review of software engineering ethics (SE ethics) [2] led to the creation of two ethics-driven instruments (see Fig. 2 and Fig. 3) described below.

The Stakeholder Map. It visualizes three overarching stakeholder roles: *system users, system development organization,* and *indirect stakeholders,* each comprising various role types, as depicted in Fig. 2[1]. For example, the role of "system development organization", in the ACS, includes role types such as "IoT experts" and "architects". The stakeholder map focuses on three key aspects: (i) the different relations of stakeholders with the system, *i.e.,*using it, building it, or being impacted by it, (ii) the system's implications on stakeholders, *i.e.,*benefits and harms, and (iii) the ways in which stakeholders receive benefits and harms from the system, *i.e.,*directly or indirectly. This map helps software designers in the system design process, to identify a comprehensive range of stakeholders.

---

[1] In the stakeholder map, solid circles represent stakeholders identified before introducing the instruments, while dotted circles correspond to those identified after the introduction.

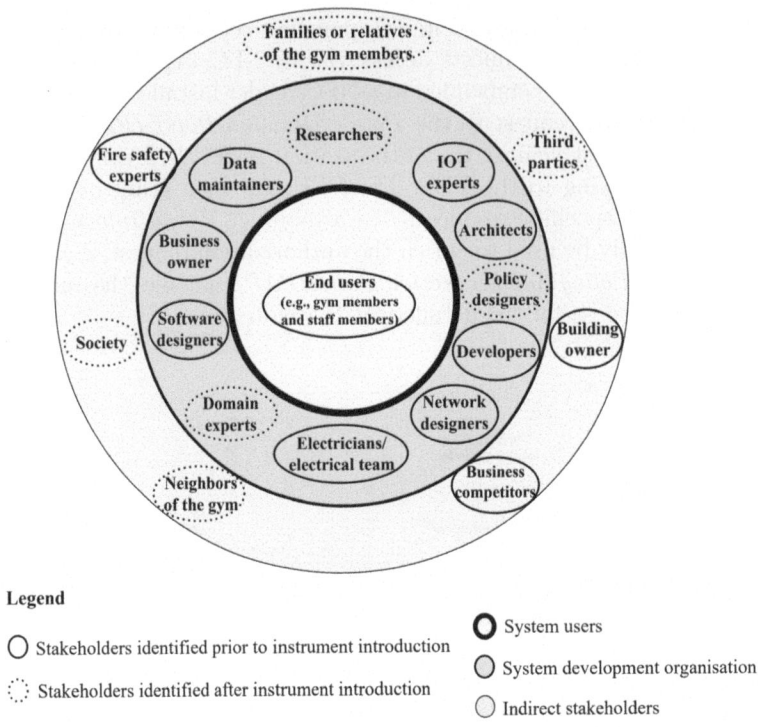

Fig. 2. The stakeholder map: A representation of the stakeholders related to the ACS based on the stakeholder map proposed in the SLR [2].

The Value Model. It categorizes ethical values commonly used in system design, along with the relations among these values, as depicted in Fig. 3[2]. This model is based on the Schwartz value structure [11,12], a widely used structure for classifying values in social sciences and ethics [13]. Software designers can utilize this model by following a series of steps. First, they should identify the relevant value categories that align with the system's goal(s), and explore subvalues w.r.t. the relevant stakeholders, assessing whether they are supported or undermined by the system. The next step involves determining the relationships among those values, including any conflicts or congruencies. To this aim designers should consider the positions of the values within *two orthogonal dimensions*, namely (i) self-enhancement vs. self-transcendence and (ii) openness to change vs. conservation. For instance, "safety" can be considered a pertinent value for gym members, in line with the system's goal. By examining its position in the value model, it becomes apparent that it conflicts with the value of "freedom", as they belong to non-adjacent categories (in *openness to change vs. conservation* dimension). The model provides designers with a guideline to identify the

---

[2] In the value model, solid circles depict values identified before introducing instruments, while dotted circles represent them after the introduction.

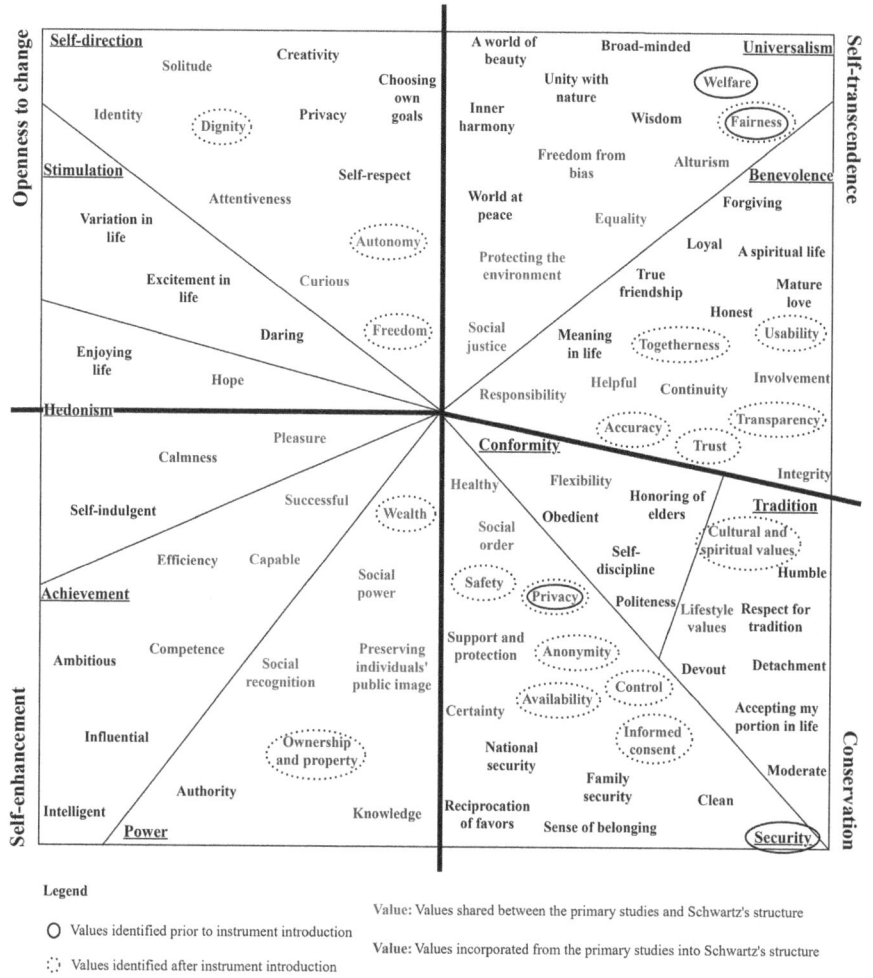

Fig. 3. The value model: A mapping of the values associated with the ACS onto the value model proposed in the SLR [2].

relevant ethical values and relations among them. This enables them to effectively manage potential conflicts and reinforce the values that align with the system's goal(s).

3   Methodology

In this section, we describe our research objective and questions, the evaluation design and execution, as well as the data collection and analysis.

Research Objective and Questions. The objective of this study is to explore the effects of the two ethics-driven instruments in supporting ethical considerations in the case of the ACS represented in Sect. 2. To achieve the research objective, we drive the study with the following research questions (RQs):

(RQ1) *How could the proposed instruments affect the identification of stakeholders with different roles and their ethical concerns?*

(RQ2) *How could the instruments affect the identification of ethical values and the potential relations among them?*

(RQ3) *How could the instruments enable decision-making to support ethical considerations?*

Evaluation Design and Execution. We conducted a retrospective study through a small-scale evaluation of the ACS [4] case. Following the guidelines proposed by Robson [10], we designed the evaluation in two steps: *initial evaluation* and *secondary evaluation* (the asked questions can be found in Appendix A[3]).

In the former, we used the focus group research method to explore the effects of the instruments on supporting ethical considerations. In the latter, we also employed a focus group to evaluate the findings from the initial evaluation.

Initial Evaluation. The focus group study was conducted in March 2023 as an online session involving four participants who had actively contributed to the design and development of the ACS. The session began with an introduction to the study objective and fundamental concepts in the context of SE ethics. The session was organized as a semi-structured discussion in two parts, lasting a total of three hours. In *part 1*, participants were asked predetermined questions categorized based on our RQs. In *part 2*, participants were introduced to the ethics-driven instruments and were asked questions regarding their usage.

The session served a twofold aim. First, understanding the current state of the ACS in terms of ethical considerations, such as stakeholders and ethical values. Second, using the instruments to uncover ethical considerations that could have been supported in the design of the ACS but were overlooked.

Secondary Evaluation. The focus group study was conducted in May 2023 as an online session lasting one and a half hours. It included two participants from the initial focus group and three additional participants who were end users of the ACS and members of the fitness center exposed to the case.

This evaluation aimed to discover the opinions and expectations of system users, regarding the ethical aspects of the ACS. The results from this phase served as an indicator of the effectiveness of the instruments in identifying ethical considerations related to the system.

Data Collection and Analysis. Focus group sessions in both evaluations were video-recorded and transcribed for further analysis. We analyzed the transcript of each session by using transcript coding as our qualitative data analysis

---

[3] Appendix A is available in the GitHub repository https://github.com/S2-group/ECSA23-SIVD-rep-pkg.git.

method. Following the approach suggested by Miles and Huberman [7], we created an initial list of codes based on the RQs, including stakeholders, ethical concerns, ethical values, value relations, and ethical decisions. Throughout the analysis process, we further expanded and refined this code list.

4 Results

In this section, we outline our research findings, by discussing the possible relation with the components making the architecture of the ACS (Sect. 2).

4.1 The Initial Evaluation Results

Finding 1. In *part* 1 of the session, participants discussed those individuals or groups who were explicitly considered in the design of the ACS, such as *the business owner* (the ACS contractor) and *the building owner*. During the stakeholder identification process, only individuals with direct relationships with the system were considered, *e.g.,* those involved in the ACS implementation, infrastructure, and usage. The participants recognized the end users of the ACS as one of the most crucial stakeholder, being the primary beneficiaries of the system (refer to the stakeholders marked with solid circles in Fig. 2). In *part* 2 of the session, as the ethics-driven instruments were introduced, the participants noted that certain stakeholders had been overlooked during the ACS design process. These stakeholders included individuals who could have a significant impact on the ethical implications of the system by, *e.g.,* establishing ethical standards and providing oversight and regulation, such as *policy designers* and *fire safety experts*. Policy designers could be directly involved in designing and implementing the PDP and policy repositories. Additionally, some could be indirectly influenced by the system's ethical implications, such as *the entire society* and *the families of end users* (refer to the stakeholders marked with dotted circles in Fig. 2). The only part of the system in which the involvement of the end users and relatives (*e.g.,* visiting the facility) maybe required is the PEP since it serves as the external interface of the ACS with the users. Table 1 reports the identified stakeholders.

> **Finding 1 (RQ1):** We observed that utilizing the ethics-driven instruments had the effect of broadening the participants' perspectives on the ethical implications associated with the system and its various interactions with stakeholders. As a result, the stakeholders that were previously disregarded, often due to their indirect or less visible relations to the system, came now into focus. This highlights the role of the instruments in considering a diverse range of stakeholders in the ACS design process.

Finding 2. During *part* 1, participants examined the possible ethical issues associated with the ACS concerning the stakeholders involved. One of the most prominent raised concerns was possible *privacy violations*. All participants were

Table 1. The list of the stakeholders identified in the two parts of the session

Stakeholder (Part1)
The business owner: The person or group who is responsible for making decisions about the implementation and use of the ACS
The building owner: Individual or organization that owns the physical building where the gym is located
The final users of the system: Individuals who require access to specific areas of the gym, including gym members, staff members, and even guests visiting the gym for a specific purpose
Software development stakeholders: The individuals involved in the system design and implementation, including designers, developers, architects, IoT experts, and network designers
Data maintainers: Individuals who are responsible for ensuring the accuracy, completeness, and security of the data used by the system
The electricians/the electrical team: Individuals responsible for installing, maintaining, and repairing the electrical components of the ACS.
Stakeholder (Part2)
Researchers: Those who inspect the existing literature to gain insight into how ACSs should be designed
Domain experts/Policy designers: Those who are specialists and have knowledge of the system's regulations, such as GDPR. They can be consulted to address queries such as "Are we performing tasks correctly?", "Is deleting the log sufficient?", or "Are we violating any legal requirements or law?"
Families or relatives of the gym members/neighbors of the gym: Those who can be indirectly affected by the ACS
Fire safety experts: Those who possess knowledge and experience in fire safety, testing, and inspection, particularly in emergency situations
Different groups of system users: The system may have diverse groups of users, including individuals and groups from different religions or cultures, transgender individuals, and other groups with unique characteristics
The entire society: A group of individuals involved in constant social interaction sharing the same social territory and cultural expectations
The business competitors: In the event of a company failing to uphold user values, such as through a violation or breach, they risk losing their customers to competing businesses that can capitalize on this loss and offer similar services
Third parties: Those who are external to the company and are not directly involved in the business's core operations. They can offer valuable insights into integrating the system with other external systems, thereby enhancing its functionality

cognizant of this issue and acknowledged its significance in the context of software systems. They also identified other ethical concerns, such as *avoiding identifiability* and *avoiding malicious activities* (see Table 2)[4]. When the system evaluates an authorization request, the PIP can enhance it with additional information such as user rights, and schedules, while the PAP is responsible for administering the authorization policies. They may be both affected by privacy issues, thus their design must consider these possible threats. In *part 2*, the participants brainstormed the system's ethical implications for different stakeholders. They discussed different scenarios to determine how ethical values in relation to the system could potentially be supported or undermined. They raised ethical concerns regarding the ACS, which they had never thought about or considered their impacts on stakeholders. For example, the risk of *violating dignity* of gym members, *e.g.*, when they are publicly denied access to gym services (by raising the alarm) due to late payment of membership fees. It could lead to feelings of embarrassment and shame. Moreover, they raised ethical concerns focused on indirect system's stakeholders, *e.g.*, *noise pollution* affecting the gym's neighbors, the potential *threats to the sense of togetherness* experienced by gym members and their families (see Table 3). Such implications emphasize the need to consider system users and indirect stakeholders when designing the components of the PEP. It is essential to properly control and configure the loudness of speakers to prevent any violation of dignity when a user is denied entrance and to ensure there are no disturbances to the gym's neighbors.

> **Finding 2 (RQ1):** We observed that using the instruments significantly enhanced the participants' ability to comprehend the possible and far-reaching ramifications of the system from an ethical perspective. It facilitated a thorough exploration of the system's capacity to impact various stakeholders, both directly and indirectly. By providing a structured framework, the instruments guided participants in uncovering the ethical concerns of the involved stakeholders and encouraged a more inclusive analysis.

Finding 3. During *part 1*, the participants discussed several values related to the system, including *privacy, security, welfare*, and *fairness* (indicated by solid circles in Fig. 3). Although not explicitly stated, they acknowledged their reliance on use cases to identify these values, guided by the functionalities requested by the business owner. Given the relations among ethical values, specified in the two parts of the session and listed in Table 4, the participants focused only on the tension between *security and privacy*, and the congruity between *fairness and well-being/welfare*. They emphasized that defining these relations was not straightforward and required reasoning, as there was no clear-cut solution. During *part 2*, following the introduction of the instruments, the participants identified several new values concerning the system (refer to the values marked with dotted circles in Fig. 3). They elucidated the relationships among these values, including tensions between values, such as *togetherness and ownership and property, freedom and safety, freedom and control, safety and anonymity, cultural*

---

[4] To enhance readability, ethical concerns identified in part 1 are presented in Table 2, while those identified in part 2 are summarized in Table 3.

Table 2. The list of the ethical concerns identified in the first part of the session

Ethical concern (Part1)
Violating privacy: During the COVID pandemic, the system barred gym entry to anyone with a temperature over 38 °C, displaying a message on the screen. But, this could potentially reveal users' confidential health information. To prevent this, the system could show a false reason, like an expired subscription, instead of the real cause
Avoiding malicious activities: The system can offer protection to users from potential harm caused by others by preventing unauthorized individuals from entering the gym
Avoiding identifiability: ACSs usually allow individuals to view information such as whether someone is inside a room or when they entered. However, this presents a privacy concern that needs to be addressed to prevent identity disclosure. In the system, only the administrator has access to users' entrance logs. Occasionally, family members of gym members may inquire about the presence of their spouse or children to monitor their activities, as they may claim to be at the gym while actually being elsewhere. With our system, users do not need to worry about such violations
Facilitating financial success: Ensuring the safety and security of users is a crucial aspect of upholding ethical principles for any gym business. By demonstrating a commitment to this principle, the business can earn a favorable reputation among users and attract more subscriptions. When users feel that their ethical concerns and values are taken into consideration, they are more likely to choose the gym over others, which can result in increased revenue and profits for the business owner
Supporting mental well-being: Mental well-being of gym members can be supported by establishing a calm and peaceful atmosphere in the gym, particularly in activities like yoga classes. When individuals enter the class and set up their mats during the final relaxation stage, it could disrupt the experience for others and trigger irritation and anxiety. To avoid such issues, limiting access to the class during a designated period before the activities begin is recommended. This approach helps promote a pleasant environment that enhances the overall mental well-being of all members
Supporting fairness: Indoor cycling and gym bikes have varying levels of quality, with newer models being superior. However, some individuals tend to monopolize the best equipment, leaving others with bad options. To address this issue, the gym owner has suggested restricting access to equipments to only 10 min before classes begin. This ensures fair equipment usage for all users

values, and congruity between *cultural values and control* (see Table 4). The ACS components are all tied to the above-mentioned value relations, highlighting the need for their consideration when designing the components.

Table 3. The list of the ethical concerns identified in the second part of the session

Ethical concern (Part2)
Noise pollution: The system can produce noise upon people entering the gym, which can be problematic, particularly at night, as it may cause disturbance to nearby residents
Controlling: There may be instances where the gym owner or staff notices that a gym member has registered for a class but did not attend. This situation can make him feel like he is being judged or controlled, even though no one is monitoring his every move. This perception can make him feel like he is not in full control of his choices and actions
Security risks: In the event of an emergency, individuals may become trapped inside or outside of the gym and feel helpless if the system does not allow them to take appropriate action
Freedom restriction: During a fire emergency at the gym, individuals may be needed to pass through rooms for which they do not have a subscription to reach the nearest security exit
Violating physical and emotional well-being: Restrictions at the gym may prevent family members from entering to provide assistance to a sick member during a lesson or retrieving a forgotten item, potentially causing undue stress and emotional problems
Violating dignity: Gym members who fail to renew their membership on time may feel a loss of dignity, as the system prompts them to make a payment and restricts access if they do not comply. This process draws attention to the fact that the payment was not made on time, potentially causing embarrassment and shame
Threatening togetherness: The system at the gym may threaten togetherness in situations where a member's family wishes to enter to witness their child's activity and show support but is restricted from doing so
Religious discrimination: Consider a scenario where users are treated differently based solely on their religious beliefs and practices, which is a form of discrimination
Violating cultural and spiritual values: In situations where a group of individuals culturally oppose monitoring, perhaps due to religious beliefs or lack of documentation, they may view it as a violation of their cultural and spiritual values
Supporting usability: The owner had a requirement to implement a system that would make it easier for users to access the facility and decrease the workload of the employees. To achieve this, gym members are allowed to use their own tags to enter and exit the room, eliminating the need for employees to constantly check the computer for subscription end dates. This results in improved usability for the system and reduced workload for the employees
Supporting trust: Users are more likely to trust a system when they can observe that it operates efficiently, provides sufficient functionalities, and does not retain sensitive information. Therefore, implementing these features can enhance the trust users have in the system
Supporting autonomy: The system notifies gym members when their memberships/subscriptions are expiring, allowing them to stay informed without seeking information from the secretary or administration. This autonomy helps them plan and avoid being rejected at the desk by choosing not to attend until the next billing cycle if they cannot pay

Table 4. The list of the potential value relations specified in the two parts of the session

Value relation (Part1)
Conflict between security and privacy: While ensuring the security of individuals, it is important to be mindful of the privacy of users and their data
Congruency between fairness and mental welfare: When a user is consistently given an older bike in the fitness area because they come from a different class, while others have enough time to choose the newer ones, it creates an unfair situation that can lead to negative emotions. This inequality may have a detrimental impact on the user's mental health.

Value relation (Part2)
Conflict between togetherness and ownership and property: The owner of the gym, who has the right of ownership, may desire to have the authority to determine who can enter the premises without necessarily considering the togetherness of the gym members and their families
Conflict between freedom and safety: Users may have to compromise some of their safety in order to gain greater freedom within the context of the ACS
Conflict between freedom and control: While it is necessary to control the entrances of various rooms within the gym, users still desire the freedom to move around the facility
Conflict between safety and privacy/anonymity: If the police require the gym to monitor all individuals entering the premises due to safety regulations, it may compromise other aspects for gym members, such as privacy and anonymity
Conflict between cultural values: While it is important to acknowledge cultural values, it may not always be feasible to satisfy all of them. Considering the prevailing culture in the region where the gym is situated can aid in determining which values to prioritize. However, applying the same approach in diverse settings may lead to challenges. In such cases, it is necessary to make compromises among cultural values
Congruency between cultural values and control: By implementing an ACS, we aim to regulate access and exert control for a specific group of individuals in order to preserve certain cultural values

> **Finding 3 (RQ2):** We observed that the instruments played a crucial role in elevating the participants' perspectives by not only expanding their awareness of affected values but also prompting a deeper understanding of the intricate relationships among these values. By focusing on stakeholders' ethical concerns, participants gained valuable insights into the complex task of identifying and balancing different ethical values within the context of the ACS.

Finding 4. Table 5 reports the list of the ethical decisions identified in the two parts of the session. During *part 1*, participants focused primarily on privacy-related design decisions, such as implementing separate internal and external

Table 5. The list of the ethical decisions identified in the two parts of the session

Ethical decision (Part1)
Ed-1: Storing sensitive user data externally, separate from internal data that could potentially be linked to user identities through building access logs. Access information is maintained externally, including the logs, which should be removed annually for security purposes

Ethical decision (Part2)
Ed-2: Designing the system that generates minimal noise, such as using biometric scanners, can foster a peaceful and supportive environment for individuals residing in the same building or nearby area. This can have a positive impact on their mental health and overall well-being
Ed-3: Reducing the amount of personal information that we need to collect. This can help to protect user privacy, as there is less data that could potentially be misused in the case of a data breach
Ed-4: Categorizing system users based on their gender, cultural background, or religious affiliation and providing tailored services to align with their cultural values
Ed-5: Providing customization options in the system to support cultural values in different contexts is certainly a good practice. However, it is important to keep in mind that releasing the system in a simulation environment and forcing it to face different cultural and ethical violations may not necessarily be the best approach. This is because it cannot fully capture the complexity of real-world cultural contexts

storage for keeping data. A scenario was derived where a user might require authorization from the PEP following another user. If the PEP includes output devices, *e.g.,* a display, the system must ensure that the PEP can provide information regarding a possible denial without causing ethical harm to the users. This highlights the importance of considering privacy concerns when designing the PDP, PIP, and PAP, even though the PEP could also be exposed. Thus, an important design decision is about how long the reason for the denial of entrance should be displayed on the screen. Alternatively, this private information could even be sent to the user confidentially, *e.g.,* by email. During *part* 2, the participants put forward various design decisions aimed at supporting different ethical aspects. They suggested, *e.g.,* a solution to reduce noise pollution at night, which could have a positive impact on the well-being of neighbors (see Table 5). When designing the PIP for the ACS, it is crucial to consider all the decisions above, as the PIP's role is to enrich the authorization with additional data.

Further, we observed that using the instruments enabled the participants to propose recommendations grounded in an understanding of the system's ethical implications on the stakeholders. These recommendations can be regarded as potential considerations for future design decisions within the context of the ACS. Below, we present the suggestions made by participants to foster ethical considerations in the context of the ACS.

– Conducting an ethical assessment using a framework/model can be crucial in evaluating the system's ethical implications. This can provide insight into potential ethical issues and conflicting values and help determine appropriate responses by the system.
– Establishing generic policies using a specific language that can articulate general invariant constraints.
– Using an ethical model to guide the design and development of the software system in a responsible and ethical manner.
– Concretizing ethical considerations during the design phase, especially in requirements and use cases, can effectively help identify potential violations. This can serve as a good starting point for improving the ethical perspective of the system.
– Deploying the system in various contexts can be useful in identifying potential ethical violations, especially those that may be associated with cultural factors.

> **Finding 4 (RQ3):** We observed that the instruments served as catalysts, elevating the participants' awareness about the vital role of ethical values in the ACS design decision process. This heightened awareness empowered the participants to actively incorporate ethical considerations into their decision-making, fostering a sense of responsibility in navigating the intricate ethical dimensions of ACS design.

4.2   The Secondary Evaluation Results

During this session, our main focus was on examining the potential ethical implications of the ACS, discovered in the initial evaluation. We delved into the opinions and perspectives of system's users (*e.g.*, gym members) regarding these implications. By analyzing the session's transcript, we found that participants acknowledged the existence of most of them within the context of the ACS. They specifically emphasized the relevance of the following implications:

– *Noise pollution:* "The gym in our specific location is situated in an isolated area, away from residential properties, and there is a hospital approximately 600 m away. Given this setting, an ACS is unlikely to cause significant problems or disruptions to the surrounding neighborhood. However, it is important to consider that in densely populated areas with numerous nearby buildings, the ACS may introduce potential disturbances."
– *Controlling:* "In relation to the system, we experienced a sense of being judged and controlled based on our understanding of how it operates. An illustration of this is when we utilize the gym's mobile app to enroll in a class, as the system administrator can track our preferences, such as attending the 7 pm guided sessions. It's worth noting that individuals may have different levels of awareness regarding data gathering and may experience varying degrees of feeling judged and controlled."

- *Violating physical and emotional well-being:* "The accessibility of the gym during emergencies is a significant concern, as it can have a detrimental impact on our physical and emotional well-being. The presence of closed doors or obstacles that impede immediate access is viewed as problematic in such situations."
- *Violating dignity:* "The experience of embarrassment is subjective and can be influenced by individual emotions and perspectives. If someone typically attends the gym with a friend, forgetting to renew a gym membership and subsequently being denied entry by the ACS can be particularly embarrassing. The presence of available staff, such as a receptionist, proves helpful in resolving access issues and reducing potential embarrassment. However, when staff is absent, especially during the early morning, it may lead to more embarrassing situations. Additionally, to avoid the embarrassment of being denied access, receiving an email reminder one or two weeks prior to the membership expiration would be preferable."
- *Threatening togetherness:* "Limitations that prevent our family members from accessing the gym can disrupt the feeling of togetherness. While granting access to parents supporting their children's activities is beneficial, it's important to consider such restrictions during the subscription process. Personal experiences illustrate the difficulties that arise when only one parent has access, especially when tasks like preparing the child after swimming lessons become challenging. Such severe restrictions can lead to dissatisfaction and subscription cancellations. Finding a balance that allows for family involvement while maintaining necessary constraints is key to ensuring a positive experience for parents and their children."
- *Violating cultural and spiritual values:* "The ACS offers a user-friendly solution, particularly for individuals struggling with technology. Using a physical bracelet as an access device enhances accessibility and transparency compared to relying on software or mobile apps. The wearable nature of the bracelet makes it well-suited for people of different ages and cultural backgrounds, including older individuals with diverse cultural habits. Moreover, this system can help prevent potential conflicts with gym staff or owners regarding membership renewals. Being rejected by an electronic device is often perceived as less aggressive than dealing with a staff member. Furthermore, in specific countries, the cultural value of unrestricted gym access may clash with the presence of an ACS. It is crucial to consider the impact on cultural values when implementing such systems."
- *Supporting usability:* "Without an ACS, entering the gym becomes challenging, especially when there is no receptionist available. The ACS is crucial as it enables self-verification and ensures a smoother experience. Manual verification with the receptionist can result in queues and delays, *e.g.,* during busy times. Additionally, relying solely on human verification increases the risk of unauthorized access. Implementing an ACS eases the workload of employees and provides valuable insights into customer preferences, allowing the gym to offer improved services based on attendance data."

– *Supporting trust:* "We favor an ACS that does not necessitate our sensitive information, as it is unnecessary for a gym or similar establishments. Having a system that does not store or utilize our sensitive data makes us feel more confident and trusting."
– *Supporting autonomy:* "While we appreciate receiving notifications about our membership status, we have concerns regarding the level of autonomy granted to us. We are uncertain if the ACS includes a feature that allows us to make membership payments. Even if we receive a notification regarding our membership expiration, we still have to visit the reception to finalize the payment process personally. Consequently, our autonomy as members remains unfulfilled in this regard."

There were also instances where participants expressed that certain implications are not deemed as significant in relation to the ACS. For instance, they believed that the system's *security risks* are not highly impactful since the system does not store sensitive information. Additionally, they believed that the system does not impose *restrictions on their freedom*, and any limitations they experience are primarily due to the gym's security measures. Furthermore, participants raised the ethical concern of *identifiability*, *i.e.,*the state of being identifiable, which had not been previously mentioned. They considered it as the most significant implication that requires to be taken into account during the design process. All the components of the ACS are clearly tied to the highlighted ethical concerns. However, since the user interaction happens through the PEP, it is crucial to design it in a way that instills a sense of trust in the end user.

> **Finding 5 (RQ1):** We observed that the opinions of the system's users regarding its ethical implications align closely with those revealed using the instruments. This suggests that the instruments have the potential to assist software designers in identifying ethical implications of the system that are important from the standpoint of stakeholders with different roles.

4.3   Threats to Validity

A potential threat to *construct validity* is related to the mediator's bias in data collection. We mitigated it by proposing predetermined questions in the two focus group sessions. A potential threat to *internal validity* is related to the reliability of the data collected from the two focus groups. To mitigate it, we used Atlas.ti [5] to code and cluster notable quotes to reduce bias and ensure reliable results. A potential threat to *external validity* is related to the experience and background of participants involved in the secondary evaluation. To mitigate it, we conducted the focus group involving participants with different experiences. A potential threat to *conclusion validity* is related to the credibility of the final findings. To mitigate it, we all discussed the study findings and drew conclusions.

5 Conclusion and Future Directions

This study highlights the dual nature of software systems, bringing substantial benefits to individuals' lives while also posing potential social and ethical challenges that may compromise ethical values. Emphasizing the significance of considering all relevant stakeholders and their values during the system design process, we introduced two ethics-driven instruments (*i.e.,*a stakeholder map and a value model) to evaluate their impact on supporting ethical considerations, illustrated through the case of an ACS. The retrospective study revealed that these instruments effectively facilitated the identification of stakeholders with different roles, their ethical concerns, values, and ethical decision-making. To further advance this line of inquiry, future research could explore a broader array of studies to comprehensively assess the effectiveness of the instruments. Another direction involves utilizing these two instruments right from the initial phases of software system design.

Acknowledgement. We would like to thank the ACS designers for their contribution to enhancing our understanding of the system from an ethical standpoint. Also, we thank the gym members for their valuable feedback. The work has been partially supported by ARS01_00540 - RASTA project, funded by the Italian Ministry of Research PNR 2015–2020. The authors De Sanctis and Iovino acknowledge the support of the MUR (Italy) Department of Excellence 2023–2027 for GSSI.

References

1. Alidoosti, R., Lago, P., Poort, E., Razavian, M.: Ethics-aware decidarch game: Designing a game to reflect on ethical considerations in software architecture design decision making. In: 2023 IEEE 20th International Conference on Software Architecture Companion (ICSA-C), pp. 96–100. IEEE (2023)
2. Alidoosti, R., Lago, P., Razavian, M., Tang, A.: Ethics in software engineering: a systematic literature review. Technical report, Vrije Universiteit Amsterdam (2022). https://tinyurl.com/39crpyn2
3. Bittner, K., Spence, I.: Establishing the Vision for Use Case Modeling, Use Case Modeling. Addison Wesley Professional, Reading (2003)
4. De Sanctis, M., Di Salle, A., Iovino, L., Rossi, M.T.: A technology transfer journey to a model-driven access control system. Int. J. Softw. Tools Technol. Transf. 1–26 (2023)
5. Friese, S.: Qualitative Data Analysis with ATLAS.ti. Sage, Thousand Oaks (2019)
6. Leong, B.: Facial recognition and the future of privacy: I always feel like... somebody's watching me. Bull. Atomic Sci. **75**(3), 109–115 (2019)
7. Miles, M.B., Huberman, A.M.: Qualitative Data Analysis: An Expanded Sourcebook. Sage, Thousand Oaks(1994)
8. Moreno, M.V., Hernández, J.L., Skarmeta, A.F.: A new location-aware authorization mechanism for indoor environments. In: International Conference on Advanced Information Networking and Applications Workshops, pp. 791–796. IEEE (2014)
9. Neudecker, T., Hayrapetyan, A., Degitz, A., Andelfinger, P.: Consideration of values in the design of access control systems. In: Informatik 2016 (2016)

10. Robson, C.: Small-Scale Evaluation: Principles and Practice. Sage, Thousand Oaks (2017)
11. Schwartz, S.H.: Universals in the content and structure of values: theoretical advances and empirical tests in 20 countries. In: Advances in Experimental Social Psychology, vol. 25, pp. 1–65. Elsevier, Amsterdam (1992)
12. Schwartz, S.H.: Basic human values: theory, measurement, and applications. Rev. Fr. Sociol. **47**(4), 929 (2007)
13. Schwartz, S.H.: An overview of the schwartz theory of basic values. Online readings in Psychology and Culture **2**(1), 2307–0919 (2012)
14. Sicari, S., Rizzardi, A., Miorandi, D., Cappiello, C., Coen-Porisini, A.: Security policy enforcement for networked smart objects. Comput. Netw. **108**, 133–147 (2016)

Data-Driven Analysis of Gender Fairness in the Software Engineering Academic Landscape

Giordano d'Aloisio⬭, Andrea D'Angelo⬭, Francesca Marzi⬭, Diana Di Marco, Giovanni Stilo^(✉)⬭, and Antinisca Di Marco⬭

University of L'Aquila, L'Aquila, Italy
{giordano.daloisio,andrea.dangelo6}@graduate.univaq.it,
diana.dimarco@student.univaq.it,
{francesca.marzi,giovanni.stilo,antinisca.dimarco}@univaq.it

Abstract. Gender bias in education gained considerable relevance in the literature over the years. However, while the problem of gender bias in education has been widely addressed from a student perspective, it is still not fully analysed from an academic point of view. In this work, we study the problem of gender bias in academic promotions (i.e., from Researcher to Associated Professor and from Associated to Full Professor) in the informatics (INF) and software engineering (SE) Italian communities (we restricted to the Italian community since each country has specific and own promotion systems). In particular, we first conduct a literature review to assess how the problem of gender bias in academia has been addressed so far. Next, we describe a process to collect and preprocess the INF and SE data needed to analyse gender bias in Italian academic promotions. Subsequently, we apply a formal bias metric to these data to assess the amount of bias and look at its variation over time. From the conducted analysis, we observe how the SE community presents a higher bias in promotions to Associate Professors and a smaller bias in promotions to Full Professors compared to the overall INF community.

Keywords: Gender bias · Academia · Italy · Informatics · Software Engineering

This work is partially supported by European Union - NextGenerationEU - National Recovery and Resilience Plan (Piano Nazionale di Ripresa e Resilienza, PNRR) - Project: "SoBigData.it - Strengthening the Italian RI for Social Mining and Big Data Analytics" - Prot. IR0000013 - Avviso n. 3264 del 28/12/2021, by "FAIR-EDU: Promote FAIRness in EDUcation institutions" a project founded by the University of L'Aquila, 2022, and by COST Action CA19122 - European Network Balance in Informatics (EUGAIN). All the numerical simulations have been realized on the Linux HPC cluster Caliban of the High-Performance Computing Laboratory of the Department of Information Engineering, Computer Science and Mathematics (DISIM) at the University of L'Aquila.
G. d'Aloisio, A. D'Angelo and F. Marzi—These authors contributed equally to the paper.

B. Tekinerdoğan et al. (Eds.): ECSA 2023, LNCS 14590, pp. 89–103, 2024.
https://doi.org/10.1007/978-3-031-66326-0_6

Terminology

In this work, we adhere to the convention in the existing literature by using the term 'gender' to refer to the sex assigned at birth, aligning with established research practices. While the literature commonly uses the term 'gender' in this context, we acknowledge that this may differ from its more typical use referring to gender identity.

1   Introduction

Nowadays, the problem of *gender bias* has been widely considered and analysed in the literature under several contexts and domains, like health [28], justice [4], or education [24]. Concerning the latter, the problem of gender bias in education gained considerable relevance over the years, and several papers studied this issue from both a technical and sociological point of view [6,23]. However, most works focus on gender bias in students' education, not considering other relevant contexts [5]. In this work, we want to analyze the issue of gender bias in education from the academic point of view by analyzing if there is a gender bias in academic promotions (i.e., from Researcher to Associated Professor and from Associated to Full Professor) in the Italian academic context, in Italian informatics (INF) in general and software engineering (SE) in particular.

We first perform a literature review to assess how the issue of gender bias in academia has been addressed so far. Next, we perform an empirical analysis of gender bias in academic promotions in the Italian informatics (INF) community. We first extract all the needed data from several open repositories and process them to make them suitable for the analysis. We perform said analysis by investigating the gender distribution and academic productivity of each gender group. Then, by applying a formal bias metric, we show the trend of bias over the years, starting from 2018 to 2022. Finally, we compare the overall trend with the sole software engineering (SE) Italian community highlighting how the trend for the latter exhibits similar behaviour, albeit considerably more biased towards researchers and less biased towards associate professors, compared to the overall INF community.

Hence, the main contributions of this work are the following:

- We perform a literature review of the most relevant papers addressing the issue of gender bias in academia by also highlighting the main weaknesses of the current approaches (Sect. 2);
- We describe a process to collect and preprocess data useful to assess the amount of gender bias in academic promotions in Italy (Sect. 3);
- We analyse the gender distribution of each gender group in both the Italian Informatics and Software engineering Communities.
- We depict the trend of gender bias in academic promotions in Italy over the years by relying on a formal bias metric, and we compare the trend of bias of the overall INF Italian community with the sole SE Italian community (Sect. 4).

The paper concludes in Sect. 6 which describes some future works and final considerations.

2   Gender Bias in Classic Academic Systems

This section describes the literature review process, focused on those works that address the problem of gender bias in academia. The search process involved research of conference proceedings and journal papers on Google Scholar by relying on the search string shown in Listing 1.1.

Listing 1.1. Search string

```
allintitle: (gender bias OR gender discrimination) AND (academic recruitment OR
Women's faculty recruitment OR faculty equity OR career advancements OR Italian
universities OR selection processes)
```

Among the results, we selected papers that studied and analysed gender bias in the context of Italian educational systems. Papers discussing practices and techniques utilised in foreign universities were also included to gain a broader perspective and compare different approaches and methods. We mainly focus on works related to the recruitment, promotion and productivity level of academic staff, i.e., full professors, associate professors and researchers. Articles about specific faculties or that address the gender bias problem in the general working world are excluded. This process yields 21 papers that have been carefully analysed to highlight these main features: the *context* (i.e. the country where the study was conducted), the *process* (i.e., recruitment, promotions or productivity) in which the gender bias has been studied, if the data used are *public* or not, the *analytical method* employed (i.e., whether descriptive or inferential statistics are used to analyze the data), and the *year* of the paper.

Table 1 summarises such features for each paper. Note that papers with the same features have been grouped in the same row.

Concerning the context, most of the papers focus on specific countries, while the rest of them are generic and unrelated to particular academic systems. In the table, we use the official national abbreviation to specify each country, while papers with unspecified countries are labeled with *UNK*.

Concerning the process, most papers address the problem of gender bias either in *recruitment* or *promotions*, while only two papers (i.e., [3,17]) address the issue of gender bias in *productivity*. Gender bias in recruitment is mainly addressed by providing recommendations, practices, and strategies to minimize the impact of bias and reach gender equity in the recruitment process. Instead, the problem of gender bias in academic promotions is mainly addressed by estimating the probability of promotion by looking at the number of female and male academicians across different career stages or focusing on women in university leadership. Finally, the problem of gender bias in productivity is addressed by investigating the causes that lead to lower productivity by women.

Concerning the source data, public data comes mainly from institutional repositories like the *Ministero dell'Università e della Ricerca (MIUR)* (i.e., the

Table 1. Summary of the Literature Review.

Paper	Context	Process	Source Data	Analytical Method	Year
[33]	AU	Prom.	Priv.	Descr.	2000
[34]	U.K.	Prom.	Priv.	Inf.	2001
[32]	U.S.	Recr./Prom.	Priv.	Inf./Descr.	2002
[17]	U.S.	Prod.	Priv.	Inf./Descr.	2005
[7]	NL	Recr.	Priv.	Descr.	2006
[2]	IT	Prod.	Pub.	Descr.	2009
[19]	UNK	Rescr./Prom.	Priv.	Inf./Descr.	2010
[25]	IT	Prom.	Pub.	Inf./Descr.	2011
[3, 26]	IT	Recr.	Pub.	Inf./Descr.	2016, 2019
[13, 16]	IT	Prom.	Pub.	Descr.	2017, 2021
[22]	IT	Prom.	Pub.	Inf.	2018
[9, 29]	U.S.	Recr./Prom	Priv.	Descr.	2020, 2019
[31]	U.S.	Recr.	Priv.	Descr.	2019
[18]	IT	Recr./Priv.	Pub.	Descr.	2020
[8]	IT	Prom.	Priv.	Inf./Descr.	2021
[10]	IS,NO,SE	Recr.	Priv.	Inf.	2021
[20]	DE,AT,CH	Prom.	Priv.	Inf./Descr.	2022
[21]	UNK	Prom	Priv	Descr	2022

Italian Ministry of University and Research) and the National Scientific Qualification website (for Italian works) [11,27]. Private data were instead collected through different methods, for instance interviews [2,22], questionnaires [3] and compilation of surveys [7,8,31,33]. Other papers collected data directly from internal private university databases.

Concerning the analytical methods, papers using classical descriptive analysis typically measure the percentages of males and females across career stages and institutions, means, standard deviations or comparisons using t-tests between men and women. In addition to these indicators, cross-tables [19], frequency distributions and segregation indexes [18] were used. Papers that perform inferential statistical analysis use different regressions methods, such as ordinary least squares regressions, multiple logistic regressions, and multilevel logistic regressions. Works like [26] use quantitative analysis with the glass ceiling index and the glass door index to measure and compare the effects of gender practices, and [34] relies on a static discrete-choice model for rank attainment.

From this review of the existing literature, it is clear how there is an interest in analysing the issue of gender bias in academia. However, some examined works are old, and the reported conclusions may be outdated. Moreover, we have seen a lack of analyses using formal metrics to measure bias, and none of the reported papers analyses the issue of gender bias in academic promotions inside the informatics community (and thereby software engineering). In this paper, we aim to overcome these lacks by formally analysing gender bias in academic promotions in the informatics (and software engineering) Italian communities.

3   Analysis Description

This section presents the analysis conducted to evaluate the level of gender bias in the academic positions within the overall informatics (INF) and software engineering (SE) Italian communities. The informatics community is the conjunction of Areas 1 and 9 of the MIUR scientific areas classification [1]. We first report the dataset creation and filtering procedure (Sect. 3.1). Next, we describe the performed experiment (Sect. 3.2).

3.1   Data Collection and Filtering

Figure 1 reports the full data collection and filtering pipeline used to collect the datasets of the INF and SE Italian communities for our analysis[1]. In the figure, we report the different sources (Italian and international) from where we gathered the needed information, namely: Scopus [14] and Google Scholar [30] as international sources and MIUR [27] and National Scientific Qualification (ASN) [11] as Italian sources.

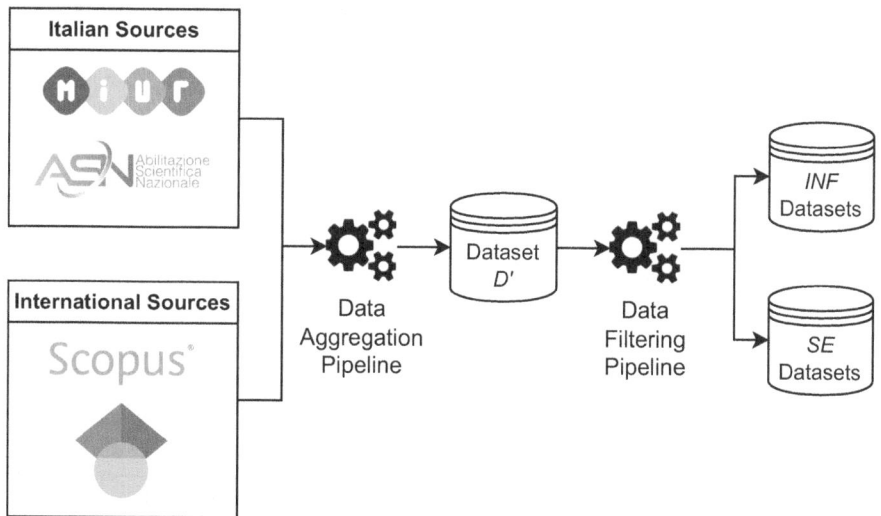

Fig. 1. Data collection and filtering pipeline

The first step of the pipeline is the dataset collection and aggregation. Specifically, data was gathered between 2015 and 2022 with the aim of identifying the following information:

---

[1] https://github.com/dangeloandrea14/Italian_SE_Fairness_Public.

- **Personal Data:** i.e., information such as age and gender. These data have been gathered from the MIUR website, which contains all the information about people employed in the Italian academia [27].
- **Academic Career:** i.e., information such as the university and department of affiliation, career advancements, academic seniority, macro disciplinary area, scientific sub-sector they belong to, area of expertise, current academic appointment, academics managerial appointments, teaching activities, funded projects, committees, salaries, and sabbatical period. These data have been gathered from the MIUR and National Scientific Qualification (ASN) websites [11].
- **Scientific Productivity:** i.e., information such as the list of publications, the total number of papers, total citations, the h-index, publication range, papers per year, citations per year, publication types, journal metrics, and research area. These data have been scraped from Scopus [14] and Google Scholar [30].

Note that not all the reported information is used in the following analysis, but we choose to gather them for future works. The data have then been aggregated into a single dataset D' using the *name, surname, email*, and *affiliation* as join keys. This aggregated dataset D' was then thoroughly anonymized to protect the University employees' privacy. As a result, no references to names, surnames, or other sensitive or personal data are stored, as they are neither relevant nor valuable for computing bias metrics. Since the licences under which some of such data are published are not clear, we prefer to not publish them, but researchers who want to analyse them can request them on-site. However, the dataset can be recreated by gathering the same data from the sources mentioned above and applying the pipeline code published at the link above.

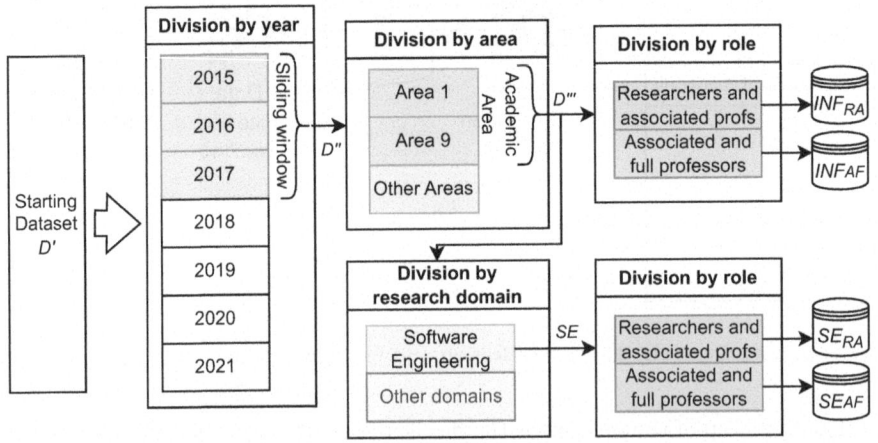

Fig. 2. Filtering pipeline of the dataset.

Starting from the anonymized dataset D', we performed a set of filtering operations to obtain the final datasets that we used to compute bias metrics yearly. The filtering procedure is depicted in Fig. 2. First, we selected from the dataset only people employed in the academic system for all the reference period (i.e., from 2015 to 2022). Next, since we are interested in the evolution of bias in academic promotions year by year, the anonymized dataset D' was split according to a sliding time window of fixed size. In particular, we considered a sliding window of three years, starting from 2015. Hence, to gather metrics for 2019, we would slice D' to obtain only the columns referencing data collected from 2016 to 2019. After this operation, we obtain a partially filtered dataset D'' for each sliding window.

The subsequent step was selecting only specific scientific areas from D''. Because different domains have different promotion criteria, it would be incorrect to consider them all together. Our study only focused on Areas 1 and 9 of the MIUR scientific areas classification, which refers broadly to Science, technology, engineering, and mathematics [1]. In this study, we refer to the conjunction of these two areas as the Informatics community. From this further filtering, we obtain a dataset D'''. From D''', we perform two different branches of operations. In the first branch, D''' is split into two versions: one without records representing researchers (INF_{AF}) and one without Full Professors (INF_{RA}). In the second phase, D''' is refined by selecting individuals who work specifically in the SE field. To achieve this, we use Google Scholar to find individuals who have expressed interest in *software engineering* or related topics. In particular, we considered people with interests in: *software engineering, software architecture, model-driven engineering, software quality*, and *software testing*. The SE dataset is then divided into two sub-datasets as done above: one consisting of only researchers and associate professors (SE_{RA}), and the other consisting of only associate and full professors (SE_{AF}). As a result of the data pre-processing pipeline, four distinct datasets were created. Two of them are for the overall Italian INF community (INF_{RA} and INF_{AF}), while the other two are for the Italian SE community (SE_{RA} and SE_{AF}). Finally, we only preserved data for people employed at an Italian university for the entire time window.

3.2 Analysis Setting

Once the final yearly datasets INF_{RA}, INF_{AF}, SE_{RA}, and SE_{AF} have been constructed, the experiments can occur. As already mentioned, the experiment aims to measure the amount of gender bias in academic promotions and analyze its variation over the years. To calculate the amount of bias, we use the *Disparate Impact (DI)* metric [15]. This metric measures the probability of having a *positive outcome* while being in the *privileged* or *unprivileged* group and is defined formally as:

$$DI = \frac{P(Y = y_p | X = x_{unpriv})}{P(Y = y_p | X = x_{priv})} \tag{1}$$

where Y is the label, y_p is the positive outcome, X is the sensitive variable, and x_{unpriv} and x_{priv} are the values identifying the unprivileged and privileged groups, respectively. The more this metric is close to one, the fairer the dataset.

In our context, the label assigned to a person represents their position for that particular year. In the analysis between Researchers and Associate Professors, the positive label is *Associate Professor*, while in the analysis between Associate and Full Professors, it is *Full Professor*. The sensitive variable is *gender*, where *men* and *women* are the privileged and unprivileged groups, respectively. Hence, the experiment is performed as follows: for each final yearly dataset (INF_{RA}, INF_{AF}, SE_{RA}, and SE_{AF}) and for each year in the considered range (2018–2022), we compute the DI between the two subsets contained in the dataset (either Researchers and Associate Professors or Associate Professors and Full Professors). We also compute the cardinality of each subset per year.

4   Experimental Results

In this section, we first present statistics on the datasets we analyzed. Then, we present and discuss the Experimental Results on the bias metric of Disparate Impact(DI).

4.1   Statistics

Figure 3 depicts the gender distribution in the Informatics and SE Italian communities, on the left and right sides respectively. For the former, the dataset size is roughly 6600 entries. For the latter, the size is around 100 entries.

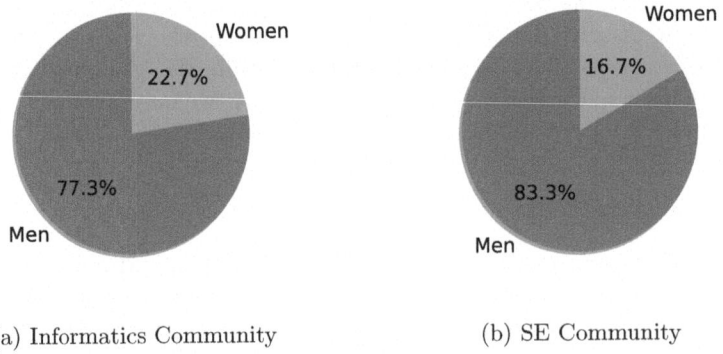

(a) Informatics Community   (b) SE Community

Fig. 3. Gender Distribution in the Italian Informatics (left side) and Software Engineering (right side) Communities in 2022.

The disparity in gender representation within both communities reveals a substantial underrepresentation of women compared to men. This disparity is indicative of a longstanding and well-documented concern within the Informatics community, which our research findings further corroborate [12]. It is noteworthy that this discrepancy becomes even more pronounced within the Software Engineering Community, with 83.3% of researchers being men.

It is also interesting to note the disparity in distribution within the single groups of Researchers, Associate Professors, and Full Professors. Please note that the following data refer to the year 2022. Figure 4 depicts them on the subfigures (a), (b), and (c) respectively. The number of total researchers is 628 (452 men and 176 women), the number of Associate Professors is 3222 (2332 men and 890 women), and the number of Full Professors is 2737 (2311 men and 426 women). It is important to note that, as described in Sect. 3.1, we only consider researchers who have been inside the Italian academic system for the entire time window that we consider. For this reason, the cardinality of the sets is skewed towards higher academic roles.

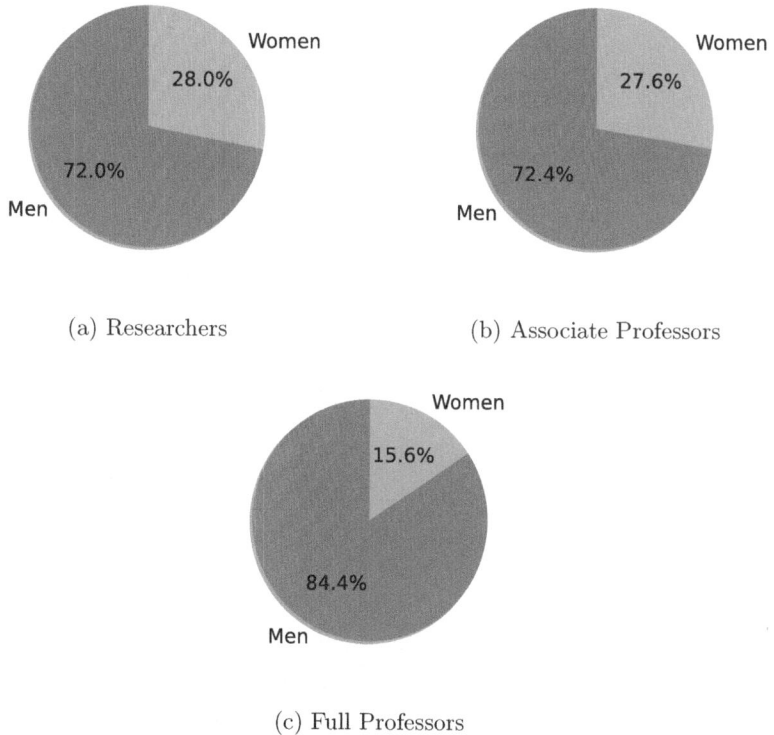

(a) Researchers   (b) Associate Professors

(c) Full Professors

Fig. 4. Gender Distribution in the Italian Informatics community, within Researchers (left side), Associate Professors (center) and Full Professors (right side) in 2022.

For the informatics community, the gender groups' size disparity increases as we progress to higher academic roles. The lower representation of female Full Professors suggests a gender-based disparity in the attainment of Full Professorship, indicating that women face greater challenges in achieving promotion to this academic rank compared to their male counterparts. However, the higher percentage of female researchers within the informatics community may lead to the inference that there is a relatively more balanced representation at the earlier career stages. This suggests that the gender-based disparities in academic roles become more pronounced as individuals progress towards higher positions, such as Associate Professors and Full Professors, indicating the need for targeted interventions to address these disparities at advanced career levels.

Figure 5, on the other hand, shows the gender distribution within roles in the Software Engineering Community. The cardinality of these sets is much lower: researchers are only 6 (6 men), Associate Professors are 32 (25 men and 7 women), and Full Professors are 34 (29 men and 5 women).

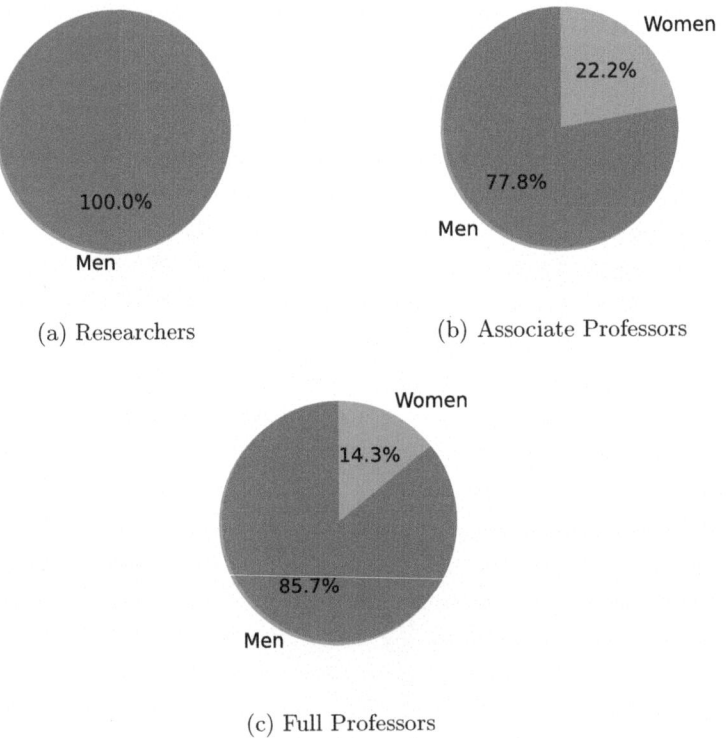

(a) Researchers   (b) Associate Professors

(c) Full Professors

Fig. 5. Gender Distribution in the Italian Software Engineering community, within Researchers (left side), Associate Professors (center) and Full Professors (right side) in 2022.

Interestingly, results are significantly different with respect to the Informatics Community. The percentage of women within the Italian Informatics community shows notable variations across academic ranks. Women are least represented among Researchers, and most represented among Associate Professors, with Full Professors falling in between. Note how, at the end of our time window, only male researchers are left (Fig. 5 (a)). This means that all women were promoted to at least Associate Professors during the time window[2]. However, this middle ground for Full Professors suggests that women may encounter unique challenges in advancing to this rank. More concerning, there is a limited presence of women in the field of Software Engineering as researchers in general, which could potentially widen the gender gap in the future.

4.2 Disparate Impact

Figure 6 shows the Disparate Impact (DI) (left y-axis) and set cardinalities (right y-axis) for each of the datasets above (INF_{RA}, INF_{AF}, SE_{RA}, and SE_{AF}) on a yearly basis in the reference period (2018–2022). In the figure, the charts on the left side show results for the Informatics (INF) Community datasets (INF_{RA}, INF_{AF}), while the ones on the right side show results for the Software Engineering (SE) Community (SE_{RA}, SE_{AF}).

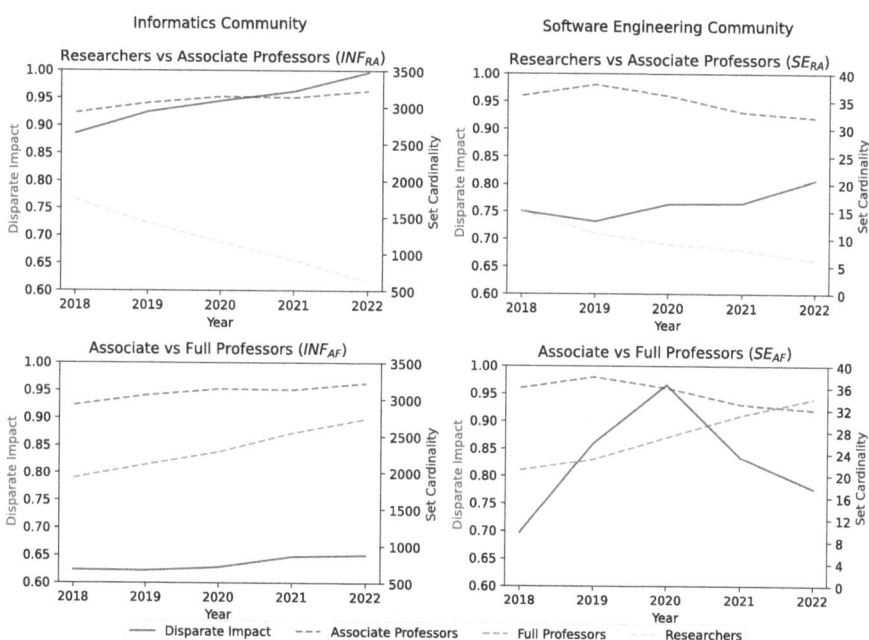

Fig. 6. Year-by-year Disparate Impact and Set Cardinality for the Informatics Community (left column) and Software Engineering Community (right column).

Concerning the full set cardinalities (i.e., of both men and women), they exhibit the same trend across all datasets. Since we only consider people that

---

[2] Since, as explained above in Sect. 3, we consider only people employed in the academic system for all the considered period.

were in the Italian academic system for the entire reference period, we do not consider researchers that were acquired later than 2018, so their cardinality is bound to decrease. The number of Full professors is rising in both the INF and SE communities, but the increase in the SE community is significantly larger. In 2022, there are more Full professors than Associate professors specifically in the SE subset. This suggests that promotions to Full professorship are occurring at a higher rate among professors in the field of SE compared to the INF community.

Concerning the gender bias in promotions to Associate Professor (INF_{RA} and SE_{RA} in the figure), in both the Informatics and Software Engineering communities the trend of Disparate Impact (DI) appears to be on an upward trajectory. However, the SE community seems to suffer from a higher bias w.r.t. the overall INF community. The DI for the SE community starts from a value of 0.75 in 2018 to a value of 0.8 in 2022. In contrast, the DI of the INF community starts from a value of 0.9 in 2018 to a value of almost 1 in 2022, meaning a nearly complete absence of bias in academic promotions. In general, we observe how the amount of bias in the SE community is about 20% higher than in the overall INF community.

In contrast, concerning bias in promotions to Full Professors (INF_{AF} and SE_{AF} in the figure), the SE community exhibits a much lower bias concerning the INF community. DI for the SE community starts from 0.7 in 2018, then reaches a peak of 0.95 in 2020, to a final value of almost 0.8 in 2022. This downtrend from 2020 to 2022 can be partially explained by the small set cardinality, which makes the DI more sensitive to small changes (i.e., additions or deletions) in the groups. Instead, the DI for the overall INF community presents a slight increase over the period, starting from a value of 0.63 in 2018 to a value of 0.65 in 2022. In this case, the amount of bias in the INF community ranges from 15 to 35% greater than in the SE community throughout the observed period.

5   Threats to Validity

This section discusses possible threats that can hamper the results of the performed evaluation.

Internal Validity concerns factors that can impact the results of our evaluation. Firstly, we want to acknowledge that we are considering gender as a binary variable in our analysis despite being aware that some individuals may not identify with this classification. However, the data sources from which we have extracted gender information present it as a binary variable, limiting our ability to perform a more detailed gender analysis. Secondly, we have chosen to restrict our analysis of the Italian SE and informatics communities to individuals within the Italian academic system for all the year ranges assessed. This decision was made to ensure that our analysis of gender bias in academic promotions is accurate and not influenced by individuals leaving or joining the academic system.

Construct Validity concerns factors that can jeopardise how the experimental evaluation has been performed. One threat could be that there might be other confounding factors impacting the results that are not related to gender. In this sense, we plan to extend our analysis considering also the number of publications and citations of each academic.

Conclusion Validity concerns threats about the conclusions that are derived from our evaluation. In this context, we observe that the low number of data samples might impact the visualized results, causing a high fluctuation of the metrics curves. The low number of samples is caused by the filtering procedure we apply to the collected data and, in particular, by the fact that we select only people employed in academia for all the considered time ranges.

External Validity concerns the generalizability of our results. Our analysis is focused on the Italian academic system and is not applicable to countries having a different academic system.

6   Conclusion and Future Work

In this paper, we have studied the issue of gender bias in academic promotions. First, we performed a literature review to observe how the literature has addressed this issue so far. Then, we formally analyzed gender bias in academic promotions in the informatics (INF) and software engineering (SE) Italian communities. From the analysis, we observed that gender bias has been improving over the years in both communities, even though the SE community has a higher trend in promoting professors from Associated to Full compared to the broader INF community. In the future, we plan to extend this analysis to other countries by identifying valuable data sources to retrieve all the needed information. Next, we plan to analyze the behaviour of a Machine Learning classifier trained on such data to predict the position of a person. In particular, we want to study how a classifier is subject to learning a possible gender bias in the data and how we can mitigate it by relying on proper fairness methods.

References

1. MIUR - Italian Higher Education guide. https://www.miur.it/guida/capitolo3.htm
2. Abramo, G., D'Angelo, C., Caprasecca, A.: Gender differences in research productivity: a bibliometric analysis of the Italian academic system. Scientometrics **79**, 517–539 (2009). https://doi.org/10.1007/s11192-007-2046-8
3. Abramo, G., D'Angelo, C.A., Rosati, F.: Gender bias in academic recruitment. Scientometrics **106**(1), 119–141 (2016)
4. Angwin, J., Larson, J., Mattu, S., Kirchner, L.: Machine bias. ProPublica **23**(2016), 139–159 (2016)
5. Baker, R.S.: Learning analytics: an opportunity for education. XRDS: Crossroads ACM Mag. Students **29**(3), 18–21 (2023)
6. Baker, R.S., Hawn, A.: Algorithmic bias in education. Int. J. Artif. Intell. Educ. (2021). https://doi.org/10.1007/s40593-021-00285-9

7. van den Brink Marieke, B., Margo, B., Waslander, S.: Does excellence have a gender? A national research on recruitment and selection procedures for professorial appointments in the Netherlands. Empl. Relat. **28**, 523–539 (2006). https://doi.org/10.1108/01425450610704470

8. Calabrese, A., Fede, M.C., Naciti, V., Rappazzo, N.: Female careers in Italian universities: the role of gender budgeting to achieve equality between women and men. Zeszyty Naukowe Uniwersytetu Ekonomicznego w Krakowie/Cracow Rev. Econ. Manag. **5**(989), 31–47 (2021)

9. Cardel, M.I., et al.: Turning chutes into ladders for women faculty: a review and roadmap for equity in academia. J. Womens Health **29**(5), 721–733 (2020). https://doi.org/10.1089/jwh.2019.8027

10. Carlsson, M., Finseraas, H., Midtboen, A.H., Rafnsdottir, G.L.: Gender bias in academic recruitment?: Evidence from a survey experiment in the Nordic region. Eur. Sociol. Rev. **37**(3), 399–410 (2021). https://doi.org/10.1093/esr/jcaa050

11. MIUR, Cineca: Abilitazione Scientifica Nazionale. https://abilitazione.mur.gov.it/public/index.php

12. Research and Innovation - European Commission: Innovation: bridging the gender gap in STEM - strengthening opportunities for women in research and innovation. Publications Office of the European Union (2022). https://doi.org/10.2777/774922

13. De Paola, M., Ponzo, M., Scoppa, V.: Gender differences in the propensity to apply for promotion: evidence from the Italian Scientific Qualification. Oxford Econ. Papers **69**(4), 986–1009 (2017). https://doi.org/10.1093/oep/gpx023

14. Elsevier: Scopus. https://dev.elsevier.com/

15. Feldman, M., Friedler, S.A., Moeller, J., Scheidegger, C., Venkatasubramanian, S.: Certifying and removing disparate impact. In: Proceedings of the 21th ACM SIGKDD International Conference on Knowledge Discovery and Data Mining, pp. 259–268. ACM, Sydney, NSW, Australia, August 2015. https://doi.org/10.1145/2783258.2783311

16. Filandri, M., Pasqua, S.: 'Being good isn't good enough': gender discrimination in Italian academia. Stud. High. Educ. **46**(8), 1533–1551 (2021). https://doi.org/10.1080/03075079.2019.1693990

17. Fox, M.F.: Gender, family characteristics, and publication productivity among scientists. Soc. Stud. Sci. **35**(1), 131–150 (2005)

18. Gaiaschi, C., Musumeci, R.: Just a matter of time? women's career advancement in neo-liberal academia. an analysis of recruitment trends in Italian universities. Soc. Sci. **9**(9) (2020). https://doi.org/10.3390/socsci9090163

19. Glass, C., Minnotte, K.L.: Recruiting and hiring women in stem fields. J. Divers. High. Educ. **3**(4) (2010). https://doi.org/10.1037/a0020581

20. Henningsen, L., Eagly, A.H., Jonas, K.: Where are the women deans? The importance of gender bias and self-selection processes for the deanship ambition of female and male professors. J. Appl. Soc. Psychol. **52**(8), 602–622 (2022). https://doi.org/10.1111/jasp.12780

21. Kenney, J., et al.: A snapshot of female representation in twelve academic psychiatry institutions around the world. Psychiatry Res. **308**, 114358 (2022). https://doi.org/10.1016/j.psychres.2021.114358

22. Marini, G., Meschitti, V.: The trench warfare of gender discrimination: evidence from academic promotions to full professor in Italy. Scientometrics **115**(2), 989–1006 (2018). https://doi.org/10.1007/s11192-018-2696-8

23. Mengel, F., Sauermann, J., Zölitz, U.: Gender bias in teaching evaluations. J. Eur. Econ. Assoc. **17**(2), 535–566 (2019). https://doi.org/10.1093/jeea/jvx057

24. Moss-Racusin, C.A., Dovidio, J.F., Brescoll, V.L., Graham, M.J., Handelsman, J.: Science faculty's subtle gender biases favor male students. Proc. Natl. Acad. Sci. **109**(41), 16474–16479 (2012)
25. Paola, M.D., Scoppa, V.: Gender discrimination and evaluators' gender: evidence from the Italian academy. In: Working Papers 201106, Università della Calabria, Dipartimento di Economia, Statistica e Finanza "Giovanni Anania" - DESF (2011). https://ideas.repec.org/p/clb/wpaper/201106.html
26. Picardi, I.: The glass door of academia: unveiling new gendered bias in academic recruitment. Soc. Sci. **8**(5) (2019). https://doi.org/10.3390/socsci8050160
27. dell'Istruzione dell'Università e della Ricerca, M.: Cerca Università, http://cercauniversita.cineca.it/php5/docenti/cerca.php
28. Ruiz, M.T., Verbrugge, L.M.: A two way view of gender bias in medicine. J. Epidemiol. Community Health **51**(2), 106 (1997)
29. Russell, J., Brock, S., Rudisill, M.: Recognizing the impact of bias in faculty recruitment, retention, and advancement processes. Kinesiol. Rev. **8**, 1–5 (2019). https://doi.org/10.1123/kr.2019-0043
30. Google Scholar. https://scholar.google.com/
31. Sekaquaptewa, D., Takahashi, K., Malley, J., Herzog, K., Bliss, S.: An evidence-based faculty recruitment workshop influences departmental hiring practice perceptions among university faculty. Int. J. Equal. Divers. Inclus. (2019)
32. Sonnad, S.S., Colletti, L.M.: Issues in the recruitment and success of women in academic surgery. Surgery **132**(2), 415–419 (2002). https://doi.org/10.1067/msy.2002.127694
33. Todd, P., Bird, D.: Gender and promotion in academia. Equal Opportunities Int. **19**(8) (2000). https://doi.org/10.1108/02610150010786166
34. Ward, M.E.: Gender and promotion in the academic profession. Scott. J. Polit. Econ. **48**(3), 283–302 (2001). https://doi.org/10.1111/1467-9485.00199

DeMeSSA

Sarch-Knows: A Knowledge Graph for Modeling Security Scenarios at the Software Architecture Level

Jeisson Vergara-Vargas[1,2]([✉]) [iD], Felipe Restrepo-Calle[1] [iD], Salah Sadou[2] [iD], and Chouki Tibermacine[3] [iD]

[1] Universidad Nacional de Colombia, Bogotá, Colombia
{javergarav,ferestrepoca}@unal.edu.co
[2] IRISA & CNRS, Université Bretagne Sud, Vannes, France
salah.sadou@irisa.fr
[3] LIRMM & CNRS, Univ Montpellier, Montpellier, France
chouki.tibermacine@lirmm.fr

Abstract. Security, as a software quality attribute, needs to be addressed from different perspectives and at different levels of the software life-cycle. One of these perspectives is the one that focuses on design decisions at the highest level, that is, at the architectural level. This paper presents a knowledge graph, called "Sarch-Knows", that models security scenarios based on the architectural design of a software system. The knowledge graph is based on different paths called scenarios, where each scenario covers the fundamental elements to meet a security property and the architectural elements on which the properties fall. This knowledge graph is being implemented as a Neo4j database on which queries can be issued to extract aggregated knowledge about security and architecture. This knowledge is scattered over many sources of documentation, like NIST, MITRE, databases, books and papers; which is why this graph can be considered as a starting option to establish an ordered scheme of this knowledge.

Keywords: Software Architecture · Security · Modeling · Knowledge Graph · Sarch

1 Introduction

The architecture of a software system is defined from a series of elements and relationships, which constitute the most important structures of the system, fundamental to reason about it [1,13]. These structures are essential to ensure compliance with the functional and non-functional requirements of the system. However, from the non-functional point of view, these structures are essential when it comes to ensuring quality attributes [12]. Although there is a wide variety of quality attributes, there are some that are indisputably relevant to all types of software systems. One of these is security. Security is the ability of a software

B. Tekinerdoğan et al. (Eds.): ECSA 2023, LNCS 14590, pp. 107–119, 2024.
https://doi.org/10.1007/978-3-031-66326-0_7

system to protect the elements of the system, including data, from unauthorized access [1,18]. Likewise, it is the ability to provide access to the different system actors that are authorized (users, components and external systems). Security as a software quality attribute is covered by the same fundamental elements of cybersecurity, among which are threats, weakness, attacks and risks. It can be identified that some contributions have been made in the identification of specific elements, at the architecture level, that can affect the security of a software system, among them the classifications of architectural weaknesses and vulnerabilities related to the application of security tactics [14,16]. Although some methodological proposals have been presented to support the secure software development process, as in [20], there is currently no comprehensive contribution that provides a transversal description of the essential security concepts as well as specific concepts related to the architecture of a software system. In this context, this paper presents a knowledge graph where it is possible to model a complete security scenario, involving elements associated with cybersecurity and elements associated with software architecture. This conceptual modeling approach makes it possible to identify the flow of a possible security risk, from the identification of the threat and the respective weakness, to the architectural elements that are subject to this risk.

The remainder of this paper is structured as follows. Section 2 describes the related work to the context of the proposed work. Section 3 specifies and details the characteristics of the knowledge graph proposed. In Sect. 4 the approach of security scenarios is presented. Section 5 analyzes the applicability of the proposed work. Finally, Sect. 6 presents the conclusions and future work.

2   Related Works

Software architecture, as a field of knowledge, poses different strategies when designing and building a software system. On the one hand, architecture is responsible for defining the structure of the system, that is, the elements that make it up and the way in which they are related [13]. On the other hand, the architecture is responsible for defining mechanisms to meet non-functional requirements, particularly quality attributes. Security, as a software quality attribute, is addressed from the architectural point of view through two fundamental concepts. In the first place, the use of architectural tactics has been proposed [4,11], as sets of design decisions that seek to guarantee the quality attribute. In the case of security, architectural tactics have been classified in different ways; however, the taxonomy is highlighted where the moment on which the tactic acts in the system to deal with an attack is taken into account [1,8]. In this case, this can be seen at the level of detection, resistance, reaction and recovery. Moreover, the use of architectural patterns is also proposed to address recurring design problems. For security, these patterns seek to specify a concrete solution on the architecture, through the implementation of a particular architectural tactic [1,5,19].

At the level of the basic elements of cybersecurity, several works have been proposed, in which a relationship between these elements and the elements of

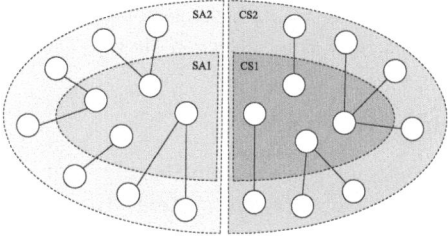

Fig. 1. Knowledge graph overview (SA: Software Architecture, CS: Cybersecurity).

the architecture of a software system is considered [10, 14–17]. In this case, the information registered by NIST in the National Vulnerability Database (NVD) is identified as one of the most relevant [9], where specific records can be found on vulnerabilities identified over time, associated with multiple types of computer systems, including software systems. In the same way, the information published by MITRE is highlighted, through the Common Weakness Enumeration (CWE) [6], where a particular mapping of architectural concepts is presented with a set of weaknesses identified over time, associated with poor implementation (or null) of an architectural tactic in a software system [7].

3   Sarch-Knows: Knowledge Graph

The proposed knowledge graph is modeled from two fundamental perspectives: the *field of knowledge* and the *level of detail*. In the first place, the perspective by field of knowledge divides the graph into two parts; the first that includes the elements associated with software architecture, and the second that includes the elements associated with cybersecurity.

On the other hand, the level of detail perspective divides the graph into two other parts; the first that includes the abstract elements (lower level of detail), and the second that includes specific elements, corresponding to instances of the abstract elements (higher level of detail).

Figure 1 presents a general overview of the knowledge graph structure, taking into account the two described perspectives. The green region corresponds to the field of knowledge: Software Architecture (SA), and the blue region corresponds to the field of knowledge: Cybersecurity (CS). Likewise, each region by field of knowledge presents the two levels of detail. SA1 and CS1 correspond to the minimum level of detail (abstract elements), and SA2 and CS2 correspond to the maximum level of detail (specific elements). The details of the graph are described below, based on the fields of knowledge. It is important to mention that both the abstract elements and the specific elements are presented in the graph as nodes. Likewise, the relationships between the abstract elements and specific elements are presented in the graph as edges/arcs. Abstract elements establish conceptual relationships between them. Abstract elements and specific elements establish instantiation relationships between them. While the specific elements establish security scenarios between them.

3.1 Software Architecture (SA)

The first part of the graph groups the relationships between different concepts related to the architecture of a software system. To comprehend the principles of software architecture, it is important to understand the generalities of the related abstract elements:

- *Architectural Element:* The fundamental unit of construction of a software system. Among its basic characteristics are: a set of responsibilities, a boundary, and a set of interfaces. These elements can include components, connectors, modules, layers, services, and messages [13].
- *System Structure:* A particular organization and arrangement of architectural elements within a software system. It can be considered as a set of architectural elements and their respective relationships [1,13].
- *Component-and-Connector Structure:* structure of the system that groups those architectural elements that are present at runtime [2].
- *Component:* a computational element or data store that is present at runtime. [2,18].
- *Connector:* a path of interaction at runtime between two or more components. [2,18].
- *Architectural Tactic:* a design decision that influences the fulfillment of a quality attribute [1,8].
- *Architectural Pattern:* an architectural solution to solve a recurring software design problem [18].

Figure 2 (a) presents the abstract elements associated with the software architecture perspective in the graph.

The software architecture perspective presents the basic idea of architecture responsibility. On the one hand, it presents the definition of the system structures, composed of a set of architectural elements and emphasizing the structure of components and connectors. On the other hand, it presents architectural tactics and architectural patterns, fundamental to achieving quality attributes; in this case, security.

3.2 Cybersecurity (CS)

The second part of the graph groups the relationships between the basic concepts of cybersecurity. These concepts are essential to understand and attend to the aspects related to the security quality attribute, from any point of view, including the architectural. Thus, to comprehend the principles of security, it is important to understand the generalities of the related abstract elements [9]:

- *Weakness:* a defect or deficiency in the design, construction or configuration of a software system.

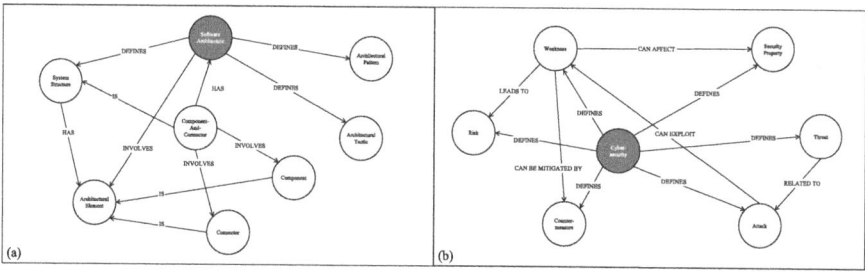

Fig. 2. First perspective: Software Architecture (a), and second perspective: Cybersecurity (b).

- *Risk:* the possibility of an undesired occurring event or incident that has a negative impact on the security of a software system.
- *Attack:* a malicious attempt to compromise the security of a software system.
- *Threat:* any event, action or entity that has the potential to cause damage or compromise the security of a software system.
- *Countermeasure:* A measure or action taken to prevent, mitigate or neutralize an identified threat or risk. Its main objective is to protect a software system against possible attacks or security incidents.
- *Security Property:* a system's ability to protect the elements that compose the system, including data, from any event that may mainly generate a confidentiality, integrity and availability risk.

Figure 2 (a) presents the abstract elements associated with the cybersecurity perspective in the graph.

The security perspective presents the basic idea of treatment of the security quality attribute from the general perspective of cybersecurity. On the one hand, it presents the concept of weakness of a software system, which can affect a security property. This weakness can be exploited by an attack, and therefore can cause a risk. Attack that will always be associated with a threat. On the other, the concept of countermeasure is presented, as the element that can prevent the attack and therefore remedy the weakness so that the risk does not become effective.

3.3 SA-CS Connection

From the two perspectives presented (Software Architecture and Cybersecurity) the graph presents a main characteristic related to the connection point between the two fields of knowledge. Particularly, the concepts of architectural tactic and architectural pattern are taken, both for the security quality attribute, which support decisions and design solutions at the architectural level. In this way, both a tactic and a pattern can be considered as forms of implementation of countermeasures at the architecture level to guarantee security properties. Figure 3

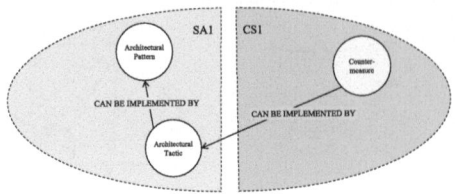

Fig. 3. Connection between the abstract elements of the two perspectives of the graph: Software Architecture (SA1) and Cybersecurity (CS1).

presents the connection between the two perspectives and their respective elements.

This figure shows the relationship that exists between the two perspectives. Fundamentally, the relationship is given in terms of the concept of countermeasure, which is what will allow to remedy the vulnerability (a weakness instance) in the system, and therefore, mitigate the risk. Since the graph has a focus on the architecture of the system, in addition to providing the specification of the architectural elements on which the possible risk falls, the graph also provides the definition of security tactics and security patterns that can be taken to address some security requirement. Thus, the graph works on the idea that tactics and patterns support the necessary countermeasures to address security requirements. In conclusion, the relationship between the two perspectives is created from the analysis of architectural tactics and patterns that can be taken at the design stage, in order to ensure a software system before and during its implementation.

4   Security Scenarios

4.1   Scenario Overview

Based on the general characteristics of the knowledge graph presented, the concept of *security scenario* is presented below. The security scenarios are based on the general scenario model for quality attributes presented by Bass et al. [1], which is composed of the following parts:

- **Source:** a *threat*.
- **Stimulus:** an *attack* that seeks to exploit a *vulnerability* (associated with a *weakness*).
- **Artifact:** the *system structure* (or part of it), composed by a set of *architectural elements*.
- **Environment:** normal execution of the system.
- **Response:** *Countermeasures* defined from *architectural tactics* and *architectural patterns*. Mechanisms used to control response.
- **Response Measure:** Evidence of the effectiveness of the applied *countermeasures*. Evidence that the *risk* became effective or not.

Based on the above, the knowledge graph presented allows the description of a security scenario from a subgraph composed of a initial set of nodes, associated with the abstract elements of the two perspectives: software architecture (SA1) and cybersecurity (CS1); and a second set of nodes, associated with the specific elements defined from the abstract elements. This last set of nodes represents a specific security case on the architecture of a software system (SA2, CS2). Specific elements are classified as *SASE* (Software Architecture Specific Elements) and *CCSK* (Current Common Security Knowledge).

4.2   Using Neo4j for Knowledge Modeling

With the purpose of making use of the knowledge graph, it has been modeled by means of a Neo4j database[1]. It is a database management system oriented to persistence and data query, through an approach of graph-based data model. Neo4j offers several advantages for graph databases. It provides efficient storage and retrieval of complex, interconnected data, enabling flexible, high-performance queries. With its native graph processing capabilities, Neo4j enables easy relationship traversal and analysis, making it ideal for applications involving knowledge graphs [3].

For the creation of the database, the characteristics of the knowledge graph described in Sect. 3 were taken into account. In this way, the database is made up of a set of nodes (and their respective relationships) associated with the abstract elements, both at the software architecture level and at the cybersecurity level. These nodes belong to a category (a label in Neo4j) called *abstract*. In addition, the complementary nodes of the database are created from the specific elements, that is, from the specific elements for each concept and that describe the security scenario. This means that a single node of an abstract element, can have multiple relationships with nodes that represent specific elements. These nodes belong to a category (a label in Neo4j) called *specific*.

In this way, a security scenario corresponds to a subgraph, formed from a logical relationship between specific elements of the software architecture and specific elements of cybersecurity. Thus, through the Neo4j query language (Cypher[2]) it is possible to filter a security scenario, and to obtain its respective subgraph, looking for all nodes corresponding to specific elements that have a logical relationship. A particular example of a security scenario is presented below. Table 1 summarizes the relationship between the abstract elements and the specific elements associated with the security scenario to be described.

The presented security scenario is related to a common weakness in different software systems designed as a Service-Oriented Front-End Architecture (SOFEA). This architecture (*system structure*) is generally composed of the following elements: a front-end component (presentation), a back-end component (business logic), a database component (data persistence), an HTTP connector for communicating a web browser with the front-end component, a REST

---

[1] https://neo4j.com/.

[2] https://neo4j.com/docs/getting-started/cypher-intro/.

connector for communicating the front-end component with the back-end component, and a database connector for communicating the back-end component with the database component. In this case, the weakness is related to the HTTP connector and refers to the fact that the protocol may not have a mechanism that allows verifying the integrity of the message that travels through that channel.

Table 1. Example of a particular security scenario for a software system with a Service-Oriented Front-End Architecture (SOFEA).

Perspective	Abstract Element(s)	Specific Element(s)	
SoftwareArchitecture(SA)	System Structure	SOFEA (Service Oriented Front-End Architecture)	
	ArchitecturalElement	HTTP connector between a web browser component and the Front-End component of the system	**sase1**
Cybersecurity(CS)	Weakness	CWE-353: Missing Support for Integrity Check	**ccsk1**
	Security Property	Integrity	**ccsk2**
	Attack	CAPEC-389: Content Spoofing Via Application API Manipulation	**ccsk3**
	Threat	Malicious User	**ccsk4**
	Risk	A08:2021 - Software and Data Integrity Failures	**ccsk5**
SA/CS	Countermeasure	Implement a Mechanism for Verifying Message Integrity	**ccsk6**
	Architectural Tactic	Detect Attacks >Verify Message Integrity	**sase2**
	Architectural Pattern	Intercepting Validator	**sase3**

The *weakness*, called "Missing Support for Integrity Check"[3] is part of the Common Weakness Enumeration (CWE) published by MITRE, in its mapping on Architectural Concepts. In this case, the weakness falls on an *architectural element* of the architecture: the HTTP connector, which allows communication between a web browser and the front-end component, connector in charge of sending messages coming from the client. Additionally, this scenario poses the *threat* of a malicious user attempting an *attack* called "Content Spoofing Via Application API Manipulation"[4] and which is part of the Common Attack Pattern Enumeration and Classification (CAPEC), also published by MITRE. The weakness leads to a *risk* called "Software and Data Integrity Failures"[5] mapped in the OWASP Top Ten classification.

Finally, the scenario presents an *architectural tactic* and an *architectural pattern* that serve as *countermeasures* to mitigate the risk generated by the weakness. In this case, the architectural tactic "Verify Message Integrity" proposes the use of techniques such as checksum and hash values to verify the integrity of

---

[3] https://cwe.mitre.org/data/definitions/353.html.

[4] https://capec.mitre.org/data/definitions/389.html.

[5] https://owasp.org/Top10/A08_2021-Software_and_Data_Integrity_Failures/.

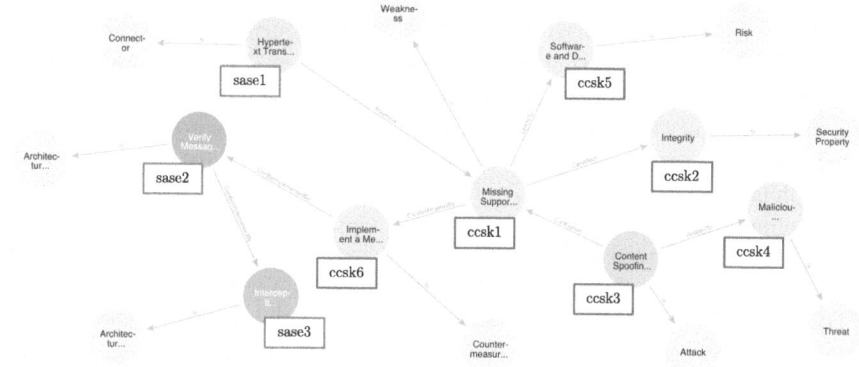

Fig. 4. Security scenario subgraph as a Neo4j database query.

the messages that travel through the HTTP connector. It is important to mention that this tactic is part of the "Detect Attacks" category. On the other hand, the architectural pattern "Intercepting Validator" is based on the addition of a new software element upfront the destination of messages (the front-end component), whose responsibility is to implement the described architectural tactic. Figure 4 presents the subgraph associated with the described security scenario, based on a query made on the Neo4j database. Here, the yellow nodes represent the abstract elements and the nodes with different colors represent the specific elements of the security scenario. See Table 1 for details of these elements.

The Cypher (Neo4j's graph query language) request made to return the described security scenario is:

MATCH p =
(a:sase {short_name: "HTTP"})-[*]-(b:ccsk {name: "Missing Support for Integrity Check"})
RETURN p;

This means that the database is being searched the subgraph (p) containing all interrelated nodes that have the "HTTP" architectural element and the weakness "Missing Support for Integrity Check" in its path.

5   Discussion

Guaranteeing the quality of a software system involves dealing with different quality attributes, among which security is one of the most important, and the architecture of the software system is essential to meet the related requirements. In this way, due to the complexity when dealing with this attribute and the number of possible scenarios that fall on a software system and where it is necessary to meet the security requirements, it is very important to have a source that synthesizes the fundamental elements. That contributes to the treatment of these security scenarios.

However, despite the fact that there are different sources of information where the elements that contribute to the description of a security scenario are related, there is no single resource that comprehensively covers and relates all the elements. For this reason, our knowledge graph proposal comprehensively conceives all the fundamental elements necessary to fully describe a scenario in which security in the architecture of a software system is sought to be addressed. The knowledge graph is implemented manually, from different sources of information, where the following stand out: the Common Weakness Enumeration (CWE) and the Common Attack Pattern Enumeration and Classification (CAPEC), provided by MITRE, the official documentation and the National Vulnerability Database (NVD) by NIST, different databases and the main bibliographical references on software architecture and cybersecurity.

At the implementation level, the base model of the graph is highlighted, which includes abstract elements of the two fields: software architecture and cybersecurity. This guarantees that all security scenarios are structured in the same way, keeping the formalism between the elements of the architecture and the solidity of the control scheme over the security of the software system. In the same way, each specific element is rigorously described, based on the identified sources of information and a corresponding analysis that allows the generation of logical relationships between each part of the scenario.

Based on the above, the applicability of the knowledge graph can be observed as follows. In the first place, the knowledge graph allows analyzing a security scenario at the level of the architecture of a software system. In analysis, it is based on the contribution of the graph when it comes to identifying vulnerabilities in a set of elements of the architecture. This can generate a security risk in the system, as well as the countermeasures that can be applied in the system to mitigate this risk. This is based on the point of view of a set of architectural tactics and patterns. In second place, all the specific elements modeled in the graph, based on the abstract elements, can have one or more security scenarios associated to them. This allows multiple security scenarios to be consulted, performing a filter by the scenario identifier, allowing multiple specific elements to be part of multiple security scenarios.

It is important to mention that vulnerabilities are not modeled in the knowledge graph since they are considered instances of weaknesses, that is, weaknesses identified or reported in real software systems.

The proposed knowledge graph can be used as a primary tool when carrying out the architectural design of a software system that requires meeting a set of security requirements, and therefore, serves as a basis to guide the construction of the system. The maintenance of the knowledge graph is based on the appearance of new reports of vulnerabilities and weaknesses in the sources of information taken as reference. The addition to the database is done using the Cypher query language, building the query from the abstract elements and the specific elements analyzed, equivalent to a new security scenario.

Finally, the works presented in Sect. 2 generally describe independent classifications when dealing with security. On the one hand, precise classifications of weaknesses at the architectural level are presented, but without a deep level of detail towards the architectural elements involved. On the other hand, works are presented that describe the different design decisions that can be taken to deal with security, but do not delve into the vulnerabilities that are sought to be remedied. For this reason, our knowledge graph proposes a joint perspective where, under the concept of security scenario, it is possible to detect vulnerabilities in a more precise way, thanks to the structure of the graph and the knowledge vocabulary that it incorporates.

6   Conclusions and Future Work

In this paper, we presented a knowledge graph for modeling security scenarios from the point of view of a software system architecture. This graph, implemented as a Neo4j database, models abstract elements in two fields: software architecture and cybersecurity, as well as specific elements that allow describing a security scenario in a software system architecture. The scenarios start from the weakness that can be exploited and that falls on a set of architectural elements, up to the countermeasures that can be applied to the system to mitigate the risk generated in terms of tactics and architectural patterns for security. The graph is created from different sources of information and allows a general overview of the elements involved when dealing with a security requirement at the software system architecture level.

As a future work, three paths are proposed. The first one is related to the definition of the strategy so that relevant security scenarios at the architectural level can be loaded into the database in a collaborative way, guaranteeing the rigor of the concepts involved, the guarantee of the sources of information and the precision of the new data. Secondly, it is pertinent to include a detailed and comparative evaluation of the proposed approach with other approaches, in order to analyze the real utility of this approach for decision-making at the architectural level, both in small and large software systems. This is due to the fact that in large software systems the number of security scenarios will grow exponentially and it is important to complement the proposal with data loading schemes and more automated data analysis, which make this tool very useful for a software architect. Finally, the possibility of extending this same knowledge graph idea to other quality attributes such as scalability, availability, among others, is raised.

References

1. Bass, L., Clements, P., Kazman, R.: Software Architecture in Practice, 4th edn (2022)
2. Clements, P., et al.: Documenting Software Architectures - Views and Beyonds, 2nd edn (2011)
3. Fernandes, D., Bernardino, J.: Graph databases comparison: allegrograph, arangoDB, infinitegraph, neo4j, and orientDB (2018). https://doi.org/10.5220/0006910203730380

4. Fernandez, E.B., Astudillo, H., Pedraza-García, G.: Revisiting architectural tactics for security. In: Weyns, D., Mirandola, R., Crnkovic, I. (eds.) ECSA 2015. LNCS, vol. 9278, pp. 55–69. Springer, Cham (2015). https://doi.org/10.1007/978-3-319-23727-5_5

5. Fernandez, E.B., Yoshioka, N., Washizaki, H.: Evaluating the degree of security of a system built using security patterns. In: ACM International Conference Proceeding Series (2018). https://doi.org/10.1145/3230833.3232821, https://dl.acm.org/doi/10.1145/3230833.3232821

6. MITRE: Common weakness enumeration (CWE). https://cwe.mitre.org/data/index.html

7. MITRE: Common weakness enumeration (CWE) - architectural concepts. https://cwe.mitre.org/data/definitions/1008.html

8. Márquez, G., Astudillo, H., Kazman, R.: Architectural tactics in software architecture: a systematic mapping study. J. Syst. Softw. **197**, 111558 (2023). https://doi.org/10.1016/J.JSS.2022.111558

9. NIST: NVD - national vulnerability database. https://nvd.nist.gov/

10. Orellana, C., Villegas, M.M., Astudillo, H.: Mitigating security threats through the use of security tactics to design secure cyber-physical systems (CPS). In: ACM International Conference Proceeding Series, vol. 2, pp. 109–115 (2019). https://doi.org/10.1145/3344948.3344994, https://dl.acm.org/doi/10.1145/3344948.3344994

11. Pedraza-Garcia, G., Astudillo, H., Correal, D.: A methodological approach to apply security tactics in software architecture design. In: 2014 IEEE Colombian Conference on Communications and Computing, COLCOM 2014 - Conference Proceedings (2014). https://doi.org/10.1109/COLCOMCON.2014.6860432

12. Richards, M., Ford, N.: Fundamentals of Software Architecture: an Engineering Approach (2020)

13. Rozanski, N., Woods, E.: Software Systems Architecture, 2nd edn. Addison-Wesley, Boston (2012). https://doi.org/10.1017/CBO9781107415324.004

14. Santos, J.C., Peruma, A., Mirakhorli, M., Galstery, M., Vidal, J.V., Sejfia, A.: Understanding software vulnerabilities related to architectural security tactics: an empirical investigation of chromium, PHP and Thunderbird. In: Proceedings - 2017 IEEE International Conference on Software Architecture. ICSA 2017, pp. 69–78 (2017). https://doi.org/10.1109/ICSA.2017.39

15. Santos, J.C., Suloglu, S., Ye, J., Mirakhorli, M.: Towards an automated approach for detecting architectural weaknesses in critical systems. In: Proceedings - 2020 IEEE/ACM 42nd International Conference on Software Engineering Workshops. ICSEW 2020, pp. 250–253 (2020). https://doi.org/10.1145/3387940.3392222, https://dl.acm.org/doi/10.1145/3387940.3392222

16. Santos, J.C., Tarrit, K., Mirakhorli, M.: A catalog of security architecture weaknesses. In: Proceedings - 2017 IEEE International Conference on Software Architecture Workshops. ICSAW 2017: Side Track Proceedings, pp. 220–223 (2017). https://doi.org/10.1109/ICSAW.2017.25

17. Santos, J.C., Tarrit, K., Sejfia, A., Mirakhorli, M., Galster, M.: An empirical study of tactical vulnerabilities. J. Syst. Softw. **149**, 263–284 (2019). https://doi.org/10.1016/J.JSS.2018.10.030

18. Taylor, R.N., Medvidovic, N., Dashofy, E.M.: Software Architecture - Foundations, Theory, and Practice. Wiley, New York (2009)

19. That, M.T.T., Sadou, S., Oquendo, F.: Using architectural patterns to define architectural decisions, pp. 196–200 (2012). https://doi.org/10.1109/WICSA-ECSA.212.28
20. Uzunov, A.V., Fernandez, E.B., Falkner, K.: Assessing and improving the quality of security methodologies for distributed systems. J. Softw. Evol. Process **30**, e1980 (2018). https://doi.org/10.1002/SMR.1980, https://onlinelibrary.wiley.com/doi/full/10.1002/smr.1980, https://onlinelibrary.wiley.com/doi/abs/10.1002/smr.1980, https://onlinelibrary.wiley.com/doi/10.1002/smr.1980

Threat Modeling: A Rough Diamond or Fool's Gold?

Anh-Duy Tran$^{(\boxtimes)}$, Koen Yskout, and Wouter Joosen

imec-DistriNet, KU Leuven, Leuven, Belgium
{anh-duy.tran,koen.yskout,wouter.joosen}@kuleuven.be

Abstract. Threat modeling is a process to identify security threats and propose effective solutions for mitigating them. Numerous resources emphasize the importance of threat modeling in the secure software development lifecycle, particularly during the design phase. In this paper, we collect and discuss the (scarce) empirical evidence from the literature that provides insights into the adoption and utilization of threat modeling. Based on our observations, we also formulate a number of open challenges related to gaining a better empirical understanding of the use of threat modeling in practice.

Keywords: Threat modeling · Empirical study · Effectiveness · Adoption · Open challenges

1 Introduction

Threat modeling is a process to identify security flaws and propose effective solutions for mitigating them based on architectural models of the system, actively involving software development team members. Numerous resources emphasize the importance of threat modeling in the secure software development lifecycle, particularly during the design phase. Specifically, threat modeling is among the techniques suggested to address the (newly introduced) A04:2021 - Insecure Design entry in the OWASP Top Ten 2021 [22]. Moreover, the Software Assurance Maturity Model (SAMM) offers an effective and measurable framework for analyzing and enhancing the secure development lifecycle, including the incorporation of threat modeling as a criterion for assessing software security posture during the Design phase [23]. SAMM stipulates that achieving Maturity Level 3 in threat modeling requires its integration into the SDLC and its adoption as an integral part of the developer security culture. Other comprehensive frameworks, such as the Microsoft SDL [19] and NIST SSDF [20], also recommend the use of threat modeling to identify architectural flaws and security threats.

With these numerous recommendations advocating for the implementation of threat modeling, we must wonder which concrete evidence exists for its practical effectiveness, especially in an industrial context. This question holds significant importance as it enables evidence-based decision-making and empowers organizations to make informed choices regarding its adoption and integration into their software development processes [12,16].

B. Tekinerdoğan et al. (Eds.): ECSA 2023, LNCS 14590, pp. 120–129, 2024.
https://doi.org/10.1007/978-3-031-66326-0_8

It is thus necessary to gather scientific evidence and insights on the precise circumstances and assumptions under which adopting threat modeling is the right choice, as well as the most effective form of threat modeling. This paper makes a first step in this direction, by asking *"What are the main insights on the effectiveness and adoption of threat modeling processes and techniques from empirical studies currently available in the literature?"*, and suggests future research directions to explore.

2   Empirical Studies on Threat Modeling

We first describe how we selected the articles with empirical studies on threat modeling for our study, followed by a brief summary of the insights they provide. For this paper, we interpret empirical studies as studies that involve systematic observations and measurements of real-world phenomena to derive knowledge from practical experience rather than relying solely on theory or belief [17,24]. Empirical studies encompass two main types: qualitative research, which gathers non-numerical data, and quantitative research, which gathers numerical data. The weaknesses of both qualitative and quantitative paradigms are somewhat balanced by the strengths of the other [28].

2.1   Article Selection

To compile the list of relevant studies, we have conducted searches across five digital libraries, namely IEEE [3], ACM [1], Google Scholar [2], Semantic Scholar [5], and Scopus [4]. In each library, we perform 32 searches, each query combining one keyword from a collection of 4 related to threat modeling (*threat modeling, threat model, threat analysis, risk assessment*) and one from a collection of 8 related to empirical evidence (*in practice, case study, empirical study, comparison, adoption, experience, effectiveness, industry*). These keywords were chosen based on their estimated relevance and applicability for the intended search, as well as their occurrence in a set of relevant papers already known by the authors. We acknowledge that this keyword selection yields a possible threat to validity by introducing bias into the set of included papers, and some relevant papers may have been overlooked.

Subsequently, to identify the relevant articles for our study, we started from the top 20 results for each library, sorted by relevance (i.e., 3200 non-unique results in total). We removed duplicates and manually reviewed the abstracts, introductions, and conclusions to select those that empirically examine the effectiveness or adoption of threat modeling processes or techniques in software systems or industry. We excluded papers that propose new methods for threat modeling where the evaluation consists solely of the authors demonstrating it on an example. This results in 20 articles, listed in Table 1. For each article, we mention the year of publication, the study method (qualitative or quantitative), the study object (adoption of threat modeling or evaluation of threat modeling), and the type of system for which the study was performed (general software or a more specific system type).

Table 1. Selected Empirical Studies on Effectiveness of Threat Modeling

Reference	Year	Methods		Objects		System Addressed
		Qualitative	Quantitative	Adopting[+]	Evaluating[-]	
Bernsmed and Jaatun[7]	2019	●	○	●	○	General Software
Bernsmed et al.[6]*	2022	●	●	●	●	General Software
Bygds et al.[8]	2021	●	●	○	●	General Software
Cruzes et al.[9]	2018	●	○	●	○	General Software
Dewitte et al.[10]	2019	○	●	●	●	Governmental Regulations
Dhillon[11]	2011	●	●	●	●	General Software
Galvez and Gurses[13]	2018	●	○	●	○	General Software
Granata et al.[14]	2023	●	●	○	●	General Software
Jamil et al.[15]	2021	●	○	●	○	Cyber-Physical Systems
Opdahl and Sindre[21]	2009	○	●	○	●	General Software
Scandariato et al.[25]	2015	○	●	○	●	General Software
Shostack[27]	2008	●	○	●	○	General Software
Stevens et al.[29]	2018	●	●	●	○	Enterprise Security
Tuma and Scandariato[32]	2018	●	●	●	●	General Software
Van Landuyt and Joosen[33]	2020	○	●	○	●	General Software
Van Landuyt and Joosen[34]	2021	○	●	○	●	General Software
Williams et al.[35]	2015	●	●	○	●	General Software
Wuyts et al.[36]	2014	●	●	○	●	General Software
Yeng et al.[38]	2020	○	●	●	●	Cloud Computing
Yskout et al.[39]	2020	●	○	●	○	General Software

* The work of Bernsmed et al.[6] also includes the results of Cruzes et al.[9] and Bernsmed and Jaatun[7]. When referring to [6], we only consider the results that have not been reported in the other papers.

[+] Adopting Threat Modeling

[-] Evaluating Threat Modeling Methods and Tools

2.2   Empirical Insights

We analyze the selected articles to gain insight into the available evidence for the effectiveness of threat modeling from two primary perspectives: (1) the adoption of the threat model process in practice, and (2) the comparison and evaluation of threat modeling methods or tools. We provide observations and suggestions related to these two perspectives.

Adopting Threat Modeling. Several studies [6,7,11,15,29] already investigated the adoption of threat modeling to enhance system or software security and identify known threats. This adoption comes with certain limitations and challenges, though.

Typically, threat modeling is carried out by developers who possess extensive knowledge about the software system they are responsible for [6,11]. Yet integrating security and privacy threat modeling into the software development processes, and agile processes in particular, poses significant challenges [6,9,13]. Threat modeling is not yet integrated into daily activities [6] and is often scheduled as a separate session, involving brainstorming and potentially requiring a significant amount of time [6,7,27]. Also, the execution of threat modeling can be hindered by, for example, the initial difficulty in understanding and using certain terminology and missing background knowledge [7,9,13,29]. Various resources are needed for effective threat modeling, such as asset identification [6], software requirements [9], technical insight into the system [10], and a deep understanding of system or component design [11]. However, these resources are sometimes not brought into the threat modeling process or have no up-to-date documentation. The created threat models may not always be up-to-date or accurately reflect the current state of systems [9,15], and they may also face challenges when being transferred to other domains [15]. Finally, scalability represents a significant challenge in threat modeling, particularly as software systems grow in complexity and size [9,11,13]. Organizations face difficulties in effectively scaling threat modeling activities to accommodate large and intricate systems, potentially resulting in gaps in threat identification and mitigation.

The selected articles provide numerous suggestions for improving the integration of threat modeling into the software development life cycle, particularly within agile methodologies [6,13]. They emphasize the importance of establishing a precise scope for threat modeling activities and defining the criteria for completion, often referred to as the Definition of Done [6,7,9]. Effective threat modeling requires proper training, skills, and guidelines. It is essential to find ways to bring relevant focus and expertise into the process with minimal effort, ensuring that individuals involved are equipped with the necessary knowledge and capabilities to perform threat modeling effectively [9,27,29,39]. Further attention should be given to the role of humans within the threat modeling process, as well as human factors engineering issues pertaining to the design of security modeling methods, processes, and tools [27]. While the involvement of a security expert is recognized as a best practice in threat modeling [6], Shostack [27] presented two reasons why it may be reasonable to perform threat modeling without experts, namely (1) a scarcity of experts, and (2) the potential benefits of engaging individuals responsible for building the system, allowing them to develop a sense of ownership and understanding of the security model.

Moreover, the articles mention several other possible enhancements to improve the effectiveness and adoption of threat modeling. These include: fostering better communication and collaboration to understand the software system better and highlight important threats [6,29] which can be supported by agile [13]; integrating multiple threat modeling techniques to provide an alternative viewpoint on system weaknesses and have a complete picture about the threats of a given software [9,15,38]; extending the impact of modeling to the source code [9], and incorporating automated threat analysis or dynamic threat modeling

[9,39]. These improvements aim to enhance the overall efficacy and acceptance of threat modeling practices. Additionally, one suggestion is to develop a standardized reference model for threat modeling, enabling the sharing and reuse of threat modeling artifacts [39]. Another improvement involves enhancing modeling support to track the iterative creation of the model and the associated assumptions, rather than solely focusing on the final model [10,11,39].

Evaluating Threat Modeling Methods and Tools. Besides insights about the adoption of threat modeling itself, we also look in to empirical evaluations of threat modeling methods and tools, for example regarding their usefulness and accuracy.

Two papers mention that developers often lack motivation to perform threat modeling techniques or utilize threat modeling tools [6,7], which may indicate the low (perceived) usefulness of these methods. While threat modeling techniques are generally perceived as learnable and practical, and yielding accurate threat identification, their usage can be time-consuming [25,36]. Certain techniques may prove more effective, accurate, and comprehensive in identifying threats under specific circumstances [14,21,32]. The review of Yeng et al. found that none of the evaluated threat modeling methods provided a comprehensive assessment of all threats and vulnerabilities [38]. Some studies indicate that threat modeling techniques heavily rely on human interpretation, such as making assumptions about the system while identifying threats [33,34].

In terms of tool support, different tools exhibit varying learning curves, with some being more challenging than others [8]. Additionally, tool selection can be influenced by factors such as simplicity, configurability, usability, and the generation of comprehensive reports [6,8,14,35,38].

Several suggestions arise from the reviewed literature. Firstly, there is a need for improved tooling that assists developers in creating Data Flow Diagrams (DFDs) and facilitates the identification and analysis of relevant threats, while promoting collaboration [6]. Secondly, involving a security expert during the DFD drawing process is considered a best practice. Additionally, combining different threat modeling techniques can enhance the effectiveness of the process [38]. STRIDE is useful for generating an initial set of threats which developers could then build upon. Lastly, utilizing DFDs as a means of documenting systems or providing additional documentation can be advantageous [6].

3   Open Challenges

While several studies have investigated the integration and effectiveness of threat modeling, there is a strong recommendation for further research to provide more concrete evidence regarding its effectiveness and other influential factors [21,25,27,32]. This section presents research questions that can guide future investigations and potential experimental studies in the field.

3.1 How Effective Is Threat Modeling in Delivering More Secure Software in Practice?

Providing compelling and specific evidence of the effectiveness of threat modeling in practical applications can increase the persuasive power for companies and enterprises to adopt and implement threat modeling in their software development processes. However, there is still a lack of existing studies that provide conclusive results regarding the effectiveness of threat modeling in an industrial context. One of the key pieces of evidence for this is demonstrating the benefits of conducting threat modeling in producing more secure software products. Research should aim to provide concrete data to assess the extent to which the application of threat modeling can reduce the number of security vulnerabilities and threats, or employ metrics to demonstrate that software development assisted by threat modeling results in more secure products, particularly in terms of architectural security.

Multiple experiments can be conducted to address this question. A comparison can be made between the number of security flaws, including security bugs, identified and remediated in a software product when threat modeling is applied versus when it is not applied within specific software development processes (e.g., agile [6,7,9,13]). The selection of effective threat modeling methods and tools for specific systems is also an important consideration. Software development teams can rely on the results of experiments, case studies, and observational methods to choose suitable methods and tools for the domain they are working in (such as CPS, Blockchain, AI, etc.). Furthermore, conducting studies on threat modeling across various scopes and sizes of systems can reveal the scalability of this approach. By exploring different contexts and dimensions, researchers can gain a better understanding of how threat modeling scales and adapts to diverse software development scenarios.

3.2 What Is the Impact of Threat Modeling on the Software Development Process?

It would be irrational to encourage companies to adopt threat modeling without providing reasonable evidence of the impact on time and cost. For businesses, time to market and production costs are crucial factors that are always considered during software development. Demonstrating that threat modeling does not excessively or reasonably impact time and cost, or showing that the time and cost invested in threat modeling are worthwhile, can partially indicate the effectiveness of threat modeling in practice and recommend its adoption by teams.

Currently, there are some studies addressing the issue of time in threat modeling implementation [6,7,27,32]. However, there is a lack of research that analyzes in detail the changes in time and cost [18]. Future research should focus on quantitative research methods to provide specific data. Researchers can compare the time and effort required for threat modeling through experiments with real-world projects or collect surveys from companies. Additionally, measuring the security level of the product is essential to assess the corresponding value in relation to the time and effort invested. Evaluating the differences in time and cost required for threat modeling in each software development phase through a longitudinal study or comparing the time and cost of different threat modeling methods and tools in specific contexts through causal-comparative research are empirical studies that need to be explored.

3.3 How Easily Can Threat Modeling Be Learned?

Demonstrating that the learning curve for adopting threat modeling is not significant and highlighting its practicality can serve as compelling evidence for increased adoption of threat modeling in practice. While some studies have evaluated the learning curve and usability of threat modeling [6,8,25,29,35], they have been limited in detail and primarily focused on student subjects. Further research is needed to provide more comprehensive and diverse evaluations in real-world settings.

Conducting training sessions on threat modeling for individuals with diverse backgrounds and skillsets, followed by pre- and post-training assessments, interviews, and surveys, can provide valuable insights into the ease of perceiving and operating threat modeling. The assessments and practical exercises help evaluate participants' knowledge and skills, while qualitative data from interviews and focus groups offer deeper understanding of their experiences and challenges. Surveys can provide quantitative data on satisfaction, usefulness, and confidence levels. By analyzing these findings, researchers can gain insights to improve the ease of use and comprehension of threat modeling techniques, ultimately enhancing its effectiveness in practice.

3.4 How Does the Human Mind Apply Threat Modeling?

The human factor plays a crucial role in understanding the effectiveness of any tool or technique. Conducting detailed evaluations of the mindset, perception, and handling of threat modeling operations can maximize the efficiency of this technique and provide valuable insights for future improvements. Currently, comprehensive assessments regarding the human thought processes involved in threat modeling are lacking, and there is a need to extend ongoing research in this area for future advancements [31].

To address this question, several experiments can be designed involving individual engineers or groups with diverse backgrounds and experiences. Games or challenges can be developed to engage participants in threat modeling activities, allowing for the observation and evaluation of their behavior and outcomes using both quantitative and qualitative methods. Controlling the participants, exercises, as well as the experimental techniques and environment, will enable researchers to provide valuable insights for the initial research objectives. Investigating the communication and collaboration among developers during threat modeling can provide valuable insights into the human factors involved.

4   Related Work

The main purpose of this paper is the collection and review of the existing empirical evidence on the effectiveness of threat modeling found in the scientific literature. Other researchers have already systematically surveyed the literature on threat modeling, albeit with a different focus. Xiong and Lagerström [37] have performed a systematic literature review on threat modeling, focusing on the different definitions and methods for threat modeling. They also investigate the validation provided for such methods, concluding that "validation methods need to be developed and enhanced for assuring the outcomes of threat modeling (less examples and more empirics)". Similarly, the systematic literature review of Tuma et al. [30] lists and compares 26 methodologies for threat analysis. Based on their findings, they also call for a more thorough empirical evaluation of threat modeling techniques. Finally, Shi et al. [26] investigate tool support for threat modeling by providing a taxonomy for such tools to classify them based on their features and characteristics. While their research is primarily focused on the features offered by such tools, they too call for more research (including a benchmark) to assist with quantitative evaluations. Neither these systematic reviews, nor the collection of existing empirical evaluations of threat modeling composed in paper, is sufficient to address the open challenges outlined in the previous section at this point. In other words, we conclude that the threat modeling community would profit from a clear demonstration of the benefits and drawbacks the existing techniques when they are applied in practice, with particular attention to human, organizational, and other non-technical factors.

5   Conclusion

In this paper, we present a review of empirical studies that investigate practical aspects of threat modeling. Our study collects several studies that provide indications for the benefits and challenges of adopting threat modeling, as well as empirical evaluations of existing threat modeling methods and tools. Based on our analysis of the collected papers, we identify open challenges, including the effectiveness, impact, learning, and human factors of threat modeling, which should be addressed in future research to generate more compelling evidence for organizations when making decisions regarding its adoption.

Acknowledgements. This research is partially funded by the Research Fund KU Leuven, and by the Flemish Research Programme Cybersecurity.

References

1. ACM Digital Library — dl.acm.org. https://dl.acm.org/. Accessed 04 Jul 2023
2. Google Scholar — scholar.google.com. https://scholar.google.com/. Accessed 04 Jul 2023
3. IEEE Xplore — ieeexplore.ieee.org. https://ieeexplore.ieee.org/Xplore/home.jsp. Accessed 04 Jul 2023

4. Scopus Preview — scopus.com. https://www.scopus.com/. Accessed 04 Jul 2023
5. Semantic Scholar — AI-Powered Research Tool — semanticscholar.org. https://www.semanticscholar.org/. Accessed 04 Jul 2023
6. Bernsmed, K., Cruzes, D.S., Jaatun, M.G., Iovan, M.: Adopting threat modelling in agile software development projects. J. Syst. Softw. **183**, 111090 (2022)
7. Bernsmed, K., Jaatun, M.G.: Threat modelling and agile software development: Identified practice in four norwegian organisations. In: 2019 International Conference on Cyber Security and Protection of Digital Services (Cyber Security), pp. 1–8. IEEE (2019)
8. Bygdås, E., Jaatun, L.A., Antonsen, S.B., Ringen, A., Eiring, E.: Evaluating threat modeling tools: microsoft tmt versus owasp threat dragon. In: 2021 International Conference on Cyber Situational Awareness, Data Analytics and Assessment (CyberSA), pp. 1–7. IEEE (2021)
9. Cruzes, D.S., Jaatun, M.G., Bernsmed, K., Tøndel, I.A.: Challenges and experiences with applying microsoft threat modeling in agile development projects. In: 2018 25th Australasian Software Engineering Conference (ASWEC), pp. 111–120. IEEE (2018)
10. Dewitte, P., et al.: A comparison of system description models for data protection by design. In: Proceedings of the 34th ACM/SIGAPP Symposium on Applied Computing, pp. 1512–1515 (2019)
11. Dhillon, D.: Developer-driven threat modeling: lessons learned in the trenches. IEEE Secur. Privacy **9**(4), 41–47 (2011)
12. Fitzgerald, B., Musiał, M., Stol, K.J.: Evidence-based decision making in lean software project management. In: Companion Proceedings of the 36th International Conference on Software Engineering, pp. 93–102 (2014)
13. Galvez, R., Gurses, S.: The odyssey: modeling privacy threats in a brave new world. In: 2018 IEEE European Symposium on Security and Privacy Workshops (EuroS&PW), pp. 87–94. IEEE (2018)
14. Granata, D., Rak, M.: Systematic analysis of automated threat modelling techniques: comparison of open-source tools. Softw. Quality J., 1–37 (2023)
15. Jamil, A.-M., Ben Othmane, L., Valani, A.: Threat modeling of cyber-physical systems in practice. In: Luo, B., Mosbah, M., Cuppens, F., Ben Othmane, L., Cuppens, N., Kallel, S. (eds.) CRiSIS 2021. LNCS, vol. 13204, pp. 3–19. Springer, Cham (2022). https://doi.org/10.1007/978-3-031-02067-4_1
16. Kitchenham, B.A., Dyba, T., Jorgensen, M.: Evidence-based software engineering. In: Proceedings of the 26th International Conference on Software Engineering, pp. 273–281. IEEE (2004)
17. Library, C.: Qualitative and quantitative research: What is "empirical research"? Website. https://library.lasalle.edu/c.php?g=225780&p=3112085
18. Mbaka, W., Tuma, K.: A replication of a controlled experiment with two stride variants. arXiv preprint arXiv:2208.01524 (2022)
19. Microsoft: Microsoft Security Development Lifecycle — microsoft.com. https://www.microsoft.com/en-us/securityengineering/sdl. Accessed 30 Jun 2023
20. NIST: Secure Software Development Framework — CSRC — CSRC — csrc.nist.gov. https://csrc.nist.gov/Projects/ssdf. Accessed 30 Jun 2023
21. Opdahl, A.L., Sindre, G.: Experimental comparison of attack trees and misuse cases for security threat identification. Inf. Softw. Technol. **51**(5), 916–932 (2009)
22. OWASP: A04 Insecure Design - OWASP Top 10:2021 — owasp.org. https://owasp.org/Top10/A04_2021-Insecure_Design/. Accessed 30 Jun 2023
23. OWASP: OWASP SAMM — OWASP Foundation — owasp.org. https://owasp.org/www-project-samm/. Accessed 30 Jun 2023

24. Patten, M.L., Galvan, M.C.: Proposing empirical research: A guide to the fundamentals. Routledge (2019)
25. Scandariato, R., Wuyts, K., Joosen, W.: A descriptive study of microsoft's threat modeling technique. Requirements Eng. **20**, 163–180 (2015)
26. Shi, Z., Graffi, K., Starobinski, D., Matyunin, N.: Threat modeling tools: a taxonomy. IEEE Secur. Privacy **20**(4), 29–39 (2022). https://doi.org/10.1109/MSEC.2021.3125229
27. Shostack, A.: Experiences threat modeling at microsoft. MODSEC@ MoDELS **2008**, 35 (2008)
28. Steckler, A., McLeroy, K.R., Goodman, R.M., Bird, S.T., McCormick, L.: Toward integrating qualitative and quantitative methods: An introduction (1992)
29. Stevens, R., Votipka, D., Redmiles, E.M., Ahern, C., Sweeney, P., Mazurek, M.L.: The battle for new york: A case study of applied digital threat modeling at the enterprise level. In: USENIX Security Symposium, pp. 621–637 (2018)
30. Tuma, K., Calikli, G., Scandariato, R.: Threat analysis of software systems: a systematic literature review. J. Syst. Softw. **144**(May), 275–294 (2018). https://doi.org/10.1016/j.jss.2018.06.073
31. Tuma, K., Mbaka, W.: Human aspect of threat analysis: A replication. arXiv preprint arXiv:2208.01512 (2022)
32. Tuma, K., Scandariato, R.: Two architectural threat analysis techniques compared. In: Cuesta, C.E., Garlan, D., Pérez, J. (eds.) ECSA 2018. LNCS, vol. 11048, pp. 347–363. Springer, Cham (2018). https://doi.org/10.1007/978-3-030-00761-4_23
33. Van Landuyt, D., Joosen, W.: A descriptive study of assumptions made in linddun privacy threat elicitation. In: Proceedings of the 35th Annual ACM Symposium on Applied Computing, pp. 1280–1287 (2020)
34. Van Landuyt, D., Joosen, W.: A descriptive study of assumptions in stride security threat modeling. Software and Systems Modeling, pp. 1–18 (2021)
35. Williams, I., Yuan, X.: Evaluating the effectiveness of microsoft threat modeling tool. In: Proceedings of the 2015 Information Security Curriculum Development Conference, pp. 1–6 (2015)
36. Wuyts, K., Scandariato, R., Joosen, W.: Empirical evaluation of a privacy-focused threat modeling methodology. J. Syst. Softw. **96**, 122–138 (2014)
37. Xiong, W., Lagerström, R.: Threat modeling – a systematic literature review. Comput. Secur. **84**, 53–69 (2019). https://doi.org/10.1016/j.cose.2019.03.010
38. Yeng, P., Wolthusen, S.D., Yang, B.: Comparative analysis of threat modeling methods for cloud computing towards healthcare security practice (2020)
39. Yskout, K., Heyman, T., Van Landuyt, D., Sion, L., Wuyts, K., Joosen, W.: Threat modeling: from infancy to maturity. In: Proceedings of the ACM/IEEE 42nd International Conference on Software Engineering: New Ideas and Emerging Results, pp. 9–12 (2020)

FAACS

Declarative Representation of UML State Machines for Querying and Simulation

Zohreh Mehrafrooz[✉], Ali Jannatpour, and Constantinos Constantinides

Department of Computer Science and Software Engineering, Concordia University,
Montreal, Canada
zohreh.mehrafroozmayvan@mail.concordia.ca,
{ali.jannatpour,constantinos.constantinides}@concordia.ca

Abstract. Among the various aspects of the Unified Modeling Language, state machines are utilized to model the dynamic behavior of reactive systems. In this paper we present a platform where we transform a state machine into a declarative model, implemented as a database of clauses in Prolog. To tackle the complexity of composite states, we propose an algorithm for flattening the state machine's representation. Both initial and flattened declarative models allow for querying on the quality attributes, the behavior and the well-formedness of the underlying machine. To complement the query-based analysis, we present a simulation process and we describe its automation and tool support. We demonstrate the analysis through a case study. The approach can assist software developers while performing validation of requirements.

Keywords: UML state machines · Model transformation · Declarative modeling · Simulation · Automation

1 Introduction and Motivation

Originally introduced by Gill in 1962 [7] and later proposed by Harel in 1987 [8] as a significant extension over traditional finite state machines, statecharts are a visual formalism for modeling the dynamic behavior of components at various levels of abstraction. The Unified Modeling Language (UML), an industrial de facto standard that supports software modeling, adopted Harel's statecharts in its specification and extended them. This study is based on the extended statechart model, referred to in the literature as "UML state machine" (or "UML statechart"). A state machine can model the behavior of a reactive system at any level of abstraction. In this study, we define a declarative representation of a state machine, and construct a platform to analyze the machine through queries and simulation. The objective is to assist in the validation of system requirements captured by the machine and the methodology entails the study of quality attributes, behavior and well-formedness of the machine as well as simulation.

© The Author(s), under exclusive license to Springer Nature Switzerland AG 2024
B. Tekinerdoğan et al. (Eds.): ECSA 2023, LNCS 14590, pp. 133–150, 2024.
https://doi.org/10.1007/978-3-031-66326-0_9

A declarative model is a powerful and intuitive way to represent state machines, offering numerous advantages in terms of maintainability, scalability, and analysis. In fact, declarative representation expresses the behavior and transitions of the state machine using logical clauses and rules. This model can be implemented in Prolog, which provides capabilities like pattern matching and backtracking, making it well-suited for modeling complex behavior in state machines [16]. Sheng et al. [15] present a Prolog-based consistency checking for UML class diagrams and object diagrams. They formalize the elements of the model and then convert the model into Prolog facts along with some consistency rules that enable querying of the properties, elements, and subsequent parts of the model. Similarly, Khai et al. [12] propose a Prolog-based approach for consistency checking of class and sequence diagrams. State machines are widely utilized in software testing to evaluate performance and quality against predefined requirements. Hashim and Dawood [11] conduct a review of test case generation methods that use UML statecharts. Chen and Lin [3] propose a test case generation strategy that enhances efficiency and guarantees high test coverage and accuracy. Aktaş and Ovatman [1] discuss statechart anti-patterns which may occur in software development process.

Using a declarative model, the static behavior of a system can be studied and the system requirements can be validated. Additionally, statecharts are a widely-used notation for representing the dynamic and executable behavior of complex systems [5]. This highlights the significance of having tools for visualizing and simulating statecharts. Mens et al. [13] introduce a technique to improve statechart design using specialized tools including a modular Python library called Sismic [5]. Van Mierlo and Vangheluwe [17] present an approach for modeling, simulating, testing, and deploying statecharts. Balasubramanian et al. [2] introduce Polyglot, a framework for analyzing models described using multiple statechart formalisms. Their approach involves translating the structure and behavior of statechart models into Java and analyzing them using pluggable semantics. Modeling state machines with nested composite states and flattening the model has been a challenge. One major issue is the potential occurrence of unwanted non-determinism which has also been studied in the literature [9,10], and [17]. E. V. and Samuel [6] describe a technique to transform hierarchical, concurrent, and history states into Java code using a design pattern-based methodology.

We structure the remainder of this paper as follows: We provide a background to the mathematical specification of a state machine in Sect. 2. We present an overview of our approach and the case study in Sect. 3. We present our initial declarative model in Sect. 4 and describe our query system in Sect. 6. We present our flattened declarative model in Sect. 5; and the simulation process in Sect. 7, together with a discussion on the results of a given scenario. We finally present our conclusion.

2   Background and Assumptions

UML 2.5.1 [14] provides numerous complex features, such as composite and nested states; entry and exit pseudostates; entry, exit, and do state behavior;

as well as implicit region completion transitions. These features lead to a complex behavioral analysis. We simplify the machine by converting it into a modified Extended Finite State Machine EXTENDED FINITE STATE MACHINE (EFSM), as specified in the subsequent section. Moreover, the standard UML does not allow ϵ-transitions. An ϵ-transition is a transition whose *event* and *guard* are empty. Observe that ϵ-transitions are only allowed in pseudostates (i.e. entry and exit), as well as region completion (i.e. in the case of the completion of a *do* behavior, or reaching a final substate).

2.1   Modified Extended Finite State Machine (EFSM)

The EFSM is formally defined as a 7-tuple [4]. Our definition of EFSMs adapts this 7-tuple, with a slight modification on the inputs of the transition. An EFSM M, is defined as a 7-tuple $(Q, \Sigma_1, \Sigma_2, q_0, V, \Gamma, \Lambda)$, where

Q is a finite set of *states*,
$\Sigma_1 = \{e_i : i \in \mathbb{Z}\}$, is a non-empty finite set of *events*,
$\Sigma_2 = \{a_i : i \in \mathbb{Z}\}$, is a finite set of *actions*,
$q_0 \in Q$ is the *starting state*,
$V = \{v_i : i \in \mathbb{Z}\}$ is a finite set of *mutable* global *variables*,
$\Gamma = \{g_i : i \in \mathbb{Z}\}$ is a finite set of *guards*,
$\Lambda = \{\lambda : q \xrightarrow{e_i[g_i]/a_i} q', i \in \mathbb{Z}\}$, is a finite set of *deterministic* transitions defined on $Q \times \overset{\circ}{\Sigma_1} \times \overset{\circ}{\Gamma} \to Q \times \overset{\circ}{\Sigma_2}$, where $\overset{\circ}{\Sigma_1} = \{\epsilon\} \cup \Sigma_1$, $\overset{\circ}{\Gamma} = \{\epsilon\} \cup \Gamma$, $\overset{\circ}{\Sigma_2} = \{\epsilon\} \cup \Sigma_2$, ϵ denotes *null*, $q, q' \in Q$, $e \in \overset{\circ}{\Sigma_1}$, $g_i \in \overset{\circ}{\Gamma}$, and $a_i \in \overset{\circ}{\Sigma_2}$ are all *bindable* string literals.

A guarded ϵ-transition is represented by $\lambda : q \xrightarrow{e_i[g_i]/a_i} q'$ where $e_i = \epsilon$. In the case where $g = \epsilon$, the transition is referred to as ϵ-transition. In order for Λ to be deterministic, for every state $q \in Q$, at most one possible transition must exist. In other words, $\forall q \forall \lambda_i : q \xrightarrow{e_i[g_i]/a_i} q'$, the satisfiability of (e_i, g_i) must be exclusive. While this property holds for all EFSMs, we enforce the following restrictions:

1. If state q has an outgoing ϵ-transition, no other outgoing transitions are allowed on q.
2. If state q has an outgoing guarded ϵ-transition, only other guarded ϵ-transitions are allowed on the state. Let $\{g_i\}$ be the set of all guards for all guarded ϵ-transitions on state q. i) $\cup g_i = \text{True}$; ii) $\forall i \forall j \neq i \ (\neg(g_i \land g_j))$.

3   Overview of the Approach and Case Study

An overview of our approach is illustrated in the UML activity diagram of Fig. 1, and the various aspects of the diagram will be discussed in the subsequent sections through a case study that models an alarm system, shown in Fig. 2 and Fig. 3.

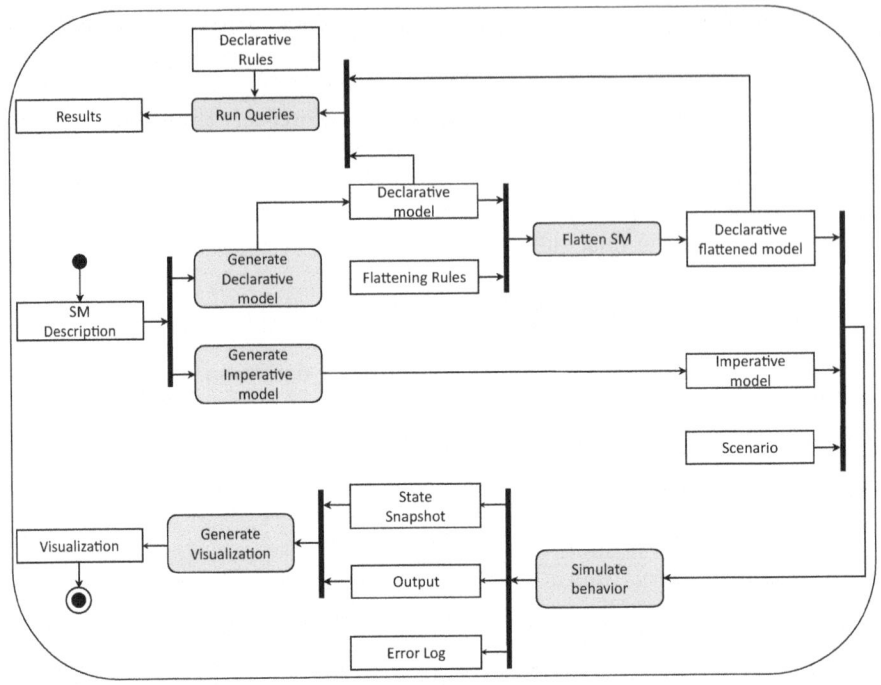

Fig. 1. UML activity diagram of the approach.

4   Transformation of the State Machine into a Declarative Model

The first part of this task is to provide a platform that can serve as a *virtual machine* for analysis of a state machine. The model consists of a declarative representation of a machine, following a defined structure of clauses, implemented as Prolog facts, that represent the state machine as a cyclic directed multigraph, where states are modeled as nodes and where transitions are modeled as edges. Unary clauses such as `state/1`, `pseudostate/1`, `initial/1`, `final/1` model their respective language element and `proc/1` defines a *do* behavior. Binary and multi-arity clauses are defined in Table 1.

4.1   Modeling Events

In this declarative model, events are represented by the `event/2` clause, implemented as `event(type, argument)`. The supported event types in accordance with the UML specification include *call*, *signal*, *time* and *change*. Additionally, we introduce three new event types: *inactivity*, *update* and *completion*. A brief description of all event types is shown below:

call: An external event that triggers a transition. Makes use of keyword `call`.

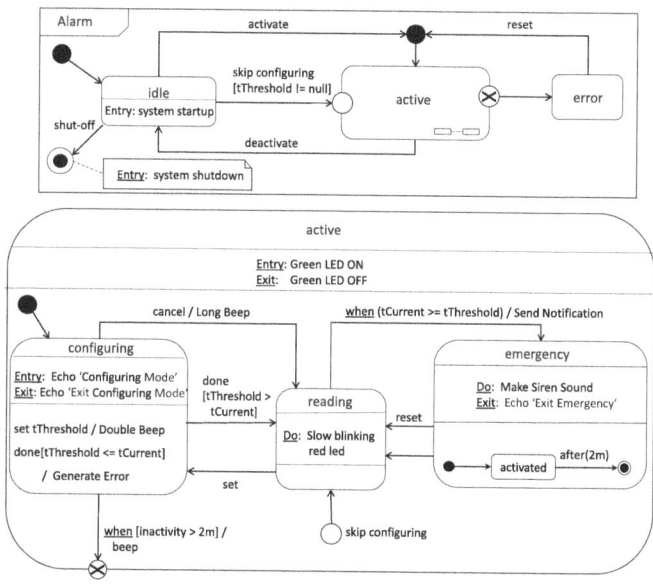

Fig. 2. Case study: Alarm.

```
% top level
state(idle).     state(active).   state(error).
state(final).    initial(idle).   final(final).   alias(final, "").
entry_pseudostate(active_skip_config_entry, reading). % active superstate is implied
exit_pseudostate(active_exit, active).
transition(idle, active, event(call, activate), nil, nil).
transition(idle, active_skip_config_entry, event(call, "skip configuring"), nil, nil).
transition(error, active, event(call, reset), nil, nil).
transition(active, idle, event(call, deactivate), nil, nil).
transition(idle, final, event(call, shutoff), nil, nil).
transition(active_exit, error, nil, nil, nil). % see exit_pseudostate
onentry_action(idle, action(log, "System Startup")).
onentry_action(final, action(log, "System Shutdown")).
% level 2
initial(configuring).              superstate(active, configuring).
superstate(active, reading).       superstate(active, emergency).
onentry_action(active, action(log, "Green LED ON")).
onexit_action(active, action(log, "Green LED OFF")).
onentry_action(configuring, action(exec, "echo('Configuring mode');")).
onexit_action(configuring, action(exec, "echo('Exit configuring mode');")).
do_action(reading, proc("Slow blinking red LED")).
transition(configuring, reading, event(call, cancel), nil, action(exec, "longBeep();")).
transition(configuring, active_exit, event(timeout, "2:00"), nil, action(exec, "beep();")).
transition(reading, emergency, event(when, "tCurrent >= tThreshold"),
    nil, action(exec, "sendNotification();")).
transition(reading, configuring, event(call, set), nil, nil).
transition(emergency, reading, event(call, reset), nil, nil).
transition(emergency, reading, nil, nil, nil). % completed emergency
transition(configuring, reading, event(call, done), "tThreshold > tCurrent", nil).
internal_transition(configuring, event(set, tThreshold), nil, action(exec, "doubleBeep();")).
internal_transition(configuring, event(call, done),
    "tThreshold <= tCurrent", action(exec, "generateError();")).
% level 3
initial(activated).     final(efinal).    alias(efinal, "").
superstate(emergency, activated).   superstate(emergency, efinal).
do_action(emergency, proc("Make Siren Sound")).
onexit_action(emergency, action(exec,"echo('Exit Emergency');")).
transition(activated, efinal, event(after, "2:00"), nil, nil).
```

Fig. 3. The initial declarative model of the alarm case study.

signal: Triggered by an internal or external clock, which indicates a specific time for triggering a transition. Makes use of keyword `at`.

time: When the source state has been active for a specified length of time, the transition occurs if its guard evaluates to true. If no guard is present (nil), a transition occurs automatically. Makes use of keyword `after`.

change: Triggered by a constantly evaluated condition once true. Makes use of keyword `when`.

inactivity: The system is expected to be inactive over a given amount of time, specified by the argument. Though treated as a time event, it makes use of keyword `timeout`.

update: Updates the value of a variable or attribute, which may subsequently trigger a transition if the new value satisfies the conditions for the transition. Makes use of keyword `set`.

completion: Occurs when a region concludes or a do behavior completes, modeled as `event(completed, ?state)`, where `?state` represents the current state (or region). Makes use of keyword `completed`.

4.2   Modeling Actions

We classify actions into `EXEC` and `LOG`. This classification provides the means to manage each action type differently, allowing for greater flexibility in the model. This classification is particularly useful when we need to flatten the model (see Sect. 5), as it allows us to easily identify and apply the appropriate processing to each type. Finally, the model introduces `action/2` to codify actions. The case study illustrates actions that are executed by the script engine (e.g. invoking the `echo()` method) as well as actions that are logged by the system (e.g. `Green LED OFF`). Note that a *do* behavior is a *process* that is *started* when the machine enters a state and may be *stopped* (upon successful termination) or *aborted* (triggered by an *exit* event). Finally, in Fig. 2, `system shutdown` is implemented as an entry behavior of the final state, since a final state cannot have an exit behavior.

5   Flattened Representation of UML State Machines

We extend the initial declarative model and develop an algorithm that flattens the machine. We believe that a flattened model can provide a platform for deeper analysis as well as a simulation of behavior (see Sect. 7). The flattened model provides the same semantic model as the initial model, though at a lower level of abstraction, being analogous to the bytecode platform for languages such as Java and Clojure, which is a seamless virtual machine. The flattened model can also be extended with rules that target the three aspects of our analysis (quality attributes, behavior, and well-formedness).

Table 1. Major clause signatures of the initial declarative model.

FACT	DESCRIPTION
`entry_pseudostate/2`	`entry_pseudostate(?Entry, ?Substate)` implies that `?Substate` is the target inner-state whose superstate is already defined by `superstate(?Superstate, ?Substate)`
`exit_pseudostate/2`	`exit_pseudostate(?Exit, ?Superstate)` implies that `?Exit` is an exit state within the superstate `?Superstate`
`superstate/2`	`superstate(?Superstate, ?Substate)` implies that `?Superstate` is a composite state with `?Substate` being a nested state
`onentry_action/2`	`onentry_action(?Name, ?Action)` implies that `?Name` defines `?Action` as an entry behavior
`onexit_action/2`	`onexit_action(?Name, ?Action)` implies that `?Name` defines `?Action` as an exit behavior
`do_action/2`	`do_action(?Name, ?Proc)` implies that `?Name` defines `?Proc` as a do behavior
`transition/5`	`transition(?Source, ?Destination, ?Event, ?Guard, ?Action)` indicates that while the system is in state `?Source`, should `?Event` occur and with `?Guard` being true, the system performs a transition to state `?Destination` while performing `?Action`. All elements of the triple (`?Event`, `?Guard`, `?Action`) are optional, and the absence of an element is codified as `nil`
`internal_transition/4`	`internal_transition(?State, ?Event, ?Guard, ?Action)` indicates that while the system is in `?State`, should `?Event` occur and with `?Guard` being true, the system performs `?Action`. In the triple (`?Event`, `?Guard`, `?Action`), only `?Guard` is optional, the absence of which is codified as `nil`
`event/2`	`event(?Type, ?Argument)` indicates an event where `?Type` shows event type and `?Argument` is a literal
`action/2`	`action(?Type, ?Argument)` indicates an action where `?Type` shows action type and `?Argument` is a literal

5.1   The Flattening Process

In a complex UML machine, transitions can trigger various sequences of actions. For example, when transitioning from *idle* to *active*, while the transition itself has no action, the *activate* event triggers the *entry* action on *active* before transitioning into *configuring*. Similarly, when transitioning from *activated* (substate of *active*) to *idle*, a sequence of actions is executed: *aborting* 'Make Siren Sound', *executing* `echo('Exit Emergency')`, and *logging* 'Green LED OFF'.

To analyze the behavior of the UML state machine, we convert it into a *flattened* EFSM by chaining the subsequent actions using ϵ-transitions. Our flattening algorithm consists of 4+1 passes, progressively eliminating complex UML features such as composite states, pseudostates, state behaviors, and internal transitions. Each pass involves multiple steps, modifying facts and reducing complexity until the machine is fully flattened. Finally, the resulting machine is minimized by reducing the number of states and combining equivalent transitions. Prolog queries are used as selectors to process the working database. An outline of the flattening algorithm is presented on the next page:

Procedure *Flatten*(Input: UML in decl. DB, **Output:** EFSM in decl. DB)
Pass 0: *Preprocessing*
1: Convert all outgoing `nil`-events form state s to *event(completed, s)*.
2: Convert all actions to action-lists.
Pass 1: *Processing pseudostates, entry, exit, and do behaviors*
1: *Resolving do behaviors:* For each state s with *do* behavior with process p: i) Append "start p", insert "abort p" notification actions to the *entry* and *exit* actions of state s, respectively; ii) For every *completed* event on state s, insert "stop p" notification action to transition's actions; iii) Remove the *do* behavior from s.
2: *Resolving entry/exit pseudostates:* i) Replace all `entry_pseudostate(s, t)` clauses with `transition(s, t, nil, nil, [])` and `superstate(p, s)` where `superstate(p, t)`; ii) Change all `exit_pseudostate(s, p)` clauses to `superstate(p, s)`.
3: *Resolving entry behaviors:* Starting from top to bottom, for every state with *entry* behavior: i) Find `onentry_action(s, a)` and remove it; ii) For each incoming transition from an external state x to s: append s to the transition's action list; iii) For each incoming transition from an external state x to a substate b of s, append a to the transition's action list; iv) If s is a top-level initial state, create a new state ps, add `state(ps)`; change `initial(s)` to `initial(ps)`, and add `transition(ps, s, nil, nil, a)`; v) Otherwise if s is a non-top-level initial state, find p where `superstate(p, s)`; add `superstate(p, ps)`; change `initial(s)` to `initial(ps)`, and add `transition(ps, s, nil, nil, a)`.
Pass 2: *Full State Resolution*
1: For each composite state p do the following: i) Obtain the list of immediate substates of p into l; Obtain the exit behavior of p into ea; ii) Change the target state of all incoming transitions to p, to the initial substate of p; iii) For each non-final substate s of p repeat: a) Inherit all outgoing `nil`-transitions from the superstate, if the child state does not contain a `nil`-transition; b) For every outgoing transition from the state s to a state that is not in l, including the above; insert ea to the transition's action list, if $ea \neq$ `nil`; c) Replace `superstate(p, s)` with `state(s)`.

iv) Find inner final state f (if applicable); remove both `superstate(p, f)` and `final(f)`; add `state(f)`; for each `transition(p, t, e, g, a)` from p to the target state t where e is a *region completion* event on p: add `transition(s, t, nil, g, a)`; insert ea to a, if $ea \neq$ `nil`; v) Remove the composite state p, its behaviors, and all its outgoing transitions.
2: For each remaining state s with *exit* behavior e, insert e to all outgoing transitions' actions list and remove the *exit* behavior clause.

3: For each internal transition on state s, convert `internal_transition` to `transition` to self.

Pass 3: *Post-Processing*

1: For all action lists containing "stop p", find corresponding "abort p" in the list; remove "stop p", and change "abort p" to "stop p".

2: For all `transition(s, t, e, g, l)`, where length(l) > 1, create intermediary state i, replace the original transition with `transition(s, i, e, g, head`$(l))$ and `transition(i, t, nil, nil, tail`$(l))$; Resolve `transition(i, t, nil, nil, tail`$(l))$, recursively. 3: Replace all `transition(s, t, e, g, [])` with `transition(s, t, e, g, nil)`.

Pass 4: *State Reduction/Minimization*

For each `transition(s, t, e, g, a)`: Find all `transition(`s_2`, t, e, g, a)` where s_2 is not initial and $s_2 \neq s$. Replace all `transition(`x`, `s_2`, `e_2`, `g_2`, `a_2`)` with `transition(`x`, s, `e_2`, `g_2`, `a_2`)`. Remove all instances of `state(`e_2`)` and `transition(`e_2`, t, e, g, a)`. Repeat until no more transitions can merge.

Having produced a flattened model, we perform a model transformation into a (new) declarative representation, deploying only the clause structures `state/1`, `initial/1`, `final/1`, `transition/5`, `event/2`, and `action/2`.

```
state(pre_idle).     state(idle).       state(configuring).
state(error).        state(active_exit).
final(final).        alias(final, "").
state(s71).          state(s41).        state(s31).
state(s12).
    . . .

transition(pre_idle, idle, nil, nil, action(log, "System Startup")).
transition(idle, s12, event(call, "skip configuring"), nil, action(log, "Green LED ON")).
transition(idle, s71, event(call, activate), nil, action(log, "Green LED ON")).
transition(s71, configuring, nil, nil, action(exec, "echo('Configuring mode');")).
transition(configuring, configuring, event(set, tThreshold), nil, action(exec, "doubleBeep()
transition(configuring, configuring, event(call, done),
      "tThreshold <= tCurrent", action(exec, "generateError();")).
transition(configuring, s31, event(timeout, "2:00"), nil,
      action(exec, "echo('Exit configuring mode');")).
transition(s31, active_exit, nil, nil, action(exec, "beep();")).
transition(active_exit, error, nil, nil, action(log, "Green LED OFF")).
transition(error, s71, event(call, reset), nil, action(log, "Green LED ON")).
transition(configuring, s41, event(call, cancel), nil,
      action(exec, "echo('Exit configuring mode');")).
transition(s41, s12, nil, nil, action(exec, "longBeep();")).
transition(configuring, s12, event(call, done),
      "tThreshold > tCurrent", action(exec, "echo('Exit configuring mode');")).
transition(idle, s12, event(call, "skip configuring"), nil, action(log, "Green LED ON")).
transition(s12, reading, nil, nil, action(log, "START 'Slow blinking red LED'")).
transition(reading, s71, event(call, set), nil, action(log, "ABORT 'Slow blinking red LED'")
    . . .
```

Fig. 4. Partial flattened declarative model of the alarm case study.

Figure 4 includes a partial model capturing transitions from states *idle* and *configuring* to *reading*. Consider the transition from *idle* to *configuring* in Fig. 2. Such transition causes `system startup` notification upon entry to *idle*. The reception of the event `activate` causes a transition to the *active* super-state which is now collapsed. Upon reaching *active*, the transition causes `echo` `configuring` mode upon entry to the *configuring* substate. Such sequence of actions are implemented in the flattened model by sequence of transitions starting from *initial*, to *pre_idle*, *idle*, *s71*, and finally to *configuring*. Note that one may extend the model to support transition with multiple actions, in which case, an extra step in pass 4 may reduce the total number of states by following and merging all outgoing `nil`-transitions into a single transition. We intentionally avoided this to make the model compatible with the definition of EFSMs (Fig. 5).

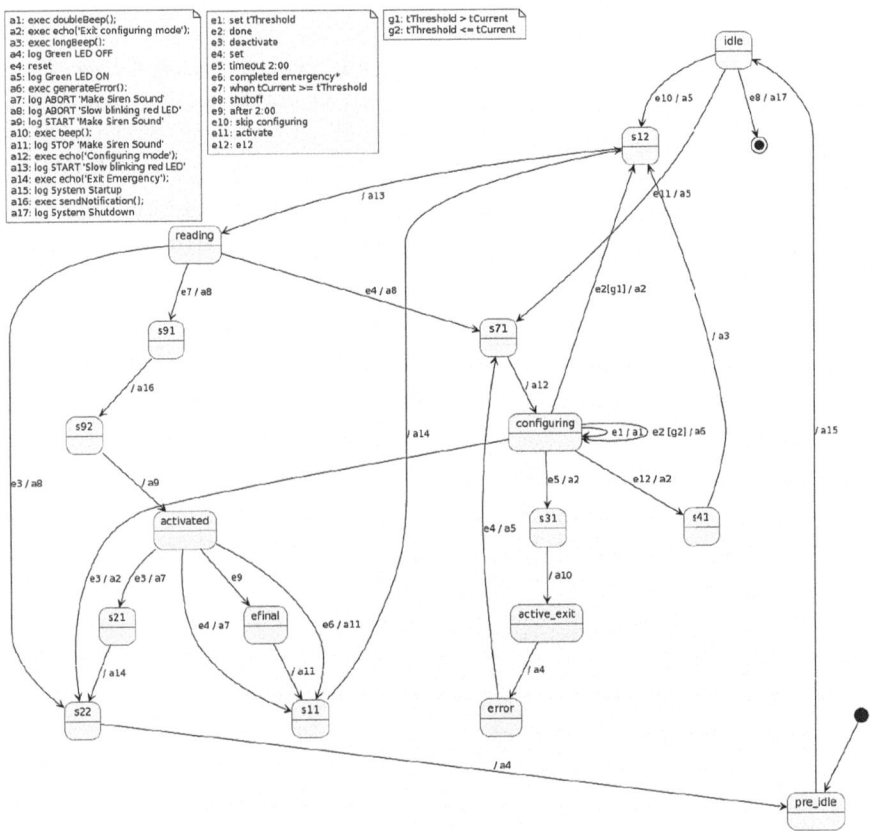

Fig. 5. The flattened UML diagram

6 Building a Query Platform

With the declarative model as is, we can execute simple ground queries that can give us some basic knowledge of the machine such as *"Is there a transition from state idle to state configuring?"*

```
? transition(idle, configuring, _, _, _).
Yes.
```

We can also execute non-ground queries such as *"Under what conditions, if any, would the state machine perform a transition to the emergency state?"* This would entail capturing any and all **state-event-guard** triples that can cause such a transition.

```
? transition(State, emergency, event(_,Event), Guard, _).
Event = "tCurrent >= tThreshold",  Guard = null,   State = reading
```

6.1 Extending the Declarative Model with Rules

We can extend the declarative model by introducing rules. We can identify three types of rules: (1) We have rules that reason about the *behavior* of the state machine by examining the traversal of the underlying graph under various different conditions. When we study behavior, we want rules that reason about elements such as the exposed interface and legal event sequences. (2) We have rules that reason about the *quality attributes* of the state machine by examining the properties and measurements of the underlying directed graph. When we study graph (machine) complexity we want rules that provide knowledge about aspects such as connectivity and (global and nodal) measurements. We argue that the above two types of rules roughly correspond to the state machine's functional and non-functional requirements. (3) We have rules that reason about the well-formedness of the machine, such as the presence of infinite loops, dead ends, or conflicts with the UML specification e.g. the existence of an internal transition without an action association.

6.2 Studying Behavior

Exposed Interface: The *call* and *set* events correspond to messages sent to the system and they collectively constitute the exposed interface of the system. Rule **get_interface/1** succeeds by collecting any and all such events.

```
get_interface(Interface) :- %% Consults: Initial model.
   findall(E, (transition(_, _, E, _, _),
           (E = event(call, _); E = event(set, _)));
        (internal_transition(_, E, _, _),
           (E = event(call, _); E = event(set, _))),
        EventList), list_to_set(EventList, Interface).
```

Legal Events at a Given State: Given the system exposed interface, it is important to note that not all events can be acted upon unconditionally. An event can be accepted based on the system's current state. It will be acted upon provided the associated guard (if one is present) evaluates to true.

```
is_legal(State, Event) :- %% Consults:  Initial model.
  transition(State, _, event(_, Event), _, _);
  internal_transition(State, event(_, Event), _, _).
```

6.3   Studying Complexity

We provide rules for properties and measurements. Measurements in graphs can be global or nodal. Global measurements refer to global properties of the graph and consist of a single number for any given graph. Nodal measurements refer to properties of the nodes and consist of a number for each node for any given graph.

Order of Graph: This measurement refers to the number of nodes in a graph. In the context of state machines, we believe that the initial model may not give us an accurate picture due to the presence of composite states. The flattened model would be more accurate for this measurement. For the initial and flattened models the corresponding rules are shown below:

```
order(N) :- %% Consults:  Initial model.
  findall(State, (state(State); superstate(_, State)), StateList),
  list_to_set(StateList, States), length(States, N).

%% Consults:  Flattened model.
order(N):- findall(S, state(S), Length), length(Length, N).
```

Number of nil Transitions: The number of *nil* transitions in a flattened model can be a measure of the complexity of a state machine. The following rule succeeds by returning the number of *nil* transitions:

```
nil_transition(N) :- %% Consults: Flattened model.
  findall(Nilevents,
    (transition(_, _, Nilevents, _, _), Nilevents=nil), Transitions),
  length(Transitions, N).
```

Size (or Length) of Graph: This measurement refers to the number of edges in a graph. In the context of state machines, we believe that the initial model may not give us an accurate picture due to the fact that in the presence of composite states, their nested states inherit the transitions of their superstate. The flattened model would be more accurate for this measurement.

```
size(N):- %% Consults: Flattened model.
  findall(S, transition(S,_,_,_,_), Length), length(Length, N).
```

6.4   Studying the Well-Formedness of the State Machine

We define rules to study the design of the state machine and find cases such as dead ends, conflicts, or inconsistencies among the state machine's elements, considering issues such as (1) Dead ends and infinite loops, (2) Internal transition without an action, (3) Multiple change events originating from the same state, (4) Non mutually exclusive guards originating from the same state, (5) The absence of a do behavior in the presence of an external transition with no event, and (6) As the previous item for a composite state, in the absence of an exit substate.

Dead Ends: We are interested in finding out if the machine can enter a state from which the final state is not reachable. Rule `dead_end/0` succeeds by obtaining a non-empty list of states from each of which there is no path to state `final`.

```
%% Consults:  Initial model.
path(X, Y) :- path(X, Y, [X]).
path(X, Y, V) :- transition(X, Y, _, _, _), \+ member(Y, V).
path(X, Y, V) :- transition(X, Z, _, _, _), \+ member(Z, V),
   path(Z, Y, [Z|V]).
dead_end :-findall(State, \+path(State, final), L), L \= [].
```

7   Simulating State Machine Behavior

The query system provides a level of analysis that is complemented with a simulation of the machine. The flattened model serves as the platform for simulation. A simulation reads in a machine representation and a scenario under which the machine is traversed and its state and behavior is monitored and recorded. The question we ask here is *"Is the Machine behaving according to its specification?"* During simulation, we need to be able to identify issues perhaps not having been identified by the query system, e.g. *"Has the simulator encountered an ambiguous transition?"*, in which case we need to report such issues.

Structure of Scenario: A scenario is a sequence of commands consisting of three types of tags: EVENT, EXECUTE, and TIME. EVENT tags can be of type `call`, `set`, or `completion`, and must trigger the corresponding transition. EXECUTE tags contain expressions that modify variable values, and may trigger a transition. TIME tags can be either `after` or `at`, which update time variables `duration` and `absoluteTime` (if applicable) and may trigger a transition.

Read-Evaluate-Execute Cycle: In UML, it is assumed that a state machine processes one event at a time and finishes all the consequences of that event before processing next event [14]. At the highest level of abstraction, and given a scenario, the simulation would be performed using a Read-Evaluate-Execute Cycle. When a command in a scenario is EVENT e, where $e \in \Sigma_1$, given the current state and the event, the simulator would construct a `transition` query and consult the declarative model. We query the database and find all transitions $\lambda_i \in \Lambda$ with event e. The result of the query is a set of λ_i, associated with tuples $\{(q, g, a)_i\}$ where $q \in Q$ is the target state, $g \in \Lambda$ is a guard, and $a \in \Sigma_2$ is an action. Each tuple is also associated with a set of $v_i \subset V$, containing all variables used in g_i and a_i. The query is successful only if one transition is possible. This is achieved by instantiating all variables in v_i and evaluating g_i. Upon success, a single transition is fired. The simulator consequently checks if any additional transitions can be triggered, following the most recent transition. The process continues until no further possible transition is applicable.

Simulator Architecture: To perform a simulation, we need to provide storage of all variables (machine and environment) while keeping track of any changes.

We also need to provide storage and keep track of the machine's current state. To support these requirements, we provide an imperative model in Java while deploying Java Prolog Library (JPL). We use Javascript to maintain system variables, and we deploy the GraalVM engine to evaluate events and guards, and finally to execute actions. We illustrate the architecture of the simulator in the UML component diagram shown in Fig. 6. We illustrate the interaction of the various components during simulation with the UML sequence diagram of Fig. 7. The diagram illustrates the interactions among high-level objects, including `SimulatorExecuter`, `JPLMediator` (facilitating the communication with the declarative model), `ScriptHandler` (responsible for evaluating guards, actions, and modifying variables), a `Scenario` defined as a text file containing a sequence of events for simulation, and the `Output` generated by the tool. The outer loop in the sequence diagram illustrates the `Read-Evaluate-Execute` cycle and the inner loop mostly covers ϵ-transitions in our flattened model.

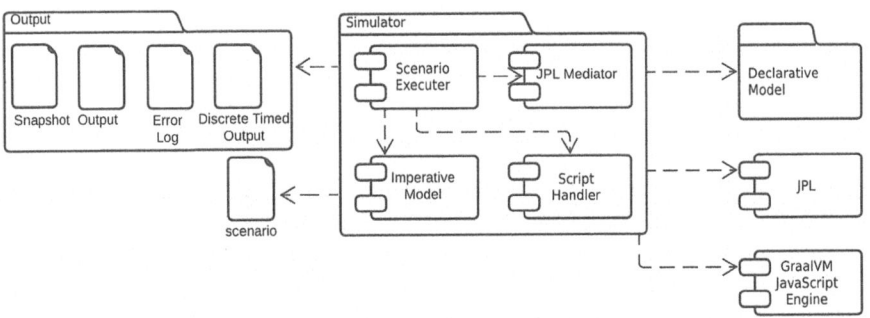

Fig. 6. UML component diagram of the simulator.

Results of Simulation in the Case Study: We applied the flattening algorithm to the declarative representation of our case study, and the resulting minimized flattened model is shown in Fig. 4. Also, Fig. 8 presents a sample scenario (top-left) along with the corresponding simulation output (top-right).

Visualization of Results: we visualize the results of simulating the scenario as the model of behavior which is shown in Fig. 8 (bottom). This diagram shows the current state of the state machine as well as state of the system in each time id.

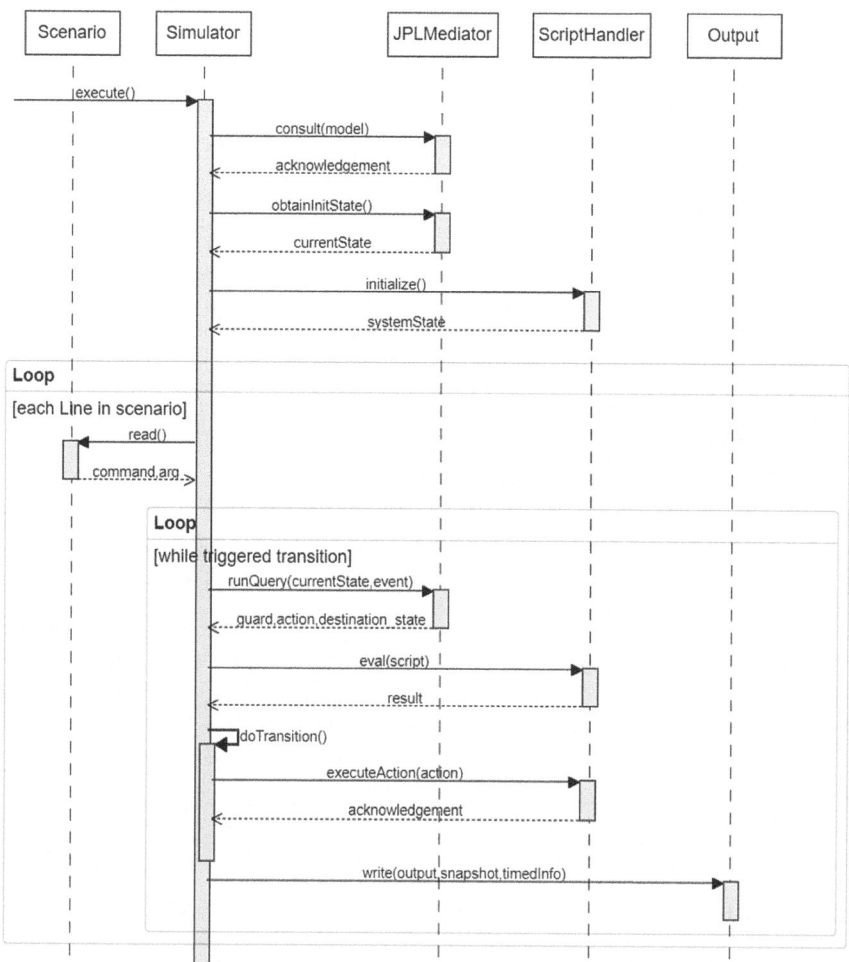

Fig. 7. UML sequence diagram of the simulation process.

Table 2. Complexity Metrics: Original vs Flattened Models

Metric	Original	Flattened
states and substates	9	18
internal initial states	2	0
transitions(+ internal)	16+2	29
entry/exit pseudostates	2	0
entry/exit (+do behaviors)	5+2	0
ϵ-transitions	2	11
actions	10	26

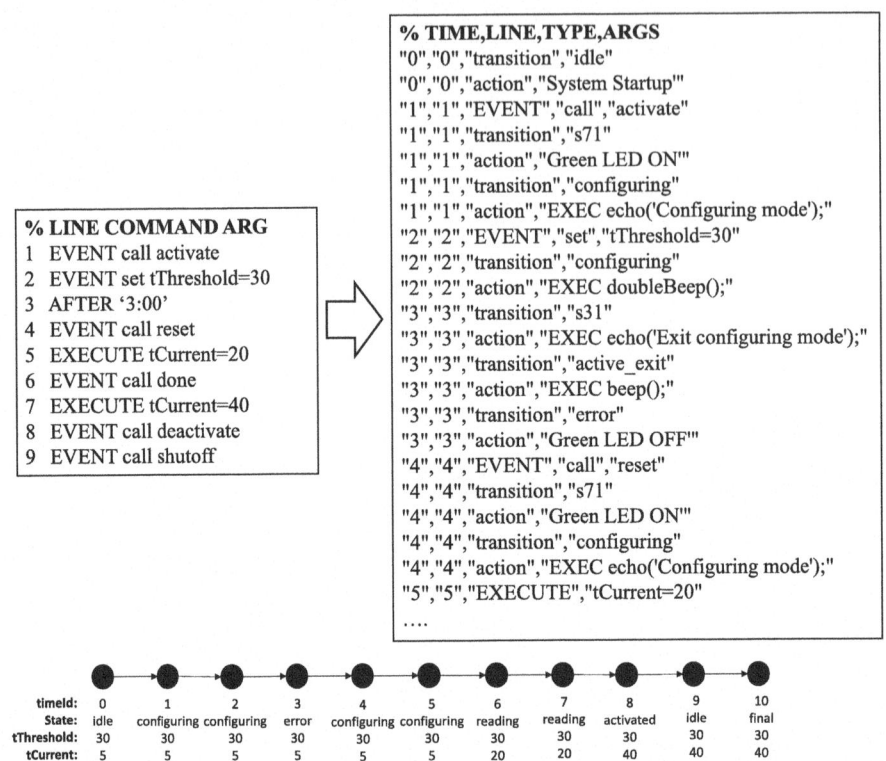

Fig. 8. Input scenario and the corresponding simulation output (top), and its model of behavior (bottom)

Conclusion

In this paper, we presented a declarative model to represent UML state machines. The model is used to study the dynamic behavior of the underlying machine. The simulation results provide insights into the machine's behavior under specific scenarios. We developed a simulation tool and a query engine that use the model in Prolog environment and run scenarios in an imperative platform. We deployed JPL for Java-Prolog interoperability. Our platform supports codified actions in JavaScript, by which developers may set or update system variables, in both the model, as well as in scenarios.

We introduced an algorithm to flatten the UML state machine and convert it into an extended finite state machine. Our algorithm supports major UML 2.5.1 features including single and composite states; exit and entry pseudostates; state behaviors including entry, do, and exit; in addition to the UML events including call, signal, time, change, as well as three newly introduced events namely inactivity, update, and completion. Table 2 lists some metrics that may be used to measure the complexity of the UML diagrams in both original and flattened models.

We used a modified version of the extended finite state machine to support guarded and unguarded ϵ-transitions that are required for handling complex sequences of actions and notifications in a non-flattened model. Future work may involve expanding the model to include contract considerations as well as other UML features such as history pseudostates and orthogonal regions.

Acknowledgments. The authors would like to thank Robin Laliberté-Beaupré and Simon Foo for their contributions to the automation and tool support for this project.

References

1. Aktaş, M., Ovatman, T.: UML statechart anti-patterns. In: 2022 IEEE 46th Annual Computers, Software, and Applications Conference (COMPSAC), pp. 413–414 (2022)
2. Balasubramanian, D., Păsăreanu, C.S., Karsai, G., Lowry, M.R.: Polyglot: systematic analysis for multiple statechart formalisms. In: Piterman, N., Smolka, S.A. (eds.) TACAS 2013. LNCS, vol. 7795, pp. 523–529. Springer, Heidelberg (2013). https://doi.org/10.1007/978-3-642-36742-7_36
3. Chen, C., Lin, W.: Research of software testing technology based on statechart diagram. In: Pan, J.-S., Li, J., Namsrai, O.-E., Meng, Z., Savić, M. (eds.) Advances in Intelligent Information Hiding and Multimedia Signal Processing. SIST, vol. 211, pp. 314–322. Springer, Singapore (2021). https://doi.org/10.1007/978-981-33-6420-2_39
4. Cheng, K.T.T., Krishnakumar, A.: Automatic generation of functional vectors using the extended finite state machine model. ACM Trans. Des. Automation Electron. Syst. **1**, May 1999. https://doi.org/10.1145/225871.225880
5. Decan, A., Mens, T.: Sismic - A Python library for statechart execution and testing. SoftwareX **12**, 100590 (2020). https://doi.org/10.1016/j.softx.2020.100590. https://www.sciencedirect.com/science/article/pii/S2352711020303034
6. Sunitha, E.V., Samuel, P.: Automatic code generation from UML state chart diagrams. IEEE Access **7**, 8591–8608 (2019). https://doi.org/10.1109/ACCESS.2018.2890791
7. Gill, A.: Introduction to the Theory of Finite-State Machines. McGraw-Hill, Electronic Science Series (1962)
8. Harel, D.: Statecharts: a visual formalism for complex systems. Sci. Comput. Program. **8**(3), 231–274 (1987). https://doi.org/10.1016/0167-6423(87)90035-9. https://www.sciencedirect.com/science/article/pii/0167642387900359
9. Harel, D., Kugler, H.: The RHAPSODY semantics of statecharts (or, on the executable core of the UML). In: Ehrig, H., Damm, W., Desel, J., Große-Rhode, M., Reif, W., Schnieder, E., Westkämper, E. (eds.) Integration of Software Specification Techniques for Applications in Engineering. LNCS, vol. 3147, pp. 325–354. Springer, Heidelberg (2004). https://doi.org/10.1007/978-3-540-27863-4_19
10. Harel, D., Naamad, A.: The STATEMATE semantics of statecharts. ACM Trans. Softw. Eng. Methodol. **5**(4), 293–333 (1996). https://doi.org/10.1145/235321.235322. https://doi.org/10.1145/235321.235322
11. Hashim, N.L., Dawood, Y.S.: A review on test case generation methods using UML statechart. In: 2019 4th International Conference and Workshops on Recent Advances and Innovations in Engineering (ICRAIE), pp. 1–5 (2019). https://doi.org/10.1109/ICRAIE47735.2019.9037786

12. Khai, Z., Nadeem, A., Lee, G.: A prolog based approach to consistency checking of UML class and sequence diagrams. In: Kim, T., Adeli, H., Kim, H., Kang, H., Kim, K.J., Kiumi, A., Kang, B.-H. (eds.) ASEA 2011. CCIS, vol. 257, pp. 85–96. Springer, Heidelberg (2011). https://doi.org/10.1007/978-3-642-27207-3_10
13. Mens, T., Decan, A., Spanoudakis, N.I.: A method for testing and validating executable statechart models. Softw. Syst. Model. **18**(2), 837–863 (2019). https://doi.org/10.1007/s10270-018-0676-3. https://doi.org/10.1007/s10270-018-0676-3
14. Object Management Group: UML® 2.5.1 (2017). https://www.omg.org/spec/UML/2.5.1/
15. Sheng, F., Zhu, H., Yang, Z., Yin, J., Lu, G.: Verifying static aspects of UML models using Prolog. In: Perkusich, A. (ed.) The 31st International Conference on Software Engineering and Knowledge Engineering, SEKE 2019, Hotel Tivoli, Lisbon, Portugal, July 10-12, 2019, pp. 259–342. KSI Research Inc. and Knowledge Systems Institute Graduate School (2019). https://doi.org/10.18293/SEKE2019-175, https://doi.org/10.18293/SEKE2019-175
16. Sterling, L., Shapiro, E.: The Art of Prolog: Advanced Programming Techniques, vol. 2. MIT Press, Cambridge (1994)
17. Van Mierlo, S., Vangheluwe, H.: Introduction to statecharts modeling, simulation, testing, and deployment. In: 2019 Winter Simulation Conference (WSC), pp. 1504–1518 (2019). https://doi.org/10.1109/WSC40007.2019.9004771

Towards Behavior-Based Analysis of Android Obfuscated Malware

Zakaria Sawadogo[1,2,3(✉)], Muhammad Taimoor Khan[2], George Loukas[2],
Jean-Marie Dembele[1], Georgia Sakellari[2], and Gervais Mendy[3]

[1] Gaston Berger University, Saint-Louis, Senegal
{sawadogo.zakaria,jean-marie.dembele}@ugb.edu.sn
[2] Centre for Sustainable Cyber Security, University of Greenwich, London, UK
{m.khan,g.loukas,g.sakellari}@greenwich.ac.uk
[3] Cheikh Anta Diop University, Dakar, Senegal
gervais.mendy@ucad.edu.sn

Abstract. In this paper, we report on the initial results of an ongoing project that aims to rigorously detect obfuscated Android malware. In fact, the detection of Android malware has become increasingly complex as malicious app developers employ various obfuscation techniques. Previous approaches have focused on addressing specific obfuscation methods, but the dynamic nature of these techniques presents challenges in accounting for all possible variations. In response to this challenge, we have developed an innovative behavioral methodology for analyzing obfuscated malware. Our approach combines model-based and AI-based techniques, making it the first effort to integrate these approaches for obfuscated malware detection. Given that deobfuscation is a computationally very challenging (i.e., NP-hard) problem, our methodology circumvents obfuscation by indirectly observing malware behavior through the runtime behavior of target services controlled and operated by the Android applications.

Keywords: Android malware · Formal model · Machine learning

1 Introduction

Ever since Google Inc. declared Kotlin[1] as the official programming language for Android app development in 2019, its popularity has been steadily growing [14]. According to Google in 2022, over 95% of major Android applications incorporate Kotlin, Java, or Java-like code. Additionally, it is more than 60% of professional Android developers opt for Kotlin, Java, or similar languages for their development projects. This demonstrates the significant adoption and usage of Kotlin and Java in the Android app development landscape. But we're also faced with a growing number of malicious apps for Android, as according to the Kaspersky Security Bulletin 2022 report [2], cyber-criminals are launching around 400,000 new malicious files a day, which is a major issue for user security.

---

[1] https://kotlinlang.org/.

B. Tekinerdoğan et al. (Eds.): ECSA 2023, LNCS 14590, pp. 151–165, 2024.
https://doi.org/10.1007/978-3-031-66326-0_10

Kaspersky's security experts have also noted a 10% increase in the number of malicious files targeting the Android platform every day.

Malware developers use obfuscation techniques such as renaming, dead code insertion, code encryption, control flow, and string encryption to transform the malware code so that it becomes more complex and less readable and can evade malicious application detection methods [17,30]. A number of efforts have proposed approaches to detect obfuscated malware using artificial intelligence, memory dumping, code analysis, and other techniques [4,21]. Though these approaches are robust and can identify unknown malware patterns, they are not practically effective mainly because they are retrospective (i.e., can only detect the already seen patterns) and suffer from high false alarms on one hand, and fail to detect the obfuscated malware due to failure in differentiating between actual malicious part and the obfuscated part of the malware code on the other hand.

In addition, various malware detection techniques have used formal approaches such as verification and model checking to analyse the source, byte-code or features of Android applications [18]. In another sense, the authors have built specific detection models for overlay banking malware [13]. In general, these approaches model the expected behaviour of the application and, possibly, known malware behaviour, then detect either by matching the malware behaviour model or by inconsistency with the expected behaviour. Although these approaches are effective at detecting modelled malware or malicious code, they fail to detect obfuscated malware because the behaviour of obfuscated malware is not known and therefore cannot be modelled. Detecting obfuscated Android applications is a complex challenge due to the variety of obfuscation techniques, the similarity of their behaviors to legitimate applications, and to constantly stay updated with the ever-evolving obfuscation techniques employed by malicious developers.

To address the aforementioned limitations, we have developed an innovative behavioral methodology for obfuscated malware analysis by combining model-based and AI-based malware analysis techniques [16]. To the best of our knowledge, this is the first effort to combine model and AI-based techniques to detect obfuscated malware. The use of obfuscation techniques makes deobfuscation classified as NP-hard, belonging to the category of challenging problems for which there is no efficient algorithm capable of providing a polynomial-time solution. As a result, the detection of obfuscated malware is also considered NP-hard [11]. Our methodology innovatively evades obfuscation by indirectly observing the malware behavior though run-time behavior of the target services that are controlled and operated by the Android applications. Based on the formal behavioral model of the critical services and operations, we perform online malware analysis based on model checking that checks consistency by comparing the observed run-time operations of the services with the known model of the services and operations, eventually raising an alarm, if inconsistency is detected. Later, AI-based offline malware analysis either learns newly identified malware behavioral patterns by the online analysis or confirms that the identified malware behavior is already known. We demonstrate our project with a simple example based on the open dataset provided by Kaggle.

The rest of the paper is organized as follows: in Sect. 2, we introduce key components of our methodology, namely, online and offline behavioral malware analysis techniques, and demonstrate the methodology based on a running example. In Sect. 3, we report on the current status of the implementation our methodology and sketch the future work. In Sect. 4, we describe state of the art related to our work. Section 5 presents the conclusions.

2   Malware Behavioural Analysis

In this section, we present the main components of the workflow (see Fig. 1) which consists of Features Extraction, Modeling, Online Malware Analysis, and Offline Malware Analysis. All the elements of the workflow enable a behavioral analysis of Android malware.

2.1   Extraction of Behavioral Features

As an initial step, we have collected, analyzed, and chosen an open (Kaggle) dataset [1] for the analysis that includes information about permissions, receivers, services, and API calls of various Android applications. Permissions, receivers, and services are related to the functionality of underlying Android phone/system features such as WiFi, Bluetooth, and Internet enabling data sharing between the phone and various applications or networks. The API calls of an application provide insights into its behavior while running on the Android platform. Considering the operational behavior of the different Android services as sketched in Fig. 2, we extracted those features from the data set that characterize dynamic but expected execution behavioral dependencies among various services. For instance, a foreground service Bluetooth service automatically starts a background Download service in an online mode, and the Download service automatically starts a bound Synchronisation service. Consequently, we enlist those features that observe execution behavioral dependencies among various services, which is a subset of the data-set features.

2.2   Modelling of Behavior

Based on the extracted behavioral features, we model their behavioral dependencies as a state transition system as sketched in Fig. 3. Our model includes selected but representative operations and services (i.e., features) of an open Kaggle data-set. The model is based on a behavioral state includes.

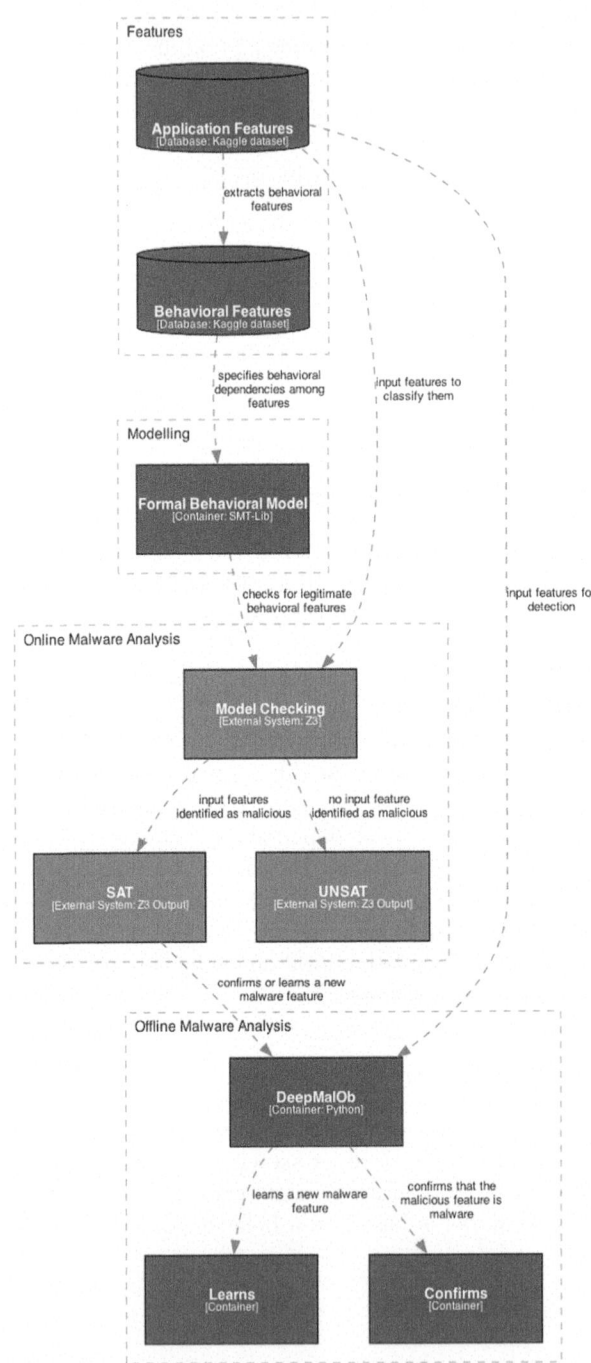

Fig. 1. Workflow of Malware Detection

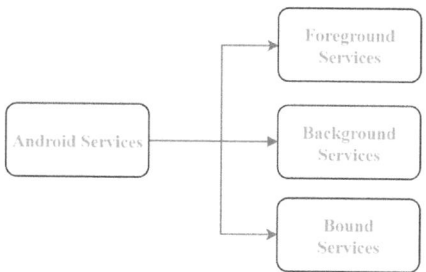

Fig. 2. Types of Android Services

- (B)luetooth service works (e.g., plays audio or video) either offline or online.
- (D)ownload service downloads data by automatically synchronizing connectivity.
- (S)ynchronisation service is required by the Download service.
- (T)ransfer service is enabled when multimedia content download is required by the Bluetooth service.

and their expected behavioral transitions to the following four states (i.e., s_0, s_1, s_2, and s_3)

- $s_0 = \langle \neg B, \neg D, \neg S, \neg T \rangle$ - in the initial and final state all the services are inactive.
- $s_1 = \langle B, \neg D, \neg S, \neg T \rangle$ - when only Bluetooth is active and working offline
- $s_2 = \langle B, D, S, \neg T \rangle$ - when Bluetooth is active and working in online mode.
- $s_3 = \langle B, D, S, T \rangle$ - when Bluetooth is active and working in online mode by transferring multimedia contents.

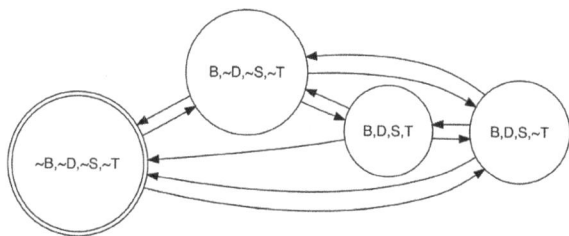

Fig. 3. Behavioural Model of Applications

All the possible expected transitions are sketched in Table 1. For the sake of modelling simplicity, the current model does not allow self-transitions.

Table 1. Possible Behavioral Transitions

Current State	Next State			
	s_0	s_1	s_2	s_3
s_0	✗	✓	✓	✗
s_1	✓	✗	✓	✓
s_2	✓	✓	✗	✓
s_3	✓	✓	✓	✗

Any transition that deviates from the described model would be considered suspicious behavior and could be classified as potentially malicious and consequently a malware. To formalize the model, we encode the model in SMT-Lib[2] format [7] as sketched in Listing 1.1.

The transition model is based on a **trans** function that declares the variables representing the four services for previous and next state (lines 3–12 of the Listing). All the possible transitions are declared as sketched in Table 1 (starting at line 56), e.g., lines 58–61 and 62–65 declare the transitions from s_0 to s_1, and s_0 to s_2, respectively. Later, the actual transitions from the previous state to the next possible state are modelled, e.g., lines 17–28 models the transition from state s_2 to s_3.

Once the dependencies are specified, we move on to defining the behavioral model of the applications (refer to the Fig. 3). This modeling enables us to establish the dependency relationships among the different features comprehensively. Subsequently, we implement our modeling approach by creating an example utilizing the Z3 framework [3]. Through this example, we explicitly outline the dependencies of each feature and the standard transitions of each state, as depicted in example transition system.

---

[2] https://ocamlpro.github.io/verification_for_dummies/trans_smt/index.html.

```
1  (define-fun trans
2      (
3          ; "Previous" state.
4          (|s.bluetooth| Int)
5          (|s.download| Int)
6          (|s.synch| Int)
7          (|s.transfer| Int)
8          ; "Next" state.
9          (|s'.bluetooth| Int)
10         (|s'.download| Int)
11         (|s'.synch| Int)
12         (|s'.transfer| Int)
13     )
14     Bool
15
16     (ite
17         (= |s'.transfer| 1)
18         (and
19             (= |s'.bluetooth| 1)
20             (= |s'.download| 1)
21             (= |s'.synch| 1)
22             (ite
23                 (= |s.download| 1)
24                 (and                        ; transition 2 to 3
25                     (= |s.bluetooth| 1)
26                     (= |s.synch| 1)
27                     (= |s.transfer| 0)
28                 )
29                 (and                        ; transition 1 to 3
30                     (= |s.synch| 0)
31                     (= |s.transfer| 0)
32                     (= |s.bluetooth| 1)
33                 )
34             )
35         )
36         ...
37     )
38 )
39
40 ; "Previous" state 0 as (0,0,0,0).
41 (declare-const bluetooth_0 Int)
42 (declare-const download_0 Int)
43 (declare-const synch_0 Int)
44 (declare-const transfer_0 Int)
45 ; "First Next" state 1 as (1,0,0,0).
46 ...
47 ; "Second Next" state 2 as (1,1,1,0).
48 ...
49 ; "Third Next" state 3 as (1,1,1,1).
50 (declare-const bluetooth_3 Int)
51 (declare-const download_3 Int)
52 (declare-const synch_3 Int)
53 (declare-const transfer_3 Int)
54
55 (assert
56     (and
57         (or
58             (trans
59                 bluetooth_0 download_0 synch_0 transfer_0
60                 bluetooth_1 download_1 synch_1 transfer_1
61             )
62             (trans
63                 bluetooth_0 download_0 synch_0 transfer_0
64                 bluetooth_2 download_2 synch_2 transfer_2
65             )
66         )
67         ...
68     )
69 )
70
```

```
72  (assert
73    (not
74      (and
75        (= bluetooth_0 0)
76        (= download_0 0);
77        (= synch_0 0)
78        (= transfer_0 0)
79        (= bluetooth_3 1)
80        (= download_3 1)
81        (= synch_3 1)
82        (= transfer_3 1)
83      )
84    )
85  )
    (check-sat)
```

Listing 1.1: SMT-Lib Model for Application Behaviour

2.3 Model-Based Online Malware Analysis

The online analysis checks if the observed behavioral pattern of different services through various Android applications is consistent with the expected behavior as described in the model (Fig. 3).

The algorithm requires (i) a sequence of run-time observations O that characterise at least one transition, and (ii) and a set of expected behaviors. The analysis works as follows:

- first it checks if each current and next observation in the sequence represents a valid behavioral state (lines 9 and 10 of the Algorithm 1) and returns the invalid state (lines 21–22 and 17–18), if so.
- if the given previous and next observations are valid behavioral states and returns the two states (line 12), if they do not represent a valid behavioral transition. Alternatively, it continues checking next possible transitions.

To implement the model, we have used model checking of the transition system using Z3, which is an Satisfiability Modulo Theory (SMT) Solver checking satisfiability of formulas in a decidable first-order theory (Fig. 4). Z3 accepts SMT-Lib format model, which implies that our previously developed model is amenable for satisfiability check by Z3. We ask the question to the solver that given the transition model, the given sequence of observed behavioral states are malicious, i.e., they do not satisfy the model. Then the solver answers

- either "SAT" which implies that the two given observed states are indeed malicious
- or "UNSAT" which implies that the two given observed states are not malicious.

To demonstrate our example, we report on checking the following two example properties using online version of Z3[3]:

1. when all the services are currently observed as active (i.e., system is in s_3 state), then in the next state all services are inactive except the Bluetooth

---

[3] https://jfmc.github.io/z3-play/.

Algorithm 1. Algorithm for Online Malware Behaviour Detection

Require: $O : (\langle b_j, d_j, s_j, t_j \rangle)_{j=1}^{n}$ s.t. $|O| \geq 2$

1:      ▷ A sequence of Observed behavioural states of services, i.e., b: Bluetooth, d: download, s: synchronisation, and t: transfer.

Require: $E : \mathbb{S}$ ▷ A set of Expected behavioural states of different services

Ensure: P : $\varnothing$ $\vee$ $(\langle b_j, d_j, s_j, t_j \rangle)$ $\sqsubseteq$ $(\langle b_j, d_j, s_j, t_j \rangle)_{j=1}^{n}$ $\vee$ $(\langle b_{j-1}, d_{j-1}, s_{j-1}, t_{j-1} \rangle, \langle b_j, d_j, s_j, t_j \rangle) \sqsubseteq (\langle b_j, d_j, s_j, t_j \rangle)_{j=1}^{n}$

2:                         ▷ Either empty, when no malware Pattern,

3:          ▷ Or a single state, when either previous or next state is not an expected behavioural state

4:          ▷ Or a sequence of two (previous and next) states, when the two states characterise a malware behavioural transition

5: $P \leftarrow \varnothing$ ▷ There is no malicious pattern, initially

6: $i \leftarrow 0$

7: $l \leftarrow |O|$

8: **while** $i < l - 1$ **do**

9:    **if** $O[i] \in E$ **then**   ▷ If the current state is an expected state

10:      **if** $O[i + 1] \in E$ **then**   ▷ If the next state is an expected state

11:        **if** $\neq$ next$(O[i], O[i + 1])$ **then**

12:          **return** $P \sqcup O[i] \sqcup O[i + 1]$

13: ▷ Return the sequence of two (previous and next) states when the transition from the previous state to the next state is unexpected

14:        **end if**

15:      **else**

16:        **return** $P \sqcup O[i + 1]$ ▷ Return the next state, if the next state is not an expected state

17:      **end if**

18:    **else**

19:      **return** $P \sqcup O[i]$ ▷ Return the current state, if the current state is not an expected state

20:    **end if**

21:    $i \leftarrow i + 1$

22: **end while**

23: **return** $\varnothing$ ▷ No malicious pattern found

and Synchronisation services. The next state is an invalid state as can be seen in Fig. 3 and indicates a malicious behavior because Synchronisation service is bound service and is only active when Download service is active as sketched in Fig. 2. The results for the verification of this property are depicted in Fig. 4a.

2. when all the services are currently observed inactive (i.e., system is in s_0 state), then in the next state all services are active (i.e., system is in s_3 state). This is again a a malicious behavior because this is not a valid behavioral transition as sketched in Table 1. The results for the verification of this property is depicted in Fig. 4b.

```
204    (assert
205        (not
206            (and
207                    (= bluetooth_3 1)
208                    (= download_3 1)
209                    (= synch_3 1)
210                    (= transfer_3 1)
211                    (= bluetooth_0 0)
212                    (= download_0 0)
213                    (= synch_0 0)
214                    (= transfer_0 0)
215            )
216        )
217    )
218    (check-sat)
```

▶ Run

sat

(a) Output of Malicious Synchronisation Service

```
189    (assert
190        (not
191            (and
192                    (= bluetooth_0 0)
193                    (= download_0 0);
194                    (= synch_0 0)
195                    (= transfer_0 0)
196                    (= bluetooth_3 1)
197                    (= download_3 1);
198                    (= synch_3 1)
199                    (= transfer_3 1)
200            )
201        )
202    )
203    (check-sat)
```

▶ Run

sat

(b) Output of Malicious Services Initialization

Fig. 4. Verification of Online Malware Analysis

Once we have identified the given sequence of behavioral observations as malicious malware, then we perform offline malware analysis as discussed in the next sub-section.

2.4   AI-Based Offline Malware Analysis

Based on the identification of malware behavioral patterns by online analysis, in this stage, we perform AI-based offline malware analysis that either confirms that the identified pattern is a known malware or learns a new behavioral pattern of malware. Online analysis only knows the valid behavioral states but in practice there are a lot of unknown but invalid behavioral states. Therefore, to make the malware analysis more efficient, the offline analysis aims to produce a list of every new malware pattern so that any given behavioral states can be directly filtered against the list before actually performing the online analysis, which otherwise will require a lot of resources and time to decide the same.

To facilitate offline malware analysis, we use DeepMalOb [22], which is a malware detection technique that addresses the detection of obfuscated malware without relying on specific obfuscation techniques. DeepMalOb uses deep learning algorithms, in particular the multilayer perceptron (MLP), which is a supervised deep learning algorithm. The dataset used to train the model was obtained by memory analysis of obfuscated malware. This allows all obfuscation techniques to be taken into account. It is a dataset that is as close as possible to a real situation because it uses malware that is widespread in the real world. DeepMalOb has achieved an accuracy performance of 99%, outperforming several works in the literature.

3   Current Status and Future Work

Currently all the different modules of the workflow (see Fig. 1 are developed independently. As a next step, we want to automate the entire workflow through

- *intra-module integration* that aims at automating the internal processing of each module. Specifically, we want to automatically generate the scalable Z3 model based on large features of the dataset in a sound way considering more complex behavioral properties, e.g., permissions that require access not only to other applications and services but to underlying hardware, e.g., memory and other peripheral interfaces.
- *inter-module integration* that aims at automating interfacing of different modules by making input/output of the modules interoperable. Specifically, we want to extend AI-based offline analysis to learn new malware patterns as identified by the model-based online analysis.

Beside the integration, we aim to assess the performance of the model on diverse datasets and real-world scenarios. This involves comparing the malware detection results obtained by our model with those achieved by other existing approaches. Through this evaluation, we aim to identify any challenges or limitations encountered during the analysis process.

4   Related Work

In this section we present related work to our behavior-based online and offline malware analysis, respectively.

More recently, AI/ML based malware detection approaches have used machine learning and deep learning algorithms to analyze Android applications, using their permissions and code structure, etc. [28]. The researchers used the learning algorithms to develop efficient models, exploiting features such as API calls, permissions, opcode, and intents. [5, 20]. A certain research focus has turned to the detection of obfuscated malware by integrating code analysis, memory dumping and machine learning techniques. By combining these methodologies, they aim to improve the efficiency of malware detection and overcome the challenges posed by obfuscation [24,25,29]. However, it is important to recognize that biases can have an impact on the reliability and robustness of models. Also, the dynamic nature of malware and the constant evolution of attack techniques are obstacles to the development of highly accurate and robust models. In addition, the presence of obfuscation and evasion techniques employed by malware developers can hamper the detection process [22].

Some other approaches have employed heuristics [18] and formal modeling techniques, to model the malicious behavior of applications. Heuristics-based approaches rely on expert knowledge and predefined rules to identify suspicious behaviors and patterns in applications. Formal modeling techniques involve mathematical or logical models to define precise specifications and analyze application behavior against these models [12]. Formal modeling of malware allows researchers to precisely define the semantics of malicious code, identify potential vulnerabilities, and analyze the impact of malware on a system [13,27]. Cimitile [10] et al., presented a method relying on formal methods to detect obfuscation in mobile applications. However, their model was developed using a limited dataset comprising trusted software and Android ransomware. Furthermore, their methodology involves model checking, which entails the translation of Java Bytecode into formal models. It should be noted that this approach may encounter challenges and potential errors when dealing with obfuscated Java Bytecode. LEILA, as presented by Canfora et al. [8], is an Android malware detection tool that utilizes model checking to analyze and validate Java bytecode derived from source code compilation. Model checking involves examining all possible system states to ensure compliance with a predefined specification. In the case of LEILA, the analyzed system is the bytecode generated by Android malware, while the specification consists of predefined rules representing the behavior of known malware families. However, it is worth noting that LEILA does not take into account potential relationships between malware from different families. Additionally, the bytecode-centric approach employed by LEILA does not consider the dynamic behavior of malware. F. Mercaldo et al. [8], presented a set of heuristics aimed at deducing the malicious nature of mobile applications by detecting whether they belong to a specific malware family. To do this, they rely on formal equivalence checks. However, it is important to note that this approach relies on signature-based detection, which means that it may not be able to identify obfuscated malware that uses techniques such as code encryption and renaming to evade detection. It is therefore possible for obfuscated malware to go undetected using this approach. Authors of these works have proposed formal methods to deepen the structure, dependencies and potential malicious attributes of malware. The formal analysis of malicious behavior is emerging as a prominent area of research in the field of Android malware detection. While formal analysis holds great potential, it is essential to acknowledge the challenges associated with its application in the realm of Android malware detection. The scalability and complexity of formal methods in handling large-scale or real-world malware scenarios remain areas of ongoing research and development.

Indeed, it is crucial to acknowledge that biases can significantly influence the reliability and robustness of models in malware detection. Biases can arise from various sources, such as imbalanced training data, biased labeling, or inherent biases in the algorithms themselves [15,23]. These biases can lead to false positives or false negatives, impacting the accuracy of the models. Moreover, the dynamic nature of malware and the continuous evolution of attack techniques pose ongoing challenges in developing highly accurate and resilient detection models [9]. Malware authors constantly adapt their strategies and employ sophisticated obfuscation and evasion techniques to evade detection. This necessitates the continuous monitoring and updating of detection models to keep pace with emerging threats. Obfuscation techniques employed by malware developers further complicate the detection process. By deliberately obscuring the code structure or employing encryption, obfuscation techniques aim to make it harder for detection models to identify and analyze malicious behavior. As a result, detecting obfuscated malware becomes more challenging and requires innovative approaches and advanced analysis techniques to overcome these obstacles. As indicated in the Table 2, the existing work in this field has certain limitations, specifically regarding the employed techniques and the approach to detecting malicious applications. Statistical techniques are unable to identify obfuscated malicious behavior effectively. Moreover, detection based on identification alone, which is commonly used, fails to detect newly obfuscated malicious behavior. In contrast, our proposed approach offers the advantage of combining multiple techniques to address the limitations found in existing literature.

Table 2. State-of-the-art Comparison

Technique	Methodology	Analysis	Required Resources	Detecting Obfuscation
AI/ML-based	DANdroid [19]	Static	Opcodes Permissions API calls	Discriminative adversarial learning
	DroidSieve [26]	Static	Syntactic features	Obfuscation family identification
	Obfuscapk [6]	Static	App code	Program analysis
	DeepMalOb [22]	Dynamic	Memory Feature	Run-time behaviour of application
Model-based	LEILA [8]	Model checking	Java Bytecode	Identifying Mobile malicious behaviour
	Mercaldo et al. [18]	Static	Java byte-code	Heuristics equivalence checking
	Iadarola et al. [13]	Static	Java Bytecode	model checking
	This work	Dynamic SMT	Memory Features App events	Dynamic features Run-time behaviour of application-controlled services

5   Conclusion

We have presented a methodology that combines model-based online malware analysis with AI-based offline malware analysis techniques to detect malware developed through obfuscation. We have demonstrated the initial results of the implementation of various modules of the workflow. Currently, we are automating the entire workflow by integrating all of the modules in a sound way.

Acknowledgment. The Partnership for Skills in Applied Sciences, Engineering, and Technology - Regional Scholarship and Innovation Fund (PASET-RSIF) provided support for this work.

References

1. Android Malware Detection|Kaggle. https://www.kaggle.com/datasets/defensedroid/android-malware-detection?select=Services+Dataset.csv
2. Kaspersky Security Bulletin 2022. Statistics | Securelist. https://securelist.com/ksb-2022-statistics/108129/
3. Z3 Theorem Prover. https://github.com/Z3Prover
4. Ahvanooey, M.T., Li, P.Q., Rabbani, M., Rajput, A.R.: A survey on smartphones security: software vulnerabilities. Malware Attacks 8(10), 30–45 (2017)
5. Alazab, M., Alazab, M., Shalaginov, A., Mesleh, A.: Intelligent mobile malware detection using permission requests and API calls. Futur. Gener. Comput. Syst. **107**, 509–521 (2020). https://doi.org/10.1016/j.future.2020.02.002
6. Aonzo, S., Georgiu, G.C., Verderame, L., Merlo, A.: Obfuscapk: an open-source black-box obfuscation tool for Android apps. SoftwareX **11**, 100403 (2020). https://doi.org/10.1016/j.softx.2020.100403
7. Barrett, C., Stump, A., Tinelli, C., et al.: The smt-lib standard: version 2.0. In: Proceedings of the 8th International Workshop on Satisfiability Modulo Theories (Edinburgh, UK), vol. 13, p. 14 (2010)
8. Canfora, G., Martinelli, F., Mercaldo, F., Nardone, V., Santone, A., Visaggio, C.A.: LEILA: Formal Tool for Identifying Mobile Malicious Behaviour; LEILA: Formal Tool for Identifying Mobile Malicious Behaviour (2019). https://doi.org/10.1109/TSE.2018.2834344
9. Carrier, T., Victor, P., Tekeoglu, A., Lashkari, A.H.: Detecting Obfuscated Malware using Memory Feature Engineering. https://doi.org/10.5220/0010908200003120
10. Cimitile, A., Martinelli, F., Mercaldo, F., Nardone, V., Santone, A.: Formal methods meet mobile code obfuscation identification of code reordering technique. In: 2017 IEEE 26th International Conference on Enabling Technologies: Infrastructure for Collaborative Enterprises (WETICE), pp. 263–268 (2017). https://doi.org/10.1109/WETICE.2017.23
11. Dunaev, D., Lengyel, L.: Complexity of a special deobfuscation problem
12. Ezekiel, O.O., Oluwasola, O.A., Martins, I.: An Evaluation of some Machine Learning Algorithms for the detection of Android Applications Malware (January 2021) (2020). https://doi.org/10.25046/aj0506208
13. Iadarola, G., Martinelli, F., Mercaldo, F., Santone, A.: Formal methods for android banking malware analysis and detection. In: 2019 6th International Conference on Internet of Things: Systems, Management and Security, IOTSMS 2019, pp. 331–336, October 2019. https://doi.org/10.1109/IOTSMS48152.2019.8939172
14. Inc, G.: Kotlin and Android | Android. https://developer.android.com/kotlin
15. Khan, M.T., Serpanos, D., Shrobe, H., Yousuf, M.M.: Rigorous machine learning for secure and autonomous cyber physical systems. In: 2020 25th IEEE International Conference on Emerging Technologies and Factory Automation (ETFA), vol. 1, pp. 1815–1819 (2020). https://doi.org/10.1109/ETFA46521.2020.9212074
16. Khan, M.T., Shrobe, H.: Security of cyberphysical systems: chaining induction and deduction. Computer **52**(7), 72–75 (2019). https://doi.org/10.1109/MC.2019.2913138
17. Liu, K., Xu, S., Xu, G., Sun, D., Liu, H.: A review of android malware detection approaches based on machine learning, pp. 124579–124607 (2020)
18. Mercaldo, F., Santone, A.: Formal equivalence checking for mobile malware detection and family classification. IEEE Trans. Softw. Eng. **48**(7), 2643–2657 (2022). https://doi.org/10.1109/TSE.2021.3067061

19. Millar, S., McLaughlin, N., Del Rincon, J.M., Miller, P., Zhao, Z.: DANdroid: a multi-view discriminative adversarial network for obfuscated android malware detection. In: CODASPY 2020 - Proceedings of the 10th ACM Conference on Data and Application Security and Privacy, pp. 353–364, March 2020. https://doi. org/10.1145/3374664.3375746
20. Razgallah, A., Khoury, R., Hallé, S., Khanmohammadi, K.: A survey of malware detection in Android apps: recommendations and perspectives for future research. Comput. Sci. Rev. **39**, 100358 (2021). https://doi.org/10.1016/j.cosrev. 2020.100358
21. Salah, Y., Hamed, I., Nabil, S., Abdulkader, A., Mostafa, M.s.M.: Mobile malware detection: a survey **17**(1) (2019)
22. Sawadogo, Z., Dembele, J.M., Tahar, A., Mendy, G., Ouya, S.: DeepMalOb: deep detection of obfuscated android malware. In: Ngatched Nkouatchah, T.M., Woungang, I., Tapamo, J.R., Viriri, S. (eds.) Pan-African Artificial Intelligence and Smart Systems, pp. 307–318. Springer, Cham (2023). https://doi.org/10.1007/978-3-031-25271-6_19
23. Sawadogo, Z., Mendy, G., Dembele, J.M., Ouya, S.: Android malware detection: Investigating the impact of imbalanced data-sets on the performance of machine learning models. In: 2022 24th International Conference on Advanced Communication Technology (ICACT), pp. 435–441 (2022). https://doi.org/10. 23919/ICACT53585.2022.9728833
24. Sawadogo, Z., Mendy, G., Dembelle, J.M., Ouya, S.: Android malware classification: updating features through incremental learning approach (UFILA). In: International Conference on Advanced Communication Technology, ICACT 2022-February, pp. 544–550 (2022). https://doi.org/10.23919/ICACT53585.2022. 9728977
25. Sharma, T., Rattan, D.: Malicious application detection in android - a systematic literature review. Comput. Sci. Rev. **40**, 100373 (2021). https://doi.org/10.1016/ J.COSREV.2021.100373
26. Suarez-tangil, G., Dash, S.K., Ahmadi, M., Kinder, J., Giacinto, G., Cavallaro, L.: DroidSieve: Fast and Accurate Classification of Obfuscated Android Malware, pp. 309–320 (2017)
27. Taimoor Khan, M.: Towards practical and formal security risk analysis of iot (internet of things) applications. In: IEEE International Conference on Emerging Technologies and Factory Automation, ETFA, September 2022. https://doi. org/10.1109/ETFA52439.2022.9921511
28. Wang, Z., Liu, Q., Chi, Y.: Review of android malware detection based on deep learning **8** (2020). https://doi.org/10.1109/ACCESS.2020.3028370
29. Xu, Y., Wang, G., Ren, J., Zhang, Y.: An adaptive and configurable protection framework against android privilege escalation threats. Futur. Gener. Comput. Syst. **92**, 210–224 (2019). https://doi.org/10.1016/j.future.2018.09.042
30. Zhang, X., Breitinger, F., Luechinger, E., O'Shaughnessy, S.: Android application forensics: a survey of obfuscation, obfuscation detection and deobfuscation techniques and their impact on investigations. Forensic Sci. Int. Digital Investigation **39**, 301285 (2021). https://doi.org/10.1016/j.fsidi.2021.301285

QUALIFIER

Towards a Prediction of Machine Learning Training Time to Support Continuous Learning Systems Development

Francesca Marzi[ID], Giordano d'Aloisio[✉][ID], Antinisca Di Marco[ID], and Giovanni Stilo[ID]

University of L'Aquila, L'Aquila, Italy
{francesca.marzi,antinisca.dimarco,giovanni.stilo}@univaq.it,
giordano.daloisio@graduate.univaq.it

Abstract. The problem of predicting the training time of machine learning (ML) models has become extremely relevant in the scientific community. Being able to predict *a priori* the training time of an ML model would enable the automatic selection of the best model both in terms of energy efficiency and in terms of performance in the context of, for instance, MLOps architectures or learning-enabled architectures. In this paper, we present the work we are conducting towards this direction. In particular, we present an extensive empirical study of the Full Parameter Time Complexity (FPTC) approach by Zheng *et al.*, which is, to the best of our knowledge, the only approach formalizing the training time of ML models as a function of both dataset's and model's parameters. We study the formulations proposed for the Logistic Regression and Random Forest classifiers, and we highlight the main strengths and weaknesses of the approach. Finally, we observe how, from the conducted study, the prediction of training time is strictly related to the context (i.e., the involved dataset) and how the FPTC approach is not generalizable.

Keywords: Machine Learning · Training Time · Formal Analysis · Learning-enabled Architectures

1 Introduction

The problem of energy efficiency and sustainability of machine learning (ML) systems is becoming increasingly important within the scientific community [7, 8,

This work is partially supported by "ICSC - Centro Nazionale di Ricerca in High Performance Computing, Big Data and Quantum Computing", funded by European Union - NextGenerationEU, by "Data-quality-driven estimation of computational complexity of Machine Learning systems" project, funded by University of L'Aquila, 2023, and by European Union - NextGenerationEU - National Recovery and Resilience Plan (Piano Nazionale di Ripresa e Resilienza, PNRR) - Project: "SoBigData.it - Strengthening the Italian RI for Social Mining and Big Data Analytics" - Prot. IR0000013 - Avviso n. 3264 del 28/12/2021.

B. Tekinerdoğan et al. (Eds.): ECSA 2023, LNCS 14590, pp. 169–184, 2024.
https://doi.org/10.1007/978-3-031-66326-0_11

24], as also highlighted by the ONU's Sustainable Development Goals (e.g., Goal 9 or Goal 12) [18]. Generally, the energy consumption of ML models is directly related to the *training phase time complexity*. This means that the longer it takes to train a model, the more energy is required by the system. For this reason, predicting *a priori* the training time of an ML model will be a significant advance in such direction, enabling the automatic selection of the efficient ML model. The training time prediction of ML models also becomes highly relevant in the context of MLOps and, in general, *continuous learning* or *learning-enabled* systems, where the ML model is constantly re-trained with new data [3]. As highlighted in [17], engineering such kind of system is always very challenging since the development processes are often ad-hoc and specific to the use case. For this reason, having an *a priori* estimation of the training time can help in standardizing some phases of the development process in contexts where, for instance, the computational power for training the model is very limited (e.g.,, IoT devices [26]). In addition, selecting the most efficient ML model can help stakeholders satisfy other relevant quality properties of software architectures, like *performance* [13].

In this paper, we present the work we are conducting towards a prediction of ML training time. In particular, we present an extensive empirical evaluation of the Full Parameter Time Complexity (FPTC) approach proposed by Zheng *et al.* in [25], which is, to the best of our knowledge, the only approach so far that formulates the ML training time as a function of dataset's and ML model's parameters. Specifically, differently from what has been done in [25], where the authors use only one dataset, we use the FPTC approach to predict the training time of a Logistic Regression [15] and Random Forest [21] classifier on a heterogeneous set of data, and we compare the predicted time with the actual training time of the method, highlighting the main strengths and weaknesses of the approach[1].

The paper is structured as follows: in Sect. 2 we discuss some related works in the context of training time prediction; Sect. 3 describes in detail the FPTC approach; Sect. 4 presents the conducted experiment and the research questions we want to answer; Sect. 5 shows the experiment's results and discuss them w.r.t. the research questions; finally Sect. 6 presents some future works and concludes the paper.

2   Related Work

Nowadays, the estimation of the running time of the training phase of ML models is primarily conducted through empirical analysis relying on a set of common characteristics.

In [12], the authors performed empirical analyses to assess the impact of different dataset characteristics, such as sample size, class type, missing values and dimensionality, on the performance of classification algorithms, considering both

---

[1] The replication package of the experiments is available here: https://bit.ly/3G4m5rF.

accuracy and elapsed time. In [2], a rule-based learning algorithm was derived through an empirical evaluation of the performance of eight classifiers on 100 classification datasets, comparing them based on various accuracy and computational time measures. The empirical results were combined with the dataset characteristic measures to formulate rules to determine which algorithms were best suited for solving specific classification problems. Finally, in [16], a model was developed to predict the running time of ML pipelines through empirical analysis of different ML algorithms with a heterogeneous set of data. The approach was used to predict the timeout of an ML pipeline.

Considering non-empirical analyses, to the best of our knowledge, [25] is the first attempt to provide an a priori estimation of the training time for various ML models without actually running the code. In this work, the authors propose a method to quantitatively evaluate the time efficiency of an ML classifier called Full Parameter Time Complexity (FPTC). The authors derive FPTC for five classification models, namely Logistic Regression, Support Vector Machine, Random Forest, K-Nearest Neighbors, and Classification and Regression Trees. FPTC depends on several variables, including the number of attributes, the size of the training set, and intrinsic characteristics of the algorithms, such as the number of iterations in Logistic Regression or the number of Decision Trees in a Random Forest. A coefficient ω was introduced to establish the relationship between the running time and FPTC. The coefficient ω can be obtained through a preliminary experiment on a small sampled dataset under different execution environments. When the physical execution environment changes, the coefficient ω should be reevaluated to reflect the new conditions.

Based on this state-of-the-art analysis, we observe that most of the studies concerning the training time of ML models tend to rely on empirical approaches. The only approach formalizing the training time as a function of datasets' and ML models' parameters is [25]. In this paper, we aim to highlight the strengths and weaknesses of this approach by conducting an extensive evaluation of the method.

3 Background Knowledge

In this section, we describe in detail the FPTC method [25] where the training time of several ML models is defined as a function of different parameters of the dataset, of the model itself, and of a coefficient (ω) that reflects the influence given by the execution environment on the actual training time of the model. This value should vary only when an ML model runs on a different execution environment. We detail better in Sect. 4 how ω has been computed in our experiment. In this work, we focus on the formulation of the training time for two particular ML models, i.e., Logistic Regression (*LogReg*) [15] and Random Forest (*RF*) [21], while we leave the analysis of other methods to future works.

The FPTC for the Logistic Regression classifier is defined as:

$$FPTC_{LogReg} = F(Qm^2vn) * \omega_{LogReg} \tag{1}$$

where n is the number of rows of the dataset, v is the number of dataset's features, m is the number of classes of the dataset, Q is the number of model's iterations during the training phase, and ω_{LogReg} is the slope of a regression function computed comparing the results of the first part of the Eq. 1 with the actual training time of a Logistic Regression model using a subset of the training datasets.

The FPTC for the Random Forest classifier is defined instead as:

$$FPTC_{RF} = F(s(m+1)nv \log_2(n)) * \omega_{RF} \tag{2}$$

where n, m, and v are the same variables as above, while s is the number of trees of the random forest. ω_{RF} is again defined as the slope of a regression function computed comparing the results of the first part of the Eq. 2 with the actual training time of a Random Forest classifier on a set of synthetic datasets.

Concerning ω, the authors state that this variable reflects the influence given by the execution environment on the actual training time of the model. Hence, this value should vary only when an ML model runs on a different environment. We detail better in Sect. 4 how ω has been computed in our experiment.

4 Experimental Setting

This section describes the experiments we conducted to evaluate the FPTC method. In particular, with our experiments, we aim to answer the following two research questions:

RQ1. Is the slope (ω) parameter of FPTC only dependent on the execution environment?
RQ2. Is the FPTC able to predict the training time of an ML model?

In Sect. 4.1, we describe the experimental setting conducted to compute the slope parameter. While in Sect. 4.2, we describe the experiment led to predict the training time of the Logistic Regression and Random Forest models. All the experiments have been executed on a DELL XPS 13 2019 with a processor Intel Core i7, 16 GB of RAM and Ubuntu 22.04.2 LTS.

4.1 Slope Computation

To answer RQ1, we must assess if the slope computation only depends on the execution environment. That is, given the same environment and the same ML model, the slope should not change significantly if the dataset used to compute the slope changes. To answer this question, we performed an experiment that computes a set of slopes using a synthetic dataset D_s with 6,167 rows and 10,000 features. In particular, we calculate a set of slopes corresponding to 19 subsets of D_s, each one with a different subset of features. Next, we compared the different slopes obtained. It is worth noticing that, in [25], the authors compute the slope on the same dataset on which they want to predict the training time.

In this experiment, we use a synthetic dataset different from the ones on which we predict the training time. We have chosen a synthetic dataset instead of a real one to have better control over its number of features and instances. In addition, a synthetic dataset can be easily released and used for computing the slopes in further experiments.

Algorithm 1: Slope computation

Input: (Synthetic dataset D_s, ML Model M, Number of starting features
$\quad\quad f = 501$, Number of features to add $a = 501$, Number of starting rows
$\quad\quad s = 100$, Number of rows to add $p = 1,000$)
Output: (List of slopes at increasing number of features)
n = number of rows of D_s // in our case 6.167
m' = number of features of D_s // in our case 10.000
$slopes = \{\}$
for $i \in 20$ **do**
$\quad$ D'_s = subset of D_s with f features
$\quad$ **while** *features of $D'_s < m'$* **do**
$\quad\quad$ $tt = []$
$\quad\quad$ $fptcs = []$
$\quad\quad$ m = features of D'_s
$\quad\quad$ /* split D' into sub-datasets and get training times and fptc
$\quad\quad$ */
$\quad\quad$ **for** *($r = s; r < n; r+ = p$)* **do**
$\quad\quad\quad$ D''_s = dataset of r rows from D'_s
$\quad\quad\quad$ train M on D''_s
$\quad\quad\quad$ t = training time of M
$\quad\quad\quad$ $fptc = getFPTC(D''_s, M)$
$\quad\quad\quad$ add t to tt
$\quad\quad\quad$ add $fptc$ to $fptcs$
$\quad\quad$ $reg = LinearRegression()$
$\quad\quad$ train reg on tt and $fptcs$
$\quad\quad$ ω = slope of reg
$\quad\quad$ append ω to $slopes[m]$
$\quad\quad$ $D'_s = D'_s + a$ other features from D_s
for $m \in slopes$ *keys* **do**
$\quad$ $slopes[m]$ = median of $slopes[m]$
return $slopes$

Algorithm 1 shows the procedure we followed to compute the slopes. The algorithm takes as input a synthetic dataset D_s, an ML model M (in our case, M is either a Logistic Regression or a Random Forest classifier), and a set of parameters useful for the analysis: f, i.e., the number of starting features of the synthetic dataset D_s; a, i.e., the number of features to add at each iteration; s, i.e., the number of rows of the first sub-dataset used to compute the slope; and p, i.e., the number of rows to add to each other sub-dataset. In our case,

$f = 501$, $a = 501$, $s = 100$, and $p = 1.000$. The algorithm returns a list of slopes, each one corresponding to a subset D'_s of D_s with a number of features lower or equal to the ones in D_s. At the first iteration, D'_s has 501 features. Next, D'_s is split into a set of sub-datasets D''_s with an increasing number of rows ranging from 100 to the total number of rows. Each sub-dataset has a delta of 1000 rows. These sub-datasets are used to compute the training time of the model M and the relative $FPTC$ prediction using Eqs. 1 and 2 for Logistic Regression and Random Forest, respectively. After computing the training times and the $FPTC$ predictions for each sub-dataset D''_s, the training times and the $FPTC$ predictions are used to train a *Linear Regression* model and to get its slope ω. The obtained slope is added to a dictionary of slopes with the key equal to the number of features of D'_s. Finally, the number of features of D'_s is increased by 500. This procedure continues until the number of features of D'_s equals the number of features of D_s. This whole process is repeated 20 times, and the median slope of each subset D'_s is finally returned.

4.2   Training Time Prediction

To answer the RQ2, we conducted a set of experiments to predict, using the FPTC method, the training time of a Logistic Regression and a Random Forest classifier using 7 heterogeneous datasets. Then we compared the predicted training time with the actual training time of the method. Algorithm 2 reports the experiment's pseudo-code. The algorithm takes as input a dataset D, the ML model M, and the list of slopes S computed with the procedure described in Algorithm 1, and returns a list of Root Mean Squared Errors $RMSE$ [5] and Mean Absolute Percentage Errors $MAPE$ [6], one for each slope. The experiment can be divided into two steps. In the first step, the algorithm computes 100 times the training time of the ML model M on D and then calculates the mean of the times. In the second step, for each slope, ω, the algorithm computes the $FPTC$ and the RMSE and MAPE between the actual training time and the $FPTC$. Finally, the list of errors is returned.

In the evaluation, we have employed 7 heterogeneous datasets which differ in terms of dimensions to evaluate if the FPTC method works better under datasets[2]. The involved datasets are reported below:

- **Adult Income (Adult)** [11]: this binary dataset comprises 30,940 instances by 101 features. The goal is to predict if a person has an income higher than 50k a year;
- **Malicious Executable Files (Antivirus)** [22]: this binary dataset comprises 373 instances and 531 features to predict if an executable file is malicious or not;

---

[2] Before running Algorithm 2, following the guidelines reported in [19], all the data has been scaled by removing the mean (μ) and by dividing the variance (σ) from each feature.

Algorithm 2: Training time prediction

Input: (Dataset D, ML Model M, List of slopes S)
Output: (List of Root Mean Squared Errors $RMSE$, List of Mean Absolute
         Percentage Error $MAPE$)
$trainingTimes = []$
for $i \in 100$ **do**
   | train M on D
   | $t = $ training time of M
   |___ add t to $trainingTimes$
$tt = mean(trainingTimes)$
$RMSE = []$
$MAPE = []$
for $\omega \in S$ **do**
   | $FPTC = getFPTC(D, M, \omega)$
   | $rmse = getRMSE(tt, FPTC)$
   | $mape = getMAPE(tt, FPTC)$
   | add $rmse$ to $RMSE$
   |___ add $mape$ to $MAPE$
return $RMSE, MAPE$

- **APS Failure at Scania Trucks (APS)** [1]: a dataset of 6000 instances and 162 features to predict if the failure of a Scania Truck is related to a failure in the APS system or not;
- **Arcene Dataset (Arcene)** [9]: this binary dataset comprises 100 instances and 10,000 features to distinguish cancer versus normal patterns from mass-spectrometric data;
- **ProPublica Recidivism (Compas)** [4]: this binary dataset is made of 6,167 instances by 399 features. The goal is to predict if a person will recidivate in the next two years;
- **Dexter Dataset (Dexter)** [10]: a dataset of 300 instances and 20,000 features to predict which Reuters articles are about *corporate acquisitions*;
- **German Credit (German)** [20]: this dataset consists of 1,000 instances and 59 features and is used to predict if a person has good or bad credit risk.

Concerning the ML classifiers, we used the implementations from the *scikit-learn* library [19] and, following the hyper-parameters settings of [25], we set the *l2* penalty and *sag* solver for the Logistic Regression, while we set the number of trees of the Random Forest classifier to 80. Finally, we set the maximum number of iterations of the Logistic Regression to 10.000.

Table 1 synthesizes, for each dataset, the values of the different parameters of the two FPTC formulations for Logistic Regression and Random Forest classifiers. In particular, together with the dimensions of the datasets, we also report the number of iterations required by the Logistic Regression to train and the number of trees of the Random Forest.

Table 1. Values of FPTC parameters for each dataset

Dataset	Dataset Coefficients			ML Methods Coefficients	
	Instances	Features	Classes	LogReg Iters	RF Trees
Adult [11]	30940	101	2	635	100
Antivirus [22]	373	531	2	840	100
APS [1]	60000	162	2	5068.73	100
Arcene [9]	100	10000	2	1089	100
Compas [4]	6167	400	2	721	100
Dexter [10]	300	20000	2	855.91	100
German [20]	1000	59	2	33.93	100

5   Experimental Results and Discussion

In this section, we present the results of our experimental evaluation and discuss them with respect to the research questions defined in Sect. 4. Finally, we present some threats to the validity of our evaluation.

5.1   Addressing RQ1

Figure 1 reports the boxplot of the variation of the slopes computed with an increasing number of features of the synthetic dataset. In particular, Fig. 1a reports the slopes computed for the Logistic Regression classifier, while Fig. 1b reports the slopes computed for the Random Forest classifier.

Concerning the Logistic Regression model, it can be seen (in Fig. 1a) how the slopes have generally low variability. An exception is given by the slopes computed with 501 and 1002 features which are, on average, higher than the others. In particular, the median of the slopes computed using 501 features is around 0.02 points higher than the others, while the median of the slopes calculated using 1002 features is about 0.04 points higher than the others. In all the other cases, the median slope ranges from $1.83 * 10^{-9}$ to $1.85 * 10^{-9}$.

Concerning the Random Forest classifier, it can be seen from Fig. 1b how the slopes present a higher variability among them, starting from a value around $8.5 * 10^{-10}$ using 501 features to a value of $2 * 10-10$ using 9519 features. In particular, it can be noticed from the figure that the value for the slope tends to decrease with an increase in the number of the dataset's features.

Moreover, we study the significance of the results of the slopes by performing the ANOVA test [14] for both experiments. This test checks for the null hypothesis that all groups (i.e., all the slopes computed using the same number of features) have the same mean; if the confidence value (p-value) is > 0.05, the null hypothesis is confirmed. Concerning the Logistic Regression classifier, the test returned a p-value of 0.002, meaning the groups do not have the same mean. However, performing the same ANOVA test excluding the slopes computed with

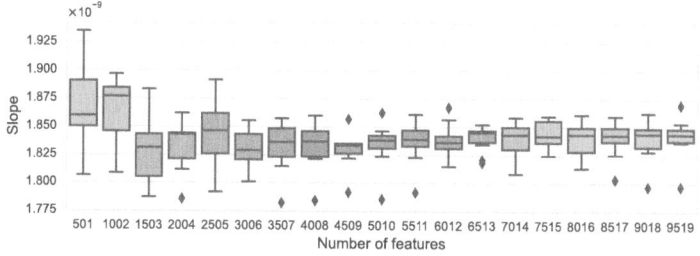

(a) Logistic Regression

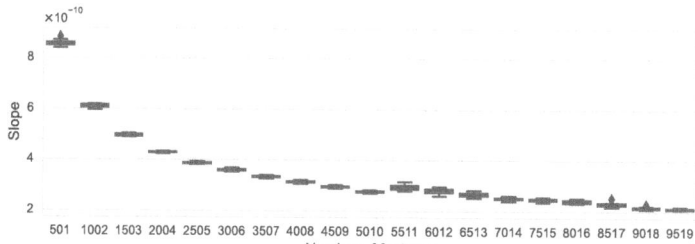

(b) Random Forest

Fig. 1. Slope variation with an increasing number of dataset's features

501 and 1,002 features returns a *p-value* of 0.352, accepting the null hypothesis of the same mean. This means that, excluding the slopes computed with 501 and 1.002 features, all the others have the overall same mean. Concerning the Random Forest classifier, the *p-value* returned is $9.022 * 10^{-222}$, confirming the high variability of the slopes.

From this analysis of the slope variations, we can conclude how, differently from what is stated in [25], the slopes do not change only when the execution environment changes, but they are also related to the number of features of the dataset used to compute them, in particular when using a Random Forest classifier.

Answer to RQ1: The slopes computed under the same execution environment but using an increasing number of features are pretty stable for the Logistic Regression classifier. Instead, they present a higher variance for the Random Forest classifier. Hence, we can conclude how the slope is also related to the number of features of the dataset used to compute them.

5.2 Addressing RQ2

Figures 2 and 3 report the errors in the predictions of the FPTC method compared to the actual training time of the Logistic Regression and Random Forest

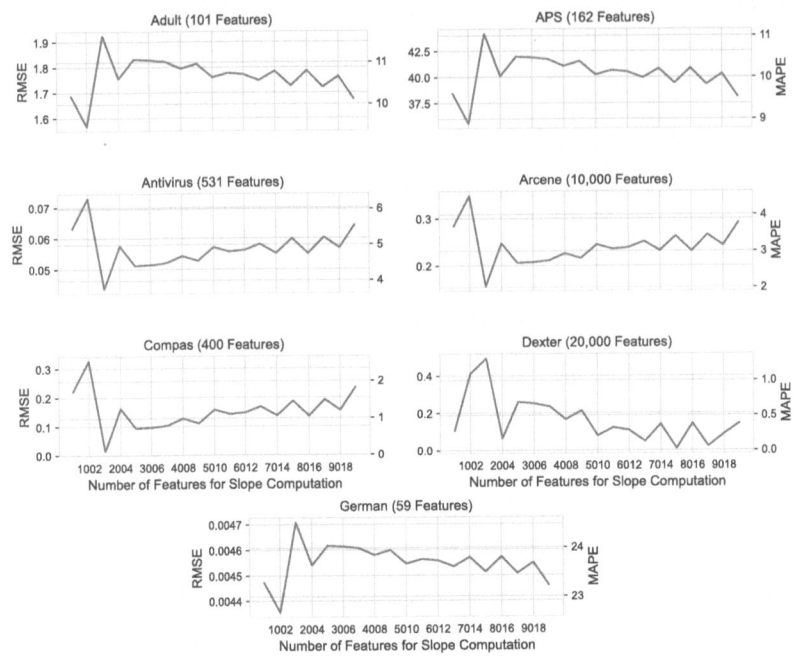

Fig. 2. RMSE and MAPE at different slope values for LogReg

Classifier, respectively, for all the datasets described in Sect. 4. In particular, in each figure, the left y-axis reports the RMSE, while the right y-axis reports the MAPE. On the x-axis, we report the number of features of the synthetic dataset used to compute the relative slope. Near each dataset name, we also report its number of features.

Concerning the Logistic Regression classifier, it can be seen from Fig. 2 how the FPTC method can predict the training time of the model under some datasets while it fails in the prediction of others. In particular, the FPTC method can predict the training time of the LogReg under the *Antivirus* dataset (with an RMSE and MAPE almost equal to 0 using the slope computed with 9,009 features of the synthetic dataset), *Arcene* (with an RMSE and MAPE almost equal to 0 using the slope computed with 6,006 features), *Compas* (with an RMSE and MAPE almost equal to 0 using the slope computed with 4,004 features), and *Dexter* (with an RMSE and MAPE almost equal to 0 using the slope computed with 501 features). In contrast, the FPTC method is not able to predict the training time of the LogReg under *Adult* (with the lowest MAPE equal to 9.5 using the slope computed with 1,503 features), and *APS* (with the lowest MAPE equal to 9.0 using the slope computed with 1,503 features). It is worth noting that the high MAPE for the *German* dataset may be influenced by the low values of FPTC and true running time, causing this metric to increase [6]. This is also supported by a low value of the RMSE.

Table 2. Mean and stand. dev. of training time and FPTC for LogReg model

Dataset	Training Time (seconds)	FPTC (seconds)
Adult	16.54 ± 0.042	14.77 ± 0.066
Antivirus	1.15 ± 0.012	1.214 ± 0.006
APS	400.156 ± 1.126	356.81 ± 1.803
Arcene	7.711 ± 0.012	7.953 ± 0.006
Compas	12.802 ± 5.366	12.956 ± 0.065
Dexter	37.597 ± 0.403	37.5 ± 0.188
German	0.019 ± 0.003	$0.015 ± 7.342 * 10^{-5}$

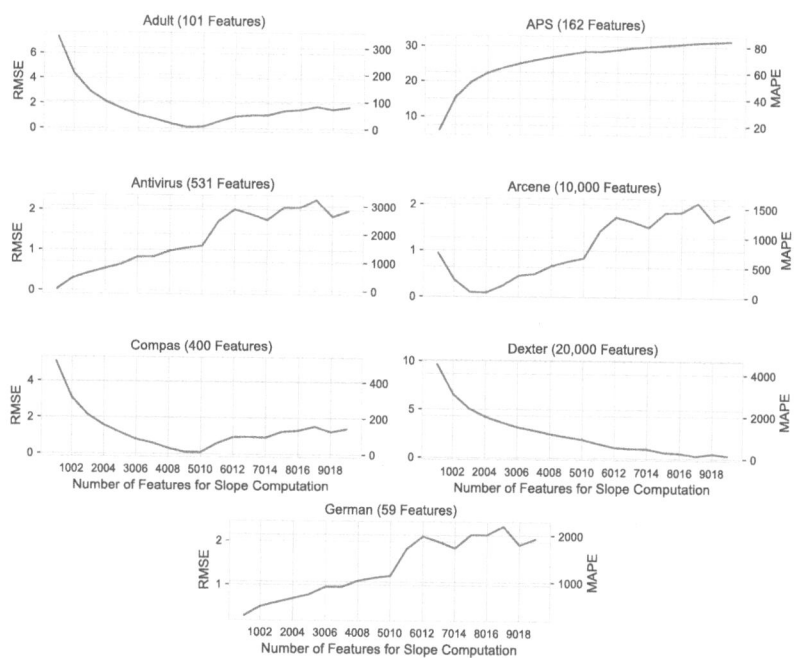

Fig. 3. RMSE and MAPE at different slope values for Random Forest

Table 2 reports the mean and standard deviation of the training time and FPTC in seconds for each selected dataset. From this table, it can be seen how the FPTC method tends to underestimate the real training time, especially in *Adult* (with a delta of almost 2 s between the actual training time and the predicted one), and *APS* (with a delta of almost 50 s between the actual training time and the predicted one). Finally, following the low variability of the slopes computed in Sect. 5.1, we notice how the slopes' variation does not much influence the FPTC predictions.

Figure 3 reports the same metrics computed for the Random Forest classifier. Differently from the Logistic Regression classier, here we notice how the FPTC method is more sensitive to the variation of the slopes, which lets the prediction increase or decrease significantly. This behaviour is explained by the high variability of the slopes shown in Sect. 5.1. In addition, it can be seen from the charts that the FPTC method can always predict real training time under a specific slope value achieving a value of zero for both RMSE and MAPE. However, we also notice how the value of the slope leading to the optimal predictions is not constant and varies between the datasets. The only dataset on which the FPTC method is not able to correctly predict the training time is the *APS* dataset, with the lowest MAPE of around 15 points. Table 3 reports the mean and standard deviation of the actual training time and the predicted one for the Random Forest classifier. Differently from above, in this case, we notice a higher variability among the predicted training times, especially in *Adult*, *APS*, *Compas*, and *Dexter*. In addition, we notice how for the *APS* dataset (which is the one letting the worse performances), the FPTC method underestimates the real training time. Finally, as noticed above, the low training time of some datasets (namely, *Antivirus*, *Arcene*, *Dexter*) explains the high value of the related MAPE metric for them.

Table 3. Mean and stand. dev. of training time and FPTC for RF model

Dataset	Training Time (seconds)	FPTC (seconds)
Adult	2.15 ± 0.012	2.60 ± 2.383
Antivirus	$0.07 \pm 8.368 * 10^{-17}$	1.20 ± 0.711
APS	37.54 ± 0.698	11.49 ± 6.469
Arcene	0.13 ± 0.004	0.79 ± 0.874
Compas	0.99 ± 0.009	1.23 ± 1.758
Dexter	0.217 ± 0.005	2.76 ± 2.452
German	0.11 ± 0.004	1.3 ± 0.677

Finally, Fig. 4 reports the Pearson correlation coefficient [23] between the FPTC parameters and MAPE for Logistic Regression (Fig. 4a) and Random Forest (Fig. 4b)[3]. Concerning LogReg, we notice how MAPE is negatively correlated with the number of features of the dataset (with a value of -0.51). This means that, on average, there is a lower error in the training time predictions for datasets with a higher number of columns. On the contrary, MAPE is lightly positively correlated with the number of instances of the dataset (with a value of 0.18), meaning that, datasets with a high number of rows have a slightly higher error in the predictions. Eventually, we notice a low correlation of

---

[3] The number of classes and the number of trees for the RF are not considered because their values are constant.

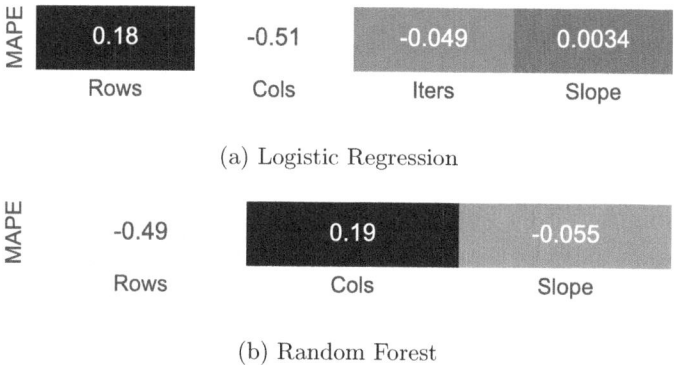

(a) Logistic Regression

(b) Random Forest

Fig. 4. Pearson correlation coefficient between FPTC parameters and MAPE for LogReg and RF

MAPE with the number of iterations and the values of the slope. In particular, the low correlation between MAPE and slope can be explained by the fact that the value of the slope leading to optimal predictions is not constant and varies with the datasets. Concerning RF, it can be seen from Fig. 4b how there is an opposite correlation between MAPE and the number of instances and features with respect to LogReg. In fact, MAPE is negatively correlated with the number of rows (−0.49), while it is lightly positively correlated with the number of columns (0.19). This means that datasets with a high number of rows have, on average, a lower prediction error, while datasets with a high number of columns have a slightly higher prediction error. Finally, as for the LogReg, we observe a low correlation between MAPE and the values of the slope. This can be again explained by the fact that the slope value leading to optimal predictions is not constant and changes with the dataset.

From this analysis, we can conclude how the FPTC method is able to predict the training time of a Logistic Regression and Random Forest classifier under certain circumstances (i.e., datasets) while it is not working in others. However, as shown in Fig. 4, we do not notice any high correlation between the FPTC parameters and the correctness of the predictions. Moreover, we see how the correctness of the predictions is directly related to the value of the slope, which is again not only dependent on the execution environment but also varies with the variation of the dataset used to compute it, as shown in Sect. 5.1. In addition, the value of the slope leading to optimal predictions is not constant and varies between the different datasets (especially with the RF classifier).

> **Answer to** RQ2: The FPTC method is able to predict the training time of the Logistic Regression and Random Forest classifiers under certain circumstances (i.e., datasets), while it fails in others. The correctness of the predictions (especially for the Random Forest classifier) is strongly related

to the value of the slope, which, however, depends on the dataset used to compute it and is not constant. Finally, we observe how, for both LogReg and RF, there is no high correlation between the FPTC parameters and the correctness of the predictions.

5.3 Threats to Validity

Internal Validity: We adopted a synthetic dataset to compute the slopes to answer RQ1. In contrast, a real-world dataset could include more complexity and variability not considered in this experiment. To answer this threat, we clarify that the goal of our experiment was to prove that the value of the slope is not only dependent on the execution environment. Hence, any dataset (synthetic or not) that proves this hypothesis is effective.

External Validity: The results of our experiments may apply only to the selected ML models and datasets. Concerning the selection of the dataset, we selected several datasets heterogeneous in their dimensions, making our results enough general. Concerning the ML models, we analysed two of the most adopted ML models for classification, while we will analyse the others in future works.

6 Conclusion and Future Work

In this paper, we have presented the work we are conducting towards predicting the training time of ML models. In particular, we have extensively evaluated the work proposed in [25], which is the only approach so far that formulates the training time as a function of the dataset's and model's parameters. In this paper, we have considered the formulations proposed for the Logistic Regression and Random Forest classifiers, and we have shown how the proposed approach is not always able to predict the training time successfully. Further, from the results shown in Sect. 5.2, there is no evidence of any correlation between the dataset size and the correctness of the predictions. Instead, from the results shown in Sect. 5.1, there is a correlation between the number of dataset features and the value of the slope used in the FPTC formulation (which is, again, not only dependent on the execution environment as stated in [25]).

In the future, we want to deeper analyse the formulations proposed for the different ML models and overcome the observed limitations. In particular, we want to investigate if some specific characteristics of the dataset or ML model influence the training time and are not considered in the current formulation.

References

1. APS Failure at Scania Trucks: UCI Machine Learning Repository (2017). https://doi.org/10.24432/C51S51
2. Ali, S., Smith, K.A.: On learning algorithm selection for classification. Appl. Soft Comput. **6**(2), 119–138 (2006)
3. Alla, S., Adari, S.K.: What is mlops? Beginning MLOps with MLFlow: Deploy Models in AWS SageMaker, Google Cloud, and Microsoft Azure, pp. 79–124 (2021)
4. Angwin, J., Larson, J., Mattu, S., Kirchner, L.: Machine bias. ProPublica, May **23**(2016), 139–159 (2016)
5. Chai, T., Draxler, R.R.: Root mean square error (rmse) or mean absolute error (mae)?-arguments against avoiding rmse in the literature. Geoscientific Model Dev. **7**(3), 1247–1250 (2014)
6. De Myttenaere, A., Golden, B., Le Grand, B., Rossi, F.: Mean absolute percentage error for regression models. Neurocomputing **192**, 38–48 (2016)
7. Fischer, R., Jakobs, M., Mücke, S., Morik, K.: A unified framework for assessing energy efficiency of machine learning. In: ECML PKDD 2022. LNCS, pp. 39–54. Springer, Cham (2022). https://doi.org/10.1007/978-3-031-23618-1_3
8. García-Martín, E., Rodrigues, C.F., Riley, G., Grahn, H.: Estimation of energy consumption in machine learning. J. Parallel Distrib. Comput. **134**, 75–88 (2019)
9. Guyon, I., Gunn, S., Ben-Hur, A., Dror, G.: Arcene. UCI Machine Learning Repository (2008). https://doi.org/10.24432/C58P55
10. Guyon, I., Gunn, S., Ben-Hur, A., Dror, G.: Dexter. UCI Machine Learning Repository (2008). https://doi.org/10.24432/C5P898
11. Kohavi, R., et al.: Scaling up the accuracy of naive-bayes classifiers: A decision-tree hybrid. KDD **96**, 202–207 (1996)
12. Kwon, O., Sim, J.M.: Effects of data set features on the performances of classification algorithms. Expert Syst. Appl. **40**(5), 1847–1857 (2013)
13. Lewis, G.A., Ozkaya, I., Xu, X.: Software architecture challenges for ml systems. In: 2021 IEEE International Conference on Software Maintenance and Evolution (ICSME), pp. 634–638. IEEE (2021)
14. McDonald, J.H.: One-way ANOVA, vol. 2. sparky house publishing Baltimore, MD (2009)
15. Menard, S.: Applied logistic regression analysis, vol. 106. Sage (2002)
16. Mohr, F., Wever, M., Tornede, A., Hüllermeier, E.: Predicting machine learning pipeline runtimes in the context of automated machine learning. IEEE Trans. Pattern Anal. Mach. Intell. **43**(9), 3055–3066 (2021)
17. Nahar, N., Zhang, H., Lewis, G., Zhou, S., Kästner, C.: A Meta-Summary of Challenges in Building Products with ML Components – Collecting Experiences from 4758+ Practitioners, March 2023. https://doi.org/10.48550/arXiv.2304.00078, http://arxiv.org/abs/2304.00078, arXiv:2304.00078 [cs]
18. ONU: ONU Sustainable Development Goals. https://www.un.org/sustainabledevelopment/
19. Pedregosa, F., et al.: Scikit-learn: machine learning in Python. J. Mach. Learn. Res. **12**, 2825–2830 (2011)
20. Ratanamahatana, C.A., Gunopulos, D.: Scaling up the naive bayesian classifier: Using decision trees for feature selection (2002)
21. Rigatti, S.J.: Random forest. J. Insur. Med. **47**(1), 31–39 (2017)
22. Rumao, P.: Detect Malacious Executable (AntiVirus). UCI Machine Learning Repository (2016). https://doi.org/10.24432/C5531V

23. Sedgwick, P.: Pearson's correlation coefficient. Bmj **345** (2012)
24. Wenninger, S., et al.: How sustainable is machine learning in energy applications?– the sustainable machine learning balance sheet (2022)
25. Zheng, X., et al.: Full parameter time complexity (fptc): a method to evaluate the running time of machine learning classifiers for land use/land cover classification. IEEE J. Sel. Top. Appl. Earth Observ. Remote Sens. **14**, 2222–2235 (2021)
26. Zikria, Y.B., Afzal, M.K., Kim, S.W., Marin, A., Guizani, M.: Deep learning for intelligent iot: Opportunities, challenges and solutions (2020)

Performance Comparison of Monolith and Microservice Architectures
An Analysis of the State of the Art

Helena Rodrigues[1]([✉]) [ID], António Rito Silva[2] [ID], and Alberto Avritzer[3] [ID]

[1] Centro Algoritmi/LASI, University of Minho, Braga, Portugal
`helena@dsi.uminho.pt`
[2] INESC-ID, Técnico Lisboa, University of Lisbon, Lisbon, Portugal
`rito.silva@tecnico.ulisboa.pt`
[3] eSulabSolutions, Inc., Princeton, USA
`beto@esulabsolutions.com`

Abstract. The migration of monolith systems to the microservices architecture is becoming common due to the promised advantages of the latter. In this paper, we do a state-of-the-art analysis of the performance, throughput, and deployment infrastructure costs associated with the migration of monoliths to microservices. We analyze existing studies using a reference model of the relevant architectural elements used to design a microservices architecture. We identified the conflicting results that were already reported in the literature and we propose some aspects that we consider to be relevant to be addressed in future studies.

Keywords: Monolith System · Microservice Architecture · Performance

1 Introduction

The migration from monolith to microservice-based systems has become increasingly popular in the last decade. This migration is even more critical in the context of cloud-native applications. Identifying the most suitable software architecture for a cloud-native application is an important but complex task because it affects the development and execution of the application in the future [19]. By decomposing applications into independent stateless components, and communicating through REST-based distributed communication mechanisms or RPC, systems architects promote development team autonomy, fast deployment pipelines, the support for multiple technology stacks, and segregation by characteristics that improve qualities such as scalability, availability, maintainability, and security [11,25].

This work was supported by Fundação para a Ciência e Tecnologia (FCT) through projects UIDB/50021/2020 (DOI:10.54499/UIDB/50021/2020), PTDC/CCI-COM/2156/2021 (10.54499/PTDC/CCI-COM/2156/2021) and UIDB/00319/2020.

B. Tekinerdoğan et al. (Eds.): ECSA 2023, LNCS 14590, pp. 185–199, 2024.
https://doi.org/10.1007/978-3-031-66326-0_12

Research has been done on the comparison of performance, scalability, and infrastructure costs between a system monolith architecture and its microservice-based architecture alternative. These papers present different aspects of the selected metrics, and the results differ from each other. For example, some present contradictory results [22, 26], others do not discuss complex service interactions [4, 16, 21, 22, 24], present very few details on the benchmark used for the experiments [2], are evaluated using simple systems [7] or use different metrics of a microservice system [1, 6]. Additional research has also been done on understanding and addressing the quality attributes of microservice-based architectures, such as in [15, 25].

In this paper, we do a state-of-the-art analysis of the performance and infrastructure costs associated with the migration of monoliths to the microservice architecture.

Our work differs from previous research because it focuses on the comparison of microservice-based and monolith architectures and on a state-of-the-art analysis of the performance and infrastructure costs associated with the migration between these two architecture styles. Research that compares the impact on the performance of migration of monoliths to microservice architecture does not use a reference model that identifies possible architectural variations [4, 15, 22].

We start by defining an architectural reference model for microservice architectures in Sect. 2, where we identify and relate the main architectural elements that are used in the related work studies. Then, in Sect. 3 we present the configuration in which the experiment studies are designed, such as the test workload. An analysis of the identified studies is done in Sect. 4, followed by a discussion of the results in Sect. 5. Finally, we conclude the paper in Sect. 6.

2   Reference Model

The adoption process for a microservice-based architecture is complex and is shaped by many factors [9, 18, 23]. In this paper, we focus on the problem of comparing the performance, scalability, and costs of monolith and microservice-based software architectures. To do so, we first introduce a reference model that will frame our analysis of state-of-the-art research works. This model will be the base for our discussion on open issues concerning the impact of each of the elements of the reference model on the mentioned qualities. In addition, it will allow us to identify the extent to which each of the case studies analyzed addresses the different architectural aspects of microservice architecture.

Figure 1 presents the architectural software elements considered in the reference model that are relevant to the design of microservice systems. These software elements are grouped into two views, according to the categorization of Clements et al. [5]: component-and-connector and deployment. The former captures the run-time aspects of the system, while the latter is deployment in the execution infrastructure.

The software elements of the component and connector view are distributed software elements that correspond to the basic types of components and

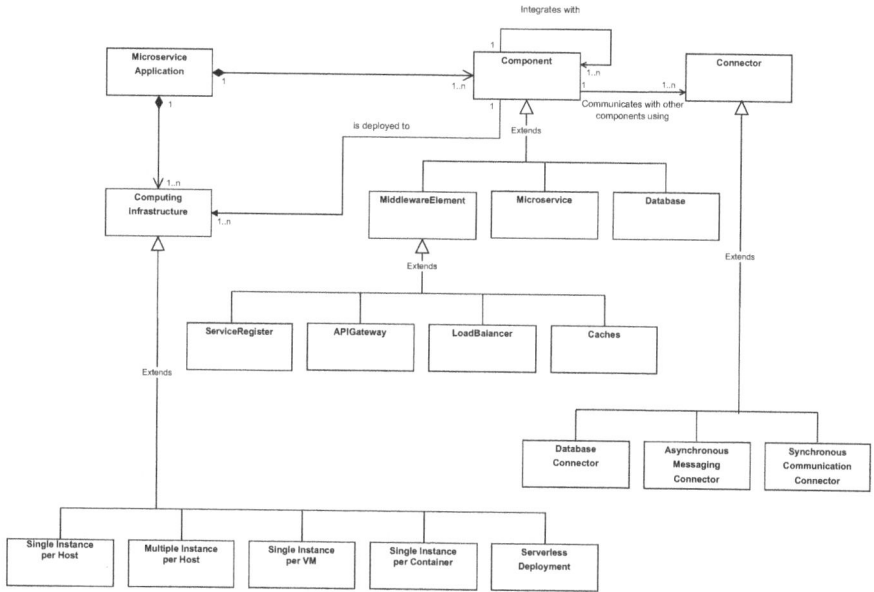

Fig. 1. Microservices architecture reference model

connectors found in the microservice-based architecture style. It includes the microservice component, which implements the application business logic, and additional specialized components that act as intermediaries or provide infrastructure services.

Microservice is the core component type of the microservice architecture. It is an independently deployable, loosely coupled component that provides a set of application functionality. In a typical microservice architecture, each microservice has its own database server, which stores the data model managed by the team responsible for the microservice. Besides this data access connector with its database component, microservices can be connected to other microservices using two different types of connectors:

– Synchronous communication: The caller microservice waits synchronously by the response of the called microservice. The most common implementation of this connector in the microservices architecture is REST. These requests are based on the four basic HTTP commands to create, retrieve, update, or delete a resource. Resources have a well-defined representation in JSON, or a similar language notation.
– Asynchronous messaging: components exchange asynchronous messages where the caller does not wait for the message to be processed by the called microservice. The messaging connector can be point-to-point or publish-subscribe, depending on whether the caller knows the address of the called or not. The called microservice can only respond to the caller using a callback.

Microservices components may be part of a more complex topology where additional components perform management activities. Some of these components are:

- API Gateway: Controls the access to the microservices network through a single entry point for all clients. It is responsible to manage authentication, access control, and other security aspects. Requests are then routed to the appropriate microservice.
- Load Balancer: This component is responsible for deciding how the workload is distributed among different microservice replicas. It can also be responsible for provisioning new instances of microservice components on demand, based on the number of requests submitted by users. It is located in front of the microservice replicas.
- Service Registry: Provides transparency in the location of microservice components. It allows services to be registered, discovered, and accessed at runtime, such that new microservices may be added and removed transparently to their clients, which can be other microservices. It is located as an intermediary between the microservices invocations.
- Caches: Implementing caches for faster information retrieval speed and to reduce the number of remote invocations for faster performance. These caches can be owned by a single microservice or shared by several microservices.

A microservices system executes functionalities. Execution of these functionalities may require the cooperation of several microservices. When this is the case, the execution of the functionality corresponds to the execution of a distributed transaction. This occurs because each microservice accesses its own database, which raises problems of isolation. Therefore, to handle this type of problem several patterns have been suggested:

- SAGA [10,20]: Each functionality is implemented as an SAGA. An SAGA is a sequence of local transactions, where each local transaction is a microservice invocation, that updates the database and publishes a message or event to trigger the next local transaction in the SAGA. Changes can be undone if any local transaction fails. This process may be coordinated by choreography or orchestration. Using choreography, local transactions are triggered by events produced by local transactions in other services. Using orchestration, an orchestrator component requests participant services to execute the involved local transactions.
- Command Query Responsibility Segregation (CQRS) [20]: Separates query services from update services, so that reads can be optimized. Defines read-only replicas of databases (database views) that join data from multiple services. The application keeps the replica up-to-date by subscribing to events published by the service that owns the data.

To address the problem of scalability, microservices can use several strategies:

- Vertical Scaling: Increases the overall application capacity by increasing the resources (computation and storage) within existing computing and storage nodes.

– Horizontal Scaling: Increases the overall application capacity by adding microservice replicas. It requires a load balancer to manage the workload of each of the replicas. This is the strategy that is more common in the microservices architecture because it allows independent scaling based on particular microservice demand.

Relevant for the analysis of the performance and scalability of the microservice architecture is how it is deployed in the communication and computation infrastructure. Therefore, it is important to describe the mapping between the software's components and connectors and the hardware of the computing platform on which the software executes. The following types of deployment are considered:

– The Single Service Instance per Host: Each microservice instance is deployed on its own host.
– The Multiple Service Instances per Host: Run multiple instances of different microservices on a host.
– The Service Instance per Virtual Machine: Each microservice is packaged with a virtual machine image and deployed as a separate virtual machine.
– The Service Instance per Container: Package the microservice as a container image and deploy each microservice instance as a Docker container.
– The Serverless deployment: Each microservice is deployed in a deployment infrastructure that hides any concept of servers. The infrastructure receives the microservice's code and runs it.

3   Test Design

The test design defines the architectural configuration under test. For instance, what are the microservices involved in the test, whether they have replicas, or if there is a service registry involved? Additionally, the test design also defines the operational profile associated with the test.

An operational profile characterizes the services invoked, their test inputs, and their frequency. Several aspects must be considered:

– Type of Request: The performance of a microservices architecture can significantly depend on the type of request. Therefore, it is important to distinguish between requests that result in accesses to the database (create, read, update, and delete) or whether they are computationally intensive.
– Multi-Service Invocations: Distributed applications have a latency overhead associated with remote invocations. Therefore, to analyze this overhead, it is important to design test variations in which a single service can fulfill the request or it is necessary to invoke several services. The latter may consider whether the service interactions follow one of the patterns: orchestration or choreography, as mentioned in the discussion on Sagas. On the other hand, it is also relevant to consider the type of connector used in interactions between services, such as synchronous communication or asynchronous messaging.

– Workload: The frequency of requests also helps characterize the performance and scalability qualities of a microservice architecture. Therefore, it is necessary to define several types of test workload, from sequential to concurrent, defining, for instance, the number of parallel requests and the maximum expected load. The payload used in the tests may also be relevant.

Another aspect to consider in test design is how the results are going to be evaluated. In terms of performance and scalability, the following metrics can be considered:

– Latency: measures the time taken to fulfill a request.
– Throughput: measures the number of successfully processed requests per unit of time.
– Cost: measures the infrastructure cost associated with the processing of requests.

Note that it may not be possible to optimize all these metrics, but analyzing the best trade-offs permits us to discuss the advantages and drawbacks of migrating a monolith system to a microservice architecture. For instance, even though the microservices architecture may perform better in terms of throughput, what is the trade-off in terms of having a more complex architecture that consumes more resources and may have a higher cost per processed request?

4   Analysis

We identified thirteen studies that compare the performance of two different architectural implementations of the same system: monolith and microservices. The analysis of these studies is done according to variations in the test design and the architectural elements of the implementation. These variations were described in the previous sections.

To search for a relevant bibliography, we used Google Scholar, a major bibliographic database, recognized as suitable for a variety of tasks, including the selection of journal and conference literature. Our search strategy consisted of one query that included a seven-year time frame and used *performance microservices monolith* as the selection keywords. The results were then refined to extract English-written peer-reviewed papers that focused on the evaluation of microservices vs monolith architectures regarding performance, throughput, and deployment infrastructure costs. Table 1 presents the list of selected case studies.

In Table 2 we present a summary of the aspects analyzed in the reviewed studies, specifically a summary of objectives and approaches. Then, we summarize the analysis in the following tables:

– Table 3: Studies Test Design.
– Table 4: Architectural Elements.
– Table 5: Deployment and scalability.
– Table 6: Performance and cost metrics.

Table 1. Selected Studies.

Study	Year	Title
Villamizar et al. [26]	2017	Cost comparison of running web applications in the cloud using monolithic, microservice, and AWS Lambda architectures
Flygare et al. [8]	2017	Performance characteristics between monolithic and microservice-based systems
Eriksson et al. [7]	2020	A case study of performance comparison between monolithic and microservice-based quality control system
Mangwani et al. [16]	2023	Evaluation of a Multitenant SaaS Using Monolithic and Microservice Architectures
Blinowski at al. [4]	2022	Monolithic vs. Microservice Architecture: A Performance and Scalability Evaluation
Ueda et al. [24]	2016	Workload characterization for microservices
Al-Debagy et al. [2]	2018	A Comparative Review of Microservices and Monolithic Architectures
Tapia et al. [22]	2020	From Monolithic Systems to Microservices: A Comparative Study of Performance
Singh et al. [21]	2017	Container-based Microservice Architecture for Cloud Applications
Costa et al. [6]	2022	Performance Evaluation of Microservices Featuring Different Implementation Patterns
Akbulut et al. [1]	2019	Performance Analysis of Microservice Design Patterns
Bjorndal et al. [3]	2021	Benchmarks and performance metrics for assessing the migration to microservice-based architectures
Jayasinghe et al. [13]	2021	An Analysis of Throughput and Latency Behaviours Under Microservice Decomposition

From Table 3 we can observe that most of the tests done considered requests with access to the database, while only two studies analyze the performance of requests that do not access a database. On the other hand, most studies analyzed requests that are fulfilled by a single microservice. This does not explore the migration of complex requests. Finally, in terms of payload, only two test studies discuss this variation. Note that some studies do not provide clear information about the type of request and multi-services invocations, which shows the importance of using an explicit reference model [2].

Table 4 shows that the API Gateway and Load Balancer were the components most frequently used in the microservice architecture of the studies. On the other hand, the Service Registry and Caches where only applied in two studies. Regarding connectors, most of the studies analyzed synchronous requests, whereas only two studies considered asynchronous requests. Interestingly, systems that have a high number of requests, like Facebook or Twitter, do a significant part of their request processing asynchronously.

Table 5 shows that most of the deployments used docker containers. Villamizar et al. [26] compare the deployment in virtual machines with the deployment using serverless. Blinowski et al. [4] experiments with a large range of

Table 2. Summary of Studies Comparing Monolith and Microservice Architectures

Study	Objective	Approach
Villamizar et al. [26]	Compare infrastructure costs of monolith vs. microservice-based architecture with different deployment scenarios	Evaluate latency and costs in service instances per virtual machine and serverless deployment
Flygare et al. [8]	Compare the performance of a microservice-based system with the monolith version on a single machine and computer cluster	Evaluate performance differences in varying deployment setups
Eriksson et al. [7]	Compare the performance of a microservice architecture versus a monolithic architecture for a specific case study	Analyze the impact of caches in migration to microservice architecture
Mangwani et al. [16]	Compare factors (performance, scalability, load balancing, reliability, resource utilization, infrastructure cost) between monolith and microservices with increasing concurrent requests	Investigate multiple factors under varying load conditions
Blinowski at al. [4]	Compare the performance of monolith and microservices architectures with similar infrastructure costs	Explore performance in equivalent cost settings
Ueda et al. [24]	Compare the performance of monolith and microservices architectures under different language environments	Analyze the behavior of AcmeAir benchmark versions (microservice-based vs. monolith) using Node.js and Java
Al-Debagy et al. [2]	Compare the performance of monolith and microservices architectures under different test scenarios	Emphasis on service discovery and its variations
Tapia et al. [22]	Analyze monolith and microservice architectures, assessing performance and resource consumption (CPU, RAM, bandwidth)	Explore resource usage in different architecture types
Singh et al. [21]	Discuss deployment of social network application in monolith and microservices architectures, considering deployment time	Explore deployment metrics in different application setups
Costa et al. [6]	Compare the performance of monolith and microservices architectures	Explore performance under different microservice implementation patterns
Akbulut et al. [1]	Compare CPU and RAM requirements of microservice vs. monolith implementation	Investigate resource usage in different architectures
Bjorndal et al. [3]	Present methodology and performance indicators for assessing migration from monolith to microservices	Investigate performance metrics in migration scenarios
Jayasinghe et al. [13]	Investigate the effect of service decomposition on microservice application performance	Explore performance impact of different microservice types and decomposition strategies

Table 3. Studies Test Design. Type of Request indicates if the request execution accesses the database (C - create, R - read, U - update, D - delete), considers whether there are computationally intensive requests (CI), or do not require any access to the database (NODB). Multi-Service Invocations indicates if more than a microservice is required to fulfill the request, when that is the case we distinguish between the use of microservice patterns like SAGA and CQRS, or whether it is only a chain of invocations (CHAIN). Workload characterizes the concurrent tests and their payload.

Study	Type of Request	Multi-Service Invocations	Workload
Villamizar et al. [26]	R,CI	No	Concurrent 1..MAX
Flygare et al. [8]	R,U	No	Concurrent 1..1000 Payload 10 properties
Eriksson et al. [7]	R,U,D,CI	CHAIN	Concurrent 1..120 Payload small..high
Mangwani et al. [16]	R,U,D,CI	No	Concurrent 100..500
Blinowski at al. [4]	R,CI,NODB	No	Concurrent10
Ueda et al. [24]	R,U	No	Concurrent 30
Al-Debagy et al. [2]	-	-	Concurrent 100..7000
Tapia et al. [22]	R,U	No	Concurrent 5Payload 10.000,20.000
Singh et al. [21]	-	No	Concurrent 1..2000
Costa et al. [6]	R,U,CI	SAGA,CQRS	Concurrent 1..MAX
Akbulut et al. [1]	CI,NODB	CHAIN	Concurrent 10..50
Bjorndal et al. [3]	C,R	CHAIN	Concurrent 1..MAX
Jayasinghe et al. [13]	R,CI,NODB	CHAIN	Concurrent 1..1000Payload 50..1024 bytes

Table 4. Architectural Elements. Besides the microservices components, the components and connectors used in the microservice architectural implementation in each of the studies.

Study	Components				Connectors
	APIGateway	LoadBalancer	Service Registry	Caches	
Villamizar et al. [26]	Yes	Yes	No	No	Synchronous (REST)
Flygare et al. [8]	No	No	No	No	Synchronous (REST)
Eriksson et al. [7]	Yes	No	No	Yes	Synchronous (REST)
Mangwani et al. [16]	Yes	Yes	No	No	Synchronous (REST)
Blinowski at al. [4]	Yes	Yes	Yes	No	Synchronous (REST)
Ueda et al. [24]	No	No	No	No	Synchronous (REST)
Al-Debagy et al. [2]	Yes	No	Yes	No	Synchronous (REST)
Tapia et al. [22]	Yes	No	No	No	Synchronous (REST)
Singh et al. [21]	Yes	Yes	No	No	Synchronous (REST)
Costa et al. [6]	Yes	Yes	No	No	Synchronous (REST) Asynchronous
Akbulut et al. [1]	Yes	Yes	No	No	Synchronous (REST)
Bjorndal et al. [3]	No	Yes	No	No	Synchronous (REST) Asynchronous
Jayasinghe et al. [13]	No	No	No	Yes	Synchronous (REST)

Table 5. Deployment and Scalablility. The deployment of the architectural elements and the use of scalability strategies.

Study	Deployment	Scalability
Villamizar et al. [26]	Virtual machinesServerless	Horizontal
Flygare et al. [8]	Docker containers	No scaling Vertical
Eriksson et al. [7]	Docker containers	No scaling
Mangwani et al. [16]	Docker containers	Horizontal
Blinowski at al. [4]	Azure Spring Cloud VMsAzure APP service VMs	HorizontalVertical
Ueda et al. [24]	Docker containers	Vertical
Al-Debagy et al. [2]	Docker containers	No scaling
Tapia et al [22]	Docker containers	No scaling
Singh et al. [21]	Docker containers	Horizontal
Costa et al. [6]	Docker containers	Horizontal
Akbulut et al. [1]	Docker containers	Horizontal
Bjorndal et al. [3]	Docker containers, Kubernets	Horizontal
Jayasinghe et al. [13]	Bare metal	No scaling

deployment variations, in terms of the number of servers, CPUs, and memory used in each of the deployment configurations, for monolith and microservices.

Not all studies address scalability. Only one study [4] compares Vertical scalability with Horizontal scalability, while another [8] compares Vertical scalability with No scalability.

The results obtained in each of the studies for the performance and cost metrics are presented in Table 6. There is a large diversity of analysis results, which reflect the objectives of each of the studies.

Concerning latency, we can observe some variation in the results. The expected result would be that, due to the introduction of a more complex architecture, the request latency would increase. The use of load balancers, for instance, or the migration of procedure calls to remote calls, would introduce an overhead in the request processing. However, some studies conclude to a decrease in latency [21,22] while others [2,3,16,26] observe a decrease in some circumstances or that the latency is not significantly different from the monolith.

The first relevant aspect for the analysis of the studies in which latency decreases for microservice architecture is that none of these studies considered multi-services invocations. This means that all the possible overhead associated with microservices execution would be restricted to interactions with additional architectural components. Actually, these studies add some components, and [2] even consider a service discovery that can be penalizing. However, studies that report an increase in latency also use these components. Therefore, we can consider the results to be somehow contradictory. Finally, two other interesting results are [16,26] where they observe the decrease in latency for particular conditions, the former for a serverless implementation and the latter for highly computationally intensive requests.

Similar contradictory conclusions can be observed for the throughput. While the expectation would be an increase in throughput, there are a large number of studies that conclude on a decrease [2, 6–8]. Note that some of them do not apply scaling techniques, though there are studies that do not apply scaling and obtained an increase in throughput [1, 22].

Table 6. Metrics. The performance and cost metrics used in the studies and the obtained results. MS stands for Microservice, SV for serveless, LCI for low computationally intensive, HCI for highly computationally intensive, NODB for no database operations, LC for low concurrency, and HC for high concurrency. The comparison is always done against the monolith, e.g. "MS <" means the microservice implementation has lower values than the monolith implementation. On the other hand, the microservice implementation can be characterized, e.g. "MS Cache <<" means that the microservice implementation used a cache and has much lower values when compared with another term in the same cell. Besides the microservices, the requests can also be characterized.

Study	Metrics (Microservice vs Monoltith)		
	Latency	Throughput	Costs
Villamizar et al. [26]	MS >SV ~=	No	MS < SV <<
Flygare et al. [8]	MS 1 Machine > MS Cluster (2) >>	MS 1 Machine < MS Cluster (2) <	No
Eriksson et al. [7]	MS No Cache >> MS Cache >	MS No Cache <<MS Cache <	No
Mangwani et al. [16]	Requests LCI > Requests HCI <	No	No
Blinowski at al. [4]	No	Requests LCI Horizontal > Requests LCI Vertical >> Requests HCI NODB >>	MS >
Ueda et al. [24]	No	-	No
Al-Debagy et al. [2]	MS ~=	Requests LC < Requests HC ~=	No
Tapia et al. [22]	MS <	MS >	No
Singh et al. [21]	Requests LC <Requests HC <<	>	No
Costa et al. [6]	MS Sync >MS Async >>	MS Sync ~= MS Async <	No
Akbulut et al. [1]	No	No	MS <
Bjorndal et al. [3]	MS Sync > MS Async >>	MS Sync <MS Async <	No
Jayasinghe et al. [13]	Requests LCI > Requests HCI <	Requests LCI < Requests HCI < MS No Cache < < MS Cache >	No

Finally, only three studies perform a cost analysis [1, 4, 26]. Also in this case the results are contradictory. Akbulut et al. [1] evaluated costs based on the consumption of RAM and CPU for monolith and microservices configurations that offer the same throughput. The costs are lower for microservices configuration as it consumes fewer resources in total. This seems to happen because the microservice architecture allows for scaling the services independently leading to less resource consumption. This seems to be also the case for the case study discussed in [26]; for the monolith configuration to obtain the same throughput as the microservices configuration, it was necessary to create additional replicas of the monolith application so that memory and CPU consumption was higher. On the other hand, Blinowski et al. [4], by experimenting with several deployment configurations, were able to find monolith configurations that have a lower cost than microservice configurations, while providing similar throughput. Furthermore, a recent result from the gray literature shows a case where a 90% cost reduction was achieved by migrating a microservice system back to the monolith architecture [14].

A more thorough analysis is presented in [4] where it compares the performance of monoliths and microservices configurations that exhibit similar infrastructure costs for both high and low-intensive computation requests, and Java Spring cloud and Azure App services. The authors conducted several experiments with different deployment configurations, with variations in the number of machines and their capabilities (horizontal and vertical scaling). They concluded that when one considers simple and short request applications, it is more advantageous to horizontally scale them by increasing the number of instances in a moderate manner. However, further increases in the number of replicas result in excessive communication overhead due to load balancing and the need for request passing. Conversely, the impact of vertical scaling is more pronounced compared to horizontal scaling. In situations involving intensive computation, the impact of both horizontal and vertical scaling is visible; the higher the configuration and the larger the number of microservice instances, the better throughput.

5   Discussion

From the previous analysis, we identified several aspects of existing case studies:

- Contradictory results for the three qualities;
- Large variation of the conditions of each study;
- An emphasis on single microservice request fulfillment;
- An emphasis on synchronous implementations of requests in the microservice architecture;
- An emphasis on docker-based deployments.

A large number of variations occur in the test conditions, although there is a set of decisions that most studies repeat. On the other hand, studies ignore that migration of a monolith to a microservice architecture may require a change of the type of request, from synchronous to asynchronous, because throughput is a quality that is mostly relevant for scalability, and latency problems are solved by returning intermediate results in response to the request.

Previous work identified open issues in microservice performance testing, monitoring, and modeling [12]. Interestingly, we identified some of the same concerns when comparing monolith with microservices. In our opinion, the literature is scarce and difficult to compare because each study is conducted in a different context and the complexities associated with infrastructure deployment were not explored. Furthermore, we believe that a new proposal for a benchmark is needed to serve as a reference model for future studies. Also, since any of the architectures do not provide the best results for all conditions, it is relevant to identify and measure the trade-offs.

This is particularly relevant because a recent industry report [14] shows that by migrating a microservice system back to the monolith architecture a reduction cost of 90% is obtained. The authors conclude that microservices and serverless components are tools designed to operate at a high scale, but the decision to adopt them instead of a monolithic architecture must be carefully evaluated on a per-case basis.

Consequently, there exist some open issues that necessitate further investigation and clarification:

- How can we define a benchmark to analyze monolith and microservices performance that covers most of the contextual variations identified in the current studies?
- Can we identify a performance and scalability threshold where the migration of a monolith to a microservice architecture becomes worthwhile?
- When should a monolith synchronous request be implemented as an asynchronous request in the microservice architecture?
- What are the trade-offs between cost and performance?

6   Conclusion

Although the migration of monolith systems to microservice architectures has become a common trend in the industry, there are also reports suggesting that the microservice architecture may not necessarily be the best solution [17]. Therefore, there are trade-offs that have to be evaluated when deciding to do the migration.

In this paper, we examine the performance and scalability qualities when comparing the monolith with the microservice architecture. Therefore, we have done an analysis of published studies that compare these qualities in both types of architecture. The results of the analysis show that the studies have contradictory results. This is due to the contextual variations in which the studies are performed.

From the analysis of the different case studies, we concluded that more research is needed to define a suitable benchmark that takes into account a large number of architectural variations. This benchmark can help in the identification of relevant trade-offs for evaluating the migration of monolith to microservice architecture. We also identified the need to give more relevance to request asynchrony when migrating monolith to microservices architecture.

References

1. Akbulut, A., Perros, H.G.: Performance analysis of microservice design patterns. IEEE Internet Comput. **23**(6), 19–27 (2019). https://doi.org/10.1109/MIC.2019. 2951094

2. Al-Debagy, O., Martinek, P.: A comparative review of microservices and monolithic architectures. In: 2018 IEEE 18th International Symposium on Computational Intelligence and Informatics (CINTI), pp. 000149–000154 (2018). https://doi.org/10.1109/CINTI.2018.8928192

3. Bjorndal, N., Araujo, L., Bucchiarone, A., Dragoni, N., Mazzara, M., Dustdar, S.: Benchmarks and performance metrics for assessing the migration to microservice-based architectures. J. Object Technol. **20**(2), 2:1–17 (2021). https://doi.org/10.5381/jot.2021.20.2.a3

4. Blinowski, G., Ojdowska, A., Przybyłek, A.: Monolithic vs. microservice architecture: a performance and scalability evaluation. IEEE Access **10**, 20357–20374 (2022). https://doi.org/10.1109/ACCESS.2022.3152803

5. Clements, P., et al.: Documenting Software Architectures: Views and Beyond, 2nd edn. SEI Series in Software Engineering, Addison-Wesley, Upper Saddle River (2010)

6. Costa, L., Ribeiro, A.N.: Performance evaluation of microservices featuring different implementation patterns. In: Abraham, A., Gandhi, N., Hanne, T., Hong, T.-P., Nogueira Rios, T., Ding, W. (eds.) ISDA 2021. LNNS, vol. 418, pp. 165–176. Springer, Cham (2022). https://doi.org/10.1007/978-3-030-96308-8_15

7. Eriksson, M.: A case study of performance comparison between monolithic and microservice-based quality control system. Bachelor's thesis, Linköpings Universitet (2020)

8. Flygare, R., Holmqvist, A.: Performance characteristics between monolithic and microservice-based systems. Bachelor's thesis, Blekinge Institute of Technology (2017)

9. Fowler, M.: Microservices. Web page (2014). http://martinfowler.com/articles/microservices.html. Accessed 06 July 2023

10. Garcia-Molina, H., Salem, K.: Sagas. SIGMOD Rec. **16**(3), 249–259 (1987). https://doi.org/10.1145/38714.38742

11. Gysel, M., Kölbener, L., Giersche, W., Zimmermann, O.: Service cutter: a systematic approach to service decomposition. In: Aiello, M., Johnsen, E.B., Dustdar, S., Georgievski, I. (eds.) ESOCC 2016. LNCS, vol. 9846, pp. 185–200. Springer, Cham (2016). https://doi.org/10.1007/978-3-319-44482-6_12

12. Heinrich, R., et al.: Performance engineering for microservices: research challenges and directions. In: Proceedings of the 8th ACM/SPEC on International Conference on Performance Engineering Companion, ICPE 2017 Companion, pp. 223–226. Association for Computing Machinery, New York (2017). https://doi.org/10.1145/3053600.3053653

13. Jayasinghe, M., Chathurangani, J., Kuruppu, G., Tennage, P., Perera, S.: An analysis of throughput and latency behaviours under microservice decomposition. In: Bielikova, M., Mikkonen, T., Pautasso, C. (eds.) ICWE 2020. LNCS, vol. 12128, pp. 53–69. Springer, Cham (2020). https://doi.org/10.1007/978-3-030-50578-3_5

14. Kolny, M.: Scaling up the prime video audio/video monitoring service and reducing costs by 90%. Web page (2023). https://www.primevideotech.com/video-streaming/scaling-up-the-prime-video-audio-video-monitoring-service-and-reducing-costs-by-90. Accessed 06 July 2023

15. Li, S., et al.: Understanding and addressing quality attributes of microservices architecture: a systematic literature review. Inf. Softw. Technol. **131**, 106449 (2021). https://doi.org/10.1016/j.infsof.2020.106449. https://www.sciencedirect.com/science/article/pii/S0950584920301993

16. Mangwani, P., Mangwani, N., Motwani, S.: Evaluation of a multitenant saas using monolithic and microservice architectures. SN Comput. Sci. **4**, Mar 2023. https://doi.org/10.1007/s42979-022-01610-2

17. Mendonca, N.C., Box, C., Manolache, C., Ryan, L.: The monolith strikes back: Why istio migrated from microservices to a monolithic architecture. IEEE Softw. **38**(05), 17–22 (2021). https://doi.org/10.1109/MS.2021.3080335

18. O'Hanlon, C.: A conversation with werner vogels. Queue **4**(4), 14–22 (2006). https://doi.org/10.1145/1142055.1142065

19. Pahl, C., Jamshidi, P., Zimmermann, O.: Microservices and containers - architectural patterns for cloud and edge. In: Lecture Notes in Informatics (LNI), Proceedings - Series of the Gesellschaft fur Informatik (GI). vol. P-300, p. 115–116 (2020)

20. Richardson, C.: Microservices Patterns. Manning (2019)

21. Singh, V., Peddoju, S.K.: Container-based microservice architecture for cloud applications. In: 2017 International Conference on Computing, Communication and Automation (ICCCA), pp. 847–852 (2017). https://doi.org/10.1109/CCAA.2017.8229914

22. Tapia, F., Mora, M.A., Fuertes, W., Aules, H., Flores, E., Toulkeridis, T.: From monolithic systems to microservices: a comparative study of performance. Appl. Sci. **10**(17) (2020). https://doi.org/10.3390/app10175797. https://www.mdpi.com/2076-3417/10/17/5797

23. Thönes, J.: Microservices. IEEE Softw. **32**(1), 116–116 (2015)

24. Ueda, T., Nakaike, T., Ohara, M.: Workload characterization for microservices. In: 2016 IEEE International Symposium on Workload Characterization (IISWC), pp. 1–10 (2016). https://doi.org/10.1109/IISWC.2016.7581269

25. Vale, G., et al.: Designing microservice systems using patterns: an empirical study on quality trade-offs. In: 2022 IEEE 19th International Conference on Software Architecture (ICSA), pp. 69–79. IEEE Computer Society, Los Alamitos, CA, USA, March 2022. https://doi.org/10.1109/ICSA53651.2022.00015

26. Villamizar, M., et al.: Cost comparison of running web applications in the cloud using monolithic, microservice, and AWS lambda architectures. SOCA **11**, 233–247 (2017)

Towards a Sustainability-Aware Software Architecture Evaluation for Cloud-Based Software Services

Iffat Fatima$^{(\boxtimes)}$ (ID) and Patricia Lago (ID)

Vrije Universiteit Amsterdam, Amsterdam, The Netherlands
{i.fatima,p.lago}@vu.nl

Abstract. The ubiquity of digital solutions integrating cloud-based software services necessitates sustainability awareness of such solutions. The integration of sustainability needs evaluation early in the software development life-cycle; preferably at the software architecture level. Although extensive literature is available for software architecture evaluation, not so much is observed for sustainability awareness, in general, and specifically for cloud-based software service architectures. In this study, we aim to create a blueprint of a software architecture evaluation method that has the potential to guide the sustainability-aware software architecture evaluation of cloud-based software services. Based on previous work, we identify 11 general steps grouped into 3 phases. We address challenges and provide recommendations for software architecture evaluation, emphasizing sustainability. Additionally, we propose sub-steps for trade-off analysis, impact analysis, and prioritization with a sustainability focus. The blueprint can be customized to evaluate cloud-based software services using specific sustainability criteria. Future work involves identifying sustainability metrics and testing the blueprint in an industrial setting for cloud-based software services.

Keywords: software architecture · sustainability · architecture evaluation · cloud-based software services

1 Introduction

The ubiquity and rapid growth of cloud-based digital solutions reinforce the need to study the sustainability of digital ecosystems. In the context of software, the sustainability needs of these ecosystems should be ensured as part of the Software Development Lifecycle (SDLC).

Designing Software Architecture (SA) is one of the most crucial stages of the SDLC, as it lays a foundation for the whole software. Bass *et al.* [5] describe the importance of SA in terms of its role in inhibiting or enabling quality attributes (QAs). Hence, evaluating SA for the fulfillment of required QAs is the first checkpoint to ensure conformance to quality.

Lago *et al.* [18] create a case for treating sustainability as a property of software quality. To ensure the conformity of software to sustainability quality requirements, sustainability awareness needs to be evaluated. Therefore, an SA evaluation method would aid in ascertaining the fulfillment of the sustainability quality of a software system.

The literature includes several studies that present a comparative analysis of SA evaluation methods [29,34]. None of these methods, however, consider sustainability as a criterion for SA evaluation. Koziolek [9] presents a review of SA evaluation methods for sustainability and catalogs architecture-level sustainability metrics. However, some of these metrics are determined by source code analysis and hence, the analysis is at a more granular level. These metrics can directly be mapped to the technical dimension of sustainability, however, further analysis and validation are needed to evaluate how these metrics may contribute to sustainability across other dimensions (social, economic, environmental) and if new metrics are required to fulfill the sustainability requirement.

Our objective is to explore the support of current SA evaluation methods in the analysis of CBSS SA. Building upon our previous work [11], which conducted a systematic literature review of SA evaluation methods, in this study, we leverage its findings and data to build an overarching SA evaluation blueprint, independent of the evaluation technique and type of software architecture. We further instantiate this blueprint to add steps to assess sustainability and present an example to apply it to CBSS architectures. Our vision for this blueprint is to help practitioners integrate sustainability into the existing SA evaluation process and make informed decisions in the context of the impact of design decisions on sustainability.

The structure of the paper is as follows: Sect. 2 presents the background of our research. Section 3 covers related work. Section 4 outlines our methodology. Section 5 presents the results of the study and discussions. Section 6 addresses the threats to the validity of the study and their mitigation. Lastly, Sect. 7 concludes with future work.

2   Background

In the context of software engineering research, software sustainability has a lot of variation in terms of its definitions. One of the early mentions of software sustainability in literature appears in a study by Robert *et al.* [31], who introduce a sustainability attribute to measure sustainability in software in terms of its potential for evolution and maintainability. Penzenstadler *et al.* [27] compare sustainability definitions in the literature and conclude that defining sustainability is relative to the context of the system and the researcher. They define sustainability as "preserving the function of a system over a defined time period".

Lago *et al.* [18] address sustainability with a broader scope and provide a comprehensive definition of sustainability dimensions embracing the aspects covered in previous definitions with economic, environmental, social and technical dimensions, which we refer to as *4D-sustainability*. *Economic (Ec)* dimension is related to the software's ability to preserve and create financial value for the stakeholders. *Environmental (E)* dimension is related to the ability of the software to impact natural resources. *Social (S)* dimension is related to the ability of the software to produce sociological impacts by its use in communities. *Technical (T)* dimension is related to the ability of the software to be used over a long period of time through its evolution. Based on the definitions of Hilty *et al.* [13], three levels of impacts are defined that affect temporal aspects of sustainability (i) *Direct impact* refers to the impact that is produced during the production and operation of ICT-based solution (ii) *Enabling impact* refers to the indirect impact of ICT on using the services (iii) *Systemic Impact* refers to the structural socio-economic impact of ICT at a macro level, over a long period of time.

To perform a sustainability assessment of CBSS architectures, it needs to be evaluated across all dimensions considering the over-time impacts (i.e. direct, enabling, and systemic) [13], of design decisions. Here CBSS architecture refers to the both the SA of the service itself and the SA of a combination of services operating on the cloud as a system. Several architecture evaluation methods, like Architecture Trade-off Analysis Method (ATAM) [14], exist that can aid in SA assessment. However, these methods do not explicitly provide support for sustainability assessment. Using sustainability criteria as a quality requirement of the system can enable sustainability assessment at the architectural level. In the context of our research, evaluation criteria specific to CBSS architectures need identification. Moreover, the SA evaluation needs to be carried out while making informed trade-offs considering the over-time impacts of design decisions on 4D-sustainability, in the context of CBSS architectures.

3   Related Work

In this section, we present work related to ours, summarising what is missing for the sustainability evaluation of CBSSs.

Comparison of State of the Art in SA Evaluation. Several SA evaluation methods are available in the literature for analyzing SA for certain QAs [4,21, 29,33,34]. These works reveal extensive literature on SA evaluation methods. Scenario-based approaches, often rooted in ATAM, are more prevalent. Existing methods offer detailed insights into evaluation steps, artifacts, and the overall process. This information enables the creation of a generic blueprint for SA evaluation, adaptable for assessing sustainability in CBSSs. Most studies focus on a few QAs, but as QAs increase, trade-off decisions become more complex. Thus, the SA evaluation method's capacity for accommodating trade-off analysis with a larger set of QAs needs study, specifically for sustainability. However, there is insufficient information for sustainability-aware SA evaluation.

State of the Art in Sustainability Evaluation of SA. Koziolek *et al.* [16] employ a metric-based SA evaluation concluding that addressing architectural erosion requires analysis by code metrics at the architectural level while requirement and technology-based changes need to be addressed through scenario analysis. Condori-Fernandez *et al.* [9] employ a software sustainability assessment framework (SAF) to evaluate a software product based on a reference architecture, identifying QAs contributing to sustainability dimensions and unidentified

QAs that can potentially trigger product evolution. The results of the study show that a criterion is needed, to qualify a QA for its over-time impact (direct, enabling, or systemic). Furthermore, all types of inter-QA effects need evaluation for a well-rounded trade-off analysis.

From the related work, we observe an emerging trend in the literature for the sustainability evaluation of SA. However, the sustainability evaluations are limited to the technical dimension of sustainability. Hence, the conformance to sustainability across other dimensions needs to be studied and appropriate metrics need to be identified. No study evaluates the long-term sustainability impact of architectural decisions on the SA over time.

SA Evaluation of Specific Architecture Types. Regarding specific architecture types, some evaluation methods are tailored for certain software architectures. For example, Nurani et al. [24] present an evaluation method for Service Oriented Architecture using a metric-based approach.

Adjepon-Yamoah et al. [1] adapt ATAM for cloud-specific QA trade-offs but acknowledge the need for exploring other cloud-specific QAs. Different SA types may require specific QAs and associated metrics for their evaluation.

4   Methodology

In this section, we provide an overview of our research objectives, highlighting the identified problems, the goals we aim to achieve, the research questions we seek to answer, and the methodologies employed for each research question.

Problem Statement. Existing SA evaluation processes lack a mechanism for incorporating sustainability as a quality criterion. CBSS architectures need thorough exploration to incorporate sustainability effectively into evaluations.

P1: Lack of uniform SA evaluation artifacts: pre-requisite and post-requisites.

P2: Lack of criteria for sustainability-aware SA evaluation.

P3: Lack of SA evaluation methods specialized for CBSS architectures.

Goals. To elaborate on the possibilities of solving this problem, we present the following four goals as a guide for our research methodology:

G1: To identify the requirements for sustainability-aware SA evaluation.

G2: To exploit the available knowledge about SA evaluation methods for sustainability awareness.

G3: To present a blueprint of a SA evaluation method equipped with sustainability-aware SA evaluation of CBSS architectures.

Research Questions. Based on the above goals, we define a set of research questions (RQs) and describe the methodology used to answer each RQ.

RQ1: What are the required input and output artifacts for SA evaluation? From the data[1] obtained from our preliminary study, we use open

---

[1] Online Material [https://github.com/S2-group/ECSA23-TSSAE-rep-pkg].

coding [35] to extract the elements about the inputs and outputs of SA evaluation methods. This step aims to identify what artifacts are used for SA evaluation and how evaluation results are represented.

RQ2: What are the Steps of Existing SA Evaluation Methods? We use axial coding [35] and a visualization-based technique to systematically categorize the steps of the existing SA evaluation methods. We illustrate these steps in activity diagrams[1] and color-code them based on similarity. Upon need, colors are merged to form a single generic category. Steps are grouped by color, representing categories in the SA evaluation blueprint. A similar technique is employed to identify order of steps and iteration patterns. The results are unified as an SA evaluation blueprint.

RQ3: What are the Challenges Associated with SA Evaluation; in General and in the Context of Sustainability? For RQ3, we reflect on (i) the results of RQ1 and RQ2, (ii) sustainability literature, and (iii) the discussion of related works. Based on this reflection we identify limitations and recommendations for developing a sustainability-aware SA evaluation blueprint for CBSSs.

RQ4: How Can Existing SA Evaluation Method be Tailored for 4D-Sustainability Evaluation of CBSS Architectures? To answer this RQ, we identify the QAs specific to the quality of CBSSs. We run a Google Scholar search with the following search string: `software AND cloud AND (''quality attribute'' OR ''non-functional requirement'')`. As a result of this search query, we filter relevant studies by title and analyze the full text of those studies and identify the quality attributes within those studies, important for CBSSs. The data is available in the Online Material[1]. We use this information as an exercise for our future work, where we aim to develop comprehensive CBSS-specific evaluation criteria. To enable a sustainability-aware evaluation, we leverage the reflections from RQ3 to provide sub-steps to enable sustainability evaluation as an additional part of the SA evaluation blueprint.

5   Results and Discussion

In this section, we present our findings per each research question (RQ). Based on these findings, we present a blueprint of the SA evaluation method and identify the challenges and recommendations, in general, and specifically in the context of the 4D-sustainability of CBSS architectures.

RQ1 - Input & Output Artifacts
We answer RQ1, in light of the findings from our preliminary work consisting of a systematic literature review [11]. We identify the common input and output artifacts of the SA evaluation methods, their limitations and possible improvements.

Most SA evaluation methods are not clear about the type of input information they need for the initiation of the SA evaluation process. We identify these inputs from the description of SA evaluation methods in the reviewed studies (see Table 1). The completion of the SA evaluation process produces output artifacts, which are normally included in an evaluation report (see Table 2). Many

Table 1. Types of inputs used for SA Evaluation

Input Type	Study ID
SA Description	S1, S5, S7, S8, S11, S17, S20, S21, S22, S30, S33, S36, S37, S39, S42, S44, S48, S55, S62, S64, S66, S69, S70
Scenarios	S5, S6, S7, S10, S12, S15, S21, S34, S37, S38, S41, S42, S50, S51, S65
Requirements	S24, S25, S28, S39, S44, S45, S48, S50, S53, S64
QAs	S6, S24, S35, S36, S46, S59, S60, S68
Goals	S5, S6, S15, S19, S33, S39, S59
SA Specification	S2, S16, S26, S29, S43, S52, S57
UML	S14, S31, S40, S49, S63
Source Code	S4, S23, S44, S47
Quality Concerns	S8, S17, S18
SA Candidates	S46, S68
Metrics	S11, S54
Design Properties	S56, S57
Documentation	S9, S32
SA Drivers	S20
Context Diagrams	S31
SA Strategies	S65
Architecture Views	S42
Simulation Model	S67
Usability Profile	S27
Fault Domain Model	S30
Risks	S15
Usage Profile	S10
SA and SC* Models	S13
Execution profiles of UML scenarios	S3
UI Prototype	S3

*SC=Source Code. See Online Material[1] for Study IDs

methods skip initial SA evaluation steps and require an input that might be an output of one of the SA evaluation steps. For example, scenarios are produced as a part of the SA evaluation process. However, some methods rely on scenarios as input without performing scenario identification [25].

> *A structured template for the inputs/outputs per step, would aid in structuring the evaluation process. The inclusion of decision rationale as an output artifact would aid architects in better decision-making for future changes.*

Table 2. Types of Outputs of SA Evaluation

Output Type	Study ID
Quantified QAs	S37, S49, S54, S55, S56, S57, S59, S60, S61, S63, S67
Metric Values	S19,S53,S29,S30,S23,S26
QA Conformance	S2, S12, S50, S48, S36
Risks	S1, S6, S38, S58
Architectural Approaches	S32, S33, S69, S70
Component Interactions	S14, S16, S18
Cost Benefit	S15, S34, S65
Impact of Architectural Decisions	S25, S28, S66
Probability of achieving quality	S40, S43
Scenario classification and ranking	S7, S39
Architectural Recommendations	S11, S66
Risk Factors	S3, S31
Uncertainty Levels	S35, S68
Evaluation Report	S13, S44
Decision Rationale	S15, S16
Scenario Description	S51, S71
Design goal violations	S4
Dependency Model	S23
Improvements	S8
Strong and weak points	S9
Acceptance Levels	S10
SA Rating	S17
Prioritized ASRs*	S45
Impact of modifiability	S5
Dependency Graph	S47
Prioritized Architectural Views	S46
Warnings	S52
Evolvability Guidelines	S20
Evolvability Points	S20
Suitability	S68

*ASR = Architecturally Significant Requirement. See Online Material[1] for Study IDs

RQ2 - SA Evaluation Blueprint

To answer RQ2, we analyze the studies presenting SA evaluation methods, to elicit the evaluation steps and the process organization.

Types of Processes. Our analysis shows that existing SA evaluation methods can be grouped into 3 categories based on the type of process they follow to carry out the evaluation activities.

1. *Sequential.* All evaluation steps are performed in a sequence, one-time each.
2. *Iterative.* All steps or a set of steps, are performed iteratively. An iteration is usually confined to the steps of the analysis phase. This iterative nature of the SA evaluation methods enables the evaluators to ponder over the implications of the design decisions. It further aids them in performing an improvement-driven trade-off- and impact- analysis.
3. *Phase-based.* Such methods divide the evaluation process into multiple phases. Based on the type of method, the steps can be either, (i) *Unique.* All steps are divided into several phases, or (ii) *Common.* The same steps are repeated in each phase with different goals and architectural artifacts per each phase [26].

Certain methods combine iterative and phase-based methods, where iterations can occur at the phase level or within individual steps of a phase.

SA Evaluation Steps. We identify the SA evaluation steps from the studies presenting SA evaluation methods. These steps are further analyzed in terms of (i) Commonalities in steps, (ii) Phases of evaluation, and (iii) Sequence of steps and iteration patterns. The data of the SA evaluation steps can be found in Online Material[1].

Common Steps. In our analysis, we observe that ATAM [14] is the baseline that, to various extents, other SA evaluation methods follow. Based on the analysis of SA evaluation steps and their comparison with steps of ATAM, we identify 11 common steps and present them as a blueprint for SA evaluation (see Fig. 1).

Phases of Evaluation. Inspired by ATAM [14], we divide the common steps of SA evaluation methods into three phases, (i) Pre-Evaluation (ii) In-Evaluation (iii) Post-evaluation (see Fig. 1 for the steps within each phase).

Sequence of Steps and Iteration Patterns. In Fig. 1, we illustrate the SA evaluation steps divided into multiple phases. We further represent the iteration and change in the sequence of steps during evaluation.

SA evaluation process naturally starts with a `Pre-Evaluation` phase consisting of two steps; `Preparation` and `Requirement Identification`. However, these steps are found missing in the majority of SA evaluation methods.

Next, comes the `In-Evaluation` phase. The first three steps in this phase are quite consistent in their placement among the sequence of steps in all evaluation methods. These are `Goal Identification`, `Method Presentation` and `Architecture Presentation`. Instead of the `Pre-Evaluation` phase, many methods use at least one or all of the above three steps, as a starting point.

In our analysis, two types of `Prioritization` steps are observed.
(a) Prioritization **of** *evaluation criteria.* It refers to an early prioritization of QAs, requirements, or evaluation perspectives (e.g. a specific architectural view).

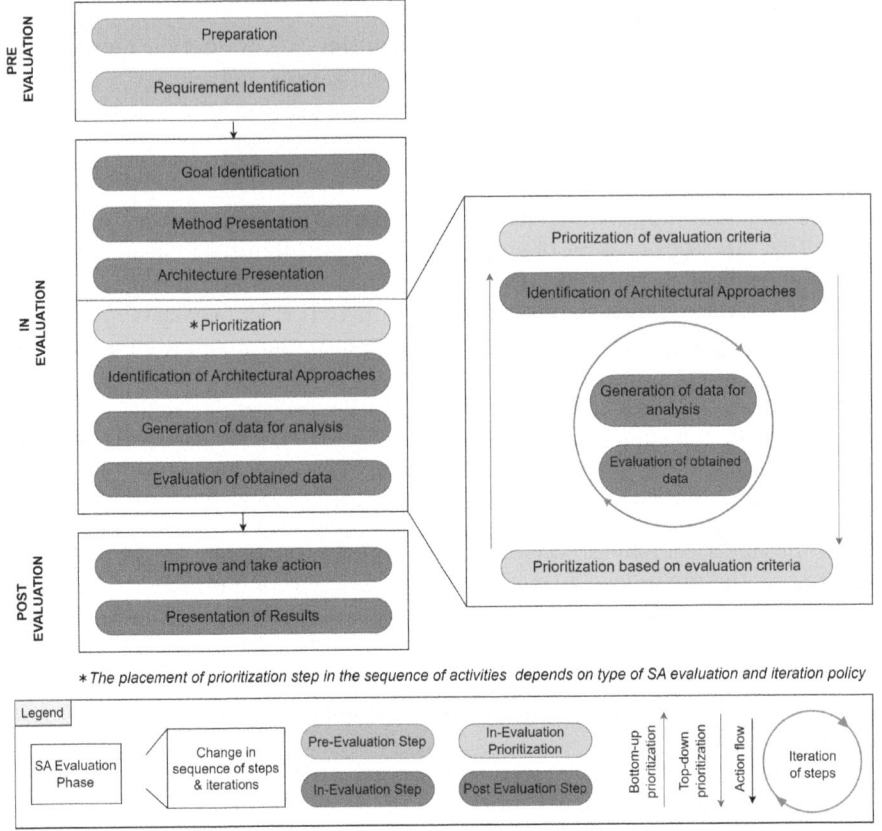

Fig. 1. Blueprint of SA Evaluation Methods

This prioritization is performed to narrow down the scope and focus of SA evaluation to high-priority QAs/requirements etc.

(b) Prioritization **Based on** *the Evaluation Criteria.* It involves prioritizing architectural decisions for scenario ranking, QA ranking, trade-off decisions, and impact analysis. For example, design decisions with positive effects on high-priority QAs may receive higher priority, or trade-off decisions may be prioritized based on their impact on critical requirements like sustainability.

The position of prioritization steps can oscillate between different steps, on an as-needed basis, facilitating a continuous improvement of the SA.

After presenting the SA, the `Identification of Architectural Approaches` takes place. The architectural approach representation can range from abstract (e.g., textual description, component diagram) to concrete (e.g., sequence diagram, source code).

Next, `Generation of data for analysis is performed`. In our blueprint, this step is independent of the evaluation technique being used. Data is generated from the identified architectural approaches based on the chosen evaluation technique. E.g., data can entail utility trees for scenario-based methods, metric computations for metric-based methods, prototypes for simulation-based methods, and Petri-net generation and execution for formal-modeling-based methods.

For `Evaluation of obtained data`, the data can be in the form of scenarios, metric values, etc. The evaluation is based on the (prioritized) requirements and goals. At this stage, some methods perform prioritization *based on* evaluation criteria. For example, one design decision may be prioritized over the other *based on* the priority *of* a scenario or a quality requirement.

Once this prioritization is completed, either the evaluation is finalized or another iteration is performed. This iteration can go back to either the generation of data or the evaluation of obtained data. This process continues until all goals have been met or the evaluators have agreed on the achieved trade-offs (see Fig. 1 - Right). For SA evaluation, prioritization can be conducted in one of two ways: (i) *Top-down* - where evaluation criteria are prioritized first, followed by prioritizing design decisions based on the established criteria, or (ii) *Bottom-up* - where the evaluation is initially carried out without prioritizing any specific criterion. Subsequently, design decisions are prioritized based on the analysis results, potentially leading to updates in the priorities of evaluation criteria.

In the `Post-evaluation` phase, analysis results are interpreted and appropriate actions are taken if needed, such as modifying the SA in the `Improve and take action` step. The `Presentation of results` concludes the process, generating a comprehensive report with all necessary output artifacts.

RQ3 - Challenges and Recommendations

To answer RQ3, we identify challenges for defining an SA evaluation method in general, and for the 4D-sustainability of CBSSs in particular. We further present recommendations that can aid in streamlining the current SA evaluation approaches.

Representation of 4D-Sustainability Needs to be Ensured By Equitable Stakeholder Representation. Our results indicate that most methods overlook ATAM (Architecture Trade-off Analysis Method) [14] Phase 0 steps, namely Partnership and Preparation. These steps involve stakeholder identification, document examination, and training. By skipping this crucial step, stakeholder identification is disregarded in the evaluation process, jeopardizing equitable stakeholder representation. In our state-of-the-art review, we found that most studies only consider technical and business stakeholders in SA evaluation. This raises concerns about the inclusion of other indirect stakeholders [3] during the evaluation. This bias in the evaluation process towards technical and economic dimensions undermines sustainability assessment. Neglecting stakeholders from social sustainability domains impedes the comprehensive 4D-sustainability awareness of SA. For example, if software users' concerns are not explicitly analyzed during SA evaluation, it can lead to unfair trade-offs and disregard the impact of design decisions on social sustainability.

> *An SA evaluation method can be stakeholder-inclusive by explicitly representing them in the process. A 4D-sustainability representation should identify indirect and hidden stakeholders.*

Heavy-Weight Methods are Prone to Non-Acceptance in Practice. In agile software organizations, incorporating heavy-weight SA evaluation methods like ATAM, which typically take at least three days for evaluation [14], can hinder fast delivery. Instead, a lightweight and continuous SA evaluation approach, as proposed by Pooley et al. [28], would be more suitable. To enhance consistency and structure in SA evaluation, standardizing the SA representation format within a project or organization can facilitate rapid adaptation to changes, while automation tools such as CSAFE [2] and SDMetrics [24] can help by extracting architectural properties, and conducting metric-based software design analysis, respectively.

> *Automation and tool-based solutions can aid in accelerating SA evaluation. A systematic process with clear templates/guides can facilitate fast(er) evaluation.*

Choice of Abstraction Level for Quantification is Complex. Scenario-based and experience-based methods are carried out at a high abstraction level (typically architecture level). Metric-based methods are carried out at a lower abstraction level (design level or code level) involving definition and collection of metrics [8,30]. Simulation-based methods evaluate the SA using ADLs [32] or source code [6], also at a lower level of abstraction.

Choosing an abstraction level for SA evaluation is complex. Hilty et al. [13] emphasize the difference between sustainability analysis at the micro- and macro-levels. They argue against performing sustainability analysis of actions at a micro-level, so to avoid missing the macro-level impact of those actions. In the context of SA, we observe this phenomenon frequently with QA trade-offs (e.g. reliability vs performance). Hence, the impact of micro-level decisions needs to be analyzed for macro-level impact; systematically.

> *An approach aggregating micro-level 4D-sustainability to macro-level 4D-sustainability is essential. Micro-level 4D-sustainability can be ensured through sustainability metrics and macro-level 4D-sustainability, through Key Performance Indicators (KPIs) and impact analysis of micro-level design decisions. Continuous impact analysis can ensure over-time sustainability impact.*

Lack of Sustainability-Specific Evaluation Criteria. The related work shows that only Koziolek [15] presents sustainability metrics that are defined at the code level and categorized based on modularization design principles, corresponding to technical sustainability. In order to provide a well-rounded view of 4D-sustainability quality, metrics are needed which provide an equitable representation of all sustainability dimensions. Liu et al. [20] present two metrics (Impact on the SA and Adaptability Degree of SA) to quantify the adaptability of SAs. In the context of over-time sustainability, similar metrics can be helpful in identifying the impact of change requirements on SA and the capacity of SA to integrate this change based on the degree of SAs adaptability and evolution.

> *Identification and measurement of comprehensive 4D-sustainability metrics is needed. In the context of over-time 4D-sustainability, architectural decisions resulting in QA trade-offs need to be analyzed for the impacts (i) on other QAs, (ii) on the sustainability dimension itself, (iii) on other sustainability dimensions, and (iv) over time, i.e., direct, enabling and systemic.*

RQ4 - Sustainability-Aware SA Evaluation of CBSS architectures. To answer RQ4, we identify CBSS-specific QAs from literature and supplement the blueprint (in Fig. 1) with additional sub-steps to ensure sustainability.

Supplementing SA Evaluation with CBSS-Specific QAs. Lee *et al.* [19] present a difference between conventional software and cloud software-as-a-service (SaaS) through the notion of quality attributes. To evaluate CBSS architectures, we identify cloud-specific QAs by conducting a small-scale systematic search as outlined in Sect. 4. Our results show that certain QAs are specifically discussed in the context of CBSSs, as having a priority (see Table 3). These CBSS-specific QAs can serve as base evaluation criteria for CBSS architectures. Our future work will explore these QAs through associated metrics for quantification and design principles for ensuring their conformance.

Table 3. Quality Attributes significant for CBSSs

QAs	References	QAs	References
Availability	$[1, 10, 19, 22, 37]$	Portability	$[22]$ $[7]$
Resource Utilization	$[19, 22, 23, 37]$	Decentrality	$[7, 12]$
Functional Correctness	$[37]$	Recoverability	$[19]$
Maintainability	$[1, 19, 22]$	Usability	$[37]$
Fault Tolerance	$[10, 19]$	Compliance	$[7, 37]$
Interoperability	$[7, 19, 22, 37]$	Configurability	$[37]$
Security	$[1, 10, 37]$	Operability	$[1]$
Scalability	$[1, 19, 22, 37]$	Elasticity	$[17]$
Response Time	$[19, 22, 23, 37]$	Reliability	$[1]$

Supplementing SA Evaluation with Sustainability

To supplement sustainability, we propose to specify the *Evaluation of obtained data* step (in Fig. 1) with 3 sub-steps (see Fig. 2). The goal of introducing this supplementary support is to make these steps explicit to ensure sustainability evaluation. The steps are (i) Trade-off analysis, (ii) Prioritization of trade-offs based on evaluation criteria, and (iii) Impact analysis. In these steps, the chosen design decisions are analyzed for possible trade-offs. The choice of selecting an appropriate trade-off is carried out using a prioritization mechanism. Next, the impact (*direct, enabling and systemic*) of the chosen trade-off, on sustainability is identified. This impact analysis is classified into 3 types. (i)

Inter-QA impact of trade-offs between prioritized CBSS-specific QAs, (ii) *Inter-dimension impact* of QA trade-offs across four sustainability dimensions, (iii) *Intra-dimension impact* of QA trade-offs within one sustainability dimension. Prioritization is a crucial sub-step here as the results of impact analysis may indicate requiring a change in prioritization of QAs or their trade-offs.

This process continues in an iterative cycle until all design decisions have been agreed upon by mutual consensus of the involved stakeholders. Although ATAM already provides a trade-off analysis mechanism, it lacks an explicit mechanism for impact analysis and continuous improvement. This mechanism is provided by adding these supplementary sub-steps to the blueprint.

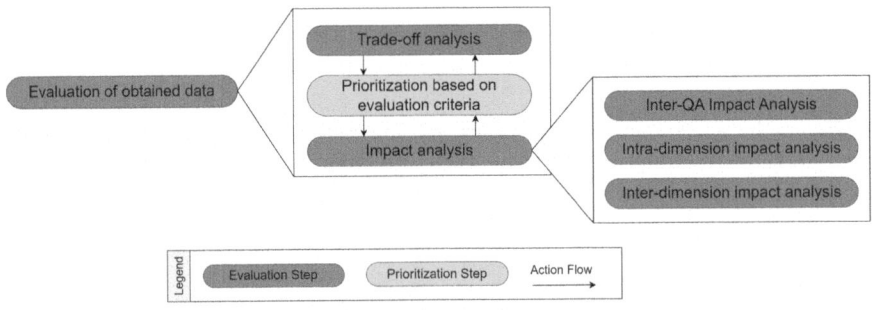

Fig. 2. Supplementary sub-steps for SA Evaluation

The blueprint itself is evaluation technique-agnostic. Evaluators have the liberty to choose a specific technique to perform impact analysis. From the results of our preliminary work [11], we find only one study by Condori-Fernandez *et al.* [9] that provides a guideline toward the impact analysis for 4D-sustainability via Sustainability Assessment Framework (SAF). We can leverage the SAF to perform this impact analysis in the context of SA evaluation.

Example. Consider the design decisions regarding scaling strategies for a CBSS architecture. Two prominent options are auto-scaling and managed scaling. Auto-scaling positively impacts availability, scalability and resource utilization with positive direct impacts across technical, economic and environmental sustainability. However, this can result in negative systemic impacts on environmental and social sustainability by fostering a mindset of infinite resource availability leading to an overall increase in the energy footprint. To perform a well-rounded SA evaluation, architects need to be equipped with an evaluation mechanism that enables them to make optimal decisions while considering sustainability dimensions and understanding the long-term impacts.

Looking ahead, our goal is to use the SA evaluation blueprint for sustainability analysis of CBSS architectures for such impacts using industrial case studies.

6   Threats to Validity

Following [36], this section explores threats to validity and mitigation strategies.

Construct Validity. The application of open coding and axial coding yields the risk of subjective bias. To mitigate this risk, the categorization is cross-reviewed by all authors. In case of inconsistencies, consensus is established through discussion, with eventual adjustments to the blueprint.

Internal Validity. To minimize internal bias, the evaluation begins with an analysis of general SA evaluation methods, which is then contextualized within the framework of sustainability and CBSS architectures. Cross-validation by the co-author is conducted to ensure objectivity and prevent any subjective bias.

External Validity. Our generic SA evaluation blueprint is enhanced for sustainability-aware evaluation using CBSS-specific QAs. This versatile blueprint can be applied to various software architectures and domains by incorporating specific QAs, and design decisions' impact on domain-specific QAs.

Reliability. The initial data for analysis was obtained through a SLR [11]. To ensure objectivity, we utilize a systematic approach to categorize and analyze SA evaluation steps, identifying common patterns and generating a blueprint. The Online Material[1] includes the data used and visualizations for categorization.

7   Conclusion and Future Work

In this paper, we leverage state-of-the-art SA evaluation methods to create a blueprint guiding SA evaluation. We (i) identify the inputs, outputs and common steps of SA evaluation methods to create a reusable blueprint (cf. RQ1-2); (ii) identify the challenges and present recommendations for a sustainability-aware SA evaluation process (cf. RQ3); (iii) supplement the blueprint with additional sub-steps for trade-offs, impact analysis and prioritization (cf. RQ4); and (iv) present preliminary results towards the evaluation criteria for CBSS architectures through CBSS-specific QAs (cf. RQ4).

In our future work, we will validate the applicability and usefulness of our blueprint. To this aim, we will conduct a case study on a CBSS-based system in the industry. We further aim to (i) identify and use evaluation criteria in terms of 4D-sustainability metrics; (ii) identify the impact of these metrics on 4D-sustainability in terms of possible trade-offs or ripple effects; and (iii) represent the sustainability-quality of CBSS architectures at a macro-level through 4D-sustainability indicators.

Acknowledgements. This publication is part of the SustainableCloud (OCENW.M20.243) project from the research program Open Competition which is (partly) financed by the Dutch Research Council (NWO).

References

1. Adjepon-Yamoah, D.E.: *cloud-ATAM*: method for analysing resilient attributes of cloud-based architectures. In: Crnkovic, I., Troubitsyna, E. (eds.) SERENE 2016. LNCS, vol. 9823, pp. 105–114. Springer, Cham (2016). https://doi.org/10.1007/978-3-319-45892-2_8

2. Admodisastro, N., Kotonya, G.: An architecture analysis approach for supporting black-box software development. In: Crnkovic, I., Gruhn, V., Book, M. (eds.) ECSA 2011. LNCS, vol. 6903, pp. 180–189. Springer, Heidelberg (2011). https://doi.org/10.1007/978-3-642-23798-0_17

3. Alidoosti, R., Lago, P., Poort, E., Razavian, M., Tang, A.: Incorporating ethical values into software architecture design practices. In: IEEE 19th Int. Conf. on Software Architecture Companion (2022)

4. Babar, M.A., Gorton, I.: Comparison of scenario-based software architecture evaluation methods. In: 11th Asia-Pacific Softw. Eng. Conference. IEEE (2005)

5. Bass, L., Clements, P., Kazman, R.: Software Architecture in Practice, 4th edn. Addison-Wesley Professional (2021)

6. Cavalcante, E., Quilbeuf, J., Traonouez, L.-M., Oquendo, F., Batista, T., Legay, A.: Statistical model checking of dynamic software architectures. In: Tekinerdogan, B., Zdun, U., Babar, A. (eds.) ECSA 2016. LNCS, vol. 9839, pp. 185–200. Springer, Cham (2016). https://doi.org/10.1007/978-3-319-48992-6_14

7. Chauhan, M.A., Babar, M.A.: Cloud infrastructure for providing tools as a service: Quality attributes and potential solutions. In: Proc. of the WICSA/ECSA Companion Volume. ACM (2012)

8. Christensen, H.B., Hansen, K.M., Lindstrøm, B.: Lightweight and continuous architectural software quality assurance using the aSQA Technique. In: Babar, M.A., Gorton, I. (eds.) ECSA 2010. LNCS, vol. 6285, pp. 118–132. Springer, Heidelberg (2010). https://doi.org/10.1007/978-3-642-15114-9_11

9. Condori-Fernandez, N., Lago, P., Luaces, M.R., Places, A.S.: An action research for improving the sustainability assessment framework instruments. Sustainability: Science Practice and Policy, vol. 12, no. 4 (2020)

10. Devata, S., Olmsted, A.: Modeling non-functional requirements in cloud hosted application software engineering. In: The 7th Int. Conf. on Cloud Computing, GRIDs, and Virtualization. IARIA (2016)

11. Fatima, I., Lago, P.: A review of software architecture evaluation methods for sustainability assessment. In: 20th Int. Conf. on Software Architecture Companion (ICSA-C). IEEE (2023)

12. Gochhayat, S.P., Shetty, S., Mukkamala, R., Foytik, P., Kamhoua, G.A., Njilla, L.: Measuring decentrality in blockchain based systems. IEEE Access **8**, 178372–178390 (2020)

13. Hilty, L.M., Aebischer, B.: ICT for sustainability: an emerging research field. In: Hilty, L.M., Aebischer, B. (eds.) ICT Innovations for Sustainability. AISC, vol. 310, pp. 3–36. Springer, Cham (2015). https://doi.org/10.1007/978-3-319-09228-7_1

14. Kazman, R., Barbacci, M., Klein, M., Carrière, S.J., Woods, S.G.: Experience with performing architecture tradeoff analysis. In: Int. Conf. on Software Engineering, IEEE/ACM (1999)

15. Koziolek, H.: Sustainability evaluation of software architectures: a systematic review. In: 7th Int. Conf. on the Quality of Softw. Architectures and 2nd Int. Symposium on Architecting Critical Systems, ser. QoSA-ISARCS '11. ACM (2011)

16. Koziolek, H., Domis, D., Goldschmidt, T., Vorst, P.: Measuring architecture sustainability. IEEE Softw. **30**(6), 54–62 (2013)
17. Kuperberg, M., Herbst, N.R., von Kistowski, J., Reussner, R.H.: Defining and quantifying elasticity of resources in cloud computing and scalable platforms. In:Karlsruhe Reports in Informatics (2011)
18. Lago, P., Koçak, S.A., Crnkovic, I., Penzenstadler, B.: Framing sustainability as a property of software quality. Commun. ACM **58**(10) (2015)
19. Lee, J.Y., Lee, J.W., Cheun, D.W., Kim, S.D.: A quality model for evaluating software-as-a-service in cloud computing. In: 7th ACIS Int. Conf. on Software Engineering Research, Management and Applications (2009)
20. Liu, X., Wang, Q.: Study on application of a quantitative evaluation approach for software architecture adaptability. In: 5th Int. Conf. on Quality Software (2005)
21. Mattsson, M., Grahn, H., Mårtensson, F.: Software architecture evaluation methods for performance, maintainability, testability, and portability. In: Int. Conf. on the Quality of Software Architectures (2006)
22. Nadanam, P., Rajmohan, R.: QoS evaluation for web services in cloud computing. In: 3rd Int. Conf. on Computing, Commun. and Networking Technol. (2012)
23. Nogueira, L., Barros, A., Zubia, C., Faura, D., Gracia Pérez, D., Miguel Pinho, L.: Non-functional requirements in the elastic architecture. Ada Lett. **40**(1) (2020)
24. Nuraini, A., Widyani, Y.: Software with service oriented architecture quality assessment. In: Int. Conf. on Data and Software Engineering (ICODSE) (2014)
25. Ojameruaye, B., Bahsoon, R., Duboc, L.: Sustainability Debt: A Portfolio-based approach for evaluating sustainability requirements in architectures. In: 38th Int. Conf. on Software Engineering Companion (ICSE-C). IEEE/ACM (2016)
26. Olumofin, F.G., Mišic, V.B.: A holistic architecture assessment method for software product lines. Information and Software Technology (2007)
27. Penzenstadler, B.: Towards a definition of sustainability in and for software engineering. In: Proc. of the 28th Annual ACM Symp. on Applied Comput. (2013)
28. Pooley, R., Abdullatif, A.: CPASA: continuous performance assessment of software architecture. In: 2010 17th IEEE Int. Conf. and Workshops on Engineering of Computer Based Systems (2010)
29. Sahlabadi, M., Muniyandi, R.C., Shukur, Z., Qamar, F.: Lightweight software architecture evaluation for industry: a comprehensive review. Sensors (Basel) **22**(3) (2022)
30. Sant'Anna, C., Figueiredo, E., Garcia, A., Lucena, C.J.P.: On the modularity of software architectures: a concern-driven measurement framework. In: Oquendo, F. (ed.) ECSA 2007. LNCS, vol. 4758, pp. 207–224. Springer, Heidelberg (2007). https://doi.org/10.1007/978-3-540-75132-8_17
31. Seacord, R., et al.: Measuring software sustainability. In: Int. Conf. on Software Maintenance. ICSM. Proc. (2003)
32. Sion, L., Van Landuyt, D., Yskout, K., Joosen, W.: SPARTA: security & privacy architecture through risk-driven threat assessment. In: Int. Conf. on Software Architecture Companion (ICSA-C). IEEE (2018)
33. Soares, R.C., Capilla, R., dos Santos, V., Nakagawa, E.Y.: Trends in continuous evaluation of software architectures. Computing (2023)
34. Sobhy, D., Bahsoon, R., Minku, L., Kazman, R.: Evaluation of software architectures under uncertainty. ACM Trans. Softw. Eng. Methodol. **30**(4), 1–50 (2021)
35. Strauss, A., Corbin, J.M., Corbin, J.: Basics of Qualitative Research: Techniques and Procedures for Developing Grounded Theory. SAGE Publications, Inc. (1998)

36. Zhou, X., Jin, Y., Zhang, H., Li, S., Huang, X.: A map of threats to validity of systematic literature reviews in software engineering. In: Asia-Pacific Software Engineering Conference, ser. APSEC. IEEE Computer Society, pp. 153–160 (2016)
37. Younas, M., et al.: Elicitation of nonfunctional requirements in agile development using cloud computing environment. IEEE Access **8**, 209153–209162 (2020)

Technical Debt in Microservices: A Mixed-Method Case Study

Roberto Verdecchia(✉)⑩, Kevin Maggi, Leonardo Scommegna⑩, and Enrico Vicario⑩

Department of Information Engineering, University of Florence, Florence, Italy
{roberto.verdecchia,leonardo.scommegna,enrico.vicario}@unifi.it,
kevin.maggi@edu.unifi.it

Abstract. *Background:* Despite the rising interest of both academia and industry in microservice-based architectures and technical debt, the landscape remains uncharted when it comes to exploring the technical debt evolution in software systems built on this architecture. *Aims:* This study aims to unravel how technical debt evolves in software-intensive systems that utilize microservice architecture, focusing on (i) the patterns of its evolution, and (ii) the correlation between technical debt and the number of microservices. *Method:* We employ a mixed-method case study on an application with 13 microservices, 977 commits, and 38k lines of code. Our approach combines repository mining, automated code analysis, and manual inspection. The findings are discussed with the lead developer in a semi-structured interview, followed by a reflexive thematic analysis. *Results:* Despite periods of no TD growth, TD generally increases over time. TD variations can occur irrespective of microservice count or commit activity. TD and microservice numbers are often correlated. Adding or removing a microservice impacts TD similarly, regardless of existing microservice count. *Conclusions:* Developers must be cautious about the potential technical debt they might introduce, irrespective of the development activity conducted or the number of microservices involved. Maintaining steady technical debt during prolonged periods of time is possible, but growth, particularly during innovative phases, may be unavoidable. While monitoring technical debt is the key to start managing it, technical debt code analysis tools must be used wisely, as their output always necessitates also a qualitative system understanding to gain the complete picture.

Keywords: Technical Debt · Microservices · Software Evolution

1 Introduction

As companies seek to take advantage of their many benefits, microservice-based architectures are becoming more and more adopted. As often referenced, the

R. Verdecchia and K. Maggi—The first two authors contributed equally to this work.

B. Tekinerdoğan et al. (Eds.): ECSA 2023, LNCS 14590, pp. 217–236, 2024.
https://doi.org/10.1007/978-3-031-66326-0_14

microservice architecture style offers several advantages, such as scalability, flexibility, and the ability to develop and deploy individual components independently [11]. Albeit the many benefits microservice-based systems offer, the architectural style also comes with its own set of challenges, including increased complexity, the need for effective management of eventual consistency, and additional effort required for integration and system testing.

In this context, we can intuitively conjecture that, in order to cope with the increased complexity and potential loss of the bigger architectural picture, developers may tend to adopt suboptimal implementation expedients. While providing temporary benefits, such expedients may tend to make future development harder or even impossible. This concept of software quality issues related to temporary expedients is commonly referred to as technical debt (TD) [5].

TD is one of the paramount factors in software development practice. If left unmanaged, TD can lead, among other consequences, to lower development speed, raise of a high number of bugs, or even completely crystallized architectures [39]. TD has been widely covered in academic literature [3,27,41] and is increasing in research popularity. Similarly, albeit the adoption of microservice architectural style could be considered as a relatively new phenomenon, its widespread adoption recently drew a considerable academic interest [12,17,34].

Surprisingly, while both TD and microservices could be considered as popular topics in current academic literature, there has been relatively little focus on the relationship between TD and microservice architectures. To date, few studies have considered how TD evolves in microservice systems and, to the best to our knowledge, none have quantitatively studied in depth the characteristics of such evolution.

With this research, through a mixed-method case study on an open-source project comprising 12 microservices (see Sect. 3.4), we make a first step towards understanding how TD changes as microservice-based systems evolve. Our goal is to pave the way for future empirical studies that investigate the evolution of this relationship. By understanding how TD evolves in microservice architectures, and gaining insights into the characteristics of such evolution, we might be able to shed light on how TD can be effectively managed in microservice architectures, with the end goal of better supporting the long-term success of software-intensive systems based on such architectural style.

The main contributions of this research are (i) a quantitative case study reporting TD measurements through the evolution of a microservice-based software system, (ii) a thorough statistical analysis complemented by a manual code inspection and discussion of the results, (iii) a qualitative assessment of the gathered results *via* an interview with the leading developer and subsequent reflexive thematic analysis, and (iv) a replication package containing the entirety of the raw, intermediate, and final data, analysis traces, and code used for this study.

This work extends the preliminary case study presented at the first International Workshop on Quality in Software Architecture (QUALIFIER) [40] by complementing the investigation with an interview with the leading developer of the case study, analyzed *via* reflexive thematic analysis, which is used to gain further insights into the results and assess our conjectures on their interpretation.

2   Related Work

By considering the academic literature that focuses on TD in microservice-based systems we can identify, to the best of our knowledge, only a handful of studies.

The research of Lenarduzzi *et al.* [25], where the effects of migrating from a monolithic to a microservice architecture can have on TD are investigated, might potentially be the most similar to this work. As our study, the research presents a case study based on repository mining and static code analysis. In contrast to such study however, we (i) do not focus on the effects of migrating from monolithic to microservice architecture, (ii) aim to study various characteristics affecting TD (*e.g.*, number of microservices), and (iii) consider as case study a software-intensive system which comprises 13 microservices instead of the 5 studied by Lenarduzzi *et al.* [25].

By inspecting the other related literature, TD in microservices appears to be investigated primarily from a qualitative point of view. In a study by Toledo *et al.* [35], a multiple case study based on 25 interviews investigating architectural TD (ATD) in microservices is reported. The results of the investigation identified ATD issues, their negative impact, and the common solutions used to repay each debt type. Differently to such study, we focus on code TD [19,27], utilize a quantitative rather than qualitative research method, and focus on a case study. In a similar work by Toledo *et al.* [16], through a qualitative analysis of documents and interviews, ATD in the communication layer of microservice-based architecture is investigated. The main contribution of the paper is a list of debt types specific to the communication layer of a microservice-based architecture, as well as their associated negative impact, and solutions to repay the debt types. Regarding the differences w.r.t. our work, the same considerations previously elicited for the other study of Toledo *et al.* [35] apply.

Bogner *et al.* [10] adopted 17 semi-structured interviews to study how the sustainable evolution of 14 microservice-based systems was ensured. Albeit from the results ATD emerged as a relevant issue, differently from our study, the work of Bogner *et al.*does not explicitly focus on TD. As additional difference w.r.t. our work, while tool-based DevOps processes were often mentioned as a mean to assure evolvability, the study is based on a qualitative rather than quantitative empirical research method. Bogner *et al.*, in a different study [9], surveyed 60 software professionals *via* an online questionnaire to learn how technical debt can be limited through maintainability assurance. Results indicated that using explicit and systematic techniques benefits software maintainability. As for the previous studies, also this work by Bogner *et al.* [9] adopts a qualitative rather than quantitative research approach. In addition, albeit both the study of Bogner *et al.* [9] and this work consider TD in microservices, the primary focus of Bogner *et al.*is on studying maintainability assurance techniques, while the one of this work is on TD evolution in microservice-based software-intensive systems.

Related to the concept of TD in microservice-based systems, Pagazz-ini et al. [31] present the extension of the tool Arcan [20] to detect microservice smells. As main difference with this work, the Arcan extension focuses on archi-tectural smells rather than focusing explicitly on TD, and does not carry out a case study on TD evolution.

A more systematic literature review on TD in microservices w.r.t. this related work section is conducted by Villa et al. [43]. Based on the analysis of 12 primary studies, Villa et al.corroborate the intuition grounding this study, namely the absence of qualitative studies focusing on the evolution of TD in microservice-based systems. From the results of Villa et al., ATD and code debt result to be the most frequently reported debt types for microservices. Such finding, which reflects the general trend observed for TD in developer discussions [2,24], pro-vides further support to the focus of this work on the evolution of code TD in microservice-based systems.

3   Study Design and Execution

In this section, we document the research design and execution of the study, in terms of research goal (Sect. 3.1), research questions (Sect. 3.2), and research process (Sect. 3.3).

3.1   Research Goal

The goal of this research is to conduct a preliminary investigation into the evo-lution of TD in software-intensive systems utilizing a microservice architecture. By using the Goal-Question-Metric framework of Basili et al. [8], our goal is:

Analyze *software evolution*
For the purpose of *studying trends and characteristics*
With respect to *technical debt*
From the viewpoint of *software engineering researchers*
In the context of *microservice-based software-intensive systems.*

In this study, we opt to focus on code TD [27], rather than other TD types (*e.g.*, ATD) guided to multiple factors, namely (i) code TD is one of the most frequent TD types appearing in microservice-based systems [43], (ii) in contrast to the other TD types, code TD is supported by a vast range of consolidated off the shelf tools, which are vastly used both in academic research and industrial practice [6], (iii) the focus on code TD allows for the natural extension of this preliminary case study to future heterogeneous case studies.

3.2   Research Questions

Based on the goal of our study, we can derive the main research question (RQ) and sub-research questions which guide our research.

The main RQ on which this study is based can be formulated as follows:

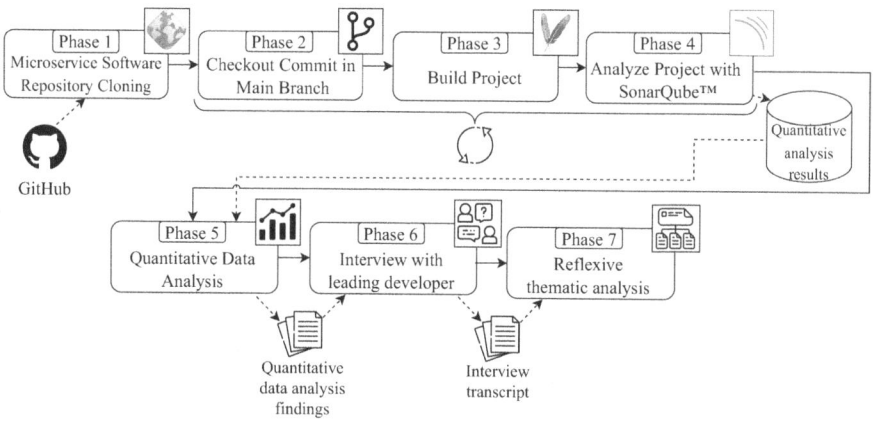

Fig. 1. Research process overview.

RQ: *How does code technical debt evolve in a microservice-based software-intensive system?*

With this main RQ, which encompasses the overall goal of the study, we broadly express our intent to study the evolution of code TD in microservice-based systems. To be more systematic, we decompose our main RQ into two sub-RQs, each one considering a different facet of TD evolution in microservice-based software intensive systems.

RQ₁: *What is the evolution trend of TD in a microservice-based software-intensive system?*

With RQ_1, we aim to understand the overall evolution trend of TD in microservice-based systems, *e.g.*, if TD is constant through the evolution of a microservice-based software-centric system, if TD showcases a growing trend in time, or if the system is characterized by a seasonal TD trend (e.g., if developers are more prone to incur in TD before/after seasonal holidays).

RQ₂: *Is there a relation between TD evolution and number of microservices?*

With RQ_2, we aim to understand if a relation exists between the evolution of TD and the number of microservices composing a software-intensive system. As example, we could conjecture that, due to suboptimal practices, as the number of microservices grows, TD grows at a higher rate (*e.g.*, TD is in superlinear or even exponential relation with the number of microservices).

3.3   Research Process

An overview of the process followed in this study is depicted in Fig. 1, and is further documented below.

The research process consists of five phases, from cloning the case study software repository containing a microservice-based software project, to the static analysis of its source code, and the concluding statistical and manual analysis of the collected data. Each research phase is described in detail in the following.

3.4   Phase 1: Microservice Software Repository Cloning

The first step of our research process consists in cloning a repository containing a microservice-based software project. For this preliminary case study, we select the software repository `Cloud Native GeoServer`.[1] The project is a microservice implementation of GeoServer, an open source server for sharing geospatial data. `Cloud Native Geoserver` splits the original GeoServer geospatial services and API offerings into individually deployable components of a microservices based architecture.

The case study is selected starting from the manually validated list of microservice-based open-source projects hosted on GitHub elicited by Baresi *et al.* [7]. The project is selected from the list by considering as selection criteria (SC_1) the real use of the application, (SC_2) the number of times the repository is forked and starred, (SC_3) the number of repository commits, and (SC_4) the number of microservices the project comprises. We use SC_1 to exclude as potential case study a toy project and demo. SC_2 instead provides us assurance on the quality and popularity of the repository. Finally, SC_3 and SC_4 guarantee us that the project is representative of a long-lived, complex, software application based on a microservie-based architecture. `Cloud Native GeoServer` to date is forked a total of 52 times and starred 176 times. The repository currently counts a total of 985 commits, comprises 13 distinct microservices, and is composed of 38k lines of code (NCLOC), and is contributed to by 10 developers.[2]

3.5   Phase 2: Checkout Commit in Main Branch

The second phase of our research consists in checking out in temporal order the commits of the selected repository. For this process, we opt to consider the commits present in the main branch of the selected repository. While we are aware of the potential pitfalls implied by considering exclusively the main branch during repository mining processes [23], we deem analyzing also other branches as out of scope for this preliminary investigation. Related threats to validity are discussed in Sect. 5.

3.6   Phase 3: Build Project

After checking out a commit, the project is built by using the build automation tool used by the case study software-intensive system, namely Maven[3]. This step is a prerequisite for the analysis of the project *via* SonarQube (Phase 4, see Sect. 3.7), as the tool requires the compiled code of the software project in order to analyze it.

During this step, 7 out of 985 builds result to fail (0.7% of all builds). Upon inspection, we identify the failure to be caused by issues related to the Project

---

[1] http://geoserver.org/geoserver-cloud. Accessed 4th July 2023.

[2] https://github.com/geoserver/geoserver-cloud. Accessed 4th July 2023.

[3] https://maven.apache.org. Accessed 4th July 2023.

Object Model (POM) of the Maven build. Rather than using a subjective heuristic to fix the issue, we opt to discard the commits associated to these failing builds. A single commit results instead to be characterized by an erroneous date in the versioning system. In order to avoid to independently estimate the correct commit date *via* some *ad hoc* heuristic, we opt to discard such commit from our analysis. Given the relatively low number of commits skipped due to build failures or dating issues (8/985 in total), we do not deem this factor to noticeably influence our results. Further considerations are reported in the threats to validity section (Sect. 5). For scrutiny and traceability purposes, the metadata of the 8 commits omitted from our analysis are documented in the replication package of this study.

To iterate and avoid possible confusion, due to the failing builds and an ill-dated commit, 977 out of the 985 total commits are considered for analysis of this study.

3.7   Phase 4: Analyze Project with SonarQube

After obtaining the compiled code of the project, the code is analyzed by utilizing the SonarQube tool. All commits are analyzed by using SonarQube version 9.9 LTS with SonarScanner for Maven version 3.9.1. During this process, in addition to the SQUALE metric measuring TD [26], other metrics and metadata of the project is collected, *e.g.,* the project size in terms of NCLOC, number of files, cognitive complexity, and committer name. To measure TD, the standard out of the box SonarQube rules configuration is used, in order to avoid subjective tempering of the tool settings.

The number of microservices appearing in each commit version is instead collected by following the method first introduced by Baresi *et al.* [7]. Such method relies on the analysis of Docker Compose files, in order to identify *via* parsing the microservices composing a software-intensive system.

Phases 2–4 are repeated for each of the 977 commits of the software project considered for this case study.

3.8   Phase 5: Data Analysis

As last quantitative step of the research process, the data collected through Steps 1–4 is analyzed to answer our RQs.

To answer RQ_1, we decompose the TD evolution trend into its seasonal, trend, and irregular components [18] by utilizing on the STL algorithm [15]. We adopt the STL algorithm as it does not assume a time series distribution, it was successfully used in previous software engineering studies [4,28], and an open-source implementation is available as an R library.[4] The resulting trend is then inspected qualitatively by graphical means. To gain further insights into

---

[4] https://stat.ethz.ch/R-manual/R-devel/library/stats/html/stl.html. Accessed 4th July 2023.

the "TD hotspots", *i.e.*, commits showcasing the most outlier values in TD measurements, the content of the outlier commits are manually scrutinized. To identify outlier values, we leverage the STL decomposition, by first removing any seasonality and trend in the TD time series, and subsequently selecting the 10 most anomalous outliers identified in the STL irregular component series for manual scrutiny.

To answer RQ_2, we first study the potential correlation between the number of microservices and TD time series. Afterwards, we analyze the potential correlation between the derivatives of such series, to understand the relation between the growth speed of TD w.r.t. microservice number. For both cases, we test the correlation by using the Multivariate Granger causality analysis [21]. To calculate the optimal lag order for the Granger analysis, we adopt the Akaike Information Criterion [1]. As the Granger test assumes the time series to be stationary, we test such assumption *via* the Augmented Dickey-Fuller test [14]. In case the time series result to be non-stationary, we make them stationary by differencing the data, *i.e.,* by subtracting the value of each observation from the value of the previous observation in the time series.

3.9   Phase 6: Interview with Leading Developer

As closing phase of our investigation, we complement the quantitative research results collected through Phases 1 to 5 *via* a qualitative research process, namely an interview with the leading developer of Cloud Native Geoserver. This final research phase is used to validate the quantitative results collected for RQ_1 and RQ_2, gain further insights into the results, and assess our conjectures on their interpretation.

To identify the leading developer of the software project, the commit authorship of the GitHub repository is analyzed, and the most recurrent committer is contacted for confirmation of being the leading developer. The interview is conducted in a semi-structured fashion [22], with the support of a slide deck which is used to guide the interview.[5] Two weeks prior the interview, the quantitative analysis findings are shared with the leading developer, to ensure the interviewee has sufficient background knowledge and time to prepare for the interview.

The interview is composed of four main portions, namely (i) introduction and background, (ii) questions on the TD evolution in Cloud Native Geoserver, (iii) questions on the relation between TD and microservices in Cloud Native Geoserver, and (iv) closing remarks. During the introductory interview portion, we verify the familiarity of the leading developer with the repository and the TD metaphor, summarize the research procedure, and outline the goals of the interview. In the second interview portion, we ask a set of questions designed to gain insights into the TD evolution trends identified in Phase 5 (see Sect. 3.8). Specifically, for each observed TD evolution trend, we inquire about the development activities conducted in that period, the awareness of the TD trend in

---

[5] For completeness, the slide deck used, including the structured questions asked during the interview, is made available in the replication package of this study (see Sect. 5.4).

that period, and the effects of the TD trend on future development activities. Additionally, we also present our preliminary conclusions on the trend nature, in order to corroborate or disprove our suppositions. In the third interview portion, which regards the relation between TD and microservices in `Cloud Native Geoserver`, we present our quantitative results on the relation and our conjectures on the interpretation of the findings. As for the previous phase, we ask a set of questions designed to gain more insights into the quantitative data collected, and verify if we reached the correct conclusions. Finally, in the closing interview portion, we give the interviewee the opportunity to provide any additional remark on the investigated topic that we might have not covered with our previous interview questions.

Due to geographical distance, the interview is conducted *via* a Google Meet video-call. To ease the interview process, webcams are utilized to observe nonverbal communication of the interviewee, *e.g.,* hand gestures, facial expressions, and posture, and provide silent feedback to the interviewee without interrupting them [13]. The interview lasts approximately 45 min.

3.10   Phase 7: Reflexive Thematic Analysis

The interview is audio-recorded and manually transcribed by utilizing the denaturalism approach, *i.e.,* grammar errors are rectified, disturbances in the interview such as stutters are eliminated, and nonstandard accents (those not belonging to the majority) are normalized while maintaining a comprehensive and accurate transcription [29]. The transcript is then analyzed *via* reflexive thematic analysis [36] based on an open and axial coding process [33]. The adopted qualitative analysis approach allows us to cluster the incidents provided by the interviewee into different themes, and subsequently map the themes to our RQs to report the interview results in an structured and systematic fashion. In addition, adopting a reflexive approach allows us to reflect and reinterpret our conjectures on our quantitative results, revising their potentially subjective interpretation, and gain a more concrete and sound understanding of the studied case.

In the following section, the quantitative results and their reinterpretation based on the qualitative insights offered by the leading developer are reported.

4   Results

In this section we report and discuss the data gathered to answer our RQs. Specifically, in the next section (Sect. 4.1) we consider the results of RQ_1, while in Sect. 4.2 we take into account the results of RQ_2.

4.1   Results RQ_1: Evolution of TD in a Microservice-Based Software-Intensive System

As described in Sect. 3.8, in order to study the TD evolution of our case study, namely the `Cloud Native GeoServer` application, we consider three different

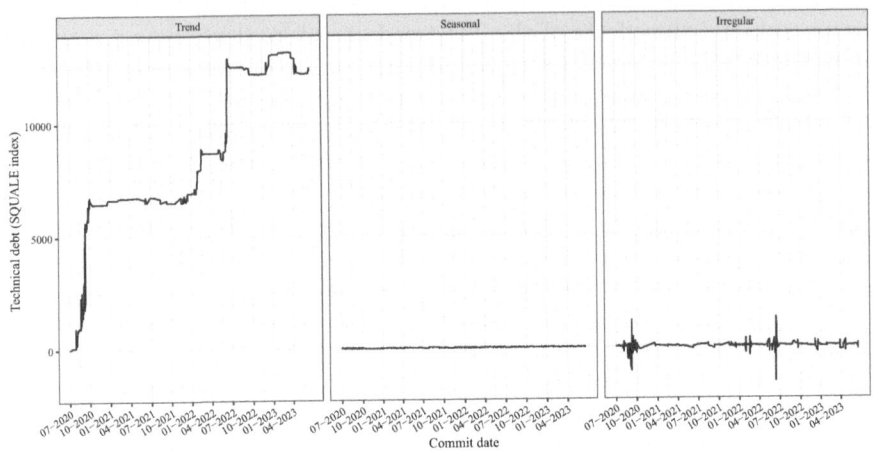

Fig. 2. Decomposition of the `Cloud Native GeoServer` application technical debt evolution *via* the STL algorithm.

components, namely the TD evolution trend, seasonality, and irregularities. An overview of such decomposition is depicted in Fig. 2.

As we can observe from the leftmost diagram of Fig. 2, the TD evolution showcases an overall growing trend. Interestingly, two outstanding jumps, *i.e.,* sudden increases in TD values, can be noticed in the plot. By comparing the trend figure with the one reporting the irregularities in TD evolution (rightmost diagram of Fig. 2), we note that such outliers are captured by the STL algorithm decomposition. The commits corresponding to such jumps are further analyzed in the second data analysis carried out to answer RQ_1, namely the manual scrutiny of the "TD hotspots" (see Sect. 3.8). Overall, as could be expected, TD tends to naturally increase during time as the application becomes bigger and more complex. From the qualitative data collected we determine that, according to the leading developer, the main reason behind the overall increasing trend is due to the lack of a systematic TD monitoring process in the development pipeline. By directly quoting the leading developer:

"The main and very actual reason for the increase of TD is the lack of monitoring it. We could have established a quality assurance policy from the beginning. For one reason or another it's something we always kept on postponing. I think that is the most relevant part."

The TD evolution trend also presents noticeable plateaus, *i.e.,* periods where the TD values remain approximately stable. The first plateau, starting from October 2020, lasts approximately one year and three months of development. By inspecting the commit dates, we note that none of the plateaus reported in the trend of Fig. 2 is due to periods of development inactivity. Therefore, we conjecture that the development periods associated to the plateaus correspond to development periods where deliberate efforts might be made to prevent a TD increase. As further discussed in the following paragraphs, spikes in TD correspond to periods of innovation and intense activity. Contrary to initial conjectures, insights from the interview reveal that the plateaus are not a result of intentional efforts to maintain TD constant. As articulated by the lead developer, these plateaus actually represent hard-earned periods of tranquil development, which followed the more tumultuous phases marked by significant jumps in TD. By quoting the leading developer:

"Seeing that almost flat line for that long period makes me happy. It means that, after all that crazyness, our development choices were not that bad."

By considering the seasonality of the time series (center diagram of Fig. 2), we can intuitively observe that no seasonal behavior is present in the TD evolution of the `Cloud Native GeoServer` application. This implies that TD is not more likely to be introduced during a certain period of the year. The leading developer confirms this conjecture by describing a general lack of seasonality in the development activities:

"We don't have an established development roadmap but we do have contracts with costumers. So it's [the release time] more based on a as needed basis and is more agile than having a six month release timeline. We actually release very often. From one week to another we can have a new release because of patching or adding new features."

As second data analysis process carried out to answer RQ_1, we manually inspect the potential "TD hotspots" (see Sect. 3.8). The most noticeable "TD hotspot" corresponds to a sudden increase in TD values recorded on June 2022 (see Fig. 2, rightmost plot). From manual scrutiny, this sudden TD variation results to be due to the upgrade of the JUnit testing framework[6]. The commit also includes the cross-microservice refactoring of test files according to the upgrade.

Other seven "hotspots", which are not graphically appreciable from the TD evolution irregularities depicted in the rightmost plot of Fig. 2, happen on the same day as the JUnit upgrade commit. Upon manual inspection, we note that the commits corresponding to these additional seven hotspots involve many microservices of the `Cloud Native GeoServer` application. The commits result to either focus on (i) further refactoring of testing artifacts, (ii) bug fixing, (iii) implementing logging mechanisms, and (iv) introducing automation processes. The leading developer confirms JUnit as being the root cause of the identified "TD hotspots", recalling the high development effort required by the upgrade:

"I did noticed as well as you did that the new JUnit 5 version provoked a jump on TD, because there are a lot of tests and we need to make all test methods and classes package private, which led to a quick [TD] spike."

Via unstructured follow up question on the TD associated to this development period, we learn that the deliberate TD taken on by upgrading JUnit paid off, by considerably easing future development activities. As described by the leading developer:

"It was refreshing. There are [in JUnit 5] new constructs... new ways to test

---

[6] https://junit.org/junit5/. Accessed 5th July 2023.

that don't require to launch the whole application. That was so time consuming. There is always a bit of a learning curve, but I would not go back to JUnit 4."

Regarding the sudden increase of TD values in October 2020 results instead, from manual inspection of the quantitative data results to be caused by the addition of 33 new files in a microservice. The commit involves the extension of the `Cloud Native GeoServer` features *via* the binding to a new JSON parser.

The last of the 10 "TD hospots" considered for manual analysis instead corresponds to a sudden increase of TD values happening in September 2020. In this case, the TD increase results to be due to a refactoring activity carried out across 70 files, which involved a considerable number of NCLOC (1.5k NCLOC additions, and 589 NCLOC deletions).

By asking about the "TD hotspost" of September and October 2020 to the leading developer, we understand that both months of noticeable TD increase are due to the early stage of the software project. During this phase, the developers get accustomed to developing the new application, learning as they go on how the project should be shaped. Taking on TD appears to be a natural consequence of this early stage development period. The lead developer recalls on this episode as follows:

"The early stages of the project were subject to a lot of activity. Figuring out mainly how to split up all GeoServer functionality into microservices, Spring Boot modules, and configurations. There was a lot of activity, and it was an intense learning period. It makes sense that until we reached some stability... we are talking about the first 3 months... it was crazy having to figure all that out."

As conclusion to RQ_1, we conclude that both working on a single microservice, or multiple ones at the same time, can drastically influence TD. Considerable TD variations can happen independently of the developer activity conducted, *e.g.,* a framework upgrade can have an unforeseen cascading impact on TD, or a refactoring activity could lead to a considerable TD increase. As could be intuitively expected, early stages of development are prone to introduce TD. In addition, taking on TD in a certain period can lead to following periods of TD steadiness, till a new cycle of development innovation is needed. As a word of caution, from the considered case study we learn that TD tool measures can be mischievous. More specifically, a steep code TD increase could also be concurrently associated with a TD decrease that is not measured by the utilized tool, as highlighted by the upgrade of JUnit in the considered case study.

RQ$_1$ answer (*TD Evolution in a Microservice-based Architecture*)
TD displays an overall increasing trend in time, albeit long periods of continued development without TD increase are noticeable. Considerable TD variations can happen by working on one or multiple microservices, and may occur regardless of the development activity conducted. Taking on in a given development phase can result in subsequent periods of TD stability, until a new wave of development innovation is needed. TD metrics can be decep-

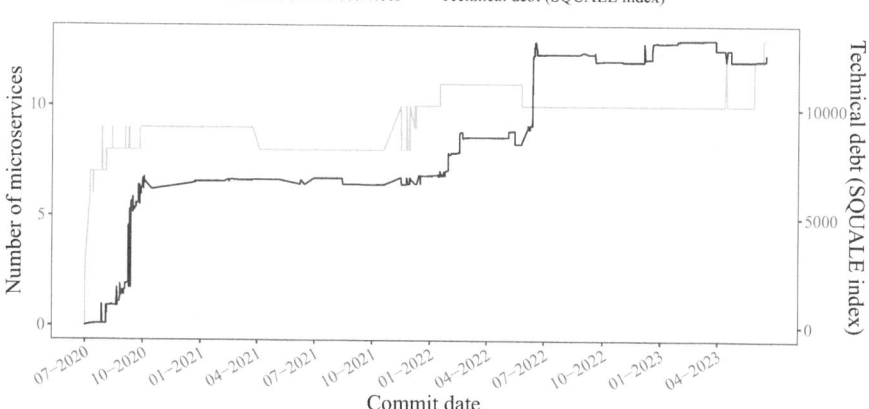

Fig. 3. Overview of the evolution of technical debt and number of microservices of the `Cloud Native GeoServer` application.

tive, as a sharp increase in code TD might coincide with an unmeasured decrease in another TD dimension.

4.2 Results RQ_2: Relation Between TD Evolution and Number of Microservices

In order to study the potential correlation between TD and number of microservices, we start by graphically inspecting the time series of the two metrics. As can be seen in Fig. 3, both TD and microservices seem to display an overall similar growth trend. However, a correlation does not appear always to be present in all commits. As example, by considering Fig. 3, we can observe that the removal of one microservice in April 2021 did not correspond to any noticeable TD decrease. In some cases, *e.g.,* April 2023, the addition of a microservice is even associated with a decrease in TD (*i.e.,* microservice number and TD are inversely proportional). This would imply that, while number of microservices could display a strong correlation of directly proportional nature, this might not always be the case.

In order to gain statistical insight into the relation, we follow the analysis process presented in Sect. 3.8. From the results of the Granger causality test we confidently reject the null hypothesis and conclude that the evolution of number of microservices and TD are strongly correlated ($p\text{-}value < 4.593^{-6}$). This implies that, albeit seldom irregularities, a growth (or decrease) of microservice number corresponds to a similar change in TD. As additional remark, this indicates that the number of microservices could be used to predict TD values.

As further analysis conducted to answer RQ_2, we study the derivatives of the two time series. This allows us to understand if the two series grow at similar rates, or if a growth in the microservice series correspond to the growth at a higher rate in the TD series. Intuitively, we could expect that, as the number of microservices increases, the software-intensive system becomes more complex, and hence TD grows at a higher rate as the system becomes bigger. From the Granger test results however, we understand that this is not the case. In fact, we observe that also the derivatives of the time series are strongly correlated ($p\text{-}value < 7.896^{-6}$), $i.e.,$ we can discard with statistical confidence the null hypothesis. This implies that the impact of adding (or removing) a microservice on TD is similar regardless of the number of microservices already present in a software-intensive system.

As subjective interpretation of this latter result, we can conjecture that this pattern indicates an appropriate adherence to the microservice architectural principles, through which microservices are developed independently by following a loosely coupled and highly cohesive architecture. From the interview with the leading developer however, we learn that this conjecture is partially inaccurate. While in fact the impact on TD of including or excluding microservice is independent of the microservices already present, the motivation behind this phenomenon is not primarily due to the microservice independence. On the contrary, as described by the leading developer, all microservices share a common architectural foundation, and each functionality implemented in the microservice heavily relies on dependencies loaded $ad\ hoc$ from the common architectural layer all microservices share. Therefore, the absent impact of microservice number on TD trends is due to the lean nature of the microservices, which enforce loose coupling by loading the functionalities from a common architectural layer. As described by the leading developer:

"It does not matter how many microservices there are in the ecosystem because architecturally there is a cross-cutting layered design. The microservice functionality itself builds up from dependencies that are usually cross-cutting. There is this cherry-picking approach on what is loaded on each microservice, but all microservices have pretty much the same dependencies on the classpath."

From the additional insights gained via the interview, we note the crucial importance of complementing quantitative source code analyses with qualitative aspects. While, during the qualitative assessment of the TD present in a software-intensive system we can conjecture on the deeper motivations behind TD values, it is only by presenting and discussing the analysis results with the developers of the system that we can get a more detailed and complete picture. Therefore, as a word of caution for software managers, product owners, and alike, it is paramount to always interpret the values provided by static analyzers with caution, and when possible qualitatively complementing the results, before taking decisions on future development activities.

RQ$_2$ answer (Relation between TD and number of microservices)
TD and number of microservices are strongly correlated, albeit in seldom cases such relation does not persist. The impact of adding (or removing)

a microservice on TD is similar, regardless of the number of microservices already present in a software-intensive system. TD tools based on source code analysis can support TD management processes. However, their results should be complemented with qualitative knowledge before making decisions on future development activities.

5   Threats to Validity

The presented results have to be interpreted in light of potential threats to validity. By following the categorization of Runeson *et al.* [32], we consider four aspects. While documented towards the end of the study, in order to avoid a common pitfall of threats to validity in software engineering research [38], threats were considered from the early stages of this investigation, as further documented below.

5.1   Construct Validity

To answer our RQs, we measured code TD by adopting the SQUALE index, a metric widely used in the literature to study TD [6,25,42]. The number of microservices was measured by utilizing the heuristic first introduced by Baresi [7] (see also Sect. 3.7). The use of the heuristic might have marginally affected our results, as it relies on the analysis of the Docker Compose file. Therefore, a service could be identified at its insertion in the Docker Compose file, which does not necessarily imply the start of its actual development. At most, this threat could have introduced a lag in the TD timeseries w.r.t. the number of microservice one (corresponding to the time elapsed from the insertion of a microservice in the Docker Compose file, and the start of its actual development). As the potential effects of this marginal threat were not noticeable in our data analysis, we do not deem the threat considerably influenced our results. The threat would at most imply a stronger correlation between microservice number and TD than the one observed. Regarding the focus on the main development branch of `Cloud Native Geoserver` (see Sect. 3.5), we note that the application possesses other two branches, which are characterized by 2 and 48 commits ahead, and 256 and 28 commits behind the master branch respectively. Given the low number of commits in such branches w.r.t. the master branch (2/985 and 48/985), we do not deem that this research design choice could have drastically influenced our results. To mitigate potential threats to construct validity due to the design of the structured interview questions, we complemented the process with follow-up questions whenever necessary, *e.g.,* when more information was required to completely understand answers. Additionally, the interviewee was frequently asked if they wanted to include any additional information on the studied topic that was not directly covered by the questions posed.

5.2   Internal Validity

To avoid potential confounding factors, we (i) discarded all failing builds, and a commit associated with an incorrect date, (ii) manually scrutinized a set of commits presenting anomalous TD values, (iii) conducted a rigorous statistical analysis on the collected data. Regarding the qualitative analysis, to avoid subjective biases during the data collection and analysis, three researchers took part to the interview, and the relevant findings were jointly discussed before including them in the paper.

5.3   External Validity

As any case study, we do not claim the complete generalizability of the obtained results. While comparable results might be observed in software-intensive systems of similar development context and characteristics as `Cloud Native GeoServer`, this could also not be the case. To partially mitigate potential threats to external validity, we selected the case study a software project developed in one of the most popular programming languages (Java), while also ensuring the representativeness of the software project *via* a set of selection criteria defined *a priori* (see also Sect. 3.4).

5.4   Reliability and Replication Package

If and to what extent the results of the study can be independently reproduced by other researchers. With exception of the manual scrutiny conducted to analyze the commits presenting the most anomalous TD values, the quantitative results are completely based on the execution of mining and data analysis scripts. We make all data, scripts, and settings available in a companion replication package[7]. Given that such results are of purely quantitative nature, we deem the reliability of such results as very high. To increase the reliability of the qualitative research process used (see Sect. 3.9), we make the guiding interview slide deck available for scrutiny in the replication package, and make extensive use of direct quotes in the manuscript to avoid subjective misinterpretation of the data collected through the interview.

6   Conclusion and Future Work

In this study, we present a preliminary case study investigating the evolution of technical debt in microservice architectures. The investigation utilizes as case study the application `Cloud Native GeoServer`, which comprises a total of 13 distinct microservices, 977 commits, and 38k NCLOC. The study is primarily based on repository mining and source code analysis. The results show that TD

---

[7] **Replication package of this study**: https://github.com/STLab-UniFI/QUALIFIER-2023-TD-microservices-rep-pkg. Accessed 6th July 2023.

evolution displays a growing trend, mostly due to development innovation periods, followed by moments of TD stability, when no disruptive change is needed. TD variation are independent of the number of microservices and development activities considered in a commit. TD and number of microservices are correlated, and adding or removing a microservice has the same impact on TD regardless the number of microservices already present.

Adhering to microservice architecture principles might keep technical debt compartmentalized within microservices, and therefore make TD more manageable w.r.t. other types of architectures (*e.g.*, monolithic ones). It is crucial for developers to remain aware of the potential TD they may incur in, irrespective of the quantity of microservices they modify or the nature of the development activity they undertake. An intuitively trivial change, such as the upgrade of a testing framework, could have a massive cascading effect on the TD of a microservice-based software-intensive system. While it is feasible to maintain a consistent level of TD during the evolution of a microservice-based application, an increase in technical debt may be inevitable as the software-intensive system grows in size and complexity.

As a word of warning for both researchers and practitioners, through the presented case study, we observe how TD metrics can be deceptive, as they may not always provide a clear and complete picture of the TD present in a software-intensive system. While conducting TD source code analyses it is therefore paramount to consider that (i) a variation in code TD may co-occur with an opposite variation in another TD aspect, (ii) code analysis results should be always complemented by qualitative knowledge (e.g., interviews or focus groups).

The leading developer however also emphasizes the importance of including TD monitoring capabilities in the development pipeline to manage TD and avoid significant consequences, *e.g.*, flaky behaviors or crystallized architectures [39]. As articulated in the interview, the leading developer states:

"It [the quantitative analysis] was quite enlightening to me. I wanted to include a static code analysis for a long time. And maybe it would have never happen or it would have taken me way too long to address if I dind't have this feedback from you".

The leading developer further reports that they are waiting for the project steering committee to integrate the repository with SonarCloud, and is currently working lowering the identified TD. From a email exchange held after the interview, we learn that the `Cloud Native GeoServer` repository underwent a considerable refactoring, leading the TD measured *via* SonarQube to be close to zero.

The presented case study has to be considered as a stepping stone for future research on TD in microservice-based systems. Several facets which could provide more information on the phenomenon are not considered in the study. As future work, we plan to (i) study the individual contribution of each microservice to the TD measured at system level, (ii) conduct a more in-depth analysis of "TD hotspots", (iii) utilize dedicated tools to measure other types of TD, *e.g.*, by combining different data sources [37] or focusing on ATD *via* the ATDx tool [30], and (iv) extend the research to a multiple-case study.

Acknowledgments. We would like to express our uttermost gratitude to Gabriel Roldan, leading developer of `Cloud Native Geoserver`, for his availability, insightful feedback, and genuine interest in the research project.

Roberto Verdecchia would like to thank Curzio Checcucci for his lighthearted yet insightful feedback on the data analysis process.

This work was partially supported by the European Union under the Italian National Recovery and Resilience Plan (NRRP) of NextGenerationEU, partnership on "Telecommunications of the Future" (PE0000001 - program "RESTART").

References

1. Akaike, H.: Information theory and an extension of the maximum likelihood principle. In: Parzen, E., Tanabe, K., Kitagawa, G. (eds.) Selected Papers of Hirotugu Akaike, pp. 199–213. Springer, Cham (1998). https://doi.org/10.1007/978-1-4612-1694-0_15
2. Aldrich Edbert, J., Jannat Oishwee, S., Karmakar, S., Codabux, Z., Verdecchia, R.: Exploring technical debt in security questions on stack overflow. In: International Symposium on Empirical Software Engineering and Measurement (2023)
3. Alves, N.S., Mendes, T.S., De Mendonça, M.G., Spínola, R.O., Shull, F., Seaman, C.: Identification and management of technical debt: a systematic mapping study. Inf. Softw. Technol. **70**, 100–121 (2016)
4. Atchison, A., Berardi, C., Best, N., Stevens, E., Linstead, E.: A time series analysis of travistorrent builds: to everything there is a season. In: 2017 IEEE/ACM 14th International Conference on Mining Software Repositories, pp. 463–466. IEEE (2017)
5. Avgeriou, P., Kruchten, P., Ozkaya, I., Seaman, C.: Managing technical debt in software engineering (dagstuhl seminar 16162). Dagstuhl Reports **6** (2016)
6. Avgeriou, P.C., et al.: An overview and comparison of technical debt measurement tools. IEEE Softw. **38**(3), 61–71 (2020)
7. Baresi, L., Quattrocchi, G., Tamburri, D.A.: Microservice architecture practices and experience: a focused look on docker configuration files. arXiv preprint: 2212.03107 (2022)
8. Basili, V.R., Caldiera, G., Rombach, D.: The goal question metric approach. In: Encyclopedia of Software Engineering, pp. 528–532. Wiley (1994)
9. Bogner, J., Fritzsch, J., Wagner, S., Zimmermann, A.: Limiting technical debt with maintainability assurance: an industry survey on used techniques and differences with service-and microservice-based systems. In: Proceedings of the 2018 International Conference on Technical Debt, pp. 125–133 (2018)
10. Bogner, J., Fritzsch, J., Wagner, S., Zimmermann, A.: Assuring the evolvability of microservices: insights into industry practices and challenges. In: 2019 IEEE International Conference on Software Maintenance and Evolution, pp. 546–556. IEEE (2019)
11. Bogner, J., Fritzsch, J., Wagner, S., Zimmermann, A.: Microservices in industry: insights into technologies, characteristics, and software quality. In: 2019 IEEE International Conference on Software Architecture Companion, pp. 187–195. IEEE (2019)

12. Bogner, J., Wagner, S., Zimmermann, A.: Automatically measuring the maintainability of service-and microservice-based systems: a literature review. In: Proceedings of the 27th International Workshop on Software Measurement and 12th International Conference on Software Process and Product Measurement, pp. 107–115 (2017)
13. Brinkmann, S.: Qualitative interviewing. Understanding Qualitative Rese (2013)
14. Cheung, Y.W., Lai, K.S.: Lag order and critical values of the augmented dickey-fuller test. J. Bus. Econ. Stat. **13**(3), 277–280 (1995)
15. Cleveland, R.B., Cleveland, W.S., McRae, J.E., Terpenning, I.: STL: a seasonal-trend decomposition. J. Off. Stat. **6**(1), 3–73 (1990)
16. De Toledo, S.S., Martini, A., Przybyszewska, A., Sjøberg, D.I.: Architectural technical debt in microservices: a case study in a large company. In: 2019 IEEE/ACM International Conference on Technical Debt, pp. 78–87. IEEE (2019)
17. Di Francesco, P., Lago, P., Malavolta, I.: Architecting with microservices: a systematic mapping study. J. Syst. Softw. **150**, 77–97 (2019)
18. Dickey, D.A., Fuller, W.A.: Distribution of the estimators for autoregressive time series with a unit root. J. Am. Stat. Assoc. **74**(366a), 427–431 (1979)
19. d'Aragona, D.A., Pecorelli, F., Baldassarre, M.T., Taibi, D., Lenarduzzi, V.: Technical debt diffuseness in the apache ecosystem: a differentiated replication. In: 2023 IEEE International Conference on Software Analysis, Evolution and Reengineering (SANER), pp. 825–833. IEEE (2023)
20. Fontana, F.A., Pigazzini, I., Roveda, R., Tamburri, D., Zanoni, M., Di Nitto, E.: ARCAN: a tool for architectural smells detection. In: 2017 IEEE International Conference on Software Architecture Workshops, pp. 282–285. IEEE (2017)
21. Granger, C.W.: Investigating causal relations by econometric models and cross-spectral methods. Econ. J. Econ. Soc. 424–438 (1969)
22. Kallio, H., Pietilä, A.M., Johnson, M., Kangasniemi, M.: Systematic methodological review: developing a framework for a qualitative semi-structured interview guide. J. Adv. Nurs. **72**(12), 2954–2965 (2016)
23. Kovalenko, V., Palomba, F., Bacchelli, A.: Mining file histories: should we consider branches? In: Proceedings of the 33rd ACM/IEEE International Conference on Automated Software Engineering, pp. 202–213 (2018)
24. Kozanidis, N., Verdecchia, R., Guzmán, E.: Asking about technical debt: characteristics and automatic identification of technical debt questions on stack overflow. In: Proceedings of the 16th ACM/IEEE International Symposium on Empirical Software Engineering and Measurement, pp. 45–56 (2022)
25. Lenarduzzi, V., Lomio, F., Saarimäki, N., Taibi, D.: Does migrating a monolithic system to microservices decrease the technical debt? J. Syst. Softw. **169**, 110710 (2020)
26. Letouzey, J.L.: The SQALE method for evaluating technical debt. In: 2012 Third International Workshop on Managing Technical Debt., pp. 31–36. IEEE (2012)
27. Li, Z., Avgeriou, P., Liang, P.: A systematic mapping study on technical debt and its management. J. Syst. Softw. **101**, 193–220 (2015)
28. Malavolta, I., Verdecchia, R., Filipovic, B., Bruntink, M., Lago, P.: How maintainability issues of android apps evolve. In: 2018 IEEE International Conference on Software Maintenance and Evolution, pp. 334–344. IEEE (2018)
29. Oliver, D.G., Serovich, J.M., Mason, T.L.: Constraints and opportunities with interview transcription: towards reflection in qualitative research. Soc. Forces **84**(2), 1273–1289 (2005)

30. Ospina, S., Verdecchia, R., Malavolta, I., Lago, P.: ATDx: a tool for providing a data-driven overview of architectural technical debt in software-intensive systems. In: European Conference on Software Architecture (2021)
31. Pigazzini, I., Fontana, F.A., Lenarduzzi, V., Taibi, D.: Towards microservice smells detection. In: International Conference on Technical Debt., Seoul, Republic of Korea, p. 6. ACM (2020). https://doi.org/10.1145/3387906.3388625
32. Runeson, P., Höst, M.: Guidelines for conducting and reporting case study research in software engineering. Empir. Softw. Eng. **14**, 131–164 (2009)
33. Saldaña, J.: The Coding Manual for Qualitative Researchers. Sage (2021)
34. Soldani, J., Tamburri, D.A., Van Den Heuvel, W.J.: The pains and gains of microservices: a systematic grey literature review. J. Syst. Softw. **146**, 215–232 (2018)
35. de Toledo, S.S., Martini, A., Sjøberg, D.I.: Identifying architectural technical debt, principal, and interest in microservices: a multiple-case study. J. Syst. Softw. **177**, 110968 (2021)
36. Vaismoradi, M., Turunen, H., Bondas, T.: Content analysis and thematic analysis: implications for conducting a qualitative descriptive study. Nurs. Health Sci. **15**(3), 398–405 (2013)
37. Verdecchia, R.: Architectural technical debt identification: moving forward. In: 2018 IEEE International Conference on Software Architecture Companion (ICSA-C), pp. 43–44 (2018). https://doi.org/10.1109/ICSA-C.2018.00018
38. Verdecchia, R., Engström, E., Lago, P., Runeson, P., Song, Q.: Threats to validity in software engineering research: a critical reflection. Inf. Softw. Technol. **164**, 107329 (2023)
39. Verdecchia, R., Kruchten, P., Lago, P., Malavolta, I.: Building and evaluating a theory of architectural technical debt in software-intensive systems. J. Syst. Softw. **176**, 110925 (2021)
40. Verdecchia, R., Maggi, K., Scommegna, L., Vicario, E.: Tracing the footsteps of technical debt in microservices: a preliminary case study. In: International Workshop on Quality in Software Architecture (2023)
41. Verdecchia, R., Malavolta, I., Lago, P.: Architectural technical debt identification: the research landscape. In: Proceedings of the 2018 International Conference on Technical Debt, pp. 11–20 (2018)
42. Verdecchia, R., Malavolta, I., Lago, P., Ozkaya, I.: Empirical evaluation of an architectural technical debt index in the context of the apache and Onap ecosystems. PeerJ Comput. Sci. **8**, e833 (2022)
43. Villa, A., Ocharan-Hernandez, J.O., Perez-Arriaga, J.C., Limon, X.: A systematic mapping study on technical debt in microservices. In: 2022 10th International Conference in Software Engineering Research and Innovation. IEEE (2022)

TQPropRefiner: Interactive Comprehension and Refinement of Specifications on Transient Software Quality Properties

Sebastian Frank[1,2]([⊠]) [iD], Julian Brott[1] [iD], Alireza Hakamian[2] [iD],
and André van Hoorn[1] [iD]

[1] University of Hamburg, Hamburg, Germany
{andre.van.hoorn,sebastian.frank}@uni-hamburg.de
[2] University of Stuttgart, Stuttgart, Germany

Abstract. Microservice-based systems are exposed to transient behavior caused, for example, by (frequent) deployments, failures, or self-adaption. The potential complexity of transient behavior scenarios makes specifying flawless transient behavior requirements challenging. Still, the required approaches and tooling to comprehend transient behavior and refine the requirements are lacking.

This paper aims to address this gap by providing a structured interactive approach that assists software architects in comprehending transient behavior and refining requirements. The prototypically implemented TQPropRefiner allows specifying transient behavior requirements using PSP. Then, TQPropRefiner uses runtime verification to evaluate requirement satisfaction on time-series data, e.g., from Chaos Experiments. TQPropRefiner visualizes the system's behavior and requirement satisfaction to foster comprehension. Based on the gathered insights, users can refine their requirements. In particular, TQPropRefiner currently supports refining timing constraints and simple predicates. Finally, we evaluated the feasibility and practical applicability of our early approach in a qualitative user study with five industry experts. All participants could interpret the results, and four solved the refinement task successfully. Despite currently limited support of PSP and refinement strategies, the preliminary results indicate that the approach can facilitate understanding transient behavior requirements among software architects and assist in the refinement process. Thus, our work is a first step toward facilitating the comprehension of transient behavior and refinement of requirements.

Keywords: Transient Behavior · Requirements · Comprehension · Refinement · Property Specification Patterns

1 Introduction

In the last decade, major software companies have tended to deploy large applications in the cloud as small (micro-)services and benefited from greater agility,

© The Author(s), under exclusive license to Springer Nature Switzerland AG 2024
B. Tekinerdoğan et al. (Eds.): ECSA 2023, LNCS 14590, pp. 237–254, 2024.
https://doi.org/10.1007/978-3-031-66326-0_15

reduced complexity, and more effective application scaling in cloud environments [27]. Due to their flexibility, microservice-based software systems are suitable for operating under frequent changes, e.g., load peaks, autoscaling, (re-)deployments, or failures. Changes in a software system usually temporarily affect the quality properties of a software system, e.g., response times increase due to a service failure. The term *transient behavior* denotes the system's behavior during the phase in which the system is not in a steady state. While it is theoretically possible to minimize transient behavior, it is practically infeasible as, for example, costly overprovisioning of resources would be necessary. Furthermore, external and unexpected events like load peaks and service failures can hardly be avoided. Thus, in practice, transient behavior is often accepted.

In an interview with experienced software engineers [4], we previously investigated whether transient behavior should be specified. Most experts stated it makes sense to specify requirements regarding transient behavior for critical systems explicitly. In such cases, it is important to make quality requirements and expectations regarding transient behavior explicit and to (in-)validate them [12]. For example, a too-long service recovery time may lead to customer frustration. Furthermore, disproving the expectation of the reaction time of an autoscaler can indicate severe problems in the system design and configuration.

However, flawlessly specifying transient behavior is challenging. This is due to the complexity involved in the changes triggering transient behavior and the dynamic nature of transient behavior. When eliciting resilience scenarios in previous work [16], we found that software architects were interested in validating that their resilience mechanisms proved helpful when transient behavior occurs, e.g., "autoscaling will be helpful". One challenge is that specifying exact parameter values involves a lot of uncertainty among software architects, i.e., they often do not know whether their overall specification is feasible. Another challenge is that user feedback must be considered to decide what transient behavior is acceptable. Thus, learning from validating and refining the requirements is necessary. Approaches like Chaos Engineering [2]—building hypotheses and experimenting on the system to (in-)validate them—tackle this problem through an iterative refinement process. However, they are unspecific in guiding comprehension and refinement with strategies and methods. Furthermore, as shown in previous work [4], there is a general lack of proper tooling to address transient behavior.

This paper presents our approach to comprehension of transient behavior and refinement of transient behavior requirements, which is an elemental part of our envisioned approach for continuous specification, verification, and refinement of resilience scenarios [14]. Thus, the presented approach aims at software architects of (business-)critical systems who want to increase confidence in their system's response to transient behavior. For single transient behavior occurrences of interest, our approach aims to help software architects decide whether and to what degree transient behavior requirements must be weakened or strengthened in cases where the initial specification turns out to be flawed or is reconsidered in the light of new information.

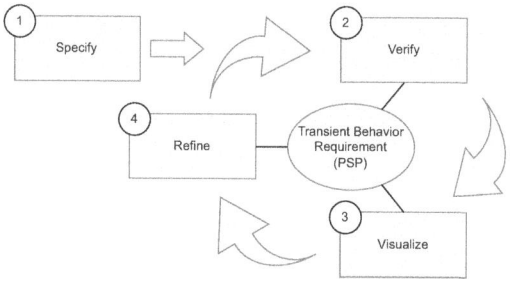

Fig. 1. Simplified overview of TQPropRefiner's refinement process.

The general process of our approach is depicted in Fig. 1. As a formalism for specifying requirements, we use PSP [1] to transform human-readable Structured English Grammar (SEG) specifications into testable Metric Temporal Logic (MTL) [23] formulas. TQPropRefiner—the early prototypical implementation of our approach—guides software architects through the three steps of (i) specifying transient behavior requirements using PSP, (ii) verifying the requirements against runtime data using runtime verification [25], (iii) presenting the requirement satisfaction using visualizations, and (iv) refining the requirements by altering time constraints or thresholds in simple predicates. Regarding refinement, our approach assists in finding satisfaction thresholds for both satisfied and unsatisfied requirements.

We conducted an expert user study with five industry participants to gather early feedback on our approach and TQPropRefiner, despite limitations in the supported PSP and refinement strategies. The participants had to solve two tasks regarding comprehension and refinement capabilities of TQPropRefiner, answer a questionnaire, and participate in an interview. The participants were able to solve the tasks, and their answers indicate that our approach was easy to use. We implemented several suggestions by the participants, e.g., alignment of the shown visualizations and initial integration with monitoring systems. However, further improvements are necessary for use in practice, e.g., closer integration with monitoring systems and persistence of specified requirements. Furthermore, the time constraint refinement needs more explanation.

In summary, the contributions of this paper comprise:

- An approach and tool (TQPropRefiner) that fosters comprehension of transient behavior to facilitate specification and refinement of transient behavior requirements. We make TQPropRefiner publicly available [7].
- Our vision and initial concept of refining transient behavior requirements. In particular, the implementation of time constraint and predicate threshold refinement strategies.
- The evaluation of our approach regarding feasibility and practicability in an expert user study. We provide the used documents and (anonymized) results as part of the supplementary material [13].

The remainder of this paper is structured as follows. Section 2 introduces the foundations used in this work, i.e., transient behavior and PSP. Next, Sect. 3 discusses the most relevant related works. Section 4 introduces our concept and the TQPropRefiner prototype, while Sect. 5 presents and discusses its evaluation by an expert user study. Finally, Sect. 6 summarizes this work.

2   Background

We first introduce Transient Behavior (see Sect. 2.1), for which we aim to acquire specifications. Then, we outline Property Specification Patterns (see Sect. 2.2), which we use as a formalism for our specifications.

2.1   Transient Behavior

Microservice-based software systems are usually complex and interdependent. Changes, e.g., failures, deployments, or self-adaptation, in one or more services may cause a system to transition from one steady state to another. This shift of states is described by the term transient behavior [5]. The concept of transient behavior originates from the field of electrical engineering. Within the state-space system model, there are two kinds of behavior: steady-state and transient. By performing transient analysis, it is possible to gain insight into the time-varying behavior of a system's Quality of Service (QoS) [28].

Since transient behavior is not focused on particular quality attributes and change types, it subsumes more specific concepts dealing with dynamic system behavior, e.g., survivability [18], elasticity [19], and resilience [24]. The quality of a system can be specified by quality requirements containing metrics such as response times. To identify occurrences of transient behavior, the actual QoS function of an underlying metric can be compared against the expected QoS [5]. Beck et al. [5] use Service-Level Objective (SLO) violations as indicators for transient behavior.

2.2   Property Specification Patterns

Transferring software system requirements to mathematical formulas to evaluate its quality can be challenging due to pragmatic barriers. To overcome this obstacle, Dwyer et al. [11] developed Property Specification Patterns (PSP) to specify temporal logic formulas for recurring requirement scenarios. A PSP represents a generalized depiction of a frequently occurring requirement that governs the allowable sequences of events and states in a finite-state model of a system. Dwyer et al. [11] introduce the two pattern categories *order patterns* and *occurrence patterns*. Each pattern also has a scope, which defines an interval during the program execution in which the pattern must remain valid [11]. The scope is established by specifying the pattern's starting and ending state/event. Five different scopes exist: *Global*, *Before*, *After*, *Between*, and *After-Until*.

The initial PSP version is qualitative, i.e., it does not consider time constraints. To address this limitation, Konrad and Cheng [22] introduced Real-Time Specification Patterns. They describe these patterns as *quantitative* as they allow for quantitative reasoning about time. Such PSP can be mapped to MTL, among others, as done in this work. Autili et al. [1] further extend and align the available qualitative and quantitative patterns.

An example of an instance of the qualitative Response pattern is: *Globally, if {response time high} then in response {instance increase} eventually holds within 5 s*. In this example, *response time high* and *instance increase* are predicates, i.e., they evaluate to either true or false at specific points in time. The *5 s* is the time constraint on how fast the autoscaler must react.

3   Related Work

To our knowledge, only a limited number of approaches and tools holistically focus on specifying and comprehending transient behavior and refining transient behavior requirements.

The Property Specification Pattern Wizard (PSPWizard) [1,26] aims to simplify the selection and creation of PSP by providing a graphical user interface to construct supported patterns. A mapping generator allows the translation of the specified pattern into various target logics. The specification is not the core contribution of our approach, so we mostly reuse the concept of the PSPWizard. We further extend it by adding capabilities to specify predicates and visualize the satisfaction of predicates for the imported runtime data.

The Transient Behavior Verifier (TBV) [15] is a tool that provides an Application Programming Interface (API) for verifying transient behavior occurrences specified as PSP or MTL on monitoring data. The requirement satisfaction is visualized using a multi-line graph for the relevant metrics and colors to indicate requirement satisfaction over time. In our approach, we reuse TBV for its verification capabilities. Further, we reuse the visualization concept to show requirement satisfaction. However, we further extend the concept by also visualizing the satisfaction of the predicates involved in the requirement.

Hoxha et al. [20] developed VISPEC, a graphical tool for eliciting MTL requirements. VISPEC utilizes a graphical formalism automatically translated to MTL to assist non-experts in creating and visualizing formal specifications. Therefore, users can easily specify requirements without requiring training in formal logic. In that regard, we share the comprehension and visualization of temporal logic on runtime data. Nevertheless, VISPEC is focused on (initial) specification, while we focus on refinement of requirements. Furthermore, VISPEC uses an MTL-based graphical formalism in the specification process, while we use PSP and internally translate to MTL. Finally, our approach has a stronger focus on visualizing the satisfaction of requirements instead of supporting the specification.

The TransVis [5] approach assists software architects and DevOps engineers in specifying and evaluating transient behavior occurrences in their microservice

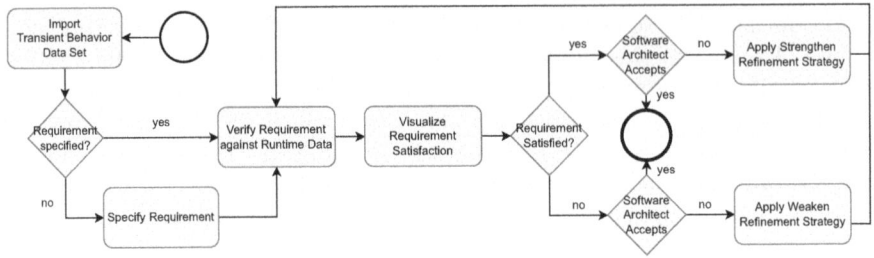

Fig. 2. Flowchart of the approach

systems. The tool displays the architecture of the assessed system and visualizes transient behavior in a graph. The user can interact with the tool via a chatbot, allowing for specifying simple requirements. The TransVis approach is based on the resilience triangle model from Bruneau et al. [8] in which transient behavior is characterized by the three indicators: initial loss of quality, time to recovery, and loss of resilience. Consequently, the specifications and visualizations are built specifically for these metrics, and there is no refinement assistance beyond visual comprehension. In contrast, we do not rely on the resilience triangle model and focus on requirement refinement.

4   Approach and TQPropRefiner

First, we outline the general concept (see Sect. 4.1) of our approach before we go into detail on the implemented refinement strategies (see Sect. 4.2). Next, we sketch our approach's intended usage and tool landscape and present how we implemented our concept into TQPropRefiner (see Sect. 4.4). Note that, due to space constraints, we only present the final version of the approach that incorporates improvements suggested by participants of the qualitative user study (see Sect. 5).

4.1   Concept

The approach presented in the following is designed to assist software architects in comprehending and refining quality requirements in the context of transient behavior occurrences. Our underlying assumption is that transient behavior occurrences have been successfully identified, and data for a specified instance of transient behavior can be provided. Thus, our approach does not provide support for identifying transient behavior occurrences beyond visual inspection.

Our general approach is depicted in Fig. 2. First, data from a detected transient behavior occurrence has to be imported. If not already available, an initial transient behavior requirement has to be specified. We use PSP as a formalism for these requirements since they are understandable to humans but also formal enough to be testable [10]. This property of TQPropRefiner is exploited in the next step, where we use runtime verification [25] to determine the satisfaction of (parts of) the requirement. Next, we visualize the runtime data and requirement satisfaction. Thus, software architects can easily decide whether the overall requirement is satisfied. Further, the software architect can consider the additional information to decide whether changes to the requirement are necessary, i.e., either because the specified requirement did not reflect the initial intention or new insights changed the expectation. A satisfied requirement can be strengthened to reflect new confidence in the system's capabilities. Vice versa, an unsatisfied requirement can be weakened to reflect the insight that the system behavior was actually good enough.

4.2 Refinement Strategies

We introduce the concept of *refinement strategies* to transform a requirement into a refined one. Besides the actual transformation, a refinement strategy has the properties (i) *type*, (ii) *target*, and (iii) *assistance*. The *type* describes whether the strategy aims to strengthen or weaken (or both) a requirement. The *target* specifies which part of the PSP the transformation affects, i.e., the overall pattern, scope, predicate, or time bound. Finally, *assistance* describes whether the strategy actively assists the software architect in making a decision or whether it just shows the software architect the effects of already applied decisions. In this work, we focus on active assistance and implemented two active refinement strategies, which we aim to extend in future work:

- **RS1: Compute Satisfying Time Constraint**
  (*type*: weaken/strengthen, *target*: time bound, *assistance*: active)
  The approach computes the threshold for the time bound so that the overall pattern is only just satisfied. Depending on whether the pattern was satisfied before, the specification is weakened or strengthened by applying the suggestion.
- **RS2: Test Predicate Threshold Values**
  (*type*: weaken/strengthen, *target*: predicate, *assistance*: active)
  For a simple predicate that involves a static threshold, e.g., *response_time* lesser than 100 ms, the approach evaluates the overall pattern satisfaction for all the available values of the predicate thresholds. The results are presented to the user, who can then select a value and, by doing so, weaken or strengthen the specification.

4.3 Envisioned Usage

TQPropRefiner is intended to be part of a process for continuous specification, verification, and refinement of resilience scenarios focusing on transient behavior as described in previous work [14]. This process is particularly useful in settings where software architects are insecure regarding the behavior and capabilities of their system regarding transient behavior. During experimentation, they can gather feedback and knowledge reflected by the increased quantity and quality

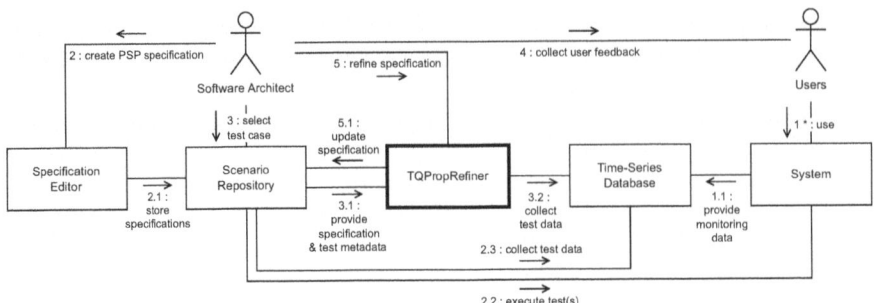

Fig. 3. Communication diagram of the envisioned technical landscape and usage

of scenarios. In our case, quality refers to the confidence of the software architect that a specified scenario makes sense. TQPropRefiner specifically aims to help software architects gain knowledge and reflect it in the specification through refinement strategies. Figure 3 depicts a simplified perspective on the role of TQPropRefiner as part of this vision and its interactions with users and other tools in practical settings.

We assume the system under test is instrumented and monitored so that monitoring data can be provided to state-of-the-art monitoring systems, e.g., Prometheus[1]. In previous works [4,16], we identified software architects as the ideal users of our approach since they possess knowledge about the system domain and system's usage as well as the applied software architecture and implemented resilience mechanisms. Therefore, they are most capable of identifying and specifying a relevant *stimulus* that leads to transient behavior and the intended *response* of the system, which both can be expressed using PSP, e.g., through specification editors as the PSPWizard [26]. The stimulus and response are the essential parts of quality scenarios as described by Bass et al. [3]. The software architects can then persist the initial scenarios in a scenario repository. Since a stimulus is specified, it can be applied to the system as part of resilience tests, and the scenario repository can collect the monitoring data associated with the tests. Note that other methods can be used instead of resilience tests at runtime to gather test data as long as the data is persisted in a time-series database by the monitoring system.

Using the scenario repository, the software architect can select a test case of interest for a scenario. The software architect can utilize scenario satisfaction and visualization approaches, e.g., Grafana dashboards[2], to decide whether a scenario and test case are interesting enough to enter the refinement phase. The specification and test metadata are then sent to TQPropRefiner, which collects the required monitoring data from the time-series database. Currently, TQProp-Refiner contains a prototypical implementation for collecting the monitoring data from a Prometheus database. Before and during the refinement process,

---

[1] https://prometheus.io/.

[2] https://grafana.com/.

the software architect is assumed to collect user feedback as the basis for the refinement decisions, particularly whether specifications or the system must be modified. When the software architect applies refinement strategies, TQProp-Refiner has to update the specification at the scenario repository to persist the newly gained knowledge.

Note that to allow an early evaluation of the approach, the first version of TQPropRefiner is deliberately designed to be useable as a standalone tool, i.e., without requiring external tools like the specification editor, scenario repository, or time-series database. However, in future work, we aim to incrementally integrate the approach into the described process and tool landscape.

4.4   TQPropRefiner

Figure 4 shows the TQPropRefiner prototype in a state where (1) a data set (see DS_2 in Sect. 5) has been imported, (2) the *Response* PSP has been selected, and (3) an initial requirement (see T_2 in Sect. 5) has been entered. The tool guides the software architect through the three-step process of importing monitoring data, selecting a PSP, and specifying & refining the requirement. Each step can be accessed via the stepper component (see Fig. 4 (A)).

Data Import. The first step is to import a Comma-separated values (CSV) file containing time series data of monitored metrics, e.g., from a chaos experiment. Alternatively, the user can retrieve monitoring data directly from a Prometheus database by specifying the time interval of interest. The imported data is displayed in a table where each row represents the monitored data for each time unit, and the columns show the metrics.

Specification. In step two, the software architect is asked to select a PSP as starting point for the initial specification. The selection is based on the pattern hierarchy introduced by Dwyer et al. [11] and the PSPWizard [26]. The software architect defines a scope, chooses a category (see Sect. 2.2), and finally picks a PSP. To provide additional context, the selected pattern is presented in the SEG as described by Autili et al. [1] and represented in a target logic of choice. However, only MTL is currently supported, and the pattern catalog is limited to three pattern variants: The *Response* pattern with the *Global* scope, and the *Universality* and *Absence* patterns with the *After* scope. We plan to add additional target logics and extend the supported patterns in the future.

The final step involves specifying the initial requirement and its refinement, as shown in Fig. 4. To provide an intuitive specification process, the selected pattern is displayed as a SEG (see Fig. 4 (C)). Each predicate of the pattern can be specified individually (see Fig. 4 (C2) & (C4)). A predicate is specified by providing (1) a meaningful name, (2) selecting a measurement source (metric), which is populated from the imported data set, (3) selecting an operator, and (4) specifying a numeric comparison value. Currently, TQPropRefiner supports

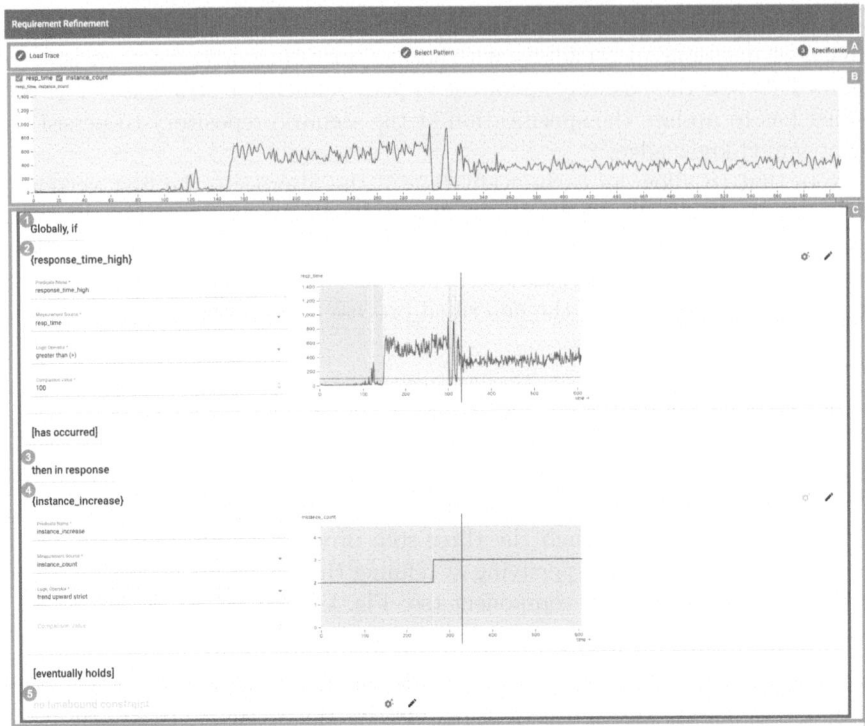

Fig. 4. TQPropRefiner showing (A) the step selection, (B) the pattern evaluation graph, and (C) the requirement specification & refinement

the same operators as TBV [15], which has to interpret these inputs. The supported operators contain basic relational operators ($<, \leq, =, \geq, >$) and (strict) upward and downward trends. While currently limited by the available operators provided by TBV, we plan to further extend the supported operators to reflect more complex and realistic use cases.

Comprehension. For verifying the PSP against the provided data set, TQPropRefiner uses the Transient Behavior Verifier [15]. We host an instance and access it via its API. The overall evaluation of the pattern is displayed in the graph at the top (see Fig. 4 (B)). An all-green graph indicates the satisfaction of the entered requirement, while a red segment marks the moment the requirement is violated. The pattern evaluation result is also visualized by a green or red rectangle around the pattern (see Fig. 4 (C)).

The predicates are individually verified against the provided data set, and the results are visualized in graphs. The time is represented on the X-axes, and the Y-axes represent the metrics. A selected metric is displayed in a black line chart, and the comparison value is a blue horizontal line. The time-dependent evaluation of the predicate is visualized by green segments for intervals the predicate is satisfied and red segments for unsatisfied intervals. In Fig. 4 (C4), the specification of the *instance_increase* predicate is shown, which is defined as *instance_count* is strictly increasing. The time-dependent evaluation of the predicate is visualized to the right in the graph. As specified, the interval is mostly marked red, while the point in time the instance count is increased to three is marked green.

Refinement. To refine the pattern specification, the software architect can tweak its predicates. TQPropRefiner provides the passive refinement strategy of updating the visualization for the selected predicate and the overall pattern. This aims to facilitate a better comprehension of how changing one or more parameters affects the satisfaction of (parts of) the requirement.

For specifying and refining the time constraints, TQPropRefiner provides the implementation of two active refinement strategies (see gear symbol in Fig. 4 (C2) & (C5)). The tool performs a binary search based on the available predicate specifications to test potential time constraints. The resulting time-dependent verification result is displayed to the user showing for which time constraint intervals the pattern is satisfied following the same color coding we use for predicates. For predicates with relational operators, the tool can evaluate the pattern satisfaction for all comparison values between the minimum and maximum values of the dataset. The tool then displays all tested values and the corresponding evaluation results indicated by red or green colors. The user can then click on a value to set it as the comparison value. Currently, these are the only two implemented refinement strategies. However, we plan to add more sophisticated strategies in future versions of TQPropRefiner, particularly ones that simultaneously modify multiple predicates.

Implementation and Technologies. TQPropRefiner has been implemented using the Angular[3] framework in conjunction with the Angular Material UI component library. Our prototype sends requests to an instance of the TBV [15] tool in order to verify the PSP specifications. The code for the prototype is publicly available [7]. The modeling of PSP has been adopted from the PSPWizard [26]. We migrated the code of selected patterns to TypeScript classes, as the PSP-Wizard is implemented in Java.

5   Evaluation

To evaluate our approach's comprehension and refinement capabilities and practical applicability, we conducted a qualitative user study with five industry experts. We provided the experts with two tasks that needed to be solved using the prototype and asked them to evaluate their experience afterward. We investigate the following research questions:

---

[3] https://angular.io/.

- **RQ1:** To what extent can our approach facilitate comprehension of transient behavior occurrences among practitioners?
- **RQ2:** To what extent can our approach assist practitioners in refining requirements?
- **RQ3:** How can the approach be improved to assist practitioners in addressing practical challenges?

In the following, the provide details on our method, the provided tasks, the study execution, the results, and the discussion of the results and our method.

5.1 Method

We decided on a qualitative evaluation for two reasons. Firstly, the research questions focus on usability and improving an early concept and prototype. We argue that this can be best achieved by promoting a dialog with the study participants. This perception is supported by Greenberg & Buxton [17], who suggest that quantitative study designs could be detrimental in evaluating new ideas, particularly during prototype design, as they may limit expert feedback. Secondly, the complexity and the specialization of the covered topic lead to the practical barrier of finding enough participants to conduct a representative study.

We designed the expert user study not to exceed 1 h and conducted it with each participant individually. In total, we gathered five participants, three working in a software company from the taxes domain and two working in a consulting and development company focusing on Application Performance Monitoring (APM). The participation did not demand any prior preparation.

Note that Sect. 4 describes the state of the prototype after the evaluation. The version used in the evaluation was less advanced, in particular, it only supported refinement strategy RS1 and only relational operators in predicates. The evaluation results led to further improvements in the tooling.

5.2 Tasks

To solve the tasks, the participants received access to a hosted version of TQPropRefiner. We also provided two CSV files containing time-series data from two chaos experiments conducted by Frank et al. [15] with Chaos Toolkit (CTK) [9]. The first data set (DS_1) provided originates from *Chaos Experiment 1*, in which an injected fault caused a service instance to crash, leading to a response times increase. The second data set (DS_2) is from *Chaos Experiment 2*, in which the workload suddenly increases, and the implemented autoscaler is required to spawn an additional service instance.

Each task demands participants to go through four steps using TQProp-Refiner. Firstly, each participant was asked to select a specific data set from a chaos experiment. Secondly, a suggested PSP from the pattern catalog needed to be selected. Thirdly, a given (initial) specification had to be entered by specifying the predicates of the selected PSP. Fourthly, a question on the requirement needed to be answered. Answering the questions may require the refinement of

Table 1. Context and SLO, initial requirement, and question for the two tasks

Task 1 (T_1): Service Failure	**Task 2** (T_2): Load Peak
Data Set 1 (DS$_1$)	Data Set 2 (DS$_2$)
– According to the SLO, response times may not exceed 150 time units – In the exceptional case of only 1 service being available, a response time of up to 400 time units is tolerated – In the experiment, 1 of in total 2 service instances has been terminated	– Response times may not exceed 100 time units. – In case the system is unable to satisfy the performance requirement, the number of instances should be increased – In the experiment, due to a load peak, service instances are scaled from 2 to 3
After {instances are smaller than 2}, it is never the case that {response times exceed 400 time units}.	*Globally, if {response times exceed 100 time units} then in response {the instance count increases to 3}.*
Is the requirement fulfilled?	How long did the system take to scale to 3 service instances?

the initial specification. For each task, the participants have been provided with context information containing (i) the SLO of the underlying system defined by stakeholders, (ii) an initial specification, and (iii) a question as shown in Table 1.

We designed Task 1 (T_1) to evaluate to which degree participants are able to enter a given requirement specification and correctly interpret the verification result without any necessary refinement. Thus, T_1 is designed to address RQ1. Task 2 (T_2) aims to evaluate to which degree participants can refine a given specification to examine a related requirement question. The answer to this question had to be derived from refining the time constraint of the selected specification. Therefore, T_2 addresses RQ1 and RQ2. To address RQ3, we conducted an interview with the participant to discuss potential improvements and required developments for practical use.

5.3 Execution

We conducted the evaluation online, with participants sharing their screens during the entire study. At the beginning of the session, we explained the study procedure. Afterward, we provided a link to a Google Form containing all information necessary for the study participation. This included seven questions on the participants' background knowledge, the two tasks to solve using TQProp-Refiner, and 20 questions. The study host was present to answer potential questions from participants but did not actively intervene while the participants were going through the information on the Google Form.

After solving the given tasks, we asked each participant to evaluate their experience concerning feasibility, usability, practical applicability, and potential improvements. To evaluate the prototype's feasibility, we asked the participants to rate their interaction with the tool on a Likert scale (one to five, one: strongly disagree; five: strongly agree; see Fig. 5). We based our useability questions on the System Usability Scale (SUS) [6] method. Finally, we gathered practical

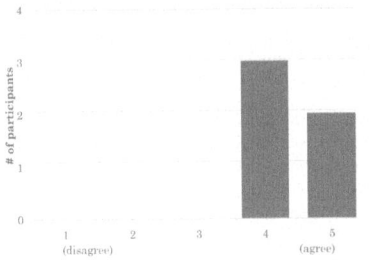

(a) ... easy to interpret the initial evaluation of a single predicate.

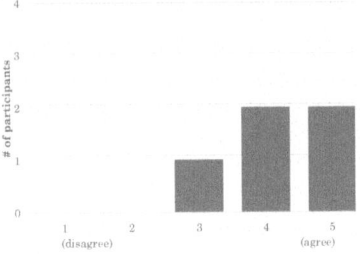

(b) ... easy to interpret the initial property evaluation.

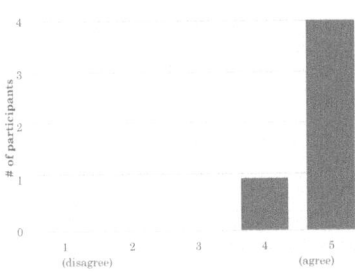

(c) ...easy to refine single predicate.

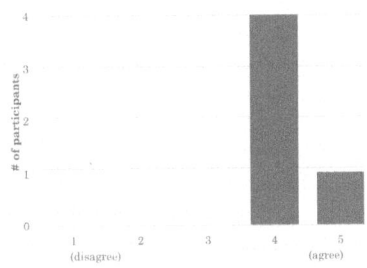

(d) ... easy to refine the property.

Fig. 5. Answers by the study participants for selected questions. It was...

applicability evaluation and potential improvement suggestions using qualitative questions as well as a discussion between the participant and the session host.

5.4 Results

RQ1. No participant encountered problems entering the given specification into TQPropRefiner. Interpreting the evaluation result of a single predicate as well as the overall property was perceived as easy by all participants, who rated the comprehensibility for both with a median value of 4 out of 5. Additionally, all five participants were able to solve the tasks correctly.

During the specification process, we observed that specifying a time constraint was not intuitive for some participants and, therefore, may require additional explanation within the tooling. Consequently, the answers to the ten SUS questions indicate that the tool overall was generally perceived as easy to use with a low entry barrier.

RQ2. All participants perceived the refinement of a single predicate as simple and rated it as easy with a 5 out of 5 median value. Refining the overall property was perceived as more difficult but was still rated with a median value of 4 out of 5. As part of the qualitative evaluation, we asked the participants whether they would have been able to solve the given task without TQPropRefiner. Two participants answered yes (they would just use the data visualization and manual inspection), two with no, and one with maybe. Also according to the results, T_2 has been solved correctly by four of the five participants. The wrong answer was due to the challenges of correctly interpreting the time constraint in the context of the overall pattern. However, the existence and the functionality of the tool's time constraint refinement feature were not intuitive to the participants, i.e., they did not understand the feature solely by seeing the gear icon. The refinement needs better presentation and explanation in future versions of TQPropRefiner.

RQ3. In open feedback, participants stated various ideas and requirements for potential production use of TQPropRefiner. Multiple participants pointed out that comprehensibility could be increased by horizontally aligning the predicate graphs. In the used version of TQPropRefiner, the two predicate graphs were not aligned, which made identifying dependencies between various metrics difficult. As depicted in Fig. 4 (C2) & (C4), we have aligned the graphs and provided a blue line that highlights the same point in time for all predicate graphs.

One participant elaborated that importing time series data as CSV files would be infeasible in production environments. Instead, an API integration of standard monitoring systems for trace import is required. Based on the suggestion, we have implemented a database connection that obtains monitoring data directly from a Prometheus database. For the question of whether the participants would frequently use the tool, the answers varied. Some participants agreed, but others pointed out that this depends on the precondition that they face tasks in their jobs where a tool like this would be beneficial.

Finally, participants provided some general potential improvements, e.g., adding a feature to save and load specifications, adding support for time units, providing additional explanations on the color coding, and improving the tool's responsive design.

5.5 Discussion

The findings of RQ1 and RQ2 indicate that our approach is able to assist practitioners in comprehending and refining transient behavior requirements. The participants were able to enter a given specification, interpret verification results, and refine requirements. The tool's usability was perceived positively, and has a low entry barrier. This is supported by the fact that the participants (mostly) solved the given tasks using the tool. Still, our approach must be improved, extended, and evaluated in a more exhaustive user study and applied to more complex use cases. To avoid the influence of useability issues on the result of potential quantitative evaluations in the future, we also have to improve features that are considered not intuitive by the participants, i.e., the time refinement and the color coding.

5.6 Threats to Validity

As a result of the evaluation, we have identified three validity concerns. Firstly, the group of participants was small and lacked heterogeneity. The five participants were employed at only two companies; some had similar expertise. Including software engineers without an APM background might have negatively impacted the results. Nevertheless, the number of (heterogenous) participants in qualitative studies is less critical. Studies with low (1 to 5) numbers of participants are not uncommon, according to Isenberg et al. [21].

Secondly, the tasks were designed specifically for the data sets we used for the evaluation. Since this data originates from academic experiments, they are not representative of the scenarios practitioners face in their production environments. Despite these concerns, we assume that the qualitative feedback we have received will be a first step in extending our early-stage prototype toward handling real-world challenges in the future.

Thirdly, some participants stated they could have solved the given tasks without TQPropRefiner. Thus, we must thoroughly investigate whether the comprehension and refinement of the requirement were facilitated due to using the tool, e.g., by comparing solutions obtained with and without TQPropRefiner.

6 Conclusion

This paper introduced our approach and tool TQPropRefiner for supporting software architects in comprehending transient behavior and refining requirements. In an expert user study, the participants were able to solve two tasks and confirmed the ease of use—providing evidence that our approach is a valuable step toward the interactive refinement of transient behavior requirements.

In future work, we aim to significantly extend the supported PSP, add support for more sophisticated predicates, and add more refinement strategies. In particular, we plan to support composed predicates and predicates on time intervals. We also plan to further integrate TQPropRefiner into our process for specifying, verifying, and refining resilience scenarios. Further, we aim to evaluate the approach in more realistic use cases and make the necessary improvements suggested by the participants, e.g., further improve monitoring integration and making the refinement features more intuitive to the users.

Acknowledgment. The authors thank Marvin Taube and Alexander Baur for their contributions to TQPropRefiner and the German Federal Ministry of Education and Research (dqualizer FKZ: 01IS22007B; Software Campus 2.0, Microproject: DiSpel, FKZ: 01IS17051) for supporting this work. The work was conducted in the context of the SPEC RG DevOps Performance Working Group.

References

1. Autili, M., Grunske, L., Lumpe, M., Pelliccione, P., Tang, A.: Aligning qualitative, real-time, and probabilistic property specification patterns using a structured English grammar. IEEE Trans. Software Eng. **41**(7), 620–638 (2015)

2. Basiri, A., et al.: Chaos engineering. IEEE Software **33**, 1–1 (2016)
3. Bass, L., Clements, P., Kazman, R.: Software Architecture in Practice, 4 edn. Addison-Wesley Professional (2021)
4. Beck, S., Frank, S., Hakamian, A., van Hoorn, A.: How is transient behavior addressed in practice? insights from a series of expert interviews. In: Companion of the 2022 ACM/SPEC International Conference on Performance Engineering, pp. 105–112 (2022)
5. Beck, S., Frank, S., Hakamian, A., Merino, L., van Hoorn, A.: Transvis: using visualizations and chatbots for supporting transient behavior in microservice systems. In: 2021 Working Conference on Software Visualization (VISSOFT), pp. 65–75. IEEE (2021)
6. Brooke, J.: SUS-a quick and dirty usability scale. Usability Eval. Ind. **189**(194), 4–7 (1996)
7. Brott, J.: Github project (2023). https://github.com/Cambio-Project/transient-behavior-requirement-refiner
8. Bruneau, M., et al.: A framework to quantitatively assess and enhance the seismic resilience of communities. Earthq. Spectra **19**(4), 733–752 (2003)
9. Chaos Toolkit Team: Chaos Toolkit (2023). https://chaostoolkit.org
10. Czepa, C., Zdun, U.: On the understandability of temporal properties formalized in linear temporal logic, property specification patterns and event processing language. IEEE Trans. Software Eng. **46**(1), 100–112 (2018)
11. Dwyer, M.B., Avrunin, G.S., Corbett, J.C.: Property specification patterns for finite-state verification. In: Proceedings of the Second Workshop on Formal Methods in Software Practice, pp. 7–15 (1998)
12. Eckhardt, J., Vogelsang, A., Fernández, D.M.: Are "non-functional" requirements really non-functional? an investigation of non-functional requirements in practice. In: Proceedings of the 38th International Conference on Software Engineering, pp. 832–842 (2016)
13. Frank, S., Brott, J., Hakamian, A., van Hoorn, A.: Supplementary material (2023). https://doi.org/10.5281/zenodo.8125612
14. Frank, S., Hakamian, A., Wagner, L., Von Kistowski, J., Van Hoorn, A.: Towards continuous and data-driven specification and verification of resilience scenarios. In: 2022 IEEE International Symposium on Software Reliability Engineering Workshops (ISSREW), pp. 136–137. IEEE (2022)
15. Frank, S., Hakamian, A., Zahariev, D., van Hoorn, A.: Verifying transient behavior specifications in chaos engineering using metric temporal logic and property specification patterns. In: Companion of the 2023 ACM/SPEC International Conference on Performance Engineering. ICPE '23 Companion, New York, NY, USA, pp. 319–326. Association for Computing Machinery (2023)
16. Frank, S., Hakamian, M.A., Wagner, L., Kesim, D., von Kistowski, J., van Hoorn, A.: Scenario-based resilience evaluation and improvement of microservice architectures: an experience report. In: ECSA (Companion) (2021)
17. Greenberg, S., Buxton, B.: Usability evaluation considered harmful (some of the time). In: Proceedings of the SIGCHI Conference on Human Factors in Computing Systems, pp. 111–120 (2008)
18. Heegaard, P.E., Trivedi, K.S.: Network survivability modeling. Comput. Netw. **53**(8), 1215–1234 (2009)
19. Herbst, N.R., Kounev, S., Reussner, R.: Elasticity in cloud computing: what it is, and what it is not. In: 10th international conference on autonomic computing (ICAC 13), pp. 23–27 (2013)

20. Hoxha, B., Mavridis, N., Fainekos, G.: Vispec: A graphical tool for elicitation of MTL requirements. In: 2015 IEEE/RSJ International Conference on Intelligent Robots and Systems (IROS), pp. 3486–3492. IEEE (2015)

21. Isenberg, T., Isenberg, P., Chen, J., Sedlmair, M., Möller, T.: A systematic review on the practice of evaluating visualization. IEEE Trans. Visual Comput. Graphics **19**(12), 2818–2827 (2013)

22. Konrad, S., Cheng, B.H.: Real-time specification patterns. In: Proceedings of the 27th International Conference on Software Engineering, pp. 372–381 (2005)

23. Koymans, R.: Specifying real-time properties with metric temporal logic. Real-time systems **2**(4), 255–299 (1990)

24. Laprie, J.C.: From dependability to resilience. In: 38th IEEE/IFIP International Conference on Dependable Systems and Networks, pp. G8–G9 (2008)

25. Leucker, M., Schallhart, C.: A brief account of runtime verification. J. Logic Algebraic Program. **78**(5), 293–303 (2009)

26. Lumpe, M., Meedeniya, I., Grunske, L.: Pspwizard: machine-assisted definition of temporal logical properties with specification patterns. In: Proceedings of the 19th ACM SIGSOFT Symposium and the 13th European Conference on Foundations of Software Engineering, pp. 468–471 (2011)

27. Villamizar, M., et al.: Evaluating the monolithic and the microservice architecture pattern to deploy web applications in the cloud. In: 2015 10th Computing Colombian Conference (10CCC), pp. 583–590. IEEE (2015)

28. Wang, C.Y., Logothetis, D., Trivedi, K.S., Viniotis, I.: Transient behavior of ATM networks under overloads. In: Proceedings of IEEE INFOCOM'96. Conference on Computer Communications, vol. 3, pp. 978–985. IEEE (1996)

TwinArch

Architecture for Digital Twin-Based Reinforcement Learning Optimization of Cyber-Physical Systems

Elias Modrakowski[1]([✉])[iD], Niklas Braun[2], Mehrnoush Hajnorouzi[1][iD],
Andreas Eich[3][iD], Narges Javaheri[4], Richard Doornbos[5], Sebastian Moritz[6][iD],
Jan-Willem Bikker[7], and Rutger van Beek[7]

[1] Institute of Systems Engineering for Future Mobility, German Aerospace Center
(DLR e.V.), Oldenburg, Germany
elias.modrakowski@dlr.de
[2] AVL Deutschland GmbH, Karlsruhe, Germany
[3] Liangdao GmbH, Munich, Germany
[4] Thermo Fisher Scientific, Eindhoven, The Netherlands
[5] TNO-ESI, Eindhoven, The Netherlands
[6] TrianGraphics, Berlin, Germany
[7] CQM, Eindhoven, The Netherlands

Abstract. The optimization of complex cyber-physical systems is a crucial task for their correct functioning, usability, and commercial viability. Due to their complexity, scale and resource intensiveness, conventional manual optimization is infeasible in many instances. We investigate the combination of the Digital Twin paradigm and Reinforcement Learning framework to address the long response times, limited availability of data, and the intractability of such systems. Here, the Digital Twin functions as the training environment in different development phases of the optimization. In this position paper we showcase our ongoing research on developing a reference architecture of a Digital Twin-Artificial Intelligence optimization system. This includes presenting the development process of the optimization system in terms of phases, an architecture from four viewpoints and an exemplary implementation.

Keywords: Digital Twin · Reinforcement Learning · System Optimization · Cyber-Physical System · Reference Architecture · System Architecture · Training Data Generation

The research is carried out as part of the ITEA4 20216 ASIMOV project. The ASIMOV activities are supported by the Netherlands Organization for Applied Scientific Research TNO and the Dutch Ministry of Economic Affairs and Climate (project number: AI211006). This research is also partially funded by the German Federal Ministry of Education and Research (BMBF) within the project ASIMOV-D under grant agreement No. 01IS21022B [AVL], 01IS21022D [Liangdao], 01IS21022F [TrianGraphics] and 01IS21022G [DLR] based on a decision of the German Bundestag.

B. Tekinerdoğan et al. (Eds.): ECSA 2023, LNCS 14590, pp. 257–271, 2024.
https://doi.org/10.1007/978-3-031-66326-0_16

1   Introduction

Complex high-tech Cyber-Physical Systems (CPSs) often have an unattainable scale (e.g., number of controls, settings, and usage scenarios) with limited availability for tests combined with high costs. The optimization in terms of adjustment of their configuration for proper functionality, usability, and commercial viability is required. However, achieving optimization objectives, due to indirect and long-term materializing optimization goals or complex high-dimensional system states, usually is challenging for conventional automated methods. Consequently, manual intervention becomes necessary which demands experts to spend valuable time and resources.

Typically, this process is slow, costly, and inexperienced personnel may inadvertently place the CPS in a non-optimal state, or disrupt the system. One solution to these problems is to determine optimal system settings by the use of Artificial Intelligence (AI), or more precisely, Reinforcement Learning (RL) techniques [31] which would yield these settings from system-generated data [7]. However, RL is known for demanding large amounts of training data making it incapable of being parameterized using the high-tech CPSs directly and therefore models and simulations are necessary for data generation [18].

To illustrate the challenge, let us assume a robot arm in a factory with a PID-controller regulating one of the actuators. In this case, the RL optimizes the CPS, i.e., the robot arm, by adjusting controller's parameters, guided by higher level objectives such as precise positioning of the robot arm's attachment or minimizing the failure rates on factory level. A human operator would need to adjust these parameters for every robot arm commissioned (as they all differ slightly from each other) and readjust them over time (aging of the machinery, changing of the attachment or manufacturing product, etc.). New controller settings may be suggested by the optimization AI and tested in simulation to minimize the downtime of the robot arm. While this example is simple, it showcases the potential of the idea as these optimizations may be done in an automated way.

In this position paper, we propose an approach of optimizing CPSs that incorporates two technologies; (i) Digital Twin (DT) to mitigate long response times and limited availability of CPS; (ii) RL to address complex systems optimization. The expected result is a setup that performs the optimization of a CPS quicker, safer, and less expensive compared to a human. More concretely, we address the question: How does an architecture look like that leverages RL training data generation using DT? This research is unique by outlining the key factors on the DT side necessary for RL training throughout a CPS's life cycle in form of a reference architecture. It is directed to system developers searching for a solution to slow, manual and expensive optimization of such systems. Subsequently, we introduce a DT-RL optimization framework, a reference architecture supporting its development, outline the application to an exemplary use case, and conclude by outlining the shortcomings resulting into future avenues of work.

2   Prerequisites and Related Work

2.1   Combining DTs and RL

Figure 1 depicts the overall interactions during the DT-based optimization-RL life cycle that shall be enables by the architecture. First, DT of a typical system is modelled with the capability of representing variations of the system. It represents the environment with which the optimization-RL Agent (RLA) is then trained. In continuation, the optimization-RL is applied to actual system(s) where further data can be collected for fine-tuning purposes. Consequently, we derived three iterative phases:

Training phase In this phase, the RLA is trained using multiple varying instances of a typical CPS. This is done to prevent the problem of overfitting and to increase generalization to enable transfer learning (see [7,25]).

Operational phase Once the RLA has matured enough, it is deployed on an actual CPS to perform system optimization. Here, the RLA is assumed to interact directly with the CPS or is part of the CPS. During this period, data from the CPS is gathered for the next phase.

Fine-tuning phase Periodically, the RLA is fine-tuned using the CPS's data from the operational phase to improve and specialize the learned policy w.r.t. the CPS instance by twinning the related real system. In addition, the variant agnostic RLA (result of the training phase) is also further trained, e.g., by using federated learning [20]. An extensive testing of the RLA adjustment is necessary, yet the frequency of the fine-tuning phase depends on the use case.

2.2   Fundamental Considerations

A DT is defined as a virtual duplicate of a system built from a fusion of models and data [32]. The essential role of DT is to represent the behavior of real system by periodically adapting to the actual system. This differentiates a DT from a

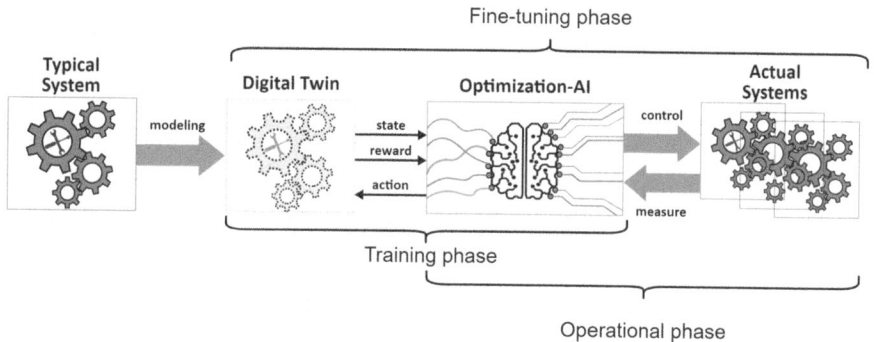

Fig. 1. Overview of the development process of DT supported RL training.

digital model [5, 12, 29, 32]. We adopt the notion of different integration levels by [2]. Different phases of system optimization apply varying degrees of integration, i.e., digital model up to DT. While a digital model of a generic CPS is sufficient for the training phase, the operational and fine-tuning acquire higher levels of integration, to the degree of twinning [17]. It is important to note that in this context, the DT encompasses the CPS itself and its surrounding environment and how it imposes influence on the CPS. With respect to the robot arm example, this would be the room temperature or properties of the manufacturing product the arm should process.

RL [31] is broadly applied in various disciplines for the purpose of system optimization or optimized control, e.g., [8, 13, 21, 33]. RL is well-suited to the problems that include learning from unlabeled data, e.g., due to long-term materialization of optimality [13].

Several challenges arise from the proposed DT-RL approach, aiming to establish simulation-based training capabilities and enable a continual enhancement of optimization RL algorithm exploiting the advantages of DTs. It is crucial to meet RL-specific demands, namely result accuracy, efficient execution, standardized simulation input/output (state, action, reward) and managing variations for policy transfer into the real world. An additional focus lies in facilitating the model re-usability throughout its life-cycle.

2.3   Literature on DT-Based RL

Recent research has delved into combination of these challenges across diverse domains. [25] introduces a RL training approach through simulations. The domain of application in this case are driving functions for automated vehicles. Nevertheless, it lacks an architectural view and continuous RLA refining. [8] emphasizes training RLA for fusion reactor control with architectural aspects taking a backseat in training consideration. [3] adopts a DT strategy for robot arm control including architectural specifications, akin to our proposal, but overlooks the post-initial learning. [18] and [11] provide insights into real-world transfer of RL policies and DT-based RL scheduling strategy training, respectively. However, architectural and, yet again, post-deployment learning aspects are under-explored. Similarly, [27] advocates DT and RL fusion for unmanned aerial vehicle control and proposes a DT-based "continuous evolution" in this context [28]. However, the work is domain-specific and generalizable architecture considerations are not present in this work.

In the field of "life-long" RL [19], scholars deal with continuous learning and policy transfer (e.g., from simulation to real world or adjustments from one system to the next). To the authors' best knowledge, availability of training data is assumed in most of the relevant studies. In context of continuous learning, Federated Learning (FL) [16] is a common practice for pre-training and consequent fine-tuning of AI. [30] showcases the combination of DT and FL but leaves the design of these DTs open for interpretation. In general, application independent DT architectures are rare as a high percentage of solution-oriented architectures [10] show that every application context requires their own interpretation.

From the cited research, it is evident that the comprehensive exploitation of the DT paradigm's capabilities has not yet been fully realized in RL training. In all of the aforementioned literature, RL is utilized for system control, wherein we see system optimization a sub-field. Our objective is to delineate the essential considerations required on the DT side for RL training across the various stages of its life-cycle. We aim to provide an architectural recommendation that goes beyond mere building block descriptions.

3   Architecture

A multi-sided description is required to plan an architecture that considers a multitude of aspects. Among various architectural view models like [14], we have adopted four viewpoints similar as in SPES (Software Platform Embedded Systems) [26]. In spite of minimizing the number of viewpoints, namely requirements, functional, logical and technical views, they are capable of covering all relevant layers and aspects [6].

3.1   Requirements View

The main objective of our approach is to realize a self-optimizing solution for complex CPSs which can be then applied to analogous systems without necessitating extensive re-development, e.g., re-modelling of interfaces, or re-training the AI from scratch. The specific requirements of our approach mostly derived from the RL requirements on the training and fine-tuning data. All requirements mentioned in this view are on the system. However, the fulfillment of some requirements is facilitated by the architecture (see Table 1).

The functional requirements of the DT in general include (i) to model the components that contribute to the observable outputs/behavior sufficiently, (ii) to model the potential influences of the CPS's environment, and (iii) to possess parameters that determine its behavior, analogous to the corresponding physical counterpart.

Moreover, in the context of RL-training, the set of requirements of DT as the training data generator model, need to be expanded by minimized calculation time (time to result) and satisfactory data accuracy. While the previous comes naturally, defining "sufficient" accuracy is not straight forward. As a general principle, more information with higher quality results in improved decision making. However, machine learning algorithms can bridge the gap and transfer whatever they learned from a less accurate model to the actual operating system (see [9,18]). As an example, the autonomous driving functions trained by simulated data, can be applied successfully to the real-world use cases [25]. This relaxes the constraints on DT's requirements and improves execution efficiency on the way. Therefore, the required accuracy level of DT within the proposed approach is highly dependent on the AI capabilities. As long as the RL model can bridge the gap, the accuracy of the DT is sufficient.

To effectively train the RLA, it is important to mitigate the impacts of noise and irrelevant information during training phase. Overfitting on these effects can hinder the trained RLA's adaptability and resilience to slightly changed circumstances comparing to the training data [4]. To address this issue, one approach is to train the RLA by higher-level features of the data, specifically by "averaging out" system-specific behavior. To this end, we propose to use a fleet of digital models or DTs representing the CPSs. These models should encompass multiple variants, each incorporating slight differences to represent the variations in real-world. The variation can be introduced by altering virtual environment effects and configuration changes within a predefined valid parameter space. This approach allows the RLA to learn from a spectrum of possible CPS variants instead of only from one specific instances. By training on a diverse set, the RLA is enabled to perform across multiple systems without requiring re-training [7].

The non-functional requirements can be summarized in footprint (minimization of resource usage), integrability (the ability to integrate heterogeneous systems and IP-protection), re-usability, and maintainability.

Table 1. Overview of key requirements and considerations at a high level, assessing their reflection by the architecture.

No.	Requirement	Description	Reflected in architecture
1	Execution efficiency	Calculation time needs to be minimized to make training time manageable	No
2	Accuracy of result	The system must accurately enough simulate real-world behavior for successful RL-driven optimization in the operational phase	No
3	Variants representation	The DTs must be able to represent real or virtual variants of a system w.r.t. to its environment and configuration	Yes
4	Twinning	The system must be able to retrieve data from its physical twin and parametrize itself accordingly	Yes
5	Footprint	The resource usage for training and fine-tuning shall be minimized	No
6	Re-Usability	To reduce resource and time consumption, developed models and infrastructure shall be reusable	Yes
7	Maintainability	The system shall be easily maintainable	Yes
8	Integrability	The integration of heterogeneous models and IP-protection shall be facilitated	Yes

3.2 Functional View

The functional view describes the specification of solution-independent functional system, i.e., it describes the functionality that the system intended to provide in order to fulfill its purpose. Figure 2 shows the functional model of optimization using data from DT and CPS during the training phase and operational

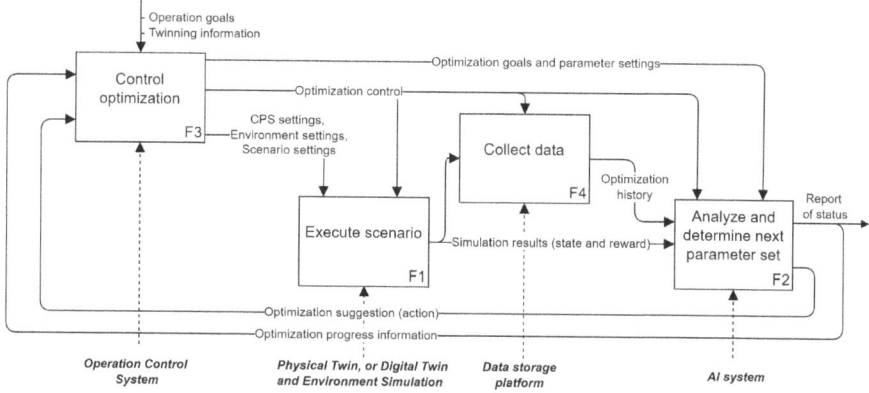

Fig. 2. Generic functional model of the system's optimization in form of IDEF0 (Integration Definition for Process Modelling).

phase, respectively. As mentioned earlier, the model shall be used interchangeably for different phases without requiring major adjustments to the architecture (requirement No. 6 in Table 1). Initially, operational goals and the twinning information are given to the system which initializes and "controls" the optimization by executing a scenario. An initial batch of parameters containing the parameters that shall be optimized as well as the parameters that define the model variants (fulfilling requirement No. 3 in Table 1) are given to an entity that performs the optimization. This might be the actual CPS or its DT. Optimization metrics and system defining information (e.g., previous parameter configuration) in form of state and reward according to the RL paradigm shall be collected one hand and also analyzed. Based on this and possibly the history of prior states, an improved configuration is proposed and returned to be executed again. It can be seen that the four major functionalities needed can be assigned to four main sub-systems: A control system, a CPS/DT within its environment, a data storage platform and an AI system.

Regarding functional capabilities of the DT as represented in Fig. 3, it must be able to control (Control simulation) and represent and execute simulation of system features (Simulate features) to mimic the CPS's behavior accurate enough and output relevant simulation results for further training. The features must be configurable to enable adaptation to a real or synthetic CPS variant.

3.3 Logical View

The logical view describes the design solution, providing functional building blocks by communicating components [26]. Due to the already stated variety of RL training algorithms, we showcase the simulation environment and the contained DT only. The simulation environment is not meant the context in which the CPS is located in, but rather the digital infrastructure for performing simulations. Both modules' structure is expressed in accordance with the SysML

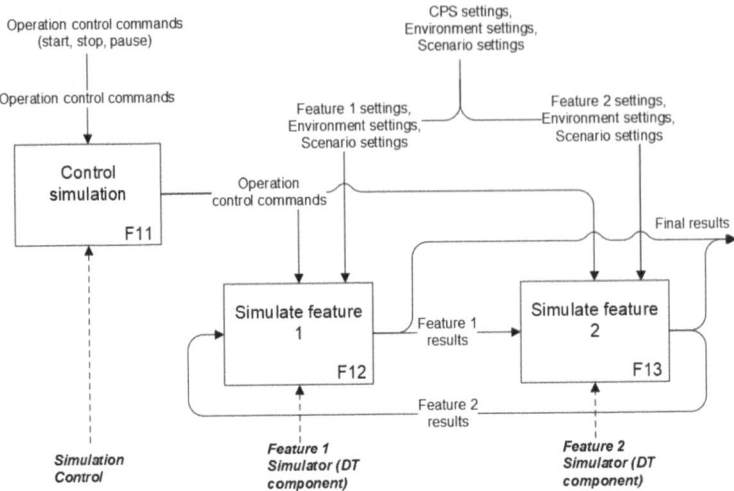

Fig. 3. Generic functional model of DT in form of IDEF0, exemplary with two simulation features.

language as internal block diagrams (ibd) in the following. The simulation environment in Fig. 4 consists of a flow of data from the action port via a pre-processing component into the DT as a simulation input, and after computing from the DT's output via a post-processing component to the state and reward output of the simulation environment. The pre- and post-processing components serve the goal of conversion of the RLA/DT output to an adequate format. A controller manages the processing and optional databases providing additional information. In case of the operational and fine-tuning phase, a twinning block is implemented to orchestrate the retrieval of CPS data as necessary according to the requirements (requirement No. 4 in Table 1). During the training phase, as no physical counterpart exists, it is replaced by a variation generator within the DT mimicking the existence of multiple, slightly different CPS instances. The simulation environment interacts through five ports: (i) control inputs from controller that manages RL training, (ii) connection to the CPS and (iii) action, (iv) reward and (v) state ports for the communication with RLA.

The DT represented in Fig. 5, consists of none or more submodule-DTs and one or more logic block(s). The latter calculates the behavioral output of the DT by using (i) simulation data input to the DT itself, (ii) and/ or simulation data output of hierarchically nested sub-DTs, (iii) static configuration parameters sourced from persistent databases, and (iv) dynamic configuration parameters, obtained through the adaptation model.

Adaptation to changing behavior of the CPS is handled by the adaptation model. It identifies any emerging differences DT and CPS data comparison and compensate them via providing a set of dynamic configuration parameters to the DT logic block. Hierarchically nested sub-DTs get their CPS output data via a twinning port, to provide adaptation on multiple levels of the DT. It is impor-

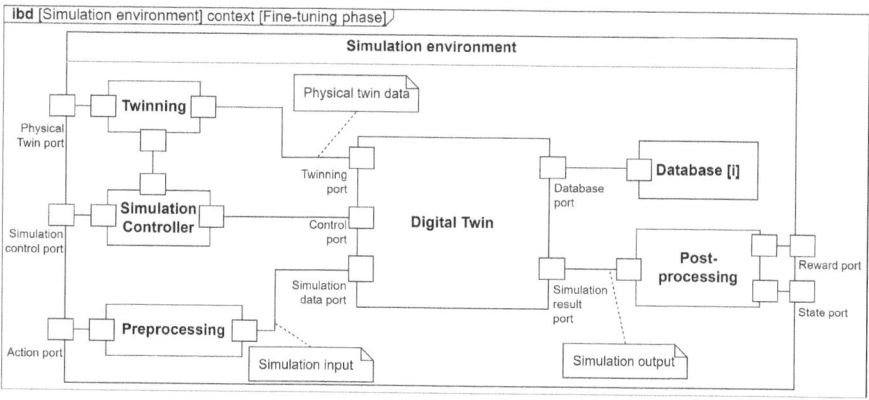

Fig. 4. Logical components and communication of the simulation environment.

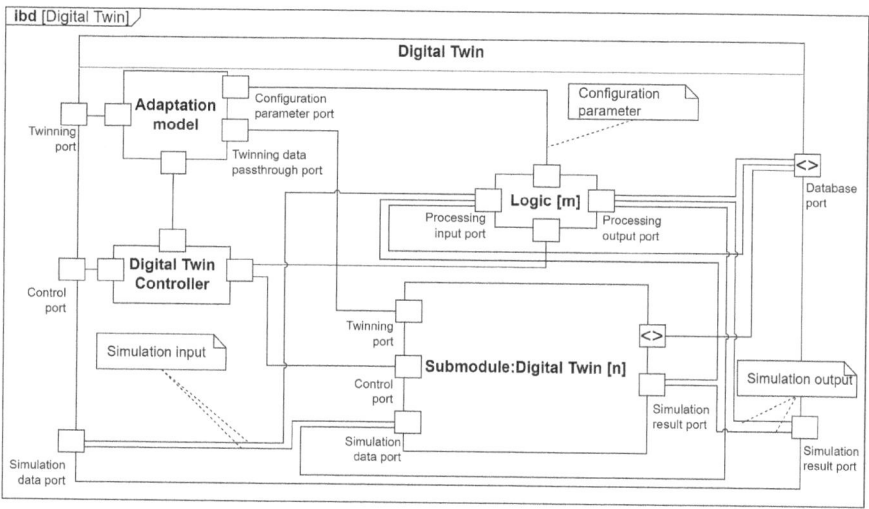

Fig. 5. Logical components and communication of the Digital Twin.

tant to define the configuration parameters that can (and cannot) be changed by every (sub-)DT to leverage the explainability and traceability provided by the architecture. The digital twin controller is used to control the adaptation model and the pass-through to sub-DTs. The logic of the adaptation model is hereby dependent on the current phase while the remainder of the architecture persists. During the training phase, the DT is used to create RL training data in a controlled manner for specified variants of the CPS but without synchronization to a CPS. Creating multiple instances of an adapted static DT representing a CPS variant for parallel RL training is possible. Slight derivatives of the adapted DT are possible to generate, via a configuration parameter generator. Generation of these parameters can be sampled from parameter distributions. These parameter

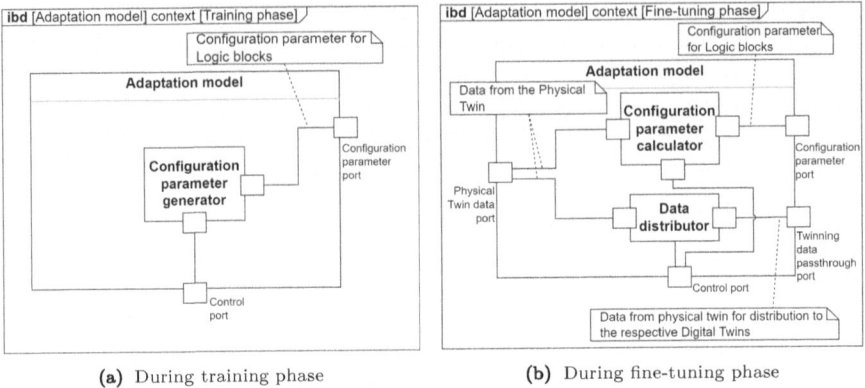

(a) During training phase   (b) During fine-tuning phase

Fig. 6. Logical components of the adaptation model.

distributions can either be estimated or measured based on one or more CPS that have already been synchronized during the fine-tuning phase. This operating mode is depicted in Fig. 6a. The fine-tuning phase sees a connected CPS, leading to the ability to synchronize behavior of the DT again. The main logical components can be seen in Fig. 6b. Twinning data from the CPS is used for calculating respective configuration parameters. This is in contrast to the training phase, where configuration parameters are generated or sourced from a parameter distribution. To realize the hierarchical DT structure, data pass-through is also handled inside the adaptation model via the data distributor.

In context of the robot-arm example, during the training phase parameter distributions are initially estimated e.g., for the room temperature, robot arm attachments properties, and manufacturing product's mass while the mechanical and electronic characteristics of the arm itself would typically be quite invariant. During the fine-tuning phase not only the optimization-RL can be improved with the DT twinned with data specific robot arm, but also the above mentioned parameter distributions can be adjusted with data from multiple robots arms. The latter is relevant for the training phase of a next iteration of the generic RLA.

3.4 Technical View

The concrete technical solution for the combination of DT and RL mainly depends on the specific demands of the use case. However, the integrability, re-usability and maintainability are the biggest drivers for a standardized solution on a technical realization level as well as execution-efficiency (requirements No. 2, 6, 7 and 8 in Table 1).

On the DT level (see Fig. 5), co-simulation is an ideal approach for simulating DTs of multiple system components to provide the possibility of creating a modular architecture where all models interact with a central control unit. Examples are HLA [15], FMI [23] or proprietary software solutions such as

Model.CONNECT[1]. They can enable the execution of simulations and calculations in a distributed computing manner using cloud-solutions and multiple on-site workstations. A benefit is increased execution speed of training data sampling which is, as already stated, a major requirement.

On a higher level, the development and integration of the architecture benefits from containerization with tools such as Docker[2]. It enables seamless and consistent deployment of the components across diverse environments by encapsulating them along with their dependencies. As the communication between the containers is via network and well defined thanks to the architecture, maintainability and scalability (multiple simulation environments for parallel sampling) is non-issue, and distributed computing between multiple workstations or in the cloud is possible.

With respect to the linkage between the DTs and their physical counterpart, infrastructure is needed that enables reliable and straightforward communication between the DT and the CPS. It is needed for (I) retrieval of physical twin data and (II) execution of optimization configurations. The level of sophistication of the applied framework depends on the use case characteristics. For this, an example is Basys4[3] where the communication between the physical asset and digital applications is managed by an Asset Administration Shell (AAS) which provides standardized communication interfaces (HTTP/REST interface) via network to applications. This makes a cloud-based deployment of the optimization RLA non-complex. In context of the presented architecture, the AAS represents the "Twinning" block (see Fig. 4) while the simulation environment can be seen as an application to the Basys4 framework. The simulation controller (see Fig. 7) can request from the AAS/Twinning block (which is connected to the physical system via a sub model) to send data to the twinning port of the DT. In principle, a profound integration of the Basys4 framework into the proposed approach is possible when considering simulation models including their sub-modules as the DT. However, this potential integration is not reflected in the given architecture.

4   Exemplary Application

The architecture is developed in conjunction with a use case from the highly-automated vehicle testing domain that aims for automatic creation of a 3D-environment for vehicle tests. The system to be optimized is the testbed including a virtual environment in conjunction with a vehicle. For development of automated vehicle driving functions, critical scenarios are to be optimized to ensure testing time is used for the most insightful tests in order to find e.g., weaknesses in the functions. Also, this approach could be used as open-exploration to build a database of scenarios. A scenario is usually characterized by specific criticality

---

[1] https://www.avl.com/en/simulation-solutions/software-offering/simulation-tools-z/modelconnect.

[2] https://www.docker.com/.

[3] https://www.basys40.de/ and https://github.com/eclipse-basyx.

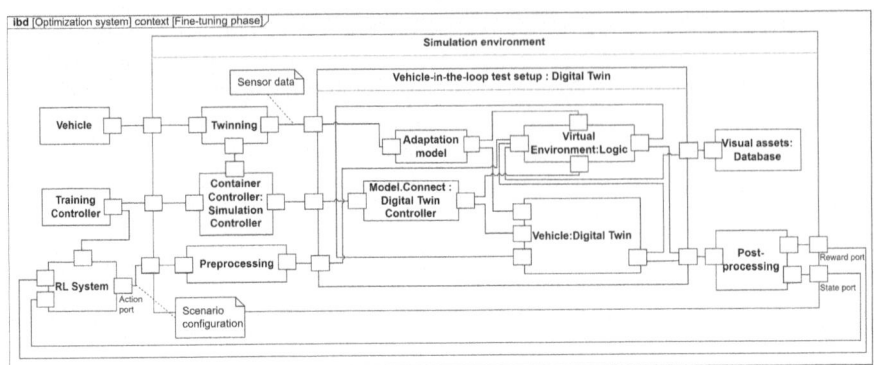

Fig. 7. Exemplary application of the architecture to a vehicle-in-the-loop test setup during the operational and fine-tuning phase wherein scenarios are optimized and additional data are gathered for further improvement of RLA.

metrics that indicate its significance and potential impacts [24]. The RLA proposes concrete scenarios with concrete parametrization/state values from logical scenarios with parameter ranges of state values (see [22]) which are executed on the virtual or real testbed, and the results are then computed to evaluate the scenarios.

Figure 7 showcases the logical view on the optimization system during the fine-tuning phase. Thanks to the reference architecture enabling hierarchical DTs, the DT of the vehicle test setup contains a virtual environment simulating e.g., the street as a logic block, and the DT of a vehicle enables a black-box integration of this sub-module. The vehicle DT can also contain other DTs as sub-modules e.g., of sensors or the chassis. A database is integrated to hold libraries of the virtual environment's assets. The simulation environment is connected to a vehicle its behavior it shall mimic. While in Fig. 7 the fine-tuning phase is depicted, the only difference to the training phase is the substitution of the adaptation model by a parameter generator as seen in Fig. 6. This results in the minimization of necessary adjustments to the system including data formats as the variation generator and the twinning function output data in identical format.

On a technical level, a Docker-based architecture is used for continuous development and prototyping. As a DT's co-simulation framework, Model.CONNECT was selected due to its features designed for automotive domain. As this example is a prototypical implementation, simple Python scripts are used to enable the function of the twinning and adaptation model. The implemented RL algorithm ("RL System" block in Fig. 7) is Maximum a Posteriori Policy Optimization (MPO) [1] inspired by [8]: an off-policy actor-critic approach.

Although a comprehensive assessment of the architecture's effectiveness and efficiency in facilitating the creation of a system capable of training and fine-tuning an optimization-RLA is ongoing, initial findings indicate favorable outcomes in terms of maintainability and reusability (see Table 1). The development process has been notably streamlined, for the incorporation of new features proving to be a straightforward task. However, a crucial aspect of the architecture and the system yet to be validated pertains to the representation capabilities of the variants, including the assessment of twinning.

5   Conclusion and Future Work

This position paper presents our work-in-progress regarding a reference architecture for DT-based AI-training for CPS optimization. In four viewpoints we highlighted the necessary considerations and requirements on the simulation environment including the DT as the virtual representation of the CPS, a model view of its functionality, a design-solution and technical considerations for the implementation. The differences of the architecture over the life-cycle of RL optimization (training-, operational- and fine-tuning phase) are highlighted and exemplary implementation in an automotive use case is shown.

In the future we will focus on improving the level of detail putting a strong focus on the differences between phases. The current state lacks detail on the requirements on data type and considerations of the twinning and variation generator. Further validation and integration are necessary in the above-mentioned use case to evaluate the improvement of the approach beyond the state of the art and verification of the broader applicability by utilizing it for the development of an alternative use case is needed. In addition, we will increase the research on behavioral modelling and the impacts on the architecture.

References

1. Abdolmaleki, A., Springenberg, J.T., Tassa, Y., Munos, R., Heess, N., Riedmiller, M.: Maximum a posteriori policy optimisation (2018). https://doi.org/10.48550/arXiv.1806.06920
2. Aheleroff, S., Xu, X., Zhong, R.Y., Lu, Y.: Digital twin as a service (DTAAS) in industry 4.0: An architecture reference model. Adv. Eng. Inform. **47**, 101225 (2021). https://doi.org/10.1016/j.aei.2020.101225
3. Alexopoulos, K., Nikolakis, N., Chryssolouris, G.: Digital twin-driven supervised machine learning for the development of artificial intelligence applications in manufacturing. Int. J. Comput. Integr. Manuf. **33**(5), 429–439 (2020). https://doi.org/10.1080/0951192X.2020.1747642
4. Amiranashvili, A., Argus, M., Hermann, L., Burgard, W., Brox, T.: Pre-training of deep RL agents for improved learning under domain randomization. eprint arXiv:2104.14386 (2021). https://doi.org/10.48550/arXiv.2104.14386
5. Barricelli, B.R., Casiraghi, E., Fogli, D.: A survey on digital twin: definitions, characteristics, applications, and design implications. IEEE Access **7**, 167653–167671 (2019). https://doi.org/10.1109/ACCESS.2019.2953499
6. Brankovic, B., Binder, C., Draxler, D., Neureiter, C., Lastro, G.: Towards a cross-domain modeling approach in system-of-systems architectures. In: Boy, G.A., Guegan, A., Krob, D., Vion, V. (eds.) CSDM 2019, pp. 164–175. Springer, Cham (2020). https://doi.org/10.1007/978-3-030-34843-4_14

7. Cobbe, K., Klimov, O., Hesse, C., Kim, T., Schulman, J.: Quantifying generalization in reinforcement learning. In: 36th International Conference on Machine Learning, vol. PMLR 97. PMLR, Long Beach, USA (2019)
8. Degrave, J., et al.: Magnetic control of tokamak plasmas through deep reinforcement learning. Nature **602**(7897), 414–419 (2022). https://doi.org/10.1038/s41586-021-04301-9
9. Dulac-Arnold, G., et al.: Challenges of real-world reinforcement learning: definitions, benchmarks and analysis. Mach. Learn. **110**(9), 2419–2468 (2021)
10. Ferko, E., Bucaioni, A., Behnam, M.: Architecting digital twins. IEEE Access **10**, 50335–50350 (2022). https://doi.org/10.1109/ACCESS.2022.3172964
11. Gan, X., Zuo, Y., Zhang, A., Li, S., Tao, F.: Digital twin-enabled adaptive scheduling strategy based on deep reinforcement learning. Sci. China Technol. Sci. 1–15 (2023)
12. Grieves, M., Vickers, J., (None): Digital twin: mitigating unpredictable, undesirable emergent behavior in complex systems. In: Kahlen, F.J., Flumerfelt, S., Alves, A. (eds.) Transdisciplinary Perspectives on Complex Systems, pp. 85–113. Springer, Cham (2016). https://doi.org/10.1007/978-3-319-38756-7
13. Haj-Ali, A., Ahmed, N.K., Willke, T., Gonzalez, J., Asanovic, K., Stoica, I.: A view on deep reinforcement learning in system optimization
14. Hankel, M., Rexroth, B.: Das Referenzarchitekturmodell Industrie 4.0 (RAMI 4.0)
15. IEEE: IEEE standard for modeling and simulation (m&s) high level architecture (HLA): Framework and rules (2010). https://standards.ieee.org/ieee/1516/3744/
16. Jamil, S., Rahman, M.: Fawad: a comprehensive survey of digital twins and federated learning for industrial internet of things (IIOT), internet of vehicles (IOV) and internet of drones (IOD). Appl. Syst. Innov. **5**(3), 56 (2022)
17. Jones, D., Snider, C., Nassehi, A., Yon, J., Hicks, B.: Characterising the digital twin: a systematic literature review. CIRP J. Manuf. Sci. Technol. **29**, 36–52 (2020). https://doi.org/10.1016/j.cirpj.2020.02.002
18. Ju, H., Juan, R., Gomez, R., Nakamura, K., Li, G.: Transferring policy of deep reinforcement learning from simulation to reality for robotics. Nature Mach. Intell. **4**(12), 1077–1087 (2022). https://doi.org/10.1038/s42256-022-00573-6
19. Julian, R., Swanson, B., Sukhatme, G.S., Levine, S., Finn, C., Hausman, K.: Never stop learning: the effectiveness of fine-tuning in robotic reinforcement learning. arXiv preprint arXiv:2004.10190 (2020)
20. Kairouz, P., et al. (eds.): Advances and Open Problems in Federated Learning, Foundation and Trends in Machine Learning, vol. 14. Now Publishers Inc. (2021). https://doi.org/10.1561/2200000083
21. Matulis, M., Harvey, C.: A robot arm digital twin utilising reinforcement learning. Comput. Graph. **95**, 106–114 (2021). https://doi.org/10.1016/j.cag.2021.01.011
22. Menzel, T., Bagschik, G., Maurer, M.: 2018 IEEE Intelligent Vehicles Symposium (IV): 26–30 June 2018, Piscataway, NJ. IEEE (2018)
23. Modelica Association Project FMI: Functional mock-up interface for model exchange and co-simulation (2019)
24. Neurohr, C., Westhofen, L., Henning, T., de Graaff, T., Möhlmann, E., Böde, E.: Fundamental considerations around scenario-based testing for automated driving. In: IEEE Intelligent Vehicles Symposium Proceedings, pp. 121–127 (2020). https://doi.org/10.1109/IV47402.2020.9304823
25. Osiński, B., et al.: Simulation-based reinforcement learning for real-world autonomous driving. In: 2020 IEEE International Conference on Robotics and Automation (ICRA), pp. 6411–6418. IEEE (2020)

26. Pohl, K., Broy, M., Daembkes, H., Hönninger, H. (eds.): Advanced Model-Based Engineering of Embedded Systems. Springer, Cham (2016). https://doi.org/10.1007/978-3-319-48003-9

27. Shen, G., et al.: Deep reinforcement learning for flocking motion of multi-UAV systems: learn from a digital twin. IEEE Internet Things J. **9**(13), 11141–11153 (2021)

28. Shen, G., Lei, L., Zhang, X., Li, Z., Cai, S., Zhang, L.: Multi-UAV cooperative search based on reinforcement learning with a digital twin driven training framework. IEEE Trans. Veh. Technol. **72**, 8354–8368 (2023)

29. Stark, R., Damerau, T.: Digital twin. In: Chatti, S., Tolio, T. (eds.) CIRP Encyclopedia of Production Engineering, pp. 1–8. Springer Berlin Heidelberg, Heidelberg (2019). https://doi.org/10.1007/978-3-642-35950-7_16870-1

30. Sun, W., Lei, S., Wang, L., Liu, Z., Zhang, Y.: Adaptive federated learning and digital twin for industrial internet of things. IEEE Trans. Industr. Inf. **17**(8), 5605–5614 (2021). https://doi.org/10.1109/TII.2020.3034674

31. Sutton, R.S., Barto, A.: Reinforcement Learning: An Introduction. Adaptive Computation and Machine Learning, 2nd edn. The MIT Press, Cambridge, Massachusetts and London, England (2018)

32. Wagg, D.J., Worden, K., Barthorpe, R.J., Gardner, P.: Digital twins: state-of-the-art and future directions for modeling and simulation in engineering dynamics applications. ASCE - ASME J. Risk Uncertainty Eng. Syst. **6**(3) (2020). https://doi.org/10.1115/1.4046739

33. Zhang, Z., Zahng, D., Qiu, R.C.: Deep reinforcement learning for power system: an overview. CSEE J. Power Energy Syst. **6**(1) (2020). https://doi.org/10.17775/CSEEJPES.2019.00920

Towards an Urban Digital Twins Continuum Architecture

Sergio Laso[1](✉) , Lorenzo Toro-Gálvez[2] , Javier Berrocal[1] ,
Javier Troya[2] , Carlos Canal[2] , and Juan Manuel Murillo[1]

[1] University of Extremadura, Badajoz, Spain
{slasom,jberolm,juanmamu}@unex.es
[2] ITIS Software, Universidad de Málaga, Málaga, Spain
{lorenzotoro,jtroya,carloscanal}@uma.es

Abstract. In the era of smart cities, where the integration of Internet of Things devices and the need to efficiently manage urban environments have generated considerable interest, the Digital Twin concept emerges as a key solution. This technology allows us to study and simulate the behavior of complex urban dynamics. However, conventional Digital Twin architectures face significant challenges, such as limited scalability, inherent latency, and data privacy concerns stemming mainly from their centralized nature. In response to these challenges, this paper proposes an innovative distributed architecture for the so-called Urban Digital Twins, implemented on top of the Computing continuum. The main objective is to establish a more efficient and scalable framework, specifically designed for the demands of smart cities. To support the feasibility of this proposal, two case studies are presented: one focused on urban public transportation systems, and the other focused on a pollution monitoring system. These case studies illustrate how a distributed architecture can effectively address existing challenges, providing a solid foundation for the smart and sustainable management of urban environments.

Keywords: Urban Digital Twins · Architecture · Smart City · Computing continuum

1 Introduction

In recent years, we have witnessed a significant increase in the use of Internet-connected devices, which has led to the emergence of the IoT paradigm [20]. This approach has been applied in various fields, such as smart homes, healthcare, industry 4.0, and smart cities. However, making adjustments to the operation in these largely distributed systems can lead to unexpected problems. For example, in a smart city scenario, managing traffic based on air quality values to alleviate congestion in one area may inadvertently lead to traffic jams in other places.

To try to solve this kind of problems, Digital Twins [22] have recently emerged as a powerful technology to replicate the behavior of real systems. A Digital Twin

B. Tekinerdoğan et al. (Eds.): ECSA 2023, LNCS 14590, pp. 272–286, 2024.
https://doi.org/10.1007/978-3-031-66326-0_17

(DT) is a digital representation of a system, service, or product. To create such a digital representation, it must receive the status of the physical system, which allows it to replicate the real environment. In a DT system, there is a bidirectional communication between the two twins that allows keeping the digital twin updated and proposing changes on the physical twin [13]. DTs become fundamental tools for monitoring, predicting, and integrating data from IoT devices.

However, conventional DT implementations have several limitations on scalability [18], latency [12], and privacy [6]. These limitations become evident when we want to represent highly-distributed systems such as smart cities, with a large variety of data sources from IoT devices, people, etc. Conventional DTs are highly-coupled systems where all collected data is centralized in one single place. Creating a so-called Urban Digital Twin (UDT) this way is practically unfeasible due to its size and complexity.

To try to overcome these challenges, the Computing continuum paradigm [2] has been gaining importance in recent years. The Computing continuum represents an evolution of Cloud computing that extends from cloud environments to IoT devices, located closer to people, for the purpose of storing and processing information. The Fog and Edge computing paradigms have brought cloud computing environments and data processing closer to information sources. By processing information closer to its source, it is possible to reduce infrastructure load, improve the quality of service, and preserve privacy.

In this paper, we propose a distributed architecture on the low-coupling Computing Continuum [3, 7] composed of different DTs that simulate the behavior of different entities in a highly-distributed system, so that altogether they compose a UDT. Due to their low coupling, the DTs work independently but can interact with each other to enrich their models allowing greater scalability and flexibility. Their distributed nature and proximity to users allow for improved data privacy as well as faster responsiveness, as it minimizes data transmission. To demonstrate the feasibility of our proposal, two case studies focused on smart cities are considered in this work, one focused on an urban public transportation system, and the other focused on a pollution monitoring system.

The paper is organized as follows. Section 2 provides an introductory context on the current state and need for an Urban Digital Twin (UDT) in the computing continuum. In Sect. 3, some related work is examined in detail. Section 4 provides a detailed explanation of the proposed Digital Twins architecture for the Computing Continuum. Section 5 presents in detail the two case studies that addressed transportation and pollution in a smart city. Section 6 discusses how our proposal addresses the current challenges and also its limitations. Finally, in Sect. 7, the conclusions derived from the study are presented and some directions for future research are outlined.

2   Motivation

In the context of smart cities, it encompasses a diversity of systems and applications aimed at optimizing their governance. These include fundamental areas such as transportation [14], whose main objective is to offer an efficient service of the arrival times of public transport, as well as in the identification of traffic patterns to improve urban mobility. Also, in the field of pollution control [5], new regulations are emerging due to the problems generated by air quality, intending to monitor them to avoid penalties and improve air quality.

The implementation of Digital Twins in these strategic areas would not only improve operational efficiency but also contribute to the sustainability and resilience of cities. By providing a real-time digital representation of the infrastructure, Digital Twins facilitate a detailed understanding and analysis of urban systems, enabling data-driven decision-making to address critical challenges such as traffic congestion, environmental pollution, and public transportation planning.

Digital Twins represent essential tools [1] in monitoring, predicting, and integrating data from IoT devices. They continuously exchange data, including dynamic physical twin data and environmental data, and store it in a data storage system (the so-called *data lake*). They use ontologies for data comprehension, high-dimensional data analysis, and data fusion algorithms to integrate multiple data sources. With artificial intelligence (AI) algorithms, DTs can perform feature selection, pattern recognition, and optimization. In addition, they enable closed-loop optimization, allowing the physical entity to respond to changes based on the DT's analysis and optimization. DTs have self-adaptation and self-parametrization capabilities, allowing them to resemble the physical twin throughout their lifecycle. They employ predictive analytics to forecast future statuses and use prescriptive analytics to make data-driven decisions.

The Digital Twins in the context of smart cities are referred to as Urban Digital Twins (UDTs) [4]. An Urban Digital Twin (UDT) is a Digital Twin that acts as a virtual representation of a city's physical resources, making use of data, analytics, and AI to generate real-time, adaptive simulation models. This digital twin captures both the present state and historical context of various aspects of a smart city. Moreover, additional applications provide practical intelligence, contributing to the construction of a collective picture of urban reality. UDTs facilitate more informed decision-making, foster collaborative governance, and improve urban planning by providing a safe environment for environmental sustainability [26].

To achieve the development of a UDT, it is essential to collect data from a variety of sources that are produced by a smart city, ranging from sensors to contextual information and the experience of users interacting with different services such as the transportation system. In previous work [9, 15], we proposed innovative models such as *People-as-a-Service (PeaaS)* and *Human Microservices* designed specifically for IoT environments. The purpose of these models lies in the collection and detailed analysis of user habits and routines. By implementing these models, we can effectively integrate citizen information into UDT models. This approach would give us the opportunity to enrich the UDT to make it more accurate and adapted to the context of the citizens who make use of it.

However, a traditional approach would involve implementing a centralized and monolithic UDT, usually deployed in the cloud. Inevitably, this comes with significant drawbacks. First, there is the complexity and lack of scalability of the system, as all information and processes are concentrated in a single location. Storing data generated by the entire city would require extremely large data transmission and storage capacities, generating considerable costs. As an example, consider the Los Angeles Department of Transportation [23], which processed more than 7 Terabytes of real-time data daily in 2022 from different sources like traffic lights signals, traffic sensors, bus signals, etc. In addition, there are concerns about user privacy when storing sensitive data about individuals, which compromises the integration of data from various sources. By concentrating all information at a single point, considerable computing power would be required to integrate all sources of information. Since the processing capabilities of a centralized model may be limited, this would adversely affect system performance and the quality of results, or greatly increase operational costs.

To overcome these drawbacks, a solution is to use distributed architectures such as Computing continuum [17] to deploy a UDT. With this type of architecture, different entities (citizens, buses, air monitoring stations, etc.) deploy their own DT providing low coupling, allowing them to work independently but interact with each other to enrich their models allowing for greater scalability and flexibility. By adopting this distributed architecture, concerns associated with centralized storage and processing on a single node, as well as high coupling between entities, are overcome. In addition, this strategy addresses privacy concerns, as personal information is handled and processed in a decentralized manner on individual devices, ensuring anonymization and preservation of data privacy.

To carry out this initiative, in this paper, we present a detailed proposal of an architecture designed in the framework of the Computing continuum to implement a UDT. To demonstrate the feasibility of this proposal, we provide a description of its application in two specific contexts: a transportation system and a pollution control system. We explain in detail how this architecture would be implemented in each of these scenarios, highlighting its adaptability to complex and dynamic urban environments, materializing the usefulness and practical applicability of a distributed UDT in concrete cases of great relevance for the improvement of the quality of life in urban environments.

3   Related Work

In this section, we present and analyze some related works on Urban Digital Twins, and we detail the requirements of this kind of system.

Lehtola et al. [11] study the impact of digital twins in smart cities. They argue that UDTs must address the specific needs of a city, offering high-fidelity content. In addition, continuous updating of the UDT—using devices like IoT sensors—is essential to reflect the constant urban changes. The authors emphasize the necessity of taking humans into consideration to ensure successful implementation in order to improve decision-making, which is a concern that we also share. They also highlight the incorporation of AI techniques for automatically updating models through the utilization of sensor data.

Schrotter and Hurzeler [21] present a UDT for the city of Zurich, which is defined as a digital and spatial model of the city that integrates 3D spatial data and models for different themes. We have chosen this work because it shows diverse applications of digital twins in smart cities: analyze city growth, visualize construction projects, assess the impact on urban climate, and enable active public participation in planning, among others. The authors also highlight the availability of open data, which is an essential component for the success and usefulness of the UDT.

Ruiz et al. propose BODIT [19], a UDT of the public transportation system in the city of Badalona (Spain). They use a traffic simulator and a genetic algorithm to reproduce the city's traffic and adapt to different situations. Bus schedules are used to predict and detect a lack of punctuality at bus stops, enabling informed decision-making as a response to unusual situations such as accidents.

Although these works present interesting UDT initiatives, there are several significant concerns that they do not properly address. In particular, all of them describe a monolithic and centralized UDT architecture. A smart city is a complex system composed of a large set of subsystems, devices, people, etc. Therefore, centralized UDTs may be unmanageable and unfeasible due to its sheer scale and complexity.

One example of a distributed architecture is given in Villalonga et al. [25], in which the authors present a distributed DT framework that improves local decision-making in the manufacturing industry. The integration of local and global digital twins enables more accurate fault detection, notifying the system for reconfiguration and scheduling actions. This distributed approach offers the advantage of increasing efficiency in decision-making by using improved predictive models and performing simulations at different levels.

After reviewing and analyzing these and other related works, we have identified several limitations that we aim to address with our approach. Some of the proposals [11,19,21] primarily focus on monolithic and centralized architectures for UDTs, ignoring the potential advantages of a distributed architecture as discussed in [25]. We can go further and consider this distribution of UDTs over the Continuum to solve the problems that centralized architectures present, such as scalability, response time, and structural complexity, among others. Taking these concerns into consideration, we advocate that DT proposals for smart cities and other complex systems follow a hierarchical and distributed architecture over the Continuum, addressing the following requirements:

- **Scalability and flexibility.** The DT architecture must rest on weakly coupled systems, which operate independently and interact and coordinate with each other. A distributed architecture allows for the storage and processing of information in the entities where it is generated or consumed. This provides greater scalability and flexibility, avoiding the complexity associated with centralized systems. Each entity manages its own information and resources, contributing to a more adaptable system.

- **Data privacy.** Personal data privacy must be prioritized by keeping sensitive information stored and processed locally on citizens' devices. This decentralized approach minimizes the need for data transmission, reducing the risks associated with centralizing sensitive data.
- **Reduction of duplicity.** By distributing computation, the system optimizes resource allocation and avoids duplicating computational tasks. Component reuse and modularization minimize duplicity by designing components that prevent redundant functionalities in different layers.
- **Reactivity and responsiveness.** By enabling local-level responsiveness, where data are computed in proximity, the system will achieve faster response times, enabling the system to react promptly to changes and events, ensuring quick processing, and providing almost instantaneous responses.
- **Adaptability to complex systems.** Smart cities are complex systems that integrate technology, interconnected infrastructures, and citizen participation to address urban challenges. Monolithic and single-deployment DTs do not address these challenges correctly. A distributed DT handles the complexity in a better way, by adapting and scaling components according to the needs. This adaptability will ensure that the DT adapts to the specific requirements and complexity of smart cities, offering flexibility and scalability as mentioned above.
- **Collaboration.** A loosely-coupled distributed DT architecture facilitates collaboration between systems or applications by providing a platform for data and knowledge exchange. Multiple applications can connect to shared twins, enabling real-time collaboration and decision-making. By leveraging a distributed architecture, DTs can be shared by different systems, leading to interoperability and resource optimization.

4   Architecture

This section presents our proposal for an Urban Digital Twin architecture in the Continuum. We will also describe which modules and components form the different layers of the architecture.

Figure 1 illustrates the proposed architecture, where the Physical Twin (PT) and the Digital Twin (DT) establish communication through a Distributed Data Lake (DDL), following the architectural conceptualization for DT systems suggested by Muñoz et al. [13]—only two Edge nodes and one Fog node have been represented for simplicity, although this structure could be expanded. The particularity of this architecture in the Continuum lies in the flexible coupling between components, managed by the Cloud, Fog, Edge, and Things layers. Figure 1 illustrates the proposed architecture, where the Physical Twin (PT) and the Digital Twin (DT) establish communication through a Distributed Data Lake (DDL), following the architectural conceptualization for DT systems suggested by Muñoz et al. [13]—only two Edge nodes and one Fog node have been represented for simplicity, although this structure could be expanded. The particularity of this architecture in the Continuum lies in the flexible coupling between components, managed by the Cloud, Fog, Edge, and Things layers.

In this context, the DT adopts a distributed architecture in which each instance of the twin operates autonomously, avoiding dependence on a centralized replica of the entire system. This approach provides flexibility and efficiency in data management, offering different levels of information and knowledge, and avoiding unnecessary data transmission and infrastructure overload. The key to achieving this objective lies in the distribution of the data lake along the Continuum so that each layer can write to and read from the corresponding DDL module. This distribution favors system adaptability, allowing each component to contribute to knowledge generation in an autonomous and collaborative way.

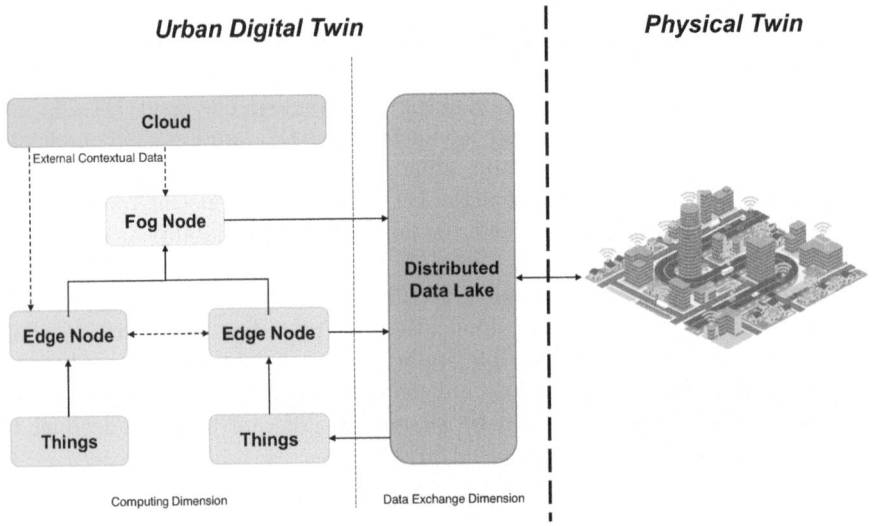

Fig. 1. Architecture proposed.

– **Things layer:** This layer focuses on the sensors that provide information to the Edge nodes. These sensors are physical devices that capture real-time data about the environment in the PT and write it in the DDL. This data is fundamental to the operation of the UDT, as it feeds the monitoring, analysis, and decision-making process. Each DT module in the Things layer gets the corresponding data from the DDL and sends it to an Edge node. This is represented in Fig. 1 with the arrow from the DDL to a Things module—only the connection with one Thing module is depicted for simplicity. Unlike Edge nodes or the Fog layer, the Things layer generally does not perform computations or data processing itself but focuses on capturing the corresponding data from the DDL and transmitting it to the Edge nodes.

– **Edge layer:** The Edge layer is composed of devices located at the periphery of the network that perform the function of collecting information from the Things layer or from other services. These Edge nodes also host DT modules that store the information collected from the Things layer that allows it to analyze and predict the behavior of the elements it monitors. Therefore, these devices must have sufficient capabilities for data collection and the provision of a DT.

The results obtained through these analyses are written in the DDL for the PT to have access to them as well as the Fog nodes for further processing. Additionally, Edge nodes also exchange information with each other. This collaboration and information sharing contribute to improving and enriching the results generated by the DTs present in each of the nodes. By working together, the Edge nodes achieve greater accuracy and quality in the results obtained. They also increase their capacity to adapt to changes and unexpected situations, as they can benefit from the experience and knowledge shared among them.

– **Fog layer:** The Fog layer serves as a crucial intermediary, tasked with gathering and retaining data sourced from the Edge nodes. This collection of data from the Edge nodes is instrumental in providing a more expansive and nuanced understanding of the system. Within each Fog node, Digital Twin (DT) modules play a pivotal role-they not only store the information acquired from the Edge nodes but also conduct in-depth analyses, unraveling the intricacies of the data. This involves identifying patterns, discerning trends, pinpointing emerging issues, and distilling this raw data into valuable knowledge and insights.

The knowledge thus amassed proves to be indispensable for anticipating events and making well-informed decisions. This reservoir of insights is not left untapped; instead, it is meticulously recorded in the DDL. This strategic move ensures that the Physical Twin (PT) has direct and immediate access to this wealth of information. By leveraging the capabilities of the Fog layer, the system not only enhances its capacity to comprehend the intricacies of the data but also empowers decision-makers with the foresight and understanding needed to navigate complex scenarios and make proactive, informed choices.

– **Cloud layer:** The Cloud layer plays a pivotal role in the system by serving as a repository for diverse external contextual data obtained from a multitude of sources including databases, APIs, and more. This layer is essential for consolidating and storing this contextual information, which is subsequently utilized to feed and enhance the functionality of the other layers within the architecture. By gathering and integrating data from various external sources, the Cloud layer ensures that the entire system has access to a comprehensive and up-to-date pool of information, facilitating more accurate analyses, predictions, and decision-making across the distributed digital twin architecture.

5   Case Studies

The proposed architecture demonstrates adaptability, allowing it to be applied
to various case studies or applications. Depending on the scenario, different elements within the architecture can assume different roles, tailored to the requirements of each application. This versatility enables the architecture to be customized based on the problem being addressed. In this section, we explore two
case studies that exemplify the adaptability of our architecture. In the first one,
the government of a smart city wants to collect data about its public transportation system and how its citizens use it, with the goal of deploying a UDT
to optimize and improve service to citizens. In the second one, the government
has to comply with current pollution regulations and wants to implement a UDT
pollution monitoring system to improve the accuracy of air quality prediction
and avoid non-compliance.

5.1   Urban Transportation System

In Fig. 2, we apply the proposed architecture to a bus transportation system,
focusing on improving the accuracy of predicting bus arrival times, detecting
potential skipped stops, and/or knowing how citizens move around the city. To
achieve this, our architecture takes into consideration both buses and passengers.
Next, we present a description of the architecture implementation:

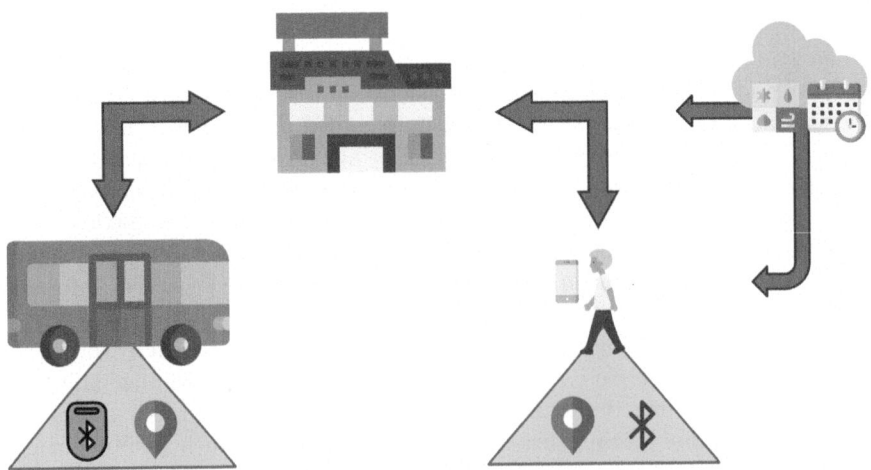

Fig. 2. Case study: Urban transportation system.

Things Layer: This layer contains Bluetooth beacons and GPS devices installed
on each bus of the transportation system, as well as the sensors (GPS and
Bluetooth) of passengers' smartphones. The bus' GPS tracks and locates the

current position, while beacons are used to detect passengers' presence through Bluetooth and count the number of people on board. These data are essential to analyze pedestrian movement patterns and calculate whether the bus will be able to make a stop at the following destinations, considering the maximum capacity allowed.

Edge Layer: The Edge nodes represent both buses and passengers, each with their own DT. Regarding the buses, each one is represented by an Edge node consisting of a DT that simulates the bus behavior. These Edge nodes are fed with the data of each bus, coming from the information of the Things layer. The information gathered allows the DTs to more accurately predict bus arrival times and identify situations where a stop may be skipped due to capacity limitations.

Similarly, each passenger is represented by an Edge node consisting of a DT that represents and simulates the user's Digital Avatar [16] that refers to the virtual representation of a person residing on their smartphone, collecting information about their habits and preferences, and allowing them to interact with the other DTs. These Edge nodes capture the information of individual passengers within the transportation system. By integrating the data from both the buses' DTs and Digital Avatars' DTs, the Edge layer improves the accuracy of arrival time predictions and overall system optimization.

Apart from their individual roles, the Edge layer facilitates horizontal communication between buses and passengers within the transportation system. Passengers can receive real-time updates and notifications about bus schedules or delays. Furthermore, buses can also communicate with other buses within the Edge layer, promoting collaboration and coordination for better efficiency.

Fog Layer: The Fog layer is essential in the bus transportation system. Each bus line is governed by a Fog node, which contains a DT representing and simulating the buses' behavior on that specific line. These Fog nodes serve as data collection and processing points for the Edge nodes, enabling the creation of an overall model for the entire line. In addition, the Fog layer is responsible for periodically distributing the federated model to other buses to update their respective DTs. This update occurs regularly or when a new bus joins the line, ensuring all buses benefit from the latest updates in the prediction model.

Moreover, the Fog nodes may be interested in incorporating information about people's habitual travel patterns to determine if a person who usually takes a specific bus line will be using it on a particular day. This information can be leveraged to provide targeted recommendations for specific buses, ensuring that the transportation system adjusts to the individual's needs and preferences.

Cloud Layer: This layer plays a crucial role in providing external contextual information, such as weather conditions, event calendars, and vacation dates. This contextual information is used to further enrich the prediction and decision-making model. For instance, considering weather conditions allows anticipating possible delays due to rain or adverse weather factors. Likewise, by taking into account the calendar of events and vacation dates, the transportation demand prediction can be adjusted and resource allocation can be optimized.

5.2   Pollution Monitoring System

In Fig. 3, we apply the proposed architecture to a pollution control system, focusing on analyzing and predicting pollution levels of CO2 and allergenic particles to improve the accuracy of air quality prediction. Next, we present a description of the architecture implementation:

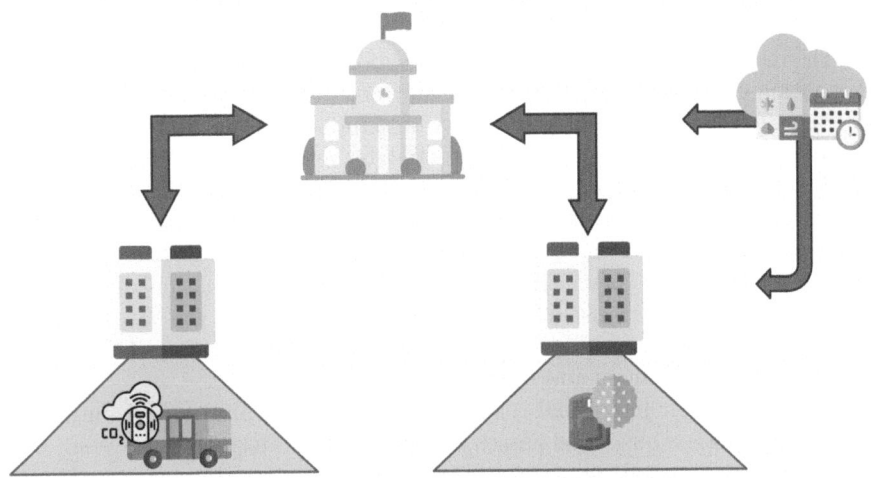

Fig. 3. Case study: Pollution monitoring system.

Things Layer: In this layer, there are sensors distributed throughout the city to measure air pollution levels, such as CO2 and suspended particles (pollutants, pollen, and other allergenic particles). CO2 sensors are located on the buses moving around the city. The data from the suspended particle sensors are strategically distributed at different points in the city.

Edge Layer: In the Edge layer, there are pollution analysis control centers distributed in different neighborhoods in the city. These centers are responsible for capturing the data coming from the Things layer. Each control center has its own DT, which represents and simulates the behavior of the center in question.

The pollution analysis control centers receive the data collected through their DTs and perform a comprehensive analysis of these data. The DTs are able to predict accurately CO2 pollution levels and suspended particle concentrations. This information is used to generate notifications and alerts to citizens through information panels. These panels display real-time and predictive information on air quality, providing relevant data on CO2 levels and allergenic particles. In this way, citizens can be informed about the air quality in their environment and receive alerts in case of risk situations or high levels of allergenic particles or activate action protocols to address the problem.

Fog Layer: The Fog layer is represented with one node by the city's air management system. Its main function is to collect and process the information coming from the different control centers. The information collected by the Fog node is essential to feed and enrich the DT present in this layer. The DT uses historical data to analyze and evaluate air quality in the city. By analyzing long-term patterns and trends, the DT can provide a complete and detailed picture of pollution and allergy levels.

The results are critical to making informed decisions. For example, if an area with high CO_2 levels is detected, authorities can take measures to regulate traffic in that area, reduce pollutant emissions, and comply with regulations set by the European Union. Regarding the concentration of allergenic particles, if high levels of allergenic particles are predicted in certain areas of the city, this will imply an increase in allergy cases in the local population. The health system can use this information to take proactive measures and provide better resource allocation and better care to affected citizens.

Cloud Layer: The Cloud layer is essential for integrating data sources from meteorological portals and event calendars to enrich the models of the different DTs. For instance, weather conditions, such as wind speed and precipitation, along with temperature and humidity, impact the dispersion of pollutants and concentration of allergenic particles in the air. Additionally, integrating event calendar data helps identify activities like sports events, concerts, or festivals that can lead to increased traffic and crowds, directly affecting air quality.

6 Discussion

In this section, we analyze the proposed architecture for the Urban Digital Twin (UDT) over the Continuum. We analyze how this proposal stands out for its scalability, flexibility, and privacy enhancement in complex urban environments. In addition, we carefully examine challenging considerations, such as implementation complexity, infrastructure requirements, and security-related issues. This critical assessment provides insight into the suitability and feasibility of the UDT architecture in the Continuum, offering a holistic perspective for consideration in smart city management. The issues addressed position it as a robust and adaptable solution for the efficient management of urban environments. However, like any proposal, it also presents certain limitations.

Firstly, the distributed architecture in the Continuum allows for efficient scalability. Each entity deploys its own Digital Twin, which facilitates the incorporation of new urban elements without affecting the existing infrastructure. This ensures exceptional adaptability as the city evolves and expands, enabling the seamless integration of new services and devices. Nevertheless, the implementation of a distributed architecture composed of different entities can be complex, requiring careful planning and coordination. This can lead to challenges in terms of integration and initial configuration, especially in urban environments already established with pre-existing systems. It is therefore important to consider economic and technological feasibility, especially for those cities with limited resources.

Secondly, the low coupling between the DTs of the different entities enables their independent operation. In addition, the architecture enables collaboration between them, thus enriching their models and improving joint decision-making. This optimizes operational efficiency while fostering collaboration and synergy between the different urban components. This low coupling brings inherent privacy improvements as information is stored and processed at the data source. This feature is fundamental to gaining the trust of citizens and ensuring compliance with privacy regulations. This low coupling in data management also poses additional challenges in terms of security and protection against threats. Careful implementation of security measures is required to ensure data integrity and confidentiality, as well as resilience to potential attacks.

The Urban Digital Twin architecture in the Continuum offers numerous advantages, from its flexibility to its privacy enhancement. However, its effective implementation requires carefully addressing the associated constraints, ensuring a smooth transition and long-term benefits for smart city management.

7   Conclusions and Future Work

Recently, Digital Twins have emerged as a powerful enabling technology for the virtualization of systems, products, and services. They represent fundamental tools for monitoring, prediction, and integration of data from IoT devices. Despite their benefits, conventional implementations face challenges such as scalability, coupling, or privacy, which can affect their ability to adapt optimally in scenarios with a high distribution of resources. To try to overcome these challenges, there are architectures such as the Computing continuum that enable the flexibility and distribution capabilities inherent to Digital Twins, thus ensuring their usefulness in diverse environments and applications.

In this paper, we have presented an architecture for Urban Digital Twins deployed in the Continuum, which addresses the limitations of conventional DTs in terms of scalability, latency, and privacy, among others. Through the distribution of DTs in the Continuum, we achieve greater flexibility and responsiveness, as well as more efficient data and privacy management. In addition, through citizen participation, we can ensure personalized data-driven decision-making. The case studies presented demonstrate the applicability and effectiveness of our architecture in the context of smart cities, enabling more accurate and participatory management of urban environments.

We are currently implementing the architecture for both case studies, setting up the necessary infrastructure, and deploying the different components across the layers. We have already obtained some preliminary implementation results, presented in [10, 24]. Furthermore, in [8] we introduce Perses, a tool that emulates different parts of the Computing Continuum, including user smartphones.

Acknowledgements. This work has been partially funded by grant DIN2020-011586, funded by MCIN/AEI/10.13039/501100011033 and by the European Union "Next

GenerationEU/PRTR", by the Spanish Ministry of Science, Innovation, and Universities (projects PID2021-125527NB-I00, TED2021-130913B-I00, TED2021-130523B-I00, and PD C2022-133465-I00), by the Regional Ministry of Economy, Science and Digital Agenda of the Regional Government of Extremadura (GR21133) and the European Regional Development Fund.

References

1. Barricelli, B.R., Casiraghi, E., Fogli, D.: A survey on digital twin: definitions, characteristics, applications, and design implications. IEEE Access **7**, 167653–167671 (2019)
2. Bendechache, M., Svorobej, S., Takako Endo, P., Lynn, T.: Simulating resource management across the cloud-to-thing continuum: a survey and future directions. Future Internet **12**(6), 95 (2020)
3. Costantini, A., et al.: Iotwins: Toward implementation of distributed digital twins in industry 4.0 settings. Computers **11**(5), 67 (2022)
4. Deng, T., Zhang, K., Shen, Z.: A systematic review of a digital twin city: a new pattern of urban governance toward smart cities. J. Manag. Sci. Eng. **6**(2), 125–134 (2021)
5. Fadda, M., Anedda, M., Girau, R., Pau, G., Giusto, D.D.: A social internet of things smart city solution for traffic and pollution monitoring in Cagliari. IEEE Internet Things J. **10**(3), 2373–2390 (2022)
6. Fuller, A., Fan, Z., Day, C., Barlow, C.: Digital twin: enabling technologies, challenges and open research. IEEE Access **8**, 108952–108971 (2020)
7. Laso, S., et al.: Elastic data analytics for the cloud-to-things continuum. IEEE Internet Comput. **26**(6), 42–49 (2022)
8. Laso, S., Berrocal, J., Fernández, P., Ruiz-Cortés, A., Murillo, J.M.: Perses: a framework for the continuous evaluation of the QoS of distributed mobile applications. Pervasive Mob. Comput. **84**, 101627 (2022)
9. Laso, S., Berrocal, J., García-Alonso, J., Canal, C., Manuel Murillo, J.: Human microservices: a framework for turning humans into service providers. Software: Practice Exp. **51**(9), 1910–1935 (2021)
10. Laso, S., Toro-Gálvez, L., Berrocal, J., Canal, C., Murillo, J.M.: Deploying digital twins over the cloud-to-thing continuum. In: 2023 IEEE Symposium on Computers and Communications (ISCC), IEEE (2023)
11. Lehtola, V.V., et al.: Digital twin of a city: review of technology serving city needs. Int. J. Appl. Earth Obs. Geoinf. **114**, 102915 (2022)
12. Lei, B., Janssen, P., Stoter, J., Biljecki, F.: Challenges of urban digital twins: a systematic review and a Delphi expert survey. Autom. Constr. **147**, 104716 (2023)
13. Muñoz, P., Troya, J., Vallecillo, A.: A conceptual architecture for building digital twins. In: Proceedings of the 3rd International Workshop on MDE for Smart IoT Systems (MeSS 2023) (2023)
14. Nikitas, A., Michalakopoulou, K., Njoya, E.T., Karampatzakis, D.: Artificial intelligence, transport and the smart city: definitions and dimensions of a new mobility era. Sustainability **12**(7), 2789 (2020)
15. Pérez-Vereda, A., Canal, C.: A people-oriented paradigm for smart cities. In: Cabot, J., De Virgilio, R., Torlone, R. (eds.) ICWE 2017. LNCS, vol. 10360, pp. 584–591. Springer, Cham (2017). https://doi.org/10.1007/978-3-319-60131-1_46
16. Pérez-Vereda, A., Canal, C., Pimentel, E.: Modelling digital avatars: a tuple space approach. Sci. Comput. Program. **203**, 102583 (2021)

17. Pujol, V.C., Raith, P., Dustdar, S.: Towards a new paradigm for managing computing continuum applications. In: 2021 IEEE Third International Conference on Cognitive Machine Intelligence (CogMI), pp. 180–188. IEEE (2021)

18. Ramu, S.P., et al.: Federated learning enabled digital twins for smart cities: concepts, recent advances, and future directions. Sustain. Urban Areas **79**, 103663 (2022)

19. Ruiz, P., Seredynski, M., Torné, Á., Dorronsoro, B.: A digital twin for bus operation in public urban transportation systems. In: Big Data Intelligence and Computing, pp. 40–52 (2023)

20. Samih, H.: Smart cities and internet of things. J. Inf. Technol. Case Appl. Res. **21**(1), 3–12 (2019)

21. Schrotter, G., Hürzeler, C.: The digital twin of the city of Zurich for urban planning. PFG - J. Photogrammetry Remote Sens. Geoinf. Sci. **88**, 99–112 (2020)

22. Singh, M., Fuenmayor, E., Hinchy, E.P., Qiao, Y., Murray, N., Devine, D.: Digital twin: origin to future. Appl. Syst. Innov. **4**(2), 36 (2021)

23. Technology, L.: LADOT. Los Angeles. Technology Action Plan; 2022. https://ladot.lacity.org/sites/default/files/documents/annual-report-2022_2023.pdf. Accessed 30 Nov 2023

24. Toro-Gálvez, L., García-Luque, R., Troya, J., Canal, C., Pimentel, E.: Towards the integration of digital avatars in urban digital twins on the cloud-to-thing continuum. In: Proceedings of the 3rd International Workshop on Big data driven Edge Cloud Services (BECS 2023) (2023)

25. Villalonga, A., Negri, E., Fumagalli, L., Macchi, M., Castaño, F., Haber, R.: Local decision making based on distributed digital twin framework. IFAC-PapersOnLine **53**(2), 10568–10573 (2020)

26. Weil, C., Bibri, S.E., Longchamp, R., Golay, F., Alahi, A.: A systemic review of urban digital twin challenges, and perspectives for sustainable smart cities. Sustain. Cities Soc. 104862 (2023)

Designing a Future-Proof Reference Architecture for Network Digital Twins

Roberto Verdecchia$^{(\boxtimes)}$ ⓘ, Leonardo Scommegna ⓘ, Enrico Vicario ⓘ,
and Tommaso Pecorella ⓘ

Department of Information Engineering, University of Florence, Florence, Italy
{roberto.verdecchia,leonardo.scommegna,enrico.vicario,
tommaso.pecorella}@unifi.it

Abstract. As the complexity, distribution, and heterogeneity of networks continue to grow, how to architect and monitor of these networking environments is becoming an increasingly critical open issue. Digital twins, which can replicate the structure and behavior of a physical network, are seen as potential solution to address the problem. While reference architectures for digital twins exist in other fields, a comprehensive reference architecture for the networking context has yet to be developed. This paper discusses the need for such a reference architecture and outlines the key elements necessary for its design. We present the findings of a preliminary survey that explores the need for a network digital twin reference architecture, the crucial information it should include, and practical insights into its design. The survey results confirm that existing standards are inadequate for modeling network digital twins, outlining the necessity of a new reference architecture. We then articulate our position on the need for a reference architecture for network digital twins, focusing on three main aspects, namely: (i) digital twins of what, (ii) for what, and (iii) how to deploy them. We then proceed to delineate the fundamental obstacles that a reference architecture must confront, in tandem with the essential characteristics it needs to embody to successfully navigate these challenges. As conclusion, we present our vision for the reference architecture and outline the main research steps we plan to take to address this open problem. Our ultimate goal is to tightly collaborate both with the networking and digital twin software architecture communities to jointly establish a sound network digital twin architecture of the future.

Keywords: Reference architecture · Digital twin · Networking

1 Introduction

In recent years, Digital Twins (DTs) gained and increasing popularity, and year after year are becoming more adopted in different and new industrial contexts. A digital twin is a virtual representation of a system, facilitating bidirectional communication between the system and its digital representation [18]. Such virtual

© The Author(s), under exclusive license to Springer Nature Switzerland AG 2024
B. Tekinerdoğan et al. (Eds.): ECSA 2023, LNCS 14590, pp. 287–306, 2024.
https://doi.org/10.1007/978-3-031-66326-0_18

representation is used, among other goals, for designing, modeling, and monitoring physical asses [11]. DTs enable to mimic the structure, context, and behavior of a single or groups of physical assets, supporting both design and runtime decision making processes of the physical counterparts. By collecting and analyzing data from multiple sources, DTs can be used to digitally gain information on various attributes, such as performance and related inefficiencies, to identify and design solutions to improve their physical counterparts.

In networking environments, DTs are commonly used to represent physical networking assets such as routers, switches, controllers, and communication channels [32]. Network DTs (NDTs) usually include information regarding operational status, performance data, and environmental conditions of their physical twins. By exchanging network data and control messages with a network of DT instances through twin-physical interfaces, network engineers can rely on DT representations to design, test, assess security, and improve the maintenance of physical networks. This allows for efficient and intelligent management of networks, with the ultimate goal of supporting the improvement of network performance, reliability, and accelerate network innovation.

The concept of DT has been largely developed in the context of Cyber Physical Systems, much promoted by the agenda of Industry 4.0 where it was also addressed and formalized in standardization initiatives [15]. In the context of future generation networks, the growing level of softwarization demands architectural paradigms that can drive the organization of functional responsibilities, their connection with data collection and intelligent processing, and their deployment and composition across network computing, storage, and connectivity resources.

While various concepts can inherit results consolidated in contexts where the DT paradigm has already reached higher maturity and readiness, application in software driven networks raises several and hard new challenges, notably including: distribution across a large-scale network, with sustainable footprint on communication and storage resources; critical need for high levels of interoperability among heterogenous resources and services managed by multiple operators; autonomic orchestration capability supporting efficient and self-adaptive placement of network functions and applications across edge-to-cloud levels and localities. The relevance of these challenges, and their scientific and technological perception is clearly testified by the level of standardization initiatives and the growing number of scientific works.

In order to architect NDTs, comprehensively model their characteristics, and manage the high complexity such systems entail, a reference architecture, *i.e.*, a template solution for an architecture of a particular domain [3], could be used. Such solution was recently introduced for manufacturing environments, with the establishment of the ISO Standard 23247 [15] (which was also picked up in recent software architecture literature [10]). To the best of our knowledge, a reference architecture to model NDTs, covering both functional and non-functional aspects of NDT architectures, is still missing in the current body of knowledge.

As note, while reference architectures and standards might have similar properties, they convey different concepts. Specifically, a reference architecture is a template architectural solution for a particular domain and context. Software engineering standards instead are a set of guidelines for the process, quality, and documentation of software development and maintenance, usually developed by industry organizations or governing bodies, *e.g.*, IEEE and ISO. Therefore while a standard can document a reference architecture (*e.g.*, in the case of the ISO Standard 23247 [15]), the opposite is not always true. Moreover, a reference architecture can leverage standards (*e.g.*, data interchange standards), but its is often independent from the particular standard being used.

The NDTs architectures are foreseen to play a critical role in the RESTART Foundation (RESearch and innovation on future Telecommunications systems and networks, to make Italy more smART)[1], funded by the European Union (EU), under the Next Generation EU (NGEU) program.[2] The RESTART Foundation is a partnership between 25 Italian universities (*e.g.*, the Sant'Anna School and the University of Rome La Sapienza.), research centers (*e.g.*, the Italian National Research Council), and companies (*e.g.*, Vodafone and Ericsson). The goal of the RESTART project is to leverage DTs to provide a structural improvement of telecommunications research and development in Italy, supporting the digital transformation of industries, and growth of related research and professional communities. Within the RESTART Foundation, the COHERENT project *"Shaping a Digital Twins future proof network architecture"* focuses explicitly on integrating the outcomes of all RESTART research activities in a comprehensive network architecture considering both a technical and a business point of view. The research project, founded for a total of 116 million euros, aims to fill a current gap in networking, namely the lack of an extensible and evolvable NDT reference architecture. Current standards and documentation related to a NDTs reference architecture result to either be too generic to effortlessly incorporate the specifics of the networking domain, *e.g.*, consider the DT framework of Josifovska *et al.* [16] or the DT archetypes of van der Valk *et al.* [30], or result to be deeply grounded in current technologies, and are therefore inherently hard to evolve according to future emerging technologies. As documented by the funding body, realizing a future proof DT network architecture and documenting its related design rationale allows to establish a set of best-practices to fully harness the potential of the implementation of projects in the networking domain.

As part of COHERENT, in this position paper we outline how, in order to comprehensively consider and integrate the various facets of NDTs, a future proof *reference architecture for network digital twins* needs to be established.

The contributions of the paper are (i) an opening survey empirically investigating the need of a reference architecture for NDTs, (ii) a grounding problem statement outlining the need of such reference architecture, and (iii) our vision on a future proof reference architecture of NDTs.

---

[1] https://www.fondazione-restart.it/. Accessed 18th June 2023.
[2] https://next-generation-eu.europa.eu/index_en. Accessed 2 August 2023.

This research builds upon the initial position paper presented at the second International Workshop on Digital Twin Architecture (Twin-Arch) [31] by (i) discussing the main challenges of designing a network digital twin reference architecture, (ii) reporting the key features the reference architecture must provide, and (iii) providing a stepping stone towards the concrete implementation of the architecture.

2   Opening Survey

In order to gain introductory empirical insights into the need for a NDT reference architecture, independent of the statements and goal set by the RESEARCH funding body (see Sect. 1), we conducted a survey involving researchers and practitioners working in the field of networking. Participants were recruited *via* convenience sampling starting from the RESTART Foundation participant list and the personal network of the authors, followed by a subsequent snowballing sampling. Survey invitation target networking experts, belonging either to academic entities, renowned large scale industrial companies, or networking standardization entities. Under the human ethics guidelines governing this study, we cannot disclose affiliations of participants to preserve their anonymity.

In total, 16 participants took part in the survey.

The survey comprised a mix of close-ended 5-point Likert scale questions (CE) and free form open-ended questions (OE). Each CE was accompanied by a OE, where respondents could further clarify their answer.[3] The survey was composed of three main parts, namely:

1. Participant demographic questions: Current job position (OE), years of experience (OE), familiarity with networking and digital twins (CE);
2. On need of a NDT reference architecture: Degree to which the ISO 23247 can be used to represent NDTs (CE), degree to which the ISO 23247 needs to be modified to represent NDTs (CE), and perceived usefulness of a NDT reference architecture (CE);
3. Further advice to establish a NDT reference architecture: expected networking components modeled (OE), expected grouping of networking components (OE), degree to which elements of standardisation groups (*e.g.,* ETSI or IETF) should appear in the NDT reference architecture (CE).

To ensure respondents have enough knowledge on DT to answer the survey, a definition of DT is provided at the beginning of the survey. Similarly, an overview of the ISO 23247 standard provided by Bucaioni *et al.* [9] is provided in the survey. Participants who acknowledge not being familiar with networking and/or DT concepts are discarded from the respondents.

---

[3] To support replicability and scrutiny, the survey and received answers are made available online at: https://github.com/STLab-UniFI/twinarch-2023-reference-architecture-rep-pkg.

From the demographic answers, the vast majority of participants resulted to work in academia (11/16), possess an average of 10 years of experience, be highly familiar with networking concepts, and moderately familiar with DT.

Regarding the ISO 23247, most participants noted that it can be applied to networking concepts only to a moderate extent (6/16) or low extent (5/16). From the supporting OE answers, we note that this is primarily due to a perceived lack of generalizability of the ISO 23247 standard. By considering the extent to which the ISO 23247 standard needs to be modified in order to be used for NDTs, respondents primarily indicated a medium, or medium-high degree (13/16). Accompanying OE questions clarified that this is mostly due to the need to model concepts specific to NDTs, *e.g.,* details regarding network virtualization functions, and other networking-related attributes, which require new abstraction levels. All participants agreed on a medium-high, or high usefulness of a NDT reference architecture (15/16).

When considering the further advice provided by participants to establish a NDT reference architecture, respondents mostly indicated basic hardware networking components, *e.g.,* routers, switches, and hubs (8/16). In contrast, virtual elements, *e.g.,* virtual machines, VPNs, and firewalls, were mentioned far less frequently (3/16). Only seldom, communication-related elements, *e.g.,* physical channels, were mentioned (3/16). Only few respondents described the expected grouping of networking components, providing heterogeneous answers, *e.g.,* "physical layer; security; services; hardware; software; protocols" and "SDN control plane; 5G-oriented data plane". Finally, respondents indicated that networking elements of presented by standardisation groups (*e.g.,* the the European Telecommunications Standards Institute (ETSI).[4]) could be used between a medium and medium-high extent to model a NDT reference architecture (15/16).

Overall, as main takeaways of the opening survey conducted for this position paper, we can conclude that, based on the opinion of mostly academic researchers experienced in networking:

1. The ISO 23247 does not fit completely the networking context, and would need to be considerably modified;
2. A NDT reference architecture is perceived as highly useful;
3. Elements to be covered in the NDT reference architecture should primarily focus on hardware networking components, could use to a moderate extent elements of existing standards.

3   On the Need of a Reference Architecture for Network Digital Twins

Albeit extensive literature considered network DT [1,19,26,27,32], the topic has been primarily addressed from a purely networking point of view. As such, aspects related to a reference architecture NDTs, *i.e.,* a reusable metamodel

---

[4] https://www.etsi.org. Accessed 18th June 2023.

that can applied to heterogeneous contexts, considering disciplines such as software engineering and software architecture, seem to have been almost completely neglected in current literature [5]. To address this point, in this position paper, we take a software engineering stance by reviewing the topic of NDTs reference architectures through the lens of software architects.

As emerges from recent reviews [1,11,32], when considering NDTs, three main aspects can be taken into account, namely *NDTs for what?*, *NDTs of what?*, and *how to deploy NDTs?*. In the following, we detail our position on these three aspects, building towards our vision on the main proprieties an NDT reference architecture needs to possess.

3.1   Network Digital Twins *for What?*

As one of the most consolidated aspects of NDTs, the related body of literature extensively describes the different application scenarios of NDT, *e.g.*, their use for network function virtualization, controlled orchestration, and reliability/security monitoring and assurance processes. For example, NDTs can be used to facilitate service placement, allowing for the efficient streaming of data from one point to another within a network [4].

Reference architectures for NDTs are available (*e.g.*, the NDTs architecture presented by the Telecommunication Standardization Sector of the International Telecommunication Union [28]). Nevertheless, such reference architectures considered primarily, if not exclusively, the functional nature of NDTs, *i.e.*, do not consider aspects related to the characteristics of the entities that have to be represented, or their concrete use/deployment (see also following sections).

Similarly, standards regarding functional aspects of DTs are widespread knowledge within the industry, as documented for example by the industry-driven effort in the Internet Research Task Force (IRTF) [35], as well as the evolution of standards relative to the network devices management planes (see for example the standards issued by the IETF NETCONF Working Group[5])

Overall, it appears as if the *"NDTs of what?"* field is a quite consolidated in the networking community. For example, the field of network function virtualization experienced a growing interest through the years, and can now be regarded as a mature, consolidated, and standardized area [34].

As more recent example of NDTs functional viewpoints, current research investigates the use of NDTs for AI model lifecycle management [17]. This topic, currently under investigation, opens for new challenges of functional NDT aspects, *e.g.*, controlling responsibilities, management of AI model lifecycle within NDTs, and consistency between models distributed *via* federated learning.

3.2   Network Digital Twins *of What?*

As less explored area, we note that often the literature on NDTs does not appear to predicate in detail and precision on the specific network elements that are

---

[5] https://datatracker.ietf.org/wg/netconf. Accessed 18th June 2023.

required to be modeled in the NDT context. As a matter of fact, frequently the nature of network components which need to be modeled within NDT architectures seem to be reported at a rather high level, with auxiliary elements left implicit, or not regarded at all. This more often than not seem to cause the unsystematic documentation of incomplete or vague NDT reference architectures, that, due to their abstract and at times speculative nature, cannot be ported into practice without making considerable assumptions.

Even in the rare cases in which the most important elements of NDTs architectures are explicitly documented, their description often lacks basic details regarding property characteristics and attributes NDTs must posses. Therefore, theoretical or even simulation results are hardly portable into practice by implementing a concrete NDT architecture. In fact, the development process would imply a considerable upfront conceptual effort, which would require *per se* an independent study and verification prior the concrete development can take place.

As a possible solution to address this issue, the information to model NDTs could be derived from standard network architecture documentation, *e.g.,* the documentation provided by ETSI. Similarly, the necessary information could be identified by porting the modeling information of network simulators (*e.g.,* ns-3[6] and OMNET++[7]) to a NDT reference architecture, documenting *via* a metamodel the NDT elements, their attributes, and relations.

3.3 *How to Deploy* Network Digital Twins?

Another area that appears to be only marginally considered from a practical standpoint is the concrete deployment of NDTs over a network.

As for DT in general, one of the challenges in the use of NDTs within a network is the distributed deployment of these virtual representations. To date, standards do not appear to provide a clear guidance on how NDTs should be deployed, distributed, and relocated. From an architectural standpoint, one approach could be to consider network elements, such as Media Access Control (MAC) addresses, as monolithic entities. Nevertheless, given the growing functional complexity of NDTs, this approach might be considered as too simplistic. As alternative, network elements could be factored into bounded contexts. This strategy would lead to the production of microservices, allowing, albeit their potential complexity increase, to take advantage of the benefits of the microservice architecture style, *e.g.,* fault tolerance and fault isolation.

By considering the adoption of a microservice architecture in the context of NDTs however, there is a special emphasis on enabling deployment and placement at different levels of the edge-to-cloud continuum at different localities.

As a double-edged sword, on one hand NDTs are responsible for resolving placement problems through their state and associated computational power (or

---

[6] https://www.nsnam.org. Accessed 18th June 2023.
[7] https://omnetpp.org. Accessed 18th June 2023.

by delegating the task at hand to other NDTs to obtain states and/or delegate the processing). However, NDTs also rise novel issues associated to how to place these responsibilities on physical and virtual resources within a network. Therefore, while DTs can resolve placement problems, they also open up new challenges in terms of the placement of NDT themselves. The challenges associated to the deployment of NDTs must be carefully managed, in order to optimize the performance of DTs within a network environment. To date, this problem appears to be marginally addressed in the literature, lacking to provide concrete guidance and reference on how NDTs should be deployed.

4   Main Challenges for a Network Digital Twin Reference Architecture

In this section, we identify the key challenges a network digital twin architecture must be capable of addressing to be considered future-proof. The ensuing list is derived from discussions and a workshop event with sector-leading experts involved in the COHERENT project, focusing on the examination of proposed standards on the topic [28,35].

4.1   Large Scale Data Collection

Considering the inherent characteristics of the network and the potential of digital twin networks, we posit that a digital twin network architecture should be equipped to manage substantial volumes of data efficiently. It is expected that the architecture will be capable of collecting and managing data of various natures originating from multiple sources.

- Recordings and event logs from all elements of the network;
- Statistics-related data like traffic throughput, latency, and packet loss;
- Data related to service usage and users;
- Monitoring data of observable entities;
- Operational and provisional data;
- Simulation and emulation results.

This information generates a continuous flow of large data sets. The digital twin should use this data to represent the current state of the entity. Additionally, it's crucial to preserve this data to maintain a historical record of the information The inherent heterogeneity of data, which encompasses both variety and volume, presents a significant challenge in its effective management.

The exponential growth of data from mobile devices and IoT applications will make this problem a central concern in network management. One of the challenges that Network Digital Twin architectures will face is managing massive network data collection from network infrastructures.

4.2   Scalability

Given the expected surge in network components and participants (*e.g.,* more sensors, clients, and applications), a Network Digital Twin architecture must effectively accommodate this growth and ensure consistent performance. As the number of network elements increases, it is crucial for a network digital twin architecture to effectively handle virtual representations of real networks, regardless of their scale. Furthermore, as network size gradually expands, the features offered by the architecture must remain efficient and effective. Therefore, features such as data collection from the network, reconfiguration, and simulations should always be available, ensuring consistent functionality irrespective of the network's size, the number of data sources, or the number of network applications. In addition to functionalities, the performance provided by the architecture should be scalable. For example, latency, the accuracy of prediction, and simulation algorithms should maintain the expected performance without depending on the size of the network that the digital twins compose.

4.3   Flexibility and Autonomous Reconfiguration

It is expected that the network will maintain a dynamic behavior, with network components, applications, and clients evolving over time and the load fluctuating in intensity. For this reason, a digital twin network should be able to cope with the network variation. Therefore, it is expected to possess the ability to execute on-demand behaviors and reconfigure itself (possibly automatically without the intervention of human operators) in response to events while maintaining Quality of Service constraints. These behaviors are moving towards the implementation of networks that are often identified with the term Zero Touch Network [8], which are envisioned to be highly autonomous networks capable of self-configuration, self-healing, and self-optimization with minimal to no human intervention. It is also expected that many of the features and constraints can be specified dynamically, thus allowing for greater system availability without taking the system online. Last but not least, given the heterogeneity of the network, the architecture must be able to provide adequate adaptability to new elements, provide functionality to new network applications, and collect and store data of various nature and format.

4.4   Heterogeneous Performance Requirements

In the near future, the network will be used to support many challenging applications. Some of these will require near real-time response requirements, *e.g.,* in the context of autonomous driving, virtual reality, gaming, and healthcare. Other applications will instead necessitate elevated levels of parallelism or data storage to execute algorithms with efficiency. Such applications typically encompass simulations, algorithms pertaining to artificial intelligence and machine learning, and, in recent developments, practices of federated learning.

The complex requirements required by network applications, sometimes in contrast with each other, will have to coexist and be natively supported in an architecture that aims to be future-proof.

4.5   Interfaces

In the context of a network digital twin architecture, we deem the selection of interfaces as a fundamental. A Network Digital Twin requires an interface to interact with the physical network. This interface is commonly called *south bound* and is responsible for establishing the ways in which digital twins exchange information with the corresponding physical entities. To ensure the architecture is accessible and open to extension, we posit that it is also crucial to establish a standard interface through which the architecture can expose its services and features externally. Beyond digital representation an control of entities, digital twins offer the significant ability to gather information and conduct analysis, emulations, and simulations based on real-world data. To execute these types of functionalities and ensure the scalability of the network architecture capabilities over time, it is crucial in the architectural design process to identify the methods through which these functions will be invoked. In this sense, we consider the definition of internal interfaces (sometimes referred to as *side bound*) to be equally fundamental to the definition of the architecture.

4.6   Digital Twin Security

Even though NDTs can be used to improve the network security of a system, *e.g.,* by analyzing and quickly applying changes related to adverse events, they have to be also resistant to attacks targeted to the NDT itself.

As a matter of fact, NDTs can be seen as a particular case of a Cyber-Physical system, and their security depends not only on the security of the NDT itself (the software component), but also on the capability to have a 'useful' knowledge of the physical counterpart, and to control it. It is fairly evident that the attack surface for NDTs is larger and more complex than the one of a traditional network, and even larger than the one of a Software-Defined Network (SDN).

In our opinion the technologies needed to address the security requirements should not be part of the NDT architecture. However, the security analysis should be part of the architecture, at least to highlight the attack surfaces and the possible threats.

For what concerns the threat agents and their capabilities, these can be considered as "normal" threat actors targeting traditional networks, as the goals and means to perform an attack are the same. The normal approach used by IETF is to define the possible attacks based on the threat actor capabilities (see [24]), *i.e.,* splitting the attacks into passive or active.

Passive attacks to NDTs are not to be underestimated, as an attacker might gather a very precise (and timely) knowledge of the network status. As a matter of fact, intercepting the data collection traffic between the physical and digital parts, an attacker can not only understand the network operational status, and perform targeted (active) attacks, but also understand the existence of particular network statuses, and correlate them with user data. Again, this can be useful to perform further actions.

Hence, the loss of confidentiality in the data collection can create serious risks, not only to the NDT itself, but also to the user data.

Active attacks are peculiar as well, as they can be targeted to the NDT software components, to the data collection mechanism, or to the network configuration elements, used by the NDT to modify the actual network setup.

The NDT components and the network elements configuration are well understood, are almost universally considered as sensitive elements, and secure-by-design architectures and network configuration protocols are generally available. On the contrary the data collection has only recently evaluated, and several protocols have been, or are in the process of being updated to add confidentiality and integrity features (see for example [7]).

Hence, we believe that a NDT architecture should contain the threat models and possible attacks to the NDT, in order to guide the implementations to use the proper security models, both in the components, and in the protocols used by the NDT.

5   Key Features of a Network Digital Twin Architecture

After identifying the challenges that the design of a network digital twin architecture will have to face (Sect. 4), we now provide the key features that, in our vision, are necessary for the architecture to adequately address these challenges.

5.1   Edge to Cloud Continuum Deployment Awareness

The increasingly pervasive spread of edge devices capable of collecting and computing data will necessitate a paradigm shift in the use of network infrastructures. The emergence of Mobile Edge Computing (MEC) represents a transformative paradigm shift [13], which is anticipated to rapidly gain prominence. This advancement is poised to facilitate the execution of algorithms and the provisioning of services in closer proximity to the end-user. MEC will enable a reduction in latency that is unthinkable in architectures that rely solely on cloud computing. Thus, MEC will enable all those applications that require near real-time requirements. In addition, by processing requests locally, the cloud and the backhaul network [25], i.e., the network that connects the edge to the cloud, will be relieved of a large number of requests.

Although mobile edge computing represents a turning point for many future applications, its use introduces complexities that must be considered. Indeed, an MEC node is characterized by a limited amount of resources, so it is not possible to deploy all functionalities on these nodes. Moreover, some particularly resource-demanding tasks, such as machine learning algorithms or simulations, are better suited to execution on the cloud where there is no problem of resource scarcity.

Another intrinsic complexity in the MEC paradigm and more generally in edge computing, is the local nature of data and services in an environment characterized by clients who typically move in space and vary over time [25]. This implies the implementation of strategies such as service placement, handover, and service offloading, should be native in a network digital twin architecture [23].

It is necessary also to consider that the duality between edge and cloud cannot be defined in a clear-cut fashion and that there is continuum between the two entities in which intermediate nodes are able to provide functionalities and data storage halfway between the two extremes. This is known as the Edge-to-Cloud continuum and is also closely related to the concept of Fog Computing [29].

Ultimately, we believe that a reference architecture for network digital twins must necessarily take into account such aspects of deployment and resource management natively. In our view, this is necessary to best manage challenges such as *large-scale data collection*, *scalability*, and *heterogeneous performance requirements*.

5.2   Digital Twin Interoperability

In our opinion, one aspect that is not adequately highlighted in the presented standards (ITU Y.3090 [28] and IRTF [35]) and which we deem central to a network digital twin architecture is the interoperability that should exist between network digital twins.

In our view, the architecture does not manage a single network digital twin but an entire ecosystem. This ecosystem, like the actual network, is not static but changes over time in terms of both elements and functionalities, and collaborates to achieve the objectives required by the network applications it uses.

The definition of an ecosystem of digital twins that collaborate with each other enables the possibility to dynamically extend the digital representation of the network. A change in the physical network does not necessitate to change the entire digital twin, but rather the addition, removal, or update of a single element. Such change does not affect the entire representation of the network but only a single part. Furthermore, this modularity allows for a more granular control of the elements.

An ecosystem of digital twin allows for extremely *flexible* management of the network with the possibility of implementing policies of distributed *auto-reconfiguration*, management of *heterogeneous requirements*, especially if combined with a deployment awareness as described in Sect. 5.1, and even *security*.

5.3   Distributed Network Digital Twin

A Network Digital Twin is anticipated to deliver a diverse array of functionalities, reflective not only of the spectrum of performance requisites but also of their inherent complexity. Considering the imperative for deployment awareness (see

Sect. 5.1) in conjunction with the diversity of functionalities each NDT furnishes, we believe that the network digital twin ought to exhibit a distributed rather than a monolithic structure.

The decentralization of the NDT is poised to facilitate performance optimization: for instance, functionalities with low latency requirements could be deployed at the edge, whereas those demanding substantial computational resources might be more aptly positioned within the cloud infrastructure. This approach is also likely to enhance network utilization, preventing the potential for data flow congestion within both the network and the cloud.

We advocate for the adoption of a distributed model for Network Digital Twins, as it promises augmented *flexibility* within the network. This model enables the dynamic reallocation of digital twin components to nodes that are optimally suited, through the implementation of strategic placement and offloading. A distributed model also permits the precise management of the *heterogeneous performance requirements* that characterize digital twins. Ultimately, this strategic framework is expected to support extensive *data collection* and *scalability*, while simultaneously reinforcing security measures, as sensitive data and functionalities can be securely housed within more secure nodes.

5.4   Composite (Hierarchical) Digital Twin

The concept of network is often associated with a composition of other subnetworks (*e.g.,*, the internet is a network of networks). We therefore naturally consider the digital twin network to be characterized by a composite and hierarchical nature. This concept, moreover, is not new to digital twins in the field of manufacturing and also appears in the seminal paper by Grieves *et al.* [12] under the term *"Digital Twin Aggregate"*. A hierarchical representation of digital twin networks enables the representation of the network at different levels of granularity, allowing for different views and functionalities depending on the type of granularity required.

At the lowest rung of the hierarchy is the digital representation of the atomic elements of the network (*e.g.,*, routers and switches). Digital twin networks with this level of granularity will therefore provide information on the status of network elements and expose functionalities aimed at their configuration. However, there are situations where it is necessary to interact with a large network like Metropolitan Area Networks (MANs) or Wide Area Networks (WANs). In such cases, it is plausible that the pertinent information extends beyond the scope of singular network components and pertains instead to an aggregated construct. Similarly, the type of actions to be performed on the network, reasonably, will not concern the individual network element but the network as a whole. In such a case, the Digital Twin Network will represent a network with aggregated information derived from Digital Twin Networks of lower granularity levels and will provide high-level functionalities that could cascade into the NDTs that compose it.

This type of representation allows bringing to the different levels of abstraction only the necessary aggregated information, ignoring data and functionalities that are too fine or too coarse. This type of hierarchical representation of digital twin networks is beneficial for many reasons and helps to address various challenges identified in this paper. The use of data of the right granularity for the level of abstraction of the digital twin network allows for *efficient data collection* and excellent *scalability*. These advantages are further enhanced when combined with deployment awareness (Sect. 5.1). Moreover, a hierarchical strategy allows for a high level of network *flexibility*. Finally, the ability to represent aggregated data combined with the presentation of high-level functionalities will greatly simplify the *interfaces* to be presented to a client (North Bound).

5.5 Prototyping

One of the main features of digital twins is to execute simulations based on real data collected in the field. Within a network context, this enables *what-if* analysis simulations and predictions, wherein hypothetical scenarios are studied based on present data. In such instances, it becomes necessary to have prototypes of network elements readily available. That is, having at disposal virtualized representations of network elements not directly associated with a physical element. A prototype is indeed a stereotypical representation of a specific type of network element and as such encapsulates default functionalities and statistical data common to the category of element it represents. The concept of a prototype is widely used in the industrial and manufacturing context, enabling procedures for product lifecycle management [12].

A prototype is a stereotypical representation of a specific type of network element and, as such, encapsulates default functionalities and statistical data common to the category of element it represents, which are based on real-world observations collected in the field. The prototype thus permits an optimized and aggregated use of data gathered during the monitoring that NDTs continuously perform.

We therefore posit that a reference architecture for network digital twins should take into account this type of representation of components. Especially, we contend that the employment and management of prototypes are fundamental, particularly for addressing challenges such as *efficient data collection*, *flexibility and autonomous reconfiguration* capabilities, and *security* through the possibility of conducting appropriate simulations.

5.6 Digital Twin of Anything

Nowadays, many network elements are digitized and programmable. The primary elements include software defined networks, virtualized network functions, and network slices [22]. However, even elements such as virtual machines and containers can be considered as integral parts of the network and contribute to its operation. We therefore believe that for a satisfactory architectural representation of the network, network digital twin should not be limited to representing physical network elements, but also those elements that inherently possess a digital nature.

Even the existing standards acknowledge this possibility [35] but without identifying its main advantages. Below we list the reasons why we consider it useful to establish a digital twin for all digital elements of the network digital twins reference architecture. The digital twin of a digital component can act as a wrapper for the component and enrich it with additional functionalities that are not natively supported by the original component. For example, a component could collect information from monitoring and perform simulations or prediction algorithms. Through the digital twin, better management of interfaces is allowed, thus improving the management by the user of the element (north bound) and the management of interoperability between different digital twins (side bound). The establishment of an interface relieves the other architectural components of the responsibility of having to know all possible elements and their specific interfaces in advance, greatly increasing the flexibility and maintainability of the network.

5.7   An Intent-Based Architecture

A network must be capable of fulfilling various requirements specified by clients and applications external to the network. These requirements change over time and are often in conflict with one another. To address the evolving nature of network requirements and ensure flexibility, self-configuration, and user-friendly interface interaction, it is crucial to adopt the concept of *Intent* as the foundation for the network configuration and specification mechanism. The concept of Intent has become increasingly prominent in recent standards [8,28,33,35]. according to IRTF NMRG [14], an intent is *"a set of operational goals (that a network should meet) and outcomes (that a network is supposed to deliver) defined in a declarative manner without specifying how to achieve or implement them"*. An intent-based network aligns with a user-centric perspective, simplifying the expression of requirements and enhancing the architecture's usability and *flexibility*. An intent can also be expressed in human language and then easily translated into machine-readable language. This simplicity in defining an intent dramatically increases the usability of the architecture and the definition of the North Bound *interface*. In addition to offering high simplicity at interface level, intent-based architectures allow for a high degree of *autonomy* and *flexibility* and *auto reconfiguration capabilities*.

In our vision, the adoption of intent-based networking techniques could be highly beneficial. Managing through intents provides several advantages, particularly when various applications are concurrently utilizing the network. The network will be capable of defining a space of possible configurations that satisfy all the intents specified by the applications. The exploration and identification of an optimal configuration can then be entrusted to algorithms and programmatic policies.

6   A Step Towards an Architecture Implementation

After identifying the set of key features deemed as essential to address the challenges posed by a network digital twin architecture, we now provide a perspective on how the architecture can be developed with a more implementational outlook. In doing so, we will also specify which key features, in our opinion, will be implemented in this manner.

In an architecture where service decoupling and high interoperability are required, as outlined in this article, a microservices ecosystem is certainly the most suitable [21]. Indeed, each microservice natively has the ability to be deployed on various network nodes while maintaining its independence and still being able to collaborate with other microservices. This characteristic thus ensures strong *interoperability between digital twins*. Furthermore, a network digital twin does not necessarily have to be confined within a single microservice. Various functionalities pertaining to the same digital twin could be represented by a set of microservices, thus implementing a *distributed digital twin*. Regarding prototyping, in our vision, just as for the network digital twin, we imagine a microservice or a set of microservices dedicated to individual prototypes. This makes the architecture both maintainable and extendable over time.

In a microservices architecture, it is simple to identify a set of microservices as "front-end" microservices, *i.e.,*, microservices that collect information and expose high-level functionalities. These microservices will therefore be the ones used by the client and will act as entry points for network functionalities. Microservices are particularly suited to defining flexible interfaces, and it would thus be possible to specify *Intents* through such entities as well (see Sect. 5.7). In networks of considerable complexity, it is conceivable that a collection of front-end microservices alone may not suffice to fulfill client intents. Under such circumstances, the front-end microservices would engage in collaboration with other microservices that operate at a more granular level of abstraction, thereby delineating a workflow of microservices: the invocation of a front-end service triggers a sequential activation of other microservice instances [2]. This cooperative mechanism thus establishes a hierarchical structure of microservices, which, in turn, facilitates the representation of *composite digital twins*.

Through specific actors and technologies commonly implied in microservices architectures (*e.g.,*, Kubernetes and its container orchestration platform [20]) it is possible to programmatically manage the scaling of individual services and also their deployment. This makes it possible to have a *deployment-aware* architecture capable of defining edge-to-cloud deployment policies and also implement dynamic service placement strategies [6].

7   Conclusions, Our Vision, and Future Work

Despite the growing adoption and complexity of network digital twins, a reference architecture for this context, which considers both functional and non-functional aspects, appears to date to be missing in the literature. From the preliminary motivating survey conducted for this position paper, we noted that (i) such reference could be highly helpful, (ii) existing standards do not totally fit the networking context, and would need to be considerably modified, and (iii) elements to be considered would be primarily of hardware nature, and could to a certain extent be modeled by leveraging existing network standards and tools.

We documented our position on the current state of the art, and what is needed to move towards a future proof reference architecture for NDTs. By considering current trends and advancements, we reasoned on the key aspects of architecting NDTs, which we formulated in terms of *NDTs for what, NDTs of what*, and *How to deploy NDTs*. Based on these three facets, we note that research and development endeavors primarily focused on the functional *"for what"* aspects of NDTs. As such, albeit crucial, which elements to be represent with NDT, and how/where to deploy NDTs, are aspects that are only marginally considered in the current state of the art. In an effort to crystallize the scenarios that a reference architecture for NDT must manage, we have pinpointed the most intricate challenges, subsequently identifying the essential key features we believe the architecture requires to address the identified issues. Ultimately, we have also provided our perspective with a more implementational outlook.

To move towards a standardized modeling of NDTs architectures, we posit that all three aspects, digital twins *of what, for what*, and how to *deploy them*, need to be considered. To do so, a reference architecture covering all three of these aspects needs to be established. Providing a standardized framework for NDTs would allow the community to move with a unified effort towards consolidated new abstractions of networking attributes, supporting the design and development of the next-generation wireless networks.

As future work, we plan to proactively build upon the position outlined in this document, by working towards the establishment of a future proof reference architecture for network digital twins. As first research step, we plan to conduct (i) a comprehensive qualitative empirical research involving network researchers and practitioners, and (ii) a systematic literature review on network digital twins. With this first step, we aim at gaining a deep and systematic understanding of the state of the art and practice of NDTs. In a second phase, we plan to design a reference architecture that comprehensively covers aspects related to NDTs *of what, for what*, and *how to deploy them*. Data and inspiration could be drawn from existing concrete artifacts to model networks, *e.g.,* the elements and attributes used by widespread simulation tools such as NS3 and OMNET++. Finally, we plan to evaluate and refine the established NDT reference architecture in a design science fashion, by gathering feedback from researchers and practitioners in the field *via* qualitative assessments and concrete case studies.

The task of establishing a NDT reference architecture is ambitious, and requires by definition interdisciplinary knowledge coming from the areas of software architecture, digital twin modeling, and networking. For this reason, we more than welcome feedback, insights, and collaboration with researchers and practitioners of any of these areas who are interested in jointly progress towards a holistic, standardized reference architecture for NDT.

With this position paper, we aim to reach out to both the networking and digital twin software architecture research and practitioners communities, in order to jointly progress towards the end goal of the RESTART mission, namely the establishment of a future proof digital twin network architecture.

Acknowledgments. This work was partially supported by the European Union under the Italian National Recovery and Resilience Plan (NRRP) of NextGenerationEU, partnership on "Telecommunications of the Future" (PE0000001 - program "RESTART").

References

1. Almasan, P., et al.: Network digital twin: context, enabling technologies, and opportunities. IEEE Commun. Mag. **60**(11), 22–27 (2022)
2. Alshuqayran, N., Ali, N., Evans, R.: A systematic mapping study in microservice architecture. In: IEEE International Conference on SO Computing and Application, pp. 44–51. IEEE (2016)
3. Bass, L., Clements, P., Kazman, R.: Software architecture in practice. Addison-Wesley Professional (2003)
4. Bellavista, P., Giannelli, C., Mamei, M., Mendula, M., Picone, M.: Application-driven network-aware digital twin management in industrial edge environments. IEEE Trans. Industr. Inf. **17**(11), 7791–7801 (2021)
5. Dalibor, M., et al.: A cross-domain systematic mapping study on software engineering for digital twins. J. Syst. Softw. **193**, 111361 (2022)
6. Detti, A.: Microservices from cloud to edge: an analytical discussion on risks, opportunities and enablers. IEEE Access (2023)
7. Elkins, N., Ackermann, M., Deshpande, A., Pecorella, T., Rashid, A.: IPv6 Performance and Diagnostic Metrics Version 2 (PDMv2) Destination Option. Internet-Draft draft-ietf-ippm-encrypted-pdmv2-05, Internet Engineering Task Force (Oct 2023). https://datatracker.ietf.org/doc/draft-ietf-ippm-encrypted-pdmv2/05/, work in Progress
8. Zero-touch network and Service Management (ZSM); Intent-driven autonomous networks; Generic aspects. Standard, European Telecommunications Standards Institute (Feb 2023)
9. Ferko, E., Bucaioni, A., Behnam, M.: Architecting digital twins. IEEE Access **10**, 50335–50350 (2022)
10. Ferko, E., Bucaioni, A., Pelliccione, P., Behnam, M.: Standardisation in digital twin architectures in manufacturing. In: 2023 IEEE 20th International Conference on Software Architecture (ICSA), pp. 70–81. IEEE (2023
11. Fuller, A., Fan, Z., Day, C., Barlow, C.: Digital twin: enabling technologies, challenges and open research. IEEE Access **8**, 108952–108971 (2020)
12. Grieves, M., Vickers, J.: Origins of the digital twin concept. Florida Inst. Technol. **8**, 3–20 (2016)
13. Haibeh, L.A., Yagoub, M.C., Jarray, A.: A survey on mobile edge computing infrastructure: design, resource management, and optimization approaches. IEEE Access **10**, 27591–27610 (2022)
14. Intent-Based Networking - Concepts and Definitions. Standard, Internet Research Task Force (Dec 2022)
15. ISO/IEC/IEEE: Automation systems and integration - digital twin framework for manufacturing - part 2: Reference architecture. ISO/IEC/IEEE ISO 23247-2:2021, pp. 1 –9 (10 2021)

16. Josifovska, K., Yigitbas, E., Engels, G.: Reference framework for digital twins within cyber-physical systems. In: 2019 IEEE/ACM 5th International Workshop on Software Engineering for Smart Cyber-Physical Systems (SEsCPS), pp. 25–31. IEEE (2019)
17. Kaur, M.J., Mishra, V.P., Maheshwari, P.: The convergence of digital twin, Iot, and machine learning: transforming data into action. In:Digital Twin Technologies and Smart Cities, pp. 3–17 (2020)
18. Kritzinger, W., Karner, M., Traar, G., Henjes, J., Sihn, W.: Digital twin in manufacturing: a categorical literature review and classification. Ifac-PapersOnline **51**(11), 1016–1022 (2018)
19. Kuruvatti, N.P., Habibi, M.A., Partani, S., Han, B., Fellan, A., Schotten, H.D.: Empowering 6G communication systems with digital twin technology: A comprehensive survey. IEEE Access (2022)
20. Li, W., Lemieux, Y., Gao, J., Zhao, Z., Han, Y.: Service mesh: Challenges, state of the art, and future research opportunities. In: 2019 IEEE International Conference on Service-Oriented System Engineering (SOSE), pp. 122–1225. IEEE (2019)
21. Lombardo, A., Morabito, G., Quattropani, S., Ricci, C.: Design, implementation, and testing of a microservices-based digital twins framework for network management and control. In: 2022 IEEE 23rd International Symposium on a World of Wireless, Mobile and Multimedia Networks (WoWMoM), pp. 590–595 (2022). https://doi.org/10.1109/WoWMoM54355.2022.00092
22. Long, Q., Chen, Y., Zhang, H., Lei, X.: Software defined 5G and 6G networks: a survey. Mobile Netw. Appl. **27**(5), 1792–1812 (2022)
23. Malazi, H.T., et al.: Dynamic service placement in multi-access edge computing: a systematic literature review. IEEE Access **10**, 32639–32688 (2022)
24. Rescorla, E., Korver, B.: Guidelines for Writing RFC Text on Security Considerations. RFC 3552 (Jul 2003). https://doi.org/10.17487/RFC3552, https://www.rfc-editor.org/info/rfc3552
25. Singh, R., Sukapuram, R., Chakraborty, S.: A survey of mobility-aware multi-access edge computing: challenges, use cases and future directions. Ad Hoc Netw. **140**, 103044 (2023)
26. Tang, F., Chen, X., Rodrigues, T.K., Zhao, M., Kato, N.: Survey on digital twin edge networks (diten) toward 6G. IEEE Open J. Commun. Society **3**, 1360–1381 (2022)
27. Tao, F., Zhang, H., Liu, A., Nee, A.Y.: Digital twin in industry: State-of-the-art. IEEE Trans. Industr. Inf. **15**(4), 2405–2415 (2018)
28. Telecommunication Standardization Sector - International Telecommunication Union: Digital twin network - requirements and architecture. Series Y: Global Information Infrastructure, Internet Protocol Aspects, Next-Generation Networks, Internet of Things and Smart Cities. (Future Networks), 1–26 (2022)
29. Tuli, S., et al.: AI augmented edge and fog computing: Trends and challenges. J. Netw. Comput. Appl. **216**, 103648 (2023)
30. van der Valk, H., Haße, H., Möller, F., Otto, B.: Archetypes of digital twins. Business and Inform. Syst. Eng. 1–17 (2021). https://doi.org/10.1007/s12599-021-00727-7
31. Verdecchia, R., Scommegna, L., Vicario, E., Pecorella, T.: Network Digital Twins: Towards a Future Proof Reference Architecture. International Workshop on Digital Twin Architecture (2023)
32. Wu, Y., Zhang, K., Zhang, Y.: Digital twin networks: a survey. IEEE Internet Things J. **8**(18), 13789–13804 (2021)

33. Yastrebova, A., Kirichek, R., Koucheryavy, Y., Borodin, A., Koucheryavy, A.: Future networks 2030: architecture and requirements. In: 2018 10th International Congress on Ultra Modern Telecommunications and Control Systems and Workshops (ICUMT), pp. 1–8. IEEE (2018)
34. Yi, B., Wang, X., Li, K., Huang, M., et al.: A comprehensive survey of network function virtualization. Comput. Netw. **133**, 212–262 (2018)
35. Zhou, C., et al.: Digital Twin Network: Concepts and Reference Architecture. Internet-Draft draft-irtf-nmrg-network-digital-twin-arch-03, Internet Engineering Task Force (Apr 2023), https://datatracker.ietf.org/doc/draft-irtf-nmrg-network-digital-twin-arch/03/, work in Progress

Tools and Demos

Evolution and Anti-patterns Visualized: MicroProspect in Microservice Architecture

Lauren Adams[1], Amr S. Abdelfattah[1], Md Showkat Hossain Chy[2],
Samantha Perry[2], Patrick Harris[1], Tomas Cerny[2(✉)],
Dario Amoroso d'Aragona[3], and Davide Taibi[3,4]

[1] Baylor University, Waco, Texas, USA
[2] SIE, University of Arizona, Tucson, Arizona, USA
tcerny@arizona.edu
[3] Tampere University, Tampere 33720, Finland
[4] University of Oulu, Oulu 90520, Finland

Abstract. A microservice architecture has become the dominant direction for designing the building blocks of large-scale, distributed software systems. However, the dynamic and changing microservices within decentralized systems in contrast to available static tracing tools presents challenges for comprehending its impact on the overall architecture. Existing tracing tools uncover service call graphs but have limitations in visualizing historical changes; moreover, they are not meant to aid with architecture assessment where developers seek potential design anomalies. With the ever-growing system complexity, developers likely resort to focusing on specific subsets of the system, especially given the lack of tools to analyze the impacts of system evolution. To address these challenges, we introduce the MicroProspect tool that provides a high-level, holistic visual perspective on the system's service view, tracks its structural changes throughout system evolution, and detects and visualizes anti-patterns that could lead to architectural degradation.

Keywords: Microservices · Evolution · Degradation · Visualization

1 Introduction

Microservices are a mainstream approach to building large and scalable systems [37]. Microservice architecture offers increased flexibility and autonomy in system evolution involving independent development teams following Conway's law [17]. However, development teams typically deal with the evolution of individual microservices without paying attention to the greater system perspective as the effect of decentralization. Without instruments to advise developers about continuous changes and the system's evolution as a whole, the system becomes susceptible to architectural degradation.[1][2]

---

[1] MicroProspect Source Code: https://github.com/cloudhubs/mvp.
[2] MicroProspect Demo: https://youtu.be/HXSB4uAxRH4.

© The Author(s), under exclusive license to Springer Nature Switzerland AG 2024
B. Tekinerdoğan et al. (Eds.): ECSA 2023, LNCS 14590, pp. 309–325, 2024.
https://doi.org/10.1007/978-3-031-66326-0_19

`Architectural degradation` is defined as the process of the persistent inconsistency between the descriptive software architecture as implemented and the prescriptive software architecture as intended [5,16]. The example of architecture degradation in open-source software is evident as over time, software architecture erodes, deviating from its intended conceptual structure due to factors like requirement changes and new features. This divergence, termed architecture erosion or drift, introduces inconsistencies between the implemented architecture and the originally planned architecture, negatively impacting software quality and potentially necessitating a redesign of the system [5]. It is typically an outcome of the gradual injection of code anomalies (i.e., anti-patterns, poor design choices, lack of maintenance, accumulated technical debt [7,27], etc.) as the software evolves. Degradation occurs when the critical quality attributes are violated [30].

Common detection strategies to identify degradation [5] base on design quality *metrics* (e.g., instability, cohesion, coupling) [8,31], or on the prioritization of *architecture anomalies* referred to as smells or anti-patterns [19,33]. `Anti-patterns` [36] are recurring design *practices, choices, or solutions to common problems* despite appearing reasonable and effective, leading to negative consequences and undermining the system's overall quality. `Bad smells` [35] describes a design characteristic that indicates a potential problem or violation of good practices, a warning sign that suggests potential issues in the design. These both prompt further analysis and consideration to identify the underlying problems and propose appropriate design improvements. To refer to both anomalies, we use the term anti-pattern.

With microservices, the system complexity easily grows to the point where system evolution becomes hard to trace, requiring new methods and tools to support history tracking for the system architecture [20]. Detecting and rectifying microservice anti-patterns apparent from the system's holistic perspective throughout the development and evolution process is crucial to avoid undesirable outcomes [4,13,29]. Even though distributed tracing tools (i.e., Jaeger [1], Dapper [34]) derive service call graphs, there is no visualization support for evolution, making it challenging to observe system changes. As many microservice anti-patterns are elusive within individual microservices, traditional tools like SonarQube [10] fail. The holistic system perspective (i.e., service call graph) is necessary for such analysis; however, even then, complex graphs in large systems pose difficulties in identifying issues due to information overload and distractions from numerous connections and nodes.

To address these limitations, we introduce a MicroProspect tool to provide developers with a comprehensive and interactive visualization fueled with the capability to compare system versions, highlight anti-patterns, and provide detailed architectural insights to identify design issues. By analyzing the system's historical data (i.e., from repositories), developers can visually identify degradation trends over time, leading to informed decisions leading to wise design choices.

This paper is organized as follows: Sect. 2 details the software architecture reconstruction process. Section 3 introduces our tool and Sect. 4 gives details on how to practically use the tool. The evaluation of the tool on a microservice system is described in Sect. 5 and related work is briefed in Sect. 6. Finally, Sects. 7 and 8 concludes the paper.

2   Software Architecture Reconstruction (SAR)

To accurately represent the system's architecture, the process of Software Architecture Reconstruction (SAR) aims at extracting the architecture from an existing software system [9]. It involves reverse-engineering the system's structure, components, and interactions based on its implementation artifacts, such as source code and configuration files. Automating the process requires constructing a system Intermediate Representation (IR) that captures the system structure and component dependencies [9]. Such a representation can be extracted from the system by various means (i.e., static or dynamic analysis).

Our target result is a visualized system service view perspective [11] decorated with information pertaining to the occurrence of anti-patterns and the system evolution. The service view represented by a service call graph is the mostly adopted visual approach for microservices [23]. In such a graph, services are represented as nodes, and requests between services as links. The overall SAR process phases are detailed in Fig. 1 and described in the following subsections.

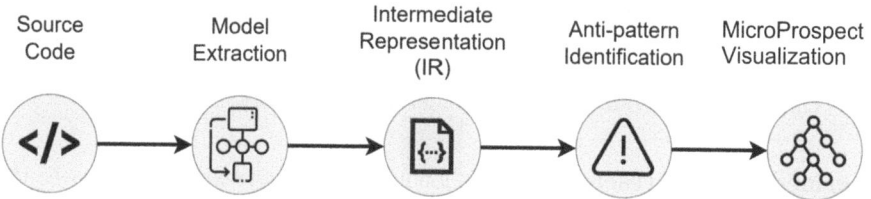

Fig. 1. Generalized SAR process for service call graph extraction and visualization used in MicroProspect processing

Model Extraction: The first phase involves static analysis of the microservices codebase to extract architectural components to construct the model representation of the system. The two-phase process involves the analysis of individual microservice codebases and then their interconnections.

The first phase analyzes the individual microservices, it can be assumed that component-based development frameworks are used to develop microservices. Resorting to low-level language use would lead to wheel reinvention and bring significant disadvantages to system evolution [32]. Therefore, our methodology assumes that the framework follows enterprise communication standards, organizing components into Controller, Service, and Data Repository within projects

[15]. We scrutinize microservices' codebases, extracting source files and parsing them to pinpoint method declarations and bodies. This extracted content encompasses an individual microservices component call graph, depicted in Fig. 2. It illustrates that endpoint calls are received from the Controller component and then delegated to the implemented Service component. The Service component is tasked with communicating with the data sources of the Data Repository component and other microservices, initiating remote calls to fulfill the required tasks. Schiewe et al. [32] demonstrated the identification of high-level constructs and components from abstract syntax trees. This approach reveals controllers and their endpoints with specific REST properties, along with identifying remote REST calls within the code.

The second phase interconnects the individual microservices with each other. The extracted remote calls from component call graphs reveal the connections between the microservices, forming the foundation for constructing service dependencies. The process combines individual component call graphs using merging ingredients like call signature match to endpoints or data simulates [3]. For extracting system interconnections, we consider the Prophet static analysis tool [9]. For explicit dependencies, Prophet uses approximation via signature matching between the REST endpoint and remote REST calls to identify connections. This approach has shown to be reliable through repeated experimentation, yet, it must be understood that static analysis provides only an approximation. However, the requisite cost is low, given no system execution is necessary, as in the case of dynamic system analysis.

The result then follows in the format of endpoint and rest call interconnections which, with the trace to their original microservices, leads to derived dependencies across microservices. A similar approach is possible for asynchronous calls (i.e., messaging) but was not considered in this work.

Intermediate Representation: Following the model extraction phase, the extracted component call graphs evolve into the IR, which represents the system components and their interconnections. From this IR, we can derive information about services, types, and dependencies which can be used to demonstrate the interconnections between services to construct a service view. Its format describes a composite structure listing the component call from endpoints within all its microservices and links between services throughout the particular endpoint route, as shown in Fig. 3. Such information makes it possible to render a service dependency graph of the system at a high level as a directed network.

Anti-pattern Identification: From the IR, we can seek to identify various anti-patterns within the microservice system that are traceable from the service dependency perspective. We can traverse the intermediate representation and label nodes with information pertaining to anti-patterns they may be a part of. We demonstrate the detection of selected anti-patterns based on information derived from the structure of the service call graph. In particular, we targeted the following:

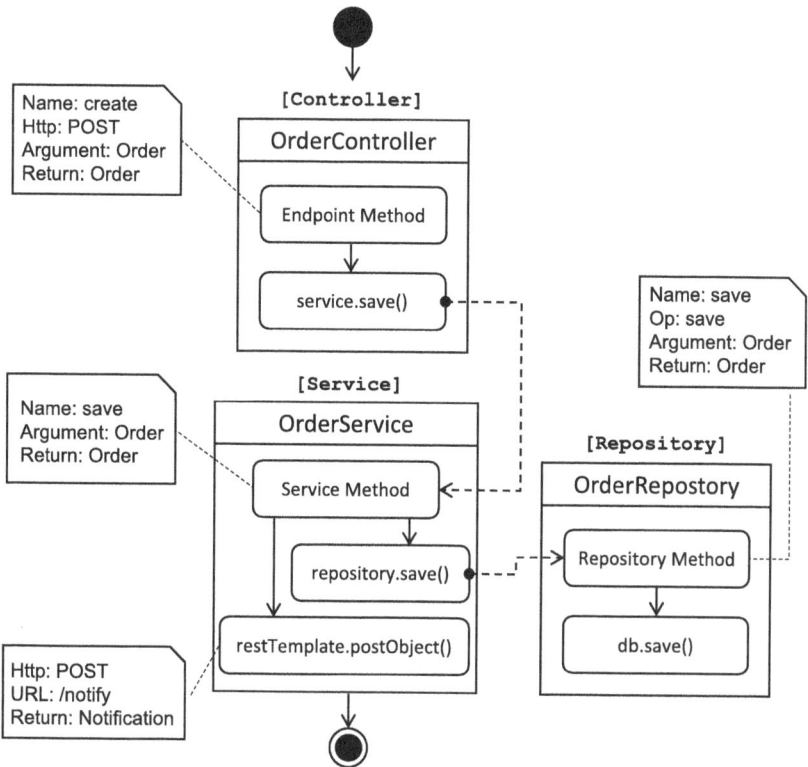

Fig. 2. Component Call Graph example

```
"source": "ts-preserve-other-service",
"target": "ts-security-service",
"requests": [
    {
        "type": "GET",
        "argument": "@PathVariable String accountId, @RequestHeader HttpHe
        "msReturn": "org.springframework.http.HttpEntity",
        "endpointFunction": "security.controller.SecurityController.check"
    }
```

Fig. 3. Example intermediate representation of service dependency graph from the train ticket system benchmark

- **High outgoing coupling**(variable threshold) - Service (outgoing connections) is interconnected or dependent on too many other services.
- **Cyclic dependency** - A cyclic chain of calls between two or more services that depend on each other directly or indirectly. Various cyclic dependency shapes can be recognized. Involved services can be hard to release and maintain. Likely, responsibilities are not separated correctly across services. This leads to problems with deployment, scalability, and co-change coupling. [13]
- **Bottleneck service** (variable threshold) - A service that is highly used (incoming connections) by other services. Its response time can be high because too many services use it. Service availability may go down due to the traffic.
- **Megaservice** (variable threshold) - Services should be small, independent, independently deployable units and serve a single purpose. A mega service has a high number of endpoints and a high fan-in. It is a result of poor system decomposition when a service combines multiple functionalities that multiple services should handle. [13] Creates maintenance issues, reduced performance, and difficult testing.

The decorated version of the graph JSON can then be used by the Micro-Prospect tool to display information pertaining to anti-patterns within and across system versions, highlighting changes.

3   MicroProspect Tool

We sought to develop a comprehensive visualization approach to enable developers to view the system service dependency graph regardless of the system scale. This necessitated an interactive tool that allows for various features suggested by Abdelfattah et al. [2], such as search, tracking, and isolation of particular services and their neighbors to successfully divide large microservice systems into manageable components. Additionally, Abdelfattah et al. found that a 3D visualization enabled novices to perform on the same level as experts in identifying relationships between services and outperform those using a 2D tool [2]. As a result of this and the service dependency graph's focus on relationships among services, we targeted a 3D visualization. Moreover, to understand system degradation, we desired to incorporate a fourth dimension in comparing system versions and anti-patterns over time. To further understand the system degradation, we can also display how anti-patterns change between system versions by comparing the individual occurrences between the two versions. Tracking system degradation can be accomplished by repeating the aforementioned SAR process for several system iterations and ordering them on a timeline that can be paged through.

Interactivity: MicroProspect offers interactive navigation of a visual service dependency graph in 3D space. The graph can be rotated, panned, zoomed, and rearranged via dragging nodes. Services are visualized as nodes in the graph and

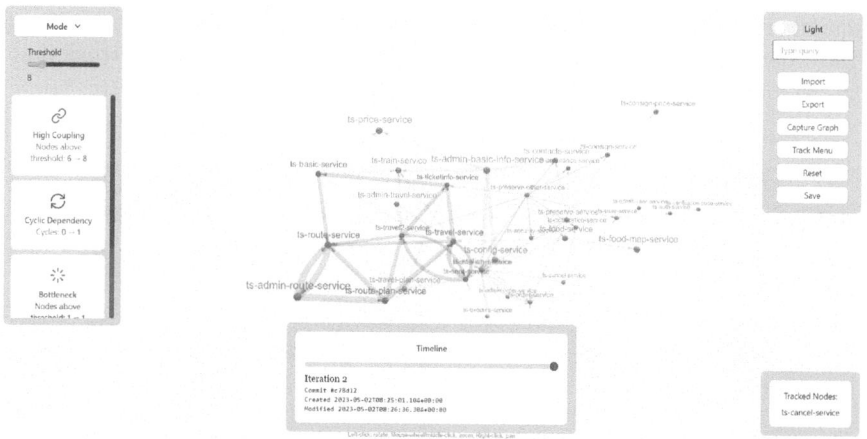

Fig. 4. Capture of the Train Ticket system in the MicroProspect tool

can be focused on via click to obtain specifics and to isolate the service and its neighbors visually. Requests between services are visualized as arrows of width dependent on request quantity and have the flow direction animated on hover. The tool offers many visualization options that can be toggled from menus on the left side of the screen, in addition to search functionality to isolate services by name for easier navigation of complex graphs.

All of these features serve to enable navigability despite graph complexity, which necessitated this 3D interactive approach. Figure 4 illustrates the Train Ticket benchmark in MicroProspect[3].

Anti-pattern Visualization: Previously mentioned anti-patterns are visualized by MicroProspect, including High outgoing coupling, Cyclic Dependency, Bottleneck, and Mega service. The anti-pattern information is extracted from the labeled system IR and used to highlight services and interactions based on the selected anti-pattern. Anti-pattern information is compared to the previous graph instance across system evolution as well to address the need to understand when and how anti-patterns developed in the system. Figure 4 highlights Cyclic Dependency in purple, and the left panel informs that a cycle did not appear in the previous system version.

System Evolution: A timeline slider enables linear paging through major graph versions over time that was extracted and uploaded to the tool. Graph versions are grouped by a unique named identifier and include metadata about creation and update time, as well as a mock git commit number. This is to be utilized in future tool iterations to extract the system timeline from a continuous integration pipeline using our SAR process. The timeline enables us to page

---

[3] https://dblp.uni-trier.de/rec/conf/icse/ZhouPX0XJZ18.html?view=bibtex.

through versions and compare anti-pattern occurrences between system iterations to determine degradation sources. This can also pair with the 'track node'
menu to focus on specific services in the graph across versions.

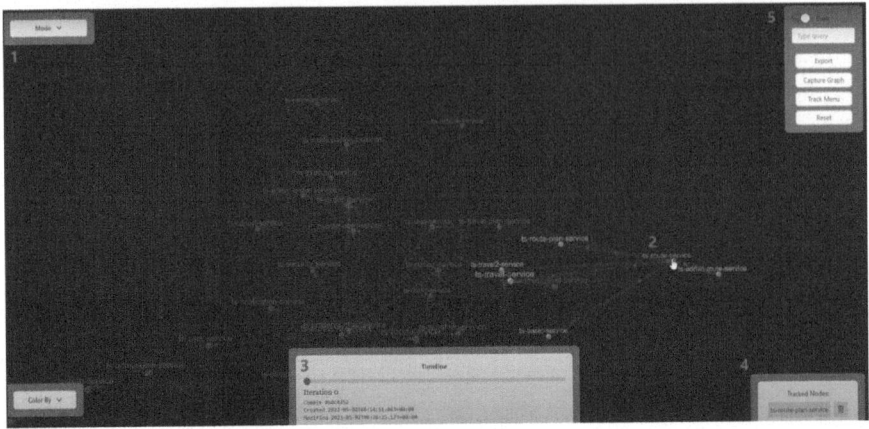

Fig. 5. MicroProspect capture with tools labeled

4   System Use Overview

The system provides two primary modes of operation that can be toggled
between in the top left corner menu (Fig. 5 ref 1). Visual Mode and Anti-Pattern
Mode each equipped with distinctive tools and capabilities. This subsection offers
an in-depth overview of these modes and their features.

Visual Mode: Visual Mode is designed to provide users with a comprehensive
visualization of the system's microservices and their dependency relationships.
Key features of Visual Mode include:

- **3D Visualization:** Users can explore the system in a 3D environment with
  six degrees of freedom.
- **Interactive Controls:** Features such as rotation, panning, and zooming in
  and out offer intuitive navigation.
- **Node Interaction:** Users can interact with nodes by clicking and dragging
  them for enhanced visualization (Fig. 5 ref 2).
- **Relationship Insight:** Hovering over nodes reveals dependency relationships. Purple links represent incoming dependencies, while yellow links represent outgoing dependencies.
- **Cyclic Dependency Visualization:** Cyclic dependencies are easily identified when a node is selected.

- **Node Details:** Clicking on nodes provides access to the following information (Fig. 6):
  - Dependency relationships.
  - Endpoints encapsulated by relationships.
  - Antipatterns detected on the node.
  - Threshold settings, if applicable.

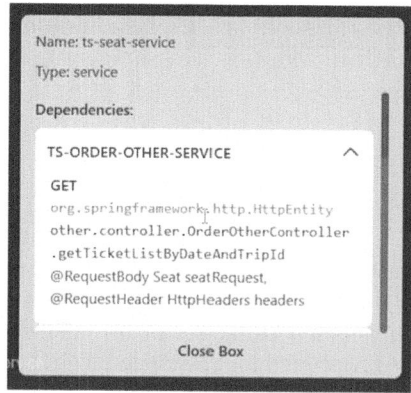

Fig. 6. Example of a selected Node's details

Furthermore, Visual Mode offers a set of tools and capabilities to enhance the user's experience:

- **Timeline:** The timeline tool allows users to explore the system's evolution by sliding between timeslices of development (Fig. 5 ref 3). Timeslices per commit provide insights into changes and evolution over time.
- **Track Nodes:** Users can track specific nodes across different timeslices by right-clicking on a node and adding it to the time slice menu (Fig. 5 ref 4). Tracked nodes are marked in green and persist through various timeslices. Users can access in-depth data for each time node by clicking on a tracked node, and they have the option to remove it from the menu.
- **Upper Right Panel:** This panel provides several toggles and options, including light and dark mode, the ability to switch between 2D and 3D views, reactive search to filter nodes based on queries, JSON schema export, capturing screenshots of the current camera angle, a track menu toggle, and a reset option to return to the default camera angle (Fig. 5 ref 5).

Anti-Pattern Mode: Anti-Pattern Mode focuses on the identification of various anti-patterns within the system. Users can set specific thresholds for anti-pattern detection. Notable features of Anti-Pattern Mode include:

- **High Coupling Detection:** The system highlights high coupling by shifting affected nodes to green, orange, and red colors. Red nodes indicate high coupling, green nodes represent low coupling, and orange nodes indicate medium coupling. The coloring is controlled by user-defined thresholds or dependency relationships. Additionally, the system provides a count of nodes above the specified threshold.
- **Cyclic Dependency Identification:** Cyclic dependencies are highlighted in purple for easy recognition.
- **Bottleneck Detection:** Services at risk of becoming bottlenecks or having dependencies above the threshold are displayed in purple.
- **Megaservice Indication:** Megaservices are identified and displayed in purple.

5   Evaluation

MicroProspect renders a service dependency graph by analyzing the IR of microservices and interconnections between endpoints and REST calls. For an assessment, we deployed our MicroProspect tool[4] with a microservice benchmark Train Ticket [38] and considered thirty-six of its microservices in our analysis since we considered only Java-based microservices. Table 1 presents the outcomes of manual code analysis versus our tool, including the number of microservices and REST Calls and their corresponding service dependency graph representations.

Table 1. Service Dependency Graph Data Analysis

Numbers/Approaches	Manual extraction	MicroProspect
Microservices	36	36
REST calls	135	135
Nodes in SDG	36	36
Links in SDG	87	87
Cycles in SDG	2	2
Highly-Coupled Nodes in SDG	8	8

The above analysis depicts that our tool successfully extracted all services and REST calls from the Train Ticket system we chose to visualize. Our representation combines multiple REST calls between the same two microservices into one singular link, which explains the different number of REST calls and links in the service dependency graph. This comparison between manual analysis and our tool shows that MicroProspect can provide an accurate representation of a system through the use of a service dependency graph.

---

[4] MicroProspect Tool: https://cloudhubs.ecs.baylor.edu/mavp.

Our tool is novel in the idea of incorporating a measure of system evolution in visualization and anti-pattern detection, allowing for distinctive use cases. Scrolling through a timeline of all the commits in a codebase would allow developers to quickly identify changes and the commit associated, which could greatly reduce the costs associated with debugging. Similarly, the automatic detection and visualization of anti-patterns is a great aid in locating the causes of deficiencies at a glance. Thus, resources could be focused more on the service being provided rather than on troubleshooting a faulty or ill-performing system.

Prior Evaluation of MicroProspect: Our prior research [25] yielded insightful data that emphasized the need for our tool when applied to microservice systems. We performed a user study involving 28 participants. The study considered the detection of two anti-patterns: cyclic dependency and knot in service-dependency graphs. The outcomes revealed that manual detection of cyclic dependencies resulted in only 66% to 70% accuracy, even dropping to as low as 32% for complex systems, despite the participants' experience levels. Similarly, in knot detection, practitioners achieved only 72% accuracy in small systems and 53% in larger ones, with false positives reported by 22% to 39% of participants. Interestingly, even highly familiar developers struggled, with accuracy rates similar to or only marginally better than less familiar peers. Notably, the time spent on detection tasks didn't significantly decrease with increased familiarity, emphasizing the inefficiency of manual detection. Naturally, the visual highlight of the selected anti-pattern explained the problem instantly.

Our prior research [25] underscores the necessity for such tools within microservice systems. The study revealed the limitations of manual detection in identifying anti-patterns, with accuracy rates often falling short, regardless of practitioners' experience levels. Notably, the time spent on detection tasks didn't significantly decrease with increased familiarity, highlighting the inefficiency of manual approaches. These findings strongly advocate for the adoption of automated tools like MicroProspect to enhance accuracy and efficiency in identifying and addressing anti-patterns within microservice architectures as demonstrated in this evaluation.

6   Related Works

Several approaches have been proposed to address the challenges of understanding and maintaining complex microservice architectures [6].

Gaidels et al. [21] explored leveraging service call graphs to identify microservice system issues using centrality and community recognition methods. Their techniques extracted meaningful metrics and visualizations, offering valuable insights into system dynamics. However, their approach lacked tool support, potentially limiting practical implementation and wider adoption. On the other hand, our solution offers a thorough analysis with integrated tool support, making it practical and accessible for evaluating and improving systems.

In the research conducted by Gamage et el. [22], they employed dynamic analysis to retrieve the dependency graph of the microservice system. By applying various graph algorithms, such as *Degree centrality* and *Clustering coefficient*, they successfully identified five common anti-patterns in the system: *Bottleneck, Knot, Cyclic Dependencies, Nano Service, Service Chain*. This approach solely relies on dynamic information for obtaining the dependency graph. Due to the dynamic nature of data extraction, sufficient time should be allocated to collect all the communication data between services. Additionally, the tool is limited to tracking synchronous systems that communicate in a RESTful style.

Cerny et al. [11] describes use of major microservice architecture tools in industry, although microservice architecture comes primarily from practitioners, so there are limited publications on the subject.

Amazon X-Ray console utilizes a map visual representation, featuring service nodes for requests, upstream client nodes for request origins, and downstream service nodes representing web services and resources. Embedded views enable users to inspect service maps and traces [11].

Netflix interactive visualization employs a service graph to depict system-wide service dependencies, allowing users to analyze different topologies by reconstructing the services communication graph. However, this approach may not be optimal for debugging specific service issues [11].

Jaeger tracing offers a Jaeger UI that renders service dependencies with dynamic data capabilities. Visualizes Directed Acyclic Graphs (DAGs) along with call frequencies to observe system architecture [1].

Kiali provides visualization tools for Istio, producing graphs representing traffic flow through the service mesh. Graph types include application, versioned application, workload, and service, each offering different levels of aggregation for system analysis [11].

With regards to additional existing tools, Engel et al. [18] developed a tool using architectural principles to uncover architectural issues in microservice systems. Their proposed approach evaluates dependency graphs based on metrics such as synchronous and asynchronous dependencies. While the tool assists in identifying design flaws, it has limited integration of graph theory concepts, potentially restricting the analysis depth. In contrast, our proposed solution takes a comprehensive approach, enabling a thorough understanding of architectural degradation and effective mitigation strategies.

MicroART [24] stands out as a tool that extracts both static and dynamic data to create a visual representation of the system's architecture. By leveraging model-driven engineering concepts, MicroART primarily focuses on recovering the system's deployment architecture and subsequently improving it. However, MicroART does not possess the capability to highlight issues and anti-patterns within the system. Hence, manual effort is required to analyze the system and identify architectural design problems.

Ma [28] introduces a tool that automatically generates the system's dependency graph for a microservice system by analyzing the source code through reflection. The tool identifies cyclic dependencies using Tarjan's Strongly

Connected Component graph technique. However, its capability is limited to detecting only the cyclic dependencies anti-pattern. In contrast, our proposed method enables the analysis and comparison of multiple versions, facilitating efficient monitoring and management of architectural changes and degradation.

Several software tools are available for visualizing architecture, such as Appdash, Datadog, Dynatrace, ElasticAPM, Hypertrace, Honeycomb.io, Instana, Jaeger, Kamon, LightStep, Logit.io, Lumigo, OpenCensus, OpenTelemetry, Splunk, Signoz, Site24 × 7, Uptrace, Victoriametrics, and Zipkin. These tools vary in their supported programming languages, licensing models, pricing, and functionalities. For instance, Datadog is renowned for its broad language support and comprehensive monitoring capabilities, while Zipkin and Jaeger offer free distributed tracing with simplicity in visualization. On the other hand, tools like Appdash and Grafana Tempo emphasize simplicity and are available for free, although they might lack certain advanced features. Janes et al. [26] delve into a comparative analysis of these tools, discussing their features, performance, and limitations, offering valuable insights into their effectiveness in diverse architectural contexts. Nevertheless, they reveal limitations in processing visualization to identify and incorporate anti-patterns, a gap addressed by our proposed tool. Moreover, our tool emphasizes the evolutionary aspect, providing complementary features that align with the dynamic nature of architectural changes, further enriching the toolset.

Recently, Cerny et al. introduced *Microvision* [12], a cutting-edge tool that offers the ability to reconstruct and visualize microservice systems in a captivating 3D virtual reality (VR) environment. By leveraging Prophet static analysis tool [9], *Microvision* can automatically reconstruct the architecture of Java-based microservice systems. However, it's important to note that *Microvision* only relies on static analysis and is limited to Java-based microservice systems, potentially overlooking the dynamic aspects of system behavior. Similarly, our tools share the same limitations.

7 Conclusion

The evolution of microservice systems faces multiple challenges related to decentralized development teams operating at individual microservice levels, focusing little on the overall system perspective. Such and many other factors might lead to system architecture degradation. In this work, we present a MicroProspect tool that uses a service call graph extracted from microservice systems to provide developers with a system-centered view of the system's dependencies. Given the extraction of the graph happens statically, they do not need to wait for the system to deploy and undergo comprehensive testing as common for established instruments. To mitigate architecture degradation, MicroProspect goes beyond presenting the system-centered view to developers expecting them to reason about the system. It utilizes the service dependency graph to detect and visualize selected anti-patterns. While we demonstrated a few examples, there are no limitations to continuing the effort by adding more anti-patterns to be detected.

Furthermore, the evolution aspect is considered as the tool takes into account service call graphs from multiple system versions to detect differences in and inform on newly formed anti-patterns. All these aspects are integrated through an intuitive visual approach using a 3D perspective that is more likely to better cope with more complex systems. The benefit of such a visualization approach is that it points developers to the specific place in the system's architecture that needs their attention rather than presenting a plain message that the system has a certain issue, which allows developers to analyze the problem in a greater context and make an informed decision on evolution. It is our belief that this approach has the potential to significantly improve the maintainability and evolvability of microservice systems and can be integrated into existing developer tools for wider adoption.

We aim to present the advancements our tool provides to the scientific community to join efforts to aid the maintenance and evolution of infrastructure for microservice systems. There are many avenues for future work extension, including dynamic analysis integration, mining software repository integration, more experimentation, and broader anti-pattern support. In ongoing works, efforts are made to catalog over 50 microservice anti-patterns [14] and some of these can be detected and visualized to bring direct utility to developers.

Acknowledgements. This material is based upon work supported by the National Science Foundation under Grant No. 2409933, and a grant from the Academy of Finland (grant n. 349488 - MuFAno).

References

1. Jaeger: Open source, distributed tracing platform. https://www.jaegertracing.io/. Accessed Nov 17 2023
2. Abdelfattah, A.S., Cerny, T., Taibi, D., Vegas, S.: Comparing 2D and augmented reality visualizations for microservice system understandability: A controlled experiment. In: 2023 IEEE/ACM 31st International Conference on Program Comprehension (ICPC), pp. 135–145 (2023). https://doi.org/10.1109/ICPC58990.2023.00028
3. Abdelfattah, A.S., Cerny, T.: The microservice dependency matrix. In: Papadopoulos, G.A., Rademacher, F., Soldani, J. (eds.) Service-Oriented and Cloud Computing: 10th IFIP WG 6.12 European Conference, ESOCC 2023, Larnaca, Cyprus, October 24–25, 2023, Proceedings, pp. 276–288. Springer Nature Switzerland, Cham (2023). https://doi.org/10.1007/978-3-031-46235-1_19
4. Abdelfattah, A.S., Cerny, T.: Roadmap to reasoning in microservice systems: a rapid review. Appl. Sci. **13**(3), 1838 (2023)
5. Baabad, A., Zulzalil, H.B., Hassan, S., Baharom, S.B.: Software architecture degradation in open source software: a systematic literature review. IEEE Access **8**, 173681–173709 (2020). https://doi.org/10.1109/ACCESS.2020.3024671
6. Bakhtin, A., Li, X., Soldani, J., Brogi, A., Tomas, C., Taibi, D.: Tools reconstructing microservice architecture: A systematic mapping study. In: Agility with Microservices Programming, co-located with ECSA 2023 (2023)

7. Bogner, J., Fritzsch, J., Wagner, S., Zimmermann, A.: Limiting technical debt with maintainability assurance - an industry survey on used techniques and differences with service- and microservice-based systems. In: 2018 IEEE/ACM International Conference on Technical Debt (TechDebt), pp. 125–133 (2018)

8. Bogner, J., Wagner, S., Zimmermann, A.: Automatically measuring the maintainability of service-and microservice-based systems - a literature review (10 2017). https://doi.org/10.1145/3143434.3143443

9. Bushong, V., Das, D., Cerny, T.: Reconstructing the holistic architecture of microservice systems using static analysis. In: Proceedings of the 12th International Conference on Cloud Computing and Services Science-CLOSER (2022)

10. Campbell, G.A., Papapetrou, P.P.: SonarQube in Action, 1st edn. Manning Publications Co., USA (2013)

11. Cerny, T., Abdelfattah, A.S., Bushong, V., Al Maruf, A., Taibi, D.: Microservice architecture reconstruction and visualization techniques: A review. In: 2022 IEEE International Conference on Service-Oriented System Engineering (SOSE), pp. 39–48. IEEE (2022)

12. Cerny, T., Abdelfattah, A.S., Bushong, V., Al Maruf, A., Taibi, D.: Microvision: Static analysis-based approach to visualizing microservices in augmented reality. In: 2022 IEEE International Conference on Service-Oriented System Engineering (SOSE), pp. 49–58 (2022). https://doi.org/10.1109/SOSE55356.2022.00012

13. Cerny, T., Abdelfattah, A.S., Maruf, A.A., Janes, A., Taibi, D.: Catalog and detection techniques of microservice anti-patterns and bad smells: a tertiary study. J. Syst. Softw. **206**, 111829 (2023). https://doi.org/10.1016/j.jss.2023.111829, https://www.sciencedirect.com/science/article/pii/S0164121223002248

14. Cerny, T., Maruf, A., Janes, A., Taibi, D.: Microservice anti-patterns and bad smells. how to classify, and how to detect them. a tertiary study. SSRN Electronic Journal (01 2023). https://doi.org/10.2139/ssrn.4328067

15. Cerny, T., et al.: On code analysis opportunities and challenges for enterprise systems and microservices. IEEE access **8**, 159449–159470 (2020)

16. Cerny, T., Taibi, D.: e static analysis: opportunities, gaps, and advancements. In: Joint Post-proceedings of the Third and Fourth International Conference on Microservices (Microservices 2020/2022). Schloss Dagstuhl–Leibniz-Zentrum für Informatik GmbH (2023)

17. Conway, M.E.: How do committees invent? Datamation (April 1967)

18. Engel, T., Langermeier, M., Bauer, B., Hofmann, A.: Evaluation of microservice architectures: a metric and tool-based approach. In: Mendling, J., Mouratidis, H. (eds.) Information Systems in the Big Data Era: CAiSE Forum 2018, Tallinn, Estonia, June 11-15, 2018, Proceedings, pp. 74–89. Springer International Publishing, Cham (2018). https://doi.org/10.1007/978-3-319-92901-9_8

19. Fontana, F.A., Roveda, R., Zanoni, M.: Tool support for evaluating architectural debt of an existing system: an experience report. In: Proceedings of the 31st Annual ACM Symposium on Applied Computing, pp. 1347–1349. SAC '16, ACM (2016). https://doi.org/10.1145/2851613.2851963

20. de Freitas Apolinário, D.R., de França, B.B.N.: Towards a method for monitoring the coupling evolution of microservice-based architectures. In: Proceedings of the 14th Brazilian Symposium on Software Components, Architectures, and Reuse, pp. 71-80. SBCARS '20, ACM (2020). https://doi.org/10.1145/3425269.3425273

21. Gaidels, E., Kirikova, M.: Service dependency graph analysis in microservice architecture. In: Buchmann, R.A., Polini, A., Johansson, B., Karagiannis, D. (eds.) Perspectives in Business Informatics Research: 19th International Conference on Business Informatics Research, BIR 2020, Vienna, Austria, September 21–23, 2020, Proceedings, pp. 128–139. Springer International Publishing, Cham (2020). https://doi.org/10.1007/978-3-030-61140-8_9

22. Gamage, I.U.P., Perera, I.: Using dependency graph and graph theory concepts to identify anti-patterns in a microservices system: a tool-based approach. In: 2021 Moratuwa Engineering Research Conference (MERCon), pp. 699–704 (2021). https://doi.org/10.1109/MERCon52712.2021.9525743

23. Gortney, M.E., et al.: Visualizing microservice architecture in the dynamic perspective: a systematic mapping study. IEEE Access (2022)

24. Granchelli, G., Cardarelli, M., Francesco, P., Malavolta, I., Iovino, L., Di Salle, A.: Towards recovering the software architecture of microservice-based systems, pp. 46–53 (04 2017). https://doi.org/10.1109/ICSAW.2017.48

25. Huizinga, A., Parker, G., Abdelfattah, A.S., Li, X., Cerny, T., Taibi, D.: Detecting microservice anti-patterns using interactive service call graphs: effort assessment. In: Han, H., Baker, E. (eds.) Next Generation Data Science: Second Southwest Data Science Conference, SDSC 2023, Waco, TX, USA, March 24–25, 2023, Revised Selected Papers, pp. 212–227. Springer Nature Switzerland, Cham (2024). https://doi.org/10.1007/978-3-031-61816-1_15

26. Janes, A., Li, X., Lenarduzzi, V.: Open tracing tools: overview and critical comparison. J. Syst. Softw. **204**, 111793 (2023). https://doi.org/10.1016/j.jss.2023.111793,https://www.sciencedirect.com/science/article/pii/S0164121223001887

27. Lenarduzzi, V., Lomio, F., Saarimäki, N., Taibi, D.: Does migrating a monolithic system to microservices decrease the technical debt? J. Syst. Softw. **169**, 110710 (2020). https://doi.org/10.1016/j.jss.2020.110710

28. Ma, S.P., Fan, C.Y., Chuang, Y., Liu, I.H., Lan, C.W.: Graph-based and scenario-driven microservice analysis, retrieval, and testing. Future Gener. Comput. Syst. **100**, 724–735 (11 2019). https://doi.org/10.1016/j.future.2019.05.048

29. Parker, G., et al.: Visualizing anti-patterns in microservices at runtime: a systematic mapping study. IEEE Access **11**, 4434–4442 (2023). https://doi.org/10.1109/ACCESS.2023.3236165

30. Riaz, M., Sulayman, M., Naqvi, H.: Architectural decay during continuous software evolution and impact of 'design for change' on software architecture, pp. 119–126. Springer, Heidelberg (2009). https://doi.org/10.1007/978-3-642-10619-4_15

31. Roveda, R., Arcelli Fontana, F., Pigazzini, I., Zanoni, M.: Towards an architectural debt index. In: 2018 44th Euromicro Conference on Software Engineering and Advanced Applications (SEAA), pp. 408–416 (2018). https://doi.org/10.1109/SEAA.2018.00073

32. Schiewe, M., Curtis, J., Bushong, V., Cerny, T.: Advancing static code analysis with language-agnostic component identification. IEEE Access **10**, 30743–30761 (2022)

33. Schmitt Laser, M., Medvidovic, N., Le, D.M., Garcia, J.: Arcade: an extensible workbench for architecture recovery, change, and decay evaluation. In: Proceedings of the 28th ACM Joint Meeting on European Software Engineering Conference and Symposium on the Foundations of Software Engineering, pp. 1546–1550. ESEC/FSE 2020, ACM (2020). https://doi.org/10.1145/3368089.3417941

34. Sigelman, B.H., et al.: Dapper, a large-scale distributed systems tracing infrastructure. Tech. rep., Google, Inc. (2010). https://research.google.com/archive/papers/dapper-2010-1.pdf

35. Taibi, D., Lenarduzzi, V.: On the definition of microservice bad smells. IEEE Softw. **35**(3), 56–62 (2018). https://doi.org/10.1109/MS.2018.2141031
36. Taibi, D., Lenarduzzi, V., Pahl, C.: Microservices anti-patterns: a taxonomy. In: Bucchiarone, A., Dragoni, N., Dustdar, S., Lago, P., Mazzara, M., Rivera, V., Sadovykh, A. (eds.) Microservices: Science and Engineering, pp. 111–128. Springer International Publishing, Cham (2020). https://doi.org/10.1007/978-3-030-31646-4_5
37. Xiao, L., Cai, Y., Kazman, R., Mo, R., Feng, Q.: Identifying and quantifying architectural debt. In: Proceedings of the 38th International Conference on Software Engineering, pp. 488–498. ICSE '16, ACM (2016). https://doi.org/10.1145/2884781.2884822
38. Zhou, X., et al.: Benchmarking microservice systems for software engineering research. In: The 40th International Conference on Software Engineering, pp. 323–324. ICSE '18, ACM (2018). https://doi.org/10.1145/3183440.3194991

An Approach and Toolset to Semi-automatically Recover and Visualise Micro-Service Architecture

Nour Ali[1]([⊠]), Nuha Alshuqayran[2], Rana Fakeeh[3], Thoybur Rohman[1], and Carlos Solis[4]

[1] Brunel University London, Uxbridge, UK
{nour.ali,2026156}@brunel.ac.uk
[2] Imam Mohammad Ibn Saud Islamic University, Riyadh, Saudi Arabia
nshaqayran@imamu.edu.sa
[3] AIDA Geschäftsführungs-Organisations-Systeme GmbH, Hauptstr. 11, 75391 Böblingen, Germany
rfakeeh@aidaorga.de
[4] ION Group, London, UK
carlos.solis@iongroup.com

Abstract. This paper presents the MicroService Architecture Recovery (MiSAR) toolset for software engineers (software architects and developers) that need to semi-automatically obtain as-implemented architectural models of existing microservice-based systems. The MiSAR approach has been designed following Model Driven Architecture, and a set of components have been developed to support the semi-automatic support of MiSAR. The toolset first parses microservice-based systems and generates a Platform-Specific Model, which is an abstract representation of the system using the technology. Then, a model transformation engine automatically generates a Platform Independent Model which represents the as-implemented microservice architectural mode of a system. To support the visualization of as-implemented architectural models, the Graphical Model Generator component of the toolset can be used. The Graphical Model Generator allows the software engineer to obtain quantitative metrics of the microservice architectural model and UML diagrams representing different views of the architecture.

Keywords: Microservice · architecture reconstruction · architecture recovery · architectural views · architecture visualization · model driven engineering · model driven architecture

1 Introduction

Microservice architecture has become a popular architectural style [1]. Microservices are developed quickly and provide more agility to the system [2], which results in continuous architectural changes [3]. Therefore, it can be stated that not every system is built using a well-documented architecture, and often the documentation of the architecture is not kept up to date [4]. Keeping control of the overall architecture during development can be very difficult, especially when microservice-based systems are designed, developed and deployed by different stakeholders and teams. Moreover, these architectures follow evolutionary design, which is very hard to manage, and architectural constraints are difficult to track. Software engineers often have little knowledge of the as-implemented architecture of their systems, and often face the challenge of not knowing in detail the underlying structures of the software system architecture.

The above concerns can be solved by using software architecture recovery (reconstruction or reverse architecting) [5, 6] which is a technique that reverse engineers systems to obtain the actual (as-implemented) architectural structure and description from system artefacts such as source code.

This paper presents the MicroService Architecture Recovery (MiSAR) toolset, which aims to support the architecture recovery of microservice systems by allowing software engineers to obtain semi-automatically an up-to-date architecture of implemented microservice systems. This can be challenging to obtain manually as microservices are not first-class citizens in the software, microservice systems use different programming frameworks and technologies, and microservices are highly inter-dependent, making analysis and architecture abstraction and comprehension difficult. The MiSAR toolset, manuals, artefacts and its application to case studies can be found at [7]. The MiSAR toolset video demonstration is available at [8].

The paper is structured as follows: Sect. 2 gives an overview of the MiSAR approach. Section 3 presents the components of the MiSAR toolset. Section 4 describes how MiSAR toolset has been implemented. Section 5 presents a walkthrough of the toolset recovering the architecture of an open-source system. Section 6 evaluates the performance of the toolset. Section 7 presents related work to MiSAR and finally Sect. 8 concludes and discusses further work.

2 MiSAR Approach

MiSAR follows Model Driven Architecture (MDA) [9], to recover architectural models of existing microservice systems. The initial version of the MiSAR approach has been defined empirically in [10]. To define the MDA artefacts of MiSAR (metamodels and mapping rules), we selected microservice-based open-source systems and recovered their architectures manually. This allowed us to learn by example the architectural elements that need to be included in the metamodels and mapping rules.

The MiSAR approach analyses the microservice software artefacts and produces models at two abstraction levels (see Fig. 1). First, MiSAR analyses the source code of a microservice project represented in text files. Second, it automatically creates a Platform-Specific Model of the project. Third, MiSAR automatically creates a Platform Independent Model which represents the architectural model of the system. To support this, the MiSAR approach includes the following MDA artefacts found at [7]:

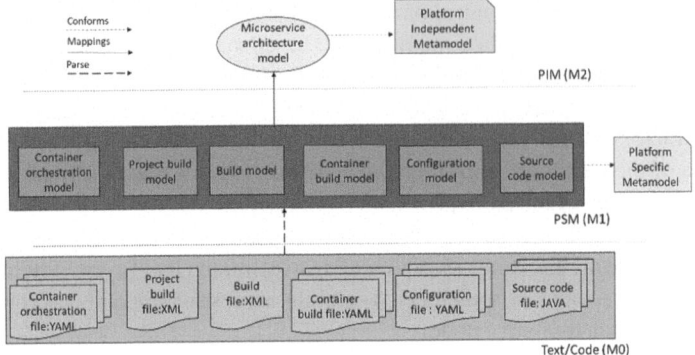

Fig. 1. MiSAR Model Driven Architecture abstraction levels

2.1 The Platform-Specific Metamodel

The Platform-Specific Metamodel defines the constructs which abstract microservice-based systems using the platforms and technologies (see Fig. 2). For each microservice-based system that needs to be recovered, a Platform-Specific Model (PSM) is generated conforming to the Platform-Specific Metamodel. The current platforms and technologies which are supported are the Java Language, Docker, and Spring boot framework and technologies which include Consul, Eureka, MongoDB, MySQL, Neo4j Graph database, OAuth2, and RabbitMQ.

Figure 2 shows the main elements of the Platform-Specific Metamodel and the PSM.ecore file can be found at [7]. As it can be seen, every PSM of a microservice application has a **DistributedApplicationProject** instance, with an application name and its root repository URI (**ProjectPackageURL**). The **DistributedApplicationProject** is composed of the architecture's development artefacts which include a multi-module project (**ApplicationProject**) and Docker containers represented by the **DockerContainerDefinition**. The **DockerContainerDefinition** elements involved in the architecture are extracted from the Docker Compose and Dockerfile files. The **DockerContainerDefinition** captures **DockerContainerPort** and DockerContainer-Link instances. An **ApplicationProject** represents one or many **MicroserviceProject** elements. A **MicroserviceProject** generalises a wide range of project artefacts implemented in any framework or language, including Java Spring Boot/Cloud. The **JavaSpringWebApplicationProject** element is a subtype of the **MicroserviceProject** element which reflects the specific characteristics of applications built with the Spring Boot/Cloud framework. Another characteristic of **JavaSpringWebApplicationProject** is that it aggregates multiple Java classes and/or Java interfaces with a means of annotation into **JavaSpringWebApplicationLayers**.

2.2 The Platform-Independent Metamodel

The Platform Independent Metamodel defines the microservice architectural elements that describe a microservice architecture in a technology independent way. The metamodel (see Fig. 3) includes 17 architectural element types. These include Microservices

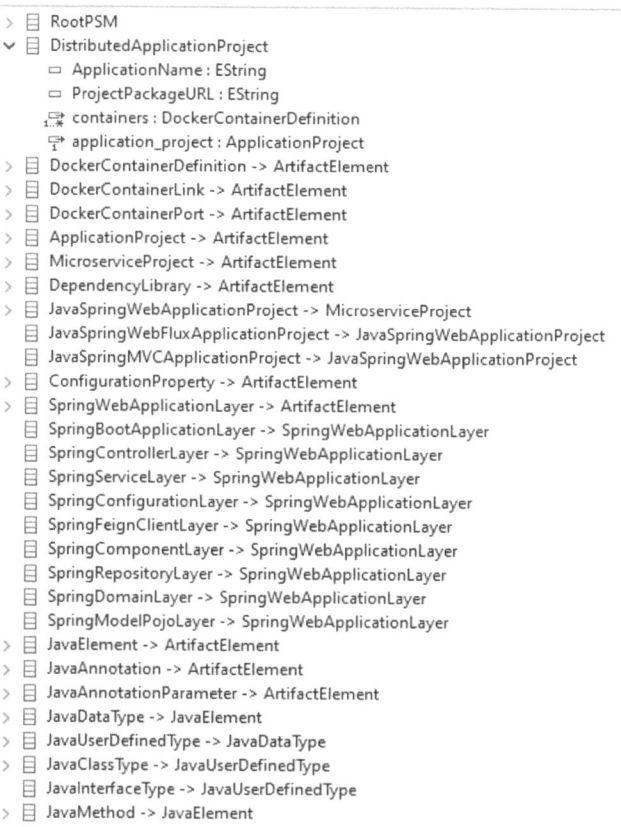

Fig. 2. MiSAR's Platform-Specific Metamodel in Ecore for the Java Language, Docker, and Spring boot

that can be classified into Functional Microservices, which realize the system's business capabilities, and Infrastructure Microservices, which realize infrastructural capabilities. Infrastructure Pattern Components which support the functionality of patterns. MessageDestination type which is an abstract element to represent communication and currently has two subtypes: Endpoints which are service URIs for synchronous remote calls and QueueListeners which are a kind of asynchronous communication. Service Dependencies which describe the communication between a consumer microservice and a provider microservice. Each architectural model recovered conforms to the Platform Independent Metamodel and is called a Platform Independent Model (PIM).

2.3 Mapping Rules

Mapping Rules map elements of PSMs into PIMs. Each mapping rule is represented with a Left-Hand Side (L-H-S) and a Right-Hand Side (R-H-S). The L-H-S includes PSM elements structured in a tree and the R-H-S indicates targeted PIM elements. The L-H-S PSM elements are checked and if they exist in a PSM instance, then the R-H-S PSM

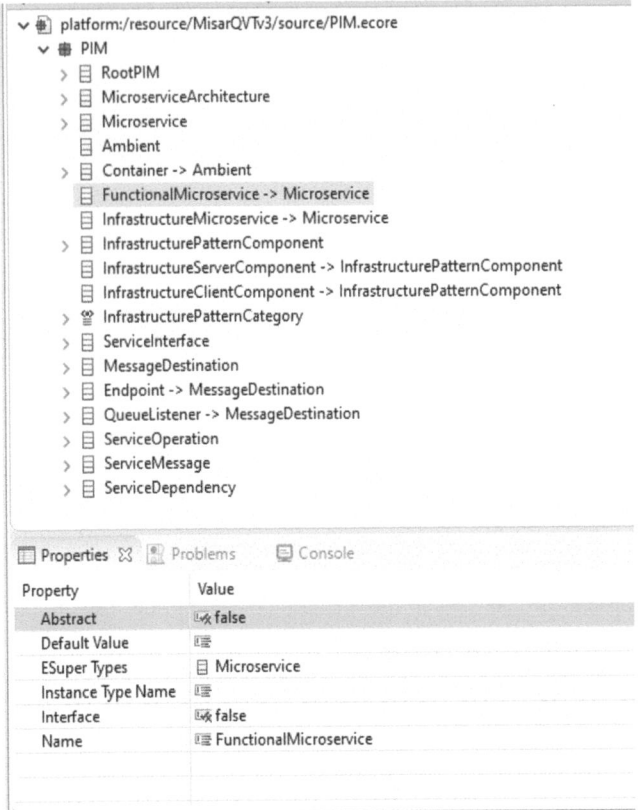

Fig. 3. MiSAR's Platform Independent Metamodel

elements are transformed into a group of target PIM elements. An example of a mapping rule is the one which identifies that a java method uses asynchronous communication:

[L-H-S] A Java Method with Element Identifier value: "convertAndSend" whose parent is a Java User Defined Type with Element Identifier value: "RabbitTemplate" or "AmqpTemplate", which has one Java Method Parameter with Parameter Order value: "2" and Field Value value: "[routing-key]" whose type is a Java Class Type with Element Identifier value: "String" such that there is a Queue Listener with Queue Name value that contains: "[routing-key]" and belongs to a Microservice with Microservice Name value: "[provider-name]" **indicates** [R-H-S] a Service Dependency with Provider Destination value: "QueueListener[QueueName:[queue-name]]".

In the above mapping rule a *Service Dependency* PIM element is created which has a QueueListener as a provider *MessageDestination*. MiSAR currently supports 275 mapping rules.

One of the benefits of MiSAR in following the MDA approach is the separation of concerns. Models can be reusable and independent of their graphical notation. As it can be noticed in the following sections, a recovered architectural model (PIM instance) can be obtained without a graphical notation. Consequently, an architectural model can be manipulated in other contexts and transformed into other forms.

Another advantage of MDA is obtaining and using models at different abstraction levels. The PSM is an abstraction that allowed MiSAR to have a structured reverse engineering process and therefore has enabled simple mapping rules (transformations) to generate an architectural model. The PSM allowed the reverse engineering process to first collect and extract which elements from the system and its technologies are needed to construct an architectural model and cluster them. The PSM instance can also be useful for users as it can allow them to trace back and identify which platform and technology elements participated in constructing a recovered architectural model.

3   Components of MiSAR Toolset

The MiSAR toolset is composed of four components which support a user to obtain an architectural model from a microservice system in a semi-automatic way. Each of the components, has as input and/or produces the MDA artefacts explained in Sect. 2. The components in the toolset are the following:

- AIO: The All In One (AIO) user interface appears when you launch MiSAR. If it is the first launch, it provides guidelines on how to install the toolset components and provides guidelines on using them.
- Parser: MiSAR includes a parser which statically analyses the source files of microservice-based software. The parser analyses these files, collects information from different artefacts, and clusters them into concepts of the PSM. The parser produces a Platform-Specific Model (PSM) of the system by instantiating the Platform-Specific Metamodel. For example, the parser to create a **JavaSpringWebApplicationProject** (explained in Sect. 2.1) object, it analyses different POM files of a system which contain a list of dependency libraries. The parser deserializes each POM file from XML format into a Python dictionary, extracting only the 'parent' and 'dependencies' elements. Each child element within the 'dependencies' element is then converted into a 'DependencyLibrary' PSM object. The information from the source element is collected and organized in attributes within this object. Finally, all the 'DependencyLibrary' objects are clustered inside one parent 'JavaSpringMVCApplicationProject' object. Currently, the parser analyses the following files:

  - **Docker Compose Files** (.yml|.yaml): These files define services, networks, and volumes for Docker containers.
  - **POM Files** (.xml): Maven POM (Project Object Model) files, specify project information, dependencies, and build configurations.
  - **Configuration Files** (.yml|.yaml|.properties): Configuration files in YAML or properties format can be parsed. These files often contain settings, properties, or environment-specific configurations.
  - **Java Source Files**: For Java source files to be parsed, the project needs to have specific libraries in the POM/build.gradle file. Specifically, include either one of the following libraries: 1) org.springframework.boot: which indicates a Java

Spring Boot project. 2) org.springframework.cloud: which indicates a Spring Cloud project.

- Model Transformation Engine: MiSAR implements bottom-up model-driven transformations to obtain architectural models. PSMs generated by the parser are fed into model transformations that automatically transform them into PIMs. The model transformations implement the mapping rules and automatically generate the as-implemented architecture model of a system.
- Graphical Model Generator: To improve the understandability of the PIMs, we have developed a Graphical Generator to enable users to visualize the PIM models of the recovered systems. For each PIM, the generator creates: 1) metrics of the PIMs (architectural models) in excel sheets, e.g., a table with the number of architectural elements in an architectural model such as the number of microservices, pattern components and service dependencies, 2) images with graphical UML diagrams of the models and 3) PlantUML [13] files of the models. We currently use the UML Component diagram to represent the microservice architecture. The architecture can also have different views at architecture level and microservice level.

4   Implementation of MiSAR

The Platform Independent and Platform-Specific Metamodels have been implemented as Ecore models using the Eclipse Modeling Framework (EMF) [11] (see Fig. 2 & Fig. 3) The MiSARParser is a python application that incorporates PyEcore, JavaLang, Yaml, XMLtoDict and other python libraries to parse YAML, XML and JAVA artefacts of a microservice-based application such as docker-compose.yml and pom.xml into a MiSAR PSM. The generated PSM is in Ecore (or XMI).

To automate the mapping rules, we have developed the model transformation engine using the Eclipse Model-to-Model Transformation (M2M) project. The 275 mapping rules of MiSAR are written using the operational QVT transformation language (QVTo) [12]. QVTo follows the structure of our mapping rules. The implementation of mapping rules into QVTo, implements the model transformation engine. The model transformation engine receives as input a PSM instance, executes the rules and then produces PIMs in Ecore (or XMI).

Finally, the graphical generator is a java application which navigates through PIMs and automatically translates them into UML graphical notations. The application uses the java Ecore implementations of MiSAR's Platform Independent Metamodel and translates each element into PlantUML textual language [13] to create the images with the diagrams. The java application also creates excel sheets with metrics of the models. We could have implemented a graphical editor by using frameworks such as Graphical Modeling Projects [14] or EcoreViz [15] which can be integrated into Eclipse. However, we made the decision to be Eclipse independent as Eclipse is heavyweight and can change its versions making our approach obsolete in the future. Since, currently, MiSAR does not require the manipulation of diagrams generated (no human interaction), then this is sufficient. This could change in the future, if MiSAR is to be extended for further software engineering activities such as manipulating models to keep them consistent with the microservice implementation.

5 A Walkthrough of MiSAR

We will demonstrate the steps and artefacts produced using the MiSAR toolset to semi-automatically generate the as-implemented architectural model of a microservice-based system. To demonstrate MiSAR, we have selected a microservice project, which is an open-source project called the MicroCompany application [16]. MicroCompany is implemented using Java Spring Boot/Spring Cloud microservice-based application that consists of 11 microservices of which 4 are business-oriented. It utilises both synchronous and asynchronous inter-service communication.

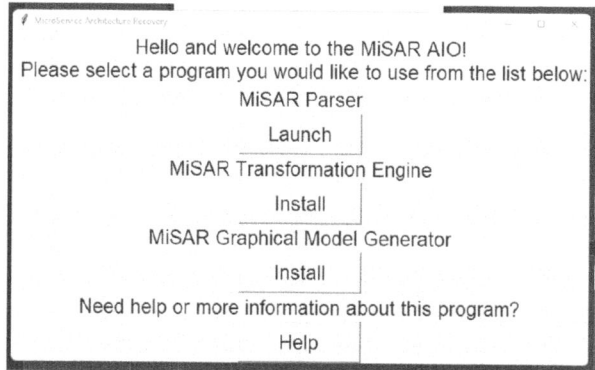

Fig. 4. User interface of MiSAR AIO

Consider that the software team, after having developed the MicroCompany application, would need to get an up-to-date architecture of their application. The software team has to follow the installation instructions and manuals found on [17]. A user can use the AIO for installation guidelines as well. Figure 4 shows the AIO when the user has already installed the parser and it is ready to be launched. To obtain the up-to-date architecture, the user follows the following steps:

Step 1- Parsing the Microservice System to Create a PSM Instance: The files from the MicroCompany GitHub are first downloaded locally. Then, the required artefacts are collected and uploaded to the existing MiSAR parser, as illustrated in Fig. 5. The parser receives as input: the Project name, Build directory of the system (multi-module) project, Path of every Docker Compose file (yml), Build directory of every microservice (single-module) project, Path of build file (POM) of the system (multimodule) project and the Path of the build file (POM) for every microservice (single-module) project. Configuration and Java Source artefacts are collected automatically by the parser with the help of the build directory of every microservice project. When the user inputs the Build Directory, the parser asks the user if they would like to import all the files automatically or whether they would like to upload them manually.

The user has the option to delete or add uploaded files. This is to allow the user to control the parts of the system which they would like to recover. Users may want to recover the architecture of the entire microservice system, whereas other users may want to only recover specific parts of the system, e.g., specific microservices.

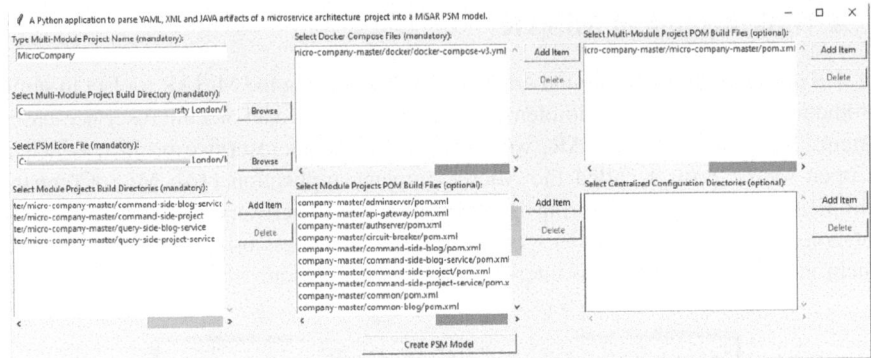

Fig. 5. User interface of Parser used to create PSM of MicroCompany

The parser produces a PSM instance for the MicroCompany application. The PSM instance can be found at [18]. Even though the PSM is not the as-implemented architecture model, it is useful, as it provides backtracking support and allows the user to understand the elements that generated the PIM, by checking the specific lines in the artefact that generated those particular PSM elements.

Step 2- Executing Model Transformations to Create the PIM Instance: The PIM architectural model is obtained by running the Eclipse QVTo project. The PIM recovered is in XMI format and can be opened as a tree view with Sample Reflective Ecore Model editor provided by the Eclipse Modeling Framework (EMF). Figure 6 shows the generated architecture of MicroCompany using EMF. It consists of 11 microservices: 6 Infrastructure microservices and 5 Functional microservices. The user can have a more detailed view of the microservices if they click on them. In Fig. 6, the user has clicked on the Infrastructure Microservice called circuit-breaker and can view its associated architectural elements: Container, Infrastructure Server Components, Infrastructure Client Components, Service Interface, Endpoint, and Service Dependencies.

In addition, the microservice view has the attributes for the microservices. Figure 7 shows attributes for the recovered microservice called query-side-blog. For instance, (a) the "query-side-blog" microservice exposes an endpoint with request URI "GET /blogposts/search/findByDraftTrue" which is handled by (b) the service operation "findByDraftTrue()" and (c) returns a response service message of model "Page(BlogPost)". As it can be noticed, one of the attributes is "Generating PSM" which indicates the element from the PSM that was used to generate the attribute. This feature provides traceability and backtracking support for the recovery.

Step 3- Transforming the PIM XMI into Graphical Architectural Diagrams: Once you have a PIM instance, you can explore it in XMI or by using EMF as explained in Step 2. However, if users are not experts in Ecore or they prefer to have an improved visualization experience, e.g., sharing diagrams with their teams, they can use the Graphical Model Generator. The user selects the PIM instance and indicates the location where the different images and excel sheets will be located once produced (see Fig. 8). Then, automatically a drop-down menu with all the microservices of the architectural model of the PIM instance will be visible under Microservice Level. The user can produce

Fig. 6. Recovered PIM model for MicroCompany

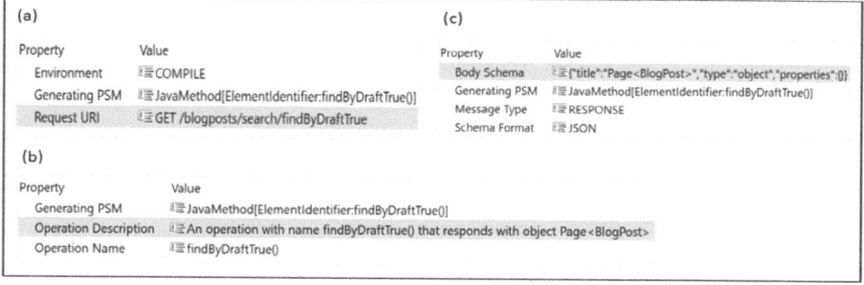

Fig. 7. Example of the recovered "query-side-blog" microservice attributes

images with UML architecture diagrams and metrics at the architecture level or at a microservice level as follows:

At Architecture Level: If the user clicks on the Architecture Metrics Excel Datasheet, an excel sheet is produced that contains the number of architectural elements for every single architectural element type. Figure 9 shows the excel sheet produced for MicroCompany. For example, there are 5 Functional Microservices and 6 Infrastructure Microservices in MicroCompany. In addition, the user can click under Dependency View and create an image (Download PNG and Download SVG buttons) or get the PlantUML

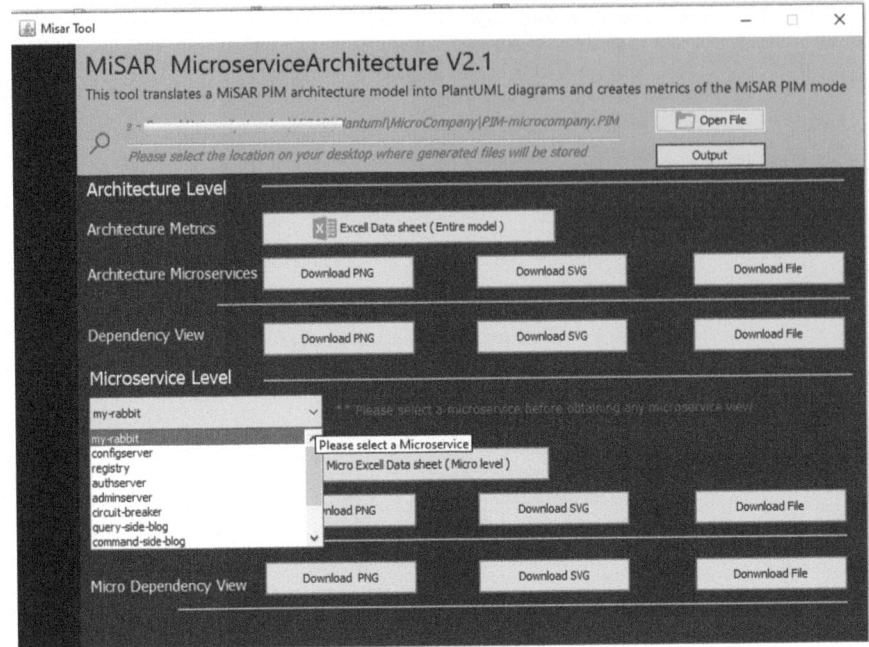

Fig. 8. Using the Graphical Model Generator for MicroCompany

file for the graphical UML diagram. Figure 10 shows the dependency diagram for the architecture of MicroCompany. The diagram shows the microservices of the architecture and their dependencies. Blue components are Functional microservices and purple components are Infrastructure microservices.

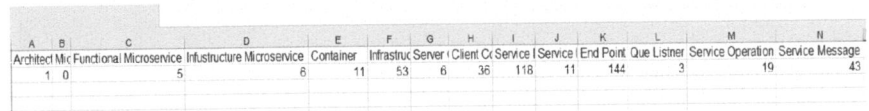

Fig. 9. Architecture Level Metrics of recovered MicroCompany

At Microservice Level: As it can be noticed from Fig. 10, it is very hard to read the architectural diagram of a medium to large architectural model such as MicroCompany. Therefore, the tool allows the user to select from the top-down menu a specific microservice. Once a microservice is selected, they can create an excel with metrics for that microservice, a microservice view which shows the pattern components, endpoints and service interfaces and a microservice dependency view diagram which shows the microservice chosen and the service dependencies it has with others. Figure 11 shows the excel sheet generated summarizing the metrics of Circuit-Breaker microservice: it has 4 Pattern Components, 1 Infrastructure Service Component, 2 Infrastructure Client components, 1 Service Interface, 1 endpoint and 7 Service Dependencies. Figure 12 shows

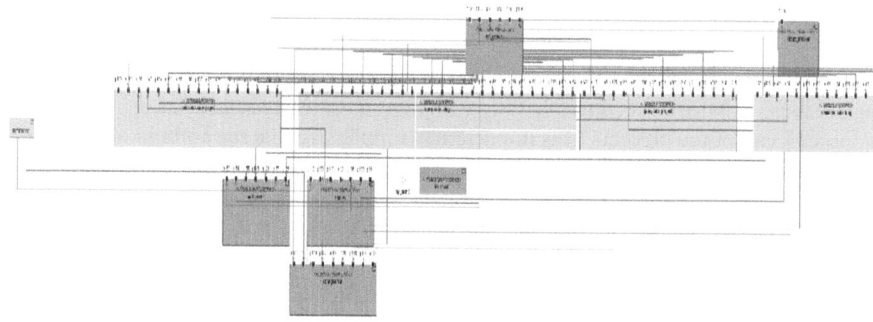

Fig. 10. Architecture Level Dependency View for recovered MicroCompany

the microservice view for Circuit-Breaker showing that it has 4 InfrastructurePattern-Components (2 of type InfrastructureClientComponents and 1 InfrastructureServerComponent) and an endpoint. Figure 13 shows the microservice dependency view diagram for Circuit-Breaker. Circuit-Breaker has 7 dependencies with other microservices.

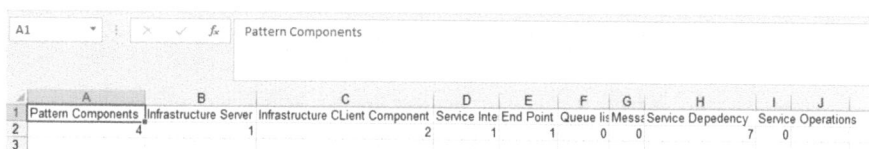

Fig. 11. Circuit-Breaker microservice metrics

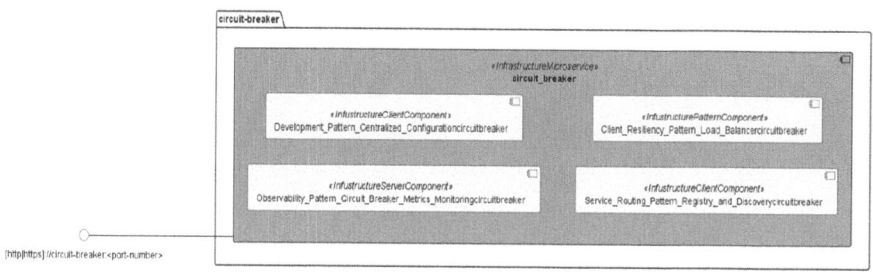

Fig. 12. Circuit-Breaker Microservice View

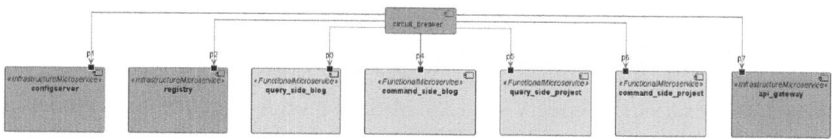

Fig. 13. Circuit-Breaker microservice Dependency View

6   Evaluation

In this section, we evaluate the performance of the tool's components to demonstrate the time it takes for MiSAR to generate the as-implemented architecture (the PIM instance) for three open-source projects. It is important to emphasize that the authors of the papers have not been involved in the development of these open-source projects. Table 1 shows the time it takes, for each toolset component, on an Intel Processor Core (TM) i5-7200U CPU @ 2.50GHz, 2701 MHz, 2 Core(s), 4 Logical Processor(s). The time for the Graphical Generator Component is not shown as this is instantaneous. It can be noticed that for a large project, such as TrainTicket, the parser takes most of the time of the recovery process. However, several days could have been taken if software engineers would want to recover the architecture manually. Manual architecture recovery typically requires the involvement of multiple stakeholders to gather knowledge about the system and its interpretation. It relies on the experience of these stakeholders and involves manual analysis of the system's source code [21]. Manual recovery could also produce an inaccurate architecture due to human errors or an architecture with not enough details.

This evaluation has several limitations. Firstly, it has only been conducted on three open-source systems, albeit including a large-scale one such as TrainTicket. Future evaluations could expand to encompass larger and industrial systems. Additionally, the evaluation did not consider the user experience of using the toolset.

Table 1. Time of MiSAR toolset to obtain as-implemented architecture models.

	LOC	Parser to generate PSM (sec)	Model Engine to Transform PSM to PIM (sec)	Total No. of Recovered elements in PIM
MicroCompany [16]	127.1K	9	3.89	490 including 11 microservices
TrainTicket [19]	507.2K	446	63.15	1341 including 69 microservices
MusicStore [20]	116.6K	1	1.07	107 including 9 microservices

7   Related Work

One of the few existing works related to ours is MicroART [22]. MicroART also uses model-driven engineering but does not follow MDA, e.g., it does not define a Platform-Specific Metamodel. In MiSAR, the architectural model is recovered automatically from the PSM, i.e., there is no human input, whereas in MicroART, a software architect needs to identify service discovery services. MiSAR produces architectural models that are richer than MicroART as MicroART only has 8 architectural concepts whereas MiSAR has 17. Therefore, the expressiveness of the MiSAR Platform Independent Metamodel has elements such as Infrastructure Pattern Components and Asynchronous communication which MicroART does not support.

MicroLyze [23] is another work which proposes an architecture recovery approach for microservices. MicroLyze, unlike MiSAR, does not adopt a model-driven approach. Instead, it utilises a distributed tracing component that dynamically monitors simulated user requests. In addition, the work of Wang et al. [24], present an automated recovery process using system source code to build a dependency graph. Like MiSAR, their approach is based on source code analysis. However, their approach does not employ model-driven architecture and does not recover many elements such as patterns.

Another approach that recovers microservice architecture is Kieker [25]. Kieker is a monitoring framework which uses dynamic analysis to discover the architecture of a system. The main elements it extracts (or recovers) are containers and methods. It does not explicitly provide a microservice as an architecture concept and infrastructure pattern components. Since Kieker uses dynamic analysis, the software engineer needs to add jar files next to docker files, execute the microservice systems and manipulate the docker files. In comparison to MiSAR which only statically analyses systems, the recovery of the architecture does not require manipulating any parts of the source code artefacts and does not require the microservice system to be executing. However, with dynamic analysis, the recovered architecture obtains dynamic information such as times of methods which are not recovered by MiSAR.

8 Conclusion

In this paper, we have introduced the MiSAR toolset that semi-automatically generates as-implemented architectural models from existing microservice systems implemented in diverse technologies. We have demonstrated how the MiSAR toolset components can be used to recover architectural models in Ecore (XMI) and if required they can be introduced to be visualized in UML Component diagrams in different views. We have also presented the evaluation of the time it takes for MiSAR to recover the architectures of 3 microservice projects.

Our further work includes improving the usability aspects of the toolset and the efficiency of the parser. As explained in the paper, currently MiSAR only supports Java Spring Boot Applications and/or Docker. We are currently working on a project to extend MiSAR to support the recovery of microservice-based systems partly (or fully) developed in Python. To do so, we need to extend the parser, the Platform-Specific Metamodel and the mapping rules. We will continue working on extending MiSAR to support its analysis of additional languages and technologies.

Furthermore, one existing limitation of our visually generated diagrams is their reliance on PlantUML, which generates static images. This restricts user manipulation of the graphical architecture models, and the layout of the diagrams cannot be controlled. To address this limitation, we plan on creating a diagramming tool. Additionally, we intend to evaluate our approach with practitioners and in industrial settings, rather than solely relying on open-source projects.

References

1. Newman, S.: Building Microservices: Designing Fine-Grained Systems. O'Reilly Media, Inc (2015)

2. Hasselbring, W., Steinacker, G., Microservice architectures for scalability, agility and reliability in e-commerce. In: IEEE International Conference on Software Architecture Workshops (ICSAW), pp. 243–246 (2017)

3. Simioni, A., Vardanega, T.: In pursuit of architectural agility: experimenting with microservices. In: 2018 IEEE International Conference on Services Computing (SCC), pp. 113–120 (2018)

4. Cerny, T., Donahoo, M.J., Trnka, M.: Contextual understanding of microservice architecture: current and future directions. ACM SIGAPP Appl. Comput. Rev. **17**(4), 29–45 (2018). https://doi.org/10.1145/3183628.3183631

5. Ducasse, S., Pollet, D.: Software architecture reconstruction: a process-oriented taxonomy. IEEE Trans. Softw. Eng. **35**(4), 573–591 (2009)

6. Ali, N., Rosik, J., Buckley, J.: Characterizing real-time reflexion based architecture recovery: an in-vivo multicase study. In: 8th international ACM SIGSOFT conference on Quality of software architectures, pp. 23–32. ACM, January 2012

7. MiSAR. https://github.com/MicroServiceArchitectureRecovery/misar

8. MiSAR Toolset video demo: https://youtu.be/sdRDkLesySO

9. Brambilla, M., Cabot, J., Wimmer, M.: Model-Driven Software Engineering in Practice, 1st ed. Morgan & Claypool (2012)

10. Alshuqayran, N., Ali, N., Evans, R.: Towards micro service architecture recovery: an empirical study. In: IEEE International Conference on Software Architecture (ICSA), pp. 47–4709 (2018)

11. Steinberg, D., Budinsky, F., Paternostro, M., Merks, E.: EMF: Eclipse Modeling Framework, 2nd edn. Addison-Wesley (2008)

12. Barendrecht, P.J.: Modeling transformations using QVT Operational Mappings, Research project report. Eindhoven University of Technology Department of Mechanical Engineering Systems Engineering Group, Eindhoven (2010)

13. PlantUML Homepage. https://plantuml.com/. Accessed 05 May 2023

14. Graphical Modeling Project. https://eclipse.dev/modeling/gmp/

15. Ecore visualization using KIELER. https://github.com/kieler/ecoreviz

16. Dugalic, I.: MicroCompany (2022). https://github.com/idugalic/micro-company. Accessed 26 Apr 2023

17. MiSAR parser and Model Transformation Engine. https://github.com/MicroServiceArchitectureRecovery/MiSAR-Parser-and-Model-Transformation

18. MiSAR PSM and PIM instances of MicroComany: https://github.com/MicroServiceArchitectureRecovery/misar/tree/main/EmpiricalStudyReplication/EvaluationOfMiSAR/microcompany-PIM%26PIM

19. Zhou, X., Peng, X., Xie, T., Sun, C.J.C., Xu, J., Zhao, W.: Benchmarking microservice systems for software engineering research. In: Proceedings of the 40th International Conference on Software Engineering Companion Proceedings - ICSE, pp. 323–324 (2018)

20. OSS, S.: MusicStore. https://github.com/SteeltoeOSS/Samples/tree/main/MusicStore. Accessed 06 July 2023

21. van Deursen, A., Hofmeister, C., Koschke, R., Moonen, L., Riva, C.: Symphony: view-driven software architecture reconstruction. In: Proceedings of Fourth Working IEEE/IFIP Conference on Software Architecture (WICSA 2004), Oslo, Norway, pp. 122–132 (2004). https://doi.org/10.1109/WICSA.2004.1310696

22. Granchelli, G., Cardarelli, M., Di Francesco, P., Malavolta, I., Iovino, L., Di Salle, A.: Microart: a software architecture recovery tool for maintaining microservice-based systems. In: IEEE International Conference on Software Architecture Workshops (ICSAW), pp. 298–302 (2017)

23. Kleehaus, M., Uludağ, Ö., Schäfer, P., Matthes, F.: MICROLYZE: a framework for recovering the software architecture in microservice-based environments. In: Mendling, J., Mouratidis, H. (eds.) Information Systems in the Big Data Era: CAiSE Forum 2018, Tallinn, Estonia, June 11-15, 2018, Proceedings, pp. 148–162. Springer International Publishing, Cham (2018). https://doi.org/10.1007/978-3-319-92901-9_14

24. Wang, L., et al.: Microservice architecture recovery based on intra-service and inter-service features. J. Syst. Softw. **204**, 111754 (2023). https://doi.org/10.1016/j.jss.2023.111754

25. Hasselbring, W., van Hoorn, A.: Kieker: a monitoring framework for software engineering research. Softw. Impacts **5**, 100019 (2020)

An Extensible Framework for Architecture-Based Data Flow Analysis for Information Security

Nicolas Boltz[✉], Sebastian Hahner, Christopher Gerking, and Robert Heinrich

Karlsruhe Institute for Technology (KIT), Karlsruhe, Germany
{boltz,hahner,gerking,heinrich}@kit.edu

Abstract. The growing interconnection between software systems increases the need for security already at design time. Security-related properties like confidentiality are often analyzed based on data flow diagrams (DFDs). However, manually analyzing DFDs of large software systems is bothersome and error-prone, and adjusting an already deployed software is costly. Additionally, closed analysis ecosystems limit the reuse of modeled information and impede comprehensive statements about a system's security. In this paper, we present an open and extensible framework for data flow analysis. The central element of our framework is our new implementation of a well-validated data-flow-based analysis approach. The framework is compatible with DFDs and can also extract data flows from the Palladio architectural description language. We showcase the extensibility with multiple model and analysis extensions. Our evaluation indicates that we can analyze similar scenarios while achieving higher scalability compared to previous implementations.

Keywords: Data Flow Diagram · Software Architecture · Security

1 Introduction

As our modern world becomes increasingly digitized, the integration of various digital services into our daily lives has become more prevalent. To enhance the quality of service, a growing amount of data is stored and processed, e.g., online shops utilizing purchase history data for recommendations. The seamless exchange of such collected data between different services or systems is a common practice. In scenarios like online shopping, sensitive information like payment details and customer addresses are involved. Consequently, security becomes a central concern in designing and building such software-intensive systems.

Information security has several definitions, e.g., as the CIA triad of confidentiality, integrity, and availability, or in ISO 27000 [17]. More recent legal regulations, like the General Data Protection Regulation (GDPR) [11], define

---

N. Boltz and S. Hahner—Both main authors contributed equally.

B. Tekinerdoğan et al. (Eds.): ECSA 2023, LNCS 14590, pp. 342–358, 2024.
https://doi.org/10.1007/978-3-031-66326-0_21

information security more broadly. For modern systems, changes and reconfiguration in the context, environment, or internal structure might occur frequently [36]. Since the protection goals are highly dependent on the system under consideration, the protection goals that must be addressed may also change. In addition to the CIA goals, other protection goals might be considered, like privacy, authenticity, non-repudiation, accountability, and auditability. A system violating confidentiality or privacy can cause costly fines, as seen in the case of H&M [16] or British Airways [4]. However, identifying such violations can be difficult, because the interconnected software systems represent complex networks of data flows. Hence, a holistic and scalable approach to analyzing them is required.

Data flow analyses based on source code, e.g., JOANA [33], KeY [1], or CodeQL [9], cannot consider context information, such as deployment. However, such information can be essential for information security, e.g., whether the application is deployed to an external cloud provider or not. In addition, source code analyses cannot be used in early design phases because of their need for existing source code. Analyzing the system during design time is beneficial because fixing issues in later phases is usually more costly [31]. Seifermann et al. [28,30] proposed an architecture-based data flow analysis to analyze software systems for confidentiality violations. Their approach considers additional context information, such as the deployment, enabling software architects to analyze confidentiality during early design phases. However, the original Prolog-based implementation of Seifermann et al. [30] is hard to maintain and has a high resource demand, which severely limits the applicability for large software systems. Although they already used a model of a data flow diagram (DFD) [10] as an intermediate representation during their analysis, they did not continue to follow the idea of using DFDs as the primary model artifact. With appropriate tool support, DFDs represent a powerful and commonly used mechanism for threat analysis [3] that helps in correctly identifying security-related issues [24].

In this paper, we present an extensible analysis framework centered around our previously presented new implementation of the aforementioned approach to data flow analysis [27]. Our framework addresses shortcomings regarding the limited input capabilities, the limited intermediate use of DFDs, and problems with maintainability, scalability, and extensibility:

C1 We propose a novel DFD metamodel. In contrast to the previous DFD model [30] we do not consider DFDs as intermediate system representations but as primary software architecture modeling artifacts. As part of our framework, we provide means to manually define DFDs as well as automatically derive them from the architecture description language Palladio Component Model (PCM) [21] and other third-party diagram representations [23,25].

C2 We present a new Java-based implementation of the analysis approach of Seifermann et al. [30], which is based on a newly developed internal data structure and alleviates the need to mix Java with other technologies like Prolog. In addition, we provide new forms of input, e.g., DFDs defined with our metamodel (**C1**), and a domain-specific language (DSL) that enables software architects to define constraints or queries for the analysis. We demonstrate how our analysis framework can be applied and extended for other security concerns, e.g., regarding the GDPR [6], or uncertainty [12].

This paper is structured as follows: Sect. 2 introduces our data flow analysis framework. Section 3 describes our new DFD metamodel (**C1**). In Sect. 4, we describe the analysis (**C2**), and in Sect. 5, we showcase existing extensions. Section 6 presents our evaluation and Sect. 7 concludes the paper.

2   Overview of the Data Flow Analysis Framework

In this section, we summarize our framework which is explained in more detail hereafter. Figure 1 gives an informal overview of the structure and the dependencies between the different parts of our data flow analysis framework. We highlight analyses and editors with a bold border; all other rectangles represent models.

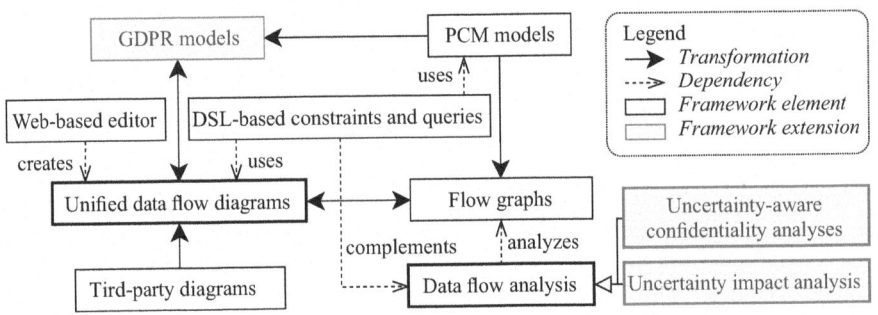

Fig. 1. Informal overview of the structure of the data flow analysis framework.

Unified data flow diagrams (DFDs) [28] play a central role in our framework (**C1**). These diagrams can be manually defined using a web-based editor or transformed from third-party diagram representations. Additionally, we enable the extraction of data flows from software architecture models described using PCM [21]. To unify the analysis process (**C2**), we transform DFD or PCM models into a set of Directed Acyclic Graphs (DAGs), called *transpose flow graphs (TFGs)*. Each vertex represents one individual data processing operation from either a DFD or PCM model, which simplifies the analysis. Using label propagation on TFGs, the analysis finds violations of predefined constraints that reflect information security objectives, e.g., confidentiality requirements. Constraints and queries can be specified using a domain-specific language (DSL), referencing PCM and DFD models. Framework extensions are possible by transforming into our DFDs or TFGs or by inheriting from the data flow analysis. GDPR models [6] are an example of the former while uncertainty impact analysis [12] and uncertainty-aware confidentiality analyses [8,14,35] showcase the latter. The framework is tool-supported and available as open source[1]. This includes

---

[1] See https://dataflowanalysis.org or https://github.com/DataFlowAnalysis.

modeling support, automated model transformations, and a DSL-supported analysis[2]. We also provide a dataset [7] including all tooling, code artifacts, and evaluation data.

3 Modeling and Deriving Data Flow Diagrams

While Seifermann et al. [28] created a unified DFD notation, they only used it as an intermediary representation for their data flow analysis [30]. However, as DFDs are an established software architecture representation [3] and are widely used to analyze various types of data security [2,30,32,34], we present an explicit DFD metamodel that can also be used as input for our analysis. The study of Bernsmed et al. [3] concludes, that, while DFDs are good for evaluating security, there exist challenges in preparing DFDs. Especially tooling that improves the effort of creating and maintaining DFDs is missing. In this section, we present our DFD metamodel (**C1**). We also provide tooling centered around our metamodel, which aims to aid in the creation of new DFDs, the import of already existing DFD notations [23,25], and the automated derivation and visualization of DFDs from system architecture models like the PCM [21].

3.1 Unified Data Flow Diagram Metamodel

DFDs, as proposed by DeMarco [10], can be represented as DAGs showing the data flow and processing in software systems. *Nodes* in these graphs represent *External* entities like users, *Processes* that can alter data, or *Stores* like databases, connected by *Flows* of data. Seifermann et al. [30] extend the notation by integrating several strands of work from different research groups into one unified metamodel. Figure 2 shows our metamodel that aligns with the unified DFD notation. It is split into the so-called *Data Dictionary* [10] and the DFD. The *Data Dictionary* does not directly depend on a modeled system and can thus be reused while DFD elements are specific to a certain system.

The central part of the unified notation is the representation of behavior and characteristics as first-class entities. *Labels* represent characteristics in the DFD, e.g., specifying the sensitivity of data, or the role of a user. They can either be defined as a characteristic of a *Node* or as a characteristic of data flowing between *Nodes*. *Labels* are grouped in *LabelTypes*. The *Behavior* of *Nodes* defines which *Labels* flow from one *Node* to the next via the connecting *Flow*. It is made up of *Pins* and *Assignments*. Input *Pins* represent required interfaces and output *Pins* represent provided interfaces of nodes. If a node has a certain *Behavior*, it also has the corresponding input and output *Pins*. A *Flow* connects two *Nodes* by connecting an output *Pin* of the source *Node* to an input *Pin* of the destination *Node*. *Assignments* define which labels flow out of a node. They reference input and output *Pins* of their corresponding *Behavior* and aggregate all *Labels* of the data flowing in through the input *Pin*. By evaluating a logical statement defined

---

[2] Video demonstration available [27]: https://youtube.com/watch?v=q3WJsMyqJcA.

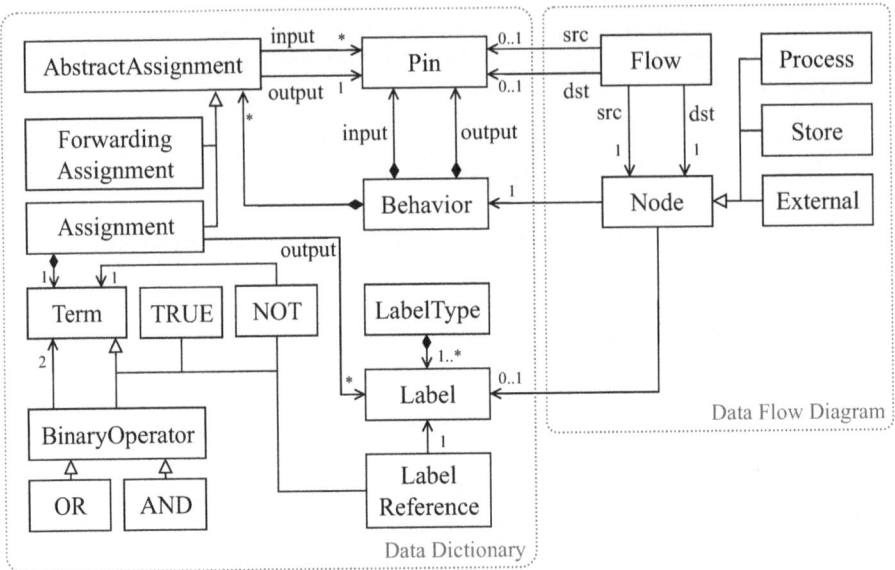

Fig. 2. Metamodel of data flow diagrams and data dictionaries.

in the assignment, it is determined how the incoming *Labels* are changed and passed on via the referenced output *Pins*, e.g., the encryption of data can be represented by an *Assignment* that adds an *encrypted* label to the flowing data.

For assignments, we define two subclasses: *Assignment* which contains a freely definable logical *Term* that is evaluated to decide if a set of *Labels* is applied to the output *Pin*. The *ForwardingAssginment* does not define a logical term but specifies that all *Labels* that flow into the input pins are combined and directly forwarded to the output pin. The logical terms can be nested with binary operators *AND* and *OR* and negated with *NOT* to express different statements. *LabelReferences* are evaluated by checking if the referenced *Label* flows into the node through one of the input pins of the *Assignment*. In this case, the *LabelReference* evaluates to true, otherwise to false. The *Assignments* of a *Behavior* are ordered. If a *Behavior* contains multiple *Assignments*, first all *ForwardingAssignments* are evaluated and the *Labels* for each output *Pin* are saved. Other *Assignments* add or remove labels for their specific output *Pin*, depending on if their *Term* evaluates to true or false. Once all *Assignments* are evaluated, the *Labels* flow to the next *Node*.

3.2 Manually Defining Data Flow Diagrams

Manual ways to define DFDs that go beyond drawing on either paper or in software are limited. With our approach, we therefore offer a ready-to-use web editor to manually define DFDs and means to import DFDs from other notations.

Our web-based editor uses a notation that is compatible with the unified DFD notation from Fig. 2. We also incorporated the concept of the data dictio-

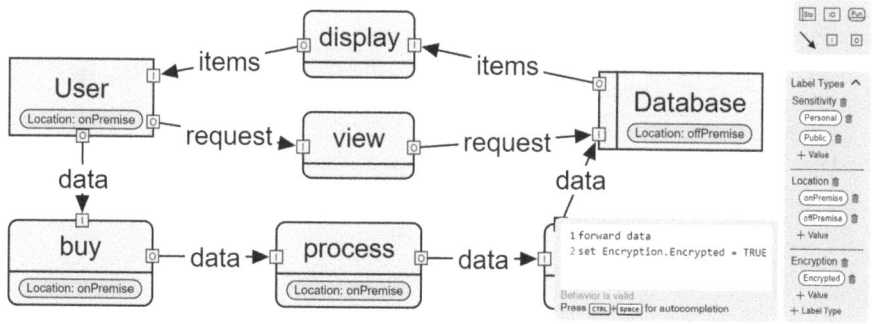

Fig. 3. Screenshot of the web-based editor showing the DFD of a simplified online shop.

naries. The graphical syntax follows earlier definitions of DFDs [10,30]. Figure 3 shows the editor with an exemplary DFD. The toolbar on the right allows the creation of the three node types, data flow edges, and input and output pins via drag and drop. The *Label Types* field allows the creation of label types and corresponding labels. Created labels can be annotated to a node by drag and drop. Double-clicking on an output pin opens an editor for specifying assignments for the corresponding output pin. Assignments can be defined in textual form using a DSL. The *forward* keyword is used to forward all labels of the corresponding input. The *set* keyword is used to define an output label and a logical term, similar to the DFD metamodel. Incoming data can be referenced via the name of the incoming edge. Labels are referenced by label type and label name. Assignments are automatically syntax-checked, and issues are reported to the user. Additionally, our web editor supports highlighting in different colors and providing tooltips for nodes. This can be used to, e.g., visualize analysis results and provide additional information regarding identified security violations.

The manually created DFDs can be exported as JSON files. To integrate the editor into our framework, we offer tooling that converts the JSON files of the web editor into an instance of our DFD metamodel. The editor is implemented in TypeScript and uses the open-source diagramming framework Eclipse Sprotty. To ease the adoption of our approach, we additionally created extensible tooling for generating instances of our DFD metamodel from various inputs. At the time of writing, we support DFD notations in PlantUML and two different types of JSON notations. To showcase this functionality, we have processed all security-enriched DFDs of the microSecEnD dataset of Schneider et al. [25]. The resulting instances of our DFD metamodel can be found in our dataset [7].

3.3   Automatically Deriving Data Flows from Architectural Models

Besides the manual modeling of DFDs, our framework also supports the automated extraction of data flows from the architecture description language PCM [21]. We choose PCM as it has already been used by previous data flow

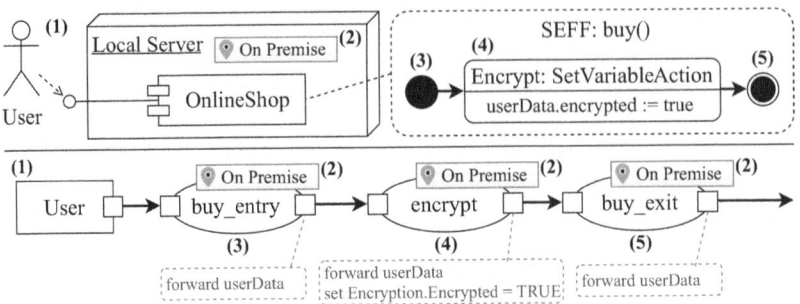

Fig. 4. Simplified PCM model of the online shop example and the corresponding data flow with annotated node labels, data labels, and numbered transformation traces.

analysis approaches [29,30]. However, the described concept of data flow extraction is also applicable to other modeling languages like UML.

Figure 4 shows a simplified PCM model of an online shop. It comprises information about components (e.g., *Online Shop*), resources (e.g., *Local Server*), deployment, usage, and system behavior as Service Effect Specification (SEFF) [21]. The model is annotated with confidentiality-related labels that represent characteristics of data storage like *On Premise* and data processing like the encryption of *userData* in the *SetVariableAction*. In the lower half, we show the extracted data flow. We annotate numbers to represent the transformation traces from PCM to DFD. Note, that this is only a simplified example; realistic software systems contain more than one data flow and several hundred nodes [12].

Every action in the usage and system behavior is transformed into one DFD node. This includes calls from the user, external calls between components, start and end nodes, and internal data processing nodes. The nodes' pins correspond to the in and outgoing data types, e.g., *userData*. For every node, we perform a lookup of node labels, which can be annotated, e.g., to resources, or usage scenarios. An exemplary lookup in the PCM model goes from the *encrypt* node to the *Online Shop* component via the deployment to the *Local Server* resource which is annotated with *On Premise*. Additionally, we convert the modeled system behavior to assignments of our DFD metamodel like the encryption of *userData* can be expressed. The default case is the forwarding of labels.

The transformation considers all information that is relevant for security analysis, e.g., data processing and characteristics. Other information is not transformed, e.g., components and servers do not cause additional elements in the DFD. This enables a system view from the perspective of the data which is especially suitable for properties like confidentiality [29]. However, we store all traces to the originating PCM elements during the transformation. This enables the evaluation of advanced queries and constraints in the data flow analysis.

4   Data Flow Analysis

The original Prolog-based analysis of Seifermann et al. [30] realized the extraction of data flows and propagation of labels by first transforming the PCM models to an explicit DFD metamodel notation, then transforming the DFD elements to Prolog. Data flow constraints were checked by defining Prolog queries that are unique to the modeled system. As one DFD element with characteristic labels is transformed into multiple Prolog statements, the Prolog code grows exponentially with the model size. The exponential growth results in high demand for memory, as the whole Prolog program needs to be fully loaded by the Prolog interpreter. As the analysis is made up of multiple chained transformations and intermediate model representations, the maintenance of the analysis was made even harder.

Additionally, the approach of modeling data flows via logical statements in Prolog can lead to increased runtimes: Due to the lazy evaluation of Prolog, the Prolog-based analysis needs to reevaluate the characteristic labels of nodes for each different constraint. For cases where very few nodes need to be evaluated, this might be an advantage. However, in using the analysis, the use case rarely occurs. For most constraints, like Role-based Access Control (RBAC), the node and data characteristic labels need to be evaluated at each node.

Due to the aforementioned reasons, we chose to implement the data flow analysis in Java and made the analysis more extensible as a central part of our framework. In this section, we first provide a general overview of the architecture of the analysis and provide a more detailed technical description of the extraction of data flows into flow graphs, label propagation, and constraint definition.

4.1   Architecture Overview

Our data flow analysis follows the general architecture of the Prolog-based data flow analysis of Seifermann et al. [30]. Figure 5 shows the analysis steps and their sequential order as an activity diagram. Initially, the input models are loaded and references between model elements are resolved. This is done automatically by the Eclipse Modeling Framework (EMF). Using the information from the models and annotations, we extract a set of *transpose flow graphs (TFGs)* that each represents one unambiguous flow of data to a data sink in the modeled software architecture, i.e., the transpose rooted directed graph, where the root is a single data sink. The extraction starts at each identified data sink and follows the modeled flow of data in the opposite direction. Afterward, we transpose the graph to represent data flows between the vertices of the graph, so each TFG connects one or multiple data sources with a single data sink. Each vertex represents one individual data processing step. If the analysis encounters an ambiguity in the data flow of the current element, it is resolved by creating copies of the current TFG, for each of the possible flows. After all TFGs are extracted, we first evaluate the node characteristic labels of the vertices. Afterward, we propagate the data characteristic labels along the edges of the TFGs. Starting with the sink vertices, we calculate the data characteristics flowing into the current vertex by recursively evaluating the behaviors of the previous vertices in the TFG and tracing back the results. How sinks are identified, how characteristic labels and vertex behavior are specified, and how they are evaluated, is specific to the input model type, e.g., DFD or PCM.

Using a set of fully propagated TFGs, data flow constraints can be checked. For example, by comparing propagated data characteristics with specified node characteristics, as described in Sect. 3.

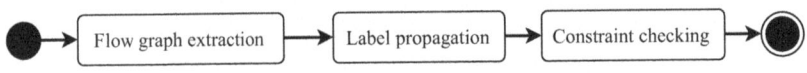

Fig. 5. Analysis architecture as performed key activities.

4.2   Flow Graph Extraction

We specify extraction logic for creating TFGs and specific subclasses of *vertex* for each element that represents a data flow node in DFDs and PCM models.

For the DFDs described in Subsect. 3.1, sinks are nodes that either have no outgoing flows or nodes whose assignments for an output pin are independent of all its input pins. Starting with these, the analysis performs a depth-first search over the DFD and creates vertices for each node. Ambiguities in the data flow exist if two or more flows point to the same input pin. To resolve the ambiguity, the analysis creates a copy of the current TFG for each path to the pin.

In the PCM, sinks are represented by the last element in usage scenarios. As the information regarding data flows is distributed across all PCM models, the analysis has to iterate over them and resolve relationships between elements. The analysis creates a vertex for all elements that can be annotated with a node characteristic label, that specifies data flow behavior, or that joins the control flow after a branch. The latter also creates a new TFG. Calls to Service Effect Specifications (SEFFs) that are defined in interfaces are also handled separately: For each call of these SEFFs, a *calling* and *returning* vertex is created, which enclose the data flows, i.e., the vertices, which make up the SEFF internally.

4.3   Label Propagation

We individually propagate the characteristic labels for each TFG. Each vertex references the input model element it represents and contains all logic regarding the calculation of node and data characteristic labels. First, we calculate the node characteristic labels and store them in the corresponding vertex. Starting from the sink of the TFG, we calculate the data characteristic labels that represent the output of the vertex and also store them in the corresponding vertex. This is achieved by recursively calling the calculation logic of all previous vertices and using the hereby calculated output labels as input. Note, that we do not consider cycles in the propagation logic because TFGs represent DAGs.

For our DFD metamodel, the calculation of node characteristic labels is trivial, as DFD nodes already contain these labels, and vertices directly represent nodes. During the calculation of data characteristic labels, each vertex first recursively evaluates its input, as described above, iterating the DFD nodes that are connected by input pins. After the input has been evaluated the labels are aggregated and saved as output of the corresponding output pin.

In PCM, node characteristic labels are directly annotated to PCM elements like resource containers or usage scenarios. For the calculation of node characteristic labels, the vertex iterates over the relationships of the PCM element it represents and stores the annotated characteristic labels relevant to the vertex. For the calculation of data characteristic labels, the PCM-specific vertices use the output of the previous vertex in the TFG. In contrast to our DFDs, the PCM does not support the definition of multiple individual data flows between two nodes that each represents a separate flowing data variable. Rather, one flow between two vertices in the TFG encapsulates all data flowing between two nodes. To evaluate the input, the vertices filter the variables with their data characteristics to only include variables that are in the scope of the element represented by the vertex. To calculate the output data characteristic labels, the vertex evaluates stochastical expressions that are used in the PCM to define propagation behavior.

4.4   DSL-Based Constraint Checking

To help in the specification and checking of constraints and queries, we define a simple domain-specific language (DSL). We follow the general structure of the DSL by Hahner et al. [15], which was defined for the original analysis of Seifermann et al. [30] but simplify the approach by implementing it in Java and fitting it to our new implementation of the analysis.

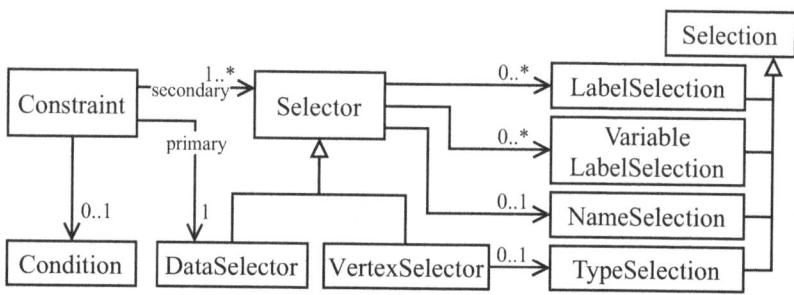

Fig. 6. Metamodel showing the abstract syntax of the DSL for the data flow analysis.

Figure 6 shows the abstract syntax of our DSL. A *Constraint* is made up of primary and secondary selectors, as well as an optional condition. *Selectors* are either specific for data or vertices. *VertexSelectors* match the properties of the vertices themselves, while *DataSelectors* match the propagated data characteristic labels of each vertex. They contain a set of *Selections* that each represent a property. A *Selection* can for example define a characteristic label or the name of a vertex or data. The *VariableLabelSelection* does not reference a specific label but defines a variable that contains all labels of a given label type that are present at either the vertex or data. These variables can be compared in the *Condition* of the constraint using set theory. Executing the constraint searches all TFGs in the modeled software architecture using the flow graph extraction, propagates all labels, and tests each vertex. The selectors return all vertices in a TFG that match the properties defined by its selections. Constraints define a *never flows* relationship between the primary *DataSelector* and secondary selectors. The results of the primary and secondary selectors represent violations. If a condition is defined, it is evaluated in addition. In this case, the violations are the results of primary and secondary selectors, for which the condition evaluates to true.

Listing 1 demonstrates the concrete syntax of our DSL for the online shop example from Subsect. 3.2. We provide a *builder* to set up the analysis with required inputs, which is simplified in line 1. We define a constraint using our DSL, starting in line 3. For our example, we specify that *personal data* (line 5) that is *not encrypted* (line 6) should *never flow* to vertices that are *off-premise* of the online shop (line 9). We execute the constraint in line 12. After the execution, the variable *violations* contains a list of all constraint-violating vertices within the modeled software architecture. If no violation has been found, the list is empty.

```
1    var analysis = new DataFlowAnalysisBuilder().build(); // simplified
2
3    var constraint = new Constraint()
4                         .ofData()
5                         .withLabel("Sensitivity", "Personal")
6                         .withoutLabel("Encryption", "Encrypted")
7                         .neverFlows()
8                         .toVertex()
9                         .withLabel("Location", "offPremise")
10                        .create();
11
12   var violations = constraint.execute(analysis);
```

Listing 1. Code snippet showing a DSL constraint for a simplified online shop.

5   Analysis Framework Extensions

We demonstrate the extensibility of our framework with several related work [5,6,8,9,12,14,26,35] that is either compatible to or already using our approach.

Boltz et al. [5,6] showcase the extension of both modeling and analysis for data protection and privacy. As shown in Fig. 1, they provide a GDPR meta-model and transformations from PCM and to and from our DFD metamodel. Regarding the consideration of uncertainty within the software architectural design and system environment, multiple black-box and white-box extensions exist. Walter et al. [35] use the data flow analysis as black-box together with PerOpteryx [20] for design space exploration regarding confidentiality under structural uncertainty. Other white-box extensions analyze access control under uncertainty [8] or trace confidentiality violations to related uncertainty sources

[14]. Our framework is also used in an uncertainty impact analysis [12] that predicts the impact of uncertainty on confidentiality based on the extracted data flows and a classification of uncertainty regarding confidentiality [13].

6   Evaluation

In our evaluation, we compare our new Java-based analysis to the Prolog-based analysis of Seifermann et al. [30]. The primary goals of this evaluation were to assess the accuracy and scalability of both analyses and to show that our Java-based analysis not only maintains the core functionalities of the Prolog-based analysis but also improves execution times and resource efficiency. Due to the lack of support for our new DFD metamodel in the Prolog-based analysis, our evaluation only focuses on PCM model instances. The evaluation of our analysis with a focus on the DFD metamodel or the extensions from Sect. 5 are considered potential future work.

6.1   Evaluation Design

To compare accuracy, we check whether both analyses correctly identify violations across various case study-based PCM models. To ensure a good base for comparison, we utilize the same case study-based models employed by Seifermann et al. [30] for evaluating the accuracy of the Prolog-based approach. The selected case studies use the default call return semantics of the current stable PCM version. We executed both analyses with semantically equivalent constraint queries, using the count of accurately identified violations as the evaluation metric.

To examine and compare scalability, we measured the full execution time of both analyses while analyzing models of increasing size. To isolate the impact of distinct model features on scalability, we generated individual minimal models incrementally increasing the number of node characteristic labels, characteristic label propagations, variable actions, or SEFF parameters. We chose these elements, as they have the highest impact on either the length of Prolog code or Java loop iterations, depending on the analysis. Each analysis was executed with a constraint designed to detect a violation at each node, thus ensuring a worst-case execution time scenario for both analyses. For each run, we increase the model feature under consideration by the power of ten, starting at 10^0 and ending with 10^5. We conducted each test 10 times and calculated the median execution time to mitigate outliers or measurement anomalies. The analyses were performed on a dedicated VM equipped with 4 AMD Opteron 8435 cores, 97 GB RAM, running Debian 11 with OpenJDK 11/17.

6.2   Evaluation Results

In terms of accuracy, both analyses successfully identified the 42 violations present in the case study-based models without returning any false positives.

Table 1 shows the results of the accuracy evaluation and size of analyzed models. As both analyses performed the same, we assume, that our Java-based analysis is functionally equivalent to the Prolog-based analysis, when analyzing models using the call return semantics of the PCM.

Table 1. Accuracy results of both analyses compared and size of the models.

Case Study	Prolog-based	Java-based	Components	Labels
ContactSMS [18]	10 violations	10 violations	3	4
FlightControl [30]	0 violations	0 violations	6	6
FriendMap [34]	0 violations	0 violations	5	12
Hospital [34]	0 violations	0 violations	4	12
ImageSharing [30]	0 violations	0 violations	1	9
PrivateTaxi [18]	0 violations	0 violations	13	20
TravelPlanner [18]	32 violations	32 violations	7	8
WebRTC [34]	0 violations	0 violations	20	12

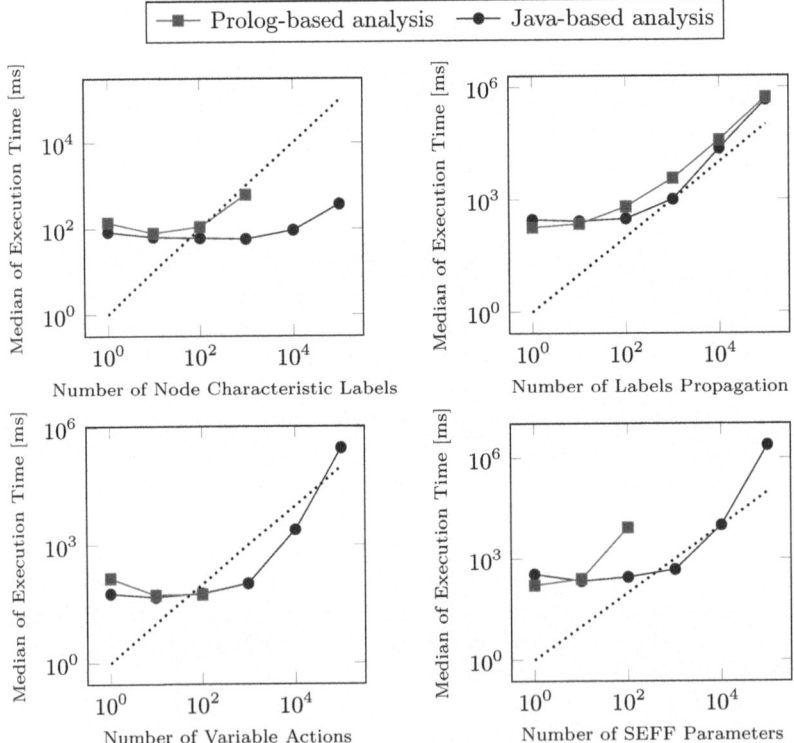

Fig. 7. Scalability results of the Prolog-based analysis and the Java-based analysis. (Color figure online)

Regarding scalability, we plotted the results of both analyses as line graphs for each examined model feature, shown in Fig. 7. Each graph contains data points from both analyses-the Prolog-based analysis (in red) and the Java-based analysis (in blue). Both axes are scaled logarithmically, with the x-axis showing the increasing number of model elements and the y-axis the median execution times in milliseconds. Our evaluation showed that the Prolog-based analysis fails to complete a run for more than 1000 node characteristic labels or 100 for variable actions and SEFF parameters, due to high memory demand (see Sect. 4). In our tests, the analysis ran in *out of memory errors* or crashed, despite the substantial *97 GB* of available memory. Regarding execution time behavior, while the Prolog-based analysis displayed an exponential increase in execution times or incomplete analysis runs for larger models, our Java-based analysis maintained nearly constant execution times up to 10^3 elements for most evaluated cases. When increasing the number of label propagations, the execution time behavior of both analyses is similar. The exponential increase in execution time of the Java-based analysis for larger models can be explained due to inefficiencies in TFG finding, and overhead during label propagation.

Overall, despite the noted increase in execution times for larger models in the Java-based analysis, we consider the time required in all scenarios feasible for design-time analyses. Our Java-based analysis, compared to the Prolog-based analysis, offers more manageable execution times and the capability to analyze large models, rendering it more suitable for real-world systems.

As parts of our evaluation are based around artificial scenarios and case studies, we discuss the external, internal, and construct validity, as well as reliability of our evaluation, as characterized by Runeson et al. [22]. Our main threat to external validity is the limited generalizability due to the case study-based evaluation. We try to mitigate this threat by using well-known case studies from literature to evaluate and compare accuracy. For the evaluation of scalability, the models were programmatically generated to only scale and focus on individual aspects of the models and analysis. A threat to the internal validity of our evaluation of scalability is that, due to the use of different technologies in both analyses, it was not possible to use the exact same constraints. We mitigate this threat by defining semantically equivalent constraints that find a violation at each node. Our main threat to construct validity of our scalability evaluation is that it does not comprehensively cover all aspects that influence the execution time. We cannot fully mitigate this threat but have chosen the examined aspects based on the execution logic of both analyses and a previous scalability evaluation of Seifermann et al. [30]. To mitigate threats regarding the reliability of our evaluation and to address the lack of replication packages in software architecture research [19], we have published a data set [7]. The dataset contains all raw and compiled code artifacts, as well as an Eclipse-based product that already includes the plugins that make up the framework. The product can be used to model DFD or PCM instances and analyze them using our data flow analysis. We also include the raw results of our scalability evaluation and the used case study models.

7   Conclusion and Future Work

In this paper, we have presented our open and extensible framework for data flow analysis. We have introduced a unified DFD metamodel as a primary software architecture modeling artifact and input for our data flow analysis framework. We have described means that we provide to manually define DFDs as well as automatically derive them from the architecture description language PCM and other third-party representations.

Based on the approach of Seifermann et al. [21], we have implemented a Java-based data flow analysis. We described the general architecture of the analysis and provided detailed technical descriptions of the core features. For the analysis, we have defined an extensible intermediate representation of data flows, called transpose flow graphs. We have described how data flows are extracted from input models and how characteristic labels are propagated using our new intermediate representation. To enable the definition of data flow constraints for the analysis, we have defined a new domain-specific language.

We highlight the problems of the Prolog-based analysis of Seifermann et al. [30] and show in our evaluation, that our Java-based analysis is functionally equivalent to the Prolog-based analysis and can analyze larger system models.

In future work, we aim to further enhance the tooling that makes up our framework. We also aim to further work on the various framework extensions, like the data protection [6] and uncertainty analyses [14] and include more cooperation points of our framework, e.g., with continuous security analysis [26]. Lastly, we aim to comprehensively evaluate the overall approach of our framework.

Acknowledgements. This publication is partially based on the research project SofD-Car (19S21002), which is funded by the German Federal Ministry for Economic Affairs and Climate Action. This work was also supported by funding from the topic Engineering Secure Systems of the Helmholtz Association (HGF) and by KASTEL Security Research Labs, the BMBF (German Federal Ministry of Education and Research) grant number 16KISA086 (ANYMOS), and the NextGenerationEU project by the European Union (EU). We like to thank Felix Schwickerath, Tom Hüller, Daniel Huber, Tizian Bitschi, Anne-Kathrin Hermann, and Nils Niehues for their support in the development of the presented work.

References

1. Ahrendt, W., et al.: Deductive Software Verification-The Key Book. Springer, Cham (2016). https://doi.org/10.1007/978-3-319-49812-6
2. Alshareef, H., et al.: Precise analysis of purpose limitation in data flow diagrams. In: ARES, pp. 1–11 (2022)
3. Bernsmed, K., et al.: Adopting threat modelling in agile software development projects. J. Syst. Softw. **183**, 111090 (2022)
4. Beverley-Smith, H., Perowne, C.H., Kelleher, F.: British airways faces significantly reduced £20M fine for GDPR breach. The National Law Review. www.natlawreview.com/article/british-airways-faces-significantly-reduced-20m-fine-gdpr-breach. Accessed 12 Nov 2023

5. Boltz, N., Walter, M., Gerking, C.: Designing Automotive Case Studies for Architectural Security Analyses (2023)
6. Boltz, N., et al.: A model-based framework for simplified collaboration of legal and software experts in data protection assessments. In: INFORMATIK 2022 (2022)
7. Boltz, N., et al.: Dataset: an extensible framework for architecture-based data flow analysis for information security. Zenodo (2024). https://doi.org/10.5281/zenodo.10794265
8. Boltz, N., et al.: Handling environmental uncertainty in design time access control analysis. In: SEAA, pp. 382–389 (2022)
9. De Moor, O., et al.: ".QL: Object-Oriented Queries Made Easy". In: International Summer School on Generative and Transformational Techniques in Software Engineering, pp. 78–133 (2008)
10. DeMarco, T.: Structure analysis and system specification. In: Pioneers and Their Contributions to Software Engineering, pp. 255–288 (1979)
11. General Data Protection Regulation (GDPR) (2016). https://gdpr.eu/tag/gdpr/
12. Hahner, S., Heinrich, R., Reussner, R.: Architecture-based uncertainty impact analysis to ensure confidentiality. In: SEAMS, pp. 126–132 (2023)
13. Hahner, S., et al.: A classification of software-architectural uncertainty regarding confidentiality. In: ICETE, pp. 139–160 (2023)
14. Hahner, S., et al.: Model-based confidentiality analysis under uncertainty. In: ICSA-C, pp. 256–263 (2023)
15. Hahner, S., et al.: Modeling data flow constraints for design-time confidentiality analyses. In: ICSA-C, pp. 15–21 (2021)
16. HmbBfDI: 35.3 Million Euro Fine for Data Protection Violations in H&M's Service Center. www.datenschutz-hamburg.de/fileadmin/user_upload/HmbBfDI/Pressemitteilungen/2020/2020-10-01-H_M.pdf. Accessed 12 Nov 2023
17. International Organization for Standardization: Information technology - Security techniques - Information security management systems - Overview and vocabulary. Standard ISO/IEC 27000:2018
18. Katkalov, K.: Ein modellgetriebener Ansatz zur Entwicklung informationsflusssicherer Systeme. doctoralthesis, Universität Augsburg (2017)
19. Konersmann, M., et al.: Evaluation methods and replicability of software architecture research objects. In: ICSA, pp. 157–168 (2022)
20. Koziolek, A., Koziolek, H., Reussner, R.: PerOpteryx: automated application of tactics in multi-objective software architecture optimization. In: QoSA-ISARCS, pp. 33–42 (2011)
21. Reussner, R., et al.: Modeling and Simulating Software Architectures - The Palladio Approach. MIT Press, Cambridge (2016). isbn: 9780262034760
22. Runeson, P., et al.: Case Study Research in Software Engineering: Guidelines and Examples. John Wiley & Sons (2012)
23. Schneider, S., Scandariato, R.: Automatic extraction of security-rich dataflow diagrams for microservice applications written in Java. J. Syst. Softw. **202**, 111722 (2023)
24. Schneider, S., et al.: How dataflow diagrams impact software security analysis: an empirical experiment. In: SANER (2024)
25. Schneider, S., et al.: microSecEnD: a dataset of security-enriched dataflow diagrams for microservice applications. In: MSR, pp. 125-129 (2023)
26. Schulz, S., et al.: Continuous secure software development and analysis. In: SSP (2021)

27. Schwickerath, F., et al.: Tool-supported architecture-based data flow analysis for confidentiality. In: arXiv preprint (2023). https://doi.org/10.48550/arXiv.2308.01645

28. Seifermann, S., et al.: A unified model to detect information flow and access control violations in software architectures. In: SECRYPT, pp. 26–37 (2021)

29. Seifermann, S., Heinrich, R., Reussner, R.: Data-driven software architecture for analyzing confidentiality. In: ICSA, pp. 1–10 (2019)

30. Seifermann, S., et al.: Detecting violations of access control and information flow policies in data flow diagrams. J. Syst. Softw. **184**, 111138 (2022)

31. Shull, F., et al.: What we have learned about fighting defects. In: METRICS, pp. 249–258 (2002)

32. Sion, L., et al.: Solution-aware data flow diagrams for security threat modeling. In: SAC, pp. 1425–1432 (2018)

33. Snelting, G., et al.: Checking probabilistic noninterference using JOANA. it - Information Technol. **56**(6), 280–287 (2014)

34. Tuma, K., Scandariato, R., and Balliu, M.: Flaws in flows: unveiling design flaws via information flow analysis. In: ICSA, pp. 191–200 (2019)

35. Walter, M., et al.: Architectural optimization for confidentiality under structural uncertainty. In: ECSA, pp. 309–332 (2021)

36. Weyns, D., et al.: Towards a research agenda for understanding and managing uncertainty in self-adaptive systems. SIGSOFT Software Eng. Notes **48**(4), 20–36 (2023)

Studying the Evolution of Library Utilization in Maven Projects: A Metric-Based Approach

Maria Kolyda, Eirini Kostoglou, Nikolaos Nikolaidis$^{(\boxtimes)}$ (iD),
Apostolos Ampatzoglou (iD), and Alexander Chatzigeorgiou (iD)

Department of Applied Informatics, University of Macedonia, Thessaloniki, Greece
nnikolaidis@uom.edu.gr

Abstract. In modern software development, usually, reuse takes place by invoking in the codebase, methods that are deployed and imported into projects as 3rd party libraries. The ease with which one can take benefit of reuse of libraries has been simplified lately, by platforms such as Maven, Gradle, etc. However, this convenient choice in many cases leads to an overwhelming number of libraries being packed in the final executable, even when not needed (e.g., the code that uses originally invoked a library is removed, or it is dead). In this paper, we propose five novel metrics that capture the extent to which each library is utilized in the codebase, providing information to the software engineers on the actual utility of the library in the final product. To automate the calculation of these metrics we have developed a corresponding tool that can be used for quality monitoring purposes. Finally, we have used the tools and metrics to study the evolution of library utilization in several Maven open-source software projects.

Keywords: libraries · metrics · maven · library utilization · app evaluation

1 Introduction

The use of third-party libraries in software development is a widely used practice to speed up the development process, and in turn reduce costs [7]. This practice only gets more popular with the rise of easy-to-use build automation tools and library repositories like Maven, Gradle, NPM, etc. Libraries provide already created and tested functionalities, so developers do not need to write code from scratch, but rather find an appropriate library. However, as any other benefit, the reuse of libraries comes with a cost, or at least with a threat of a cost—e.g., by introducing bugs or vulnerabilities. Based on the literature, the use of third-party libraries is a living part of software development, in the sense that libraries can be added, upgraded, or removed along evolution, and similarly does the code around them [17].

The excessive and unnecessary use of third-party libraries can lead to three main problems: (a) the size of the target system grows larger in size, hurting the performance and resource utilization of the software; (b) the third party library might bring vulnerabilities into the target system; and (c) the external quality of the library cannot be controlled, in the sense that in the majority of the cases, third-party library reuse is black-box. As

© The Author(s), under exclusive license to Springer Nature Switzerland AG 2024
B. Tekinerdoğan et al. (Eds.): ECSA 2023, LNCS 14590, pp. 359–374, 2024.
https://doi.org/10.1007/978-3-031-66326-0_22

examples of excessive and unnecessary use of third-party libraries, the following cases can be considered. First, along evolution, there is a chance that some *libraries* become *unused* after some source code update. In other words, either the code that was invoking a method declared from a library is removed, or it becomes dead code. However, if the development team does not remove the library from the build automation system, the library will remain a part of the build process. Therefore, it is important to keep track of the libraries that are used in the target system, and the extent of their utilization—in some cases, it might be beneficial to implement something from scratch, if a very small fraction of a library is utilized. Additionally, as an *unnecessary upgrade of the library*, we can consider an upgrade to a newer version of a library that does not offer any functional or non-functional benefit. Therefore, it is important to monitor along evolution if the level of library utilization is not decreasing over time—i.e., importing larger libraries that are not used more.

The rest of the paper is organized as follows: In Sect. 2 we present related work, while in Sect. 3 we propose five novel metrics that assess the level of library utilization in a software project. Section 4 presents the developed tool for automating the metrics calculation, to boost their adoption in practice. Moreover, in Sect. 5 we present the case study of open-source projects and the evolution of their metrics along with a validation study, while in Sect. 6, we present the results. Section 7 presents the threats of our study, and we conclude our study in Sect. 8. As supplementary material for this submission, we have added online a video presentation[1], a running instance[2], and the codebase[3,4].

2   Related Work

A lot of information about library reuse and metrics can be found in the literature, thus we try to present some of those studies in this section. Firstly, Mora et al. [4, 5] provided a way that compares libraries to help the developers with selecting the most suitable each time. To achieve this comparison, they used 9 metrics for each library and asked a total of 61 developers to evaluate them. They found out that developers are more interested in metrics related to the popularity, security, and performance of libraries. But this can change a bit depending on the domain of the application under development. A similar study was conducted by Vargas et al. [10], where they studied the factors that influence the selection process of libraries. They asked 115 developers for feedback on a total of 26 factors, which in turn could be used as metrics. Also, they grouped these factors into three categories namely: technical, human, and economic. Finally, similar types of metrics with an emphasis on performance, usability, documentation, and popularity were proposed in other studies as well [1, 8, 9, 12].

Moreover, Washizaki et al. [16] viewed the libraries as black-box reuse and focused on metrics based on the limited information that can be obtained from outside of the components without any source code. They defined five metrics and through evaluation

---

[1] https://youtu.be/m1N22F5mbHI.

[2] http://195.251.210.147:3005.

[3] https://github.com/kostoglou/LibraryUtilization.

[4] https://github.com/MariaKolyda/javaLibraryUtilization.

experiments, it was found that these metrics can effectively identify black-box components with high reusability. These metrics are EMI (Existence of Meta-Information),
RCO (Rate of Component Observability), RCC (Rate of Component Customizability),
SCCr (Self-Completeness of Component's Return Value), and SCCp (Self-Completeness
of Component's Parameter). A similar black-box approach was selected by Shatnawi
et al. [14], where they proposed a model consisting of three metrics. These metrics
are related more to the business side and are the library investment ratio, the library
investment level, and program simplicity.

In contrast to the previously mentioned studies that aim at assessing the quality of
the libraries per se, to aid developers in library selection, in this work, we focus on the
target system, and we assess the effectiveness of reuse—i.e., the level to which a library
is utilized in each system. Therefore, even for the same library, the metric scores could
be different for different systems, since the way that the library is used is being assessed,
rather than the library per se. Finally, we created a tool which is able to calculate those
metrics, and provide details on the utilization of libraries along with their evolution.

3 Proposed Metrics

In this section, we present the proposed metrics that can be used to assess the level of
library utilization in a specific project. Most of these metrics rely on the entry points of a
library, used in a specific project, as well as the call-tree that is parsed by invoking these
methods (i.e., the subsequent series of method calls made inside the library to provide
the needed functionality). Similar approaches can be found in other studies that calculate
the call tree, e.g., for assessing the Technical Debt (TD) of service, based on the entry
points of services (end-points) and the methods that are subsequently invoked by the
API call [11]. The proposed metrics are in principal novel; however, the rationale of their
inception is based on existing metrics. For example, as inspiration we have used Coupling
Factor (CF), which is calculated as a fraction of existing dependencies to the number
of possible dependencies. In that sense, some of our metrics count the utilization of a
metric as a fraction of the actual usage against the maximum allowed usage. To explain
the proposed metrics, we provide an illustrative example in Fig. 1. We should note that
each circle represents a class, while the number inside the circle represents the methods
of that class. Finally, the connection between the classes represents the called methods
from one class to another, and the different colors are used for each call-tree.

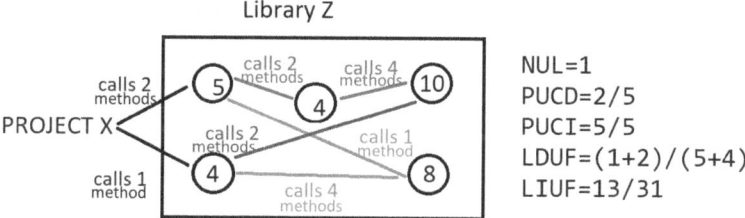

Fig. 1. Illustrative example for all metrics

Number of Used Libraries (NUL).   The first proposed metric is calculated at the project level, and as the name implies is the number of the used libraries from one project. In our example, we can see that Project X used classes only from one library (Library Z). So, the value of NUL is 1. This number provides an indication of how much the project depends on third-party code—related to the performance and resource utilization of the executable.

Percentage of Used Classes Directly (PUCD).   To measure the utilization of a library we proposed the PUCD metric, which calculates the percentage of used classes from a given project. We should note that for the calculation of this metric, we consider only the classes that are being used directly from the given target projects. So, in our example since Project X uses only two classes out of 5, the PUCD is 2/5 or 40%. This metric is related to the extent to which the quality of the target system might be affected by the third-party code.

Percentage of Used Classes Indirectly (PUCI).   To measure the usability of the whole library, by considering all the classes that are being used, we proposed the PUCI metric. For the calculation of this metric, we consider all the classes that are being accessed, even indirectly from the examined project. So, the value of PUCI is 5/5 or 100%, because in our example all 5 classes are being used. This metric is related to the extent to which the quality of the target system might be affected by the third-party code. The same discrimination between direct and indirect dependencies, can be found in traditional coupling metrics, as well (e.g., TCC and LCC [3]).

Library Direct Utilization Factor (LDUF).   To measure the utilization of a library we proposed the LDUF metric, which calculates the percentage of used methods out of the total number of methods that the used classes have. We should note that in this metric we do not consider the indirect methods that are being used. In the given example, Project X calls in total 3 methods (2 from the first class, and 1 from the second one) of Library Z, and these classes have 9 methods in total (the first one has 5, and the second one has 4). So, the value of LDUF is 3/9 or 33.3%. This metric can act as an indicator of the *"worth"* of reusing the library, based on its fraction that is reused in practice.

Library Indirect Utilization Factor (LIUF).   Finally, we created the LIUF metric, which considers the indirect utilization of a library. To achieve this, we trace all the method calls that take place, and we find the number of used methods of each class. In the same example from Library Z 13 methods are being used out of the total 31 methods, so the value of LIUF is 13/31 or 41.9%. In more detail, we can see that the red call tree calls 6 methods, the blue one calls 2 methods, and the green calls 5 methods. Also, we should note that we do not count more than once a used method. This metric can act as an indicator of the *"worth"* of reusing the library, based on the fraction that is reused.

4   Library Utilization Tool

For the calculation of the proposed metrics, we created the Library Utilization tool. This tool was created as a web application, with a front-end, written in React and a back-end written in Java and the Spring framework. The web service exposes all the necessary functionalities through a RESTful API, whereas the web app makes the appropriate requests and demonstrates the appropriate results and views to the user. We should note that both the frontend[5] and backend[6] projects can be found online, along with a video[7], which presents all the functionalities. The main functionalities of the application are the following: (a) analyze a project, (b) inspect the metrics scores, (c) inspect the call-tree of a method call, and (d) analyze the history of a project.

Analyze a project. When the users open the web application, they are greeted with the screen of Fig. 2, from where they can start a new analysis. By providing the Git URL of the project they want to analyze, they can start a new static analysis in the last commit of the project or get the last already analyzed commit (if any exist). The analysis of a project is time-consuming, especially for big projects with a lot of libraries. To calculate all the proposed metrics, we must analyze the code of the project and all the libraries that are being used. To be able to get the code of each library we had to limit our application to analyze only Maven project (at least for a first release). Moreover, we had to analyze the code of the project, to get the used methods of each library, and the code of each library, to get the call-tree of the methods. To this end, we used the *JavaParser* library [15], which is a very well-known parsing library for Java projects. Finally, we should note that once a project is analyzed it is saved in a database, so in case a user asks for an already analyzed project the results can be provided almost instantly.

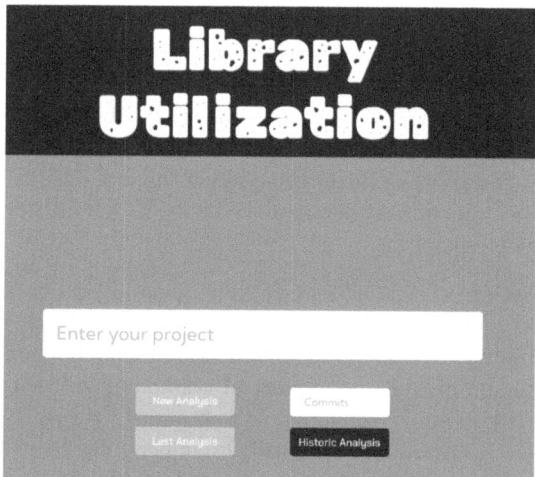

Fig. 2. Analyze Project Screen

Inspect the Metric Scores. Once the project analysis is finished, or the results are retrieved from the database, the user is presented with the metric scores (see Fig. 3).

The user can see the NUL of the project and for each library the values of the other four metrics. This feature provides a basic and bird-eye view on the analysis.

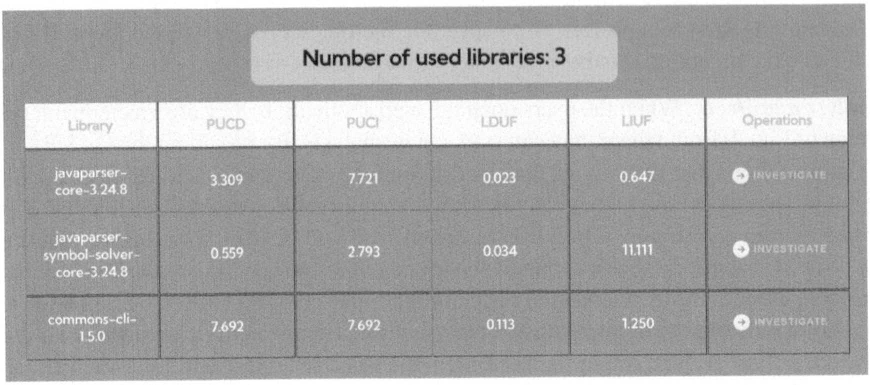

		Number of used libraries: 3			
Library	PUCD	PUCI	LDUF	LIUF	Operations
javaparser-core-3.24.8	3.309	7.721	0.023	0.647	➡ INVESTIGATE
javaparser-symbol-solver-core-3.24.8	0.559	2.793	0.034	11.111	➡ INVESTIGATE
commons-cli-1.5.0	7.692	7.692	0.113	1.250	➡ INVESTIGATE

Fig. 3. Metrics Results

Inspect the call-tree of a method call. By selecting the "Investigate" button for one library, the user can see all the methods that were used from this library. And by selecting one, the user can see the call-tree of that method (see Fig. 4). Moreover, a slider is provided from which the user can specify the number of nodes they want to see for a given call tree. The nodes are limited to a max number of 800 since after that the graph is hard to read and maybe not so useful. This function can be useful for inspecting out of which method calls, tentatively malicious or low-quality methods are being invoked, affecting the external behavior of the target system. Through this feature, the engineer can get a hint of which functionalities might need to be re-written from scratch, in case of a run-time quality problem.

Analyze Project History. The analysis of all the commits of a project is not recommended due to time constraints, and since we do not expect there to be a big change in every commit from the aspect of library utilization. For this reason, in the historical analysis, the user should provide the number of commits they want to analyze along with the Git URL. The commits that are going to be analyzed will be spread out to the history of the project according to the provided number. Once the historic analysis is completed, the user is presented with the results like in Fig. 5. The users can see the evolution of NUL in a line chart and a table with all the libraries that were used along with their commits. Finally, by selecting a specific library they can see the evolution of the four-remaining metrics. This feature can be interesting for seeing if the level of library utilization stays constant along evolution, or if the library grows or shrinks, but no additional features are being exploited.

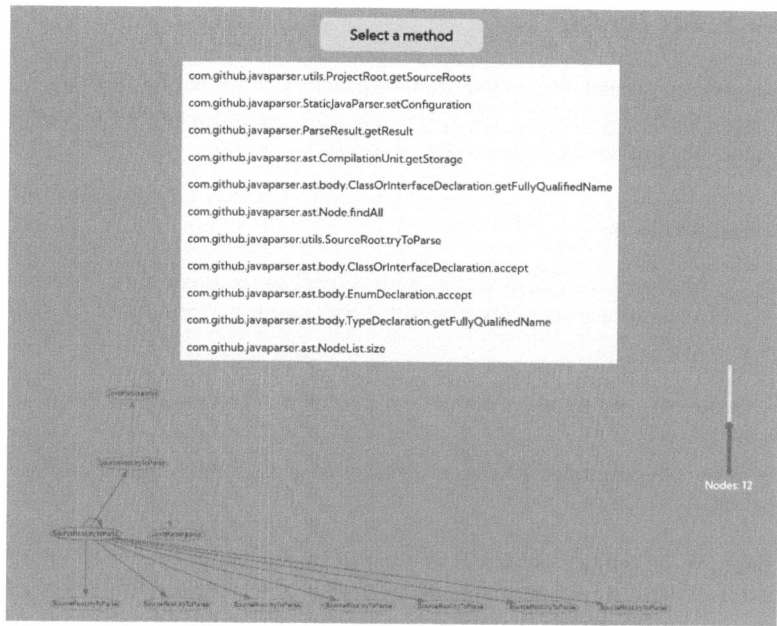

Fig. 4. Call-Graph Representation

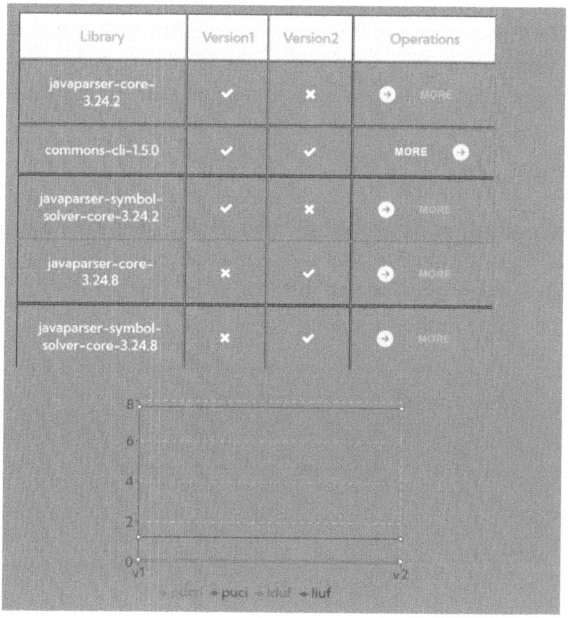

Library	Version1	Version2	Operations
javaparser-core-3.24.2	✓	✗	➡ MORE
commons-cli-1.5.0	✓	✓	MORE ➡
javaparser-symbol-solver-core-3.24.2	✓	✗	➡ MORE
javaparser-core-3.24.8	✗	✓	➡ MORE
javaparser-symbol-solver-core-3.24.8	✗	✓	➡ MORE

Fig. 5. Evolution Analysis

5   Case Study Design

In this section, we present the study design, by providing information about the research questions and the datasets that we used. The case study was designed and reported based on the guidelines provided by Runeson et al. [13].

5.1   Research Questions

To study the proposed metrics, and tool with respect to its usage in practice, in terms of real-world systems and the relevance of the idea, we have formulated the following research questions.

RQ1: What are the metrics values and evolution in open-source large-scale software projects?

RQ2: Does the developed library utilization tool meet the expectations of the practitioners?

In **RQ1**, we investigate the actual real-world values that the proposed metrics can have, and how these can change over the evolution of the project. The answer to this question will help us determine the correctness of our metrics, by cross-checking changes in the history of the projects or finding patterns and correlations that might exist between them. In **RQ2**, we focus on the usability of the tool and its characteristics. For this reason, we conducted a survey with senior software developers to get initial feedback on our tool. The answer to this question will give us an insight into the actual usage of such a tool by industry, along with some very important feedback on new features or needed improvements.

5.2   Cases and Units of Analysis

To answer the first research question, we selected several open-source projects to analyze them with our tool. The reason for selecting open-source projects was the vast amount of open data and their openness to using third-party libraries [17]. The five projects that we analyzed can be found in the following Table 1.

Table 1. Dataset Demographics

Project	Releases	Commits	Size (LoC)
apache/brooklyn-server	29	14,321	345.527
apache/incubator-baremaps	41	1,430	23.083
apache/ozone	22	6,782	466.682
apache/zookeeper	164	2,528	121.067
apache/doris	104	15,379	543.311

The selection of the projects was based on the following criteria:

- The main programming language is Java, due to the language specific tool that we created which, at the moment, works only with this language. Moreover, in this way, we will not risk having different results due to language specific characteristics.
- The automation build system is Maven, due to the specific limitations of the created tool, at the moment. This acted as criteria while selecting the projects, but we do not expect it to differentiate the results of the metrics in other Java automation build systems (Gradle, Ivy, Grape, etc.), since they all have a common repository[8].
- The project should have more than 20 releases in the form of tags in GitHub. This is important to have a sufficient number of versions to analyze with our tool.

5.3 Data Collection

For the data collection regarding the first research question, we used the created tool's backend mechanism to analyze snapshots of our choosing of each selected project. The reason for not analyzing all the commits is two-fold, firstly, we do not expect to see many changes to the libraries that a project uses in each commit, and secondly, the analysis is quite time-consuming. For this reason, we automated the process of analyzing each project as shown in the following figure.

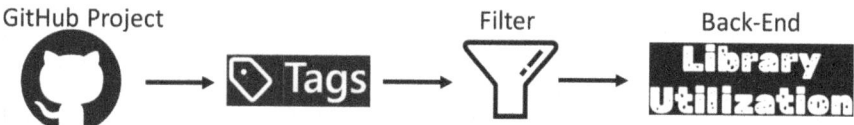

Fig. 6. Data Collection Flow

For each project, we identified the tag releases that we wanted to analyze and fed them one by one to the analyzer. The tag releases that we analyzed were different for each project and the number of them along with their versions, were relying on the versioning that each project was using. The selected tags for each project can be found in the following Table 2.

Regarding the second research question, the validation of the tool was conducted by asking 13 senior software developers from the area of software architecture, from 5 different companies based in Greece, to use and evaluate the tool in a 1-day workshop. First, the researchers have presented the tool, as well as the envisioned motivation and usage scenarios. Then, the practitioners were given a small task to familiarize themselves with the tool, and then some extra time to experiment independently. To assess the relevance and usability of the tool, we provided access to the participants to an online instance of the web application. They were asked to perform several tasks and interact with the application, to get hands-on experience. Each of the participants was asked to do the following: (a) create a new analysis; (b) inspect the results and the call tree; and (c) inspect the results of the evolution analysis. Then, they were asked to brainstorm

---

[8] https://mvnrepository.com

Table 2. Analyzed Tags per Project and NUL

Project	Analyzed Tags	Tags
apache/brooklyn-server	5	1.0.0, 0.12.0, 0.11.0, 0.10.0, 0.9.0
apache/incubator-baremaps	7	v0.7.1, v0.7.0, v0.6.0, v0.5.10, v0.5.1, v0.4.0, v0.3.0
apache/ozone	5	1.3.0, 1.2.0, 1.1.0, 1.0.0, 0.5
apache/zookeeper	5	3.9.0, 3.8.0, 3.7.0, 3.6.0, 3.5.5
apache/doris	9	2.0.0-rc01, 1.2.0-rc01, 1.1.0-rc01, 1.0.0-rc01, 0.15.0-rc01, 0.14.0-rc01, 0.13.0-rc01, 0.12.0-rc01, 0.10.0-rc03

on what they had learned from using the tool in the form of a focus group, using the whiteboard. The focus group and the discussion were moderated by the researchers.

The workshop closed with the participant filling in a small questionnaire at the end. The evaluation of the relevance of the metrics and the usability of the tool was performed based on the System Usability Scale (SUS) instrument [2].

6 Results and Discussion

In this section, we present the results of this study based on the research questions that we described in Sect. 5.1.

6.1 Metrics and Evolution

To answer RQ$_1$, we first present the values of a metric across the history of each project, along with some detailed examples with the evolution of all the metrics. Finally, we performed a correlation analysis to find patterns and correlations between our proposed metrics.

In Table 3 we present the evolution of the number of libraries for each project. We should note that here we counted only the times when a method of some library was used, like we defined the NUL method. We can observe that in most cases, the NUL slowly increases or remains the same as the project evolves. But for the "*incubator-baremaps*" project we can see that in the last two versions, the NUL was zero. For this specific instance, if we compare the two versions, we can see that big restructuring and changes overall the project took place. Along with those changes, all the libraries were removed and replaced with new code to not have so many dependencies. This practice can be seen in other projects as well, in which one library is added and in a later version it might be replaced with new code. As new libraries are continuously added, this phenomenon is not visible in Table 3. Regarding the rest of the metrics, since they are method-level specific, the report of them is a bit less trivial. The complete dataset can be found online[9]. First, by examining the evolution of the metrics (PUCD, PUCI, LDUF, LIUF), we can see that the values of the metrics, in most cases, are small and remain the same. This shows that a library is used for some specific method calls and rarely is utilized to its full potential.

Table 3. Analyzed Tags per Project and NUL

Project	Tags	Number of Libraries
apache/brooklyn-server	1.0.0	13
	0.12.0	12
	0.11.0	11
	0.10.0	11
	0.9.0	2
apache/incubator-baremaps	v0.7.1	0
	v0.7.0	0
	v0.6.0	5
	v0.5.10	3
	v0.5.1	3
	v0.4.0	4
	v0.3.0	1
apache/ozone	1.3.0	3
	1.2.0	3
	1.1.0	3
	1.0.0	2
	0.5	1
apache/zookeeper	3.9.0	9
	3.8.0	9
	3.7.0	9
	3.6.0	1
	3.5.5	1
apache/doris	2.0.0-rc01	4
	1.2.0-rc01	5
	1.1.0-rc01	4
	1.0.0-rc01	4
	0.15.0-rc01	7
	0.14.0-rc01	2
	0.13.0-rc01	0
	0.12.0-rc01	0
	0.10.0-rc03	0

---

[9] https://users.uom.gr/~a.ampatzoglou/aux_material/LibUse.rar.

However, this is not always the case, in Fig. 7 we provide some instances of specific methods metrics and their evolution. We should note that the first two charts correspond to methods from the *"brooklyn-server"* project, while the third corresponds to the *"incubator-baremaps"* project. Also, the horizontal axis labels contain the number of the version, the library, and the version of the library as follows: {project version}_{library}-{library version}.

From these charts, we can obtain information on: (a) the change in the metrics (from version to version); (b) when the developers are utilizing the libraries more (or less); and (c) when the developers update the libraries. For the changes in the libraries' version, we can focus on the first two charts where is visible that this change also affects the

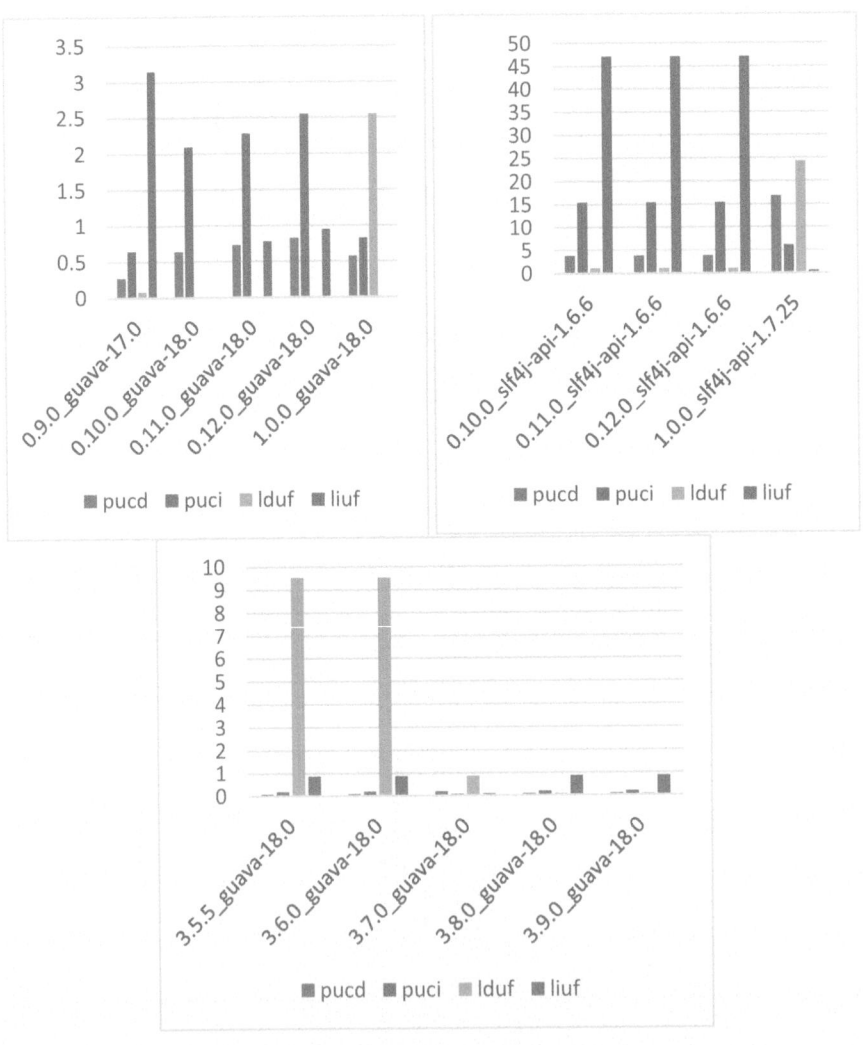

Fig. 7. Examples of metrics evolutions

metrics. We can see that the PUCD metric is changed in both of those instances and in turn, so are all the other metrics. This is mostly because the number of methods that exist in the class that is used from the source project is changed (a library change), or the user utilizes more of the provided methods of the library (a project change). This can be important feedback for the developers to differentiate between library and project-level changes and track them across the evolution of the project.

It is evident that changes in the library version, or changes in the utilization of them from the project level affect the metrics, but the correlation between them is not clear. For this reason, we performed a correlation analysis for the values of each metric using the Pearson correlation. The results of this analysis can be found in Table 4. We can see that there are two significant correlations, one positive between PUCD and PUCI, and one negative between PUCD and LDUF. First, the correlation between the PUCD and the PUCI can be explained because of the similarity of their definition, where the first one counts the number of used classes, and the second one counts the unused as well. For the second one, similarly to the previous, the correlation can be explained due to the similarity of the definitions, where the PUCD counts the number of used classes, and the LDUF considers the number of used classes (along with their methods).

Table 4. Correlations of metrics

		pucd	puci	lduf	liuf
pucd	Pearson Correlation	1	.737**	-.182*	.002
	Sig. (2-tailed)		.001	.036	.981
puci	Pearson Correlation	.737**	1	-.002	-.005
	Sig. (2-tailed)	.001		.981	.951
lduf	Pearson Correlation	-.182*	-.002	1	-.164
	Sig. (2-tailed)	.036	.981		.061
liuf	Pearson Correlation	.002	-.005	-.164	1
	Sig. (2-tailed)	.981	.951	.061	

6.2 Evaluation

The results of the evaluation from RQ_2 are presented in Fig. 6 based on SUS. We can see that all the questions received excellent responses, however, the frequency of the application usage received a little bit more unfavorable feedback. The participants seemed to understand the main disadvantage of the application, which is the time needed for a new analysis, but they were not displeased about it. In a Q&A that was followed with some of the participants, we could see the need for supporting more languages and library registries. Moreover, as for the frequency of use of the tool, the participants told us that they do not often add new libraries or change the methods that they use. So, it is normal to not have to use a tool like this in their daily routines, but mostly as a complementary analysis during quality control processes (e.g., before releases or end of sprints).

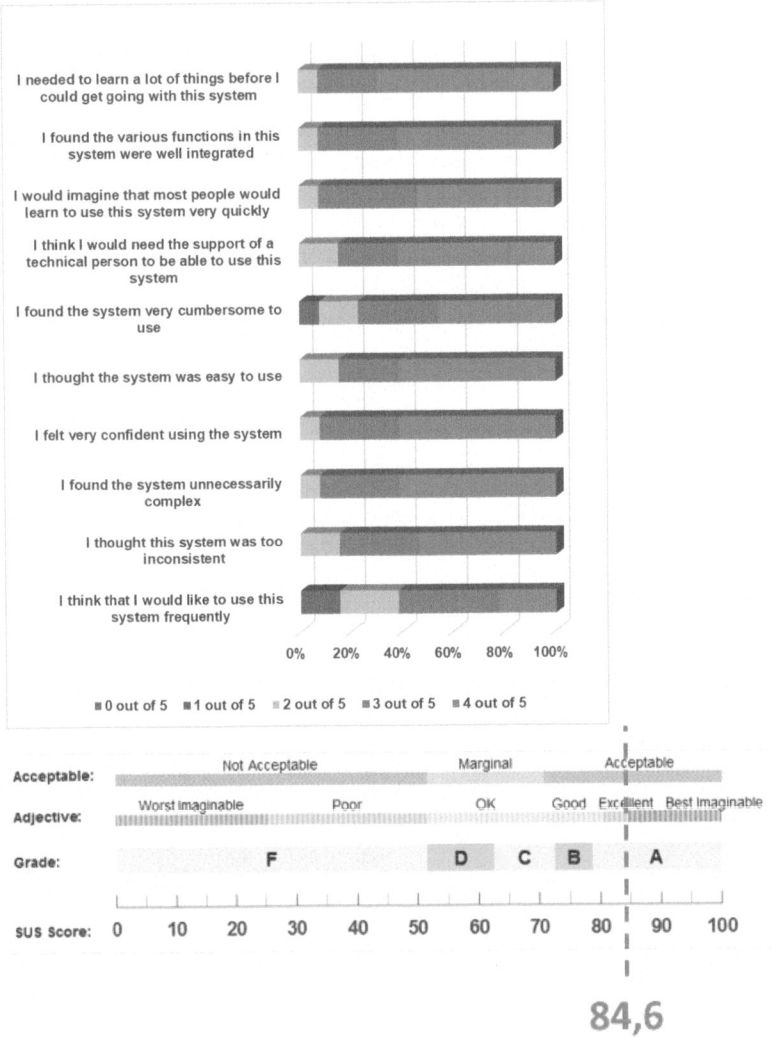

Fig. 8. Usability of Proposed Metrics and Tool

7   Threats to Validity

In this section, we present and discuss construct, reliability, and external threats to the validity of this study [13].

Construct validity is related to what extent the phenomenon under study represents what is investigated according to the research questions. In our study, the main threat is the way of evaluating the tool, without long-term usage. This can positively affect the results since the participants used the tool only for a demo session, while it can negativly affect due to the limited time and experience of the developer with the tool.

To mitigate any *reliability* threats, two different researchers were involved in the data collection of both studies. Also, all the data, from the extraction of the metrics all the way to the call trees of each method call, can be found online as already mentioned.

Finally, concerning *external validity*, we have identified two possible threats. Firstly, all the investigated projects are written in Java and it's possible that different programming languages would result in different conclusions. Even though the usage of automation tools like Maven exists for other languages (NPM for JavaScript), the programming style along with the inner workings of the libraries are different. Secondly, the study of the evolution of metrics was conducted on 5 open-source projects, which can be considered small, and the validation took place with only 13 developers. As a result, we cannot generalize our findings for the metrics to all open-source projects, or all the companies regarding the validation. The main reason for the first limitation was the time-consuming analysis of the projects. As we already mentioned, this analysis is time-consuming since it's very exhaustive and the bigger the project the more is required.

8   Conclusions

Using libraries in software engineering is a widely adopted practice, for both time and reliability reasons. The usage of many dependencies or wrong ones can lead to a lot of problems, so several metrics exist to measure some aspects of the libraries. However, there is a gap in the existing metrics, which makes the libraries unaware of their environment (project) each time, so the metrics do not consider the way that the library is being used each time. In this paper, we have introduced five metrics to fill this gap in the utilization aspect of a library for a given project. To provide a more robust solution, we also created a tool for the calculation and presentation of these metrics, and we provided it as a web application. Moreover, we performed an initial exploration of the values of these metrics across the evolution of 5 open-source projects. We found out that our metrics were in line with actual big changes in either the project level or the library level (in case of a library update). This goes to show the relevance of our metrics to the development process, and that in big revisions, releases, or tags these metrics and the tool can be useful. Finally, an industrial validation took place with 13 developers from 5 companies to assess the usability of the created tool. The results showed that the tool is usable and liked by the participants, with the only concern being the frequency with which they would use it.

Acknowledgements. Work reported in this paper has received funding from the European Union's Horizon 2020 research and innovation programme under grant agreement No. 780572 (project SDK4ED).

References

1. Abdalkareem, R., Nourry, O., Wehaibi, S., Mujahid, S., Shihab, E.: Why do developers use trivial packages? An empirical case study on NPM. In: Proceedings of the 2017 11th Joint Meeting on Foundations of Software Engineering, pp. 385–395 (2017)
2. Brooke, J.: Sus: a "quick and dirty"usability. Usabil. Eval. Indus. **189**(3), 189–194 (1996)
3. Charalampidou, S., Arvanitou, E.M., Ampatzoglou, A., Avgeriou, P., Chatzi-georgiou, A., Stamelos, I.: Structural quality metrics as indicators of the long method bad smell: An empirical study. In: 2018 44th Euromicro Conference on Software Engineering and Advanced Applications (SEAA), pp. 234–238 (2018). https://doi.org/10.1109/SEAA.2018.00046
4. De la Mora, F.L., Nadi, S.: An empirical study of metric-based comparisons of software libraries. In: Proceedings of the 14th International Conference on Predictive Models and Data Analytics in Software Engineering, pp. 22–31 (2018)
5. De La Mora, F.L., Nadi, S.: Which library should I use? A metric-based comparison of software libraries. In: Proceedings of the 40th International Conference on Software Engineering: New Ideas and Emerging Results, pp. 37–40 (2018)
6. Floven, K.F.: State management models impact on run-time performance in single page applications (2020)
7. Frakes, W.B., Kang, K.: Software reuse research: status and future. IEEE Trans. Softw. Eng. **31**(7), 529–536 (2005)
8. Gizas, A., Christodoulou, S., Papatheodorou, T.: Comparative evaluation of Javascript frameworks. In: Proceedings of the 21st International Conference on World Wide Web, pp. 513–514 (2012)
9. Hora, A., Valente, M.T.: apiwave: Keeping track of api popularity and migration. In: 2015 IEEE International Conference on Software Maintenance and Evolution (ICSME), pp. 321–323. IEEE (2015)
10. Larios Vargas, E., Aniche, M., Treude, C., Bruntink, M., Gousios, G.: Selecting third-party libraries: the practitioners' perspective. In: Proceedings of the 28th ACM joint meeting on European Software Engineering Conference and Symposium on the Foundations of Software Engineering, pp. 245–256 (2020)
11. Nikolaidis, N., Ampatzoglou, A., Chatzigeorgiou, A., Tsekeridou, S., Piperidis, A.: Technical Debt in Service-Oriented Software Systems. In: Taibi, D., Kuhrmann, M., Mikkonen, T., Klünder, J., Abrahamsson, P. (eds.) Product-Focused Software Process Improvement PROFES 2022. LNCS, vol. 13709, pp. 265–281. Springer, Cham (2022)
12. Piccioni, M., Furia, C.A., Meyer, B.: An empirical study of API usability. In: 2013 ACM/IEEE International Symposium on Empirical Software Engineering and Measurement, pp. 5–14. IEEE (2013)
13. Runeson, P., Host, M., Rainer, A., Regnell, B.: Case Study Research in Software Engineering: Guidelines and Examples. John Wiley & Sons, London (2012)
14. Shatnawi, M.Q., Hmeidi, I., Shatnawi, A.: Software library investment metrics: a new approach, issues and recommendations (2017)
15. Smith, N., Van Bruggen, D., Tomassetti, F.: Javaparser: Visited. Leanpub. (2017)
16. Washizaki, H., Yamamoto, H., Fukazawa, Y.: A metrics suite for measuring reusability of software components. In: Proceedings. 5th International Workshop on enterprise networking and computing in healthcare industry (IEEE Cat. No. 03EX717), pp. 211–223. IEEE (2004)
17. Zaimi, A., et al.: An empirical study on the reuse of third-party libraries in open-source software development. In: 7th Balkan Conference on Informatics Conference. BCI 2015, ACM (2015). https://doi.org/10.1145/2801081.2801087

Slicing and Visualizing F' Topologies with F'Prism

Jialong Li[1], Christos Tsigkanos[2], Toshihide Ubukata[1], Elisa Yumi Nakagawa[3], Zhenyu Mao[1], Nianyu Li[4(✉)], and Kenji Tei[5]

[1] Waseda University, Tokyo, Japan
lijialong@fuji.waseda.jp, {toshihide,rockmao}@akane.waseda.jp
[2] University of Athens, Athens, Greece
christos.tsigkanos@aerospace.uoa.gr
[3] University of São Paulo, São Paulo, Brazil
elisa@icmc.usp.br
[4] ZGC National Laboratory, Beijing, China
li_nianyu@pku.edu.cn
[5] Tokyo Institute of Technology, Tokyo, Japan
tei@c.titech.ac.jp

Abstract. As the barriers to entry in the aerospace industry continue to decrease, software engineering techniques are increasingly being integrated into spaceflight software development methods. F', an open-source software framework developed by JPL (Jet Propulsion Laboratory), leverages component-based architectures with a strict, fine-grained, and explicit declaration of components with typed ports, fostering compile-time correctness guarantees, modularity, and reusability. However, such declaration inevitably increases architectural complexity, leading to potential pitfalls in understandability of such component-based architectures and maintainability of systems built using F'. To mitigate the aforementioned problem, this paper presents F'PRISM, an open-source tool that incorporates automated architecture slicing into topology visualization by employing three architecture-general and three spaceflight-specific slicing criteria tailored for F' architectures. Our observation shows architecture slicing has potential to improve visualization and comprehension of such complex, critical software architectures.

Keywords: Topology Visualization · F prime · Architecture Slicing · Component-based Architectures · Flight Software

1 Introduction and Motivation

The emergence of low-cost and powerful onboard computers on small-scale flight- and space-craft has lowered the barrier to entry [43], often referred to as *New Space* [31]. Software is a core part of spaceflight missions, with its complexity increasing – mirroring other software systems. As long acknowledged in software

© The Author(s), under exclusive license to Springer Nature Switzerland AG 2024
B. Tekinerdoğan et al. (Eds.): ECSA 2023, LNCS 14590, pp. 375–389, 2024.
https://doi.org/10.1007/978-3-031-66326-0_23

engineering research, such complexity brings challenges for designing, maintaining, and understanding systems [37]. In this setting, there is an increase of interest in the availability and adoption of open development platforms, including software frameworks that can support the engineering of such systems, along with adoption of contemporary software engineering methods and techniques. While software architecture is usually reflected in representations such as models capturing architectural views, maintaining architectural knowledge beyond representations involves other factors [39], it also encompasses methods and techniques necessary to manage the often complex and sizable codebases of software systems, reflecting those representations. As such, architectural knowledge should be transferable, comprehensible, and relevant for stakeholders such as developers and project managers, who should be aided in taking in (their) system view. The latter is particularly important for e.g., onboarding new team members. For spaceflight software systems, this is particularly relevant because the cost of potential failures is typically high [33].

Regarding frameworks for the space domain, F' ("F prime") is a software framework developed by Jet Propulsion Laboratory (JPL), targeting small-scale spaceflight applications and enabling rapid development and deployment [16]. Notable real-world deployments include the Ingenuity Mars Helicopter [18], Near Earth Scout CubeSats [24,36] as well as multiple instrument and satellite software. From the software architecture perspective, F' contains components and connectors, uses typed interfaces to provide compile-time guarantees, and has built-in unit and integration testing features. The architecture of an F' software system (i.e., a system derived from F') is concretely represented in a so-called *topology*, explicitly declared through a set of component instances and their typed port connections. Ports in F' are defined as generalizations of SysML[11] flow ports, demanding the directionality, data types, and other detailed interface specifications for specifying interactions between components. Within F', ports are primarily categorized into input or output ports, and input ports are further divided into synchronous, asynchronous, and guarded. Connections are established from an output port to an input port with matching port types. Hence, F' enables modularity and separation of concerns (by virtue of its component-based approach), with key concepts being restricted visibility (via access through typed ports) and procedural/object abstraction [32].

Due to the strict and fine-grained (i.e., data-type) port declaration, F' topologies can quickly become sizable, hindering architecture comprehension and maintainability. Table 1 summarizes an investigation of topology complexity of open-source F' projects[1]. Remarkable complexity is observed even in a basic "hello world" project, which includes 219 ports and 142 connections within 25 components (one application-specific component and 24 standard components) provided by F' standard library. This complexity is also mirrored in the lines of code (LoC) metric, with 249 LoC for topology declaration (in F', the topology is not

---

[1] It is worth noting that these three (small-scale) F' projects are all sourced from the F' official website [3]. Larger-scale examples are typically unavailable due to the intellectual property constraints associated with real-world flight software.

merely "implied" but explicitly declared via XML). Moreover, merely 48 LoC are for implementation within C++ source, counting only application-specific components (and excluding standard F' components).

Table 1. Topology complexity of indicative open-source F' projects.

	#Components	#Ports	#Connections	.xml LoC	.cpp LoC
Hello World [28]	25	219	142	249	48
LED Blinker [29]	26	226	147	275	91
Ref App [27]	33	315	214	554	564

Motivated by this complexity problem, this paper presents F'PRISM, an F' topology visualization tool that leverages automated architecture slicing. The key idea is to visualize a project's F' topology with various slicing criteria, enabling relevant stakeholders such as developers, system engineers, and project managers, to better understand the topology they are involved in, and thus indirectly improving other software development life cycle facets, such as testing, maintenance, or documentation [40]. In short, our main contributions are as follows:

1. We propose new architecture slicing criteria tailored for spaceflight software ("spaceflight-specific"). We also explore established criteria such as slicing by coupling or component complexity ("architecture-general") for dealing with general architectural aspects;
2. We extend existing F' visualization tools [14,15], to support interactive slicing parameter specification and visualization, aiming to support stakeholders in architecture comprehension;
3. We realize the aforementioned in a tool artifact, available as open-source software. A demonstration video can be accessed at https://youtu.be/KbZcF-IQjlg, and the artifact is accessible at https://github.com/545659928/FPrimePrism.

The remainder of this paper is organized as follows. Section 2 presents a brief background and related work. Section 3 describes the slicing criteria. Section 4 presents F'PRISM and its demonstration. Section 5 concludes this work and discusses potential future work.

2   Background and Related Work

We briefly describe JPL's F', the software framework targetted by F'PRISM for slicing and visualization, before considering works that have an affinity with the approach presented in this paper.

2.1   JPL's F' Framework

F' (F prime), is an open-source software framework developed by the JPL specifically for embedded (space-)flight systems [16,38]. The software architecture employed by F' is component-based, enjoying well-defined interfaces which encourage reusability, analyzability, and maintainability [39]. This architectural topology is defined explicitly in XML, detailing component instances and their typed port connections. Ports in F' have types specifying data that can be transmitted through them and are primarily categorized into input or output ports, and input ports are further divided into synchronous, asynchronous, and guarded. Connections are established from an output port to an input port with matching port types.

In terms of implementation, C++ is employed to facilitate encapsulation and inheritance inherent in Object Oriented Design, enhancing both reusability and modularity. Components in F' are defined as C++ classes comprised of a set of data, and associated operations on this data, termed methods. Benefitting from its open-source nature, multiple flight-proven components are officially provided in the F' standard component library [18]. The library mainly provides two kinds of components: (i) OS features abstraction such as threads, files, and clocks, and (ii) a collection of reusable components that perform standard flight software functions such as command dispatch, event logging, and ground system support. Note that the above components are strictly designed per F' architectural principles with well-defined ports and connections, providing a solid foundation for rapid development allowing engineers to focus on application-specific components.

2.2   Related Work

Software and Architecture Slicing. Software or program slicing [42] has been employed in various software engineering activities, including for program understanding [21], debugging [9], testing [12,25], maintenance [22], model checking [41], reuse [34], reverse engineering [13], and complexity measurement [35]. Slicing methods have also been explored within software architectures. Zhao et al. [45] pioneered architecture slicing based on information flow dependency. Kim et al. [23] introduced dynamic slicing to uncover architecture's dynamic behavior. Lun et al. explored and compared the efficiency of forward and backward slicing methods [30]. Zhao et al. applied the slicing methods aiming to extract reusable architectural elements (e.g., components and connectors) from the existing architectural specifications [44]. Colangelo et al. [20] used slicing and abstraction to reduce architecture complexity for model checking in large-scale architectures.

Architecture slicing focuses on the architectural level of software and aims to better understand the high-level design of the software, how it's organized, and how its components interact. From the side of the practice, several commercial software tools have slicing features to aid engineers in modeling and visualizing software architectures, e.g., Astah [1], Papyrus [6], StarUML [7], Visual

Paradigm [8], and Enterprise Architect [2]. Observe that most of them primarily provide support for manual slicing (i.e., manual choice of hiding some components), and Enterprise Architect specially allows finer-grained manual slicing (i.e., manual choice of hiding connectors within components). However, to the best of our knowledge, these tools lack capabilities for automated architecture-driven slicing.

F' Topology Visualization. Magicdraw's F' plug-in [5] was developed for the modeling and visualization of F' software [38]; however, with the deprecation of MagicDraw support from F' version 2.0 due to limited usability and expandability [4], several initiatives have emerged to develop tools, including open-source ones, specifically for F'. The tool proposed in [19] was an initial attempt at visualizing the F' topology. Subsequently, F Prime Layout (FPL) [14] and F Prime Visualizer (FPV) [15] were proposed. FPL acts as a preprocessor, converting topology XML into JSON, while FPV is a web application developed to visualize the latter as generated by FPL. In our tool, we employ both: (i) FPL to encode the complete topology at hand (and implement slicing at the FPL JSON level) and (ii) FPV is used to visualize it.

3   Slicing Criteria

In this section, we detail the slicing criteria that are supported by F'PRISM, whose classification overview is shown in Fig. 1. The first-level classification is bifurcated into (i) spaceflight-specific slicing criteria that are specifically tailored for spaceflight software, and (ii) architecture-general slicing criteria that are suitable for generic issues of software architectures.

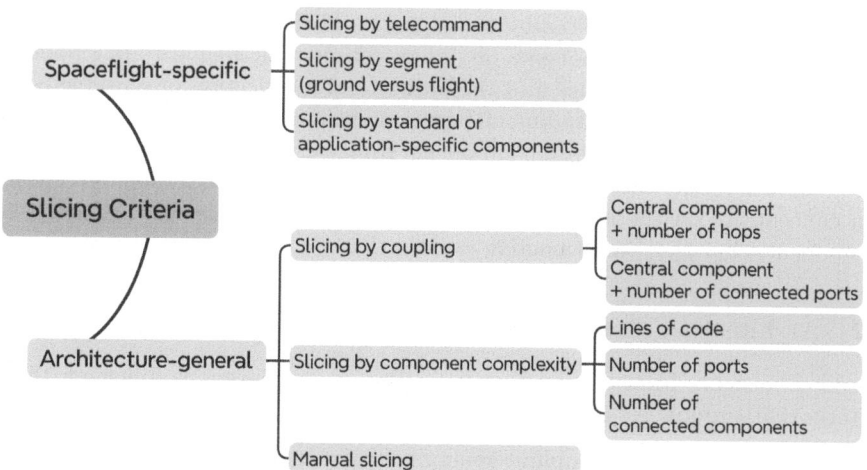

Fig. 1. Classification of Slicing Criteria.

3.1 Spaceflight-Specific Slicing Criteria

Spaceflight-specific slicing criteria aim to increase developer's comprehension by utilizing typical domain-specific concepts that spaceflight systems have in common. Based on discussions with experts and developers in the field of aerospace, we identified the following three criteria.

Slicing by Telecommand: Telecommanding is a core feature of spaceflight applications, enabling ground center staff to manipulate the spacecraft (e.g., adjusting orientation, firing thrusters, or activating scientific instruments). It sends telecommands to invoke specific logic that, in the case of F' software, are implemented in F' components. This criterion focuses on elements (components and respective connections) triggered or issued by each telecommand. Such slicing is achieved through the invocation chain, analyzed via static code from the XML (capturing topology) and C++ (containing implementation) files. This slicing criterion not only facilitates engineers in grasping the scope of each telecommand but also is beneficial in designing test cases, as command-based test cases are common patterns in spaceflight software.

Slicing by Segment: Spaceflight software contains logic pertaining to both the flight segment (running on flight-/space-craft) and the ground segment (which is responsible for ground operations). Those flight and ground software segments are often co-designed in space software, something reflected as a key feature in F' as well. To this end, this slicing criterion allows the topology to be subdivided and sliced into either flight segment or ground segment. Such a separation facilitates a clear comprehension and review of the respective responsibilities pertaining to each segment, including its components.

Slicing by Standard or Application-Specific Components: F' contains an open-source, flight-proven standard component library, which comprises more than 40 well-designed components providing various functionalities (e.g., operation system abstractions, files and threading) and a collection of reusable components (e.g., for telecommanding and system event capture). This criterion was designed to hide these standard components from the topology, avoiding showing the complexity that these components introduce. By omitting them, engineers can concentrate on the unique operational logic of their mission, i.e., bespoke components that they implemented.

3.2 Architecture-General Slicing Criteria

Based on insights from the existing literature, we organize the following three criteria that support established ways of slicing software architectures.

Slicing by Coupling: Coupling generally refers to the degree of interdependence or the measure of the connection strength between two components. F'PRISM considers two fundamental definitions of coupling: qualitative and quantitative. Given one component c as the central (or start) node, the qualitative coupling is defined as "whether a component is connected to component

c within m hops", where m ($m \geq 0$) and c are user-specified. Quantitative coupling is defined as "whether a component is connected to component c with more than n connections", where n is also defined by the user. Moreover, more complex types of coupling [23] can be supported in future work.

Slicing by Component Complexity: This criterion addresses three dimensions of component complexity: (i) LoC (in .cpp files); (ii) number of ports (in topology .xml files); and (iii) number of connected components. This criterion empowers engineers to grasp the complexity of each component intuitively, potentially providing indirect support in risk assessment and localization during the testing phase.

Manual Slicing: Alongside automated slicing, manual, user-defined slicing (as supported by most commercial tools) is beneficial. This criterion offers users the ability to choose specific components, visualizing their interactions with others. More precisely, in this case the sliced topology comprises: (i) the user-selected components; (ii) their respective ports; and (iii) the connections between them.

4   Visualizing F' Topology Slices

In the following, after a high-level view of F'Prism, we illustrate its slicing features along with their visual counterparts.

4.1   Overview of F'Prism Implementation

Figure 2 offers an overview of F'Prism. Its architecture is divided into three main parts: Front-end (left), Back-end (middle), and Source (right).

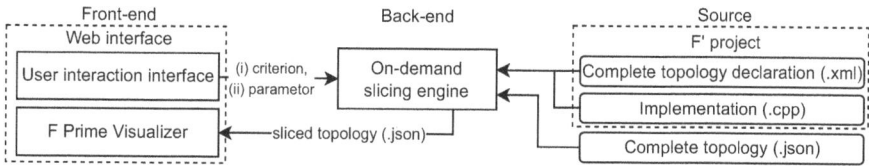

Fig. 2. F'Prism tool architecture.

- The **User interaction interface** provides a user interface that allows users to (i) upload the F' project and (ii) select slicing criteria and input necessary parameters.
- the **On-demand slicing engine** generates a sliced topology (as a .json file), upon receiving (i) user inputs; (ii) an F' project (complete topology declaration (.xml file); (iii) implementation (.cpp files); and (iv) the complete topology (.json file).

  Here, the F' project's source code is employed for static code analysis, which lays the groundwork for the slicing operation. Note that the code analysis functionality, specially designed for F', requires both .cpp and .xml files. This is because of the restricted visibility imposed by F' – a component cannot directly call methods of other components. Instead, it must invoke its own output ports (implemented within .cpp), which then indirectly trigger the connected input ports of another component (declared within .xml), thereby calling the corresponding handler functions within that component (also implemented within .cpp).

Based on the aforementioned method, the slicing engine slices the topology in an on-demand way, according to user specifications. Specifically, slicing by telecommand and coupling starts from a specific component or function, and then recursively analyzes the components, ports, and connections that meet the user condition. The remaining four criteria involve selecting components that meet user conditions by traversing all components, and subsequently analyzing their interactions.

- Ultimately, the **F Prime Visualizer** [15] parses the generated .json file and shows the resulting sliced topology. Observe that the functionality offered can be integrated within a CI/CD pipeline as well, facilitating teams working on F' projects and visualizing relevant slices upon respective relevant changes in the system's architecture.

Briefly, the project is developed using the React framework, and the programming languages used are: (i) TypeScript, a superset of JavaScript, for implementing application logic and dynamic content rendering; (ii) CSS to handle the visual styling and layout of the web pages; and (iii) JSX (JavaScript XML), which allows HTML-like syntax directly in JavaScript, serving as the basic structure for web pages.

4.2   F'Prism **Workflow and Demonstration**

Workflow. We introduce the workflow of using F'Prism, assuming that the user runs this application in a local environment. The user first starts the local server by running a bash script. After that, they can access F'Prism locally in a web browser. When using F', the user initially needs to upload the F' project files. Subsequently, the user selects the slicing criterion and provides the slicing parameters through selection boxes and/or text input. In a user experiment involving four graduate students who are familiar with F', the average time taken to set up the necessary environment for running the tool was approximately 15 min, and users typically became proficient in utilizing F'Prism within an additional 5 min.

Demonstration. Ref App [27] is a reference application part of the official F' tutorial and demonstrates key features for data transmission and reception. This application primarily employs four application-specific components to manage various types of data interactions, noting that there is no direct interaction between them. Recalling Table 1, Ref App contains 33 components, 315 ports with 214 connections, with its topology defined in 554 LoC and 564 LoC of C++ source. The application-specific components within this application are: (i) Five instances of *SignalGen* component, identified as *SG1* to *SG5*, each distinguished by their respective generation frequencies. These component instances are designed to generate a variety of signals, such as Triangle and Sine waves, with user-defined parameters like amplitude and phase; (ii) *PingReceiver*, a component that increments its counter every time a ping is received and subsequently forwards a ping; (iii) *RecvBuff*, a component receives, deserializes, and processes data buffers, further updating telemetry data like sensor values once the data is successfully processed; and (iv) *SendBuff* is responsible for creating and sending data buffers when the corresponding command is invoked. Note that these application-specific components are designed to be used to handle different types of data interactions, and there is no direct interaction between them.

Figure 3 shows (a fragment of) screenshots of six slicing criteria of the F'Prism workflow, where Figs. 3a to 3c illustrate three architecture-general slicing criteria, and Figs. 3d to 3f demonstrate three spaceflight-specific slicing criteria.

- **Manual slicing**: Figure 3a illustrates (part of) the complete topology (before slicing) of Ref App. This is also the default setting of manual slicing, where all components are initially pre-selected. Observe that dense connections span the entire visual page, significantly hampering readability and comprehensibility.

- **Slicing by coupling**: Figure 3b illustrates an example of *slicing by coupling*, where *SG1* is chosen as the central component and hop is set to 1. This pared-down sub-topology lets users focus on and intuitively understand the direct interactions between *SG1* and other components. For instance, *SG1* transmits log information from its *logOut* port to the *LogRecv* port of *eventLogger*.

- **Slicing by component complexity**: Fig. 3c shows the sub-topology which only includes the components that have more than ten ports. By adopting this criterion, we can more effectively distinguish complex components, as their complexity often implies a significant impact on overall system functionality.

- **Slicing by telecommand**: Figure 3d provides an example of *slicing by telecommand*, where the selected command is *"SB_GEN_FATAL"*, which injects fatal errors into the data buffer of *SendBuff* component. Observe that *cmdDisp* sends the command to *SendBuff* via its *cmdSequencer* port, and then *SendBuff* relays the results back through *CmdReg* and *CmdStatus* ports. This sub-topology provides engineers with two additional pieces of valuable information: (i) the command only impacts the internal behavior of *SendBuff* and does not directly engage external components; and (ii) the result of this command is not logged within the system since *eventLogger* is not displayed.

- **Slicing by segment**: Figure 3e displays the sub-topology of flight segments. This enables engineers to concentrate on the interactions of components

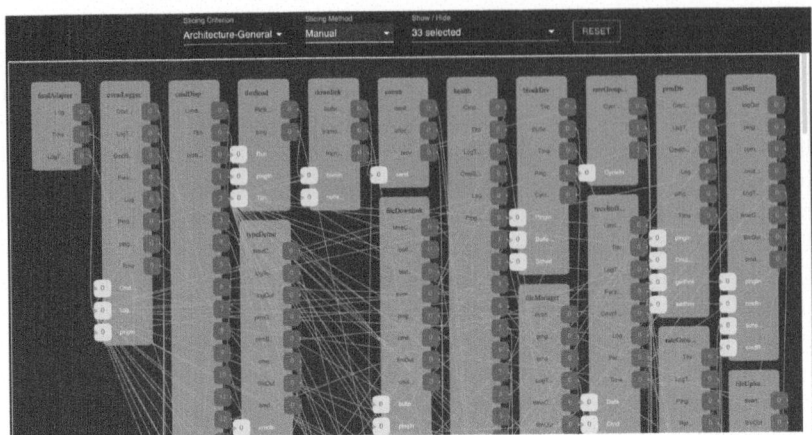

(a) Complete topology of Ref App. (default setting of manual slicing)

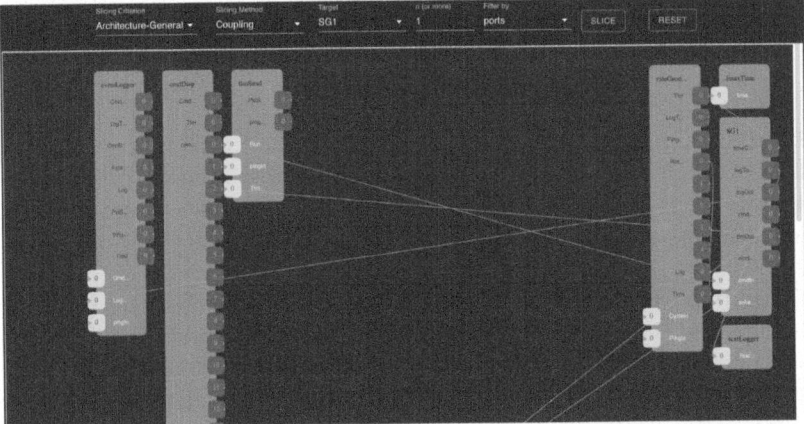

(b) Sub-topology sliced by coupling ($SG1$ as central component, hop = 1).

(c) Sub-topology sliced by component complexity (port number >10)

Fig. 3. Demonstration of Six Slicing Criteria on Ref App.

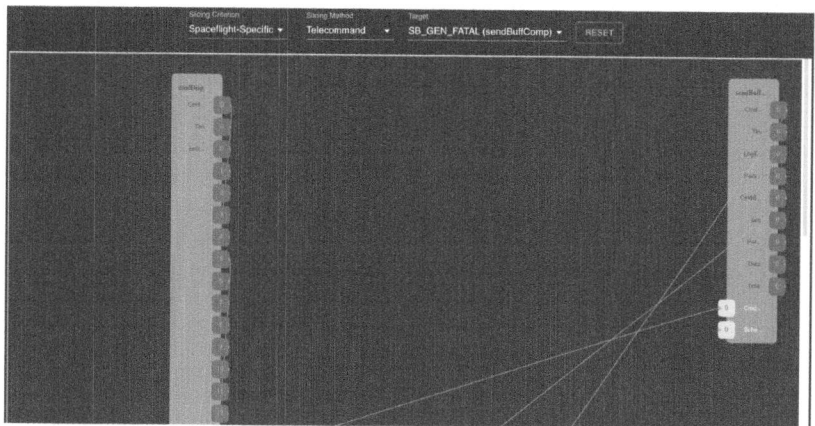

(d) Sub-topology sliced by telecommand (telecommand: SB_GEN_FATAL).

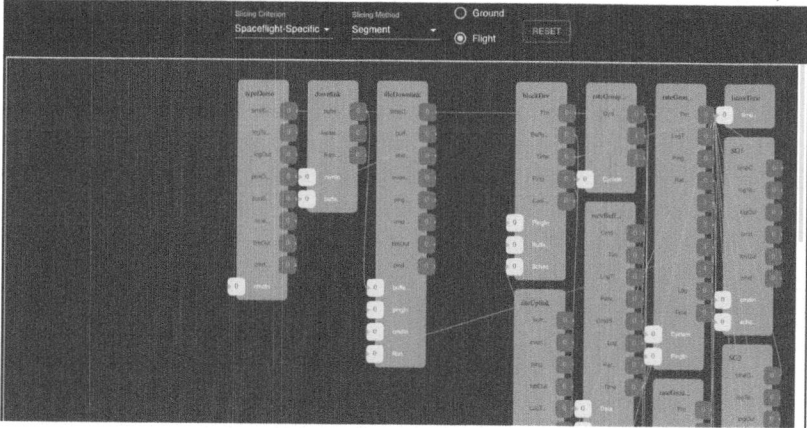

(e) Sub-topology sliced by flight segment

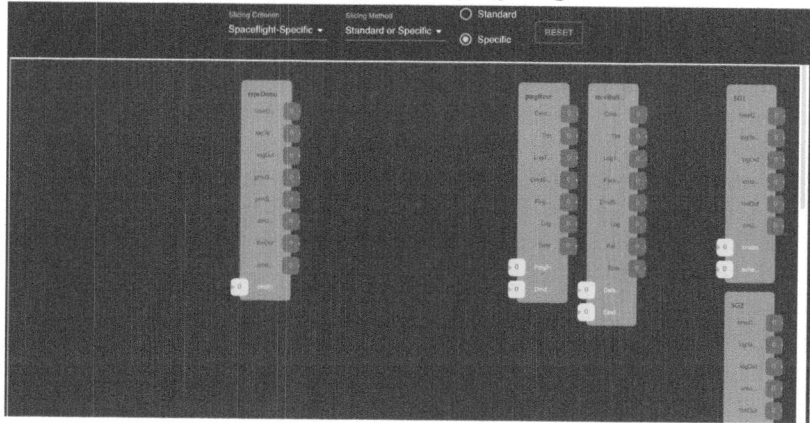

(f) Sub-topology sliced by application-specific components

Fig. 3. (*continued*)

within the spacecraft while disregarding the logic of the ground system and the interactions between the spacecraft and the ground system.

- **Slicing by standard or application-specific components**: Fig. 3f displays the sub-topology of only application-specific components. In this view, we can observe the four types of application components of Ref App (SG1 to SG5, all located in the rightmost column), as introduced earlier in this chapter. More specifically, it is evident that there is no direct interaction between these components because they are independent units responsible for the transmission and reception of different types of data.

5   Conclusion and Future Work

Architectural visualization is essential for understandability of software architectures, with important implications to software quality. This paper introduced F'PRISM, a visualization tool that incorporates automated architecture slicing for the F' space software development framework. This tool encompasses novel spaceflight-specific slicing criteria as well as slicing criteria applicable to generic issues of software architectures, also supporting interactive slicing parameter specification and visualization. Hence, this paper makes dual contributions to the field of software architectures: (i) we pioneer the integration of automatic slicing into architectural visualization, an approach not yet widely available in contemporary commercial tools; and (ii) we illustrate integration of architectural slicing and visualization, underscoring their potential in enhancing architecture comprehension. We intend this work can serve as an example for other application domains to address their large-scale and complex architectures.

Regarding future work, we intend to evolve F'PRISM in three aspects, each corresponding to each part depicted previously in Fig. 2:

- **Visualization:** Visualization has been facilitated via FPV; we aim to refine this with bespoke visualization functionality that leverages layout optimization [26] and that follows an overview + details-on-demand approach [10] to enhance readability and usability.
- **Slicing:** We intend F'PRISM to support more advanced slicing. This includes: (i) expanding the current slicing criteria, for instance leveraging other software maintenance metrics such as cyclomatic complexity or data complexity. Additionally, (ii) supporting combined criteria, such as 'flight segment + manual slicing'; considering the perspective of users requiring more comprehensive, multi-view slicing.
- **Source input:** The slicing engine was designed to support solely code analysis on XML topologies. Those can also be specified with FPP [17], a simplified language. As .xml files can be derived by compiling .fpp files, we plan to embed an automatic compiling feature within F'PRISM. This seeks to eliminate the need to compile manually .xml files, thereby improving usability.

Furthermore, as a limitation of this study, we acknowledge that the practical effectiveness of our tool has not been verified. To address this and further enhance the utility of our tool in real-world settings, we plan to gather feedback from actual F' engineers and introduce additional features. These enhancements could include IDE integration, allowing users to directly navigate to specific pieces of code by interacting with a port within the tool.

Acknowledgment. This work was partially supported by CNPq (313245/2021-5), FAPESP (2015/24144-7), RV4THINGS (HFRI/GR), and JSPS KAKENHI (JP23H03374, JP22KJ2935). The author, Jialong Li, would like to thank Tzu-Yi Pan for her inspiration on this work.

References

1. Astah: Premier diagramming, modeling software & tools. https://astah.net/. Accessed 25 Jun 2023
2. Enterprise architect. https://sparxsystems.com/. Accessed 06 Jul 2023
3. F' flight software & embedded systems framework. https://nasa.github.io/fprime/. Accessed 20 Jun 2023
4. Magic draw support (deprecated). https://nasa.github.io/fprime/v2.0.1/UsersGuide/dev/magicdraw.html. Accessed 20 Jun 2023
5. Magicdraw. https://www.3ds.com/products-services/catia/products/no-magic/magicdraw/. Accessed 20 Jun 2023
6. Papyrus. https://www.papyrus.com/. Accessed 25 Jun 2023
7. Staruml. https://staruml.io/. Accessed 25 Jun 2023
8. Visual paradigm. https://www.visual-paradigm.com. Accessed 25 Jun 2023
9. Agrawal, H., Demillo, R.A., Spafford, E.H.: Debugging with dynamic slicing and backtracking. Software Pract. Experien. **23**(6), 589–616 (1993). https://doi.org/10.1002/spe.4380230603
10. Arleo, A., Tsigkanos, C., Leite, R.A., Dustdar, S., Miksch, S., Sorger, J.: Visual exploration of financial data with incremental domain knowledge. Comput. Graph. Forum **42**(1), 101–116 (2023). https://doi.org/10.1111/cgf.14723
11. Balmelli, L.: The systems modeling language for products and systems development. J. Object Technol. **6**, 149–177 (2007). https://doi.org/10.5381/jot.2007.6.6.a5
12. Bates, S., Horwitz, S.: Incremental program testing using program dependence graphs. In: Proceedings of the 20th ACM SIGPLAN-SIGACT Symposium on Principles of Programming Languages. POPL '93, New York, NY, USA, pp. 384–396. Association for Computing Machinery (1993). https://doi.org/10.1145/158511.158694
13. Beck, J., Eichmann, D.: Program and interface slicing for reverse engineering. In: Proceedings of 1993 15th International Conference on Software Engineering, pp. 509–518 (1993). https://doi.org/10.1109/ICSE.1993.346015
14. Bocchino, R.: F Prime Layout (FPL) (2021). https://github.com/fprime-community/fprime-layout. Accessed 20 Jun 2023
15. Bocchino, R.: F prime visualizer (fpv) (2021). https://github.com/fprime-community/fprime-visual. Accessed 20 Jun 2023
16. Bocchino, R., Canham, T., Watney, G., Reder, L., Levison, J.: F Prime: an open-source framework for small-scale flight software systems. In: 32nd Annual Small Satellite Conference (2018)

17. Bocchino, R.L., Levison, J.W., Starch, M.D.: FPP: a modeling language for f prime. In: 2022 IEEE Aerospace Conference (AERO), pp. 1–15 (2022). https://doi.org/10.1109/AERO53065.2022.9843754

18. Canham, T.: The mars ingenuity helicopter - a victory for open-source software. In: 2022 IEEE Aerospace Conference (AERO), pp. 01–11 (2022). https://doi.org/10.1109/AERO53065.2022.9843438

19. cdmuhlb: Grafprime (2020). https://github.com/cdmuhlb/GraFPrime. Accessed 20 Jun 2023

20. Colangelo, D., Compare, D., Inverardi, P., Pelliccione, P.: Reducing software architecture models complexity: a slicing and abstraction approach. In: Najm, E., Pradat-Peyre, J.-F., Donzeau-Gouge, V.V. (eds.) FORTE 2006. LNCS, vol. 4229, pp. 243–258. Springer, Heidelberg (2006). https://doi.org/10.1007/11888116_19

21. De Lucia, A., Fasolino, A., Munro, M.: Understanding function behaviors through program slicing. In: WPC '96. 4th Workshop on Program Comprehension, pp. 9–18 (1996). https://doi.org/10.1109/WPC.1996.501116

22. Gallagher, K., Lyle, J.: Using program slicing in software maintenance. IEEE Trans. Software Eng. 17(8), 751–761 (1991). https://doi.org/10.1109/32.83912

23. Kim, T., Song, Y.T., Chung, L., Huynh, D.T.: Software architecture analysis: a dynamic slicing approach. ACIS Int. J Comp. Inf. Sci. 1(2), 91–103 (2000). https://doi.org/10.5555/543107.543111

24. Kolhof, M., Rawson, W., Yanakieva, R., Loomis, A., Lightsey, E.G., Peet, S.: Lessons learned from the gt-1 1u cubesat mission. In: 35nd AIAA/USU Conference on Small Satellites (2021)

25. Lalchandani, J.T., Mall, R.: Regression testing based-on slicing of component-based software architectures. In: Proceedings of the 1st India Software Engineering Conference. ISEC '08, New York, NY, USA, pp. 67–76. Association for Computing Machinery (2008). https://doi.org/10.1145/1342211.1342227

26. Larmore, L., Gajski, D., Wu, A.H.: Layout placement for sliced architecture. IEEE Trans. Comput. Aided Des. Integr. Circuits Syst. 11(1), 102–114 (1992). https://doi.org/10.1109/43.108623

27. LeStarch: Ref (2021). https://github.com/nasa/fprime/tree/master/Ref. Accessed 20 Jun 2023

28. LeStarch, h.: fprime-tutorial-hello-world (2023). https://github.com/fprime-community/fprime-tutorial-hello-world. Accessed 20 Jun 2023

29. LeStarch, kevin-f-ortega, J.A.: fprime-workshop-led-blinker (2023). https://github.com/fprime-community/fprime-workshop-led-blinker. Accessed 20 Jun 2023

30. Lun, L., Chi, X., Xu, H.: The relationship between forward slicing and backward slicing for software architecture. Comput. J. 57(5), 744–758 (2014). https://doi.org/10.1093/COMJNL/BXT025

31. Martin, G.: Newspace: The emerging commercial space industry (2017). nASA Ames Research Center

32. Halvorson, M., et al.: Model-based systems engineering and f': proof of concept via the creation of an on-orbit textual command parsing component for the abex mission. 35th AIAA Space Conference (2021)

33. Network, A.S.: Asn aircraft accident airbus a320-211 d-aipn warsaw-okecie airport (1993). https://aviation-safety.net/database/record.php?id=19930914-2

34. Ning, J.Q., Engberts, A., Kozaczynski, W.V.: Automated support for legacy code understanding. Commun. ACM 37(5), 50–57 (1994). https://doi.org/10.1145/175290.175295

35. Ottenstein, K.J., Ottenstein, L.M.: The program dependence graph in a software development environment. SIGPLAN Not. **19**(5), 177–184 (1984). https://doi.org/10.1145/800020.808263

36. Pong, C.M.: On-orbit performance & operation of the attitude & pointing control subsystems on Asteria. In: 32nd AIAA/USU Conference on Small Satellites (2018)

37. Pressman, R.S.: Software Engineering: A Practitioner's Approach, 4th edn. McGraw-Hill (1994)

38. Rich, T.: The development and application of the f prime magicdraw plug-in user handbook. In: 34th AIAA/USU Conference on Small Satellites (2020)

39. Shaw, M., Garlan, D.: Software Architecture - Perspectives on an Emerging Discipline. Prentice Hall (1996)

40. E.C. for Space Standardization: Software engineering handbook. ecss-e-hb-40a (2011). https://ecss.nl/hbstms/ecss-q-hb-80-01a-reuse-of-existing-software/

41. Tsigkanos, C., Nianyu, L., Jin, Z., Zhenjiang, H., Ghezzi, C.: Scalable multiple-view analysis of reactive systems via bidirectional model transformations. In: 2020 35th IEEE/ACM International Conference on Automated Software Engineering (ASE), pp. 993–1003. IEEE (2020). https://doi.org/10.1145/3324884.3416579

42. Weiser, M.D.: Program slicing. In: Jeffrey, S., Stucki, L.G. (eds.) Proceedings of the 5th International Conference on Software Engineering, San Diego, California, USA, March 9–12, 1981, pp. 439–449. IEEE Computer Society (1981)

43. Yost, B., et al.: State-of-the-art small spacecraft technology p. 1-366 (NASA Ames Reserach Center, 2021) (2021)

44. Zhao, J.: A slicing-based approach to extracting reusable software architectures. In: Proceedings of the Fourth European Conference on Software Maintenance and Reengineering, pp. 215–223 (2000). https://doi.org/10.1109/CSMR.2000.827330

45. Zhao, J.: Applying slicing technique to software architectures. In: Proceedings. Fourth IEEE International Conference on Engineering of Complex Computer Systems (Cat. No.98EX193). pp. 87–98 (1998). https://doi.org/10.1109/ICECCS.1998.706659

Maestro: A Deep Learning Based Tool to Find and Explore Architectural Design Decisions in Issue Tracking Systems

Jesse Maarleveld[1]([✉]) [iD], Arjan Dekker[1], Sarah Druyts[1],
and Mohamed Soliman[1,2] [iD]

[1] University of Groningen (RUG), Groningen, The Netherlands
{j.maarleveld,m.a.m.soliman}@rug.nl,
{a.j.dekker.5,s.druyts}@student.rug.nl
[2] Paderborn University, Paderborn, Germany
mohamed.soliman@uni-paderborn.de

Abstract. Software engineers commonly re-use architectural design decisions (ADDs) from their previous experience. However, in practice, software engineers still depend on adhoc mechanisms to re-use ADDs. Recent studies show that software engineers discuss ADDs in issue tracking system, which could be useful for software engineers to make new ADDs. Nevertheless, it is rather challenging to find ADDs among the big amount of issues in issue trackers. Therefore, we introduce Maestro, an open source tool for finding, annotating, and exploring ADDs in issue tracking systems. The tool allows researchers and practitioners to find and analyze issues containing ADDs in issue trackers. Maestro provides annotation mechanisms, deep learning components, keywords-based search engine and a user-interface that can be easily used by researchers and practitioners to find and analyze ADDs in issue trackers.

Keywords: Architectural design decisions · issue tracking system

1 Introduction

Software engineers tend to reuse the knowledge from previously made Architectural Design Decisions (ADDs) [14], such as ADDs on components design (e.g. through patterns ([6])), technology ADDs [22], and ADDs on tactics to address quality requirements (e.g. authentication mechanisms as security tactics) [2]. For instance, software engineers can learn from the drawbacks (e.g. performance issues) of solutions decided in previous ADDs. The re-use of knowledge from previous ADDs could help software engineers to effectively design new systems and mitigate risks.

While re-using ADDs could be useful in practice, empirical studies show that software engineers do not commonly document ADDs [14]. For instance, researchers proposed a wide variety of tools to manage and document ADDs

© The Author(s), under exclusive license to Springer Nature Switzerland AG 2024
B. Tekinerdoğan et al. (Eds.): ECSA 2023, LNCS 14590, pp. 390–405, 2024.
https://doi.org/10.1007/978-3-031-66326-0_24

[7, 26, 27]. However, software engineers still tend to maintain their knowledge on ADDs in their head (i.e. tacit) without explicit documentation [7]. On the other hand, software engineers communicate and discuss ADDs *informally* to resolve issues (e.g. new features[1] or improvements[2]) in issue tracking systems (e.g. Jira) [3, 20]. We call issues containing such discussions *architectural issues*. The discussions on ADDs in architectural issues contain useful knowledge, which software engineers could potentially re-use to make new ADDs.

While architectural issues could potentially be useful for software engineers, they are not tagged by software engineers [20], which make them hard to find and explore in between the vast majority of issues on programming and bugs. Therefore, researchers utilised different approaches (e.g. machine learning [3], source code analysis [20], and qualitative analysis [20]) to find and explore architectural issues, each with different pros and cons. However, the diversity of the different approaches require researchers and practitioners to execute each approach separately, and possibly manually combine their results to effectively find and explore architectural issues. To execute each approach separately is a complex, error prone and time-consuming process, which require expertise in different fields like machine learning and qualitative analysis.

In this paper, we propose Maestro: An open source tool[3] to find and explore ADDs in issue tracking systems. Maestro combines four different approaches to find and explore ADDs in a single process: keyword-based searches, deep learning, qualitative analysis, and statistical analysis. In addition, Maestro allows importing results from other approaches such as source code analysis. In Maestro, we distinguish between different types of ADDs according to Kruchten et al. [12]: existence (component related), executive (process and technology related), and property (quality related). Maestro is designed to be extensible and easy to use for both researchers and practitioners. For instance, software engineering researchers can train and run deep learning models without expertise on programming deep learning models. Maestro can be deployed remotely or locally, which provides flexibility for researchers and practitioners to run the tool.

The rest of the paper is organised as follows: In Sect. 2, we discuss the requirements of Maestro. In Sect. 3, we discuss the architecture of Maestro. We explain the process of developing Maestro in Sect. 4, and Maestro's limitations in Sect. 5. Furthermore, we compare Maestro with related work in Sect. 6. Finally, we conclude the paper in Sect. 7.

2   Requirements

Because software engineers informally discuss ADDs in software repositories, it is challenging for both practitioners and researchers to find ADDs within these informal discussions. Therefore, Maestro *aims to facilitate recovering ADDs from informal discussions in issue trackers*. We envisioned Maestro to be useful for

---

[1] https://issues.apache.org/jira/browse/HADOOP-13944.

[2] https://issues.apache.org/jira/browse/CASSANDRA-12245.

[3] Available from: https://github.com/mining-design-decisions/Maestro.

both researchers and practitioners. Researchers can use Maestro to search for ADDs for further empirical analysis. Additionally, researchers can use Maestro to design new deep learning models for finding ADDs in issue trackers. Practitioners can use Maestro to recover ADDs in order to understand design in pre-existing systems, and to find knowledge which might be useful in making new decisions – either when evolving the system or when designing a new system involving similar challenges. We explain the functional requirements in form of use cases, as well as non-functional requirements in the following two sub-sections.

2.1   Use Cases

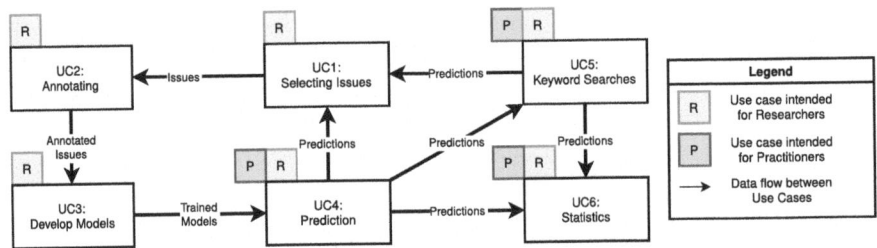

Fig. 1. Use cases supported by Maestro, annotated with relevant actors per use case (indicated with "P" for practitioner and "R" for researcher). Arrows represent the flow of data between use cases by showing how results from one use case can be used by others (e.g. issues annotated in UC2 can be used to train models developed in UC3).

Our vision of Maestro leads to six use cases. The use cases for researchers were inspired by our own research experiences (see Sect. 4). While Maestro has not yet been used or evaluated by practitioners, we hypothesise useful use cases for practitioners, which are based on our practical and research experiences [20,21]. Figure 1 shows an overview of the use cases supported by Maestro and their relationships. We explain each use-case below:

UC1 Select candidate issues for qualitative analysis: Researchers can select certain issues to be manually analysed (in UC2). The nomination of the selected issues can come from different sources: 1) predictions made by deep learning classifiers (in UC4). 2) issues resulting from keywords-searching (in UC5). 3) issues identified from other tools (e.g. source code analysis [18,20]), and 4) issues selected randomly similar to Bhat et al. [3].

UC2 Annotate issues with types of ADDs: Researchers can analyse selected issues (from UC1) using qualitative methods (e.g. grounded theory [23]), and annotate them based on the types of ADDs within issues. Using the tool, multiple remotely located researchers can discuss types of ADDs using an online conversation associated with each issue. The UI provides the researchers with the summaries and descriptions of issues, the assigned types of ADDs, and a discussion thread per issue. The conversations between researchers can be used incrementally to create a coding book for annotating architectural issues. For example, Fig. 2 shows a snapshot of a conversation between researchers to annotate an issue. Furthermore, the tool supports researchers to calculate agreement measures such as Kappa [9] to ensure high quality of the qualitative analysis. The annotated issues can be directly used to develop new deep learning models (in UC3).

UC3 **Develop deep learning models to identify types of ADDs in issues**: First, researchers can design classifiers by choosing from different types of feature generation (e.g. Word embedding [15] and Word Frequency), deep learning architectures (e.g. RNN [8,11], CNN [17], and BERT [10]), which can be automatically tuned using the flexible user interface of the tool (Fig. 3). Second, researchers can train designed classifiers using the annotated issues (from UC2), and compute their accuracy (e.g. in terms of F_1 score) to automatically identify types of ADDs in issues.

UC4 **Predict types of ADDs in issues**: Both practitioners or researchers can use the trained classifiers (from UC3) to predict types of ADDs in new, previously un-annotated, issues. Specifically, practitioners can find past ADDs in issues of existing projects, understand their rationale, and re-use their knowledge to make new ADDs. Researchers could further analyse these issues using qualitative analysis (in UC2) or statistical analysis (in UC6).

UC5 **Search for ADDs using keywords**: Both practitioners or researchers can search for architectural issues using classical keywords-based search (i.e. information retrieval). Moreover, the tool facilitates filtering search results based on the predictions of classifiers (from UC4). In this way, practitioners could effectively find issues that discuss certain types of ADDs. At the same time, researchers can focus their qualitative and statistical analysis (in UC2 and UC6) on issues that discuss certain types of ADDs. More details can be found in Fig. 4.

UC6 **Perform statistical analysis on ADDs**: Researchers and practitioners could perform statistical analysis on architectural issues. For example, practitioners could determine the duration of issues that involve certain types of ADDs. This can help practitioners to estimate the duration of future ADDs based on their type. As another example, researchers might be interested to determine the amount of knowledge on certain types of ADDs in the descriptions and comments of architectural issues.

2.2   Non-functional Requirements

In addition to the use cases of Maestro, we also explain the non-functional requirements (NFRs) with the highest priority. These non-functional requirements were based on our research experience and initial trial usage of Maestro

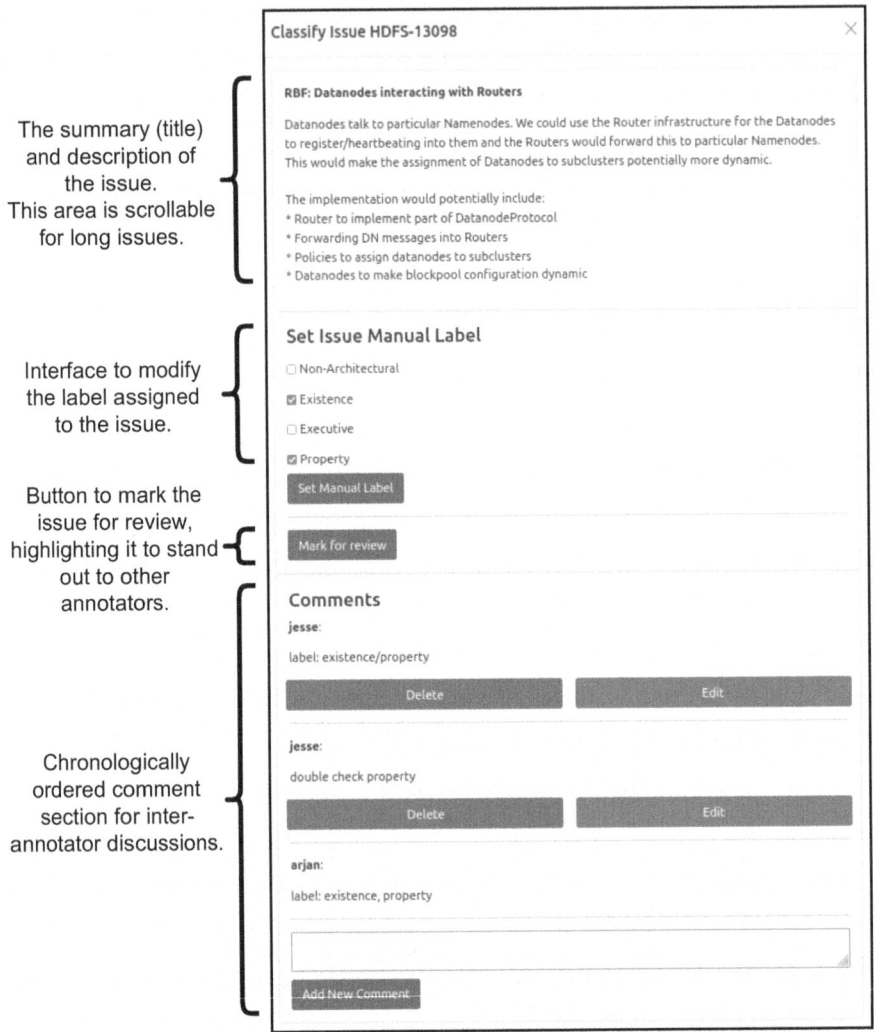

The summary (title) and description of the issue. This area is scrollable for long issues.

Interface to modify the label assigned to the issue.

Button to mark the issue for review, highlighting it to stand out to other annotators.

Chronologically ordered comment section for inter-annotator discussions.

Fig. 2. Screenshot of the annotating screen in Maestro.

(see Sect. 4), and thus describe the NFRs necessary to effectively and efficiently use Maestro in a research context. We believe that these NFRs also support the use cases from a practitioners point of view, because the use cases envisioned for practitioners are a strict subset of the research use cases. We will now describe every NFR below, with some additional details for each NFR:

NFR1 *Extensibility*: The development of deep learning models (UC3) and search approaches (UC5) should be easily extended by developers to introduce new deep learning algorithms and searching techniques. This

Different tabs
with settings

Classifier Selection
(Feed Forward
Neural Network)

Classifier Settings

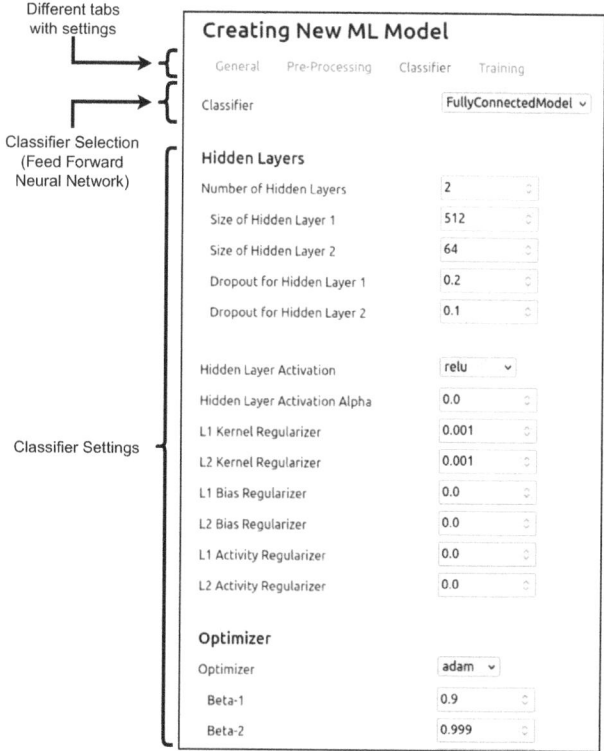

Fig. 3. Screenshot of the model creation screen in Maestro

1: Search bar with configurable amount of results.

2: Interface to optionally select a model to filter search results based on classifier predictions.
Users can filter issues based on the three decision types with fitlers "True", "False", and "Eithher".

3: Dropdown menu to select which projects in the database to search for issues.

4: List of search results.

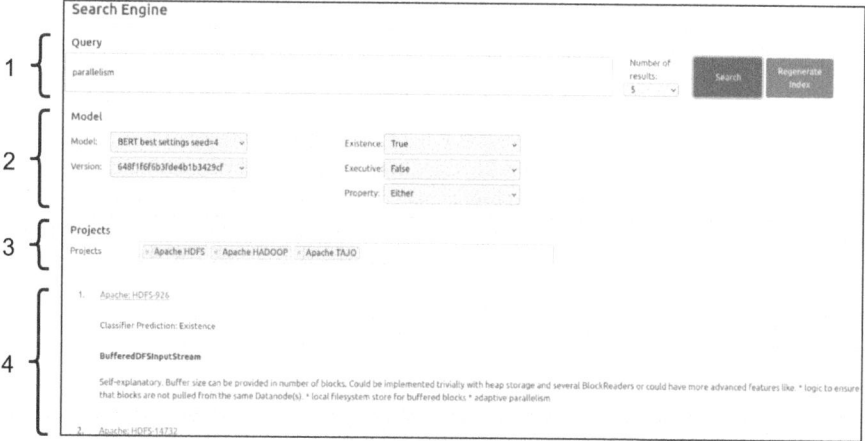

Fig. 4. Screenshot of the search screen in Maestro.

is especially important due to the fast evolution of techniques in the machine learning field.

NFR2 *Deployability*: Software engineers should be able to easily deploy Maestro's components without further guide. This is important due to the complexity of the system, and to facilitate the task for users who want to use the system without extending it.

NFR3 *Usability*: Software engineers and researchers with limited machine learning knowledge should be able to develop (UC3) and use (UC4) deep learning models, without further knowledge on programming models or libraries. This requirement is important, because many software engineering researchers and practitioners are not experts in machine learning.

NFR4 *Performance & Scalability*: The system must be able to scale to handle large amounts (millions) of issues, without experiencing malfunctions or timeouts. In particular, the size of the workload should not affect the loading times in the user interface.

NFR5 *Interoperability*: It should be possible to communicate with Maestro's components through standard interfaces without the user interface. This is important for researchers who might want to query the database or execute separate components of Maestro.

3   Architecture of Maestro

Maestro consists of four layers, each containing multiple components. The logical architecture is depicted in Fig. 5, and the physical architecture in Fig. 6. We explain below each layer in more details:

- The **Persistence Layer** contains four different databases: 1) a database that contains data on issues (e.g. summary and description), which we based on the dataset from Montgomery et al. [16]. 2) a database that contains data related to the manual annotation of issues (e.g. manual labels and discussions between researchers), and all deep learning related data (e.g. trained models, their configurations, performance scores), 3) a database that contains cached statistics data, and 4) a database for usernames and passwords.

- The **Data Access Layer** provides secure access to the databases using an API designed with authentication tactics. Furthermore, it contains components that can update the issues database with new issues from issue trackers (current only Jira is supported) to support the extensibility (**NFR1 – Extensibility**) of the system. We re-used the component created by Montgomery et al. [16], and enhanced it to be extensible.

  The **Data Access Layer** can be used by other components inside Maestro, but also by external components (**NFR1 – Extensibility**). For instance, a source code analysers meant to search for architectural design decisions in issue trackers could use the API in order to mark certain issues as likely to contain design decisions.

The API for accessing the database also provides pagination endpoints which allow the user interface to remain responsive and fast, even when dealing with large amounts of issues. Additionally, the database API uses streaming responses, which enables only loading part of the data from the database at a time, while still sending a large collection of data. This lowers the memory footprint of the program, and allows the API to scale even when large quantities of data are requested (**NFR4 – Performance & Scalability**).

– The **Processing Layer** contains two major components:

1) The *Keywords Search Engine* provides a centralised API for performing keyword searches (UC5) using Apache Lucene with additional filtering based on predictions made by classifiers and issue characteristics (e.g. number of comments on an issue). The centralised search engine interface enables the re-use of pre-computed indices for text search using Lucene.

2) The *Deep Learning Manager* acts as the backend for all deep learning related functionality outlined in UC2 and UC3. The deep learning was designed to be extensible (**NRF1 – Extensibility**) by application of the factory pattern. In Fig. 5, every "pipeline" makes use of one or more entities. (e.g. the feature generation pipeline uses feature generator entities). New entities, such as new feature generators or neural networks types, can be easily added by adding new entity classes which are instantiated through factories. By having the available entities and their configuration options exposed through a public API, other components (i.e. the UI) can adapt through dynamic run-time introspection and do not have to be modified to accommodate the addition of new functionality in the deep learning manager. This loosens the coupling between these components and improves extensibility (**NRF1 – Extensibility**) and maintainability of the system.

– The **User Interface** provides an interface for the user to fulfil all use-cases in Sect. 2.1. For instance, to achieve UC3, the UI presents different options for each deep learning model and provides a user-friendly interface to provide parameter values (**NRF3 – Usability**). Through the UI, researchers could initiate the training of machine learning models, and view accuracy scores in a concise overview. Moreover, researchers could manually view and classify issues (UC2). Further details on the UI can be viewed in our video[4]. The UI is designed according to the Model-View-Controller (MVC) pattern, and depends on the processing layer and the data access layer (see Fig. 5). Whenever possible, the UI uses pagination endpoints from the database API in order to remain responsive irrespective of the amount of data being worked with (**NFR4 – Performance & Scalability**).

Components can be deployed locally or remotely (Fig. 6), allowing data centralisation and offloading of computationally intensive tasks to other devices. By using Docker, we also improve cross-platform deployability and make installation of required software and deployment of Maestro's components easier (**NFR2**

---

[4] https://www.youtube.com/watch?v=sztY5it5Lb4.

– **Deployability**). Additionally, by separating the components into separate Docker files, subsets of components can be deployed if desired. This, combined with the fact that all back-ends components provide APIs, allows the re-use of Maestro's components with external tools and scripts (**NFR5 – Interoperability**).

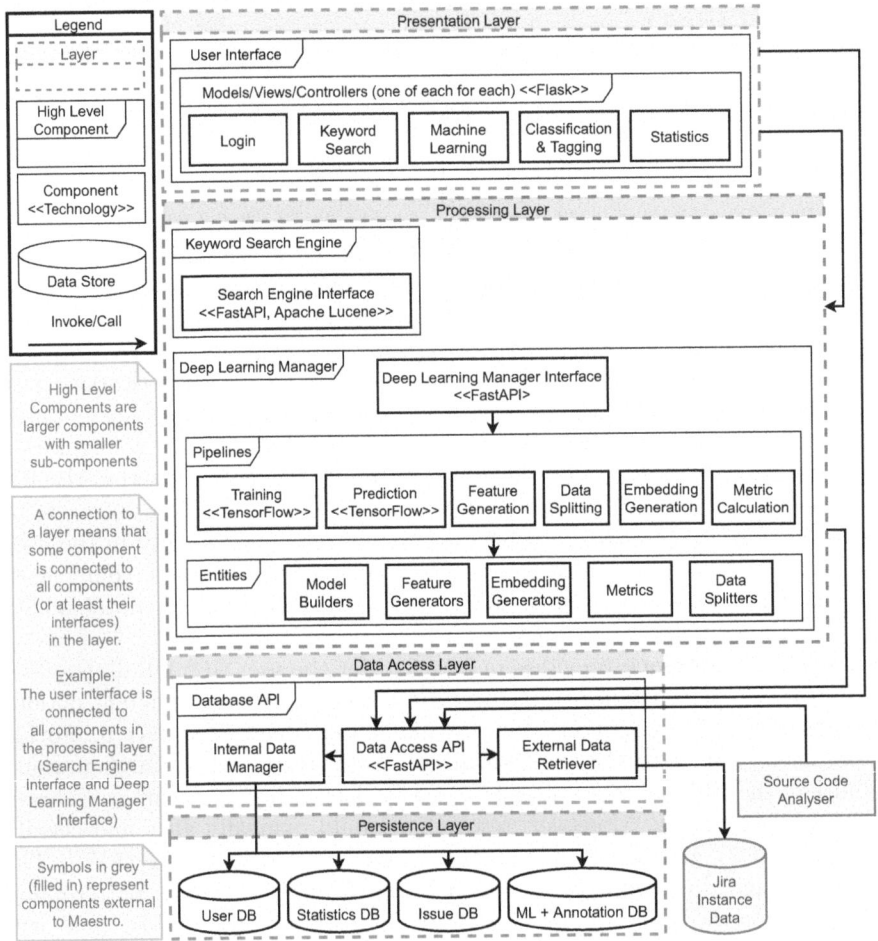

Fig. 5. The logical architecture of Maestro.

4   Research Process Leading to Maestro

Maestro is a result of a research project spanning more than 2 years of efforts ([13]) that aims to explore ADDs in issue tracking systems. The four authors

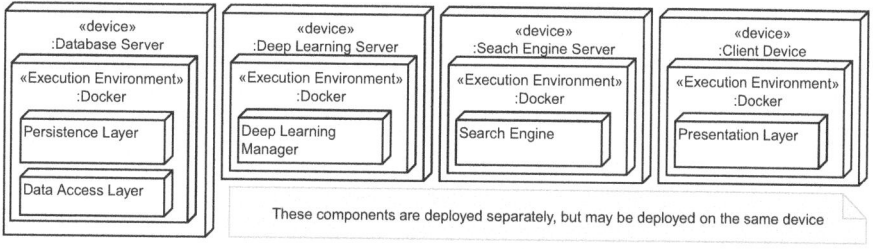

Fig. 6. The physical architecture of Maestro.

of this paper, as well as two other independent researchers, participated in this project. Our research follows an action research method [1], where researchers investigated the problem of finding and exploring architectural issues in issue trackers, evaluated in a research context (in later iterations using Maestro), and simultaneously developed approaches to find and analyse architectural issues. Various ideas, insights, and challenges encountered during this research have resulted into various custom-made solutions which ultimately ended up in the creation of Maestro. In this section, we will briefly explain the research process which formed the larger context in which – and as a result of which – Maestro was developed. This will illustrate what problems Maestro is meant to solve, how it was conceived from various challenges encountered during research, how it can improve over other methodologies, and how it can be used in research. In detail, we followed four phases, each consisting of an action and an evaluation steps. We explain below each phase and step, and associate them to the use-cases (UC) in Sect. 2.1:

– **Phase 1 - Random sampling to find architectural issues**:
  Action: We selected a random sample of 400 issues from six different open-source projects, and analysed them using qualitative analysis [23].
  Evaluation: The percentage of architectural issues range between 10–15% of the random sample, which shows that random sampling is not an effective approach to find ADDs in issue trackers; Manually finding issues containing ADDs would be too time consuming for the collection of large datasets.
– **Phase 2 - Keywords-search and source code analysis**:
  Action: Because random sampling was ineffective to find architectural issues, we experimented with two further approaches: searching using keywords from literature (**UC5**), and source code analysis [20]. Using both approaches, we selected 2179 candidate issues (**UC1**) from six open source projects from the Big Data domain (e.g. Apache Hadoop) to be manually analysed using qualitative analysis. For each issue, we downloaded its title and description in an excel sheet, and annotated the types of ADDs in their descriptions according to Kruchten et al. [12]: Existence, property and executive. Disagreements between researchers were discussed in separate meetings.
  Evaluation: Keywords searching and source code analysis were effective to find existence ADDs (precision > 50%), but suffered from low precision to find

property and executive ADDs (precision < 20%). Moreover, during the qualitative analysis, we realised that it is challenging to annotate large number of issues using Excel sheets, because some issues are long and contain formatting symbols, which cannot be correctly visualised. It was also challenging to track our discussions on issues during our meetings. These discussions were important to write and improve our coding book to annotate ADDs in issue trackers.

– **Phase 3 - Machine learning to find architectural issues**:
  Action: Because keywords-search and source code analysis were not effective (i.e. low precision) to find property and executive architectural issues, we trained different deep learning models to automatically classify architectural issues (**UC3**). We then used the model with the best accuracy (i.e. "BERT" model) to predict the types of issues (**UC4**), which have not been previously manually analysed. Accordingly, We sorted the issues identified from "BERT" model depending on the confidences obtained from the model to analyse manually (**UC1**). We developed the user interface of the tool to display and sort list of issues based on the confidences generated by deep learning models. Furthermore, we developed a dedicated user interface to annotate and tag issues based on the types of ADDs in their description (**UC2**).
  Evaluation: The tool showed significant usefulness to annotate issues, because researchers (allocated remotely) could directly view, discuss and classify issues in one process. According to our experience, using the tool was better than relying on excel sheets, especially in visualising long and complex issues. Moreover, the tool allows to discuss issues, and instantly add issues to the training set without any need to run other scripts or upload data, which prevent faults such as forgetting to include issues or inserting duplicate issues (i.e. the tool provides a consistent overview of all labelled issues for all users). Additionally, during annotations, the tool allows adding tags to issues, which helped us to mark issues that require a second opinion on their classification, and enabled us to track information about who annotated which issues, and how these issues were found (e.g. using keywords searching – **UC5**). This tagging functionality helped us to more easily identify groups of potentially miss-annotated issues. Furthermore, the UI brings notable enhancements to train deep learning models. Previously, we had to manually create configurations for each model, which was error-prone and tedious. However, the UI now clearly presents all available options for each model to facilitate creation, training and evaluation. Using this new functionality of the tool, we performed UC2-UC4 in 3 iterations to expand our dataset to reach 2210 architectural issues and 2903 non-architectural issues. The deep learning models had a precision (sometimes far) exceeding 50% for finding issues containing executive and property ADDs, making deep learning an effective method to find such ADDs.

– **Phase 4 - Find architectural issues from different domains**:
  Action: In the previous phases, we explored ADDs in six open-source projects from the Big Data domain. In this phase, we explore ADDs in projects from different domains other than Big Data. Thus, we re-used a recent dataset

from Montgomery et al. [16], which contains more than 2.7 million Jira issues from 1352 projects that belong to six different domains including Big Data, Cloud Computing, SOA, and DevOps. We trained and executed the best performing model (i.e. "BERT") to identify architectural issues and predict the types of ADDs in all issues in the dataset (**UC4**). We also developed a statistical analysis functionality in the tool (**UC6**) to visualise the types of ADDs in the different domains, as well as the characteristics of architectural issues such as time to resolve and the amount of discussion in comments.

Evaluation: Using the tool, we automatically identified 250,708 architectural issues from the six domains. Moreover, we determined the most common types of ADDs per domain, and compared characteristics of architectural issues per domain. For example, issues that discuss property ADDs were most involved and took longer time to resolve. The statistical functionality in the tool (**UC6**) shows its usefulness to explore ADDs in a massive number of architectural issues.

5 Limitations

In this section, we will cover some of the limitations of Maestro, as well as some possible proposals for improvements. We came up with these limitations by 1) considering the degree to which Maestro fulfils our desired requirements, and 2) comparing the workflow in Maestro with our old workflow using spreadsheets (see Sect. 4), focusing on the quality attributes expressed in our non-functional requirements.

- **Functionalities**
  Currently Maestro is limited to importing issues from Jira issue trackers. We aim to expand the scope of Maestro to import issues from other issue trackers, such as Git issues or Bugzilla.
- **Extensibility**
  While the deep learning manager was specifically designed to be extensible, the search engine does not fulfil this requirement to the same degree. Thus, refactoring of the search engine is required to make it extensible and flexible for changes.
- **Deployability**
  Maestro can be deployed using Docker, which enables a fairly platform-independent and quick deployment. However, the setup process is still fairly involved, requiring manually executing separate steps, which could be automated in a single process.
- **Usability**
  Few functionalities (e.g., importing issues from Jira, calculating Kappa, and adding custom tags to issues) cannot be directly executed from the user interface and require calling API functions and scripts. These functionalities require separate user interfaces.

– **Performance & Scalability**
   The deep learning manager is, as is the nature of deep learning, a resource intensive component. In some cases, this is exacerbated by the use of sub-optimal data representations (e.g. dense versus sparse arrays), and lack of streamed feature generation and learning (i.e. all data is loaded into memory at once). Both these things could be changed to improve scalability.

One final potential limitation, unrelated to our non-functional requirements, is the lack of evaluation by practitioners. Specifically, we have no prior empirical evidence – and have not yet evaluated – how practitioners would benefit from Maestro's functionalities, how they would benefit from the recovered ADDs from issue trackers.

6   Related Work

Several traditional architectural knowledge management tools have been previously proposed [24]. These tools store and document ADDs in repositories and templates, which need to be manually populated. On the other hand, our proposed tool Maestro focuses on ADDs discussed in issue tracking systems.

The closest tool to Maestro is ADeX [4], which can classify architectural issues using machine learning. Moreover, ADeX can recommend developers for making certain ADDs based on personal expertise. While both tools ADeX and Maestro aim to find and explore ADDs in issue trackers, our proposed tool Maestro is different from ADeX in the following points:

– Maestro allows researchers to apply qualitative analysis (in UC2), and add manually classified issues to the training dataset. Moreover, Maestro supports keywords-based searches (in UC5), which allows researchers to easily expand their dataset of architectural issues through a snowballing process. This process is not supported by ADeX.
– Maestro provides a user-friendly UI to train and evaluate *new deep learning models* (in UC3 and UC4), which can help researchers to evolve models for classifying architectural issues. This flexibility is not provided by ADeX, which provides pre-trained machine learning models for classification. The accuracy of the pre-trained model is fixed based on Bhat et al. [3].
– Maestro has been evaluated on a large dataset of issues with 2.7 million issues from different domains, which show its scalability and usefulness to run on projects from different domains. In contrast, ADeX has been applied on two open source projects.
– Maestro is open source[5] and is designed to be extended by other researchers or practitioners. In contrast, the source code of ADeX is not referenced by the authors of ADeX.

---

[5] https://github.com/mining-design-decisions/Maestro.

The authors are not aware of other tools to search for ADDs in software repositories. However, some approaches have been proposed to find ADDs. However, they have not been developed into tools. For instance, Shahbazian et al. [18,19] proposed a machine learning approach to identify ADDs in issue tracking system. They employed static source code analysis to identify architectural code changes between different versions of a system, identify commits in which these changes were introduced, and map these commits to the corresponding issues in the issue tracker. Shahbazian et al. assumed that these issues contain architectural discussions, and trained their prediction classifier on issues identified using this described approach. The most important difference with our work, is that all our issues were manually inspected and annotated. During this process, we also found that not all architectural changes result in architectural discussions (also not all architectural discussions lead to architectural code changes).

Other sources have also been explored as sources for architectural knowledge. In [25], Viviani et al. used machine learning to detect architectural knowledge in paragraphs of comments in GitHub pull requests. Stack Overflow has also been explored by various researchers. In [5] automatic mining of discussions on architectural tactics and quality attributes from StackOverflow was evaluated. In [21], Soliman et al. developed a search approach for architectural discussions in StackOverflow posts which is somewhat similar to the approach used by Maestro. Soliman et al. proposed a keyword search, which is then re-ranked based on predictions made by a classifier which classified posts as either "Pure programming post", "Technology identification", "Technology evaluation", or "Features and configuration". This is different from Maestro, because 1) we implemented a strict filtering and not a re-ranking, and 2) we filter based on the decision types "existence", 'executive", and "property".

7   Conclusion

We developed Maestro, an open source tool for finding, and exploring architectural issues that discuss design decisions. Our experience with Maestro showed its usefulness to find and annotate 5113 issues, and develop deep learning models that automatically classified 250,708 architectural issues. Contrary to existing tools, Maestro supports researchers to find and annotate architectural issues through keywords searching, deep learning models and snowballing. Our future work focuses on evaluating Maestro with practitioners to evaluate its usefulness to re-use ADDs from issue trackers. Furthermore, we aim to use Maestro to further expand our dataset with new issues from different projects, and different issue trackers. This can improve the accuracy and generalizability of Maestro. Finally, at the time of writing, we are working on major refactorings for the components of Maestro to mitigate some of its limitations.

References

1. Baskerville, R.L., Wood-Harper, A.T.: A critical perspective on action research as a method for information systems research. In: Willcocks, L.P., Sauer, C., Lacity, M.C. (eds.) Enacting Research Methods in Information Systems: Volume 2, pp. 169–190. Springer, Cham (2016). https://doi.org/10.1007/978-3-319-29269-4_7

2. Bass, L., Clements, P., Kazman, R.: Software Architecture in Practice. Addison-Wesley Professional, Upper Saddle River (2003)

3. Bhat, M., Shumaiev, K., Biesdorf, A., Hohenstein, U., Matthes, F.: Automatic extraction of design decisions from issue management systems: a machine learning based approach. In: Lopes, A., de Lemos, R. (eds.) ECSA 2017. LNCS, vol. 10475, pp. 138–154. Springer, Cham (2017). https://doi.org/10.1007/978-3-319-65831-5_10

4. Bhat, M., Tinnes, C., Shumaiev, K., Biesdorf, A., Hohenstein, U., Matthes, F.: ADeX: a tool for automatic curation of design decision knowledge for architectural decision recommendations. In: 2019 IEEE International Conference on Software Architecture Companion (ICSA-C), pp. 158–161 (2019). https://doi.org/10.1109/ICSA-C.2019.00035

5. Bi, T., Liang, P., Tang, A., Xia, X.: Mining architecture tactics and quality attributes knowledge in stack overflow. J. Syst. Softw. **180**, 111005 (2021). https://doi.org/10.1016/j.jss.2021.111005

6. Buschmann, F., Meunier, R., Rohnert, H., Sommerlad, P., Stal, M.: Pattern-Oriented Software Architecture, Volume 1: A System of Patterns. Wiley, Chichester, UK (1996)

7. Capilla, R., Jansen, A., Tang, A., Avgeriou, P., Babar, M.A.: 10 years of software architecture knowledge management: practice and future. J. Syst. Softw. **116**, 191–205 (2015). https://doi.org/10.1016/j.jss.2015.08.054

8. Chung, J., Gulcehre, C., Cho, K., Bengio, Y.: Empirical Evaluation of Gated Recurrent Neural Networks on Sequence Modeling (2014). https://doi.org/10.48550/arXiv.1412.3555

9. Cohen, J.: A coefficient of agreement for nominal scales. Educ. Psychol. Measur. **20**(1), 37–46 (1960). https://doi.org/10.1177/001316446002000104

10. Devlin, J., Chang, M.W., Lee, K., Toutanova, K.: BERT: pre-training of deep bidirectional transformers for language understanding (2019). https://doi.org/10.48550/arXiv.1810.04805

11. Hochreiter, S., Schmidhuber, J.: Long short-term memory. Neural Comput. **9**, 1735–80 (1997). https://doi.org/10.1162/neco.1997.9.8.1735

12. Kruchten, P.: An ontology of architectural design decisions in software intensive systems. In: 2nd Groningen Workshop on Software Variability (2004)

13. Maarleveld, J., Dekker, A.: Developing Deep Learning Approaches to Find and Classify Architectural Design Decisions in Issue Tracking Systems. M.Sc. thesis, University of Groningen (2023). https://fse.studenttheses.ub.rug.nl/31368/

14. Manteuffel, C., Avgeriou, P., Hamberg, R.: An exploratory case study on reusing architecture decisions in software-intensive system projects. J. Syst. Softw. **144**, 60–83 (2018). https://doi.org/10.1016/j.jss.2018.05.064

15. Mikolov, T., Chen, K., Corrado, G., Dean, J.: Efficient Estimation of Word Representations in Vector Space (2013). https://doi.org/10.48550/arXiv.1301.3781

16. Montgomery, L., Lüders, C., Maalej, W.: An alternative issue tracking dataset of public Jira repositories. In: Proceedings of the 19th International Conference on Mining Software Repositories, pp. 73–77 (2022). https://doi.org/10.1145/3524842.3528486

17. Ren, X., Xing, Z., Xia, X., Lo, D., Wang, X., Grundy, J.: Neural network-based detection of self-admitted technical debt: from performance to explainability. ACM Trans. Software Eng. Methodol. **28**(3), 15:1–15:45 (2019). https://doi.org/10.1145/3324916
18. Shahbazian, A., Kyu Lee, Y., Le, D., Brun, Y., Medvidovic, N.: Recovering architectural design decisions. In: Proceedings - 2018 IEEE 15th International Conference on Software Architecture, ICSA 2018, pp. 95–104 (2018). https://doi.org/10.1109/ICSA.2018.00019
19. Shahbazian, A., Nam, D., Medvidovic, N.: Toward predicting architectural significance of implementation issues. Proceedings - International Conference on Software Engineering pp. 215–219 (2018). https://doi.org/10.1145/3196398.3196440
20. Soliman, M., Galster, M., Avgeriou, P.: An exploratory study on architectural knowledge in issue tracking systems. In: Biffl, S., Navarro, E., Löwe, W., Sirjani, M., Mirandola, R., Weyns, D. (eds.) ECSA 2021. LNCS, vol. 12857, pp. 117–133. Springer, Cham (2021). https://doi.org/10.1007/978-3-030-86044-8_8
21. Soliman, M., Rekaby Salama, A., Galster, M., Zimmermann, O., Riebisch, M.: Improving the search for architecture knowledge in online developer communities. In: 2018 IEEE International Conference on Software Architecture (ICSA), pp. 186–18609 (2018). https://doi.org/10.1109/ICSA.2018.00028
22. Soliman, M., Riebisch, M., Zdun, U.: Enriching architecture knowledge with technology design decisions. In: 2015 12th Working IEEE/IFIP Conference on Software Architecture, pp. 135–144 (2015). https://doi.org/10.1109/WICSA.2015.14
23. Stol, K.J., Ralph, P., Fitzgerald, B.: Grounded theory in software engineering research: a critical review and guidelines. In: Proceedings of the 38th International Conference on Software Engineering. ICSE ', pp. 120–13116, New York, NY, USA. Association for Computing Machinery (2016). https://doi.org/10.1145/2884781.2884833
24. Tang, A., Avgeriou, P., Jansen, A., Capilla, R., Ali Babar, M.: A comparative study of architecture knowledge management tools. J. Syst. Softw. **83**(3), 352–370 (2010). https://doi.org/10.1016/j.jss.2009.08.032
25. Viviani, G., Famelis, M., Xia, X., Janik-Jones, C., Murphy, G.C.: Locating latent design information in developer discussions: a study on pull requests. IEEE Trans. Software Eng. **47**(7), 1402–1413 (2021). https://doi.org/10.1109/TSE.2019.2924006
26. Weinreich, R., Groher, I.: Software architecture knowledge management approaches and their support for knowledge management activities: a systematic literature review. Inf. Softw. Technol. **80**, 265–286 (2016). https://doi.org/10.1016/j.infsof.2016.09.007
27. Weinreich, R., Groher, I., Miesbauer, C.: An expert survey on kinds, influence factors and documentation of design decisions in practice. Futur. Gener. Comput. Syst. **47**, 145–160 (2015). https://doi.org/10.1016/j.future.2014.12.002

Industry Track

Demeter: An Architecture for Long-Term Monitoring of Software Power Consumption

Lylian Siffre[1], Gabriel Breuil[1], Adel Noureddine[2(✉)] [ID], and Renaud Pawlak[3]

[1] Constellation, Saint-Cloud, France
`lylian.siffre@impakt.iq gabriel.breuil@dlr.de`
[2] Universite de Pau et des Pays de l'Adour, E2S UPPA, LIUPPA, Pau, France
`adel.noureddine@univ-pau.fr`
[3] Cinchéo, Paris, France
`renaud.pawlak@cincheo.com`

Abstract. Quantifying and long-term monitoring of the energy consumption of software in end-user computers is a complex task. It brings multiple technical and sociological challenges. End users need to visualize their energy consumption and get a per-software feedback about their energy impact to adapt their software usage towards a greener approach. In this paper, we present our monitoring and feedback architecture: Demeter. Our distributed approach monitors energy consumption per application on runtime, provides end users with immediate feedback through a graphical user interface, and delayed feedback through an analysis email notification. We illustrate our approach with a two-week study of software usage of three different user profiles in a corporate environment.

Keywords: Power Monitoring · Measurement · Energy Consumption · Long-term monitoring · Distributed Architecture · Software Engineering

1 Introduction

Information and Communications Technology (ICT) has direct, indirect, and extended effects. The direct effects are the production, use, and disposal of hardware while the indirect effects are the effects of use (induction and obsolescence) and the extended effects (rebound and emerging risks) [8]. The indirect impacts are due to the abstract representation of software, API, browsers, networks, virtualization, and the offshoring of the manifold data centers over the world [3,9]. Thus, one has to evaluate how much is ICT energy consuming and what are the solutions to reduce its energy consumption. The impact of ICT is already at 4% of the total worldwide energy consumption, more than civil aviation [6]. It is expected that in 2030 the energy consumption of ICT will triple [13].

© The Author(s), under exclusive license to Springer Nature Switzerland AG 2024
B. Tekinerdoğan et al. (Eds.): ECSA 2023, LNCS 14590, pp. 409–425, 2024.
https://doi.org/10.1007/978-3-031-66326-0_25

Basic variants of energy consumption monitoring software, such as the task manager, are available on modern OS to inform qualitatively on the software energy consumption. Unfortunately, the given data are not always accurate nor specific. In the past ten years, scientists and practitioners have focused their research on developing more elaborate energy-probing software. Johann *et al.* [12] discussed the importance of using a generic metric to quantify energy consumption. They suggest two methods: 1) a white-box method consists in measuring the energy consumption of the source code and 2) a black-box method consists in measuring the energy consumption of the whole software. The latter allows one to perform benchmark and individual measurements on computers. Two major issues arise from the existing energy probing software: 1) they only quantify the energy consumption of a specific group of software [5,11,16] or of the general energy consumption of a computer without software specification, and 2) the probing software is not hardware specific. Even though the CPU is well known to be energy consuming, it is essential to consider the energy consumption of every hardware component [4,11,16].

Most recent monitoring software at the component and application levels, such as Jolinar and PowerJoular [10,15], are capable of monitoring hardware components for a limited number of applications (typically one application or process), and are primarily available on server environments or Linux systems. In particular, existing monitoring solutions are either limited in capabilities (*i.e.*, only monitoring specific hardware components or a particular software), or cannot scale up for multi-days or weeks of monitoring (*i.e.*, huge data collected, high CPU or energy impact of the monitoring tool, invasive monitoring interface, etc.). Moreover, end users tend to be less savvy and more reluctant to install monitoring software on their computers. The difficulty is in convincing users and administrators alike to deploy a monitoring software. Our goal is summarized in two main objectives: 1) provide a long-term monitoring software (days and weeks measurements), and 2) provide energy feedback to users with fine granularity (per-application and per-hardware component). Our presented software architecture, Demeter, implements these two objectives and allows practitioners, researchers, and industrial managers to study the energy impact of devices and users, and encourage eco-friendly software usage behavior.

In this article, we first present Demeter's architecture and its energy consumption models in Sect. 2. Then we present, in Sect. 3, a use case scenario using Demeter and aiming towards studying the energy impact of users' software usage in a corporate environment. Finally, we conclude in Sect. 4.

2   Architecture of Demeter

In this section, we present Demeter's architecture. The intended purpose is to develop a probing software capable of monitoring the energy consumption of various applications. Demeter interacts with the end user (who can view its power consumption and get immediate or delayed feedback), and with applications and the OS in order to collect statistics of usage and estimate energy consumption.

Demeter focuses on four criteria:

- *simplicity* fosters clear code comprehension, effortless software usage and installation, and streamlined data utilization.
- *energy efficiency* aims to ensure the software produces accurate results while minimizing energy consumption.
- *adaptability* refers to the capacity of the architecture to accommodate a diverse spectrum of use cases, ensuring its suitability for a wide range of applications.
- and *lightness* entails minimizing the reliance on external libraries and producing lightweight output files.

We model the architecture of Demeter using the C4 software architecture model[1]. The system context diagram of Demeter is presented in Fig. 1, showing the interactions between the end user, applications, the operating system, and Demeter itself.

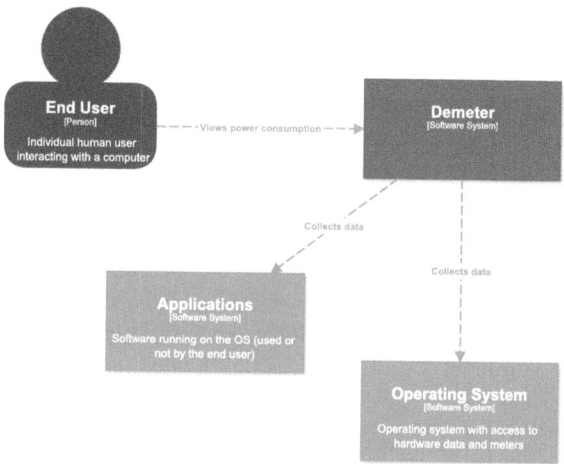

Fig. 1. System context diagram of Demeter architecture

Figure 2 presents the container diagram of Demeter with its three main parts:

- Monitoring Application (MA): responsible for the usage and power monitoring of every application and hardware component. It collects data from running applications and the OS and provides the results to the graphical user interface and to the reporting server.
- Graphical User Interface (GUI): a graphical interface software allowing per-application visualization to end users, aggregated statistics, and historical power usages.

---

[1] https://c4model.com/.

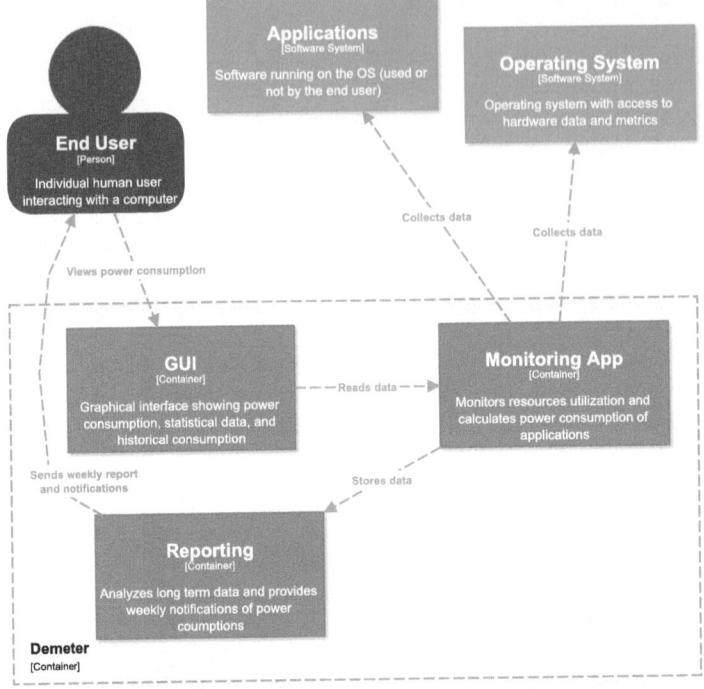

Fig. 2. Container diagram of Demeter architecture

– Reporting Server (RS): responsible for analyzing long-term power data, providing weekly summaries and notifications to end users about their energy usage and impacts.

Figure 3 presents the component diagram of the Monitoring Application. Each hardware component has a dedicated software component implementing the relevant sensors to collect usage or power data, and its associated power formulas and models to estimate its power consumption. An additional component is also implemented to collect processes and applications information and usage, and a utility component manages the input/output of the application and communications with the Remote Server. Demeter's architecture is OS-agnostic, but our initial implementation only targets Microsoft Windows as it is the most used desktop OS in corporate environments.

2.1   Monitoring Application Implementation

This section describes the implementation of the Monitoring Application (the source code is available under an open source license [2]), and the tradeoffs we made to accommodate the four criterion.

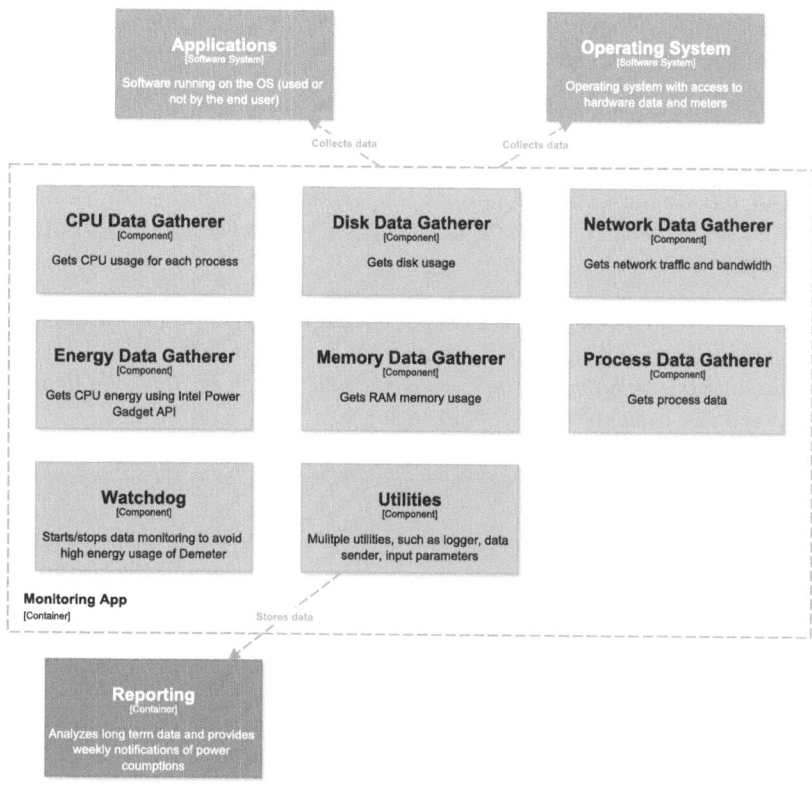

Fig. 3. Component diagram of Demeter's Monitoring Application

To satisfy the *simplicity* criterion, we decided to develop a one-agent probing software. Thus a non-Object-Oriented Programming (OOP) approach seems to be more suitable, reducing the memory footprint of Demeter and the cost of object creation and management.

Motivated by the *energy efficiency* criterion, we programmed in C++ since it is ranked among the most energy efficient programming languages [17].

To accommodate to most use cases, according to the *adaptability* criteria, each data source is handled in an independent file, thus no side effect on the software can be expected when adding or removing a data source. The behavior of Demeter is based on a unique periodic `while` loop for which the time between two iterations of this loop is at least an interval long. It will sequentially collect data from all activated sources (*i.e.*, calls to a function).

To ensure a light and low external dependency software and satisfy the *lightness* criteria, we prioritized on using system APIs. For instance, gathering memory, disk and CPU data is done through calls to the Windows Win32 API[2].

---

[2] https://learn.microsoft.com/en-us/windows/win32/api/.

However, for network and CPU energy data collection, we must rely on third party drivers as described in the next paragraphs.

CPU: The CPU is the most consuming computing component (besides the display) in a laptop without a dedicated graphics card [14]. There are two major ways to monitor CPU energy consumption from a computer: 1) using a power meter and applying a statistical approach to isolate the CPU energy, or 2) using a mathematical model to estimate the CPU energy consumption and of applications [7,15].

Implementation: In Demeter, the energy consumption is collected through Running Average Power Limit (RAPL) and Intel Power Gadget API (IPG). They are model-based software and are precise enough to rely on [18]. We define the CPU percentage usage of a process as in Eq. 1.

$$U = (\frac{t_{\text{user}} + t_{\text{kernel}}}{t_{\text{total}}})/n_{\text{cores}} \tag{1}$$

Where n_{cores} is the CPU's core amount, t_{user} is the duration during which the process runs in user mode, t_{kernel} is the duration during which the process runs in kernel mode and t_{total} is the duration during which the CPU is active and idle. These values are retrieved from PSAPI[3]. In Eq. 1, the sum between t_{kernel} and t_{user} corresponds to the invested CPU time for a process. To avoid having values above 100%, it is required to divide by n_{cores}.

Hard Drive: Modern hard drives use different technologies, such as in SSD or mechanical drives. Even drives with the same technology have different read and write operation costs. In our probe, we base our disk model on hardware specifications provided by manufacturers in order to estimate the disk energy consumption. For instance, in our experiments, we use the NVMe KBG40ZNS512G NVMe KIOXIA 512 GB disk, where the manufacturer provides detailed information about read and write costs [1].

Implementation: We use the read and write performance power ratio to calculate the disk energy consumption, in addition to the idle power consumption. This ratio is usually provided by manufacturers of modern disk drives. In addition, if the sequential read and write performance power ratio is also given, we take this ratio into consideration as it is more aligned with disk operations.

Network: Our aim is to probe the energy consumed by the network interface controller as Demeter will only estimate the energy consumed by the computer and its components.

Implementation: Gathering the bandwidth for every process is done using the Npcap driver[4]. Npcap sniffs and reads the content of every packet passing through a network interface. Every available network interface of the computer is

---

[3] https://learn.microsoft.com/en-US/windows/win32/psapi/psapi-functions.
[4] https://npcap.com.

then opened and sniffed. For each process, the upstream and downstream bandwidths are gathered by our packet parser, using Npcap. The network energy consumption of a given software is the sum of its processes energy consumption. In our approach, for each packet, we increase the bandwidth counter of the port it goes through by the size of the packet. For every loop iteration, ports are mapped to the corresponding process that has opened the port. The corresponding process accounts for each and every bit that has gone through the port since the last loop iteration.

We base our model on data from Ethernet transceiver's data sheet of manufacturers. In particular, most transceiver can negotiate multiple bitrates, such as $10/100/1000$ Mb$\cdot$s^{-1}, each with its own energy consumption.

WatchDog: Demeter has to control its CPU usage to have the smallest impact on the system. Our CPU consumption regulator is called WatchDog (WD), which can be activated or deactivated by the user.

Implementation: The WatchDog will pause Demeter's activity if it becomes too CPU-consuming. The calibration of the WD is based on the CPU average consumption of Demeter over the first hour. It pauses the software for one minute if it detects an over-consumption (*i.e.* if its energy consumption is higher than three times the energy mean value during the calibration hour). Pausing has consequences as data gathering and exporting are stopped. As the network is sniffed by our parser, all data is lost during the pause. The CPU and disk data are not impacted as they are probed continuously by external software. All network consumption data are lost, but the CPU energy consumption data is not because it is probed through IPG. Disk transfer data is metered by the operating system (Windows) and stored in counters. Therefore, pausing does not affect disk consumption data. We discuss the impact of our WatchDog function in Sect. 2.3.

2.2   Data Feedback

In this section, we discuss the two types of feedback Demeter proposes. Data can be viewed in real-time or aggregated over time, both bringing different insights. To leverage all the benefits of collecting and processing data, we decided to exploit both real-time data and aggregated data. These two types of feedback are described in the next two sections.

Immediate Feedback Through a Graphical User Interface (GUI): The GUI (shown in Fig. 4) aims to give immediate feedback to users as Demeter is also meant to be used by non-technical end users. The GUI is desktop application relying on the monitoring data provided by the Monitoring Application.

The GUI allows the user to create their own dashboard by adding, moving, and removing graphics. The graphics can be configured with two main parameters: the program to plot and the resource to plot. The user has the possibility to display its real-time energy consumption, the cumulative energy consumption of an hour of the day, and the cumulative energy per day of the current week.

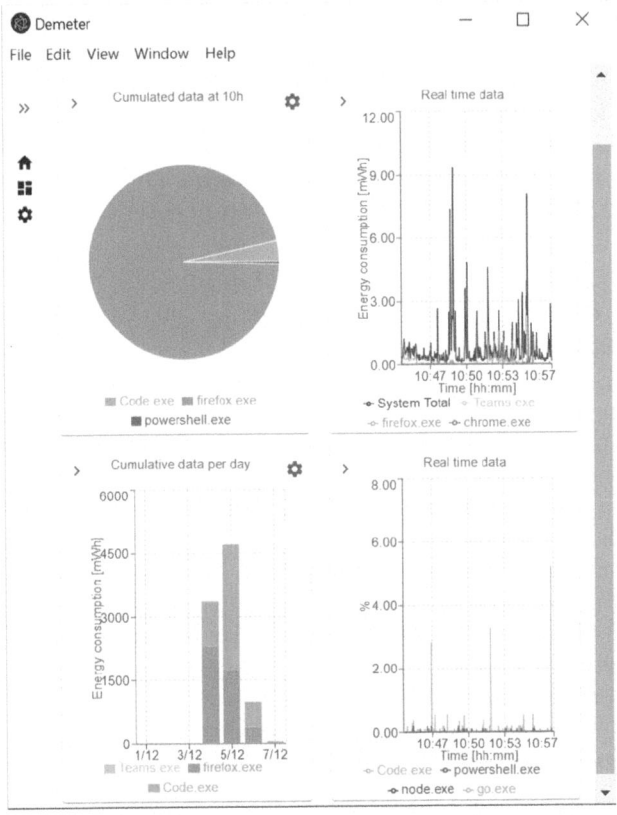

Fig. 4. Screenshot of Demeter's GUI

The GUI allows end users to monitor the power consumption of all applications. For each application, users can monitor real-time power consumption, the historical power evolution (through time), and aggregated statistics about power usage. The flexibility of the GUI (per-application and system-wide measurements and statistics), allows end users to customize the interface according to their desires and needs, thus allowing a personalized approach with the tool and in regards to power consumption. We argue that such a relationship where the user feels empowered in freely and easily choosing what to follow might lead to better engagement with power efficiency software usage best practices, and thus to an overall reduction of power consumption.

Delayed Feedback Through Cloud Notifications: The third part of Demeter is the Remote Server (RS). The server component is responsible for: 1) storing all power data sent by the Monitoring Application for all related users (for instance, one RS can handle all users in an office, a company, or a building); 2) analyzing per-user and cross-user power consumption patterns and trends, and providing an overview of a population's power profiles (for example, through a dashboard); and 3) sending recurrent notifications to users with a summary of their power consumption along with trends and recommendations for power reductions. For instance, an email notification could be sent to users in a corporate environment with the power analysis of their consumption of the prior week.

In the next section, we validate our architecture and power models, then present a real-world experiment scenario using Demeter to monitor users' software and energy usage in a corporate environment.

2.3   Validation

In this section, we validate our architecture, in particular the monitoring application, in accordance with the four criteria. Demeter uses Intel's APIs to estimate the power consumption of the CPU, and we use existing state-of-the-art power models for the other hardware components. Therefore, we consider that Demeter provides accurate power readings as far as Intel's API and existing power models are accurate.

The simplicity of Demeter is shown in the simple installation and usage of its monitoring application. The latter is built where each power model component is self-sufficient with no dependencies on other power models. Thus, it is simple to add a new energy consumption model of another hardware component. The application only depends on two external libraries: Npcap and Intel Power Gadget.

We perform benchmark tests using SilverBench[5] on a web page on Firefox. The benchmark is an online multi-core CPU benchmark that uses JavaScript and lasts around 10 min. All other applications and services are stopped during the benchmark session. Demeter's monitoring is adaptable as data is collected in a variable interval. This interval is configurable by the user, and we evaluate the value of the smallest interval that gives accurate data and is also long enough for the runtime calculations of Demeter to finish. We calculate the mean value and the standard deviation of the duration of a probing and writing loop during one benchmark with the following configuration, *no WD, 5-s time step*. We then obtain a time length t_{loop} such that:

$$t_{loop} = 1.97 \pm 1.46 \,\text{s} \tag{2}$$

The benchmark test lasted 8 min 57 s and 106 measurements are listed. Four have lasted more than five seconds (5.78 s, 6.27 s, 5.97 s, and 5.07 s). We can assess

---

[5] https://silver.urih.com.

that the lowest recommended monitoring interval is five seconds. A smaller time interval would not increase the accuracy of the measurements.

The energy efficiency of Demeter is analyzed through an empirical validation of its various configurations: the use or not of the watchdog (WD) function and the duration between two measurements (5 s, 30 s, and 60 s). We repeat the experiment 20 times with each configuration. In Table 1, we gather the mean values of the total energy ($\overline{E_{tot}}$), power consumption ($\overline{P}$), and size of the output file ($\overline{size}$). We also calculate the related standard deviations for each mean value ($\sigma_{\overline{E_{tot}}}$, $\sigma_{\overline{P}}$, and $\sigma_{\overline{size}}$). The total energy and power consumption are given for Demeter and for the Firefox web page on which the benchmark is launched.

Table 1. Mean values of the total energy ($\overline{E_{tot}}$) and power ($\overline{P}$) with their respective standard deviations ($\sigma_{\overline{E_{tot}}}$ and $\sigma_{\overline{P}}$) for the benchmark test on Firefox and with six configurations on Demeter – 5-s, 30-s, 60-s, WD and 5-s, WD and 30-s, WD and 60-s step.

Configuration	$\overline{E_{tot}}$ [Wh]	$\sigma_{\overline{E_{tot}}}$ [Wh]	$\overline{P}$ [W]	$\sigma_{\overline{P}}$ [W]	$\overline{size}$ [Ko]	$\sigma_{\overline{size}}$ [Ko]
Demeter						
WD - 5 s	$21.65 \cdot 10^{-3}$	$9.27 \cdot 10^{-3}$	$143.82 \cdot 10^{-3}$	$59.81 \cdot 10^{-3}$	621.00	43.17
WD - 30 s	$3.07 \cdot 10^{-3}$	$0.51 \cdot 10^{-3}$	$20.98 \cdot 10^{-3}$	$3.10 \cdot 10^{-3}$	104.30	3.98
WD - 60 s	$2.08 \cdot 10^{-3}$	$0.54 \cdot 10^{-3}$	$14.26 \cdot 10^{-3}$	$4.02 \cdot 10^{-3}$	56.10	3.56
WD - 5s	$10.33 \cdot 10^{-3}$	$4.20 \cdot 10^{-3}$	$71.45 \cdot 10^{-3}$	$28.28 \cdot 10^{-3}$	184.13	60.87
WD - 30s	$3.42 \cdot 10^{-3}$	$1.39 \cdot 10^{-3}$	$23.02 \cdot 10^{-3}$	$9.85 \cdot 10^{-3}$	86.80	12.79
WD - 60s	$2.49 \cdot 10^{-3}$	$1.31 \cdot 10^{-3}$	$17.42 \cdot 10^{-3}$	$9.80 \cdot 10^{-3}$	45.15	5.42
Benchmark test on Firefox						
WD - 5 s	6.86	0.67	46.56	8.12		
WD - 30 s	6.95	0.27	47.80	4.98		
WD - 60 s	6.61	0.35	47.44	6.08		
WD - 5 s	7.05	0.18	49.02	2.50		
WD - 30 s	6.61	0.58	44.99	8.31		
WD - 60 s	6.61	0.53	46.61	7.37		

The larger the time step between two measurements, the lower the energy consumption of Demeter. We see in Table 1 that the 60-s configuration is less consuming than the two others. Indeed, Demeter is consuming $\overline{E_{tot}}(60\,s) = 2.08 \cdot 10^{-3}$ Wh while it consumes $\overline{E_{tot}}(30\,s) = 3.07 \cdot 10^{-3}$ Wh and $\overline{E_{tot}}(5\,s) = 21.65 \cdot 10^{-3}$ Wh for the two other configurations, respectively. We observe a similar behavior concerning the different time steps when Demeter is used with the WD function. The WD function allows Demeter to go into sleep mode if its energy consumption is too high and so it artificially increases the time step of the software. Therefore, we observe, for the same time step, a decrease in the energy consumption of Demeter when the WD function is activated. For example, in the case of a 5-s configuration, Demeter consumes $\overline{E_{tot}}(WD-5\,s) = 10.33 \cdot 10^{-3}$ Wh when the WD is activated while it consumes $\overline{E_{tot}}(5\,s) = 21.65 \cdot 10^{-3}$ Wh without. Since the total energy decreases when the time step increases and the duration of the benchmark tests are the same, it is clear that the power related to the energy consumption of Demeter decreases as well.

When the WD puts Demeter in sleep mode, we miss data on the energy consumption of the network and of the hard disk. This is why the total energy of the Firefox web page consumes less energy than when the WD is not activated, but we still get the same order of magnitude. The benchmark test consumes with and without the WD function for a 60-s configuration $\overline{E_{tot}}(WD-60\,s) = 6.61$ Wh and $E_{tot}(60\,s) = 6.61$ Wh, respectively. As Intel Power Gadget probes the energy consumption of the CPU, and even if the data are not collected by Demeter, IPG still stores the monitored values. Whensoever Demeter will collect the CPU's energy, it will be the exact energy consumption. However, it is not possible to recover the energy consumption related to the network during the activation of the WD. Thus, we have a less accurate measurement when the duration of the step increases and with the frequency of WD activations.

Finally, the lightness of Demeter is validated where an increase in the time length or the activation of the WD function reduces the number of measurements and therefore reduces the size of the output files. When the WD function is not activated, we observe a decrease of 6 and 12 times the weight of the output file when the time step is of 30 and 60 s compared to a time step of five seconds, respectively. If the WD function is activated, the weight of the output file decreases of 2 and 4 times when the interval step is of 30 and 60 s compared to a time step of five seconds, respectively. This is due to the fact that with bigger sampling, the probabilities to exceed the WD threshold are greater.

3   Long-Term Monitoring Preliminary Study of Software Energy Consumption in a Corporate Environment

We present in this section the effect of the usage on the energy consumption of applications. We first determine good practices on the energy consumption of applications, then we examine their impacts during a two-week experiment on the overall energy consumption and on user behavior. For our study, we implement the Monitoring Application and the GUI, but we did not implement the Remote Server.

3.1   Green Good Practices

To determine precise energy consumption good practices, we measure the energy consumption of specific application usages on a laptop[6]. We evaluate the energy savings that can be made when reducing the quality of a YouTube video, reducing the quality of music streaming on Spotify, having the lowest possible number of opened tabs on Google Chrome, and deactivating the camera on Teams.

---

[6] Dell Latitude 5420.

Watching YouTube videos: All running applications were closed except Demeter and a YouTube web page on Chrome. We launched the first 30 min of the following YouTube video[7]. We measured the energy consumption of Chrome for three video resolutions: 160p (E = 27.445 mWh), 480p (E = 28.425 mWh), and 4K (E = 211.773 mWh). We observe that the energy consumption related to the video resolution at 160p and 480p are in the same order of magnitude while the energy consumption at 4K is 7.7 and 7.45 times higher, respectively. Since we do not measure the energy consumption of the GPU, we underestimate the overall energy consumption. We conclude that reducing the video resolution from 4K to 480p helps in reducing energy consumption.

Music Streaming: All applications have been closed except for Demeter and Spotify. We played each of these two tracks once for 30 min[8,9]. We measured the energy consumption of Spotify for two different audio quality: low (24 Kbits.s^{-1}, E = 7.563 mWh) and very high (320 Kbits.s^{-1}, E = 12.141 mWh). We conclude that decreasing the quality helps in reducing the overall energy consumption of Spotify of 4, 578 mWh.

Browsing Webpages on Chrome: We measured and compared the energy consumption of two different scenarios: 1) every minute we refresh one tab, in a round-robin cycle, while the 14 others are idle; and 2) every five minutes we open the tab of Wikipedia's random page[10] and close the previously browsed ones. We did both measurements during 30 min each. We observe that scenario 1 consumes E = 30.649 mWh, and scenario 2 consumes E = 17.993 mWh. Therefore, we saved 12, 656 mWh thanks to the scenario 2.

Videoconferencing on Teams: We started two 30-minute meetings on Teams, one with the cameras of both users on, and the one with cameras off. The experiment during which the cameras were activated had an overall energy consumption of E = 1 123.405 mWh while the latter consumed E = 164.059 mWh. Therefore, the deactivation of both cameras allowed a decrease in energy consumption by a factor 6.8 and we saved ΔE = 959.346 mWh.

3.2 Impact of the Good Practices During a Two-Week Experiment

We showcase the importance of our approach in a two-week experiment, studying the impact of the recommended good practices on the energy consumption and sustainability awareness of 3 corporate users. We run Demeter for two weeks on three laptops (Dell Latitude 5420) for 3 different user profiles: user 1 is a project leader in digital marketing, user 2 is a help desk technician, and user 3 is a researcher in Green IT. The three users performed their day-to-day tasks at work as usual.

---

[7] youtube.com/watch?v=XVkADAwOXnU, accessed 04/26/2023.

[8] open.spotify.com/track/2QJx8IgKSFfbMQDKxMUioZ?si=13b3e7896d82491e.

[9] open.spotify.com/track/3KtsRijwp8KunCRYlOdWEi?si=373f58f7accb47ba.

[10] https://en.wikipedia.org/wiki/Special:Random.

During the first week, no specific instructions have been given to the users. Then, users were briefed about sustainability software good practices before the second week. Users finally had to report how they used Teams, Spotify, and Chrome during the two weeks.

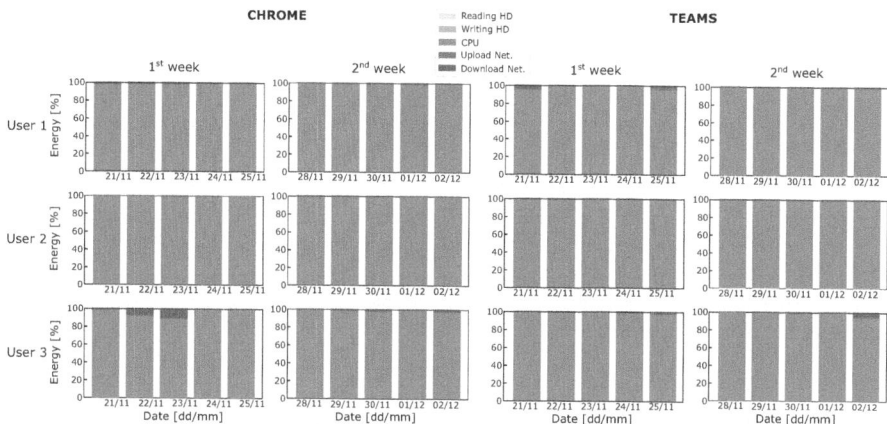

Fig. 5. Stacked bar chart of the energy consumption [Wh] of Chrome (on the left) and Teams (on the right) during two weeks for three users detailed by electric components (Hard-disk reading and writing phases, CPU, Network upload and download phases

In Fig. 5, we gather the percentage of the energy consumption per day and per component for users 1, 2, and 3, and for Chrome and Teams. We observe that the CPU consumption embodies the total energy consumption. The CPU energy is higher than 99.93% of the total energy for both applications. The upload and download stream is lower than 0.068% of the total energy. The reading and writing phase of the hard disk is the least consuming part of the laptop since their energy consumption is lower than 0.002%.

Chrome and Teams Evaluation: In Fig. 6 is gathered the total energy consumption for Chrome and Teams. Only user 1 listened to music on YouTube (720p in the first week and 140p in the second). The user 1 had an average of 10 tabs opened per day in the first week, and 2 to 3 tabs per day in the second week. He did a one-hour meeting on Google Meet on Chrome without the camera turned on during the second week (on 01/12 and 02/12). No significant variation is observed in Fig. 6 between the two weeks.

Thus, an increase of the total energy ($E_{tot} = 1.26$ Wh) is noticed in the second week in regard to the first one. User 2 had a more constant usage of Chrome. During the first week, the user had an average of 10 tabs opened per day, and in the second week, the user tried to close the tabs as soon as possible. No meeting was scheduled, and the user did not listen to music on his laptop. It led to a saving of the total energy of $E = 2.36$ Wh. User 3 listened to music on YouTube (720p in the first week, 140p in the second week), and had an average

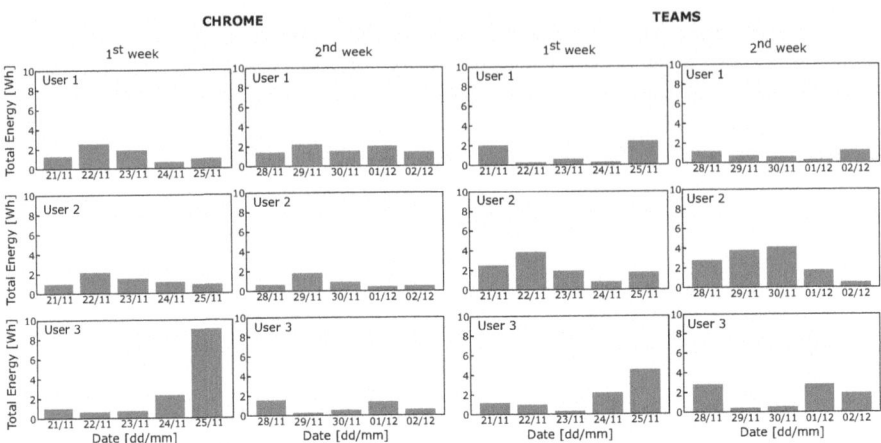

Fig. 6. Total energy consumption [Wh] of Chrome (on the left) and Teams (on the right) during two weeks for users 1, 2, and 3.

of 10 tabs opened per day in the first week while it was around 3 tabs per day in the second week. User 3 did a videoconference on 25/11 with the camera turned on and screen sharing while no meeting was done on the second week on Google Meet on Chrome.

Besides the last days of each week, we see a noticeable variation in the second week which is presumably due to the advised usages. We observe a strong difference between these two days leading to a total saving of $E = 9.79$ Wh between the two weeks.

On 21/11 and 25/11, user 1 did a videoconference with the camera turned on for 45 min and 2 h 45, respectively. Videoconferencing has been done without the camera on 22/11 (3 min), 23/11 (7 min), and 02/12 (1 h 11 min). We observe that the second week is less energy-consuming. The most significant effect is the use of the camera on 21/11 and 25/11 while it has not been used on the one-hour meeting the 02/12. Thus, it reduces the Teams total energy consumption of $E = 14.42$ Wh. User 2 did a videoconference of 22 min on 22/11 with the camera while on the 21/11 (1 h 08 min), 23/11 (1 min), 25/11 (1 h 19), 28/11 (18 min), 29/11 (23 min), 30/11 (2 h 02), 01/12 (11 min), and 02/12 (1 h 35 min) the user did a videoconference without the camera.

Therefore, Teams increases its energy consumption of $E = 2.95$ Wh on the second week compared to the first one. User 3 had a similar use of Teams during both weeks. The user did videoconferences with the camera turned on during both weeks. They were on 21/11 (10 min), 24/11 (1 h), 25/11 (2 h 45 min), 28/11 (1 h), 01/12 (1 h), and 02/12 (1 h). Since the usage of Teams was similar in both weeks, we cannot spot significant differences. Teams energy consumption of the second week is lower by $E = 0.69$ Wh than the first week. Overall, it remains quite similar to the first week. We observe that the use of the camera has an effect on energy consumption of Teams when doing videoconferences. Moreover closing tabs and reducing the quality of the music on YouTube and Spotify have a significant impact on the energy consumption of Chrome.

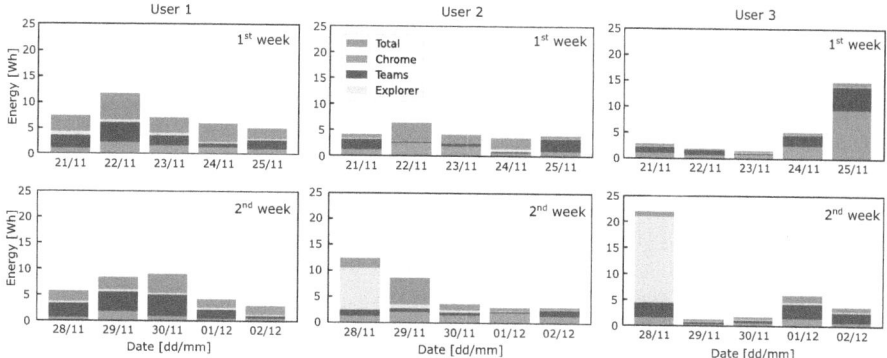

Fig. 7. Energy consumption [Wh] per application (Explorer is yellow, Teams is purple, Chrome is blue, and the total energy consumption of the computer is gray) during two weeks for users 1, 2, and 3. (Color figure online)

Total Evaluation: Figure 7 shows the energy consumption of users 1, 2, and 3 during two weeks, with the total energy of all applications (in gray), of Chrome (in blue), of Teams (in purple), and of the Windows Explorer (in yellow, a file manager in Windows).

Teams and Chrome represent a significant part of the overall energy consumption of a computer for these three users. In the first week, the sum of both applications is 57% (User 1), 48% (User 2), and 90% (User 3) of the overall energy consumption while in the second week, they represent 40% (User 1), 57% (User 2), and 37% (User 3) of the overall energy. Since Teams was less solicited for User 1 (no camera) during the second week, a reduction of energy is detected.

During the first week, Teams represent 24% of the total energy consumption while it represents 12% in the second week. Users 2 and 3 used Teams more during the second week which lead to an increase in energy consumption. It represents 30% (User 2) and 35% (User 3) of the overall energy in the first week while it represents 43% (User 2) and 25% (User 3) in the second. Finally, we see for users 1 and 3 that on 28/11 there is an energy consumption peak, $E_{tot} = 12.35$ Wh (User 1) and $E_{tot} = 21.76$ Wh. (User 3). This is due to the usage of Windows Explorer, while its energy consumption is very low during the other days.

As we didn't collect specific and detailed software usage (through our tool or the questionnaire), it is difficult to analyze why we have this peak for a specific application on 28/11. However, Demeter allows users and system administrators to get an insight into software energy consumption for multiple days and weeks, and therefore identify energy leaks or abnormal energy behavior.

3.3   Discussions and Limitations

We recommended good practices for users to modify their software behavior in order to evaluate their impact on the application's energy consumption.

All of the recommendations were simple to follow for all three users and did not require significant changes in their workflows. However, some actions were more bothering for users, such as closing the browser's tabs. Since some users are not used to frequently close their tabs, they had to constantly be aware and remember they have to close unused tabs.

This constant awareness might either fade and certain users stop applying the recommendations, or it might turn into a habit. A similar conclusion is brought on the deactivation of the camera which is not a systematic habit for some users. Moreover, this action involves other users who would like to keep their camera activated or wish to see the face of the speaker.

We also found that the two easiest recommendations to follow were reducing the music and the video quality. Both recommendations required only some actions at the beginning (such as changing YouTube's parameters). A longer experiment might give us a wider overview of the impact of good practices recommendations on the software's energy consumption and on user behavior.

Our study and our approach have a few limitations:

- Our study only consisted of three users. Although different in their user profile and role in the office, they all worked for the same company.
- The experiment lasted for two weeks, with the first week serving as a control study, and the second week aimed to study the impact of the green recommendations. Although we monitored software energy constantly for two weeks, we argue that we need to analyze usage for a longer period of time, in particular to study if behavioral changes are kept on the long run.
- Our study is the first essay into understanding user software usages in an office environment, and therefore we did not follow field studies protocol (no control group, no randomization of groups, low number of participants, etc.). However, we monitored users in normal usage for the first week, serving as a control week, and we monitored three different user profiles.

4   Conclusion and Perspectives

We presented Demeter, a software architecture capable of energy consumption long-term monitoring of software. We developed Demeter in accordance with four criteria: *simplicity, energy efficiency, adaptability,* and *lightness.* We conducted a real world experiment with three users in a corporate environment for two weeks. We observed a significant difference in energy consumption after providing users with green software good practices.

From our perspectives, we aim to reduce even further the dependencies of our probe and improve its own performance. We aim to conduct a multi-month study of multiple users in a large corporate environment using Demeter, with a goal to provide insights into their energy patterns, impact, and acceptance of green recommendations and actions.

References

1. Delivering improved performance and power efficiency with next-generation BG4 series client NVMe^{TM} SSDs. https://europe.kioxia.com/content/dam/kioxia/shared/business/ssd/client-ssd/asset/whitepaper-cSSD-BG4.pdf. Accessed 06 Oct 2022
2. Demeter GitHub repository. https://github.com/Constellation-Group/Demeter
3. Bieser, J.C.T., Hilty, L.M.: Assessing indirect environmental effects of information and communication technology (ICT): a systematic literature review. Sustainability **10**(8), 2662 (2018)
4. Chen, H., Wang, S., Shi, W.: Where does the power go in a computer system: experimental analysis and implications. In: 2011 International Green Computing Conference and Workshops, pp. 1–6. IEEE (2011)
5. Dick, M., Kern, E., Drangmeister, J., Naumann, S., Johann, T.: Measurement and rating of software-induced energy consumption of desktop PCs and servers. In: EnviroInfo, pp. 290–299 (2011)
6. Efoui-Hess, M.: Climate crisis: the unsustainable use of online video. The Shift Project, pp. 1–36 (2019)
7. Flinn, J., Satyanarayanan, M.: PowerScope: a tool for profiling the energy usage of mobile applications. In: Proceedings of the Second IEEE Workshop on Mobile Computing Systems and Applications, WMCSA 1999, February 1999, pp. 2–10 (1999). https://doi.org/10.1109/MCSA.1999.749272
8. Hankel, A., Heimeriks, G., Lago, P.: A systematic literature review of the factors of influence on the environmental impact of ICT. Technologies **6**(3), 85 (2018)
9. Horner, N.C., Shehabi, A., Azevedo, I.L.: Known unknowns: indirect energy effects of information and communication technology. Environ. Res. Lett. **11**(10), 103001 (2016)
10. Islam, S., Noureddine, A., Bashroush, R.: Measuring energy footprint of software features. In: 2016 IEEE 24th International Conference on Program Comprehension (ICPC), pp. 1–4. IEEE (2016)
11. Jagroep, E., van der Werf, J.M.E., Jansen, S., Ferreira, M., Visser, J.: Profiling energy profilers. In: Proceedings of the 30th Annual ACM Symposium on Applied Computing, pp. 2198–2203 (2015)
12. Johann, T., Dick, M., Naumann, S., Kern, E.: How to measure energy-efficiency of software: metrics and measurement results. In: 2012 First International Workshop on Green and Sustainable Software (GREENS), pp. 51–54. IEEE (2012)
13. Jones, N.: The information factories. Nature **561**, 163–166 (2019)
14. Mahesri, A., Vardhan, V.: Power consumption breakdown on a modern laptop. In: Falsafi, B., VijayKumar, T.N. (eds.) PACS 2004. LNCS, vol. 3471, pp. 165–180. Springer, Heidelberg (2005). https://doi.org/10.1007/11574859_12
15. Noureddine, A.: PowerJoular and JoularJX: multi-platform software power monitoring tools. In: 18th International Conference on Intelligent Environments (2022)
16. Ournani, Z.: Software eco-design: investigating and reducing the energy consumption of software. Ph.D. thesis, University of Lille (2021)
17. Pereira, R., et al.: Ranking programming languages by energy efficiency. Sci. Comput. Program. **205**, 102609 (2021)
18. Rotem, E., Naveh, A., Ananthakrishnan, A., Weissmann, E., Rajwan, D.: Power-management architecture of the intel microarchitecture code-named sandy bridge. IEEE Micro **32**(2), 20–27 (2012)

Experience of the Architectural Evolution of a Big Data System

Felipe Cerezo(ID) and Belén Vela(✉)(ID)

VorTIC3 Research Group, Universidad Rey Juan Carlos (URJC), Madrid, Spain
jf.cerezo.2019@alumnos.urjc.es, belen.vela@urjc.es

Abstract. This paper presents the evolution of a hybrid Big Data architecture over 7 years to adapt to changes in user requirements and technological evolution. This architecture is developed and used by one of the main telco companies in our country. Currently, the result of the presented work is used in many projects providing key information for the operation of the company.

We describe the initial architecture, its main shortcomings, and the current architecture as well as the challenges we met in the process. The main lessons learned are related to the need of modularity and flexibility in the architecture of Big Data systems.

Keywords: Architectural evolution · real-time · batch · Big Data system · technological landscape

1 Introduction

Since mid-2016 members of our research group have been collaborating in the development of several Big Data projects within one of the main telecommunications operators in our country, with more than 20 million customers. In this paper we will show the evolution over 7 years of the software architecture used for these Big Data projects to adapt it to new system requirements that were appearing, to overcome the detected shortcomings and to tackle the evolution of the relevant technologies.

Currently the result of our work is used in 21 projects with more than 130 end users, providing key information for the operation of the company.

We will start with the initial scenario and the used technologies. We will show how the architecture has evolved with new requirements, showing the most relevant changes related to the architectural elements. We present a description of the main changes made in response to the user needs in chronological order.

Finally, we include a discussion and the main conclusions obtained.

2 Initial Scenario

When these projects started, a standard architecture model was used. It could be considered a simplification of the NIST model [1]. This architecture has a hybrid model, combining real time and batch data processing. In this configuration, the information is

B. Tekinerdoğan et al. (Eds.): ECSA 2023, LNCS 14590, pp. 426–437, 2024.
https://doi.org/10.1007/978-3-031-66326-0_26

received through input files in a storage space, called the **Landing Area**. These files are **ingested** in real time into a **Data Bus**. This information is read from the Data Bus and **processed** both in real time (RT) and batch. The results of this processing are stored in two separate **Data Repositories** (RT and batch) that would be accessed by the end user by means of specific **Consumer Tools**. We can see this initial architecture in Fig. 1.

This architecture is quite similar to the Lambda architecture [2], but it implements a little modification: the batch layer does not process all the information from scratch. This batch process is executed with the information already processed by the speed layer. With this modification we optimize the use of hardware resources. Any change in the process to provide new indicators needs only to be done in the real time layer; batch layer had this information already processed [3].

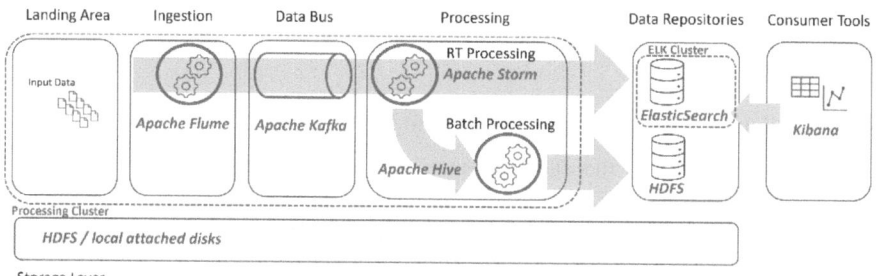

Fig. 1. Architecture of the initial scenario indicating the used technologies

The Landing Area was implemented with local disks on each server. Kafka [4]was selected as the Data Bus and Flume [5] was chosen for performing data ingestion in Kafka. For the data Processing, Apache Storm [6] was used for real-time and long term batch processing was deferred to Apache Hive [7] (YARN [8] and Tez [9] were used for process execution). For storing the results, Elasticsearch [10] is used as the repository for real-time data and HDFS [11] for batch data. To access this information, Kibana [12] is used as the end-user consumer tool, but only for Elasticsearch. Data stored in HDFS were not accessed by users at this initial stage of the project.

In Fig. 1 highlighted with green colour, we show the two different hardware clusters of our system: one only for Elasticsearch (ELK Cluster) and the other (Processing Cluster) for RT (Flume, Kafka and Storm) and for batch processing (Apache Hive and HDFS).

Initially, the platform architecture was intended to be deployed on-premise, using our own hardware infrastructure, as opposed to a public cloud or private virtualization deployment. This customer requirement was justified for different reasons:

- **Economic:** The customer, being a large operator, already has its own computing centres. Therefore, installation, maintenance and support costs are not high compared to the costs of deploying a full Big Data environment without having these facilities.
- **Security:** The information stored in the system includes calls made by the operator's customers. As required by the corresponding legislation, this information must be stored in a secure manner and accesses must be audited. The customer considers that

there is a greater security and control if this information does not physically leave its facilities.

- **Performance and Control:** The customer wants to obtain the maximum performance from the systems used, as well as the greatest possible control and monitoring in case of performance problems with the hardware.

Finally, we started with 10 servers on-premise (590 TB HDD, 3.3 TB RAM, 680 cores) in this initial scenario.

3   Main Architectural Changes and Evolution

We describe the main changes made in the 7-year of the architectural evolution in response to user needs and technological requirements. We present them, respectively affecting: 1) Data repository, 2) Processing elements and 3) Landing area. For each element, we will discuss the implemented changes in chronological order.

3.1   Evolution of the Data Repository: From One to Several Elements

As can be seen in Fig. 1, the data consumer tool accesses the RT input information stored in Elasticsearch [12]. This technology has a very good performance as a search engine and, in our environment, it can handle more than 100 billion documents. It also has analytical capabilities, aggregations, using different fields or patterns, and some quite interesting features, such as *approximate count distinct* and dynamic histograms. However, Elasticsearch presents relevant limitations in terms of analytical capabilities, such as not being able to perform joins between indexes [13] or to carry out operations with different fields of the data.

Therefore, in order to perform this kind of analytical queries, the information is also stored in a Hive datastore, which behaves as a SQL relational database. The design of the Hive architecture [14], based on HDFS, allows handling large volumes of data. In our system we have tables up to 500 billion records. The data are represented with a snowflake model [15]. With this model, the generated queries perform one or more joins between the different tables.

Response times for this type of queries in Hive are very long. This is due to Hive's own architecture, which divides each query into one or more Map-Reduce operations, which involve many disk accesses. Therefore, Vertica [16], another database management system, was initially used to store a smaller subset of the data. With Vertica we were able to perform the queries on the snowflake model much faster. However, since the cost of the required Vertica licenses is high, fully replacing Hive with Vertica was discarded.

In the resulting architecture, the information is available for the data consumer tools in three different ways, as can be seen in Fig. 2: 1) Elasticsearch for fast searches and simple analytics, 2) Vertica for fast queries on a snowflake model, but with a smaller subset of data, and 3) Hive, with higher response times but capable of handling large volumes of data with a lower cost. Each consumer tool can only access certain technologies: Elasticsearch is accessed through Kibana and MicroStrategy has been chosen to access Hive and Vertica.

Figure 2 shows the evolution of the Data Repositories and Consumer Tools elements.

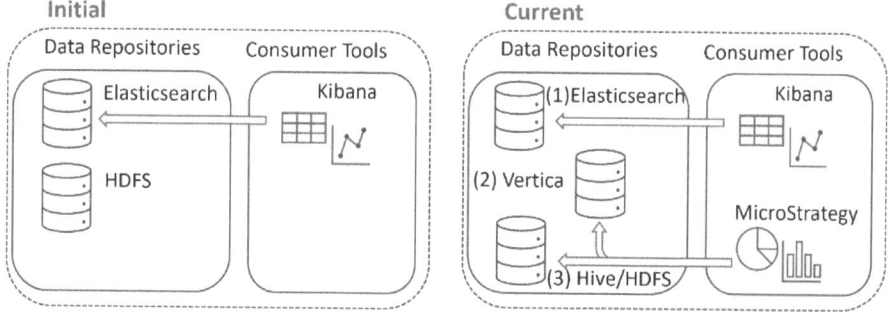

Fig. 2. Initial and current versions of the Data Repositories and Consumer Tools

3.2 Evolution of Processing Elements

Real-time applications become more and more relevant: users require information to be available within seconds or minutes after it is generated. This makes it possible to react to customers access problems, or to know which telephones are affected at a specific moment in certain geographical areas during network outages. For this reason, it was decided to expand the existing hardware. Part of that hardware expansion was used for the horizontal growth of Elasticsearch and the rest was used to build a new cluster for batch processing. The initial processing cluster was now only dedicated for real time processing. In both clusters the technologies used are the same existing in the initial configuration. With this change the resources used for real-time processing were decoupled from those used for batch processing.

After this separation into two clusters (batch and real time), the client decided to incorporate a new real time data source. This source generated a very large volume of data (400 Gb per day, 2,500 million records). Therefore, additional hardware was acquired. At the software level, this hardware was configured as a new cluster completely separated from the previous one. This prevented both clusters from competing for the same resources and allowed them to provide a completely independent service. We can see the final version of the system in Fig. 3.

Additionally, in the case of a catastrophic loss of the real-time cluster, the batch cluster is available to perform their operations, as a disaster recovery. This seemed an unlikely scenario, but it was actually used to perform a migration of the technologies in the real-time cluster without loss of service.

New services, mainly machine learning, advance analytics and AI start to be in demand by system users. These services started with the need of information about data quality (at the syntactic and semantic level) of the existing data, but soon after new requirements on clustering and segmentation also appeared. These new needs pose new architectural problems. Frequently these technologies are not familiar to the existing development and support teams, so they have no or little knowledge of installation and configuration. Also, different users often need different versions of the tools (such as Python and data libraries as Pandas), which can be incompatible.

Additionally, we need to ensure that these new services do not interfere with already existing elements in production. In this context, the most adequate solution would be to

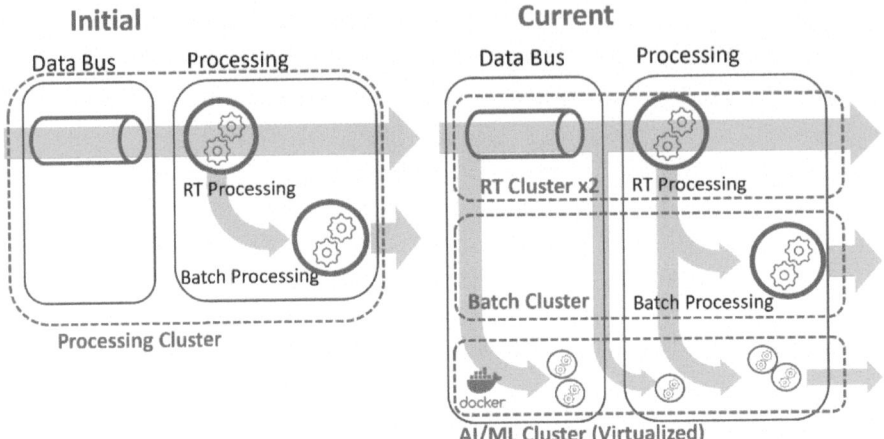

Fig. 3. Initial and current configuration of the Processing Elements

use containers or machine virtualization. Using this solution, it is possible to create different isolated environments with the tools configured for each use. Using containers, tools are installed and ready to use with little or no configuration at all. Using virtual machines, it is possible to install the tools and do all the experimentation and configuration needed in them; all of this without interference in production environments.

The introduction of virtualization was motivated by the needs of system users; the development team also started to use virtualization.

As we have seen, different tools have been introduced throughout the life of the system. These new tools must be properly and fully validated before being introduced into the system. Virtualization provides us with an environment to perform the functional validation of the tools. This can also be used for testing Big Data volumes because more hardware resources are available. This validation can be done when system users have less need of resources, e.g. weekends, holidays or when users have finished their analysis.

Virtualization has also two additional advantages in our project: first, the capability to configure and to limit hardware resource usage for every virtualization: different environments do not compete for these resources. Second, a low time to market: it is quick and easy to provide to the users with the tools they need.

In summary, the architecture of the processing module has increased in complexity; from a single cluster to four different clusters: two for real-time, one for batch and a fourth virtualized cluster, open to any kind of tools.

3.3   Evolution of the Landing Area: Diversification and Securitization

In the initial architecture, the landing area was a storage space for the reception of input data files. It was composed of local disks where several servers received the input files in a balanced way using the scp protocol [17] (a widely used mechanism for simplicity in network routing and security). Initially the received information was composed of CDR (Call Detail Records) with an uncompressed data volume of 500Gb per day.

But, as the use of the platform increased, we began to receive additional information from other sources: alarms, DNS logs, inventories, downloads from different operational databases, etc. This information was stored in Vertica and Elasticsearch for querying and was also available as files to be accessed by other users. This way, the system evolved into a Data Lake [18], where information can freely be accessed and used through a search engine, a database or directly as files.

So, it is necessary for the Landing Area to evolve from being a set of servers with local storage to a shared storage space. Therefore, the next proposal was to use HDFS as shared storage, and several servers that mount HDFS and use a FUSE driver [19]. But this was not a stable solution as the servers periodically crashed and had to be rebooted. We found out that this driver is not recommended in production environments [20].

Therefore, we need a new storage sharing element: a NAS (Network Attached Storage) using NFS to allow servers to offer a file service still compatible with scp.

Moreover, a new source of information had to be included, namely the daily reports with the setofbox [21] configuration of the operator's customers. As these reports are sent to our servers through a direct connection to the Internet, additional security measures are required. The only allowed operation must be to receive these reports. A new file reception area, local to each server, is included in the Landing Area. After reception, files are moved to a shared storage area (Secured Landing). There is a full control over the files, where only the expected ones are processed.

In summary, the Landing Area, which initially was very simple, has become quite complex due to the needs of the platform. This evolution is depicted in Fig. 4.

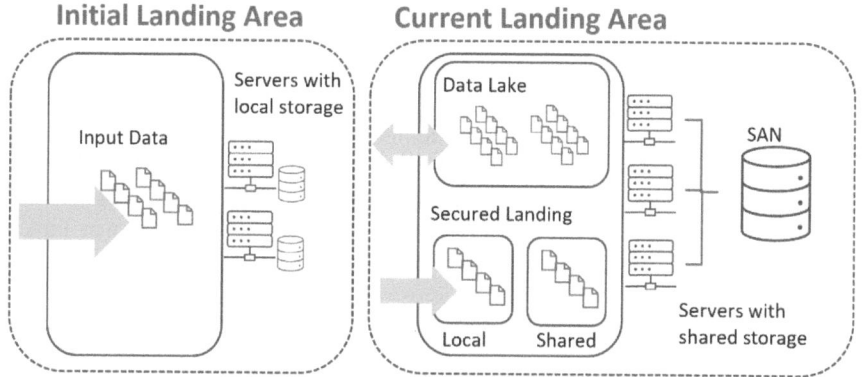

Fig. 4. Initial and current versions of the Landing Area

3.4   Current Architecture

In Fig. 5, we present the current architecture of the system. It is quite clear that compared to the initial version of the architecture, this one is much more complex.

Another indicator of the increased complexity is the volume of used resources. As can be seen in Table 1, the hardware resources have been multiplied by a factor between

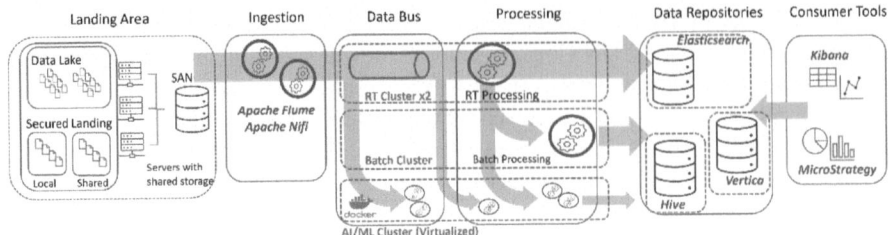

Fig. 5. Current version of the architecture of the system

10 and 13, depending on the concrete resource under consideration. It is interesting to mention that the growth of each of them (servers, cores, RAM and hard disk) has been very similar. Although it is possible that this is due to a bias of the initially purchased servers. When acquiring new hardware, the previously deployed servers would be used as a starting point.

Table 1. Evolution of resources

Resource	Initial	Current	Increase (times)
#Servers	10	103	x 10
#Cores	680	8,000	x 12
RAM (TB)	3.3	41.5	x 13
Hard Disk (TB)	322	3,434	x 11

The complexity not only involves the number of used servers (the highest level) depicted in Fig. 5. Some of these elements also has several instances or clusters to fulfil customer needs. These needs include data isolation between different projects and final end-users, and avoiding competition for resources. We show this complexity in Table 2. The total number of servers does not add up, because some are used for additional tools (head nodes for cluster control, Kibana, Microstrategy, MySQL databases).

Table 2. Number of software clusters

Element	Initial		Current	
	#Clusters	#Servers	#Clusters	#Servers
Processing Cluster	1	4	3	14
Elasticsearch	1	6	5	47
Vertica	-	-	2	6
Data Mediation (NiFi)	-	-	3	12
Virtualized environment	-	-	2	5

4 Discussion

The constant evolution of the complexity in the system is mainly caused by the addition of new user requirements. This is consequence of the well-known of Lehman's Second Law (Law of Increasing Complexity) in the context of an analytical system [22]. New needs for information and analysis arise, either because new data are incorporated or because new studies are carried out on existing data.

This growth in complexity inherently implies a growth in the required hardware resources, so it is essential that the tools are able to scale horizontally [23].

Tools do not need to be structured in a monolithic way: one architectural element does not necessarily correspond to a single technology cluster. In some scenarios, such as the ones presented here, two separate processing clusters or separate landing areas meet user requirements better than a single technology element. In the same way, other tools (Kafka, HDFS, Elasticsearch, etc.) may present similar scenarios: the same architectural element can be implemented using different clusters or technologies.

A major problem of increasing complexity in a Big Data ecosystem is that the tools have a very specific scope of use. This is because the volume of data handled forces both the design and architecture of the tool to focus on some specific functionalities. The tools can be used for other functionalities, but the large volume of data used will not allow them to work properly.

For instance, in the case of data repositories, Elasticsearch allows very fast searches but has very limited analytical capabilities. Hive does not allow fast searches but has the capability to handle large volumes of data. Vertica has great analytical capabilities and could be used for fast searches, but would require the creation and maintenance of indexes, which would not cover more than a few search cases.

Therefore, in the evolution of our Big Data architecture the choice of the right tool for each functionality has been significant. Experience has shown us that the results are not good when a Big Data tool is used outside its core functionality.

In this selection of tools there have been four key criteria. First, the tool should adequately cover the required functionality (e.g. Vertica for fast and powerful analytical queries). Second, avoid using recently released tools, as it can be very risky since their evolution is unpredictable. Third, selecting tools that are active and used by the community. And fourth, adding only tools that provide a clear benefit, since the maintenance of many tools is complex and costly.

Architecture should be **modular**. This is a regular requirement, and part of the tradition in software architecture, but it is also a specific requirement in this context. There are two main reasons for this: 1) a modular approach makes easier to support a healthy system growth, which has been required every time. 2) The constant evolution of technologies and tools in a Big Data environment is often a driver for the co-evolution of a specific part of the architecture.

With regard to the former, to integrate a new data flow or a new information analysis, both the input and output elements should be analysed in a modular approach. Once this information is available, the interfaces are clearly defined, and the implementation of a new module can focus on the processing of the information, not on the relationship with other existing elements.

This modular mechanism has an additional advantage, as it allows to study the impact of the new development within the overall system, and mainly the impact on use of hardware. The modularity makes possible to selectively activate or deactivate parts of the system in the case of some problem.

Regarding the constant evolution of technologies and tools, and the way in which they can affect the system, several situations may arise:

- New relevant tools appear, and existing tools continue to be used, even with a similar purpose. In the context of RT processing, this happens with Apache Storm, Apache Spark Streaming and Apache Flink.
- A new tool appears that causes an existing tool to "freeze" and to significantly slow down its evolution. This was the case, in our system, of Apache NiFi, that has replaced Apache Flume in new developments.
- A tool becomes stagnant, does not evolve and eventually "disappears". This was the case of the once popular Apache Sqoop [24].

Table 3 shows some data that support the above statements. Apache Storm, Apache Flink and Apache Spark are tools which include batch and streaming capabilities, and all of them are widely used by many companies. In this context, an older tool is likely to become more widespread. And even then, currently the number of companies using Apache NiFi doubles the number of companies using Apache Flume, despite having appeared three years later. Also, the number of commits on Github, a metric often used as a measure of the popularity of a technology, is eight times higher.

Table 3. Information about Big Data Apache tools usage, including the date of the first release on Apache and the number of Github commits in 2022/2023. Sources (at 2023/06/08): (1), https://enlyft.com/, (2) github.com

Tool	#Companies (1)	First Apache release	#Commits 2022/2023 (2)
Apache Flume	1,000	Jul 2012	183
Apache Nifi	2,458	Jul 2015	1.533
Apache Storm	3,065	Feb 2014	95
Apache Spark	5,257	Apr 2012	4.937
Apache Flink	1,789	Dec 2014	3.931

Modularity helps to manage the complexity caused by the evolution of technologies. When it becomes necessary to replace an older technology with a more recent one, we can control the impact on the overall system. By restricting this impact, it is possible to have more flexibility in the migration between tools, i.e., it is possible to migrate module by module or all modules at the same time, in a "big bang" mode. The coexistence between the new tool and the old one is also possible; the existing modules can remain without changes, and the new ones can be integrated already using the new tool. This strategy can not only be applied to the change of a tool, but also allows us to migrate between different versions of the same tool.

Modularity implies that the technologies able to replace each other must be interconnectable. Thus, for example, when Apache Flume is replaced by Apache NiFi to load files into Kafka or into a database, both tools must be able support this functionality. Therefore, you must have interoperable and interconnectable interfaces, which can be used interchangeably.

Considering all of the above, we find that **changes** in this kind of systems have, as already implied, two main origins, namely: new user requirements and the technologies themselves. In the first case, these are not necessarily requirements for new data analyses or the addition of new data sources. They can have a different nature, such as security requirements (as during the evolution of the landing area) or virtualization requirements (as it happened in the processing module).

Therefore, the architecture of a Big Data system can never be considered as something finished and immutable: on the contrary, it must be **flexible**. This way, it will be able to respond to changes that appear over time: the addition of new sources of information, the integration of new technologies, the total or partial disappearance of existing technologies, the adaptation to new security requirements, the modification of information access needs, etc.

5 Conclusions

In this paper we have presented the evolution of a Big Data system during a period of 7 years. The increase of complexity in the system is evident in the evolution of the hardware needs. We started with 10 on-premise servers (322 TB HDD, 3.3 TB RAM, 680 cores), and now the system is using 103 servers (3.4 PB HDD, 41.5 TB RAM, 8000 cores). That means an increase of an order of magnitude.

As already noted, there are two main sources for change: new user requirements and the evolution of Big Data technologies. The current ecosystem is significantly different from the one existing 7 year ago, which inspired the original design.

Modularity is the main key to handle the increasing complexity of the architecture, keeping elements isolated and being able to measure and control the impact of changes.

Flexibility is also a very important feature. We need flexibility in the architecture to be able to add new elements and to solve the problems arising from new scenarios proposed by the client. Flexibility is also necessary to include the new relevant technologies that appear over time.

With regard to the organization of the project, the main key to success throughout these years has been the excellent communication and transparency at the technical level among the project's stakeholders. In every architectural decision made, there was always a certain degree of uncertainty regarding the impact of changes. A clear and transparent technical study of the changes done by the stakeholders has made possible to be aware of their advantages and disadvantages.

Acknowledgments. This work was partially supported by the In-Data (Intelligent data engineering techniques for a digital society) project (M3036), and the mobiliToo (Intelligent Mobility Data Platform with a Gender Perspective) project (M3332), funded both by the Rey Juan Carlos University.

References

1. Chang, W.L., Boyd, D.: NIST big data interoperability framework: volume 6, big data reference architecture. Nat. Inst. Standards Technol., USA (2019)
2. Marz, N.: How to beat the CAP theorem. Thoughts from the Red Planet (2011), [Online]. Available: http://nathanmarz.com/blog/how-to-beat-the-cap-theorem.html
3. Cerezo, F., Cuesta, C.E., Moreno-Herranz, J.C., Vela, B.: Deconstructing the lambda architecture: an experience report. In: 2019 IEEE International Conference on Software Architecture Companion (ICSA-C), pp. 196–201 (2019). https://doi.org/10.1109/ICSA-C.2019.00042
4. Shapira, G., Palino, T., Sivaram, R., Petty, K.: Kafka: The Definitive Guide, 2nd Edition. Sebastopol, CA: O'Reilly Media (2020)
5. Flume, A.: Welcome to Apache Flume — Apache Flume. https://flume.apache.org/. Accessed 04 May 2023
6. Storm, A.: Apache Storm. https://storm.apache.org/. Accessed 23 Apr 2023
7. Hive, A.: Getting Started - Apache Hive - Apache Software Foundation. https://cwiki.apache. org/confluence/display/Hive//GettingStarted#GettingStarted-Hive,Map-ReduceandLocal-Mode. Accessed 20 Apr 20 2023
8. Hadoop, A.: Apache Hadoop 3.3.5 – Apache Hadoop YARN. https://hadoop.apache.org/docs/stable/hadoop-yarn/hadoop-yarn-site/YARN.html. Accessed 19 May 2023
9. Tez, A.: Apache Tez – Welcome to Apache TEZ®. https://tez.apache.org/. Accessed 19 May 2023
10. Near real-time search | Elasticsearch Guide [master] | Elastic. https://www.elastic.co/guide/en/elasticsearch/reference/master/near-real-time.html. Accessed 02 May 2023
11. Apache Hadoop 3.3.5 – HDFS Architecture. https://hadoop.apache.org/docs/current/hadoop-project-dist/hadoop-hdfs/HdfsDesign.html#Data_Disk_Failure.2C_Heartbeats_and_Re-Replication. Accessed 20 Apr 2023
12. Elasticsearch, Kibana: Explore, Visualize, Discover Data, Elastic. https://www.elastic.co/kibana. Accessed 11 Jun 2023
13. Elasticsearch, Joining queries | Elasticsearch Guide [8.7] | Elastic. https://www.elastic.co/guide/en/elasticsearch/reference/current/joining-queries.html. Accessed 09 May 2023
14. Hive, A.: Design - Apache Hive - Apache Software Foundation. https://cwiki.apache.org/confluence/display/hive/design#Design-HiveArchitecture. Accessed 09 May 2023
15. Levene, M., Loizou, G.: Why is the snowflake schema a good data warehouse design? Inf. Syst. 28(3), 225–240 (2003). https://doi.org/10.1016/S0306-4379(02)00021-2
16. Vertica, Enterprise Mode concepts, Vertica 12.0.x. https://docs.vertica.com/en/architecture/enterprise-concepts/. Accessed 09 May 2023
17. scp (1): secure copy - Linux man page. https://linux.die.net/man/1/scp. Accessed 11 Jun 2023
18. Gorelik, A.: The enterprise big data lake: delivering the promise of big data and data science, First edition. Sebastopol, California: iO'Reilly Media, Inc (2019)
19. FUSE — The Linux Kernel documentation. https://www.kernel.org/doc/html/next/filesystems/fuse.html. Accessed 25 May 2023
20. Cloudera, Configuring Mountable HDFS | 6.3.x | Cloudera Documentation. https://docs.cloudera.com/documentation/enterprise/6/6.3/topics/cdh_ig_hdfs_mountable.html.   Accessed 25 May 2023
21. Rath, K., Wendorf, J.W.: Set-top box control software: a key component in digital video. Philips J. Res. 50(1), 185–199 (1996). https://doi.org/10.1016/0165-5817(96)81308-8
22. Lehman, M.M.: On understanding laws, evolution, and conservation in the large-program life cycle. J. Syst. Softw. 1, 213–221 (1979). https://doi.org/10.1016/0164-1212(79)90022-0

23. Ali, A.H., Abdullah, M.Z.: A survey on vertical and horizontal scaling platforms for big data analytics. Int. J. Integr. Eng. **11**(6), 138−150 (2019). https://doi.org/10.30880/ijie.2019.11.06.015

24. Apache Sqoop - Apache Attic. https://attic.apache.org/projects/sqoop.html. Accessed 04 May 2023

Parallel and Distributed Architecture for Multilingual Open Source Intelligence Systems

Alper Karamanlioglu[1,2(✉)], Gokhan Yurtalan[1,3], and Yahya Bahadir Karatas[1,2]

[1] AI Technologies Group, HAVELSAN, 06800 Ankara, Turkey
{alperk,gyurtalan,ybkaratas}@havelsan.com.tr
[2] Department of Computer Engineering, Middle East Technical University,
06800 Ankara, Turkey
[3] Department of Computer Engineering, Çankaya University, 06530 Ankara, Turkey

Abstract. The proliferation of publicly available information across multiple languages presents both unique challenges and opportunities for Open Source Intelligence (OSINT) systems. This paper proposes a novel architecture for multilingual OSINT that is both parallel and distributed. The architecture integrates language identification and translation capabilities, enabling it to handle linguistically diverse data by transforming it into a unified format for efficient analysis. Designed specifically to address the challenges of parallel and distributed processing in OSINT systems, this architecture aims to offer scalability and performance benefits when dealing with massive data volumes. Our primary focus has been on devising strategies and tactics that address these concerns, providing a robust solution for the collection, processing and analysis of data in various languages. This work marks a significant step towards the development of more globally inclusive OSINT systems.

Keywords: data scraping · distributed systems · multilingual data processing · open source intelligence · OSINT architecture · parallel architecture

1 Introduction

Open Source Intelligence (OSINT) involves collecting and analyzing information from publicly available sources to produce actionable intelligence. This intelligence can support a range of domains, including national security, law enforcement and business intelligence. The proliferation of publicly accessible data from diverse sources, including websites, social media platforms and news articles, has significantly expanded the potential for deriving valuable predictions through OSINT. However, this expanded potential also introduces significant challenges.

Among these challenges, the linguistic diversity of the data is particularly prominent. The Internet, a global platform, hosts content in hundreds of languages. This reality introduces significant complexity into the processing and

B. Tekinerdoğan et al. (Eds.): ECSA 2023, LNCS 14590, pp. 438–450, 2024.
https://doi.org/10.1007/978-3-031-66326-0_27

understanding of such data, especially for OSINT systems designed to analyze and gather intelligence from these vast and diverse sources.

This challenge stems from many existing OSINT systems' inability to process data in multiple languages. These systems are typically designed for specific languages, limiting their applicability across different linguistic contexts. Moreover, with the growing volume of open-source data, the need for scalable and efficient processing solutions has become increasingly critical. Clearly, there is a need for an architecture capable of handling diverse linguistic data in a scalable and efficient manner.

Our research tackles this challenge by developing a novel architecture for OSINT systems, designed to effectively process data across multiple languages. The proposed architecture integrates language identification and translation techniques, facilitating the conversion of diverse linguistic data into a common language for streamlined processing and analysis. The architecture offers a solution that is not only language-independent but also scalable and reliable. Furthermore, it incorporates a continuous data crawling system, complete with a queue mechanism for managing incoming data, and reliable storage solutions to ensure data persistence.

The architecture of the system supports various language-specific NLP models, each specially designed to manage tasks including named entity recognition, classification, summarization, question answering and sentiment analysis for the respective language. This multi-model strategy enables the system to adapt flexibly to the content it processes, thereby optimizing both its performance and the accuracy of its predictions.

Employing parallelism and distribution, this architecture handles data processing both efficiently and scalably, underlining these strategies as vital to its design. Distributing the processing load across multiple nodes allows the system to manage and process larger data volumes faster. The use of Virtual Private Server (VPS) machines for web scraping not only enhances the system's capabilities but also maintains anonymity, an essential aspect of OSINT operations.

1.1   Contributions

Our research advances OSINT systems and the handling of multilingual data in several key ways:

- We propose a novel architecture for OSINT systems that can effectively handle multilingual data extracted from the scraped content.
- Strategies of parallelism and distribution are employed to enhance the efficiency and scalability of data processing.
- VPS machines are utilized for web scraping, ensuring operational security and anonymity, which are crucial for OSINT.

This paper presents a novel parallel and distributed architecture aimed at bridging this gap. The architecture integrates cutting-edge language identification and translation technologies, web scraping tools and distributed task management strategies to handle an extensive range of languages and large data volumes. Accordingly, it has the potential to markedly enhance OSINT capabilities by expanding its geographic and cultural scope.

The rest of the paper is organized as follows: Sect. 2 reviews relevant literature. In Sect. 3, we introduce the proposed architecture in detail. In Sect. 4, we present a discussion on the implications of the architecture. Finally, Sect. 5 outlines the conclusion and future directions of the paper.

2   Related Work

Multilingual OSINT is an evolving field demanding sophisticated methods and techniques to navigate the complexities of diverse and dynamic data sources [6]. Despite significant advancements, existing studies have not yet offered a comprehensive architecture capable of effectively scaling and managing the evolution of data sources for language-independent OSINT applications. This paper aims to address this gap by proposing a novel parallel and distributed architecture for multilingual OSINT.

Current research in multilingual OSINT focuses on specific aspects of the system, such as translation services or individual modules for information extraction and analysis. These works, while essential, often lack a comprehensive view of the architectural needs of large-scale, multilingual data processing in OSINT applications, such as scalability and adaptability.

In one of the earliest studies, Zavarella et al. [21] introduced a system for information extraction and analysis from multilingual web sources, consisting of modules for language identification, translation, information extraction and fusion. While this work provides a foundation for multilingual information extraction, it lacks the provisions for scalability that is required for large-scale data processing, a crucial aspect of OSINT systems.

Another system, proposed by Steinberger et al. [18], focuses on monitoring global media coverage of events in various languages using a large-scale news aggregator. This work is significant in using a news aggregator for monitoring global media coverage. However, the authors did not thoroughly discuss the architecture's scalability and adaptability, aspects which are vital for handling the growth and evolution of data sources and the ever-increasing data volumes.

More recently, Ranade et al. [14] presented a system specifically for translating multilingual threat intelligence using deep neural networks, addressing the need for translation services in private security environments. While this study highlights the importance of translation services, it is constrained to a specific application (threat intelligence) and does not propose a broader solution that could be applicable to a wide range of multilingual OSINT applications.

Quoc et al. introduced UniCrawl [13], an efficient geo-distributed crawler designed to minimize inter-site communication costs. An independent crawler is initiated for each site and applies a four-phased routine consisting of generate, fetch, parse and update. The crawled domain space is partitioned across sites and their storage and computing resources are federated in order to minimize the inter-site communication cost. The crawling logic is implemented using Apache

Nutch [11]. In order to avoid the duplication of requests to a URL, a caching solution which replicates the crawled URLs list at all nodes in a site is used. When a URL is selected in the frontier, it is first checked locally against the visited URLs. While the proposed solution resulted in a 1.75 times faster crawler system than the Apache Nutch deployment, this study focuses solely on the distributed crawling architecture and does not provide any multilingual support.

Bahrami et al. [2] proposed a cloud-based distributed crawler architecture that runs on Azure Web Services. The Cloud-based web crawler engine (CWCE) they used leverages Azure Cloud Queue for temporary URL storage and Azure Cloud Table for permanent page information. The mentioned table is based on a NoSQL database which allows flexibility without a predefined schema. As a distribution strategy, they employed the MapReduce programming technique. This study, much like [13], lacks multilingual support while introducing a well-architectured cloud-based crawler.

Heydon et al. [8] introduced one of the early scalable and extensible Web Crawlers which can be scaled up to the entire web. By their definition of extensibility, the system has two major features. Initially, it has the flexibility to introduce additional features such as incorporating new processing modules to handle downloaded documents in a personalized manner. Secondly, it can be effortlessly configured to employ different versions of its key components. For the deduplication of content, they used checksum based methods like content-seen test.

While these pioneering studies have laid the groundwork for multilingual OSINT, they highlight the necessity for a scalable, adaptable and comprehensive architecture that supports extensive language diversity and data volumes. Our proposed architecture seeks to address these critical gaps by offering scalable and efficient processing, language-agnostic design, and enhanced security measures for comprehensive OSINT applications.

3   Proposed Architecture

Understanding both the requirements and constraints is crucial for evaluating any architecture. Generally, the fundamental purpose of OSINT is to perform data acquisition by browsing billions of web URLs with optimum performance. Sufficient resources are required for this operation. However, increasing the resources does not always yield optimum results and may even lead to decreased efficiency. For this reason, there is a need for a strongly scalable system architecture in accordance with Amdahl's law [1] with a high speed-up value. In addition, constraints such as not sending more requests from a client to target websites during data acquisition and the client's compliance with politeness rules highlight the need for parallel programming.

Against this backdrop, the proposed architecture provides a parallel, comprehensive and robust solution for efficiently processing and analyzing multilingual data to generate valuable intelligence and predictions from the vast array of publicly available information. This architecture also leverages various technologies and methodologies to enhance performance, scalability, reliability and anonymity. These are important differentiating features of the proposed architecture, as it provides a practical framework for multilingual OSINT and addresses vital technical challenges associated with large-scale data processing and analysis. The capabilities of the system for multilingual content handling are shown in Fig. 1:

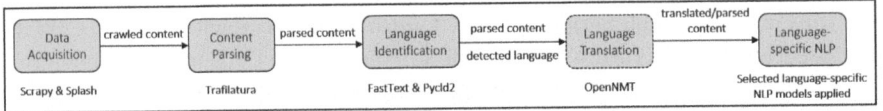

Fig. 1. Multilingual content handling.

- **Data Acquisition:** This initial phase involves scraping web content from diverse sources. We utilize Scrapy [16], an open-source web crawling framework renowned for its speed and efficiency. Scrapy is one of the ideal choices for our data acquisition needs as it is especially effective for data mining and automated testing and can be easily adapted to specific needs. According to a study by Yang and Thiengburanathum [20], Scrapy exhibits the lowest failure rate and ranks among the most scalable open-source web crawlers. Additionally, it includes abstractions that simplify various mechanisms, including authentication, session management, compression, cookie handling, caching, user-agent spoofing, concurrency support, crawl depth restrictions and rate limiting. To supplement Scrapy, we also employ Splash [17]. By using Splash, we are able to handle complex web content, including JavaScript-based elements, thereby extending the scope of our data acquisition capabilities.
- **Content Parsing:** Following data acquisition, the raw HTML content must be parsed and cleaned to extract valuable textual data. For this process, we utilize Trafilatura [3]. As a specialized library for extracting text from HTML and XML documents, Trafilatura enables accurate and efficient distilling of the raw scraped data into meaningful and usable text [4].
- **Language Identification:** Upon cleaning the data, the next crucial step is to identify the language of the content, which is essential for the subsequent processing and analysis stages. The architecture incorporates FastText [7] and pycld2 [12] for this purpose. FastText is an open-source library that uses a neural network-based model for language identification, offering superior performance even for low-resource languages. Pycld2, on the other hand, is a Python interface to Google's language-detection library (CLD2) and provides a good balance between speed and accuracy. FastText generates a confidence rate that is generally accurate for language detection. However, this rate may not be as high for content consisting of mixed languages. Such content can be fragmented with character offsets of different language parts with Pycld2. Therefore, parts to be translated into the target language can be prepared.

- **Language Translation:** Following the language identification, the architecture employs OpenNMT [10] for translation. By using OpenNMT, we can handle a wide range of language pairs and translation requirements, providing a high level of adaptability for multilingual data processing. This step converts the text into a common language, facilitating subsequent analysis and comparison across different languages. Given the security concerns associated with OSINT systems, OpenNMT emerges as the most inclusive and sustainable option, allowing for the training or fine-tuning of models rather than relying on service-like solutions. Language translation is optional when the source and target language are the same as shown in Fig. 1.
- **Language-Specific NLP:** Depending on the identified language, the system selects the relevant NLP models for tasks such as named entity recognition, classification, summarization, question answering and sentiment analysis. The language-specific models generally enable more precise processing of text data, improving the overall quality of the intelligence and predictions generated. The selected models can either be developed in-house or sourced from the HuggingFace library [19], which provides a wide range of pre-trained models for various NLP tasks.
- **Data Distribution and Task Management:** The architecture uses Celery [5], a robust asynchronous task/job manager based on distributed message passing, to manage the distribution of tasks across multiple worker nodes. This allows for effective load balancing and parallel processing, significantly enhancing the scalability and performance of the architecture. Moreover, Kafka, a distributed event streaming platform, manages high-velocity real-time data, enhancing the system's scalability and robustness.
- **Data Storage and Management:** The processed and translated data is stored and managed using PostgreSQL, a powerful, open-source relational database system. This ensures reliable and efficient storage of the large volumes of data handled by the architecture. For real-time data retrieval and analytics, the system utilizes Redis [15], a high-performance in-memory database known for its speed and flexibility.

In making the design decisions for this study, we considered interactions among the system's building blocks Manager Application, AI Application, Master Application and Web Scraper for runtime communication. To describe the runtime communications of blocks and subsystems, we use the concepts of service provision and consumption, as well as item flow interactions. The interaction diagram of the blocks and subsystems of the entire system is given in Fig. 2. The master application orchestrates the system, managing both the tasks assigned to the web scrapers and synchronously sharing content with the manager application. The manager application block processes the content to obtain analytical outputs and assists the AI application in article processing.

Manager application is the orchestrator that coordinates the system context with the data flow and functional services between the system's technical building blocks. It has business logic that meets OSINT functional requirements with its business building blocks. It is also the interface of the entire system with exter-

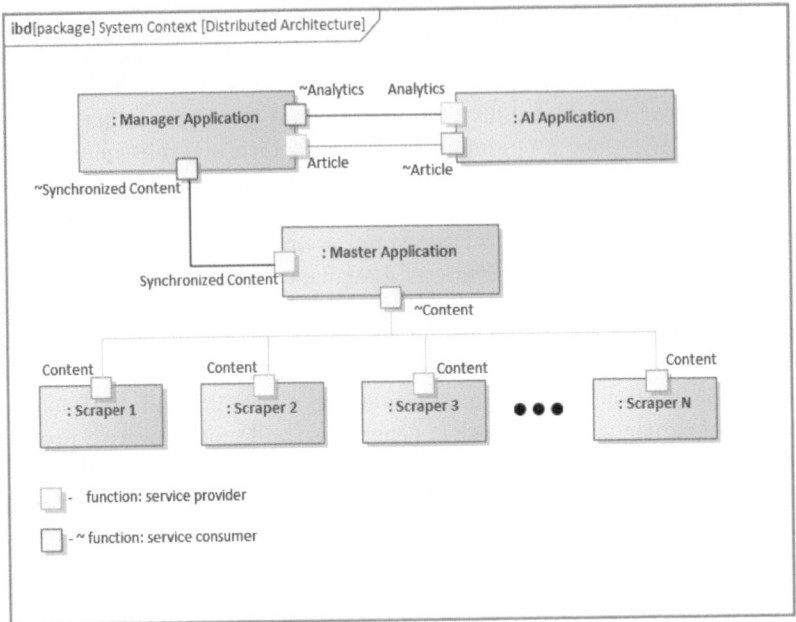

Fig. 2. System Context.

nal systems and the end user. Requests enter the system through the manager application, which also transmits all outputs aligned with the business goals as responses. As indicated in Fig. 3, it has bounded context created by query management, article management, seed URL management, system administration and duplicate detection modules for the business solutions.

The operator creates the criteria to be searched from open internet resources through query management. After the slaves complete their task given by the master application, different responses returned from the master application are combined with the article management. There may be duplication between the articles. At this stage, the duplicate detection module assesses the duplication ratio between articles, presents the results for the operator's approval and facilitates storage decision management. Finally, the seed URL management module oversees the seed URLs, crucial for query management, and determines the login information for these URLs. All these issues create the bounded context of the manager application.

In addition, it has technical system contexts such as Cross-cutting Concerns, Data Access Layer and Fault Tolerance Layer. Cross-cutting concerns not only serve modules within the manager application's bounded context but also benefit other subsystem modules. Since each of them is developed as a component, it can be used by other components in accordance with aspect-oriented programming [9]. Apart from all this, all domain components in the manager application manage the data to be stored or read through the data access service. The data

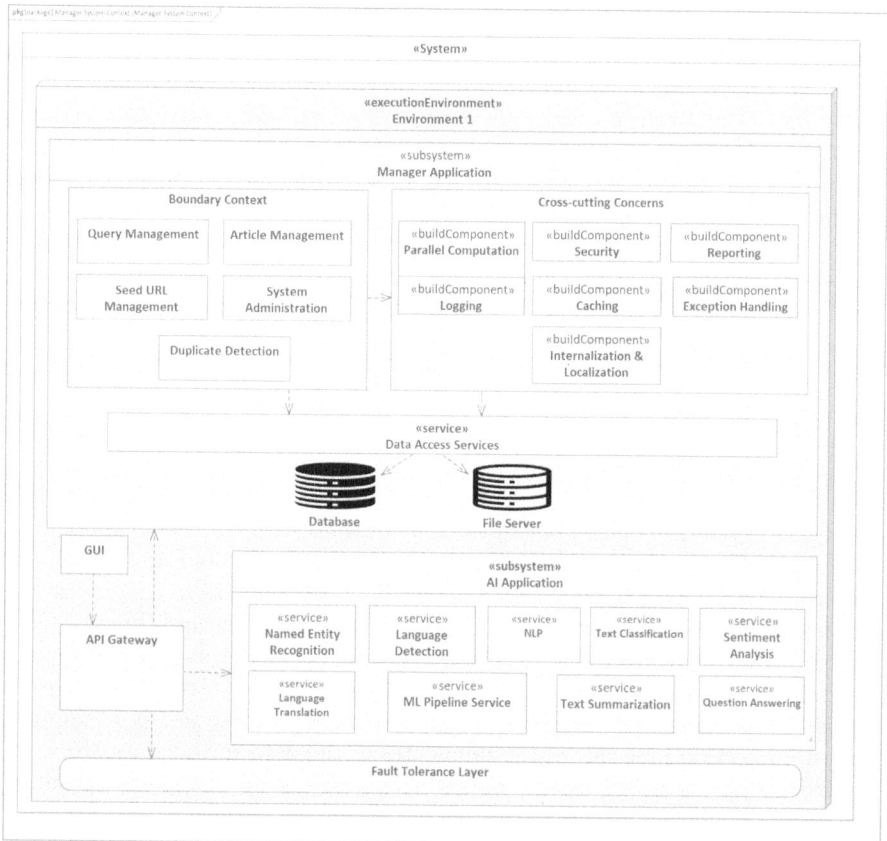

Fig. 3. Manager Application System Context.

access service, also known as the persistence framework, acts as middleware facilitating the storage and retrieval of information between applications and databases. It acts as an abstraction layer for persistent data, bridging the conceptual and technical differences between storage and usage. Within the scope of the manager application, data transfer via file server is also planned with the data access service.

The master application and external systems communicating with the manager application make requests to the system using APIs. Similarly, users make requests to the system via Graphical User Interface (GUI). Then clients receive the response to the request through API Gateway, represented as a technical component. API gateway has significantly contributed to managing, orchestrating, monitoring and maintaining APIs provided to clients in the system architecture. Orchestrated APIs are coupled with business logic via Fault Tolerance Layer rather than directly. The authentication, verification, logging, auditing and defending cyber-attack for the security of the system are performed by the fault tolerance layer. Verified and audited requests passing through the fault tolerance layer turn into meaningful responses with business logic, represented as a subsystem in Fig. 3, divided into structures according to principles.

AI application performs the analysis task of interpreting the data it receives from the manager application with text summarization, text classification, sentiment analysis, named entity recognition, question answering, language detection and language translation models. Models that analyze text may need NLP features such as tokenization and normalization. The NLP model service provides these features. All these models need an infrastructure to operate sustainably. The machine learning pipeline provides all infrastructural tools required for the model to work properly, such as data collection, data verification, feature extraction, machine resource management, process management, configuration, deployment and monitoring.

The master application does not collect and interpret information by itself. Instead, it orchestrates, synchronizes and manages the scraper tasks necessary for information creation. Briefly, it undertakes the task of master in the master-slave architecture pattern. It performs all these operations with the task orchestrator, cache and message broker services it contains, as shown in Fig. 4. The task orchestrator continuously triggers the slaves by creating tasks in each iteration. The created tasks are produced to the message broker's queue and thus the tasks are distributed asynchronously. Cache is the in-memory database used to store the contents collected by slaves. The in-memory database acts as short-term memory, enabling small-scale data manipulations and analyses. For example, duplicate detection first checks the duplicates of the data in this data store.

The message broker service balances the workload of the slaves, ensuring instantaneous, efficient system operation and leveraging parallel processing capabilities. As indicated in Fig. 4, message broker distributes tasks simultaneously by keeping the tasks processed by each VPS in the queue data structure. Tasks are distributed in configurable batches, not individually, to maximize task processing in a single batch and minimize network costs, given that VPSs operate with minimal resources and maximal internet bandwidth. This design ensures that the architecture is strongly scaling. Message broker's distributed task processing is initiated via message relay using a middleware agent such as Kafka. Task processing is performed by the slave(s) responsible for the execution of the task. Results from task processing can be stored in a backend repository such as Redis. Task processing can be triggered immediately (real-time) or scheduled (batch). The system automatically retries failed tasks to ensure robust processing. A complex pipeline of tasks can be handled by deploying tasks to different hosts. The architecture is based on a pluggable component model. For all these features, the Celery framework is used in the system of message broker service. The design of the system allows for robust handling of tasks and ensures reliable processing even in case of task failures.

Web scraper applications hosted on VPS machines carry out data collection and scraping operations. These are technically defined as slaves of the master-slave architecture pattern. They are standalone applications and their packages

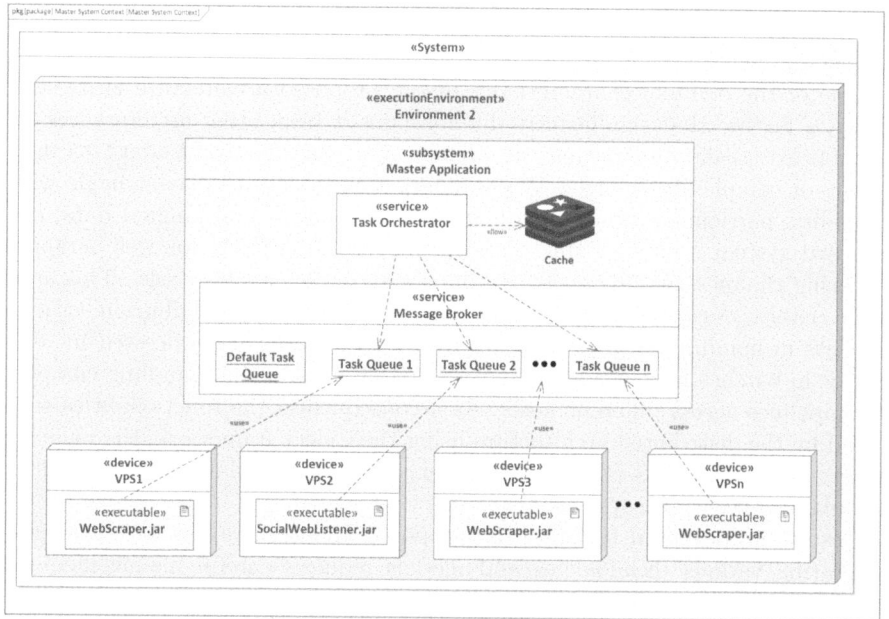

Fig. 4. Master Application System Context.

(e.g., DLL, Jar) will be deployed and executed in each VPS. The master application waits asynchronously to fulfil the scraper tasks that it shares with the slaves. Slaves will be available for new tasks by transmitting the results of the tasks they have completed to the master.

All the systems are executed in two different network environments. Environment 1 includes main components and the master application in accordance with the master-slave architecture pattern. It can be run on-premise by the organization or in the cloud network. Environment 2 includes the slaves of the master-slave architectural pattern and the message broker that enables these slaves to work efficiently. Slaves, represented as VPS devices, should work in an environment different from Environment 1 to avoid leaving a footprint for organizations. Such configurations ensure the system's flexibility and scalability, while also upholding security and privacy standards.

4   Discussion on the Implications of the Architecture

The proposed architecture can handle a significant range of languages, thus increasing the variety of data sources available. By integrating language identification and translation technologies, our architecture can process and analyze content from various sources regardless of the original language. This capability is fundamental to the system's functionality, as it ensures our architecture's applicability across a diverse range of contexts and environments. In this way, the geographic and cultural reach of OSINT systems broadens and allows for a more comprehensive and globally inclusive analysis.

One of the defining characteristics of the proposed architecture is its scalability, a feature that significantly differentiates it from other architectures. In this context, scalability means the architecture can effectively adapt to data volume or complexity changes. While different architectures may struggle with scalability, particularly when handling large volumes of multilingual data, our proposed system addresses this by leveraging multiple VPS for web scraping and using the message broker for handling distributed scraper tasks. This approach enables our architecture to exploit parallelism and distribution, crucial elements in handling large-scale data. In addition, tasks are processed in real-time or in batches for automatically retrying failed tasks and handling complex task pipelines across different hosts. As a consequence, the functionalities supported by the distributed architecture using the Celery framework, the message broker service and VPS machines together, contribute to the overall scalability and adaptability of the system.

Despite its potential benefits, the proposed architecture has its challenges. Integrating various technologies and models requires careful management to ensure seamless interoperability. Moreover, the large-scale handling of multilingual data may also raise issues related to data privacy and ethical considerations that need to be addressed. It's crucial to note that the sensitivity and potential misuse of public data makes it necessary to implement rigorous data protection measures and ensure the technology's ethical use. This includes stringent access controls, privacy-aware processing techniques and careful consideration of the data sources' legality and ethics.

5 Conclusion and Future Work

This paper presents a novel parallel and distributed architecture for multilingual OSINT systems. The architecture combines language identification and translation technologies, enabling it to handle a wide range of languages and opening up the potential for more globally inclusive data analysis. It also has a distributed software architecture with multiple VPS, message broker architectural pattern and Celery which is used for task management, ensuring efficient and reliable large-scale data handling.

This work contributes to the ongoing discourse on effectively leveraging the power of large-scale, multilingual data for intelligence purposes. The study aims to stimulate further innovation in the design and implementation of OSINT systems and related applications. This architecture is recommended for organizations needing rapid data acquisition from open sources.

For future work, we plan to develop a dynamic adaptation strategy to enhance the system's responsiveness to changes in data volume and complexity. Furthermore, we aim to conduct a comprehensive performance evaluation of the architecture, including its scalability, fault tolerance and overall effectiveness in generating valuable predictions from multilingual data sources. Additionally, future efforts will focus on establishing a framework to address privacy and ethical considerations inherent in the large-scale processing and analysis of multilingual data to ensure our proposed architecture's secure and responsible use.

References

1. Amdahl, G.M.: Validity of the single processor approach to achieving large scale computing capabilities. In: Proceedings of the April 18–20, 1967, Spring Joint Computer Conference, pp. 483–485 (1967)
2. Bahrami, M., Singhal, M., Zhuang, Z.: A cloud-based web crawler architecture. In: 2015 18th International Conference on Intelligence in Next Generation Networks, pp. 216–223. IEEE (2015)
3. Barbaresi, A.: Trafilatura: a web scraping library and command-line tool for text discovery and extraction. In: Proceedings of the 59th Annual Meeting of the Association for Computational Linguistics and the 11th International Joint Conference on Natural Language Processing: System Demonstrations, pp. 122–131 (2021)
4. Bevendorff, J., Gupta, S., Kiesel, J., Stein, B.: An empirical comparison of web content extraction algorithms (2023)
5. Celery (2023). https://docs.celeryq.dev/en/stable/userguide/workers.html. Accessed 17 May 2023
6. Coleman, S., Secker, A., Bawden, R., Haddow, B., Birch, A.: Architecture of a scalable, secure and resilient translation platform for multilingual news media. In: 1st International Workshop on Language Technology Platforms, pp. 16–21 (2020)
7. FastText (2023). https://fasttext.cc. Accessed 17 May 2023
8. Heydon, A., Najork, M.: Mercator: a scalable, extensible web crawler. World Wide Web **2**(4), 219–229 (1999). https://doi.org/10.1023/A:1019213109274
9. Kiczales, G., Hilsdale, E., Hugunin, J., Kersten, M., Palm, J., Griswold, W.G.: An overview of AspectJ. In: Knudsen, J.L. (ed.) ECOOP 2001. LNCS, vol. 2072, pp. 327–354. Springer, Heidelberg (2001). https://doi.org/10.1007/3-540-45337-7_18
10. Klein, G., Kim, Y., Deng, Y., Senellart, J., Rush, A.M.: OpenNMT: open-source toolkit for neural machine translation. arXiv preprint arXiv:1701.02810 (2017)
11. Nutch (2023). https://nutch.apache.org. Accessed 09 Dec 2023
12. PYCLD2 (2023). https://github.com/aboSamoor/pycld2. Accessed 17 May 2023
13. Quoc, D.L., Fetzer, C., Felber, P., Rivière, , Schiavoni, V., Sutra, P.: UniCrawl: a practical geographically distributed web crawler. In: 2015 IEEE 8th International Conference on Cloud Computing, pp. 389–396 (2015). https://doi.org/10.1109/CLOUD.2015.59
14. Ranade, P., Mittal, S., Joshi, A., Joshi, K.: Using deep neural networks to translate multi-lingual threat intelligence. In: 2018 IEEE International Conference on Intelligence and Security Informatics (ISI), pp. 238–243. IEEE (2018)
15. Redis (2023). https://redis.io. Accessed 17 May 2023
16. Scrapy (2023). https://scrapy.org. Accessed 17 May 2023
17. Splash (2023). https://splash.readthedocs.io/en/stable. Accessed 17 May 2023
18. Steinberger, R., Ehrmann, M., Pajzs, J., Ebrahim, M., Steinberger, J., Turchi, M.: Multilingual media monitoring and text analysis – challenges for highly inflected languages. In: Habernal, I., Matoušek, V. (eds.) TSD 2013. LNCS (LNAI), vol. 8082, pp. 22–33. Springer, Heidelberg (2013). https://doi.org/10.1007/978-3-642-40585-3_3

19. Wolf, T., et al.: HuggingFace's transformers: state-of-the-art natural language processing. arXiv preprint arXiv:1910.03771 (2019)
20. Yang, D., Thiengburanathum, P.: Scalability and robustness testing for open source web crawlers. In: 2021 Joint International Conference on Digital Arts, Media and Technology with ECTI Northern Section Conference on Electrical, Electronics, Computer and Telecommunication Engineering, pp. 197–201. IEEE (2021)
21. Zavarella, V., Tanev, H., Linge, J., Piskorski, J., Atkinson, M., Steinberger, R.: Exploiting multilingual grammars and machine learning techniques to build an event extraction system for Portuguese. In: Pardo, T.A.S., Branco, A., Klautau, A., Vieira, R., de Lima, V.L.S. (eds.) PROPOR 2010. LNCS (LNAI), vol. 6001, pp. 21–24. Springer, Heidelberg (2010). https://doi.org/10.1007/978-3-642-12320-7_3

HITA: An Architecture for System-level Testing of Healthcare IoT Applications

Hassan Sartaj[1]([✉]) [iD], Shaukat Ali[1] [iD], Tao Yue[1] [iD], and Julie Marie Gjøby[2] [iD]

[1] Simula Research Laboratory, Oslo, Norway
{hassan,shaukat,tao}@simula.no
[2] Section of Welfare Technologies, Oslo Kommune Helseetaten, Oslo, Norway
julie-marie.gjoby@hel.oslo.kommune.no

Abstract. System-level testing of healthcare Internet of Things (IoT) applications requires creating a test infrastructure with integrated medical devices and third-party applications. A significant challenge in creating such test infrastructure is that healthcare IoT applications evolve continuously with the addition of new medical devices from different vendors and new services offered by different third-party organizations following different architectures. Moreover, creating test infrastructure with a large number of different types of medical devices is time-consuming, financially expensive, and practically infeasible. Oslo City's healthcare department faced these challenges while working with various healthcare IoT applications. To address these challenges, this paper presents a real-world test infrastructure software architecture (HITA) designed for healthcare IoT applications. We evaluated HITA's digital twin (DT) generation component implemented using model-based and machine learning (ML) approaches in terms of DT fidelity, scalability, and time cost of generating DTs. Results show that the fidelity of DTs created using model-based and ML approaches reach 94% and 95%, respectively. Results from operating 100 DTs concurrently show that the DT generation component is scalable and ML-based DTs have a higher time cost.

Keywords: Healthcare Internet of Things (IoT) · Software Architecture · System Testing · Digital Twins

1 Introduction

Healthcare Internet of Things (IoT) applications follow a cloud-based architecture to create an interconnected network with various medical devices and third-party applications [11]. The primary objective of developing healthcare IoT applications is to create a central access point for medical professionals, patients, hospitals, pharmacies, and caretakers to deliver efficient healthcare services. Failure to provide timely healthcare services may lead to financial and human life loss. Therefore, automated and rigorous system-level testing of healthcare IoT applications is essential to ensure their dependability.

© The Author(s), under exclusive license to Springer Nature Switzerland AG 2024
B. Tekinerdoğan et al. (Eds.): ECSA 2023, LNCS 14590, pp. 451–468, 2024.
https://doi.org/10.1007/978-3-031-66326-0_28

This work is conducted with Oslo City's healthcare department [1], which is working with various industries to develop healthcare IoT applications to deliver patients with high-quality services. One of the primary objectives is to create a test infrastructure for the system-level testing of healthcare IoT applications. Such test infrastructure requires integrating physical medical devices (e.g., medicine dispensers) and third-party applications (e.g., pharmacies) with a healthcare IoT application. A major testing challenge is that healthcare IoT applications evolve continuously with the addition of new medical devices, new/updated medical services, and new third-party applications. Integrating several different types of medical devices from various vendors is time-consuming, costly, and not a practical solution. Moreover, each third-party application has a limit on the maximum number of allowed requests for a particular time interval. Testing healthcare IoT applications within the limitations of third-party applications is challenging.

Several architectures have been proposed in the literature for developing healthcare IoT applications [21]. A few works also utilize architectures for various software testing activities, e.g., integration testing [20]. Our work focuses on designing a test infrastructure architecture to facilitate automated system-level testing of healthcare IoT applications.

To address the above-mentioned challenges, this paper presents a real-world test infrastructure software architecture (HITA) designed for healthcare IoT applications. HITA includes the DT generation (DTGen) and test stubs generation (TSGen) components to handle the integration of medical devices and third-party applications. We evaluate HITA's DTGen component implemented using model-based and machine learning (ML) approaches. For the evaluation, we use a medicine dispenser (named Medido [17]) integrated with a healthcare IoT application as a part of the experimental apparatus provided by Oslo City. Our evaluation analyzes the fidelity of DT created using both approaches, the scalability of the DTGen component in operating 100 DTs, and the time cost involved in generating DTs. The evaluation results indicate that the fidelity of DTs created using model-based and ML approaches is 94% and 95%, respectively. Results from operating 100 generated DTs concurrently show that the DTGen component is scalable. Results also indicate that ML-based DTs have a higher time cost compared to model-based DTs. In the end, we describe our experiences and lessons learned from applying HITA in a real-world industrial context.

The remaining paper is organized as follows. The related work is discussed in Sect. 2. HITA is described in Sect. 3. Evaluation is presented in Sect. 4, and lessons learned are outlined in Sect. 5. The paper's conclusion is given in Sect. 6.

2   Related Work

Many works are available related to architectures for healthcare IoT targeting various aspects. This includes; analysis of IoT architectures for healthcare applications [21], design patterns for healthcare IoT [18], architecture for intelligent

IoT-based healthcare systems [10], architectural design decisions for developing digital twins of IoT systems [16], a tool for modeling IoT architectures [30], health monitoring architecture for IoT systems [6], an architecture for IoT-based remote patient monitoring [2], a requirements-based healthcare IoT architecture [15], distributed IoT architecture [3], health data sharing architecture [22], analyze architecture for healthcare IoT system [24], architecture for an IoT-based healthcare monitoring system [19], and architecture for blockchain-driven healthcare IoT systems [31]. In contrast to the aforementioned works, our work focuses on developing a test infrastructure architecture for healthcare IoT applications.

Several works are also available targeting architecture-based testing. This includes; analysis of architecture's function in software testing [7], architecture-based test criteria [14], architecture-driven integration testing [20], an architecture for analyzing fault tolerance [8], and reliability assessment using architecture models [9]. Compared to the above-mentioned works, our work offers a distinct contribution by presenting a test infrastructure architecture for healthcare IoT applications, which is designed to facilitate automated system-level testing of such applications.

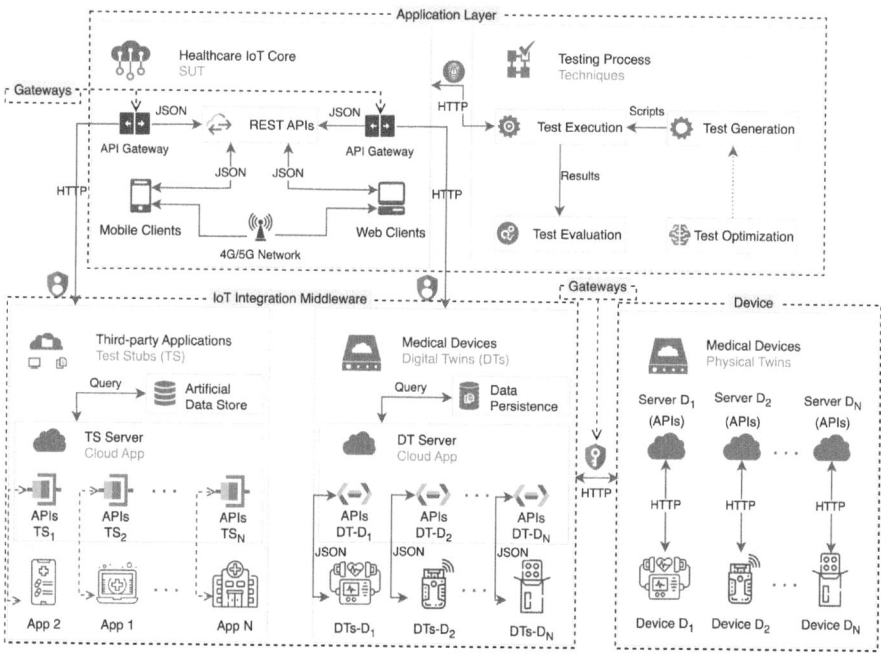

Fig. 1. An overview of HITA. The arrow (⟶) shows one-way information flow, (⟷) indicates two-way information flow, (◀-▶) exhibits behavior simulation, and (·····▶) depicts optional information flow.

3   HITA: An Architecture for Test Infrastructure

3.1   HITA Components

Fig. 1 shows a real-world test infrastructure software architecture (HITA) designed for healthcare IoT applications. HITA is designed based on two commonly used architectural patterns, i.e., *collaborative* and *centralized* for healthcare IoT [21]. HITA follows IoT reference architecture [13], which is composed of an *Application Layer* including healthcare IoT core and testing process, *IoT Integration Middleware* with the DT generation (DTGen) and test stubs generation (TSGen) components, *Gateways*, and *Device* comprising physical medical devices.

Healthcare IoT Core. The system under test (SUT) is a healthcare IoT application core that consists of several web and mobile clients for different users, such as patients, medical professionals, caregivers, and health authorities. The primary communication channel for mobile clients (including iPads/Tablets) is the 4G/5G network due to its availability and access in remote areas. WiFi is used as an alternative communication channel in rare cases. An important component of healthcare IoT applications is Application Programming Interfaces (APIs) developed according to the Representational State Transfer (REST) architecture [12]. These REST APIs allow communication among various clients, third-party applications, and medical devices. The data interchange format used for this purpose is JavaScript Object Notation (JSON). To execute the tests on SUT, several different types of medical devices and third-party applications need to be integrated. HITA utilizes the DTGen component for medical devices and the TSGen component for third-party applications to handle integration challenges. API Gateways are used for secure communication with DTGen and TSGen components using Hypertext Transfer Protocol (HTTP) and secure API keys.

Medical Devices - DTGen Component. For integration with medical devices, HITA utilizes the concept of digital twins to create a virtual representation of physical devices. Each medical device from a different vendor is connected to a server with several APIs for integration (as shown in the right-bottom of Fig. 1). The architecture for creating physical medical devices DTs consists of one *DT Server* with APIs (e.g., *APIs DT-D_1*) specific to a certain type of DTs representing a particular device (e.g., *DTs-D_1*). APIs need to be developed following REST architecture [12] to allow easy integration with SUT. DTs of medical devices can be generated with commonly used approaches [32] like model-based approach or ML approach. In the case of multiple versions of a medical device, a separate DT for each device variant is required to be generated. For the communication between the *DT Server* and DTs, JSON data interchange format is used. In case medical devices support different JSON schema, the Schema Registry can be used to ensure compatibility. The DTGen component also consists of *Data Persistence* to preserve the state of DTs among various requests. The APIs of DTs are used to integrate DTs with SUT and physical medical devices. During testing, the DTs act as middle-ware between SUT and physical medical devices. DTs handle all communication traffic from SUT and communicate (via HTTP) with their physical twins when necessary.

Third-Party Applications - TSGen Component. To handle the challenges of integrating third-party applications for testing purposes, HITA's TSGen component plays an important role. Each third-party application has dedicated servers with APIs for integration. The architecture for test stubs creation consists of one *TS Server* with APIs (e.g., *APIs TS$_1$*) simulating the behavior of various applications (e.g., *App 1*). The APIs for each test stub must be developed according to REST architecture [12] for easy integration with SUT. Test stubs play a key role in replicating the functionality of third-party applications. For APIs requiring data (e.g., health data), the architecture includes an artificial data store with multiple databases corresponding to APIs representing different applications. The data manipulation is performed using query language compliant with the database type.

Testing Process. The testing process starts with the test generation step using techniques for generating test data, test sequence, and test oracle. Before testing SUT, it is important to ensure that DTGen and TSGen components adequately represent the desired behaviors. This can be done through pilot experiments evaluating the similarity in behaviors. The similarity in outputs should ideally be close to 100% to have sufficient reliance on testing results. The generated tests in the form of test scripts are executed on the SUT. Test execution requires API keys for communicating with SUT according to test scripts. The results of test execution are evaluated to analyze errors, faults, and failures. Moreover, test optimization during test generation is required for testing in a rapid-release environment and within a short time frame.

HITA Operational Context. A tester initiates the testing process for testing a particular aspect of SUT, REST API testing, or graphical user interface (GUI) testing. This requires SUT to be integrated and operated with DTGen and TSGen components. Tests are executed on SUT through HTTP using JSON format. The SUT processes the request and communicates with medical devices DTs or third-party applications TS, depending on the test case. Finally, SUT generates a JSON response containing test execution results and sends it to the test execution module. This process continues for a specified testing budget.

3.2   Quality Attributes

Scalability. An important concern when testing a healthcare IoT application with a growing number of medical devices is *scalability* of development efforts. HITA provides a component for digital twins used in place of physical medical devices during testing. Any number of digital twins corresponding to a particular medical device can be easily created and operated in HITA, either utilizing model-based or ML practices. Digital twins eliminate the physical need to integrate several medical devices and the risk of damaging physical devices. The use of digital twins is also *cost-effective*, which is another key consideration for creating test infrastructure. In addition to digital twins, HITA has a *Device* layer for connecting medical devices in the case physical devices are required in testing.

Maintainability. Using digital twins of medical devices and test stubs of third-party applications enables achieving *maintainability* quality. Furthermore, HITA utilizes one server for DTGen and TSGen components that can operate locally or on the cloud, depending upon industrial preferences. Using one server each for both components requires less *maintainability* effort as compared to using individual servers for different applications.

Extensibility. The modular structure of HITA components allows for achieving *extensibility*. For each new medical device, digital twins and their APIs can be created using a model-based or ML approach. The APIs of digital twins are used for communication with SUT and the physical device. In the case of adding new healthcare services or features from a third-party application, a test stub is required to be created consisting of APIs for communication with SUT. The artificial dataset is created for testing if the new application is data-intensive and the data is unavailable or inaccessible.

Evolvability. HITA implicitly achieves *evolvability* quality attribute by facilitating the evolvability of medical devices and third-party applications. Whenever a new medical device is added or an existing one is upgraded, the DTGen component can be utilized to generate a new DT or calibrate an existing one. Similarly, when third-party applications undergo evolution, the TSGen component can be employed to generate or update test stubs. This leads to achieving overall *evolvability* requirements of SUT and integrated devices/applications during testing.

Heterogeneity. Creating test infrastructure for healthcare IoT applications involves integration with heterogeneous systems such as different medical devices and various types of third-party applications. HITA addresses this challenge by utilizing REST APIs, HTTP communication protocol, and the JSON data interchange format, providing a standardized method across all layers and components. This enables HITA to seamlessly support heterogeneous medical devices and third-party applications.

Security & Privacy. Using real health records (e.g., patients' health data) during the testing process may lead to security breaches and data privacy issues. To handle security concerns, HITA imposes authentication and authorization mechanisms on all components. For data privacy, the TSGen and DTGen components consist of *Artificial Data Store* and *Data Persistence*, respectively, which contain synthetic data instead of real patients' health data.

Availability. A critical problem solved by HITA is the *availability* of medical devices and third-party applications during testing. Running extensive tests with the goal of rigorous testing may lead to unavailable services. HITA uses third-party applications' test stubs in the form of APIs running on a server (*TS Server*). Similarly, digital twins have *DT Server* to handle requests during test execution. These servers are dedicated for testing purposes and hosted locally or on the cloud according to the up-time required for the testing process.

Robustness. The goal of testing a healthcare IoT application is to identify errors, faults, and failures with the assumption that integrated applications are robust. HITA instructs the development of APIs for DTGen and TSGen components following REST architecture, which provides a reliable mechanism for integration and communication among various applications [12]. Moreover, as a result of test execution, DTGen, and TSGen components generate responses with failure and success information that enables identifying errors/faults in SUT.

Portability. It is an additional feature of HITA. The architecture followed by TSGen and DTGen components can work on local machines when testing offline and remotely in different cloud environments.

4   Evaluation

We evaluate HITA's DTGen component considering the DT fidelity, scalability of operating 100 DTs, and time cost of DT generation steps. We utilize model-based and ML approaches to generate DTs. We address the following research questions (RQs) in this evaluation.

- **RQ1:** *What is the fidelity of DTs generated using model-based and ML approaches?*
  In this RQ, we analyze the fidelity DTs in terms of their similarity with corresponding physical devices.
- **RQ2:** *How do DTs operate with test infrastructure as the number of DTs scale up?*
  In this RQ, we assess the scalability of HITA by examining its ability to manage the operation of 100 DTs across various batch sizes (i.e., 10, 20, .., 100) during test execution.
- **RQ3:** *How much time is required in creating DTs using model-based and ML approaches?*
  In this RQ, we examine the time cost in various steps of model-based and ML approaches for creating DTs.

4.1 DTGen Component Implementation

We generate DTs with two common approaches, i.e., model-based and ML approaches [32]. The DTs generation steps of both approaches are described below.

Model-Based DT. To generate model-based DT, we follow the approach presented in [26], which is briefly described below. In the first step, we model the structural and behavioral aspects of a medical device for which we need to create DTs. This requires creating a domain model of a medical device to capture device concepts and properties, specifying constraints on device properties using Object Constraint Language (OCL), and modeling the device behavior in the form of state machines. Creating models and constraints in the first step is manual. The next steps are automated. In the second step, we create an instance model of the domain model using the input device property values (in JSON format) and validate the instance model using OCL constraints [27]. In the third step, we create a device state machine as the owned behavior of the device instance model. Finally, we make a device executable model to operate DT simulating the device.

ML-Based DT. Generating DTs using ML requires medical devices' data for training. Since medical devices are assigned to patients, their data is inaccessible. In the first step, we collect data using a REST API testing tool (i.e., EvoMaster [4]). For each test execution, we collect data from the API request and response. In the second step, we preprocess the data to remove outliers and handle missing values. In the third step, we define a neural network (NN) architecture with an input layer representing total features and output layers representing total classes. The number of hidden layers, dropouts, and activation functions are finalized through a pilot experiment for hyperparameter search. In the fourth step, we train the NN with the training data. For training, we use the Adam optimizer and cross-entropy loss function, which are suitable for classification tasks in ML. At the end of training, we store the trained model. Finally, to operate a DT, we load the trained model and prepare for inference.

Development Utilities. We implemented the DTGen component in Python, with different frameworks and libraries employed for both DT generation approaches. For the model-based DTs, we utilized the PyEcore[1] framework to handle modeling aspects of DT. For ML-based DTs, we used Scikit-learn [23] library and PyTorch framework. To develop a DT server for the DTGen component, we utilized the Flask[2] framework, with Flask-RESTful library for creating REST APIs of DTs. In addition, to facilitate DTs' data persistence and communication, we used JSON data interchange format.

---

[1] https://github.com/pyecore/pyecore.
[2] https://flask.palletsprojects.com/en/2.2.x/.

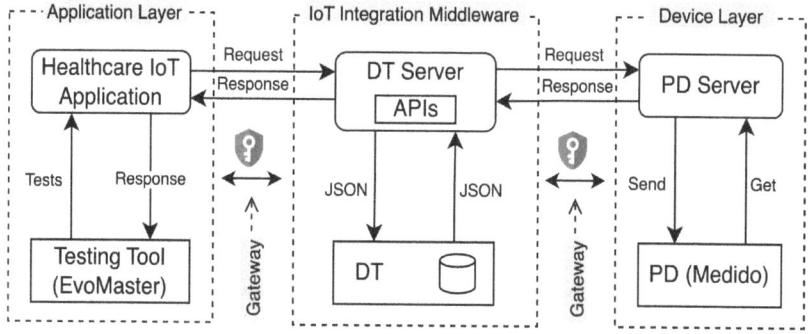

Fig. 2. Evaluation setup with a healthcare IoT application, testing tool, DTGen component, and physical device (PD).

4.2 Experiment Setup and Execution

Real-World Case Study. We used Medido [17] medicine dispenser integrated with a healthcare IoT application provided by Oslo City as a part of the experiment apparatus. Medido is a multi-featured automatic medicine dispenser that provides various functionalities to stakeholders. It enables healthcare specialists and caretakers to personalize device settings, including language, alarm, and medication plans. Its key operations are loading medication plans from the healthcare IoT application, following a plan to dispense medicine at the specified time, and notifying concerned healthcare specialists/caretakers regarding missed doses and medicine dispense problems.

Setup. Fig. 2 presents an overview of the evaluation setup. At *application layer*, we used a healthcare IoT application provided by Oslo City as a part of the experiment apparatus. We used a REST API testing tool, namely EvoMaster [4]. At *device layer*, we utilized Medido [17] medicine dispenser supplied by Oslo City. Medido is connected to its server, which manages communication with the device. For the *IoT integration middleware*, we generated DTs of Medido using model-based and ML approaches, namely MBDT and MLDT, respectively. For MBDT, we modeled the domain, constraints, and state machines of Medido. For MLDT, we performed a pilot experiment to determine the NN architecture and hyperparameters. The resulting NN has two hidden layers with dimensions eight and four, dropout rate=0.2, and a Sigmoid activation function. The remaining hyperparameters are learning rate=0.01, epochs=3000, optimizer=Adam, and loss function=Cross-entropy. For both MBDT and MLDT, we created DT APIs and configured a DT Server. We used JSON as a data interchange format for communication with DTs.

For each RQ, we executed EvoMaster to generate test data and sent this data to both MBDT and MLDT, as well as to Medido. EvoMaster was configured to run for a duration of two hours at a rate of 100 API requests per minute. In each execution, we collected responses from MBDT, MLDT, and Medido. Using responses, we analyzed the fidelity (for RQ1) of MBDT and MLDT with Medido based on the similarity in responses. For RQ2, we generated 100 MBDTs and 100 MLDTs and run them in different batch sizes, i.e., 10, 20, 30, ..., 100. We sent test data to all MBDTs and MLDTs running in different batches and to Medido and compared the responses of all DTs. For RQ3, we executed each machine-dependent automated step 10 times on one machine to analyze the average time.

Execution. We ran experiments using a machine with a macOS operating system, an 8-core CPU, and 24 GB RAM.

4.3   Metrics and Statistical Tests

We analyze DTs' fidelity in terms of their operating similarity with PD. For this purpose, we used the Cosine similarity measure. To statistically analyze DTs' fidelity, we also used the Wilcoxon test signed rank and Cliff's Delta (δ) with a significance level (α) 0.05, following guidelines by Arcuri and Briand [5].

4.4   Results and Discussion

Following, we discuss results corresponding to each RQ.

RQ1: DT Fidelity. Table 1 shows results of MBDT and MLDT fidelity in terms of their similarity with Medido PD. The similarity of MBDT and MLDT with Medido PD is ≈94% and ≈95%, respectively, indicating both types of DTs have close operational resemblance with PD. The Wilcoxon test p-values are greater than α for both MBDT and MLDT. This shows there is no significant difference between MBDT and PD and MLDT and PD. The effect size analysis indicates that the difference magnitude is negligible for both MBDT and MLDT. This indicates a high operational similarity of MBDT and MLDT with their corresponding Medido PD.

RQ1 Result

> DTs generated using model-based and ML approaches have fidelity compared to Medido.

RQ2: DTGen Component Scalability. Fig. 3 shows boxplots for fidelity comparison of MBDTs and MLDTs running in different batch sizes, i.e., 10, 20, 30, ..., 100, highlighted with increasing gradient color. It can be observed that the median fidelity level of MBDTs is approximately 94% across different batches. Similarly, MLDTs' median fidelity is approximately 95.5% for varying batch sizes. It is worth noticing that the fidelity of different batches of MBDTs and MLDTs with their corresponding Medido PD is consistent with the increase in

Table 1. RQ1: Fidelity of MBDT and MLDT compared with Medido PD

	MBDT	MLDT
Cosine Similarity	94.05%	95.54%
Wilcoxon Test($p - value$)	1.0	1.0
Effect Size (δ)	-0.12 (negligible)	-0.09 (negligible)

DTs number. Furthermore, the fidelity values reported in Table 1 for one MBDT and MLDT are in order with the median fidelity values observed while operating multiple MBDTs and MLDTs in various batch sizes. This indicates that operating different numbers of DTs has nearly identical fidelity as the number of DTs grows.

RQ2 Result

The fidelity of 100 DTs (MBDTs and MLDTs) is consistent in all batch sizes, highlighting that the DTGen component is scalable.

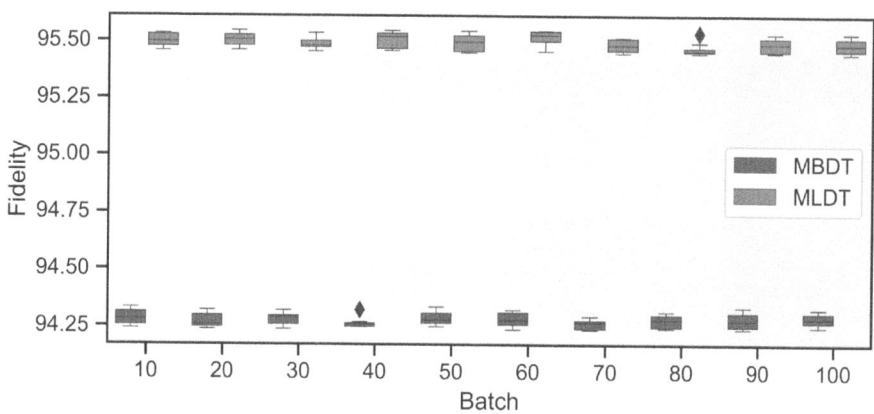

Fig. 3. RQ2: Scalability of multiple MBDTs and MLDTs running in different batch sizes

RQ3: Time Cost. Table 2 and 3 present the estimated time cost involved in various steps of creating MBDT and MLDT, respectively. To generate MBDT, modeling domain, constraints, and behavior requires significant time, approximately 1–2 hours, which can vary depending on the modelers' experience. Providing input configurations may take 2–5 minutes. It is important to note that generating one or more MBDTs is an automated step and only takes time in ms.

The time required to generate one MBDT and 100 MBDTs is, on average, ≈108 and ≈229 ms, respectively.

For MLDT, the data collection step requires integrating a testing tool and compiling data during execution. This semi-automatic step takes 2–3 hours to collect sufficient data set for training. In case more data set is required, this can take more time. Configuring ML involves identifying suitable NN architecture and hyperparameters search that can take approximately 1–2 hours. Training MLDT with 3000 epochs takes 3 min and 15 s, and with 5000 epochs it takes 5 min and 29 s. In our experiments, 3000 epochs are sufficient to obtain a well-trained model; however, training with higher epochs is not high. The time required to generate one MLDT and 100 MLDTs is, on average, ≈4 and ≈38 ms, respectively. The automatic steps' time cost varies with machine specifications, thus requiring further empirical study involving machines with different specifications.

RQ3 Result

DTs generated using ML require fewer manual steps and more time compared to model-based DT. ML approach with higher time cost generates DTs with higher fidelity compared to model-based DTs.

Table 2. RQ3: MBDT time cost considering main/sub-steps, automation level, and average time

	Steps	Automation	Time
Modeling	Domain model, OCL constraints, state machines	Manual	1–2 hrs
Inputs Configs.	Device properties, server settings, API mapping	Manual	2–5 min
DT Generation	Create executable models and DT storage, operate DT	Automatic	108.428 ms (avg)
00 DTs	Create 100 DTs	Automatic	228.931 ms (avg)

4.5   Threats to Validity

To minimize potential **external validity** threats, we evaluated HITA's DTGen component utilizing a Medido medicine dispenser integrated with a real-world healthcare IoT application. Medido is a widely used and a good representative

Table 3. RQ3: MLDT time cost considering main/sub-steps, automation level, and average time

	Steps	Automation	Time
Data Collection	Setup and run testing tool, compile data from responses	Semi-Automatic	2–3 hrs
ML Configs.	NN design, tune hyperparameters	Semi-automatic	$\approx$1–2 hr
Training	Train and save NN model	Automatic	3m 15 s - 5m 29 s
DT Generation	Load NN model, create storage, operate DT	Automatic	4.551 ms (avg)
100 DTs	Create 100 DTs	Automatic	38.208 ms (avg)

medicine dispenser. We intend to add more medical devices to conduct a large-scale evaluation in the future. To reduce **internal validity** threats, we carefully designed experiments based on device and API documentation from Oslo City. We conducted sessions with industry practitioners to showcase the setup and get their feedback. Apart from initial configurations, the MBDT generation approach involves no further parameter tuning during execution. Regarding the MLDT experiment, we conducted pilot experiments for hyperparameter search, ensuring careful consideration of hyperparameters. To handle **construct and conclusion validity** threats, we used the Cosine similarity measure, the Wilcoxon test signed rank, and Cliff's Delta. We used the suggested significance level [5] for statistical analysis. In the time cost analysis (RQ3), we executed each automated step 10 times for both MBDT and MLDT to calculate the average time, ensuring robustness in our analysis.

5 Experiences and Lessons Learned

Following we outline our experience and lessons learned while developing HITA work products and analyzing them through experiments.

5.1 DTs Role in Test Infrastructure

System-level testing of healthcare IoT applications requires different medical devices in the loop. Each type of medical device from a different vendor is linked to a web server that has certain constraints on maximum allowed requests. The test generation and execution process involves sending several requests to medical devices through a healthcare IoT application. This leads to the blocking of service or the damaging of a medical device. Further, testing with hundreds of such devices is costly and not a practical option. Based on such experiences from Oslo City, we propose the idea of using DTs in place of physical medical devices to enable testing with multiple digital representations of physical devices. Thus, DTs have an important role in this regard. DTs with dedicated *DT Server* and APIs eliminate the risk of service blockage or device damage. Virtually representing physical devices, DTs are a scalable and cost-effective solution. Our experiments with 100 DTs in different batches (i.e., 10, 20, 30, ..., 100) indicated scalability, heterogeneity, and cost-effectiveness of the DTGen component.

5.2   Trade-Off Between Model-Based and ML DTs

The model-based approach for the automated generation of DTs requires creating domain models of medical devices capturing devices' structural aspects and modeling behavioral aspects of medical devices using executable state machines. Several modeling tools (e.g., IBM RSA and Papyrus) are available for this purpose. Test engineers need to have a fundamental level of familiarity with any of the modeling tools. Models developed in this way involve a one-time effort and can be reused for testing multiple evolution phases of SUT [28,29]. In the case of adding or upgrading medical devices, only the domain model and executable state machines need to be fine-tuned.

For generating DTs using the ML approach, training data needs to be generated with medical devices in the loop. A key consideration for generating training data is a device's request processing capability. For example, if a device takes two seconds to process a request, sending many requests without delay may damage the device. With training data collected and preprocessed, identifying suitable neural network architecture and hyperparameters for training requires several experiment trials. These steps are largely automated; nevertheless, for each new/upgraded device, these steps must be repeated.

Using model-based or ML approaches for DT generation depends on the industrial application context. The model-based approach requires more manual steps compared to the ML approach. However, device data is a fundamental requirement for using the ML approach which needs to be generated using test devices. Since model-based and ML DTs have nearly similar fidelity, either approach can be employed with test infrastructure.

5.3   Fidelity Evaluation of DTs

While utilizing DTs of physical devices, an important consideration is the fidelity of DTs corresponding to physical twins. For this purpose, we empirically evaluated the fidelity of model-based and ML DTs (up to 100) in terms of their functional similarities with a physical medicine dispenser (Medido). The results highlighted the functionality of DTs was almost similar to medicine dispensers. Moreover, fidelity evaluation in terms of internal behaviors is challenging due to limited access to internal operations of physical medicine dispensers.

5.4   Testing with Third-Party Applications

We experimented with testing the REST API of a healthcare IoT application (SUT) connected to different third-party applications [25]. In our experiments, we observed that API failures of third-party applications during test execution pose a challenge in pinpointing faults within the SUT. We also noticed that services provided by third-party applications often become unavailable after numerous test executions, causing a hindrance to the rigorous testing of healthcare IoT applications. Hence, the creation of test stubs for third-party applications, as suggested in HITA, appears to be a viable solution.

5.5   Domain-Specific Testing Strategies

Our experiments with REST API testing highlighted the need for domain-specific testing strategies for healthcare IoT applications [25]. We analyzed that automated realistic test data generation is a challenging and open research problem. For example, automatically generating a valid medication plan for a patient is not a simple task. Generating a valid medication plan requires information regarding the start date, dose intake, number of days to take medicines, number of doses, and the total number of medicines allowed in a roll of a medicine dispenser. This involves understanding domain properties related to medications and the context of a medicine dispenser. There is still a need for domain-specific testing strategies.

5.6   Intelligent Test Generation Technique

Healthcare IoT applications commonly have a two-way communication mechanism with different medical devices and third-party applications. Several scenarios require an integrated medical device or third-party application to initiate the first step of the process. Automatically generating test cases for such scenarios is challenging. For instance, the steps to assign an alert (received from a patient) to concerned personnel include: (i) the patient's medical device generates an alert, (ii) the alert is received as an unassigned alert, (iii) identify an appropriate person (doctor, nurse, caretaker, etc.) to assign the alert, and (iv) assign the alert with notification to health authorities. An alert should be generated beforehand to test the alert-assigning scenario. This requires an intelligent technique for automated test case generation since HITA is designed for creating test infrastructure.

5.7   Test Optimization

Testing an industrial healthcare IoT application in production and a rapid-release environment requires a designated time budget for test generation and execution. Executing a maximum number of test cases with the aim of rigorous testing for each release is desirable but not feasible, even using test stubs and digital twins. An approach for generating and executing optimized test cases is necessary to ensure the dependability of healthcare IoT applications within a given time frame.

6   Conclusion and Future Work

In this paper, we presented real-world architectural work in collaboration with Oslo City's healthcare department. We introduced HITA – a test infrastructure architecture to facilitate automated system-level testing of healthcare IoT applications, with design considerations aligned to Oslo City's healthcare department requirements. We evaluated HITA's DTGen component by creating DTs of a Medido medicine dispenser using model-based and ML approaches. Our evaluation focused on analyzing the fidelity of DT created using both approaches, assessing the scalability of the DTGen component when operating 100 DTs in different batch sizes, and the time cost involved in creating DTs. Results show that the fidelity of DTs created using model-based and ML approaches is 94% and 95%, respectively. Results with 100 DTs also show that the DTGen component is scalable. Moreover, results indicate that DTs generated with the ML approach have fewer manual steps and higher time costs compared to model-based DTs. Finally, we presented experience and lessons learned based on experiments conducted with work products of HITA that are valuable for industry practitioners working in a similar domain. Our architecture, findings, and lessons learned are generalizable to various IoT-based systems such as activity/fitness trackers, smart homes, and smart security systems.

In the future, we plan to extend the DTGen component and create DTs of different types of medical devices. We also intend to implement HITA's TSGen component supporting third-party applications. Next, we plan to develop domain-specific testing strategies focusing on GUI testing, REST API testing, and test optimization.

Acknowledgements. This work is a part of the WTT4Oslo project (No. 309175) funded by the Research Council of Norway. All the experiments reported in this paper are conducted in a laboratory setting of Simula Research Laboratory; therefore, they do not by any means reflect the quality of services Oslo City provides to its citizens. Finally, we would like to acknowledge Kjetil Moberg for providing feedback on the initial version of this paper.

References

1. Norwegian health authority. https://www.oslo.kommune.no/etater-foretak-og-ombud/helseetaten/. Accessed 18 May 2023
2. Al-Joboury, I.M., Hemiary, E.H.: Internet of things architecture based cloud for healthcare. Iraqi J. Inform. Commun. Technol. **1**(1), 18–26 (2018). https://doi.org/10.31987/ijict.1.1.7
3. Alnefaie, S., Cherif, A., Alshehri, S.: Towards a distributed access control model for IoT in healthcare. In: 2019 2nd International Conference on Computer Applications and Information Security (ICCAIS), pp. 1–6. IEEE (2019). https://doi.org/10.1109/CAIS.2019.8769462
4. Arcuri, A.: Restful API automated test case generation with Evomaster. ACM Trans. Softw. Eng. Methodol. **28**(1), 1–37 (2019). https://doi.org/10.1145/3293455

5. Arcuri, A., Briand, L.: A practical guide for using statistical tests to assess randomized algorithms in software engineering. In: Proceedings of the 33rd International Conference on Software Engineering, pp. 1–10 (2011). https://doi.org/10.1145/1985793.1985795

6. Azimi, I., et al.: HiCH: hierarchical fog-assisted computing architecture for healthcare IoT. ACM Trans. Embed. Comput. Syst. **16**(5s), 1–20 (2017). https://doi.org/10.1145/3126501

7. Bertolino, A., Inverardi, P., Muccini, H.: Software architecture-based analysis and testing: a look into achievements and future challenges. Computing **95**, 633–648 (2013). https://doi.org/10.1007/s00607-013-0338-9

8. Morrison, R., Balasubramaniam, D., Falkner, K. (eds.): Software Architecture: Second European Conference, ECSA 2008 Paphos, Cyprus, September 29-October 1, 2008 Proceedings. Springer, Berlin, Heidelberg (2008)

9. Brosch, F., Koziolek, H., Buhnova, B., Reussner, R.: Architecture-based reliability prediction with the palladio component model. IEEE Trans. Softw. Eng. **38**(6), 1319–1339 (2011). https://doi.org/10.1109/TSE.2011.94

10. Catarinucci, L., et al.: An IoT-aware architecture for smart healthcare systems. IEEE Internet Things J. **2**(6), 515–526 (2015). https://doi.org/10.1109/JIOT.2015.2417684

11. Fiedler, M., Meissner, S.: IoT in practice: examples: IoT in logistics and health. In: Bassi, A., et al. (eds.) Enabling Things to Talk. Springer, Berlin, Heidelberg (2013). https://doi.org/10.1007/978-3-642-40403-0_4

12. Fielding, R.T.: Architectural Styles and the Design of Network-Based Software Architectures. University of California, Irvine (2000)

13. Guth, J., Breitenbücher, U., Falkenthal, M., Leymann, F., Reinfurt, L.: Comparison of IoT platform architectures: a field study based on a reference architecture. In: 2016 Cloudification of the Internet of Things (CIoT), pp. 1–6. IEEE (2016). https://doi.org/10.1109/CIOT.2016.7872918

14. Jin, Z., Offutt, J.: Deriving tests from software architectures. In: Proceedings 12th International Symposium on Software Reliability Engineering, pp. 308–313. IEEE (2001). https://doi.org/10.1109/ISSRE.2001.989484

15. Lindquist, W., Helal, S., Khaled, A., Hutchinson, W.: Iotility: architectural requirements for enabling health IoT ecosystems. IEEE Trans. Emerg. Top. Comput. **9**(3), 1206–1218 (2019). https://doi.org/10.1109/TETC.2019.2957241

16. Malakuti, S., Grüner, S.: Architectural aspects of digital twins in IIoT systems. In: Proceedings of the 12th European Conference on Software Architecture: Companion Proceedings, pp. 1–2 (2018). https://doi.org/10.1145/3241403.3241417

17. Medido, A.M.D.: https://medido.com/en/. Accessed 10 Nov 2023

18. Mezghani, E., Exposito, E., Drira, K.: A model-driven methodology for the design of autonomic and cognitive IoT-based systems: application to healthcare. IEEE Trans. Emerg. Top. Comput. Intell. **1**(3), 224–234 (2017). https://doi.org/10.1109/TETCI.2017.2699218

19. Moosavi, S.R., et al.: SEA: a secure and efficient authentication and authorization architecture for IoT-based healthcare using smart gateways. Procedia Comput. Sci. **52**, 452–459 (2015). https://doi.org/10.1016/j.procs.2015.05.013

20. Muccini, H., Inverardi, P., Bertolino, A.: Using software architecture for code testing. IEEE Trans. Softw. Eng. **30**(3), 160–171 (2004). https://doi.org/10.1109/TSE.2004.1271170

21. Muccini, H., Spalazzese, R., Moghaddam, M.T., Sharaf, M.: Self-adaptive IoT architectures: an emergency handling case study. In: Proceedings of the 12th

European Conference on Software Architecture: Companion Proceedings, pp. 1–6 (2018). https://doi.org/10.1145/3241403.3241424

22. Nguyen, D.C., Pathirana, P.N., Ding, M., Seneviratne, A.: BEdgeHealth: A decentralized architecture for edge-based IoMT networks using blockchain. IEEE Internet Things J. **8**(14), 11743–11757 (2021). https://doi.org/10.1109/JIOT.2021.3058953

23. Pedregosa, F., et al.: Scikit-learn: machine learning in Python. J. Mach. Learn. Res. **12**, 2825–2830 (2011)

24. Pise, A., Yoon, B., Singh, S.: Enabling ambient intelligence of things (AIoT) healthcare system architectures. Comput. Commun. **198**, 186–194 (2023). https://doi.org/10.1016/j.comcom.2022.10.029

25. Sartaj, H., Ali, S., Yue, T., Moberg, K.: Testing real-world healthcare IoT application: experiences and lessons learned. In: Proceedings of the 31st ACM Joint European Software Engineering Conference and Symposium on the Foundations of Software Engineering, pp. 2044-2049. ESEC/FSE 2023, Association for Computing Machinery (2023). https://doi.org/10.1145/3611643.3613888

26. Sartaj, H., Ali, S., Yue, T., Moberg, K.: Model-based digital twins of medicine dispensers for healthcare IoT applications. Softw. Prac. Experience **54**(6), 1172–1192 (2024). https://doi.org/10.1002/spe.3311

27. Nejati, S., Gay, G. (eds.): Search-Based Software Engineering: 11th International Symposium, SSBSE 2019, Tallinn, Estonia, August 31 – September 1, 2019, Proceedings. Springer International Publishing, Cham (2019)

28. Sartaj, H., Iqbal, M.Z., Khan, M.U.: CDST: a toolkit for testing cockpit display systems. In: 2020 IEEE 13th International Conference on Software Testing, Validation and Verification (ICST), pp. 436–441. IEEE (2020). https://doi.org/10.1109/ICST46399.2020.00058

29. Sartaj, H., Iqbal, M.Z., Khan, M.U.: Testing cockpit display systems of aircraft using a model-based approach. Softw. Syst. Model. **20**(6), 1977–2002 (2021). https://doi.org/10.1007/s10270-020-00844-z

30. Sharaf, M., Abughazala, M., Muccini, H.: Arduino realization of caps IoT architecture descriptions. In: Proceedings of the 12th European Conference on Software Architecture: Companion Proceedings, pp. 1–4 (2018). https://doi.org/10.1145/3241403.3241412

31. Sharma, P., Namasudra, S., Crespo, R.G., Parra-Fuente, J., Trivedi, M.C.: EHDHE: enhancing security of healthcare documents in IoT-enabled digital healthcare ecosystems using blockchain. Inf. Sci. **629**, 703–718 (2023). https://doi.org/10.1016/j.ins.2023.01.148

32. Somers, R.J., Douthwaite, J.A., Wagg, D.J., Walkinshaw, N., Hierons, R.M.: Digital-twin-based testing for cyber-physical systems: a systematic literature review. Inform. Softw. Technol. **156**, 107145 (2023). https://doi.org/10.1016/j.infsof.2022.107145

Doctoral Symposium

Pragmatic Architectural Framework to Design for Sustainability in Cloud Software Services

Sahar Ahmadisakha$^{(\boxtimes)}$ ⓘ and Vasilios Andrikopoulos ⓘ

University of Groningen, Groningen, Netherlands
{s.ahmadisakha,v.andrikopoulos}@rug.nl

Abstract. The incorporation of sustainability in cloud software services design is crucial. This paper proposes a Pragmatic Architecting Framework addressing challenges related to sustainability multi-dimensionality and cloud computing characteristics. It aims to provide guidance on handling different cloud stakeholder engagements, offer decision support, and promote sustainability as a core aspect of software architecting. This research presents also the results of a systematic literature review on the sustainability-relating concerns that can affect architectural solutions.

Keywords: Software Architecture · Cloud Software Services · Sustainability · Architecturally Significant Concerns · Decision Support

1 Introduction

Given the rapidly growing use of software-intensive systems, it is essential to recognize the significance of software sustainability. Various endeavors have been made to clarify and define software sustainability, including its four dimensions [21]: *technical, economic, social,* and *environmental,* concerning software longevity, capital preservation, community continuity, and natural resource conservation, respectively. The recognition of sustainability as a quality attribute in software systems has also prompted its integration into software architecture [21]. Additionally, research has demonstrated how software architecture can act as a valuable lever for addressing sustainability [27] in light of its potential to contribute positively to it [18]. While previous research has explored the intersection of software architecture and sustainability [9,21,29] and addressed it in the software system design [20,26], there remains a need for further work on the service orientation aspect [27], specifically on cloud software services.

The pervasive adoption of cloud computing has amplified the importance of sustainability in software services and allows a significant portion of the software market to rely on service orientation, aligning with the Everything as a Service

This work is partly funded by the project SustainableCloud (project number OCENW.M20.243) of the research program Open Competition Domain Science by the Dutch Research Council (NWO).

B. Tekinerdoğan et al. (Eds.): ECSA 2023, LNCS 14590, pp. 471–487, 2024.
https://doi.org/10.1007/978-3-031-66326-0_29

(EaaS) model [2]. However, existing studies in cloud computing have primarily focused on the environmental dimension [12], also overlooking the other cloud software service stakeholders' perspective [2].

This research project aims to develop a Pragmatic Architectural Framework built upon the Sustainability-Aware Architecting Framework (SAAF) [2] for designing sustainable cloud software services (both cloud-based and cloud-native software services). The framework consists of three pillars: (1) a sustainability body of knowledge encompassing its various dimensions and architectural knowledge on the cloud software services, (2) cloud software services' stakeholder engagement to align sustainability-affecting concerns with design choices, and (3) a decision support mechanism enabling the integration of multiple sustainability dimensions with cloud-related architecting decisions and stakeholders. For the first action, we explore the literature in the format of a systematic literature review to elaborate on creating the body of knowledge. This review offers some initial outcomes that pertain to the sustainability-related concerns that can affect the architecture.

This research proposal includes a problem statement in Sect. 2 and a problem decomposition augmented by research methods and anticipated research outcomes in Sect. 3. Section 4 reports on the initial results of a study currently under review, while Sect. 5 presents new results out of the same study. The conclusion in Sect. 6 wraps up the paper.

2   Problem Statement

Main statement: While software architects already possess the expertise to design sustainable software systems in general, there is a paucity of literature and experiences on creating software (services) that function within the cloud computing domain aimed at achieving sustainability objectives. In the following, we outline the main arguments to support our statement.

S1. Lack of a Sufficient Body of Knowledge (BoK): Although guidelines for sustainability-aware software development have been formulated in [9] with a focus on the technical and economic dimensions, the intersection of cloud computing and sustainability in the software architecture suffers from a lack of a substantial BoK, specifically given the multi-dimensional nature of sustainability. For instance, while cloud-native architectural assets have been identified in [13], the attainment of sustainability goals remains a distant objective.

S2. Unclear Effect of Cloud-Specific Stakeholders (SHs): Incorporating sustainability into software requirement engineering is of interest [4,24], with existing models and frameworks also promoting sustainability [8,25]. Gaining an understanding of the trade-offs between sustainability goals and other business goals can be instrumental in aiding SHs' decision-making, including architects, as highlighted in [26]. However, a distinct absence is observed in terms of any discernible trace regarding the various cloud-specific SHs (cloud provider, cloud broker, cloud carrier, cloud auditor as per [22]) and their potential impact on the decision-making process of designing cloud software services. For instance, cloud auditor SHs may not necessarily prioritize sustainability concerns, but their specific reports to regulatory agencies or the cloud provider can influence the overall design and preferences of other SHs on the same topic.

S3. Absence of Knowledge on Cloud Implications and Decision Making: Most works exploring the stability of design decisions as architectural knowledge [5] and as a means of achieving architectural sustainability [29] focus on technical aspects, neglecting other dimensions. Moreover, while some information exists on the positive and negative environmental impacts of cloud computing [13,19] and the sustainability impact of software systems [20], our awareness of *cloud-related architecting decisions'* (CAD) sustainability impacts, particularly across all dimensions of sustainability, is still incomplete.

These CADs can encompass, for example, the selection of the cloud provider, as well as the choice of cloud deployment and delivery model [2]. Furthermore, these decisions can be more granular, such as determining the specific cloud computing resources utilized for the range of services that the service can leverage from the provider.

S4. Lack of a Decision Support Method (DSM) Centered Around Sustainability: Given the diverse impacts of various CADs on sustainability goals, it is imperative for architects to employ appropriate decision support methods. However, existing methods focused on CADs [3,11] share common deficiencies in that they fail to prioritize sustainability as a central aspect and neglect to consider its potential (side-)effects. Additionally, these methods do not adequately incorporate the influence of SHs on the decision-making processes.

3   Problem Decomposition

The proposed research project is grounded in the design science framework [28]. It addresses *Research Questions (RQ)* that encompass design problems (RQD) and knowledge questions (RQK). The investigation of these questions will utilize empirical methods described in [10]. In the following, we provide a detailed elaboration on the decomposition of the aforementioned problem statements (S1-S4), assigning them individual objectives (OBJ). Each objective corresponds to a distinct problem and may encompass multiple RQs. Furthermore, we outline the empirical methods to be employed for each OBJ and highlight anticipated outcomes (OCMs).

OBJ1. to Establish a Comprehensive BoK Encompassing Cloud-Related Architectural Knowledge Concerning Sustainability in Cloud

Software Services, both from the Literature and Industrial Perspectives. In light of the identified S1, we pursue the attainment of OBJ1 and formulate two corresponding RQs: *RQK1) How do cloud architectural solutions address sustainability?* to be answered by a Literature Review (LR), and *RQK2) How do practitioners in cloud software services currently address sustainability?* to be addressed by a Practitioner Survey (PS) or a Multi-Case Study (MCS).

As part of this objective, we also aim to investigate and evaluate our hypothesis regarding the potential for achieving *sustainability through cloud computing* via architectural design. To address those inquiries, we anticipate asking about the sustainability concerns involved in architects' cloud usage decisions, the pros and cons of cloud computing in designing for sustainability, and the specific design decisions and solutions addressing sustainability in cloud software services' design. As **OCM1**, we envision a *BoK* for architectural knowledge in the design of sustainable cloud software services, showcasing the feasibility of achieving *sustainability through cloud computing.*

OBJ2. To explore and define the impact of cloud SHs' concerns on the design decisions (DDs). This objective aligns with S2 and is accompanied by a single research question denoted as *RQK3) What are the SH concerns that affect the sustainability of cloud software services and in what way?* This question is going to be investigated through one or more exploratory case studies (CS).

In these studies, we aim to investigate the various SH types (both cloud- and services-specific) and their concerns impacting sustainability. Subsequently, we will consider how architects' decisions are influenced by these sustainability-affecting concerns. **OCM2** is anticipated to *incorporate diverse cloud SHs perspectives within the architectural design.*

OBJ3. To acquire a more comprehensive understanding of the impact of CADs on sustainability and their interrelationships. This objective, aimed at investigating sub-problem S3, will be achieved through the formulation of two corresponding RQs: *RQK4) How do CADs impact sustainability?* (in terms of which decisions and in what way) and *RQK5) How are CADs related to each other?* Both RQs are intended to be explored through one or more exploratory CS.

Here, our research aims to identify CADs and their impact on sustainability. Subsequently, we strive to understand the interrelationship among CADs and explore strategies for managing their effect on sustainability. The **OCM3** pertains to the *identification of CADs and their impact on sustainability, as well as the examination of their interrelationships.*

OBJ4. To establish a DSM considering SHs and the sustainability implications of cloud. In the pursuit of S4, we define a design problem formulated as *RQD6) Design and validate a DSM on the impact of CADs on system sustainability.*

Our intended empirical course of action involves the validation and examination of the final DSM through confirmatory CS. We anticipate **OCM4** as a *DSM that facilitates the observability of relationships between various CADs and SHs throughout the decision-making process, with sustainability as its paramount objective*

4   Initial Results: Solutions on Sustainability

In our endeavor to address the stated problem and contribute to a comprehensive understanding, we embarked on the task of developing a body of knowledge by conducting a systematic literature review. Through this systematic review which is currently under review, we tried to answer the **RQK1) How do cloud architectural solutions address sustainability?** To provide a more detailed exploration of this query, we have formulated a set of sub-inquiries as follows:

RQ1: *What cloud architectural solutions have been proposed to address one or more sustainability dimensions?*
RQ2: *What are the building blocks of the proposed solutions and how these blocks are related to each other and to the various sustainability dimensions?*
RQ3: *To what extent sustainability dimensions are covered by the identified solutions?*
RQ4: *Which quality requirements in the proposed solutions are taken into account considering sustainability?*
RQ5: *How is the adoption of cloud computing perceived in relation to sustainability?*

Our initial aim was to discover architectural solutions that effectively address sustainability within the context of software systems utilizing the cloud computing model. To apprehend how these systems take sustainability into account, we have investigated the primary studies' solutions. Following this identification, a comprehensive evaluation should be conducted to ascertain the individual contributions of each identified solution toward sustainability objectives. By these means, we could differentiate the solutions that are most widely adopted and subsequently analyze their constituent building blocks to effectively address sustainability, specifically within the context of cloud computing.

Ultimately, our attention in this study was directed toward gaining an understanding of how cloud computing is firmly situated within the solutions space, particularly considering the significance of sustainability. This study was conducted following a widely recognized method for conducting systematic literature reviews, as outlined by [17]. For the main research question (RQK1), we conducted searches in several reputable databases, including Scopus, ACM Digital Library, IEEE Xplore, ScienceDirect, Web of Science, and Wiley Online Library, using the following query:

```
software AND architect* AND sustainab* AND cloud
```

Our initial search yielded a total of **541 papers**. After removing duplicate studies and applying our inclusion and exclusion criteria, we narrowed down the selection to **23** primary studies for the purpose of data extraction. Additionally, we conducted both backward and forward snowballing, as recommended by [16], which further expanded our sample to a total of **27** primary studies. To extract data, we used the fields marked with ID C1 to C9 as presented in Table 1.

Table 1. Data Extraction Form. Each row in this table represents a column in the main data extraction sheet.

ID	Column	Explanation/Purpose	RQ
C1	Paper ID	A unique number attaching to each primary study	-
C2	Paper Title	Title of the primary study	-
C3	Publication Year	The year that primary study is published	-
C4	Stakeholder	To identify whether the primary study proposing the solution from the cloud provider perspective or the cloud consumer one	RQ1
C5	Solution	A summary of the proposed solution and the reason for the solution is extracted here, along with the goal of such a solution	RQ1, RQ2, RQ3
C6	Sustainability Dimension	To single out which sustainability dimension is addressed by the proposal	RQ2, RQ3, RQ4
C7	Service Model	To single out which service model is covered by the proposal	RQ2
C8	Quality Requirements	To identify what quality requirements are considered by the solution	RQ4
C9	Cloud Perception	To identify how cloud computing is understood in the proposal	RQ5
C10	Concern	To identify the sustainability-related concerns mentioned in the primary study	RQ6, RQ7
C11	Viewpoint	To single out which sustainability viewpoint is considered in the primary study	RQ7

After finishing up the data extraction, the results of the data analysis provided the following insights per research question as discussed in the following. We also made the replication package of these five RQs available online.

RQ1–Solution Types: From the 27 primary studies, we successfully identified 10 distinct types of architectural solutions: *Tactics, System Architecture, Software Architecture, Patterns, Modified Cloud Architecture, Model, Infrastructure Architecture, Enterprise Architecture, Design Rules and Principles, and Cloud Management Systems*. These solutions were subsequently categorized based on the role that cloud computing plays within them. When a solution was proposed to benefit the cloud provider side, it was classified under the Cloud Architecture (CA) category. Conversely, if the solution targeted cloud customers, it was classified under the Cloud-Based Architecture (CB) category.
Insight: Reusable architectural solutions, such as *tactics* and *patterns*, are relatively underutilized among the identified solution types.

RQ2–Building Blocks: Upon thorough analysis and synthesis of the solution types, we identified 8 commonly recurring design decisions and pinpointed 11 key entities that serve as the foundational elements of the recognized solution types. The predominant design decision observed is *Application Infrastructure Provisioning*, which essentially underscores the prevalent practice of utilizing cloud computing primarily as a back-end for applications in the solutions and primary studies. In parallel, the most frequently encountered entity we identified is *Application Infrastructure*. This implies that these solutions predominantly focus their modifications and decisions on the infrastructure where the application will ultimately be deployed.

Insight: Given the paramount significance of computational resources and application infrastructure, architects should exercise caution when creating the architectural deployment views of the application.

RQ3–Sustainability Dimensions: Our analysis revealed that all four dimensions of sustainability have been considered in the primary studies. However, none of the primary studies encompasses all of these sustainability dimensions. Notably, the environmental dimension emerged as the most commonly addressed, followed by the economic dimension in second place. The technical and social dimensions took the third and fourth positions, respectively.

Insight: It was surprising to note that the patterns for addressing sustainability dimensions in our study did not align with those reported in [1]. In our research, the most addressed dimension was identified as the environmental dimension, while authors in [1] recognized the technical dimension as the most prominent. This disparity may be attributed to the contextual influence of cloud computing in our study, leading to varying emphases on sustainability dimensions.

RQ4–Quality Requirements: We compiled a list of 28 quality requirements mentioned in the studies. Interestingly, some of these requirements, such as "elasticity" which holds great significance for cloud-based applications [6], were not included in the list presented by ISO [15]. However, the majority of these requirements (22 in total) were found following [7,27]. Among this extensive list, there are five quality requirements that exhibit the strongest associations with various sustainability dimensions. These include *accessibility, compatibility, cost efficiency, energy efficiency*, and *flexibility*.

Insight: Economic sustainability has the largest contribution to different quality requirements. Additionally, cloud computing not only enforces specific quality requirements but also transforms the manner in which we address them.

RQ5–Cloud Perceptions: We delved deeper into our research to determine whether the primary studies acknowledged cloud computing as a facilitator or inhibitor to sustainability. Our findings revealed 17 distinct cloud perceptions, with the prevailing sentiment being that the cloud is most often perceived as an enabler of sustainability.

Insight: In our exploration of these perceptions, we discovered that certain cloud characteristics, as outlined in NIST's definition [23], align with the factors that enable sustainability. While cloud computing may be categorized as a promoter of sustainability, it remains imperative to discern the specific conditions and contexts under which this promotion occurs.

5   Further Results: Concerns on Sustainability

In the context of the previous section, we provided an overview of the results obtained from a systematic literature review aimed at comprehending how architectural solutions within a cloud computing context are concerned with sustainability. In the earlier series of research inquiries (RQ1-RQ5), our exploration centered on the solution space, while the central research question (RQK1) and its goal delve also into another facet, namely the problem space, which we will refer to as *concerns* here. To further expand our investigation in this space for the aim of the current study, we present the following new research questions pursued in the context of the same literature review:

> **RQ6**: *What are the architecturally significant concerns that are sustainability-related as reported by the primary studies?*
> **RQ7**: *How are the identified concerns related to the different sustainability dimensions and viewpoints?*

The aim of RQ6 is to identify the key issues highlighted in the primary studies. In this context, our aim is to isolate and categorize only those concerns that are specifically directed toward sustainability and have the potential to impact it. In other words, we compile a list of concerns that inherently encompass sustainability implications. On the other hand, RQ6 also aims to discern whether these identified concerns have the potential to impact the proposed architectural solutions. As articulated in the definition of Architecturally Significant Requirements (ASR) provided in [14], it is important to note that not all concerns are pertinent to the architectural aspect. Moreover, certain ASRs may not originate as standalone concerns but could emerge from other architectural considerations or the system's contextual factors [14].

In the end, RQ7 seeks to explore whether the identified concerns are associated with distinct *viewpoints* on sustainability, which encompass two main paradigms: Sustainable Software (SS) and Sustainability through Software (StS), as outlined in [27]. The former pertains to the objective of ensuring sustainability in software systems and their architectural design, while the latter concentrates on the delivery of sustainability to stakeholders through the utilization of software systems.

To address these research questions, the search process and the inclusion and exclusion criteria remain consistent with those outlined in the previous section. The structure and approach of the use of the data extraction form will also remain unchanged. However, the data extraction is using fields C10 and C11 in Table 1 to answer RQ6 and RQ7 this time. We introduce C10 to document quotations from primary studies indicating concerns relevant to the proposed solutions. These concerns were selected based on if they are directly related to sustainability goals, i.e. they are sustainability-related concerns. We use C11 to enable the extraction of the viewpoints on the sustainability of each primary study (SS or StS). To address RQ6, we will primarily focus on the data from the C10 row. RQ7, on the other hand, will be addressed by considering both C10 and

C11 in combination. The interested reader can find the new replication package for the last two RQs <u>online</u>. Additionally, it is worth noting that the threats to the validity of this study align with those outlined in the paper currently under review.

5.1 RQ6: Identified Concerns

We have identified a total of 22 concerns from the primary studies. Among them, 10 concerns are identified as Architecturally Significant (AS) and the rest as Non-Architecturally Significant (NAS). It is noteworthy to highlight that both types of concerns are extracted in relation to cloud architecture, as our focus is centered on primary studies related to cloud architectural solutions. In this section, we will list and explain the AS concerns only. NAS concerns are out of the scope of this paper but are available in the replication package.

AS1. Service and Resource Sharing in Communities : There is a *need for diverse services and more resources to support various communities*. This concern arises from the necessity to establish a cloud federation environment, enabling diverse communities to gather and access a wide array of services. Consequently, a multitude of services offered by different providers can be aggregated to serve a specific domain (P1). Moreover, there is also a *need for sharing computing resources across communities*. Within community networks, bandwidth sharing is a common practice, but sharing computing resources, especially storage, is equally essential for the benefit of users and economic advantages (P18).

AS2. Challenges on Data : There are situations in which there is a *large amount of data to process and store*. This data is employed to address a specific sustainability dimension and is hard to manage. This data can be used, for example, for managing economic growth and public participation (P16) or minimizing environmental impacts (P6, P23, P25). In this case, where there is a large amount of data, sometimes *the presence of a huge number of users generating data* could also be a concern. This is a sustainability issue since if systems cannot manage the number of users and the data they are creating, properly, they will end up with high energy usage. If the data production and resource demand are not managed properly, systems will face a loss of users (P2).

Sometimes *data is local and hard to process*. Current data loggers utilized for example in irrigation management systems are not energy-efficient, and they typically store data locally (P5). Additionally, retrieving and processing this data to establish an effective management system is a challenging task. Moreover, *lack of data consistency* can influence energy optimization efforts. For achieving this goal, having a performance trend is necessary, while a lack of unified data models and inconsistent data can present significant challenges to this objective (P12).

We also see *heterogeneous data formats* or *fragmented data* as potential issues. The former means that for data to be processed effectively across various systems and devices, the data must be presented in a uniform format. Without this standardization, there would be a deficiency in interoperability among these diverse systems (P21). The latter point particularly affects environmental data that frequently fails to adhere to established standards and is collected in various, mismatched formats from different sources and groups. Therefore, achieving integrated environmental monitoring necessitates both compliance with standards and service interoperability (P22, P25).

AS3. Challenges on the Network Management : This concern has two faces. First, there is a *need for unifying scheduling and allocation of network resources*. Given the presence of various types of network devices in data centers, it is crucial to achieve unified control over them to enhance energy efficiency (P3). The second network-related concern is that there is *network congestion within data centers*. Traffic congestion at the switch point between the client and server within data centers can have a detrimental impact on the sustainability of a network management system. It can also compromise the guaranteed bandwidth for other customers. To ensure sustainable management, especially within virtual private clouds, the system must be capable of handling various types of network equipment (P14). This concern will affect the physical view of the architecture on the cloud service provider side.

AS4. Lack of Energy Efficiency Support in the Cloud : This concern shows itself in different service offerings of cloud computing. In some cases, the cloud fails to show energy measures to its customers, a deficiency originating from the absence of this functionality across its diverse service layers. In other words, *cloud customers cannot measure their energy usage*. They lack full access to the energy consumption of their applications and cannot trace how their decisions affect energy usage. Additionally, they often lack knowledge on how to migrate their applications to the cloud to achieve energy efficiency (P20, P27).

This deficiency comes from the *lack of functionalities to support energy efficiency in IaaS, PaaS, and SaaS layers*. In the service offerings across different cloud layers, there is a deficiency of components designed to enhance energy efficiency in each respective layer (P26). Developing this feature is also of importance since *creating cost and energy efficiency balance in the serverless applications* is necessary. Since the pricing model is a key business driver of serverless decisions, it is important to have a balance between the cost and the energy usage of this model (P4).

AS5. Need for Architectural and Goal Continuity Across Different Cloud Layers : When it comes to the software evolution and adaptation as a goal, especially for cloud-based software, it should be considered as a multilayer affecting concern, since this software mostly uses different cloud layers (IaaS, PaaS, and SaaS) (P7).

AS6. Challenges in Managing the Resources : In some domains like e-learning, there is a *need for surviving the peaks*. In systems subject to variable loads, it is vital for them to withstand peak request levels, while a substantial amount of resources is needed (P8). The other side of this issue in general, is the *need for maximum performance with minimum computing resources*. When utilizing cloud computing, the virtualization layer can sometimes sacrifice over-all performance in favor of greater elasticity and scalability. Therefore, achieving satisfactory user performance without excessive resource consumption is essential. This not only aids in reducing energy usage but also lowers the costs paid by customers (P11).

Moreover, the *need for running fewer physical hosts* is crucial. To reduce energy consumption, it is crucial to minimize the number of physical hosts running in the data center (P9). Furthermore, increasing the number of operational physical servers leads to higher energy consumption. To minimize both energy usage and the associated costs in data centers, it is imperative to reduce the number of running servers, including the energy used for cooling purposes (P24).

This concern has another side that arises when the cloud provider starts *delivering high-quality services to the cloud customers*. To prevent financial losses for the cloud provider, it is essential to monitor and manage the quality of the service experienced by the end customer. Occasionally, customers may have a subpar experience not because the provider offers inadequate service or resources, but due to their poor network coverage or resource limitation. This aspect should be monitored, even on the customer's device (P19).

AS7. Challenges in Having a Reliable Infrastructure : This concern which can be associated with the deployment view, means that having a reliable infrastructure has some consequences considering its *economic or environmental* impact. Considering the cost, it points out that the importance of having technically and economically feasible hardware and software infrastructure becomes evident when aiming for a continuously up-to-date system that requires minimal maintenance efforts (P10). This means, in turn, that looking at *the need for cost-effective and reliable infrastructure* at the same time is crucial.

Considering the environmental impact, we also see that paying attention to the *infrastructure availability and service accessibility and environmental impact* at the same time is important. Having the infrastructure available and services accessible in the data centers needs high-performance computing which means energy-hungry facilities in data centers. These contrasting requirements must be carefully handled (P15).

AS8. Need for Preventive and Predictive Device Maintenance : To effectively manage energy and maintain a sustainable system, it must have the capability to store historical and real-time data, enabling the detection of failures in real-time or even before they occur (P13).

AS9. Designing a Multi-tenant Web App Is Time-Consuming and Expensive : Creating a multi-tenant web application is a complex endeavor that demands time and effort. This is primarily because many existing frameworks lack support for modularity and reusability, resulting in the loss of initial efforts and reduced long-term maintainability (P17).

AS10. Device Dependent Software : The cost of software design and development escalates when there is a requirement to create distinct software for each individual device (P21). It is because of the need for developing software that is embedded in a particular terminal or independent device. A lack of adopting an as-a-service model can exacerbate the situation. This concern can directly affect the economic sustainability of the system.

5.2   RQ7: Concerns and Sustainability Dimensions Viewpoints

According to the data presented in Table 2, each concern is linked to a particular viewpoint. It is worth noting that the viewpoint itself is not an attribute of the concern; instead, it pertains to the primary study that encompasses the respective concern. In summary, among the 27 studies, there are 11 studies adopting the StS viewpoint and 15 studies the SS viewpoint, with one study encompassing both viewpoints (P21). When examining the concerns, we observe 5 concerns exclusively associated with the SS viewpoint (AS: 3, 4, 5, 7, 9, and 10) and 1 concern (AS: 8) linked to the StS viewpoint.

An additional noteworthy aspect to address is concerns AS1, AS2, and AS6, which emanate from both the StS and SS perspectives. This signifies that these particular concerns can be approached via both viewpoints. For instance, for AS6, the former involves decreasing the number of operational servers by incorporating specific architectural components within the software, thereby promoting environmental sustainability through the careful allocation of virtual machines on the hosting infrastructure (SS). Alternatively, the latter entails having direct control over the active hosts within a data center by creating software to deliver this feature (StS).

It is also worth mentioning that, whenever we observe a StS viewpoint for a primary study, that study contains both AS and NAS concerns. Studies adopting the StS viewpoint often connect AS concerns to broader concerns, such as the promotion of environmental sustainability through smart irrigation systems, which fall outside the scope of AS, while it involves AS2.

Table 2. Architecturally significant concerns, along with the viewpoints and sustainability dimensions from which these concerns arise. **CR**: Concern, **PID**: Primary study ID from Table 3, **AS**: Architecturally Significant, **SS**: Sustainable Software, **StS**: Sustainability through Software.

AS CR#	SID	Viewpoint	Associated Sustainability Dimension	Temper
1	P1	SS	Social	Social
	P18	StS	Social→Economic	
2	P2	SS	Social	Social-Environmental
	P5	StS	Environmental→Economic	
	P6	StS	Environmental	
	P12	StS	Environmental	
	P16	StS	Social→Environmental, Economic	
	P21	StS	Social	
	P22	StS	Environmental→Technical, Economic	
	P23	StS	Environmental	
	P25	StS	Environmental	
3	P3	SS	Environmental	Social-Environmental
	P14	SS	Social→Technical	
4	P4	SS	Environmental→Economic	Environmental
	P20	SS	Environmental	
	P26	SS	Environmental	
	P27	SS	Environmental	
5	P7	SS	Technical→Environmental	Technical
6	P8	SS	Technical	Technical-Economic-Environmental
	P9	SS	Environmental→Economic	
	P11	SS	Environmental	
	P19	StS	Economic	
	P24	StS	Environmental→Economic	
7	P10	SS	Economic→Technical	Economic-Environmental
	P15	SS	Environmental→Technical	
8	P13	StS	Environmental	Environmental
9	P17	SS	Economic→Technical	Economic
10	P21	SS	Technical→Economic	Technical

Regarding the relationship with sustainability dimensions, we create a map connecting concerns and associated dimensions in Table 2. For this purpose looked into the study to find what sustainability dimension(s) this specific concern points to. The arrows in the sustainability dimensions column show that the dimension on the left might affect the ones after it. In this study, we lack sufficient evidence to describe the specific nature of the relationship and how addressing a concern can indirectly impact another sustainability dimension. Table 2 simply identifies a perceived relation from one dimension to another as presented in relevant primary study.

The only aspect we can determine based on the extracted data is the nature of each AS concern, as indicated in Table 2 under the "Temper" column. A concern may be discussed in various studies, and not all studies necessarily cover the same dimension. The Temper column summarizes the diverse natures of each concern, irrespective of its source study. These temper classifications are derived from the associated sustainability dimensions of the concerns. The process involves designating the sustainability dimension on the left side of the arrow in the associated dimensions column as the temperament of the concern.

In other words, the "Associated Sustainability Dimension" column provides a summary of the sustainability dimension linked to the specific concern mentioned in each study. Given that concerns in various studies may be associated with different sustainability dimensions, this column captures those associations. On the other hand, the "Temper" column aims to depict the overall sustainability association of the concern, irrespective of the specific study referencing it. To provide an example, take AS1; it consistently exhibits a social sustainability association across all the studies it originates from. Consequently, the overall temper of this concern is labeled as social, indicating its social nature. Conversely, AS7 displays an economic association in one study and an environmental association in another. This suggests that this concern has the potential to impact both economic and environmental dimensions, which are mentioned in the "Temper" column. The majority of concerns exhibit an *Environmental* temper with respect to sustainability, followed by *Economic*, *Social*, and *Technical* tempers.

6   Conclusion and Future Work

The adoption of cloud computing and the as-a-service model underscores the importance of sustainability in software systems. To effectively integrate sustainability as a quality attribute, considering it from a software architecture perspective is crucial. Three key points emerge within this context: the lack of comprehensive BoK on architectural knowledge of cloud software services encompassing all sustainability dimensions, identifying cloud SHs' sustainability concerns, and the scarcity of decision support to design for sustainability considering the cloud-related architecting decisions. To address these considerations, our proposal aims to develop a *Pragmatic Architecting Framework* tailored for software architects. This framework intends to guide architects in designing *cloud software services with sustainability goals in mind* which a part of the BoK is presented in the current study that concerns cloud architectural solution types and their associated concerns.

Future actions encompass the precise exploration of the implications of these issues on sustainability. Additionally, our objective is to investigate the *interplay* among the dimensions of sustainability linked to these concerns. We also aim to explore the notion of *reusable concerns* associated with sustainability, beginning with the most frequently recurring concerns identified in this study.

Appendix

Table 3. Selected Primary Studies. Detailed code presentations and extracted records for each primary study are available in the replication package. and the new replication package

PID	Primary Study Title and Link	Year
P1	Creating a sustainable federation of cloud-based infrastructures for the future internet	2015
P2	Green architecture for sustainable elearning systems	2017
P3	A Green and High Efficient Architecture for Ground Information Port with SDN	2020
P4	Sustainability Efficiency Challenges of Modern IT Architectures - A Quality Model for Serverless Energy Footprint	2020
P5	Irriman Platform: Enhancing Farming Sustainability through Cloud Computing Techniques for Irrigation Management	2022
P6	IoT-Aware Waste Management System Based on Cloud Services and Ultra-Low-Power RFID Sensor-Tags	2020
P7	Cloud architecture continuity: Change models and change rules for sustainable cloud software architectures	2017
P8	Scalable and elastic e-Assessment cloud solution	2014
P9	PaaS-IaaS Inter-Layer Adaptation in an Energy-Aware Cloud Environment	2017
P10	Architectural framework for implementing visual surveillance as a service	2014
P11	L3B: Low level load balancer in the cloud	2013
P12	GeoBMS: Hybrid Cloud/ On-Premise Architecture for Building Energy Optimization	2019
P13	An Enterprise Architecture based on Cloud, Fog and Edge Computing for an Airfield Lighting Management System	2020
P14	Sustainable Network Resource Management System for Virtual Private Clouds	2010
P15	Sustainable availability provision in distributed cloud services	2016
P16	A Cloud-Based Architecture for Citizen Services in Smart Cities	2012
P17	Multi-tenant web application framework architecture pattern	2015
P18	Towards Distributed Architecture for Collaborative Cloud Services in Community Networks	2014
P19	Fuzzy Logic based QoS Management and Monitoring System for Cloud Computing	2020
P20	Architectural Tactics to Optimize Software for Energy Efficiency in the Public Cloud	2022
P21	A Healthcare System as a Service in the Context of Vital Signs: Proposing a Framework for Realizing a Model	2012
P22	Experiences of Using a Hybrid Cloud to Construct an Environmental Virtual Observatory	2013
P23	An Intelligent Power Distribution Service Architecture Using Cloud Computing and Deep Learning Techniques	2018
P24	Application for modern energy efficient data center	2014
P25	An architecture for integrated intelligence in urban management using cloud computing	2012
P26	Energy efficiency embedded service lifecycle: Towards an energy efficient cloud computing architecture	2014
P27	Green architectural tactics for the cloud	2014

References

1. Andrikopoulos, V., Boza, R.D., Perales, C., Lago, P.: Sustainability in software architecture: a systematic mapping study. In: 2022 48th Euromicro Conference on Software Engineering and Advanced Applications (SEAA), pp. 426–433. IEEE (2022)
2. Andrikopoulos, V., Lago, P.: Software sustainability in the age of everything as a service. In: Next-Gen Digital Services. A Retrospective and Roadmap for Service Computing of the Future: Essays Dedicated to Michael Papazoglou on the Occasion of His 65th Birthday and His Retirement, pp. 35–47 (2021)
3. Andrikopoulos, V., Strauch, S., Leymann, F.: Decision support for application migration to the cloud. Proc. CLOSER **13**, 149–155 (2013)
4. Becker, C., et al.: Requirements: the key to sustainability. IEEE Softw. **33**(1), 56–65 (2015)
5. Capilla, R., Nakagawa, E.Y., Zdun, U., Carrillo, C.: Toward architecture knowledge sustainability: extending system longevity. IEEE Softw. **34**(2), 108–111 (2017)

6. Chauhan, M.A., Probst, C.W.: Architecturally significant requirements identification, classification and change management for multi-tenant cloud-based systems. In: Requirements Engineering for Service and Cloud Computing, pp. 181–205 (2017)
7. Condori-Fernandez, N., Lago, P.: Characterizing the contribution of quality requirements to software sustainability. J. Syst. Softw. **137**, 289–305 (2018)
8. Duboc, L., et al.: Requirements engineering for sustainability: an awareness framework for designing software systems for a better tomorrow. Requirements Eng. **25**, 469–492 (2020)
9. Durdik, Z., et al.: Sustainability guidelines for long-living software systems. In: 2012 28th IEEE International Conference on Software Maintenance (ICSM), pp. 517–526. IEEE (2012)
10. Easterbrook, S., Singer, J., Storey, M.A., Damian, D.: Selecting empirical methods for software engineering research. In: Guide to Advanced Empirical Software Engineering, pp. 285–311 (2008)
11. Farshidi, S., et al.: A decision support system for software technology selection. J. Decis. Syst. **27**(sup1), 98–110 (2018)
12. Gill, S.S., Buyya, R.: A taxonomy and future directions for sustainable cloud computing: 360 degree view. ACM Comput. Surv. **51**(5), 1–33 (2018)
13. Goniwada, S.R.: Cloud native architecture and design patterns. In: Cloud Native Architecture and Design: A Handbook for Modern Day Architecture and Design with Enterprise-Grade Examples, pp. 127–187 (2022)
14. Hofmeister, C., et al.: A general model of software architecture design derived from five industrial approaches. J. Syst. Softw. **80**(1), 106–126 (2007)
15. ISO/IEC 25010: 2011: Systems and software engineering-systems and software quality requirements and evaluation (SQuaRE)-system and software quality models. Technical report (2011)
16. Kitchenham, B., Brereton, P.: A systematic review of systematic review process research in software engineering. Inf. Softw. Technol. **55**(12), 2049–2075 (2013)
17. Kitchenham, B., Charters, S.: Guidelines for performing systematic literature reviews in software engineering, ver. 2.3. Technical report (2007)
18. Koziolek, H.: Sustainability evaluation of software architectures: a systematic review. In: Proceedings of the Joint ACM SIGSOFT Conference-QoSA and ACM SIGSOFT Symposium-ISARCS on Quality of Software Architectures-QoSA and Architecting Critical Systems-ISARCS, pp. 3–12 (2011)
19. Kumar, S., Buyya, R.: Green cloud computing and environmental sustainability. In: Harnessing Green IT: Principles and Practices, pp. 315–339 (2012)
20. Lago, P.: Architecture design decision maps for software sustainability. In: 2019 IEEE/ACM 41st International Conference on Software Engineering: Software Engineering in Society (ICSE-SEIS), pp. 61–64. IEEE (2019)
21. Lago, P., Koçak, S.A., Crnkovic, I., Penzenstadler, B.: Framing sustainability as a property of software quality. Commun. ACM **58**(10), 70–78 (2015)
22. Liu, F., et al.: NIST cloud computing reference architecture. NIST Spec. Publ. **500**(2011), 1–28 (2011)
23. Mell, P., Grance, T., et al.: The NIST definition of cloud computing (2011)
24. Mireles, G.A.G., et al.: A classification approach of sustainability aware requirements methods. In: 2017 12th Iberian Conference on Information Systems and Technologies (CISTI), pp. 1–6. IEEE (2017)
25. Mussbacher, G., Nuttall, D.: Goal modeling for sustainability: the case of time. In: 2014 IEEE 4th International Model-Driven Requirements Engineering Workshop (MoDRE), pp. 7–16. IEEE (2014)

26. Penzenstadler, B., et al.: Software engineering for sustainability: find the leverage points! IEEE Softw. **35**(4), 22–33 (2018)
27. Venters, C.C., et al.: Software sustainability: research and practice from a software architecture viewpoint. J. Syst. Softw. **138**, 174–188 (2018)
28. Wieringa, R.J.: Design Science Methodology for Information Systems and Software Engineering. Springer, Berlin, Heidelberg (2014). https://doi.org/10.1007/978-3-662-43839-8
29. Zdun, U., Capilla, R., Tran, H., Zimmermann, O.: Sustainable architectural design decisions. IEEE Softw. **30**(6), 46–53 (2013)

Author Index

A

Adams, Lauren 309
Ahmad, Isra Shafique 19
Ahmadisakha, Sahar 471
Ali, Nour 326
Ali, Shaukat 451
Alidoosti, Razieh 71
Alshuqayran, Nuha 326
Amoroso d'Aragona, Dario 309
Ampatzoglou, Apostolos 359
Andrikopoulos, Vasilios 471
Avritzer, Alberto 185

B

Bakhtin, Alexander 3
Berrocal, Javier 272
Bikker, Jan-Willem 257
Boltz, Nicolas 342
Braun, Niklas 257
Breuil, Gabriel 409
Brogi, Antonio 3
Brott, Julian 237

C

Canal, Carlos 272
Cerezo, Felipe 426
Cerny, Tomas 3, 309
Chatzigeorgiou, Alexander 359
Constantinides, Constantinos 133
Copei, Sebastian 33

D

d'Aloisio, Giordano 89, 169
D'Angelo, Andrea 89
De Sanctis, Martina 71
Dekker, Arjan 390
Dembele, Jean-Marie 151
Demirörs, Onur 19
Di Marco, Antinisca 89, 169

Di Marco, Diana 89
Doornbos, Richard 257
Druyts, Sarah 390

E

Eich, Andreas 257

F

Fakeeh, Rana 326
Fatima, Iffat 200
Frank, Sebastian 237

G

Gerking, Christopher 342
Gjøby, Julie Marie 451

H

Hahner, Sebastian 342
Hajnorouzi, Mehrnoush 257
Hakamian, Alireza 237
Harris, Patrick 309
Heinrich, Robert 342
Hossain Chy, Md Showkat 309

I

Iovino, Ludovico 71

J

Jannatpour, Ali 133
Javaheri, Narges 257
Jilderda, Hendrik 53
Joosen, Wouter 120

K

Karamanlioglu, Alper 438
Karatas, Yahya Bahadir 438
Kolyda, Maria 359
Kosiol, Jens 33
Kostoglou, Eirini 359

B. Tekinerdoğan et al. (Eds.): ECSA 2023, LNCS 14590, pp. 489–490, 2024.
https://doi.org/10.1007/978-3-031-66326-0

L

Lago, Patricia   71, 200
Laso, Sergio   272
Li, Jialong   375
Li, Nianyu   375
Li, Xiaozhou   3
Loukas, George   151

M

Maarleveld, Jesse   390
Maggi, Kevin   217
Manuel Murillo, Juan   272
Mao, Zhenyu   375
Marzi, Francesca   89, 169
Mehrafrooz, Zohreh   133
Mendy, Gervais   151
Modrakowski, Elias   257
Moritz, Sebastian   257

N

Nakagawa, Elisa Yumi   375
Nikolaidis, Nikolaos   359
Noureddine, Adel   409

P

Pawlak, Renaud   409
Pecorella, Tommaso   287
Perry, Samantha   309

R

Raibulet, Claudia   53
Razavian, Maryam   71
Restrepo-Calle, Felipe   107
Rito Silva, António   185
Rodrigues, Helena   185
Rohman, Thoybur   326

S

S. Abdelfattah, Amr   309
Sadou, Salah   107
Sakellari, Georgia   151
Sartaj, Hassan   451
Sawadogo, Zakaria   151
Scommegna, Leonardo   217, 287
Siffre, Lylian   409
Soldani, Jacopo   3
Soliman, Mohamed   390
Solis, Carlos   326
Soylu, Görkem Kılınç   19
Stilo, Giovanni   89, 169

T

Taibi, Davide   3, 309
Taimoor Khan, Muhammad   151
Tei, Kenji   375
Tibermacine, Chouki   107
Toro-Gálvez, Lorenzo   272
Tran, Anh-Duy   120
Troya, Javier   272
Tsigkanos, Christos   375

U

Ubukata, Toshihide   375
Ünlü, Hüseyin   19

V

van Beek, Rutger   257
van Hoorn, André   237
Vela, Belén   426
Verdecchia, Roberto   217, 287
Vergara-Vargas, Jeisson   107
Vicario, Enrico   217, 287

Y

Yskout, Koen   120
Yue, Tao   451
Yurtalan, Gokhan   438

GPSR Compliance

The European Union's (EU) General Product Safety Regulation (GPSR) is a set of rules that requires consumer products to be safe and our obligations to ensure this.

If you have any concerns about our products, you can contact us on ProductSafety@springernature.com

In case Publisher is established outside the EU, the EU authorized representative is:

Springer Nature Customer Service Center GmbH
Europaplatz 3
69115 Heidelberg, Germany

The manufacturer's authorised representative in the EU is Springer
Nature Customer Service Centre GmbH, Europaplatz 3, 69115 Heidelberg,
Germany. If you have any concerns regarding our products, please
contact ProductSafety@springernature.com

Printed and bound by CPI Group (UK) Ltd, Croydon, CR0 4YY
29/04/2026
02099533-0003